Communications in Computer and Information Science 2473

Series Editors

Rationale

The CCIS series is devoted to the publication of proceedings of computer science conferences. Its aim is to efficiently disseminate original research results in informatics in printed and electronic form. While the focus is on publication of peer-reviewed full papers presenting mature work, inclusion of reviewed short papers reporting on work in progress is welcome, too. Besides globally relevant meetings with internationally representative program committees guaranteeing a strict peer-reviewing and paper selection process, conferences run by societies or of high regional or national relevance are also considered for publication.

Topics

The topical scope of CCIS spans the entire spectrum of informatics ranging from foundational topics in the theory of computing to information and communications science and technology and a broad variety of interdisciplinary application fields.

Information for Volume Editors and Authors

Publication in CCIS is free of charge. No royalties are paid, however, we offer registered conference participants temporary free access to the online version of the conference proceedings on SpringerLink (http://link.springer.com) by means of an http referrer from the conference website and/or a number of complimentary printed copies, as specified in the official acceptance email of the event.

CCIS proceedings can be published in time for distribution at conferences or as post-proceedings, and delivered in the form of printed books and/or electronically as USBs and/or e-content licenses for accessing proceedings at SpringerLink. Furthermore, CCIS proceedings are included in the CCIS electronic book series hosted in the SpringerLink digital library at http://link.springer.com/bookseries/7899. Conferences publishing in CCIS are allowed to use Online Conference Service (OCS) for managing the whole proceedings lifecycle (from submission and reviewing to preparing for publication) free of charge.

Publication process

The language of publication is exclusively English. Authors publishing in CCIS have to sign the Springer CCIS copyright transfer form, however, they are free to use their material published in CCIS for substantially changed, more elaborate subsequent publications elsewhere. For the preparation of the camera-ready papers/files, authors have to strictly adhere to the Springer CCIS Authors' Instructions and are strongly encouraged to use the CCIS LaTeX style files or templates.

Abstracting/Indexing

CCIS is abstracted/indexed in DBLP, Google Scholar, EI-Compendex, Mathematical Reviews, SCImago, Scopus. CCIS volumes are also submitted for the inclusion in ISI Proceedings.

How to start

To start the evaluation of your proposal for inclusion in the CCIS series, please send an e-mail to ccis@springer.com.

Jagadeesh Kakarla · R. Balasubramanian ·
Subrahmanyam Murala ·
Santosh Kumar Vipparthi · Deep Gupta
Editors

Computer Vision and Image Processing

9th International Conference, CVIP 2024
Chennai, India, December 19–21, 2024
Revised Selected Papers, Part I

Springer

Editors
Jagadeesh Kakarla
IIITDM Kancheepuram
Chennai, Tamil Nadu, India

R. Balasubramanian
IIT Roorkee
Roorkee, Uttarakhand, India

Subrahmanyam Murala
Trinity College Dublin
Dublin, Ireland

Santosh Kumar Vipparthi
IIT Ropar
Rupnagar, Punjab, India

Deep Gupta
VNIT Nagpur
Nagpur, Maharashtra, India

ISSN 1865-0929 ISSN 1865-0937 (electronic)
Communications in Computer and Information Science
ISBN 978-3-031-93687-6 ISBN 978-3-031-93688-3 (eBook)
https://doi.org/10.1007/978-3-031-93688-3

This Springer imprint is published by the registered company Springer Nature Switzerland AG
The registered company address is: Gewerbestrasse 11, 6330 Cham, Switzerland

Preface

The 9th International Conference on Computer Vision & Image Processing (CVIP 2024), a premier annual conference focused on Computer Vision and Image Processing, was held during December 19–21, 2024 at Indian Institute of Information Technology, Design and Manufacturing, Kancheepuram (IIITDM Kancheepuram), India. CVIP provides a great platform for students, academics, researchers and industry persons. Previous editions of CVIP were held at IIT Jammu (CVIP 2023), VNIT Nagpur (CVIP 2022), IIT Ropar (CVIP 2021), IIIT Allahabad (CVIP 2020), MNIT Jaipur (CVIP 2019), IIITDM Jabalpur (CVIP 2018) and IIT Roorkee (CVIP 2017 and CVIP 2016). All editions of CVIP have been endorsed by the International Association for Pattern Recognition (IAPR).

This year, CVIP 2024 received a record-breaking 647 submissions, the highest in the conference's history. After a rigorous two-round review process, 178 papers were accepted. Submissions came from nearly all premier Indian institutions, including IITs (Kharagpur, Guwahati, Roorkee, Madras, Delhi, Bombay, Kanpur, Patna, Goa, Tirupati, Ropar), IISc Bangalore, ISI, IIITs (Allahabad, Hyderabad, Gwalior, Jabalpur, Kalyani, Vadodara), and several NITs (Trichy, Hamirpur, Calicut, Warangal, Nagpur). Additionally, we received contributions from prestigious international institutions such as the Norwegian University of Science and Technology, Cardiff Metropolitan University, the University of Auckland, and HSE University, spanning eight countries.

A single-blind review policy was followed, ensuring that each manuscript received a minimum of three independent reviews before a final decision. The accepted papers cover a diverse range of emerging topics in image processing, computer vision applications and advanced deep learning and machine learning techniques. Many selected works also address real-world, impactful challenges, demonstrating the practical significance of research in this domain.

The technical program committee was led by Deepak Mishra (IIST Trivandrum), Ananda S. Chowdhury (Jadavpur University), Nidhi Goel (IGDTUW), Shitala Prasad (IIT Goa), Surya Prakash (IIT Indore), Rama Krishna Sai Gorthi (IIT Tirupati), Vivekraj V. K. (IIIT Dharwad), Korra Sathya Babu (IIITDM Kurnool), Amitesh Singh Rajput (BITS Pilani), Pushpendra Kumar (MANIT Bhopal), Mamta Juneja (Panjab University) and Suvendu Rup (NIT Raipur). The CVIP 2024 conference was successfully conducted with the support of core organizing members P. K. Biswas (IIT Kharagpur), Umapada Pal (ISI Kolkata), Mohan Kankanhalli (NUS Singapore), R. Balasubramanian (IIT Roorkee), R. Venkatesh Babu (IISc Bangalore), Subramanyam Murala (Trinity College Dublin, Ireland), Sanjeev Kumar (IIT Roorkee), Santosh Vipparthi (IIT Ropar), Gaurav Bhatnagar (IIT Jodhpur), Puneet Goyal (IIT Ropar), Aparajita Ojha (IIITDM Jabalpur), Pritee Khanna (IIITDM Jabalpur), Shiv Ram Dubey (IIIT Allahabad), Deep Gupta (VNIT Nagpur), Harkeerat Kaur (IIT Jammu), Sambit Bakshi (NIT Rourkela), Manisha Verma (IIT (ISM) Dhanbad), Prashant Patil (IIT Guwahati), B. Surendiran (NIT Puducherry) and P. Prakash (MIT, Anna University).

The successful completion of the event was made possible through the dedicated efforts of IIITDM Kancheepuram faculty members—Masilamani V., B. Chitti Babu, Sadagopan N., Priyanka Kokil, Krishna Priya, Umarani Jayaraman, Rahul Raman, Jaishree Mayank, Sanjeet Kumar Nayak, Santhanam Raghavan, and Preeth R. Their contributions, under the mentorship of M. V. Kartikeyan (General Chair and Director, IIITDM Kancheepuram), played a pivotal role in the event's success.

CVIP 2024 was a remarkable convergence of academia, industry and entrepreneurship. The conference featured insightful keynote talks by Yasushi Yagi (Osaka University, Japan), Laurent Najman (Gustave Eiffel University, France), Fahad Khan (Mohamed bin Zayed University of Artificial Intelligence, UAE), Dinesh Kumar (RMIT University, Australia), Venkatesh Babu (IISc Bangalore), A. N. Rajagopalan (IIT Madras), Chandra Sekhar (IISc Bangalore), Vikram M. Gadre (IIT Bombay) and Nikita Pinto (MathWorks).

Additionally, a challenge on Multi-Class Abnormality Classification for Video Capsule Endoscopy attracted 150 teams, fostering innovation in medical image analysis. MathWorks further enriched the event by organizing a workshop titled "AI for Computer Vision," covering practical steps in AI modelling, verification, validation, code generation, model compression and deployment to edge devices.

CVIP 2024 presented high-quality research works with innovative ideas. To acknowledge and promote the spirit of research and participation, six different awards were announced: IAPR Best Paper Award, IAPR Best Student Paper, CVIP 2024 Best Paper Award, CVIP 2024 Best Student Paper Award, CVIP 2024 Best Poster Award and CVIP 2024 Best Industry Paper Award. Three prizes were awarded to the challenge winners who secured first, second and third positions. Moreover, to celebrate outstanding work the committee nominated Vikram M. Gadre, IIT Bombay, for the CVIP 2024 Lifetime Achievement Award for his remarkable research in the field of Image Processing and Computer Vision.

We extend our best wishes for the continued success of the CVIP conference series as the baton is proudly passed to IIT Ropar for CVIP 2025, carrying forward the spirit of excellence and innovation.

December 2024

Jagadeesh Kakarla
R. Balasubramanian
Subrahmanyam Murala
Santosh Kumar Vipparthi
Deep Gupta

Organization

Patron

B. B. Chaudhuri	Indian Statistical Institute, Kolkata, India

General Chairs

M. V. Kartikeyan	IIITDM Kancheepuram, India
P. K. Biswas	IIT Kharagpur, India
Umapada Pal	Indian Statistical Institute, Kolkata, India
Mohan Kankanhalli	National University of Singapore, Singapore

General Co-chairs

R. Balasubramanian	IIT Roorkee, India
R. Venkatesh Babu	Indian Institute of Science, India

Conference Chairs

Jagadeesh Kakarla	IIITDM Kancheepuram, India
Subrahmanyam Murala	Trinity College Dublin, Ireland
Sanjeev Kumar	IIT Roorkee, India
Sriparna Saha	IIT Patna, India

Conference Co-chairs

Priyanka Kokil	IIITDM Kancheepuram, India
Ram Prasad Padhy	IIT Bhubaneswar, India
Santosh Vipparthi	IIT Ropar, India
Gaurav Bhatnagar	IIT Jodhpur, India
Puneet Goyal	IIT Ropar and NIMS University, India

Conference Conveners

Aparajita Ojha	IIITDM Jabalpur, India
Pritee Khanna	IIITDM Jabalpur, India
Masilamani V.	IIITDM Kancheepuram, India
Satish Kumar Singh	IIIT Allahabad, India
Shiv Ram Dubey	IIIT Allahabad, India
Deep Gupta	VNIT Nagpur, India

Conference Co-conveners

Partha Pratim Roy	IIT Roorkee, India
Harkeerat Kaur	IIT Jammu, India

Sponsorship Chairs

Sadagopan N.	IIITDM Kancheepuram, India
B. Chitti Babu	IIITDM Kancheepuram, India
Krishna Priya	IIITDM Kancheepuram, India
Jiji	Shiv Nadar University, India
S. Chandrakala	Shiv Nadar University, India

Publicity Chairs

Sambit Bakshi	NIT Rourkela, India
Noor Mahammad	IIITDM Kancheepuram, India
Manisha Verma	IIT ISM Dhanbad, India
Prashant Patil	IIT Guwahati, India
Pankaj Pratap Singh	Central Institute of Technology, Kokrajhar, India
B. Surendiran	NIT Puducherry, India
U. Srinivasulu Reddy	NIT Tiruchirappalli, India
B. Yogameena	Thiagarajar College of Engineering, India
P. Uma Maheswari	Anna University, India
P. Prakash	MIT, Anna University, India
T. Nagarajan	Shiv Nadar University, India

TPC (Technical Program Committee) Chairs

Deepak Mishra	IIST Trivandrum, India
Ananda S. Chowdhury	Jadavpur University, India
Nidhi Goel	Indira Gandhi Delhi Technical University for Women, India
Vinit Jakhetiya	IIT Jammu, India
Shitala Prasad	IIT Goa, India
Surya Prakash	IIT Indore, India
Rama Krishna Sai Gorthi	IIT Tirupati, India
Maheshkumar H. Kolekar	IIT Patna, India
Vivek Kanhangad	IIT Indore, India
Anil B. Gonde	Shri Guru Gobind Singhji Institute of Engineering and Technology, India
Vivekraj V. K.	IIIT Dharwad, India
Korra Sathya Babu	IIITDM Kurnool, India
Amitesh Singh Rajput	BITS Pilani, India
Pushpendra Kumar	MANIT Bhopal, India
Mamta Juneja	Panjab University, India
Suvendu Rup	National Institute of Technology, Raipur, India

Local Organizing Committee

Umarani Jayaraman	IIITDM Kancheepuram, India
Rahul Raman	IIITDM Kancheepuram, India
Jaishree Mayank	IIITDM Kancheepuram, India
Sanjeet Kumar Nayak	IIITDM Kancheepuram, India
Santhanam Raghavan	IIITDM Kancheepuram, India
Preeth R.	IIITDM Kancheepuram, India

National Advisory Committee

S. Sadagopan	IIIT Bangalore, India
Ganapati Panda	IIT Bhubaneswar, India
Santanu Choudhary	IIT Jodhpur, India
Banshidhar Majhi	VSSUT, India
D. V. L. N. Somayajulu	NIT Manipur, India
A. G. Ramakrishnan	IISc, India
Sharat Chandran	IIT Bombay, India
A. N. Rajagopalan	IIT Madras, India

Balaraman Ravindran	IIT Madras, India
Ram Bilas Pachori	IIT Indore, India
C. Krishna Mohan	IIT Hyderabad, India
Jayanta Mukhopadhyay	IIT Kharagpur, India
Sushmita Mitra	ISI Kolkata, India
Phalguni Gupta	IIT Kanpur, India
Sundar Balakrishna	Government of Andhra Pradesh, India
V. M. Gadre	IIT Bombay, India
Anil Kumar Singh	IIITDM Jabalpur, India
Sumohana S. Channappayya	IIT Hyderabad, India
Sanjay Kumar Singh	IIT BHU, India
Chetan Arora	IIT Delhi, India
Yegnanarayana B.	IIIT Hyderabad, India
Ujjwal Maulik	Jadavpur University, India
Rajeev Srivastava	IIT BHU Varanasi, India
Dharmendra Singh	IIT Roorkee, India
Brajesh Kumar Kaushik	IIT Roorkee, India
Ram Sarkar	Jadavpur University, India
S. Sivasathya	Pondicherry University, India
Soma Biswas	Indian Institute of Science, India
D. Ram Rajak	Indian Space Research Organisation, India
D. S. Guru	University of Mysore, India
Suresh Sundaram	IIT Guwahati, India
Vinod Pankajakshan	IIT Roorkee, India
Bhardwaj Alok	IIT Roorkee, India
Koteswar Rao Jerripthula	IIT Kanpur, India
Pravendra Singh	IIT Roorkee, India
Kalidas Yeturu	IIT Tirupati, India
Tharun Kumar Reddy	IIT Roorkee, India
Satyajit Nayak	Valeo India Private Limited, India

International Advisory Committee

Anil K. Jain	Michigan State University, USA
Ishwar K. Sethi	Oakland University, USA
Vincenzo Piuri	University of Milan, Italy
Raghavendra Ramachandra	NTNU, Norway
Jonathan Wu	University of Windsor, Canada
Barbara Zitova	Academy of Sciences of the Czech Republic, Czechia
Fabio Dellacqua	University of Pavia, Italy

Yongmin Li	Brunel University London, UK
Rangaraj M. Rangayyan	University of Calgary, Canada
Gaurav Sharma	University of Rochester, USA
Daniel P. Lopresti	Lehigh University, USA
Nalini K. Ratha	State University of New York at Buffalo, USA
Dilip K. Prasad	UiT The Arctic University of Norway, Norway
Satish E. Viswanath	Case Western Reserve University, USA
Paula Brito	University of Porto, Portugal
Henry Leung	University of Calgary, Canada
B. S. Manjunath	University of California, Santa Barbara, USA
Lianwen Jin	South China University of Technology, China
Kiran Raja	NTNU, Norway
Vishal M. Patel	Johns Hopkins University, USA
Richard Hartley	Australian National University, Australia
Bir Bhanu	University of California, Riverside, USA
Sudeep Sarkar	University of South Florida, USA
Xiaoyi Jiang	University of Münster, Germany
M. Omair Ahmad	Concordia University, Canada
Xingquan Zhu	Florida Atlantic University, USA
Anup Basu	University of Alberta, Canada
Kidiyo Kpalma	INSA, France
Sukalpa Chanda	Østfold University College, Norway
Pradeep K. Atrey	University at Albany, USA
Pitikhate Sooraksa	King Mongkut's Institute of Technology Ladkrabang, Thailand
Xiaobai Li	Zhejiang University, China
Yogesh S. Rawat	University of Central Florida, USA
Shivakumara Palaiahnakote	University of Salford, UK
Taposh Banerjee	University of Pittsburgh, USA
George Azzopardi	University of Groningen, Netherlands
Aparna Bharati	Lehigh University, USA
Barbara Zitova	Academy of Sciences, Czech Republic
Fabio Dellacqua	University of Pavia, Italy
Yongmin Li	Brunel University London, UK

Reviewers

Nitin Gupta	NIT Hamirpur, India
A. Eashaan Rao	IIT Tirupati, India
Abhilasha Chaudhuri	NIT Surat, India
Abhilasha S. Jadhav	IIT Ropar, India

Abhilasha Sharma	NIT Kurukshetra, India
Abhimanyu Sahu	MNNIT Allahabad, India
Abhisek Ray	IIT Patna, India
Aditi A. Shetkar	IIT Goa, India
Ajay Kumar Mallick	NIT Hamirpur, India
Akoramurthy Balasubramaniam	NIT Puducherry, India
Amardeep Gupta	Amity University, India
Ambika M. Mani	IIIT Tiruchirappalli, India
Amirhossein Panahi	University of California San Diego, USA
Amit Kumar	IIIT Kota, India
Amit Raghunath Shewale	IIIT Nagpur, India
Amit Verma	Tezpur University, India
Amitesh Singh Rajput	BITS Pilani, India
Ananda S. Chowdhury	Jadavpur University, India
Anish Natekar	IIT Goa, India
Anjali Gautam	IIIT Allahabad, India
Anjan Kumar Ray	NIT Sikkim, India
Ankit Ashokrao Bhurane	VNIT Nagpur, India
Ankit Kumar	MANIT Bhopal, India
Ankur Gupta	IIT Roorkee, India
Anshul Pundhir	IIT Roorkee, India
Ansuman Mahapatra	NIT Jamshedpur, India
Anushka Joshi	IIT Roorkee, India
Aparajita Ojha	IIITDM Jabalpur, India
Aravinda Reddy P. N.	IIT Kharagpur, India
Arijit De	Jadavpur University, India
Arnav Bhavsar	IIT Mandi, India
Arpita Gupta	KL University, India
Arup Kumar Pal	IIT(ISM) Dhanbad, India
Ashish Phophalia	IIIT Vadodara, India
Ashish Soni	Thapar University, India
Ashish Yadav	NLIU Bhopal, India
Ashutosh C. Kulkarni	IIT Ropar, India
Ashwini Y. Mate	VNIT Nagpur, India
Atal Tewari	IIT Gandhinagar, India
Aurpan Majumder	NIT Durgapur, India
Avinash Reddy Avuthu	VIT Chennai, India
B. Shameedha Begum	NIT Trichy, India
Badal Soni	NIT Silchar, India
Bala Krishna Thunakala	IIITDM Kancheepuram, India
Bala Venkateswarlu Isunuri	SRM University, India
Balaji Banothu	NIT Trichy, India

Bhaskar Mukhoty	Mohamed bin Zayed University of Artificial Intelligence, UAE
Bhavana Singh	MANIT Bhopal, India
Bhukya Krishna Priya	IIITDM Kancheepuram, India
Bindu Avadhani	Amrita Vishwa Vidyapeetham, India
Chalavadi Vishnu	IIT Tirupati, India
Chandra V. Sekhar	Samsung Electronics, India
Chhavi Dhiman	Delhi Technological University, India
Daniel Lopresti	Lehigh University, USA
Debbrota Paul Chowdhury	NIT Silchar, India
Deep Gupta	VNIT Nagpur, India
Deepak Kumar Dewangan	IIITM Gwalior, India
Deepak Gupta	NIT Arunachal Pradesh, India
Deepak Kumar	IIT Roorkee, India
Deepak Mishra	IIST Trivandrum, India
Deepak Singh	NIT Raipur, India
Deepika Agrawal	NIT Raipur, India
Deval Verma	Bennett University, India
Dhakshayani J.	NIT Puducherry, India
Dhiraj Sangwan	CSIR-CEERI, India
Dhivya Bharathi P.	NIT Puducherry, India
Dibyasundar Das	NIT Rourkela, India
Diksha Rangwani	IIT(ISM) Dhanbad, India
Dinesh Kumar Tyagi	MNIT Jaipur, India
Divya Sinshu Lekha	IIIT Kottayam, India
Doli Uppal	IIT Indore, India
Krishan Berwal	NIT Kurukshetra, India
Palak Mahajan	Central University of Jammu, India
Satyendra Singh Yadav	NIT Meghalaya, India
Soubhagya Barpanda	VIT Amaravati, India
Subidh Ali	IIT Bhilai, India
Sumit Hazra	KL University, India
Abhishek Sharma	IIIT Naya Raipur, India
Anoop Jacob Thomas	IIIT Tiruchirappalli, India
B. Surendiran	NIT Puducherry, India
Debanjan Sadhya	ABV-IIITM Gwalior, India
G. Devasena	IIIT Trichy, India
Himanshu Agarwal	Jaypee Institute of Information Technology, India
Jasvinder Pal Singh	Central University of Jammu, India
Lavanya Madhuri Bollipo	NIT Srinagar, India
Mohammed Javed	IIIT Allahabad, India
Nagesh Bhattu	NIT Andhra Pradesh, India

Oishila Bandyopadhyay	IIIT Kalyani, India
Parveen Kumar	NIT Kurukshetra, India
Sanjoy Pratihar	IIIT Kalyani, India
Saran Raj Sowrirajan	Vel Tech, India
Shirshendu Layek	IIIT Dharwad, India
Varun Prakash Saxena	Government Women Engineering College Ajmer, India
Vikram Kumar Pudi	IIT Tirupati, India
Umarani Jayaraman	IIITDM Kancheepuram, India
Figlu Mohanty	IIIT Bhubaneswar, India
G. Sankara Raju Kosuru	IIT Ropar, India
G. Sreelekha	NIT Calicut, India
Gargi Gupta	Technological University Dublin, Ireland
Geet Sahu	Amity University, India
Gireesh Kumar T.	Amrita Vishwa Vidyapeetham, India
Gopakumar G.	Amrita Vishwa Vidyapeetham, India
Gorthi Rama Krishna Sai Subrahmanyam	IIT Tirupati, India
Gourav Kumar	Central University of Jammu, India
Gurinder Singh	Cleveland State University, USA
Hadia Showkat Kawoosa	IIT Ropar, India
Hemant Kumar Kathania	NIT Sikkim, India
Hemkumar D.	VNIT Nagpur, India
Hima Bindu Kommanti	NIT Andhra Pradesh, India
Himashree Kalita	IIT Guwahati, India
Jagat Sesh Challa	BITS Pilani, India
Jaishree Mayank	IIITDM Kancheepuram, India
Jasdeep Singh	IIT Ropar, India
Jaya Pathak	BITS Pilani, India
Jaya Sreevalsan-Nair	IIIT Bangalore, India
Jayant Mahawar	IIT Jodhpur, India
Jayendra Kumar	NIT Jamshedpur, India
Jignesh N. Sarvaiya	SVNIT Surat, India
Jitendra Tembhurne	IIIT Nagpur, India
Joe Dhanith P. R.	VIT Chennai, India
Joohi Chauhan	MNNIT Allahabad, India
Josep Lladós	Universitat Autònoma de Barcelona, Spain
Joy Dhar	IIT Ropar, India
Kalidas Yeturu	IIT Tirupati, India
Kamal	IIT Guwahati, India
Kapil Rana	IIT Ropar, India
Karthick Seshadri	NIT Andhra Pradesh, India

Karthik N.	NIT Puducherry, India
Kasthuri P.	Madras Institute of Technology, India
Katta Ranjith	IIT Ropar, India
Kavitha Muthusubash	Nagasaki University, Japan
Kiruthika S.	VIT Chennai, India
Kishore Babu Nampalle	IIT Roorkee, India
Kopal Rastogi	IIT Jodhpur, India
Krishan Gopal Sharma	Scaledge India Pvt. Ltd., India
Krishna Kumar Yadav	UNSIET, Veer Bahadur Singh Purvanchal University, India
Krishna Kumar Mohbey	Central University of Rajasthan, India
Kuldeep Biradar	MNIT Jaipur, India
Kushall Pal Singh	MNIT Jaipur, India
Lidiya Thampi	IIIT Kottayam, India
M. Mohammadha Hussaini	Government College of Engineering Erode, India
Machavaram Venkata Raghunadh	NIT Warangal, India
Mahendra Pratap Yadav	IIIT Pune, India
Malaya Kumar Nath	NIT Puducherry, India
Mamatha E.	IIIT Dharwad, India
Mamta Juneja	UIET, Panjab University, India
Manish Okade	NIT Rourkela, India
Manisha Verma	IIT (ISM) Dhanbad, India
Manjunath V. Joshi	DA-IICT, India
Manoj Kumar Somesula	NIT Jalandhar, India
Mayank Chopra	Central University of Himachal Pradesh, India
Mayuri A. Digalwar	IIIT Nagpur, India
Md. Raqib Khan	Trinity College Dublin, Ireland
Md. Sarfaraj Alam Ansari	NIT Sikkim, India
Min-Ling Zhang	Southeast University, China
Mohan Karnati	Amity University, India
Mohd Ubaid Wani	IIT Ropar, India
Mohit Kumar	NIT Hamirpur, India
Mrityunjay Singh	IIIT Una, India
Muhammad Suhaib Kanroo	IIT Ropar, India
Nancy Mehta	IIT Ropar, India
Neeraj Goel	IIT Ropar, India
Neetu Sood	NIT Jalandhar, India
Neha Gour	Khalifa University, UAE
Nikita Yadav	MANIT Bhopal, India
Niladri B. Puhan	IIT Bhubaneswar, India
Nitin Arora	IIT Roorkee, India
Nitin Singhal	Samsung Research, India

Nitin Tyagi	IIT Roorkee, India
Nitish Kumar Mahala	MANIT Bhopal, India
Niyati Baliyan	NIT Kurukshetra, India
Om Prakash Singh	IIIT Bhagalpur, India
P. S. Latha Kalyampudi	Central Tribal University of Andhra Pradesh, India
Panchatcharam Mariappan	IIT Tirupati, India
Pankaj Kumar Keserwani	NIT Sikkim, India
Pankaj P. Singh	Central Institute of Technology Kokrajhar, India
Parshuram M. Kamble	Central University of Karnataka, India
Parul Sahare	IIIT Nagpur, India
Pavan Kumar	IIIT Dharwad, India
Pisharody Harikrishnan Gopalakrishnan	IIT Palakkad, India
Piyush Kumar	NIT Patna, India
Poornima Singh Thakur	IIITDM Jabalpur, India
Pournami P. N.	NIT Calicut, India
Prabir Roy Chowdhury	IIT Kharagpur, India
Pradeep Singh	IIT Roorkee, India
Pradyut K. Biswal	IIIT Bhubaneswar, India
Praful Hambarde	IIT Ropar, India
Prafulla Saxena	MNIT Jaipur, India
Prakash P.	Madras Institute of Technology, India
Prakash Pawar	IIIT Dharwad, India
Pramit Mazumdar	IIIT Vadodara, India
Prasad P. Kanhegaonkar	IIT Indore, India
Prashant Pathak	IIT Indore, India
Prashant D. Pathak	Government College of Engineering Aurangabad, India
Prashant Patil	IIT Guwahati, India
Pratap Turimerla	VR Siddhartha Engineering College, India
Pratishtha Verma	NIT Kurukshetra, India
Praveen Kumar Chandaliya	SVNIT Surat, India
Preeth R.	IIITDM Kancheepuram, India
Preeti Mehta	NIT Delhi, India
Prerana Mukherjee	Jawaharlal Nehru University, India
Pritee Khanna	IIITDM Jabalpur, India
Prithwijit Guha	IIT Guwahati, India
Pritpal Singh	National Taipei University of Technology, Taiwan
Priyanka Kokil	IIITDM Kancheepuram, India
Priyanka Mishra	IIT Ropar, India
Priyavrat Chauhan	Central University of Punjab, India

Protyay Dey	IIT Ropar, India
Puneet Goyal	IIT Ropar & NIMS University Jaipur, India
Pushpendra Kumar	MANIT Bhopal, India
R. Malmathanraj	NIT Trichy, India
Rahul Bhardwaj	IIT Guwahati, India
Rahul Raman	IIITDM Kancheepuram, India
Rajib Ghosh	NIT Patna, India
Rakesh Chandra Balabantaray	IIIT Bhubaneswar, India
Rakshith Basavaraju	CIDC Private Limited, India
Ram Prasad Padhy	IIT Bhubaneswar, India
Ram Prakash Sharma	NIT Hamirpur, India
Raviteja Sista	IIT Kharagpur, India
Rejoy Chakraborty	IIT Ropar, India
Richa Makhijani	IIIT Nagpur, India
Ritu Raj Singh	Netaji Subhas University of Technology, India
Romi Banerjee	IIT Jodhpur, India
Rukhmini Bandyopadhyay	University of Texas MD Anderson Cancer Center, USA
S. Sastry	IIT Hyderabad, India
S. Sumitra	IIST Trivandrum, India
Sabyasachi Patra	IIT Bhubaneswar, India
Sandeep Kumar	NIT Delhi, India
Sandeep Raj	IIIT Bhagalpur, India
Sania Bano	IIT Ropar, India
Sanjay Ghosh	IIT Kharagpur, India
Santosh Ku Behera	NIT Calicut, India
Santosh U. Kumar	IIITDM Kancheepuram, India
Santosh Kumar	IIIT Naya Raipur, India
Saquib Mazhar	IIT Guwahati, India
Sasikala Dhamodaran	NIMS University, India
Sasithradevi Anabalagan	VIT Chennai, India
Satya Narayan	Government Engineering College Ajmer, India
Satya Verma	NIT Raipur, India
Satyajit Das	IIT Palakkad, India
Satyajit Nayak	Valeo India, India
Scindhiya Laxmi	IIT (ISM) Dhanbad, India
Shanmuganathan Raman	IIT Gandhinagar, India
Shashikala Tapaswi	ABV IIITM Gwalior, India
Sheeba Rani J.	IIST Trivandrum, India
Shitala Prasad	IIT Goa, India
Shiv Ram Dubey	IIIT Allahabad, India
Shivdutt Sharma	IIIT Una, India

Shree Prakash	VIT Chennai, India
Shruti S. Phutke	IIT Ropar, India
Shubhi Srivastava	IIT Roorkee, India
Shveta Mahajan	NIT Jalandhar, India
Siddharth R.	IIIT Dharwad, India
Sneha Singh	IIT Mandi, India
Somaraju Suvvari	NIT Patna, India
Soumen Bag	IIT Dhanbad, India
Soumya Shamarao Jahagirdar	IIIT Hyderabad, India
Sree Rama Vamsidhar S.	IIT Tirupati, India
Srikantaiah K. C.	Central University of Karnataka, India
Srimanta Mandal	Dhirubhai Ambani University, India
Srinivas Pinisetty	IIT Bhubaneswar, India
Srishti Yadav	IIT Roorkee, India
Subin Sahayam	Shiv Nadar University, India
Subrahmanyam Murala	Trinity College Dublin, Ireland
Subrajeet Mohapatra	BIT Mesra, India
Subrato Bharati	Concordia University, Canada
Sudhakar C. H.	IIITDM Kancheepuram, India
Sudhakar Kumawat	Osaka University, Japan
Sudharson S.	VIT Chennai, India
Sujata Goswami	Oak Ridge National Laboratory, USA
Sujit Das	NIT Warangal, India
Sujithra Alias Kanmani	VIT Chennai, India
Sumalakshmi C. H.	KL University, India
Sumit Mishra	IIIT Guwahati, India
Sunil C. K.	IIIT Dharwad, India
Supratim Gupta	NIT Rourkela, India
Suresh Sundaram	IIT Guwahati, India
Sushanta Kumar Sahu	Jadavpur University, India
Sushil Kumar	NIT Kurukshetra, India
Sweeti Sah	NIT Kurukshetra, India
T. Veerakumar	NIT Goa, India
Tanmay Kumar Behera	NIT Jalandhar, India
Tanushree Meena	IIT BHU Varanasi, India
Thurimerla Prasanth	IIITDM Kancheepuram, India
Tirath Prasad Sahu	NIT Raipur, India
T. P. Sharma	NIT Hamirpur, India
Tusarkanta Dalai	NIT Rourkela, India
Udai Pratap Rao	NIT Patna, India
Umamaheswara Sharma Bhutamapuram	NIT Calicut, India

Umesh Chandra Pati	NIT Rourkela, India
Upendra Pratap Singh	LNMIIT Jaipur, India
Upendra Kumar Sahoo	NIT Rourkela, India
Usha Rella Rani	CVR College of Engineering, India
V. K. Gupta	IIITDM Jabalpur, India
Veningston K.	NIT Srinagar, India
Venkata Phanikrishna	IIITV-ICD, India
Venkatesh Pandiri	IIITDM Kancheepuram, India
Venkateswara R. Kagita	NIT Warangal, India
Vijay M. Galshetwar	Punjab Engineering College, India
Vijayalakshmi M.	VIT Chennai, India
Vikram Singh	NIT Kurukshetra, India
Vinayak S. Nageli	CAIR DRDO, India
Vipin Gautam	IIT Goa, India
Vipin Milind Kamble	VNIT Nagpur, India
Vishal Satpute	VNIT Nagpur, India
Vivek Singh Baghel	National Taipei University of Technology, Taiwan
Vivek Singh Verma	HBTU Kanpur, India
Vivekraj K.	IIIT Dharwad, India
Vrinda Yadav	IIIT Nagpur, India
Watanabe Osamu	Takushoku University, Japan
Yogendra Prajapati	MNNIT Allahabad, India

Contents – Part I

Navigating the Night: Robust Night Scene Semantic Segmentation for Autonomous Driving

G. Murari, Prabha C. Nissimagoudar(✉), Nalini C. Iyer, and H. M. Gireesha

School of Electronics and Communication Engineering, KLE Technological University, Hubli, Karnataka, India
{pcnissimagoudar,nalinic,gireesh_hm}@kletech.ac.in

Abstract. In the dynamic field of autonomous driving, the study explores the crucial yet underexplored realm of night scene semantic segmentation. Despite advancements in daytime scenarios, challenges persist in nighttime scenes due to insufficient exposure and a scarcity of labeled data. To address these issues, the NightCity dataset was enriched by creating labeled nighttime images with diverse low-light conditions. Techniques such as adjusting illumination, contrast, brightness, and introducing blur were employed to enhance the dataset's complexity. This augmented dataset was then used to train an existing model, incorporating Dual Image-Adaptive Learnable Filters (DIAL-Filters). Comprising a Context-Aware Image Processing Module (CAIPM) and a Learnable Guided Filter (LGF), the DIAL-Filters aim to enhance semantic segmentation under varying illuminations during nighttime driving conditions. The CAIPM module integrates differentiable image filters within a compact neural network, adaptively improving images for enhanced segmentation under diverse illuminations. The Learnable Guided Filter (LGF) also refines the segmentation network output, contributing to the final segmentation result. The model underwent end-to-end hybrid supervised training using both the augmented and Cityscapes datasets, producing noteworthy results in night scene semantic segmentation. This dual-module approach optimizes the model for effective semantic segmentation in various nighttime driving conditions.

Keywords: Augmentation · Autonomous Driving · Semantic Segmentation · Learnable Guided Filter (LGF)

1 Introduction

In the domain of autonomous driving, accurate and precise scene understanding is paramount for safe and reliable navigation, particularly in challenging environments such as nighttime conditions. Despite significant advancements in daytime scene perception, the transition to nighttime presents unique challenges due to reduced visibility and varying lighting conditions. In this context, semantic segmentation of night scenes plays a critical role in enabling vehicles to interpret

J. Kakarla et al. (Eds.): CVIP 2024, CCIS 2473, pp. 1–14, 2026.
https://doi.org/10.1007/978-3-031-93688-3_1

their surroundings by categorizing image regions according to their object class. While instance segmentation and object detection techniques offer significant benefits in comprehending scenes, semantic segmentation offers a fine-grained understanding of the scene by categorizing each pixel into meaningful classes. This approach provides autonomous vehicles with richer contextual information essential for making informed decisions during navigation.

However, the predominant focus of research on daytime scenarios has left a gap in addressing the specific challenges of low-light environments. The limited availability of labeled nighttime datasets impeded the development and evaluation of robust segmentation algorithms tailored for night scenes. To address this issue, researchers have explored methodologies to adapt models trained during the day to nighttime conditions, employing techniques like domain adaptation and transfer learning. These efforts aim to enhance the generalization capabilities of semantic segmentation models across diverse lighting conditions, thereby improving performance in real-world autonomous driving scenarios.

Establishing benchmarks specific to nighttime segmentation is crucial for evaluating algorithm effectiveness and fostering collaboration within the research community. Standardized evaluation metrics and datasets empower researchers to compare the performance of various approaches and drive innovation in nighttime scene understanding. This paper introduces an innovative approach to semantic segmentation of nighttime scenes, designed to overcome the challenges posed by low-light conditions. By leveraging recent developments in deep learning techniques for image enhancement, this approach enhances the robustness and generalization capabilities of semantic segmentation models in nighttime scenarios. The method is evaluated on a newly curated nighttime dataset, demonstrating significant improvements in segmentation accuracy and robustness compared to baseline approaches. Through this research, the study aims to contribute to the advancement of autonomous driving by enabling vehicles to navigate safely and effectively in challenging nighttime conditions.

In this paper, the challenges of nighttime semantic segmentation for autonomous driving are addressed. The main contributions of this research are as follows:

1. **Dataset Enhancement:** An augmented version of the NightCity dataset is presented, incorporating a diverse range of labeled nighttime images with varying low-light conditions. This enhancement addresses the scarcity of labeled nighttime data and improves the robustness of models trained on it.
2. **Dual Image-Adaptive Learnable Filters (DIAL-Filters):** A novel framework is introduced, comprising two key components: (a) A Context-Aware Image Processing Module (CAIPM) that adaptively improves image quality for segmentation under diverse illuminations, and (b) A Learnable Guided Filter (LGF) that refines the segmentation network output.
3. **Hybrid Training Approach:** The effectiveness of a hybrid supervised training method is demonstrated, leveraging both the augmented NightC-

ity dataset and the Cityscapes dataset, resulting in improved performance in various nighttime driving conditions.

4. **Comprehensive Evaluation:** Extensive experimental results are provided, including comparisons with state-of-the-art methods, and generalization tests on unseen nighttime scenarios.

2 Related Work

2.1 Semantic Segmentation

Over the decades, extensive research efforts have been dedicated to semantic segmentation, particularly with the emergence of deep learning methodologies and convolutional neural networks (CNNs), proving its utility across numerous real-world applications. Finding multi-scale context and producing high-resolution representations are the two main design tenets that were adhered to when constructing architectures for this purpose.

FCN-based strategies, DeepLab variations, and multi-scale-sensitive architectures such as HRNet, and PSPNet have prominently advanced semantic segmentation and stand out as significant advancements within this domain. Moreover, the output of the segmentation network was enhanced with the addition of Atrous Convolution and Atrous Spatial Pyramid Pooling by deepLab and its variations. While existing methods have primarily addressed segmentation tasks in daytime conditions, this paper uniquely shifts the focus to night-time scenes. In particular, this study investigates how well the suggested DIAL filters work for segmenting driving scenes at night. For this evaluation, well-established segmentation networks are chosen, with RefineNet serving as the baseline for the semantic segmentation task. This adjustment allows us to assess the performance of our approach in challenging low-light conditions, offering insights into its potential applicability in nighttime scenarios.

2.2 Image Enhancement

Image enhancement techniques, such as those found in [1–4], are used to remap pixel values to make an image more visible. Wang et al. introduced a dynamic brightness configuration function [5] that adjusts the enhancement parameters based on the lighting distribution aspects of an input image. Xueqing Deng et al. [6] proposed a Regulated Light Adaptation Module as a means to enhance the evening images. Xu et al. proposed a frequency decomposition technique as a solution to mitigate the issue of under-exposure combined with noise in practical scenarios. Motivated by these techniques, this study implements an image enhancement network that uses a CNN-based parameter predictor network as part of a context-aware processing module to forecast the filter parameters of the differentiable filters for segmentation in nighttime driving scenarios.

2.3 Data Augmentation

According to recent research, data augmentation is essential for improving the volume, quality, and diversity of training data used in machine learning models. Data augmentation becomes an important regularization strategy in the search for massive amounts of annotated data, which are frequently collected and annotated manually. This approach seeks to improve the effectiveness of the model by adding more data to capture more broad characteristics of the underlying issue.

Among the three types of data augmentation—Affine Transformations, Non-Affine Geometric Transformations, and Photometric Transformations this paper focuses on Photometric Transformations. Specifically, it addresses real-world challenges in computer vision tasks caused by photometric effects, such as motion blur, optical noise, distortions, low illumination, and color artifacts. Photometric transformation methods simulate these effects through established digital image processing techniques, allowing the generation of diverse training images that enhance the model's visual understanding.

Unlike geometric methods, photometric image augmentation modifies pixel content while preserving spatial structure, often involving changes in RGB channel composition through classical image processing functions. The intuitive goal is to alter visual properties like color, brightness, sharpness, contrast, and saturation. This approach proves essential for deep learning models, boosting their robustness against variations in environmental conditions, including illumination, weather, and imaging device artifacts. By accounting for these factors, photometric data augmentation contributes to more resilient and adaptable deep learning models.

2.4 Nighttime Scene Parsing

Several researchers used domain adaptation-based techniques [7–9] to move the model trained in typical settings to the target domain to contribute to Nighttime Scene Parsing. A gradual adaption method was put forth in [10] to make the transition from day to night via the twilight time bridge. Based on DMAda [10], Sakaridis et al. [8] introduced a guided curriculum adaption approach that uses both annotated synthetic imagery alongside unannotated real-world images to iteratively refine segmentation models across day-night transitions. Before training the semantic segmentation models, some studies [11–13] trained additional style transfer networks, such as CycleGAN [14], to execute the day-to-night or night-to-day picture transfer. An illumination adjustment network is positioned at the forefront of the segmentation network in Wu et al.'s recently suggested unsupervised one-stage adaption technique [15]. In this study, segmentation network performance in diverse lighting conditions is enhanced by incorporating a pre-training image enhancement network. The model is trained in a hybrid manner, enabling it to adapt effectively to both daytime and nighttime scenes. This approach aims to improve overall segmentation accuracy and robustness across varying environmental conditions.

3 Methodology

To effectively address challenges related to poor visibility in nighttime driving scenarios, our proposed methodology focuses on mitigating exposure differences to enhance semantic output. A key element of our approach involves the integration of robust data augmentation techniques to augment the training dataset's diversity. This augmentation process strategically modifies image properties. In this study, segmentation network performance in diverse lighting conditions is enhanced by incorporating a pre-training image enhancement network. The model is trained in a hybrid manner, allowing it to adapt effectively to both daytime and night-time scenes. This approach aims to improve overall segmentation accuracy and robustness across varying environmental conditions by modifying properties such as contrast, and illumination, and introducing blur, thereby creating a more extensive and varied dataset. This diversity enables our Image Enhancement Network to learn from a wide range of image conditions and complexities.

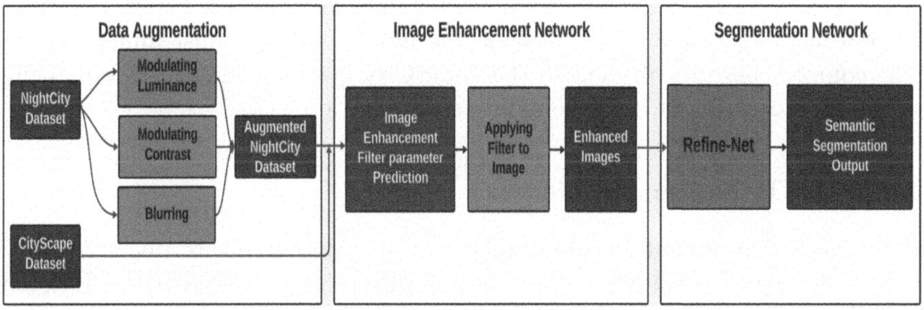

Fig. 1. "System Methodology: A concise overview outlining the key steps in our approach for Night Scene Semantic Segmentation"

As shown in Fig. 1, our methodology comprises three blocks: Data Augmentation, Image Enhancement Network, and the Segmentation Block. The Image Enhancement Network comprises a Context-Aware Image Processing module, which includes a CNN-based parameter predictor network and a set of differentiable filters. These filter parameters adapt to each image within the network and the network provides optimized parameter values, enhancing the image quality. The Segmentation Block includes a pre-trained segmentation model and a learnable guided filter, which enhances the segmentation output.

3.1 Data Augmentation

The Data Augmentation block is implemented before model training to enhance the NightCity dataset through precise transformations. Each transformation contributes to the model's resilience in night scene semantic segmentation. Luminance modulation involves scaling pixel values, and adjusting image brightness to account for variations in ambient lighting during different nighttime periods. This enables the model to effectively differentiate objects and structures in low-light situations. Contrast modulation sharpens the model's ability to distinguish between objects by adjusting the difference in pixel brightness, proving crucial in revealing subtle details in typically low-contrast night scenes. The introduction of controlled blur mitigates visual artifacts common in low-light environments, assisting the model in distinguishing relevant features from noise. Additionally, temporal augmentation exposes the model to images captured at different nighttime periods, enhancing its adaptability and generalization across diverse temporal conditions in night scenes.

Our data augmentation process applies these four individual transformations to each randomly selected set of 500 images from the NightCity dataset, adding complexity to the dataset. The complete dataset comprises 4,998 images for training and 1,299 for validation. Luminance, contrast, and blur modulation within the dataset are executed by adjusting values within the range of 0.3–0.7 for variability. This ensures a diverse set of images with modified luminance, contrast, and blur properties, enriching the training dataset and improving the model's ability to generalize across various lighting conditions during the night. The goal of this approach is to provide the model with a robust understanding of the complex features present in the NightCity Dataset, ultimately enhancing its performance in night scene semantic segmentation tasks.

3.2 Image Enhancement Network

The Image Enhancement Network consists of a "Context-Aware Image Processing Module" which comprises differentiable filters and a CNN-based Parameter predictor network to dynamically enhance image quality by adjusting filter parameters based on individual image content.

In the context of training the CNN-PP (CNN-based Parameter Predictor) network through gradient-based optimization, the filters need to be differentiable. This allows the network to undergo training via backpropagation. The differentiable filters in our technique, namely exposure, gamma, contrast, and sharpen, are the DIFs (differentiable image filters) having hyperparameters that may be adjusted. An input pixel value (r_i, g_i, b_i) is transformed into an output pixel value (r_o, g_o, b_o) by these pixel-wise filters, where (r, g, b) represents the values of the three color channels, correspondingly, red, green, and blue.

The main goal of the CNN-based parameter prediction network is to predict the parameters of the Dual Image Filters (DIF) by analyzing the overall content of the image, including aspects such as brightness, color, tone, and exposure level. Notably, it efficiently achieves this by utilizing a downscaled version of the input image, thereby significantly reducing computational requirements. The architecture of CNN based parameter prediction network comprises five convolutional blocks, leading to a dense layer that generates the image transformation parameters of the DIF filters. The CNN-PP model is remarkably effective, and it still has a lightweight design with only 278K parameters and a small portion of all the DIF hyperparameters 4. Training this network with a low-resolution iteration of the input image (downsampled to 256×256 resolution) helps to adeptly estimate the hyperparameters of the DIF.

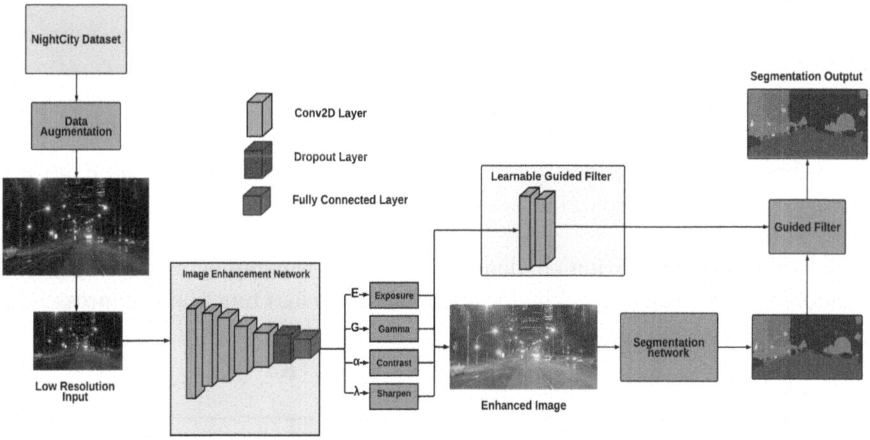

Fig. 2. Our end-to-end training pipeline incorporates a compact CNN-PP for hyper-parameter prediction, along with data augmentation before processing high-resolution images through the DIF module, unlocking enhanced segmentation performance.

3.3 Segmentation Network

The Segmentation Block in this methodology is a pivotal component that utilizes the RefineNet architecture, with ResNet-101 serving as its backbone. ResNet-101 provides the foundational architecture for feature extraction within the RefineNet framework. For the implementation of the Segmentation Block, a pre-trained RefineNet model is employed, which has been trained for 150,000 epochs on the Cityscapes dataset. The decision to use a pre-trained model is driven by the complexities involved in training such intricate architectures from scratch, which typically require significant computational resources and time.

A learnable guide filter (LGF) is added behind the segmentation network to improve segmentation outcomes even more, similar to [16]. The segmentation network produces an output with 19 channels, and the guided map generated by the learnable guided filter from the enhanced image is employed to refine the segmentation output. The LGF layer operation includes two convolutional layers with 64 and 19 output channels, comprising a total of 1,491 parameters. To address the challenge of uneven pixel distribution, particularly for small-sized objects in driving scene images, a re-weighting scheme based on a prior approach [15] is employed during training.
In particular, for every category $p \in C$,

$$w'_p = -\log(a_p) \tag{1}$$

where a_p is the percentage of all valid pixels in source domain C that are assigned the category p label.

The above equation assigns higher weights to categories with a lower proportion of annotated pixels in the labeled Cityscapes dataset. This facilitates the segmentation of smaller objects.

To normalize the weights w'_p an additional adjustment is made using the equation

$$w_p = \frac{w'_p - \bar{w}}{\sigma(w)} \cdot \mathrm{std} + \mathrm{avg} \tag{2}$$

where the mean and standard deviation of w'_p are represented by $\bar{w}$, $\sigma(w)$ and *std*, an adjustable hyperparameter. *std* is initially set to 0.05 and average = 0.01 during training.

To address segmentation challenges effectively, we employ a commonly used weighted cross-entropy loss. The formulation of the loss function is expressed as:

$$L_{\mathrm{seg}} = -\frac{1}{|P|} \sum_{n \in P} w_p \| \mathrm{GT}^{(n)} \cdot \log(K^{(n)}) \|_1 \tag{3}$$

where the n-th channel of the segmentation result is indicated by $K^{(n)}$, w'_p is the weight determined according to (Eq. 1), N denotes the count of valid pixels within the respective segmented image, $|P|$ signifies the number of labeled categories in the Cityscapes dataset and $GT^{(n)}$ stands for the one-hot encoding of the ground truth for the n-th category. This loss function plays a crucial role in guiding the training process towards accurate segmentation results

The transfer learning of the Segmentation Block is performed in a hybrid manner, incorporating both CityScape and NightCity datasets. The combination includes images captured during both day and night times, allowing the model to adapt to the challenges posed by varying lighting conditions. This hybrid learning approach enables the segmentation network to generalize well and effectively handle the transition from day to night, contributing to improved semantic segmentation performance in nighttime driving scenes.

Table 1. Comparing individual class Intersection over Union (IOU) scores on the NightCity test dataset across various state-of-the-art methods and our proposed approach, emphasizing the superior results in bold.

Method	road	sidewalk	building	wall	fence	pole	light	scene	vegetation	terrain	sky	person	rider	car	truck	bus	train	motorcycle	bicycle	**mIOU**
Pix2PixHD	85.9	33.5	68.8	**50.0**	42.9	27.0	13.8	34.6	47.9	20.1	82.8	35.5	12.1	72.7	53.5	58.3	42.6	17.3	25.0	43.38
DIAL	**89.56**	**47.02**	**82.23**	44.37	44.0	**32.47**	**28.49**	**51.01**	**57.78**	**22.78**	**86.53**	**50.14**	13.03	**78.57**	**63.98**	**68.96**	**46.37**	**25.68**	**38.96**	51.21
Ours	89.33	45.93	82.18	43.75	**44.11**	30.0	26.41	49.3	57.66	21.22	86.3	47.99	**14.01**	78.52	63.28	65.91	37.84	22.5	36.48	49.62

4 Dataset and Evaluation Metrics

In assessing our experiments, we opted for the mean of category-specific Intersection over Union (mIoU) as the metric for evaluation. The evaluation process involves utilizing the following datasets for both training and evaluating the model performance.

Cityscapes Dataset: Cityscapes plays a crucial role as a semantic understanding dataset, with a specific emphasis on capturing daytime urban street scenes. Widely acknowledged as a standard dataset for semantic segmentation tasks, which consists of 19 categories of pixel-level semantic annotations. With a size of $2{,}048 \times 1{,}024$ pixels, the dataset consists of 2,975 training photos, 500 validation snapshots, and 1,525 testing images. In our research, Cityscapes is employed as the labeled dataset for hybrid supervised training in daytime scenarios.

NightCity Dataset: NightCity stands as a comprehensive dataset specifically designed to capture nighttime city driving scenes, featuring pixel-level semantic annotations ideal for supervised semantic segmentation. The original dataset comprises 2,998 images for training and 1,299 images for validation or testing, each annotated with 19 categories identical to Cityscapes. Through the application of Data Augmentation techniques, the NightCity dataset is expanded to include 4,998 images for training and 1,299 images for validation. This augmentation ensures a diverse representation of images under various lighting conditions.

5 Implementation Details

In our execution, we embedded DIAL filters within the segmentation network, thus molding our methodology for nighttime semantic segmentation. Figure 2 depicts the arrangement of the Context-Aware Image Processing Module Modulation (CAIPM) and Learnable Guided Filters (LGF) components, positioned at the head and end of the segmentation network, respectively. To refine the training procedure further, we utilized random cropping at dimensions of 512×512, adjusting the scale between 0.5 and 1.0 for variation. Additionally, random horizontal flipping was employed to augment the training data. The input images underwent pre-processing through the CNN-PP network for image enhancement. This hybrid enhancement process generated feature maps for four filters, enhancing the images at the pixel level. The resulting enhanced images were then fed into the segmentation network for transfer learning, utilizing a pre-trained RefineNet model trained on the Cityscapes dataset for 150,000 epochs.

We conduct end-to-end training for our model over 50,000 steps. We apply a 5×10^{-4} weight decay and a momentum of 0.9 to the Stochastic Gradient Descent (SGD) optimizer to optimize the model. The initial setting for the learning rate is at 2.5×10^{-4}, we incorporate a polynomial learning rate policy, progressively decreasing it with a power of 0.9. The entire training procedure is carried out on an Nvidia GeForce RTX T5000 GPU equipped with 16 GB of memory.

6 Results

In our detailed analysis of model contributions for each class, as depicted in Table 1, it becomes evident that our methodology leads to significant improvements across various classes when compared to other methods. Notably, our model excels, particularly in two classes, outperforming the DIAL Method. Specifically, our model demonstrates strong performance in segmenting challenging classes such as "rider" and "fence" compared to other methods.

For instance, after implementing our methodology, the mIOU score for the "rider" class increases from 13.03 to 14.01, while the mIOU score for the "fence" class increases from 44.0 to 44.11. The corresponding qualitative results are illustrated in Fig. 3. However, it is crucial to acknowledge that certain classes did not exhibit improvement, such as "wall" and "train". This lack of improvement is attributed to the similarity between "wall" and "building", leading to potential confusion, especially in dark environments. Additionally, the similarity between "train" and "bus" in the NightCity dataset is confusing. Nevertheless, our approach proves more effective for other similar classes.

To assess the robustness of our model, we conducted evaluations on the established NightCity Dataset. We present the mean Intersection over Union (mIoU) results of various methods, all trained on both Cityscapes and NightCity datasets in a hybrid manner. The evaluation is done on the validation set of NightCity, and the outcomes are documented in Table 2. We assessed our model by a comparison analysis against several cutting-edge scene parsing techniques, including SegNet [17], FCN-8s [18], PSPNet [19], BiSeNet [20], PSANet [21], ESPNet [22]and the most widely used baseline models such DeepLabv2 [23] and RefineNet [24]. The results presented in Table 2 demonstrate that our model consistently outperforms these methods.

Table 2. Evaluation of our approach against state-of-the-art methods on the NightCity test dataset, where "(C + N)" denotes models trained with combined Cityscape and NightCity data and "N(t)" denotes NightCity test set.)

Methods	mIOU % on $N(t)(C+N)$
SegNet [17]	18.1
FCN-8s [18]	28.1
PSANet [21]	28.8
ESPNet [22]	34.2
BiseNet [20]	46.2
DeepLabv2 [23]	46.39
PSPNet [19]	47.29
RefineNet [24]	48.70
Ours (RefineNet)	49.62

Figure 3 provides a visual representation of the results obtained through our methodology. The images exhibit varying degrees of under- or over-exposures, making recognition and segmentation challenging. The visual sequence illustrates multiple stages, starting from input through enhancement to segmentation, offering a comprehensive understanding of the process.

(a) Input Image (b) Enhanced Input Image (c) Segmented Image (d) Ground-Truth Image

Fig. 3. Visual Representation of qualitative results obtained from our methodology on the NightCity+ test set.

The effectiveness of our model is attributed to the data augmentation performed before training, enabling it to handle diverse images under varying night conditions with different illuminations. This augmentation facilitated the learning of complex and critical features for light enhancement, contributing to precise segmentation.

The results demonstrate the capability of our methodology to finely segment input images, even in challenging lighting conditions, showcasing the robustness and effectiveness of our approach.

7 Conclusion

In conclusion, our proposed approach for semantic segmentation in nighttime driving conditions demonstrates notable advancements in accuracy and performance. By adaptively enhancing input images through data augmentation and introducing dual image-adaptive learnable filters (DIAL filters), we address the challenges associated with low-light scenarios. The incorporation of a differentiable Context-Aware Image Processing module, guided by a small convolutional neural network, further refines the segmentation process. The end-to-end training, with weak supervision guiding parameter prediction, ensures the effective learning of the DIF module. Experimental results on supervised datasets underscore the superiority of our method over existing nighttime driving-scene semantic segmentation techniques. The adaptability and robustness of our approach position it as a promising solution for real-world applications, contributing to the advancement of computer vision in challenging nighttime environments. This work contributes to the advancement of perception-based autonomous applications, enhancing vehicle safety and paving the way for further innovations in the field of autonomous driving technologies.

References

1. Yan, Z., Zhang, H., Wang, B., Paris, S., Yu, Y.: Automatic photo adjustment using deep neural networks. ACM TOG **35**(2), 1–15 (2016)
2. Wang, S., Zheng, J., Hu, H., Li, B.: Naturalness preserved enhancement algorithm for non-uniform illumination images. IEEE Trans. Image Process. **22**(9), 3538–3548 (2013)
3. Li, C., Guo, J., Porikli, F., Pang, Y.: LightenNet: a convolutional neural network for weakly illuminated image enhancement. Pattern Recogn. Lett. **104**, 15–22 (2017)
4. Ying, Z., Li, G., Ren, Y., Wang, R., Wang, W.: A new low-light image enhancement algorithm using camera response model. In: IEEE ICCV (2017)
5. Wang, J., Zhuang, W., Shang, D.: Light enhancement algorithm optimization for autonomous driving vision in night scenes based on YOLACT++. In: 2022 3rd International Conference on Information Science, Parallel and Distributed Systems (ISPDS), pp. 417–423. IEEE (2022)
6. Deng, X., Wang, P., Lian, X., Newsam, S.: NightLab: a dual-level architecture with hardness detection for segmentation at night. In: Proceedings of the IEEE/CVF Conference on Computer Vision and Pattern Recognition, pp. 16938–16948 (2022)
7. Sakaridis, C., Dai, D., Van Gool, L.: Map-guided curriculum domain adaptation and uncertainty-aware evaluation for semantic nighttime image segmentation. IEEE Trans. Pattern Anal. Mach. Intell. **44**(6), 3139–3153 (2020)
8. Sakaridis, C., Dai, D., Gool, L.V.: Guided curriculum model adaptation and uncertainty-aware evaluation for semantic nighttime image segmentation. In: Proceedings of the IEEE/CVF International Conference on Computer Vision, pp. 7374–7383 (2019)

9. Hu, Y., He, H., Xu, C., Wang, B., Lin, S.: Exposure: a white-box photo post-processing framework. ACM Trans. Graph. (TOG) **37**(2), 26 (2018)
10. Dai, D., Van Gool, L.: Dark model adaptation: semantic image segmentation from daytime to nighttime. In: IEEE Intelligent Transportation Systems Conference, pp. 3819–3824 (2018)
11. Sun, L., Wang, K., Yang, K., Xiang, K.: See clearer at night: towards robust nighttime semantic segmentation through day-night image conversion. In: Artificial Intelligence and Machine Learning in Defense Applications, vol. 11169, p. 111690A. International Society for Optics and Photonics (2019)
12. Nag, S., Adak, S., Das, S.: What's there in the dark. In: International Conference on Image Processing, pp. 2996–3000. IEEE (2019)
13. Romera, E., Bergasa, L.M., Yang, K., Alvarez, J.M., Barea, R.: Bridging the day and night domain gap for semantic segmentation. In: 2019 IEEE Intelligent Vehicles Symposium, pp. 1312–1318 (2019)
14. Zhu, J.Y., Park, T., Isola, P., Efros, A.A.: Unpaired image-to-image translation using cycle-consistent adversarial networks. In: Proceedings of the IEEE/CVF International Conference on Computer Vision, pp. 2242–2251 (2017)
15. Wu, X., Wu, Z., Guo, H., Ju, L., Wang, S.: DANNet: a one-stage domain adaptation network for unsupervised nighttime semantic segmentation. In: Proceedings of the IEEE/CVF Conference on Computer Vision and Pattern Recognition, pp. 15769–15778 (2021)
16. Liu, W., Li, W., Zhu, J., Cui, M., Xie, X., Zhang, L.: Improving nighttime driving-scene segmentation via dual image-adaptive learnable filters. IEEE Trans. Circ. Syst. Video Tech. (2023)
17. Badrinarayanan, V., Kendall, A., Cipolla, R.: SegNet: a deep convolutional encoder-decoder architecture for scene segmentation. IEEE Trans. Pattern Anal. Mach. Intell. (2017)
18. Long, J., Shelhamer, E., Darrell, T.: Fully convolutional networks for semantic segmentation. In: IEEE CVPR, pp. 3431–3440 (2015)
19. Zhao, H., Shi, J., Qi, X., Wang, X., Jia, J.: Pyramid scene parsing network. In: IEEE CVPR (2017)
20. Yu, C., Wang, J., Peng, C., Gao, C., Yu, G., Sang, N.: BiSeNet: bilateral segmentation network for real-time semantic segmentation. In: ECCV 2018, pp. 325–341 (2018)
21. Zhao, H., et al.: PSANet: point-wise spatial attention network for scene parsing. In: ECCV 2018, pp. 267–283 (2018)
22. Mehta, S., Rastegari, M., Caspi, A., Shapiro, L., Hajishirzi, H.: ESPNet: efficient spatial pyramid of dilated convolutions for semantic segmentation. In: ECCV (2018)
23. Chen, L.-C., Papandreou, G., Kokkinos, I., Murphy, K., Yuille, A.L.: DeepLab: semantic image segmentation with deep convolutional nets, atrous convolution, and fully connected CRFs. PAMI **40**(4), 834–848 (2017)
24. Lin, G., Milan, A., Shen, C., Reid, I.: RefineNet: multi-path refinement networks for high-resolution semantic segmentation. In: IEEE CVPR, pp. 1925–1934 (2017)
25. Tan, X., Xu, K., Cao, Y., Zhang, Y., Ma, L., Lau, R.W.: Night-time scene parsing with a large real dataset. IEEE Trans. Image Process. **30**, 9085–9098 (2021)
26. Wang, H., et al.: SFNet-N: an improved SFNet algorithm for semantic segmentation of low-light autonomous driving road scenes. IEEE Trans. Intell. Transp. Syst. **23**(11), 21405–21417 (2022)

27. Wang, Q., Gao, J., Li, X.: Weakly supervised adversarial domain adaptation for semantic segmentation in urban scenes. IEEE Trans. Image Process. **28**(9), 4376–4386 (2019)
28. Wang, W., Chen, Z., Yuan, X., Guan, F.: An adaptive weak light image enhancement method. In: Twelfth International Conference on Signal Processing Systems, vol. 11719, p. 1171902. International Society for Optics and Photonics (2021)
29. Hu, P., Shuai, B., Liu, J., Wang, G.: Deep level sets for salient object detection. In: Proceedings of the IEEE Conference on Computer Vision and Pattern Recognition, pp. 2300–2309 (2017)

DiverseCeph19: A Cephalometric Landmarks Annotation Dataset

S. Rashmi[1(✉)], S. Srinath[2], Seema Deshmukh[3], Karthikeya Patil[4], and S. Prashanth[3]

[1] Dept. of School of Computer Science, RV University, Bangalore, India
rashmibe.nayak@gmail.com
[2] Dept. of Computer Science & Engineering, JSS Science & Technology University, Mysuru, India
[3] Dept. of Pediatric and Preventive Dentistry, JSS Dental College & Hospital, Mysuru, India
[4] Dept. of Oral Medicine and Radiology, JSS Dental College & Hospital, Mysuru, India

Abstract. Automation of cephalometric landmark annotation holds significant importance within the domain as a research area. This article presents a dataset consisting of 1692 cephalometric radiograph images, along with manually annotated data on 19 anatomical cephalometric landmarks. The data is available in individual text files corresponding to individual radiographic image files. Along with this, the latest annotation formats like COCO JSON and YOLO file formats for artificial intelligence (AI) model training are also available. Annotations are performed by experienced medical professionals with more than twenty years of experience and technical professionals with 6 years of research experience in the domain. The images are pre-processed and segregated based on resolution, image quality, dental structure, and other artifacts. The final image data is saved in BMP format with 0.127 mm/pixel resolution. The images refer to cephalometric analysis performed between 2011 and 2022 in patients treated at JSS Dental College and Hospital (JSS DCH), with patients age between 5 to 60 years. The demographic information of patients is not available with individual image data. Ethical clearance is obtained from the Institutional Ethical Committee of JSS DCH. Various levels of experimentation are carried out using the dataset, and the results demonstrate robust performance. Landmark annotation based on segregation type is one of the first types in this area of cephalometric landmark annotation. The availability of this dataset offers researchers a robust platform for investigating and conducting experiments using machine learning and deep learning techniques.

Keywords: Cephalometric radiographs · Anatomical Landmarks · Dataset · Machine Learning · Deep Learning

1 Introduction

Cephalometric images are radiographic images of the human head and neck region, predominantly used in dentistry and orthodontics for various diagnostic and treatment planning purposes. These radiograph images help in understanding the skeletal and

J. Kakarla et al. (Eds.): CVIP 2024, CCIS 2473, pp. 15–27, 2026.
https://doi.org/10.1007/978-3-031-93688-3_2

soft tissue structure of the craniofacial region, assisting in the easy understanding of the dental and skeletal relationship, craniofacial growth pattern, and other anatomical abnormalities [1]. Lateral cephalometry represents a specific category of cephalometric imaging, involving the acquisition of radiographs depicting the lateral view of the human skull. Using these lateral cephalometric images, a series of anatomical landmarks are identified, followed by the computation of predetermined linear and angular measurements. This comprehensive procedure is commonly referred to as a cephalometric analysis. Dentists and orthodontists utilize cephalometric analysis to assess a range of conditions, including classifications of skeletal structure, issues related to tooth alignment, and other facial proportion discrepancies [2]. The initial phase of cephalometric analysis, wherein landmarks are localized, assumes paramount importance, as it significantly influences the entirety of the analysis. The conventional method employed for anatomical landmark identification is manual localization on the cephalometric radiographs. This standard method of annotation does not withstand its inherent limitations such as subjectivity, susceptibility to errors, and time-intensive nature [3, 4]. Moreover, the burgeoning integration of artificial intelligence into the medical sciences domain presents ample opportunities for automating the landmark localization process.

Since the early 1990s, efforts to automate cephalometric landmark identification have been underway. Initial methodologies were trialled on datasets ranging from 2 to 200 images, predominantly leveraging statistical approaches [5–11]. However, these methods exhibited a wide spectrum of detection accuracies, ranging from 50% to 95%, rendering direct comparisons between them impractical due to variations in dataset size and characteristics. Moreover, these solutions demonstrated strong correlations with factors such as image noise, radiographic exposure, biological variability [12], and limited adaptability to accommodate larger sets of landmarks due to their ad-hoc nature [7]. Additionally, variations existed in dataset curation, annotation protocols, landmark count, and quantitative evaluation metrics among these methods. During the early 20s, a transition occurred towards classic machine learning approaches employing diverse feature extraction methods. These methodologies further diverged in dataset handling, annotation techniques, landmark quantity, and evaluation metrics. To address these disparities, a unified dataset was introduced by ISBI in 2015 [13, 14], prompting subsequent experimentation with modern machine-learning techniques [14–18]. In recent years, despite the availability of benchmark datasets, the quantity of images contained within them has proven inadequate for the requirements of contemporary deep-learning methodologies. Consequently, researchers have resorted to utilizing private datasets, yielding higher landmark detection accuracies [19–22]. However, despite promising results obtained from private datasets with varying image and landmark counts, a comprehensive performance comparison remains elusive due to the absence of publicly available datasets. Consequently, the need arose for the aggregation of a comprehensive dataset and corresponding annotations to facilitate standardized research practices. The public availability of such a dataset would streamline research efforts, enabling direct comparisons and advancements in the performance of state-of-the-art AI methodologies.

The precise localization of cephalometric landmarks plays a crucial role in quantifying and classifying skeletal structures. However, the manual process of localizing landmarks is laborious. Despite continuous efforts to develop automated cephalometric landmark detection systems, their effectiveness in orthodontic applications remains limited. This inadequacy can be attributed to the insufficient publicly available datasets and training images for training AI models. Robust AI software, particularly those based on deep learning, necessitates large and diverse datasets. To address the scarcity of relevant datasets, this article presents a dataset containing diversified cephalometric landmark annotation data. This dataset aims to alleviate the shortage of openly accessible data in the field, potentially serving as a solution for developing more effective AI software. By leveraging this comprehensive dataset, researchers and developers in the orthodontic domain can enhance automated cephalometric landmark detection, thereby improving the accuracy, efficiency, and reliability of diagnosis and treatment planning processes. The major contributions of our dataset are outlined as follows:

- Our dataset boasts the largest annotated collection to date, comprising 1692 lateral cephalometric images. Each image features annotations for 19 cephalometric landmarks, meticulously annotated and validated by a team of three medical professionals and two technical experts.
- The dataset includes novel segregation of images based on resolution, image quality, dental structure, and the presence of artifacts, representing a pioneering approach to dataset organization.
- The annotation labels are provided in three distinct formats namely individual text format, COCO JSON format, and YOLO format to facilitate experimentation and analysis.

The paper is structured as follows: Sect. 2 provides an extensive examination of existing datasets, emphasizing the disparities between the current dataset and other publicly accessible datasets. Section 3 outlines the procedures involved in dataset collection and annotation. In Sect. 4, we delineate the dataset, elucidating the complete specifications of the dataset. Finally, Sect. 5 delves into the application and potential use of the dataset.

2 Existing Datasets

Dataset 1[1]: The IEEE International Symposium on Biomedical Imaging (ISBI) initiated the grand challenge on cephalometric images in 2014 [23], extending it into the following year [13]. As part of this challenge, a benchmark dataset was released in two stages. This dataset comprised 400 lateral cephalometric images, each annotated with 19 landmarks by both senior and junior professionals. The mean values of these annotations served as the ground truth data. Additionally, the individual annotation files included eight significant measurements pertinent to cephalometric analysis. The primary objective of the challenge was to automate the annotation task and subsequently compute linear and angular measurements, along with performing skeletal structure classification. The images had a resolution of 1935×2400 pixels, with a pixel resolution of 0.1 mm/pixel, obtained using the Soredex CRANEX Excel cephalometric X-ray machine. The radiograph images are collected from subjects age ranging between 6 to 60 years, from the Dental Department, Tri-Service General Hospital, Taiwan. However, notable observations emerged from the experimentation results of this dataset. The dataset was divided

[1] https://figshare.com/s/37ec464af8e81ae6ebbf.

into three subsets: train (150 images), test1 (150 images), and test2 (100 images). While experimentation reports consistently demonstrated high success detection rates (SDR) and low mean radial error (MRE) for the test1 dataset, the test2 set exhibited relatively lower SDR and higher MRE. This discrepancy suggested that the annotation models trained on the training images failed to accurately generalize to the test2 images [14–18, 24]. To address this issue, several methods deviated from the train/test split suggested by ISBI and employed cross-validation techniques to report results [25, 26]. These approaches succeeded in achieving higher detection accuracy compared to previously reported results. However, despite these advancements, the limited number of images in the dataset posed a challenge for experiments utilizing latest deep learning models with foundational architecture.

Dataset 2[2]: In 2020, Zeng et al. publicly released another dataset known as the PKU Dataset, as detailed in their work [24]. This dataset comprises 102 images, each with a resolution of 2089 × 1937 pixels and a pixel resolution of 0.125 mm/pixel. The radiograph images were captured using the Planmeca ProMax 3D cephalometric X-ray machine. These images were sourced from patient data within the Fourth Clinical Division, School and Hospital of Stomatology, Peking University, spanning an age range from 9 to 53 years. Similar to the previous dataset, the PKU Dataset features annotations for 19 landmarks, performed by two experienced professionals. Experimental results conducted on this dataset demonstrate reasonable predictions, with a reasonable mean radial error [24, 27]. Given its size, this dataset can only serve as an auxiliary dataset to validate the latest methods trained on larger datasets, as it may not be sufficient to train the latest deep learning models.

Dataset 3: In 2023, Khalid et al. made a significant contribution to cephalometric analysis by releasing a CEPHA29 dataset comprising 1000 images. These images were gathered from patients undergoing orthodontic treatment at Islamic International Dental College, Riphah International University, Islamabad, Pakistan, utilizing seven different image-capturing devices with varying pixel resolutions [28]. The dataset was made available as part of the ISBI 2023 grand challenge [29]. It includes annotation information for 29 landmarks, along with labels for the cervical vertebral maturation (CVM) stage classification. The dataset is divided into 700 test images, 150 validation images, and 150 test images. While the dataset is not currently freely accessible, interested parties may request access from the corresponding author. To date, neither the ISBI grand challenge committee nor any other individual researcher has reported results using this dataset.

After examining all the datasets mentioned above, it becomes evident that there is a lack of Indian-based cephalometric annotation datasets. This absence is significant as skeletal structure can vary based on factors such as race and region. Furthermore, it is noted that the existing datasets do not include images with mixed dentition, soft tissue profiles that are not commonly observed, images with artifacts, or images with dental braces. Flexibility in including these images can be given for experiments, as each piece of data in medical science holds significant informational value. Incorporating such diverse images into the dataset would enhance its variability, and training with this complex dataset would contribute to the development of robust and generic models.

[2] https://doi.org/10.6084/m9.figshare.13265471.v1.

3 Data Collection and Annotation

The dataset prepared comprises 1692 radiographic images of lateral cephalograms sourced from the JSS DCH, affiliated with the JSS Academy of Higher Education and Research (JSS AHER) in Mysuru. The work is part of a collaborative research effort involving cooperation between the Department of Computer Science and Engineering, JSS Science and Technology University, and JSS DCH.

The images were derived from a cohort of 1557 subjects, consisting of 763 females and 794 males, spanning an age range from 5 to 60 years. The lateral cephalometric scans conducted over the period from 2011 to 2023 are considered for work. Utilizing the Planmeca Promax- Scara 3 machine with Romexis software, the images were originally saved in JPEG format, exhibiting varying image resolutions, with a pixel resolution of 0.127 mm/pixel. Patient names were used for image identification. To ensure anonymity and streamline the dataset for research purposes, the images underwent initial cropping to remove patient information located at the bottom of the cephalometric image which contained the subject's details, age, and date of capture of the radiograph. Subsequently, the images are renamed with consecutive numerical identifiers. Following these preprocessing steps, the images are filtered based on different resolutions. Two major resolutions, 1341x1938 and 1257x1672, were selected to accommodate the diverse research requirements. These images were then converted and stored in BMP format. Additionally, the images are segregated based on complexity from a deep learning perspective. The categorization is based on the presence of dental braces and metal holding, the visibility of soft tissue landmarks, and whether the subject is wearing ornaments, etc. These categorizations aim to support the comprehensive nature of the research and enable more targeted investigations. The visual representation of images distributed in the dataset containing Normal, Full Ceph, Soft Tissue Clarity, Complex Teeth Structure, Ornaments, and Dental Braces in both resolution sets is shown in Fig. 1.

Fig. 1. Data distribution graphs

Each image was sequentially numbered according to the segregation categories. Details regarding the segregation and corresponding image numbering are provided in the accompanying Table 1.

Annotation commenced subsequent to image preprocessing and categorization. A total of 19 landmarks were chosen for annotation, representing a standard set utilized

Table 1. Distribution and Descriptive Categories of data segregation.

Resolution	Category	Image Number		Description
		Start	End	
SET1 1341x1938	1_Normal	1	1246	Images without any complexities are mentioned below
	2_Soft_Tissue_Clarity	1247	1269	Radiographs where the soft tissue profile is indistinct
	3_Complex_Teeth_Structure	1270	1406	Radiographs depicting mixed dentition
	4_Ornaments	1407	1450	Radiographs displaying nose pins or earrings
	5_Dental_braces	1451	1565	Radiographs of patients wearing dental braces or metal holdings
SET2 1257 × 1672	1_Normal	1566	1668	Images without any complexities are mentioned below
	2_Soft_Tissue_Clarity	1669	1671	Radiographs where the soft tissue profile is indistinct
	3_Complex_Teeth_Structure	1672	1679	Radiographs depicting mixed dentition
	4_Ornaments	1680	1684	Radiographs displaying nose pins or earrings
	5_Dental_braces	1685	1692	Radiographs of patients wearing dental braces or metal holdings

across numerous studies. These landmarks provide important reference points for analyzing and evaluating craniofacial structures in cephalometric radiographs. Figure 2 illustrates a sample image annotated with these 19 landmarks, each labeled with its respective name. Initial annotation tasks were conducted by two experienced practitioners, each possessing more than 20 years of expertise in the relevant field. Subsequently, these annotations underwent thorough review and validation by a third professional with more than 25 years of experience. The final landmark coordinates were determined through consensus among the three experts. Initially, attempts were made to obtain annotation pixel coordinates using Nemoceph and Webceph software. However, these software solutions did not provide satisfactory results for accurate landmark ground truth collection, as they required manual adjustments by professionals. Subsequently, individual landmarks were manually annotated using the ImageJ labeling tool, with annotation information primarily exported to a text file. Subsequently, the annotations were converted into COCO JSON and YOLO formats for enhanced usability. As all the images had the same pixel spacing, there was no need for image-level calibration adjustments. Bounding box values for COCO format and YOLO format are calculated by considering minimum and maximum x and y coordinates among all keypoints. These coordinates define the top-left (x_min, y_min) and bottom-right (x_max, y_max) corners of the bounding box.

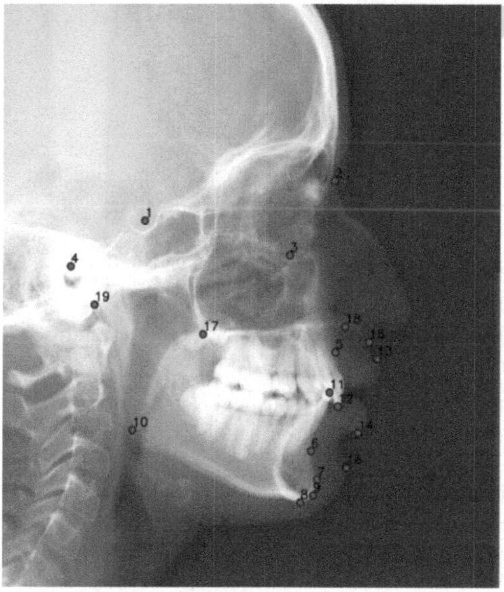

Number	Abbreviation	Name
L1	S	Sella
L2	Na	Nasion
L3	Or	Orbitale
L4	Po	Porion
L5	A	Subspinale
L6	B	Supramentale
L7	Pog	Pogonion
L8	Me	Menton
L9	Gn	Gnathion
L10	Go	Gonion
L11	L1	Incision Inferius
L12	U1	Incision Supirius
L13	UL	Upper Lip
L14	LL	Lower Lip
L15	Sn	Subnasale
L16	Pog'	Soft Tissue Pogonion
L17	PNS	Posterior Nasal Spine
L18	ANS	Anterior Nasal Spine
L19	Ar	Articulare

Fig. 2. Sample image with a list of 19 landmarks annotated on radiograph.

Ethical clearance for the collection and annotation of the dataset is obtained from the Institutional Ethical Committee of JSS Dental College and Hospital (JSSDCH IEC Research Protocol No. 78/2023). Additionally, the committee waived the necessity for patient consent, given the retrospective nature of the study focusing solely on radiographs. Subsequent to insightful discussions and recommendations from the review meeting, a decision was made to crop out patient information from the cephalometric images and rename them. This precautionary measure was implemented to safeguard the privacy and confidentiality of patient data.

4 Dataset Specification

The complete specification of the dataset prepared is shown below in Table 2.

By incorporating the expertise of technical and medical professionals and the review process by senior medical professionals, the annotation process aimed to achieve precise and reliable results. During the annotation phase, a collaborative effort between a technical professional with technical research experience and a medical professional with professional experience was undertaken. Their combined expertise contributed to accurately labeling the data. Individual images are carefully observed, categorized, and annotated, as shown in Fig. 3. Additionally, the resolution of the collected data is adjusted to 2 distinct resolutions to maintain consistency throughout the dataset.

Table 2. Dataset Specifications.

Subject	Dentistry, Oral Surgery and Medicine, Computer Vision and Pattern Recognition, Artificial Intelligence
Title	DiverseCeph19: Diverse Dataset of Cephalometric Radiographs with 19 landmarks
Type of data	Images (JPEG format)
How the data were acquired	Images are acquired using Panmeca Promax-Scara 3 machine with Romexis software, pixel size of 0.127 mm/pixel with different resolutions Landmarks are annotated using ImageJ software
Data format	Image: BMP format Labels: Individual text format, COCO JSON format, and YOLO format
Description of data collection	• Each image collected from the hospital is first cropped to eliminate the patient-related information like name, sex, age, and date of image capture • Images are cropped to 2 distinct resolutions: 1341x1938 and 1257x1672 based on the lateral cephalometric region covered in the raw images and are saved in BMP format • Further, within individual resolution, images are segregated based on various factors, like 1. Teeth structure (supernumerary teeth, unerupted teeth) 2. Visibility of soft tissue profile 3. Presence of orthodontic braces 4. Presence of earrings or a nose pin • Segregated image data is annotated by technical and medical professionals using ImageJ software (v1.53q). Identified landmarks are reviewed by experienced medical professionals, and finally, the landmark pixel locations are extracted into a text file
Data source location	Institution: JSS DCH, JSS AHER City: Mysuru Country: India
Related research article	Preliminary experiment findings are published in the articles [30]
Data availability	Data reposited in Indian Biological Image Archive with ID:IBIAP_1000000015

Three standard evaluation metrics are defined for the cephalometric landmark annotation task: success detection rate (SDR), mean radial error (MRE), and standard deviation (SD). These metrics can be used to evaluate the performance of models using the dataset. SDR is the ratio of landmarks accurately localized within the allowed radial precision (2 mm, 2.5 mm, 3 mm, 4 mm) to the total number of landmarks. A higher SDR indicates better performance in accurately localizing landmarks. The SDR is calculated as shown in Eq. 1.

$$SDR = \frac{Count\ of\ Landmarks\ located\ within\ Radial\ Error\ Range}{Total\ count\ of\ Landmarks\ (N)} * 100 \quad (1)$$

MRE is an average of the Euclidean error between the prediction coordinates and ground truth coordinates. MRE indicates the overall localization error in terms of mm, as shown in Eq. 2.

$$MRE = \frac{1}{N}\sum\nolimits_{i=1}^{N} \|Predictection\ Coordinates_i - Groundtruth\ Coordinates_i\| \quad (2)$$

SD quantifies the variability or dispersion of the landmark localization errors as given in below Eq. 3, where $error_i$ represents the individual distance error for each landmark in mm. MRE and SD are calculated without considering any precision range. The lower the MRE and SD values, the higher the performance of the prediction model.

$$SD = \sqrt{\frac{1}{N}\sum\nolimits_{i=1}^{N}(error_i - MRE)^2} \quad (3)$$

5 Applications and Potential Uses

- The dataset, comprising images and corresponding annotation data, holds immense potential for automating landmark annotation through artificial intelligence (AI) research. Specifically, researchers in the field of cephalometry can utilize this dataset to develop AI-based methods that automate the process of landmark annotation. By doing so, they can enhance the efficiency and accuracy of cephalometric analysis, a vital aspect of their research and clinical practice.
- The dataset offers significant opportunities for medical and technical professionals to delve into a wide range of image processing, machine learning, and deep learning techniques. These professionals can leverage the dataset to explore and apply diverse feature extraction, feature learning, and deep learning methods, thereby advancing their understanding and expertise in the field.
- The dataset offers an extensive range of image categorization based on factors such as resolution, dental formation, visibility of soft tissue landmarks, and more. This categorization provides researchers with a higher level of variety and volume compared to existing public datasets available for research experiments. By utilizing this dataset, researchers can access a diverse set of images that cover a wide spectrum of characteristics, enabling more comprehensive and robust experimentation in their research endeavors.
- Further, the dataset can serve as a valuable resource for conducting further research, enabling the calculation of various angular and linear measurements. These measurements can be extracted from the annotations and utilized for investigations related to skeletal structure classification.

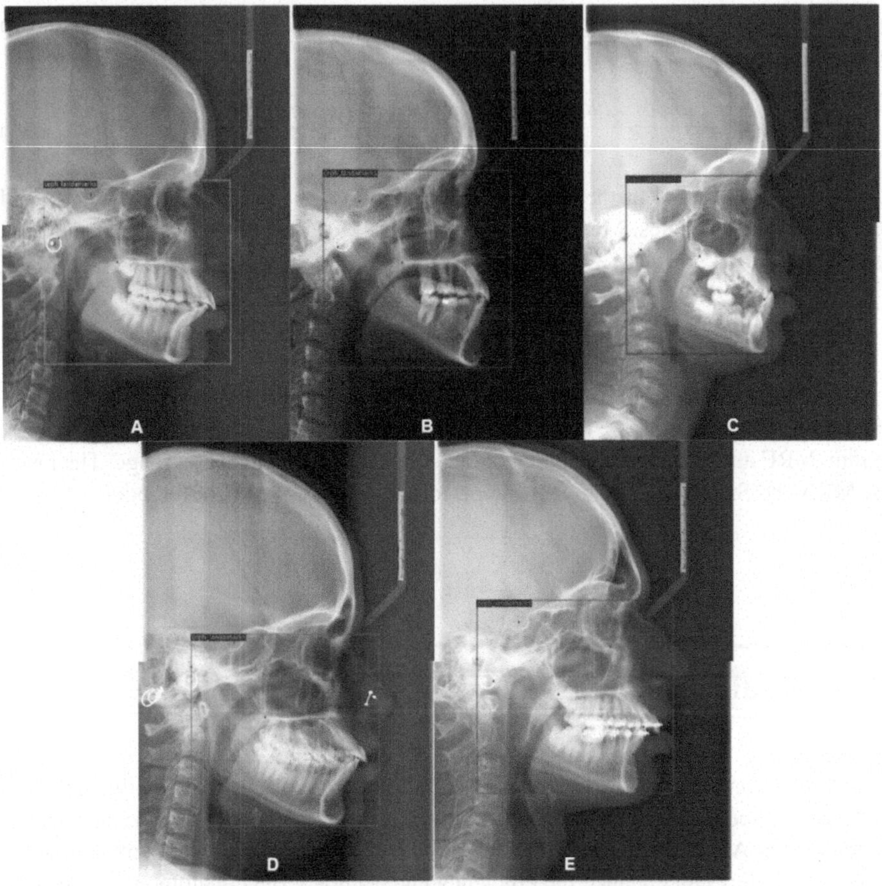

Fig. 3. Showing data annotation for diverse data samples. A. Normal, B. Soft Tissue Visibility, C. Complex Teeth Structure, D. Ornaments, E. Dental Braces.

- The presence of artifacts such as jewelry or dental holdings in a few radiographic images could warrant a separate research endeavor aimed at eliminating these artifacts. By addressing and mitigating these artifacts, the overall landmark annotation process can be greatly facilitated and enhanced.
- The dataset serves as a powerful resource that empowers researchers to develop and refine AI-assisted software tools, particularly in the field of orthodontics. They can train and fine-tune algorithms, apply advanced machine learning techniques, and optimize software performance to create more efficient and accurate tools for orthodontic analysis, treatment planning, and diagnosis.

6 Conclusion

The field of cephalometric landmark annotation automation currently faces a challenge due to the lack of diverse datasets, which are essential for the development of generalized and robust models. To address this gap, the present study has prepared a comprehensive and novel dataset, DiverseCEPH19 comprising diverse categories of lateral cephalometric images, each annotated with landmark annotations. The dataset consists of 1692 images, provided in two varying resolutions: 1341x1938 and 1257x1672. Furthermore, images are meticulously categorized based on factors such as radiograph visibility quality, dental structure, and other relevant criteria. The annotation of 19 landmarks was conducted by three experienced professionals in the field. To the best of our knowledge, this dataset represents the largest collection in the field of cephalometric analysis and is the first dataset to include radiographic images from patients in India. It is publicly available to the research community, offering significant potential to enhance the accuracy and reliability of automated cephalometric landmark detection systems. Ultimately, this advancement can lead to more informed decisions in orthodontic treatment planning and execution.

Acknowledgments. We thank the JSS Dental College and Hospital, JSS AHER, and the Institutional Ethical Committee for supporting the data collection and annotation.

CRediT Author Statement. Rashmi S: data Curation, Possible Available Software Exploration, Data Annotation, Original Draft; Srinath S: data Curation, Methodology, Supervision, Review, & Editing; Seema Deshmukh: data Collection, Data Annotation, Supervision, Review, & Editing; Karthikeya Patil: Data Collection, Review, & Editing; Prashant S: Data Annotation, Supervision, Review, & Editing;

Declaration of Competing Interest

The authors declare that there are no known competing financial interests or personal relationships that might have influenced or could be perceived to have influenced, the work presented in this article.

References

1. Proffit, D.M.. Fields, W.R., Larson, H.W., Sarver, B.: Contemporary orthodontic (proffit, 2019). Contemporary orthodontics-e-book. Elsevier Health Sciences., pp. 5–24 (2019)
2. Doff, M.H.J., Hoekema, A., Pruim, G.J., Huddleston Slater, J. J. R., Stegenga, B.: Long-term oral-appliance therapy in obstructive sleep apnea: a cephalometric study of craniofacial changes. J. Dent. 38(12,) 1010–1018 (2010). https://doi.org/10.1016/j.jdent.2010.08.018
3. Kamoen, A., Dermaut, L., Verbeeck, R.: The clinical significance of error measurement in the interpretation of treatment results. Eur. J. Orthod. **23**(5), 569–578 (2001). https://doi.org/10.1093/EJO/23.5.569
4. da Silveira, H.L.D., Silveira, H.E.D.: Reproducibility of cephalometric measurements made by three radiology clinics. Angle Orthod. **76**(3), 394–399 (2006). https://doi.org/10.1043/0003-3219(2006)076[0394:ROCMMB]2.0.CO;2
5. Lévy-Mandel, A.D., Venetsanopoulos, A.N., Tsotsos, J.K.: Knowledge-based landmarking of cephalograms. Comput. Biomed. Res. **19**(3), 282–309 (1986). https://doi.org/10.1016/0010-4809(86)90023-6
6. Liu, J.-K., Chen, Y.-T., Cheng, K.-S.: Accuracy of computerized automatic identification of cephalometric landmarks. Am. J. Orthod. Dentofac. Orthop. **118**(5), 535–540 (2000). https://doi.org/10.1067/mod.2000.110168
7. Cardillo, J., Sid-Ahmed, M.A.: An image processing system for locating craniofacial landmarks. IEEE Trans. Med. Imaging **13**(2), 275–289 (1994). https://doi.org/10.1109/42.293920

8. Rudolph, D.J., Sinclair, P.M., Coggins, J.M.: Automatic computerized radiographic identification of cephalometric landmarks. Am. J. Orthod. Dentofac. Orthop. **113**(2), 173–179 (1998). https://doi.org/10.1016/S0889-5406(98)70289-6
9. Shahidi, S., Oshagh, M., Gozin, F., Salehi, P., Danaei, S.M.: Accuracy of computerized automatic identification of cephalometric landmarks by a designed software. Dentomaxillofacial Radiol. 42(1) (2013). https://doi.org/10.1259/dmfr.20110187
10. Kafieh, R., Mehri, A., Sadri, S.: Automatic landmark detection in cephalometry using a modified Active Shape Model with sub image matching. In: 2007 International Conference on Machine Vision, pp. 73–78. IEEE (Dec. 2007). https://doi.org/10.1109/ICMV.2007.4469276
11. Vucinic, P., Trpovski, Z., Scepan, I.: Automatic landmarking of cephalograms using active appearance models. Euro. J. Orthodontics **32**(3), 233–241 (2010). https://doi.org/10.1093/ejo/cjp099
12. Davis, D.N., Taylor, C.J.: A blackboard architecture for automating cephalometric analysis. Med. Inform. **16**(2), 137–149 (1991). https://doi.org/10.3109/14639239109012123
13. Wang, C.-W., et al.: A benchmark for comparison of dental radiography analysis algorithms. Med. Image Anal. **31**, 63–76 (2016). https://doi.org/10.1016/j.media.2016.02.004
14. Ibragimov, B., Likar, B., Pernuš, F., Vrtovec, T.: Automatic cephalometric X-ray landmark detection by applying game theory and random forests. In: ISBI Int. Symp. Biomed. Imag. 2014, Automat. Cephalometric X-Ray Landmark Detection Challenge (2014)
15. Chen, C., Xie, W., Franke, J., Grutzner, P.A., Nolte, L.-P., Zheng, G.: Automatic X-ray landmark detection and shape segmentation via data-driven joint estimation of image displacements. Med. Image Anal. **18**(3), 487–499 (2014). https://doi.org/10.1016/j.media.2014.01.002
16. Lindner, C., Cootes, T.: Fully Automatic Cephalometric Evaluation using Random Forest Regression-Voting (Dec. 2015)
17. Wang, S., Li, H., Li, J., Zhang, Y., Zou, B.: Automatic analysis of lateral cephalograms based on multiresolution decision tree regression voting. J. Healthc. Eng. **2018** (2018). https://doi.org/10.1155/2018/1797502
18. Wirtz, A., Lam, J., Wesarg, S.: Automated cephalometric landmark localization using a coupled shape model. Current Directions Biomed. Eng. **6**(3) (2020). https://doi.org/10.1515/cdbme-2020-3015
19. Song, Y., Qiao, X, Iwamoto, Y., Chen, Y.-W.": Automatic Cephalometric Landmark Detection on X-ray images using a deep-learning method. Appli. Sci. (Switzerland) **10**(7) (2020). https://doi.org/10.3390/app10072547
20. Bulatova, G., Kusnoto, B., Grace, V., Tsay, T.P., Avenetti, D.M., Sanchez, F.J.C.: assessment of automatic cephalometric landmark identification using artificial intelligence. Orthod. Craniofac. Res. **24**(S2), 37–42 (2021). https://doi.org/10.1111/ocr.12542
21. Hwang, H.-W., et al.: Automated identification of cephalometric landmarks: Part 2-Might it be better than human? Angle Orthod. **90**(1), 69–76 (2020). https://doi.org/10.2319/022019-129.1
22. Qian, J., Luo, W., Cheng, M., Tao, Y., Lin, J., Lin, H.: CephaNN: a multi-head attention network for cephalometric landmark detection. IEEE Access **8**, 112633–112641 (2020). https://doi.org/10.1109/ACCESS.2020.3002939
23. Wang, C.-W., et al.: Evaluation and comparison of anatomical landmark detection methods for cephalometric X-Ray images: a grand challenge. IEEE Trans. Med. Imaging **34**(9), 1890–1900 (2015). https://doi.org/10.1109/TMI.2015.2412951
24. Zeng, M., Yan, Z., Liu, S., Zhou, Y., Qiu, L.: Cascaded convolutional networks for automatic cephalometric landmark detection. Med. Image Anal. **68** (2021). https://doi.org/10.1016/j.media.2020.101904

25. Rashmi, S., Ashok, V.: A novel method for cephalometric landmark regression using convolutional neural networks and local binary pattern. Commun. Comput. Inform. Sci. (2021). https://doi.org/10.1007/978-981-16-1086-8_28
26. Lindner, C., Wang, C.-W., Huang, C.-T., Li, C.-H., Chang, S.-W., Cootes, T.F.: Fully automatic system for accurate localisation and analysis of cephalometric landmarks in lateral cephalograms. Sci. Rep. **6**(1), 33581 (2016). https://doi.org/10.1038/srep33581
27. Rashmi, S., Srinath, S., Patil, K., Murthy, P.S., Deshmukh, S.: Lateral cephalometric landmark annotation using histogram oriented gradients extracted from region of interest patches. J Maxillofac Oral Surg **22**(4), 806–812 (2023). https://doi.org/10.1007/s12663-023-02025-z
28. Khalid, M.A., et al.: Aariz: A Benchmark Dataset for Automatic Cephalometric Landmark Detection and CVM Stage Classification. Electr. Eng. Syst. Sci. Image and Video Process. (2023)
29. Khalid, M.A., et al.: CEPHA29: Automatic Cephalometric Landmark Detection Challenge 2023. Compute. Vis. Pattern Recogn. (Dec. 2022)
30. Rashmi, S., Srinath, S., Murthy, P.S., Deshmukh, S.: Landmark annotation through feature combinations: a comparative study on cephalometric images with in-depth analysis of model's explainability. Dentomaxillofacial Radiol. (2023). https://doi.org/10.1093/dmfr/twad011

Automatic Segregation of Chest X-Ray Posterior-Anterior (PA) and Anterior-Posterior (AP) Projection Images Using NLP

Menaka Pushpa Arthur(✉) and Vaibhav Sharanabasappa Gadag

School of Computer Science and Engineering, Vellore Institute of Technology, Chennai Campus, Chennai 600127, Tamil Nadu, India
menakapushpa.a@vit.ac.in

Abstract. Chest X-ray is a prime imaging test in the healthcare sector to detect and treat abnormalities and diseases in the lungs, heart, and bones. Proper interpretation and annotation of chest radiographs by the radiologist or Artificial Intelligence Clinical Assistant Diagnosis system should be ensured for high-accuracy computer-aided diagnosis. By treating chest X-ray projections Posterior-Anterior (PA) and Anterior-Posterior (AP) as separate datasets to train the deep learning models, the accuracy of disease prediction can be improved. Automatic segregation of AP and PA view CXR images reduces the burden and time of manual process. Also in a Healthcare Digital Archiving System, the chest radiographs can be maintained separately as AP and PA groups under frontal view. The proposed work exploits the major techniques in Natural Language Processing (NLP) i.e., Optical Character Recognition (OCR) and pattern matching to detect the projection type of the labeled chest X-ray images and then classify them into two views, AP and PA. We created the dataset with chest X-ray images collected from various dataset sources including NIH etc. This work also compares the proposed NLP-based CXR view classification system with a transfer learning-based system to classify chest X-ray images into PA and AP projections.

Keywords: Chest X-ray projection · Posterior-Anterior (PA) · Anterior-Posterior (AP) · Natural Language Processing · Optical Character Recognition (OCR) · transfer learning model · Artificial Intelligence Clinical Assistant Diagnosis System · Healthcare Digital Archiving System

1 Introduction

The frontal view of chest radiographs can be captured by projecting X-ray beams in a posterior and anterior direction over the patient. In the Postrio-Anterior

V. S. Gadag—These authors contributed equally to this work.

J. Kakarla et al. (Eds.): CVIP 2024, CCIS 2473, pp. 28–42, 2026.
https://doi.org/10.1007/978-3-031-93688-3_3

(PA) projection, X- ray beams are projected on the posterior side of the patient and then it is captured by the X-ray detector at the anterior side of the patient. In the Antero-Posterior (AP) projection, X-ray beams travel from the anterior to posterior side of the patient and to captured by the X-ray detector. The PA view of chest radiographs is a gold standard for radiologists to analyze tho- racic cavity organ abnormalities. The patient may stand or lie down while taking the chest X-ray depending on his medical condition or a need for different imaging to analyze the tho- racic cavity well. Under some medical conditions of the patient such as unconscious or life support unit or disabled, the chest AP view radiograph is generated. According to the patient's standing direction toward the X-ray detector, the radiographs are labeled as AP erect and PA erect. The erect PA view can be produced if the patient faces the X-ray detector in a standing position. If he faces the X-ray source in a standing or sitting position the erect AP will be generated. The AP supine view is captured when the patient lying on his back to generate chest radiographs. Recently, medical analysts recommended chest- prone position radiographs for seriously ill patients to improve the monitoring of lung diseases. Under various circumstances and better imaging, different types of chest radiograph positions are recommended by the specialist. The various positions of the chest radiographs are given in Fig. 1.

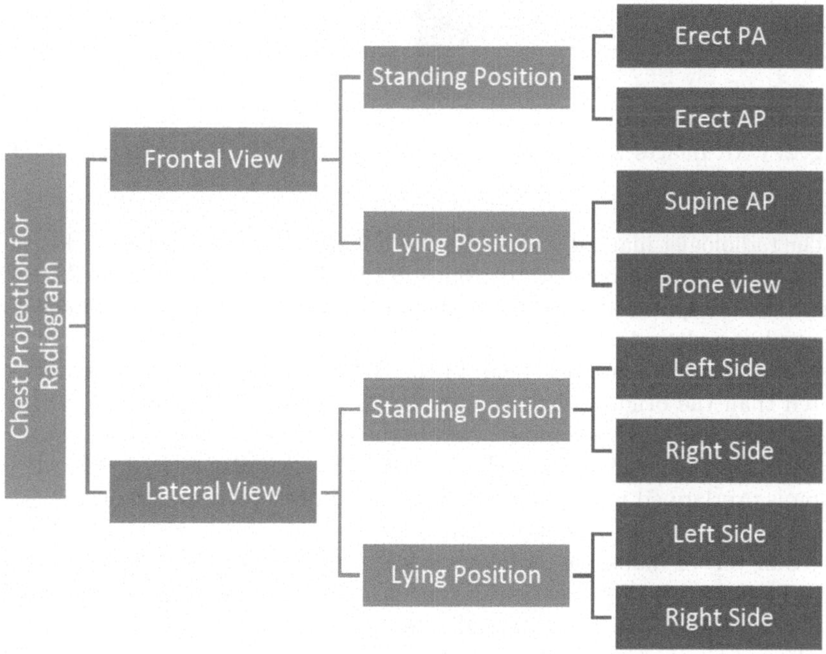

Fig. 1. Various Positioning for Chest Radiographs

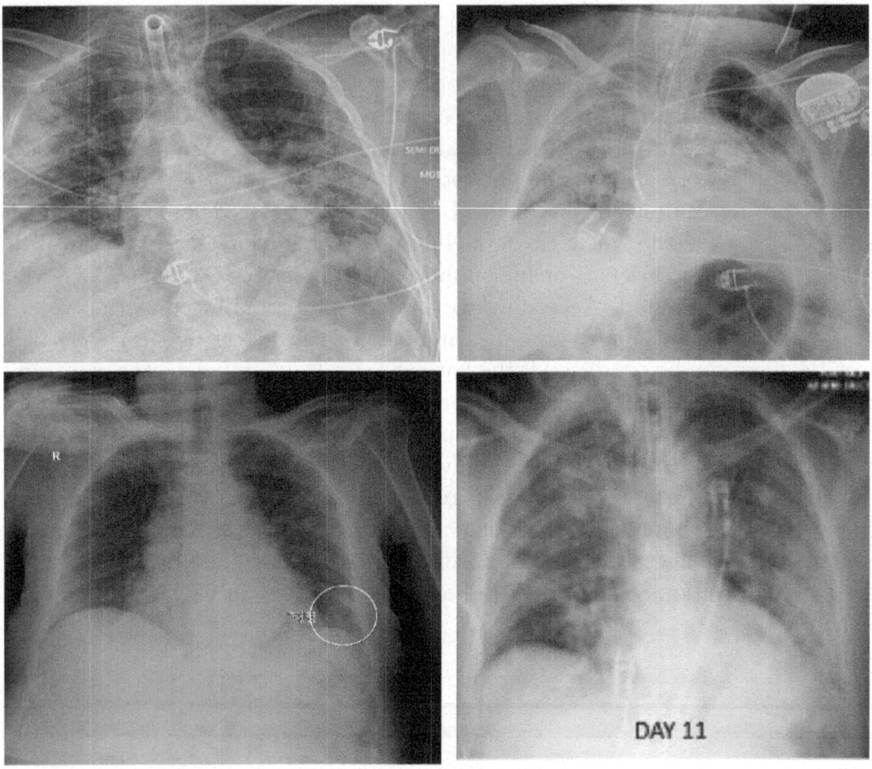

Fig. 2. CXR Images with various issues collected from the Public Dataset [14–17]

The radiologist manually identifies the AP and PA views of chest radiographs and classifies them into separate groups in the Digital Medical Image Archiving System for computer-aided disease diagnosis. With the help of cardio-thoracic ratio and scapular edge, radiologists can differentiate AP and PA views of chest X-ray images and then label them. In the AP view, the heart size is more exaggerated than the original size because the X-ray source is located closer to the body in this capture. A magnified view of the heart in the radiographs shows the difference between AP and PA chest views. The scapular edge in the AP projection is overlapped with the lungs. Whereas, in the PA view, the lungs can be clearly visible without overlapping the scapula. This kind of AP and PA labeling process is very tedious for radiologists if the number of chest X-ray images is more. The labeling of projection in the chest radiographs is marked as 'AP' or 'ap' for AP view. The PA view radiographs are mostly not labeled or labeled as 'PA' or 'pa'. The marking of position, projection view, and other details of the radiographs such as patient name, date, and time are carried out by the radiologist. Sample PA and AP view CXRs are shown in Fig. 3.

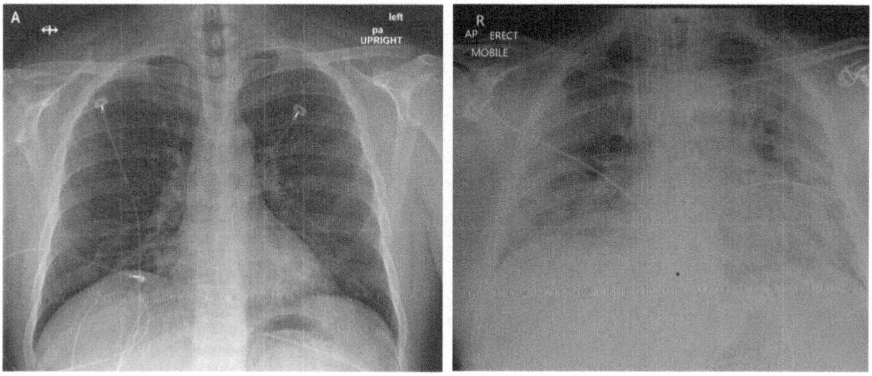

Fig. 3. Sample PA and AP views of CXR Images collected from the Public Dataset [14–17]

1.1 Why Do We Need Our System?

- The chest X-ray benchmark datasets such as NIH, VinDr- CXR, Shenzhen CXR set, PadChest, CRADI, Covid-19 CXR, and MIMIC-CXR contain both frontal views PA and AP. The percentage of AP view CXR images is very low in the combined dataset. Only a few datasets Montgomery County Chest X-ray set, Mendeley Covin 19, PediCXR and Chest X-ray datasets contain all images in PA view. The datasets only with AP view chest radiographs are rarely found. We can see a clear separation folder for frontal and lateral view CXRs at the same time AP and PA views are maintained under a single folder frontal. Manual segregation is tedious and it becomes complicated when CXR images are collected from multiple sources.
- Recent research works on lung disease detection have been carried out in order to find the superior projection view among PA and AP for accurate disease prediction [1–3]
- Clinical information on CXR images is not clearly visible due to blurring, distortion, or tilt. In Fig. 2, (a) CXR with slit labels (b) Tilted CXR with no label visibility and (c) CXR Image with small size label (d) blurred Image

The organization of the paper is as follows. Section 2 discusses the relevant works that have been done in this problem statement. Section 3 explains the proposed system and Sect. 4 discusses its implementation results. Finally, this research work concludes in Sect. 5.

2 Existing Works

The taxonomy of the existing works based on the adapted techniques is shown in Fig. 4. Figure 5 explains the methodologies that have been used to classify PA and lateral views and Frontal and lateral views in the state-of-the-art works.

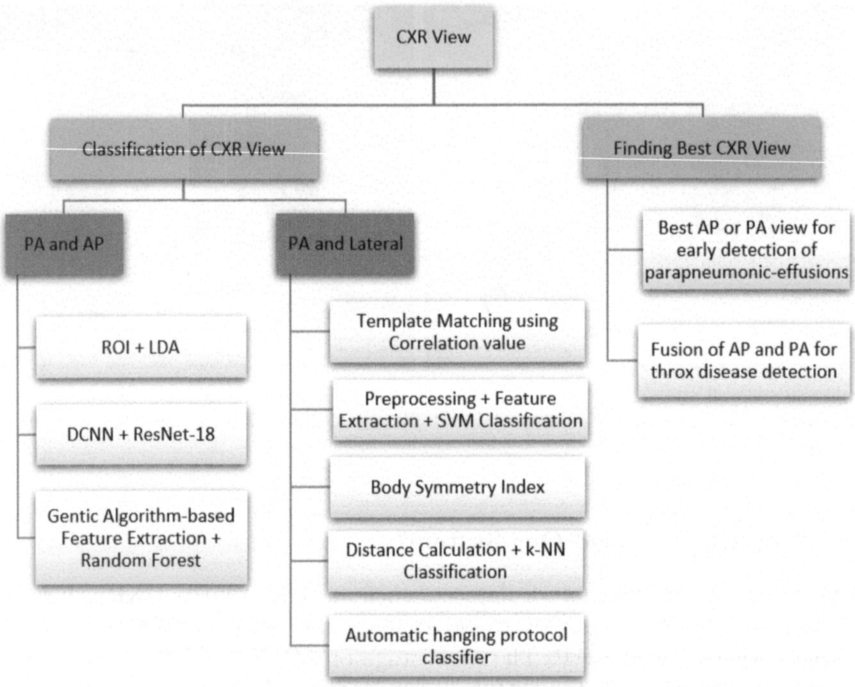

Fig. 4. Taxonomy of Chest X-Ray View Classification

The chest X-ray projection images are automatically classified into lateral and frontal (AP/PA) using machine learning algorithms with efficient feature selection or Region of Interest (ROI) extraction [1,2,4–6] or deep learning technique [3,7,8]. The importance of CXR frontal view classification into AP and PA is highlighted in the studies [3,9]. Instead of using PA and AP view CXR in a single dataset, [9] has used two different datasets to detect parapneumonic effusions in an early stage. This work identified that the highest classification accuracy 84% is achieved by PA lateral view than 67% of AP view. The lateral and frontal different datasets are used as the separate input for MVC-Net [3], a Back Projection Transposition (BPT) deep fusion network to detect thorax diseases.

The primary CXR view classification into frontal and lateral research work was actually initiated in the year 2002 [10]. Using the cross-correlation coefficient similarity score, the unknown chest image is compared with 9 templates of lateral and frontal chest images. For the template matching technique, 6 templates were generated for PA view and 3 templates were generated for lateral views. They have used 647 samples in the dataset and achieved 100% for automatic classification of chest CXR into frontal PA and lateral. In the year 2003 [1], the four main distances between reference and sample radiographs were calculated by the Euclidean distance formula after that using the k-NN classification algorithm

CXR View Classification Type	Ref No.	Year of Publication	Classification Method	Dataset Size
PA and Lateral	[10]	2002	Similarity score of Test Chest Image Vs Template of PA and lateral Chest Images. 9 Template Images. Obtain Cross-Correlation Coefficient similarity score (-1, 0, +1).	Department of Radiology, University of Chicago. 447 PA + 200 Lateral = 647
	[5]	2015	Contour-based shape descriptor and SVM classification algorithm. Generates 99% of accuracy.	8200 images from the National Library of Medicine (NLM)
	[11]	2006	Body symmetry and background percentage index values are identified for the image profile.	2000 Frontal + 1000 Lateral = 3000 from Kaohsiung Medical Univ
	[1]	2003	The distance vector with four features between reference and sample radiographs is calculated by the Euclidean distance formula. Then apply the k-NN classification algorithm	1866
	[2]	2006	Features are extracted from CXR projection views before applying the automatic hanging protocol for image classification.	
Frontal and Lateral	[4]	2011	Three indices from the scapula, clavicle, and lung are generated by observing the tilt angle and extension of radiolucence in the lung. Linear Discriminant Analysis (LDA) is applied and then RoC is observed.	600 PA + 600 AP = 1200
	[7]	2019	DCNN and ResNet-18 models. ROC and AUC metrics are observed.	1,12,120 from NIH dataset
	[6]	2019	Histogram of Orientation Gradients (HOG) and image profile are obtained using Genetic Algorithm based feature selection. Then Random Forest classification is used to give 96.39% accuracy.	24000

Fig. 5. Analysis of Existing Works

frontal and lateral images were classified. Automatic hanging protocol was used as the classifier [2] for the same in the year 2006.

The frontal and lateral view has been classified using SVM [5] with a high accuracy of 99% for the NLM dataset. The image profile, body size ratio, and pyramid of histograms of orientation gradients are considered the major features extracted by contour-based shape descriptor for the classification algorithm SVM. Hence, Kaohsiung Medical University chest radiographs [11] have been classified into frontal and lateral using the body symmetry index and background percentage index methods. In the year 1992 [12], a simple 2-layer Neural Network was used to detect 8 different orientations of chest radiographs. They have considered 8 different orientations for PA images and 89% of classification accuracy is achieved. As per the technology development over the years, the techniques used to classify the PA and AP view CXR images updated from ROI-specific feature extraction for Linear Discriminant Analysis (LDA) [4] to Genetic Algorithm-based feature extraction for Random Forest algorithm [6] and DCNN with transfer learning model [7]. The study [13] automatically annotates the labels from AP images using the sentence clustering NLP technique.

3 OCR-Based AP/PA View Detection System

The chest radiographs are marked with basic clinical information such as patient name, date, time, and projection views such as AP or PA. For Posterior–anterior (PA) chest X-ray projection, the label is marked as 'pa', 'PA' 'p-a', 'P-A', or not mentioned. Whereas, Anterior-Posterior chest X-ray, the label is given as 'AP', 'ap', 'a-p', or 'A-P'. For Computer-Aided Diagnosis, radiologists manually go through the label printed on the CXR image to classify them into AP and PA views. This manual process is tedious because of the low-quality CXR images, missing labels, or labels cropped by image boundary. For creating large image repositories, this process should be repeated which consumes more time. Hence, an automatic CXR view detection system is proposed to classify the CXR digital images into frontal views such as anterior-posterior (AP) and posterior-anterior (PA) based on the clinical information marked on it. The following issues in the projection of chest radiographs induce major challenges in the proposed system design.

1. Mostly the view label is not mentioned for the Posterior–Anterior (PA) CXR view. In this case, the Radiologist assumes that the CXR which does not contain any view label is considered a PA projection. This gives confusion to differentiate standard PA CXR and CXR which is not actually labeled.
2. Different patterns used for marking the projection label in the chest X-ray images such as PA, P-A, and posterior-anterior, AP, A-P, and anterior-posterior in lower and upper cases.
3. Poor quality CXR images and marked clinical information in poor visibility
4. Along with the projection label, other clinical information is also marked on CXR. These labels may contain the sequence of characters/letters 'pa' or 'ap' that will create ambiguity at the time of view detection

The proposed system shown in Fig. 6 contains three major components; (a) Preprocessing of CXR image (ii) Optical Character Recognition (OCR) and (c) Pattern matching. The first component can solve the (iii) issue in the CXR i.e., image quality. The image Preprocessing component contains two sub-components; image type conversion and resizing. The CXR image is converted into a grayscale image that improves the quality of the image reasonably. The chest radiographs are in different sizes since they are collected from different

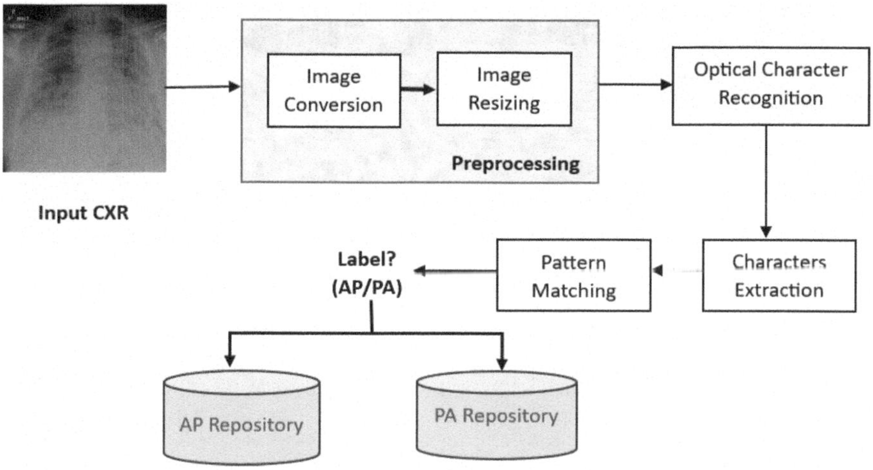

Fig. 6. Automatic Detection of AP/PA Frontal View of CXR

repositories. The image resizing sub-component resizes the grayscale CXR image into 1800×1800 pixels. This process makes input images are in equal size before applying the OCR technique to it. Also, this image resizing increases the label font of the CXR digital image. That improves the visibility of the label to be extracted by the Optical Character Recognition (OCR) component from the CXR with less ambiguity. The quality-enhanced CXR is sent to the OCR component to extract the patterns from the image. The sample chest X-ray image and its pattern generated by the OCR are given in Fig. 7. The actual view of the CXR is 'AP Sitting'. The label is sliced in half by the image border. The label identified by the OCR is 'Ar oilling' i.e., highlighted in the OCR-generated right-hand side pattern. Totally, 5 patterns are generated for this input image such as 'L0p? 707ee ad'. 'Ar oilling', 'D', 'Portal', and 'R'. Each pattern is represented by three values; 4 corner coordination points of bounding box over text, text identified, and its confidence level. In this CXR, the text 'R' is clearly visible. Hence, its confidence level is nearly 1 when compared to 'L' with a very low confidence value of 0.0004. Figure 6 CXR image is a very challenging input to detect the correct projection view.

The texts in the CXR are extracted by the Character Extraction component by maintaining a separate list for coordinates and confidence values. The Character Extraction component provides the list of texts in the image. For Fig. 8, the list ['L0p? 707ee ad'. 'Ar oilling', 'D', 'Portal', and 'R'] with texts are generated by this component. Finally, the Pattern Matching component uses the application-specific regular expression to find the possible labels that represent the projections Anterior-Posterior (AP) and Posterior-Anterior (PA) in the chest radiographs. The extracted characters from the CXR are mostly incorrect or misinterpreted due to the poor quality of the image and the invisibility of the labels. This induces challenges in the design of regular expression to find

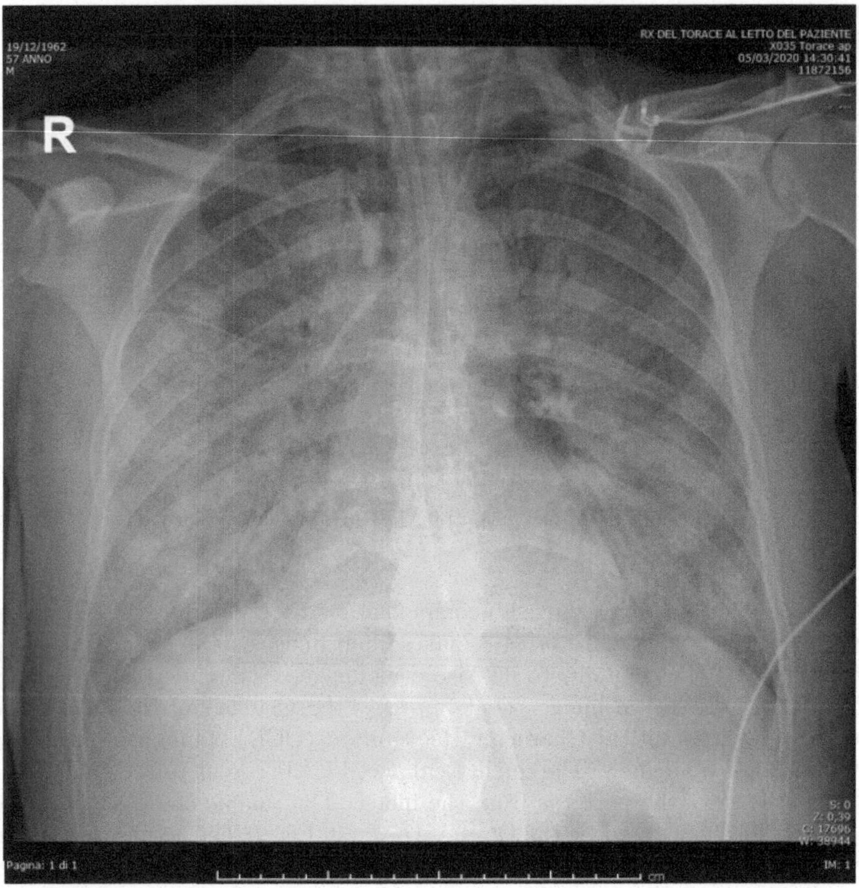

Image Name: 067.jpeg
Pattern Observed: [([[1526, 54], [2042, 54], [2042, 84], [1526, 84]], 'RX DEL TORACE AL LETTO DEL PAZIENTE', 0.7766351883780056), ([[6, 84], [162, 84], [162, 114], [6, 114]], '19/12/1962', 0.9732877904813358), ([[1836, 82], [2038, 82], [2038, 112], [1836, 112]], 'X035 Torace ap', 0.7525758859060978), ([[6, 112], [122, 112], [122, 140], [6, 140]], '57 ANNO', 0.7939532009295226), ([[1760, 110], [2038, 110], [2038, 142], [1760, 142]], '05/03/2020 14.30.41', 0.8963292689720946), ([[4, 140], [34, 140], [34, 168], [4, 168]], 'M', 0.9992125393085907), ([[1389, 121], [1427, 121], [1427, 171], [1389, 171]], '2', 0.3960383679664723), ([[1904, 140], [2040, 140], [2040, 168], [1904, 168]], '11872156', 0.9999939308461857), ([[88, 252], [188, 252], [188, 356], [88, 356]], 'R', 0.9999916553671397), ([[1982, 1852], [2038, 1852], [2038, 1878], [1982, 1878]], 'S: 0', 0.5560554371613731), ([[1942, 1878], [2040, 1878], [2040, 1910], [1942, 1910]], '2:0,39', 0.9250465579808564), ([[1916, 1908], [2040, 1908], [2040, 1936], [1916, 1936]], '017696', 0.7361970284286419), ([[1910, 1934], [2040, 1934], [2040, 1962], [1910, 1962]], 'W: 38944', 0.6757717974670536), ([[2, 1990], [184, 1990], [184, 2022], [2, 2022]], 'Pagina: 1 di 1', 0.7271855017030839), ([[1968, 1992], [2040, 1992], [2040, 2018], [1968, 2018]], 'IM: 1', 0.9170238223121061), ([[521, 2009], [727, 2009], [727, 2048], [521, 2048]], '1!', 0.03179622779301162), ([[1253, 2009], [1537, 2009], [1537, 2048], [1253, 2048]], 'JL!]] ', 0.00612524949297488), ([[1544, 2020], [1590, 2020], [1590, 2046], [1544, 2046]], 'cr', 0.8907975895331438)]

Fig. 7. Pattern generated by OCR from Chest X-Ray – Positive Test Case collected from the Public Dataset [14–17]

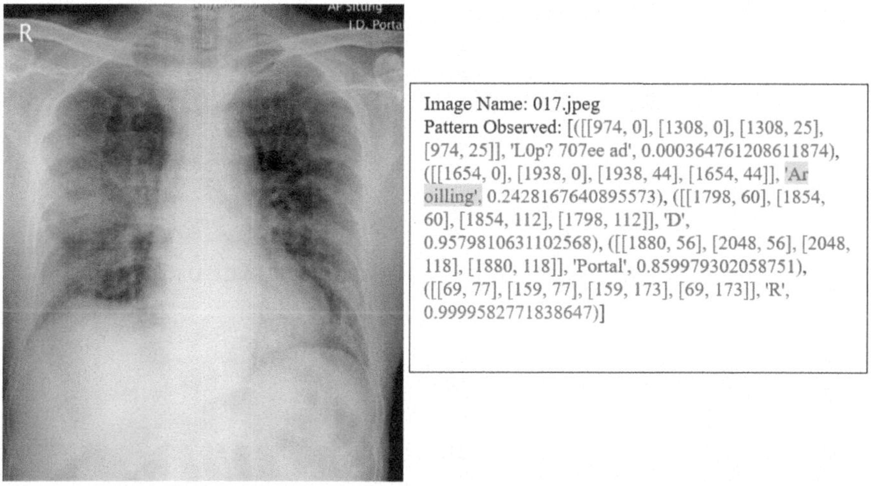

Fig. 8. Pattern generated by OCR from Chest X-Ray – Challenging Test Case collected from the Public Dataset [14–17]

the targeted patterns related to two frontal projections. The regular expression supports upper and lower cases in the view label also formed to find misinterpreted labels using other clearly visible labels. After detecting the projection view of the chest X-ray, the image will be moved to either AP digital repository or PA digital repository. Based on the misclassified CXR projections, the regular expression gets kept updated to improve the accuracy and robustness of the system.

4 Results Discussion

The implementation of the proposed system is carried out under two major purposes; Evaluate the OCR-based Proposed System and Comparison between proposed system transfer learning models.

4.1 OCR-Based CXR View Detection System

Python programming language is used to implement the project in the Google Colaboratory Notebook environment. The number of CXR images used for the proposed system and transfer learning model varied depending on their requirement. Optical Character Recognition (OCR) is implemented using three well-known Python packages Tesseract, Keras OCR, and Easy OCR and their results are observed to find the best model for our proposed system. The PA and AP chest X-ray images are collected from various sources [14–17] under different representations of views in the clinical information marker. The total images used for evaluating our system process are 4350 with PA 4000 and AP 350. The

Table 1. Input Image Data Set

Category	Number of Samples
PA	4000
AP	350
Total	4350

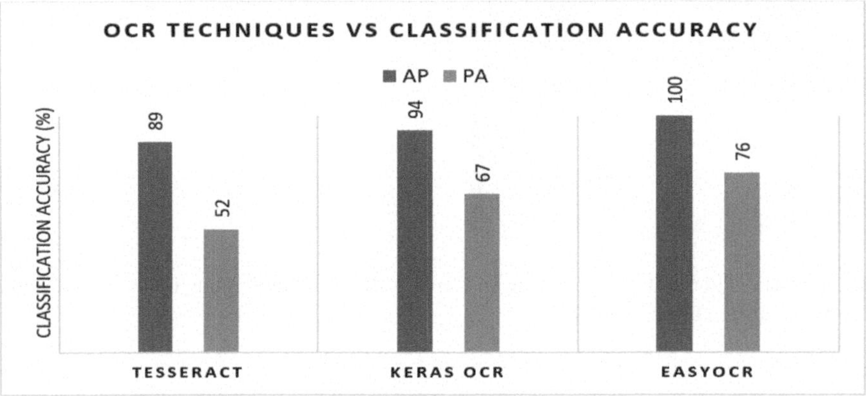

Fig. 9. Classification Accuracy of OCR-based CXR View Detection System

number of input images under each view class used for system evaluation is given in Table 1. We have used more input images to tune the regular expression to find the target pattern such as AP or PA with high precision. We could collect more PA CXRs than AP from the publicly available datasets. The input images regulate the proposed system and evaluate the performance of the same. Three well-known OCR Python packages such as Tesseract, Keras OCR, and Easy OCR are used for character extraction from the chest radiographs and the result of the system is given in Fig. 9.

4.2 Transfer Learning Model-Based CXR View Detection System

The chest X-ray dataset consists of 700 images with two categories AP and PA. We have manually identified the AP and PA chest radiographs from the public dataset [14–17] to form our own dataset for the evaluation of the transfer learning model-based CXR view classification system. Data augmentation is not appropriate in chest X-ray image processing. Hence, our system is built without image augmentation techniques. The dataset has split into train and test datasets using an 80:20 ratio. The training dataset gets 280 under each class i.e., PA and AP view. The test dataset is created with 70 chest radiographs and class labels are equally distributed among them. The validation dataset contains 80 images i.e. 40 CXR images in each class. The pre-trained VGG transfer learning model was then tested on the entire training dataset i.e. 560 images and we achieved

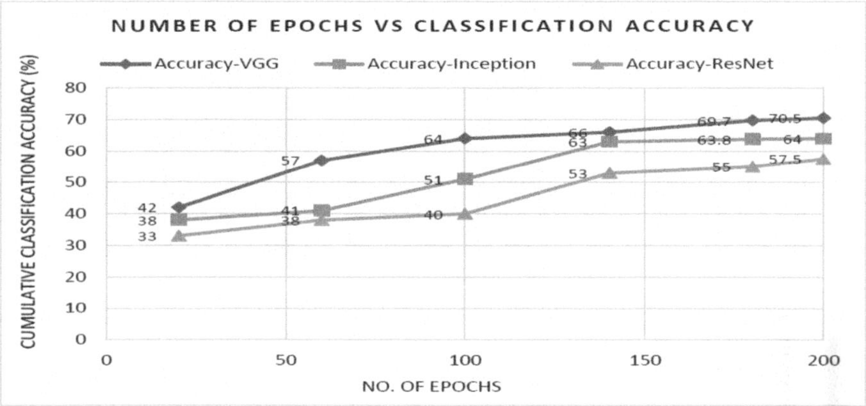

Fig. 10. Training Classification Accuracy Vs Number of Epochs in the Transfer Learning Model

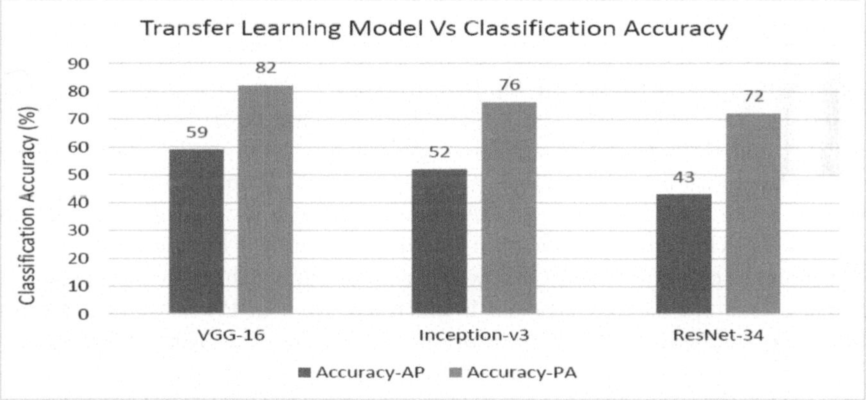

Fig. 11. Testing Phase Classification Accuracy Vs Transfer Learning Models

the following results. We used VGG16, Inception-v3 and ResNet-34 transfer learning models. The classification accuracy in the training phase of the transfer learning models is presented in Fig. 8 by increasing the number of epochs. The accuracy projected in this Fig. 10 graph is cumulative by considering PA and AP view classes. The testing phase classification accuracy is presented in Fig. 11 for three transfer learning models. VGG-16 outperforms well with a 70.5 cumulative classification percentage when compared to Inception and ResNet models at the training phase. In the testing dataset, VGG-16 gives a classification accuracy of 82% for PA and 59% for PA images.

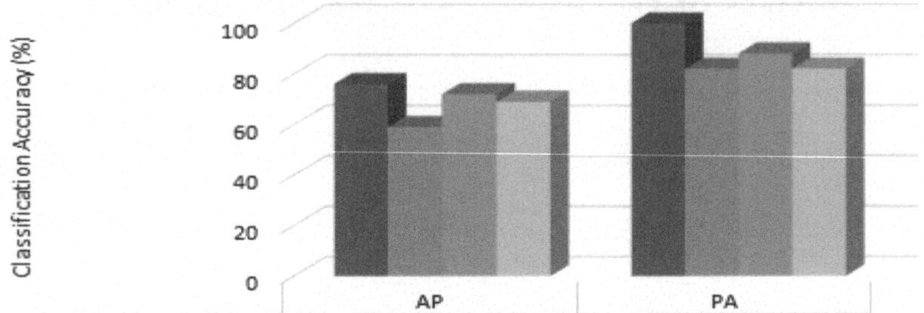

	AP	PA
OCR-based System	76	100
VGG-16 based System	59	82
DCNN[7]	72	88
LDA[3]	69	82

Fig. 12. CXR View Classification Accuracy of OCR-based and Transfer Learning (VGG) and Existing Systems

4.3 OCR vs Transfer Learning Model-Based Proposed System

The classification accuracy of Optical Character Recognition (OCR) implemented by EasyOCR gives the highest accuracy for both views AP and PA with 76% and 100% than the VGG-16, a transfer learning model. A comparison between the four major techniques is given in Fig. 12. From the state-of-the-art, ResNet-18 based DCNN [7] and LDA [3] are applied to evaluate the considered dataset for CXR image classification based on the projection view PA and AP. All techniques classify the PA CXR with better accuracy than the AP CXR. The number of samples in the AP class is much less than in PA chest radiographs. The image augmentation is inappropriate and reduces the overall performance of computer-aided disease diagnosis systems. Hence, the system is implemented with fewer samples in AP chest X-ray images. Due to this undersampling issue in the AP class samples, the classification accuracy is much less than PA in both OCR and transfer learning-based CXR projection/view detection systems.

5 Conclusion

The proposed system uses Optical Character Recognition (OCR) to automatically segregate chest radiograph projections such as Posterior-Anterior (PA) and Anterior-Posterior (AP) into separate sections in the digital medical imaging repositories. The manual checking of clinical information on the chest X-ray consumes more time and effort to classify the AP and PA view images. Our system outperforms well in detecting the PA CXR by 100% and the AP CXR by 76%. The EasyOCR technique achieves this accuracy more than Tesseract and Keras. The OCR-based CXR view detection system is compared with transfer learning models VGG, Inception, and ResNet. OCR precisely detects view labels from the chest X-ray when compared to the feature extraction of the transfer learning model for classification.

Declarations

- Competing Interests: Nil
- Funding Information: Not Applicable
- Author contribution: All authors contributed equally
- Data Availability Statement: Used existing datasets
- Research Involving Human and /or Animals: Not Applicable
- Informed Consent: Not Applicable

References

1. Lehmann, T.M., Güld, O., Keysers, D., Schubert, H., Kohnen, M., Wein, B.B.: Determining the view of chest radiographs. J. Digit. Imaging **16**(3), 280-291 (2003). https://doi.org/10.1007/s10278-003-1655-x. Accessed 15 Dec 2003. PMID 14669063; PMCID PMC3045251
2. Luo, H., Hao, W., Foos, D.H., Cornelius, C.W.: Automatic image hanging protocol for chest radiographs in PACS. IEEE Trans. Inf. Technol. Biomed. **10**(2), 302–311 (2006). https://doi.org/10.1109/titb.2005.859872. PMID 16617619
3. Zhu, X., Feng, Q.: MVC-NET: multi-view chest radiograph classification network with deep fusion. In: 2021 IEEE 18th International Symposium on Biomedical Imaging (ISBI), Nice, France, pp. 554–558 (2021). https://doi.org/10.1109/ISBI48211.2021.9434000
4. Kao, E.F., Lin, W.C., Hsu, J.S., Chou, M.C., Jaw, T.S., Liu, G.C.: A computerized method for automated identification of erect posteroanterior and supine anteroposterior chest radiographs. Phys. Med. Biol. **56**(24), 7737–7753 (2018). https://doi.org/10.1088/0031-9155/56/24/004. Accessed 18 Nov 2011. PMID 22094308
5. Xue, Z., et al.: Chest X-ray image view classification. In: 2015 IEEE 28th International Symposium on Computer-Based Medical Systems, Sao Carlos, Brazil, pp. 66–71 (2015). https://doi.org/10.1109/CBMS.2015.49
6. Reza,S., Amin, O.B., Hashem, M.M.A.: A novel feature extraction and selection technique for chest X-ray image view classification. In: 2019 5th International Conference on Advances in Electrical Engineering (ICAEE), Dhaka, Bangladesh, pp. 189–194 (2019). https://doi.org/10.1109/ICAEE48663.2019.8975457
7. Kim, T.K., et al.: Deep learning method for automated classification of anteroposterior and posteroanterior chest radiographs. J. Digit. Imaging **32**(6), 925–930 (2019). https://doi.org/10.1007/s10278-019-00208-0. PMID 30972585; PMCID PMC6841900
8. Park, D., Kim, M., Kim, H., Lee, J., Chun, S.Y.: Domain adaptation from posteroanterior to anteroposterior X-ray radiograph classification via deep neural converter with label recycling. In: 2023 International Conference on Electronics, Information, and Communication (ICEIC), Singapore, pp. 1–4 (2023). https://doi.org/10.1109/ICEIC57457.2023.10049919
9. Moffett, B.K., et al.: Comparing posteroanterior with lateral and anteroposterior chest radiography in the initial detection of parapneumonic effusions. Am. J. Emerg. Med. **34**(12), 2402–2407 (2016). https://doi.org/10.1016/j.ajem.2016.09.021. ISSN 0735-6757

10. Arimura, H., Katsuragawa, S., Li, Q., Ishida, T., Doi, K.: Development of a computerized method for identifying the posteroanterior and lateral views of chest radiographs by use of a template matching technique. Med. Phys. **29**(7), 1556–1561 (2002). https://doi.org/10.1118/1.1487426. PMID 12148738
11. Kao, E.F., Lee, C., Jaw, T.S., Hsu, J.S., Liu, G.C.: Projection profile analysis for identifying different views of chest radiographs. Acad. Radiol. **13**(4), 518–525 (2006). https://doi.org/10.1016/j.acra.2006.01.009. PMID 16554233
12. Boone, J.M., Seshagiri, S., Steiner, R.M.: Recognition of chest radiograph orientation for picture archiving and communications systems display using neural networks. J. Digit. Imaging **5**(3), 190–193 (1992). https://doi.org/10.1007/BF03167769. PMID 1520746
13. Syeda-Mahmood, T.F., et al.: Building a benchmark dataset and classifiers for sentence-level findings in AP chest X-rays. In: 2019 IEEE 16th International Symposium on Biomedical Imaging (ISBI 2019), pp. 863–867 (2019)
14. Cohen, J.P., Morrison, P., Dao, L., Roth, K., Duong , T.Q., Ghassemi, M.: COVID-19 image data collection: prospective predictions are the future. arXiv:2006.11988. https://github.com/ieee8023/covid-chestxray-dataset (2020)
15. Wang, X, Peng, Y., Lu, L., Lu, Z., Bagheri, M., Summers, R.M.: ChestX-ray8: hospital-scale chest X-ray database and benchmarks on weakly-supervised classification and localization of common thorax diseases. In: IEEE CVPR (2017). ChestX-ray8_Hospital-Scale_Chest_CVPR_2017_paper.pdf
16. NIH News release: NIH Clinical Center provides one of the largest publicly available chest x-ray datasets to scientific community
17. Original source files and documents. https://nihcc.app.box.com/v/ChestXray-NIHCC/folder/36938765345

Object-Based Quadrant Triggering for Smart Energy Management System

M. Saravanan[1(✉)], M. Bennish[1], and Rahul Raman[2]

[1] Department of Networking and Communications, School of Computing SRM Institute of Science and Technology Kattankulathur, Chennai, India
{saravanm7,bm9887}@srmist.edu.in

[2] Department of Computer Science and Engineering, Indian Institute of Information Technology Design and Manufacturing Kancheepuram, Chennai, India
rahul@iiitdm.ac.in

Abstract. The escalating demand for energy efficiency and sustainability underscores the pressing need for advanced technologies to optimize energy consumption across diverse domains. Energy wastage has emerged as a critical challenge, contributing to the inability to fulfill the surging consumer need for electrical energy. The paper introduces a cutting-edge approach, proposing a system that leverages advanced object detection techniques to monitor and dynamically control energy consumption in real-time. The system employs a distributed architecture integrating edge devices and computer vision to enhance energy management efficiency. Smart computer vision devices deployed at the edge capture real-time environmental data, utilizing instance and semantic segmentation algorithms for zone segmentation and accurate identification and counting of individuals within these zones. The counted persons determine threshold values, governing the operation of electrical appliances via a relay mechanism. This integration of object detection and smart IoT edge devices facilitates real-time energy monitoring, enabling users to take proactive measures to reduce electricity consumption based on the identified number of persons. When compared with the existing method of Faster- RCNN, the custom YOLOv8 model achieves an accuracy of 92.3%, with a difference of 12.3% and a fast detection rate of 0.92ms. Furthermore, the system provides precise energy forecasting, facilitating proactive load management and optimal resource allocation. This paper delves into the confluence of YOLO-based Region of Interest (ROI) Object Detection and Quadrant Triggering for a Smart Energy Management System, presenting a cutting-edge approach to cut costs, conserve electricity, and foster environmental sustainability.

Keywords: Deep neural network · Deep Learning · Object Classification · Computer vision · YOLOv8 · Region of Interest · Internet of Things · edge computing · energy conservation

J. Kakarla et al. (Eds.): CVIP 2024, CCIS 2473, pp. 43–57, 2026.
https://doi.org/10.1007/978-3-031-93688-3_4

1 Introduction

The inexorable reliance on electrical appliances in our daily lives has engendered a surge in energy consumption, precipitating heightened demands on urban and rural energy infrastructures. This escalating demand, especially in critical institutions such as hospitals, schools, and businesses, has accentuated the need for innovative solutions to manage energy resources efficiently [1]. In response, countries worldwide are investing extensively in research and development endeavors, striving to create sustainable, renewable, and alternative energy sources to meet the burgeoning electricity requirements [2]. Recognizing the imperative to curtail energy waste and manage consumption judiciously, educational institutions emerge as focal points for addressing this challenge. Object detection, an increasingly prominent research domain, is pivotal in optimizing energy utilization [3]. Traditional methods for counting crowds based on images have yielded numerous research outcomes. An extensively examined demographic and behavioral aspects through video analysis, specifically focusing on the computation for estimating population size and density [4].

In computer vision technological advancements, researchers have shown a keen interest in leveraging Object classification-based techniques for population detection [5]. Employing machine learning models, particularly adept at addresing non-linear challenges [6], becomes instrumental in processing such data. In certain scenarios of densely populated crowds, objects exhibit diminutive dimensions, substantial scale variations, and considerable occlusions [7], presenting formidable challenges for object detection methodologies that concurrently ascertain the positions and dimensions of objects in a picture [9]. The proliferation of deep neural networks (DNN) introduces a pressing concern regarding the substantial demand for annotated data [10]. However, the advent of YOLO architecture [8], has a significant advantage over object recognition techniques.

The proposed system operates on a fundamental premise rooted in computer vision [11], which will segment the target environment into quadrants and be specifically designed to identify individuals within a classroom environment [12]. Through meticulous custom-trained YOLO V8 object detection algorithms [8], the system dynamically assesses the presence of people in the particular quadrant [1], subsequently determining threshold values for controlling the activation and deactivation of fans across the classroom's four zones [15]. By harnessing the capabilities of the Raspberry Pi 4 Model B board [26], this innovative methodology exemplifies a pragmatic application of deep learning in addressing the escalating current energy demands of our society [13]. The methodology and principles of our system [14], reveal its capacity to initiate enduring beneficial transformations in the realm of energy conservation. Through empirical validation and comprehensive evaluation, this research seeks to establish the system's efficacy, scalability, and potential [11] to significantly contribute to smart and sustainable energy management practices.

2 Related Works

2.1 Traditional Person Detection Approaches

In response to escalating security concerns, the deployment of Closed-Circuit Television (CCTV) systems across urban landscapes has become pervasive for surveillance purposes [22]. Numerous object detection applications rely on the copious motion pictures and frames produced by these CCTV installations [21]. The utilization of computer vision technology greatly facilitates the identification and detection of objects within videos or frames [24]. Conventional object detection techniques involve numerous procedural steps, which include segmentation, processing, item occurrence evaluation, characteristic extraction, and structural evaluation [15]. Despite the efficacy of machine learning techniques [19], their limitation in handling large volumes of data poses a significant challenge.

Traditional machine learning models face performance issues within this system, necessitating extensive training and learning of intricate features for improved prediction. Sparse head detection, an approach grounded in machine learning, identifies individuals' heads within an image [7]. The detection process is deemed sparse as it selectively identifies a subset of heads rather than every individual's head present in the image [13]. This technique serves the purpose of ascertaining the overall headcount within a given gathering. Notably, the model doesn't attempt to detect every head in the image, given the impracticality stemming from the high population density. In summary, this approach seamlessly integrates into existing crowd-tracking systems, augmenting their precision and overall performance.

2.2 Person Counting in Crowd Denser Region

Leveraging the strides in Deep Neural Networks (DNN), contemporary object detection frameworks like Faster R-CNN, Retina Net, and Center Net demonstrate commendable efficacy [28]. Despite notable advancements, these methodologies face challenges in accurately enumerating petite and densely obscured entities within congested visual contexts [14]. Employing a derived clustering network approach addresses the complexities associated with overlapping objects in densely populated scenes [15]. While the detectors mentioned above exhibit commendable performance, it is imperative to acknowledge that they necessitate training and supervision [16] through annotated with bounding boxes.

The single-focused point-level annotations result in an absence of information regarding object sizes [18]. Consequently, contemporary object detectors grounded in DNN face non-trivial challenges when applied to such point-based supervision [19]. However, these approaches encounter difficulties in scenarios characterized by highly congested objects within the crowd, posing additional hurdles to accurate counting processes [23]. Evading traditional localization and counting-by-regression strategies [21], alternative methodologies have been introduced to tackle the occupant enumeration challenges [24].

The YOLO community model is comparatively well-known in the object detection field due to its output layer that provides sophistication-unique chances and bounding container coordinates [25]. However, as the literature points out, there are some flaws and knowledge gaps in earlier YOLO fashion iterations:

- YOLOv2 may encounter difficulties identifying objects in photos with complex backgrounds or low lighting, potentially requiring an in-depth extent of facts is required for fine training [25].
- YOLOv3 may demand more computational resources [28].
- YOLOv4 could necessitate even greater computational resources than its predecessors [34].
- YOLOv5 might still struggle with identifying small or intricately shaped objects, requiring extensive data for training [40], and may be susceptible to spurious regressions.

The YOLOv8 model deviates from the standard practice of using anchors by explicitly estimating the item's middle rather than estimating the object's distance from a considered anchor container [28]. This reduction in the field prediction relies on anchor-free detection to speed up a complex post-processing step that eliminates any detectable signal following inference.

3 Significant Objectives of the Proposed System

In developing nations like India, the predominant reliance on electrical fans within educational institutions, particularly conventional ceiling fans in every classroom, presents a challenge of discerning and mitigating unnecessary fan operation [24]. Typically running continuously from the beginning to the end of the working day, this continuous operation in unoccupied or minimally occupied classrooms contributes significantly to energy wastage and elevated operational costs [23]. The objectives of the proposed system are addressed by the deployment of an Object-based quadrant triggering for a smart energy management system, encompassing the following key aspects:

- Object classification is employed for quantifying the number of electrical fans and individuals present within the classroom, utilizing an advanced custom- trained YOLO-P deep learning algorithm.
- Classrooms are segmented into quadrant zones or regions of interest based on the spatial distribution of electrical fans, leveraging computer vision method- ologies for effective delineation.
- Automatic activation of fans situated within the designated quadrant zones in the classroom is facilitated through intelligent algorithms, optimizing energy utilization.
- Utilizing deep learning approaches, specifically the round-robin method, the activation sequence of each quadrant region is determined based on head counts of individuals within the classroom, ensuring an energy-efficient and responsive system.

4 YOLO-P Based Enumeration

We obtain a set of CCTV video recordings that display exceptional conditions, lights, and crowd sizes in school room settings. The dataset is separated into subsets for checking out, validation, and schooling, and it has bounding boxes around every man or woman with annotations. The CCTV footage ought to be pre-processed via varying body rates, standardizing pixel values, and the use of augmentation techniques like brightness, rotation, and flipping. We think about the YOLOv8 deep getting-to-know architecture for person detection due to its velocity, accuracy, and complexity. Using pre-skilled weights from a large-scale dataset like COCO, we initialize the YOLO model. Then, we use transfer studying strategies to pleasant-song the version on our custom annotated dataset. We examine the detection effects and regulate the parameters to enhance the performance of the model.

We developed a system that examines the monitored individuals to count the number of persons within the quadrant zones and those leaving areas of interest (ROI) zones and track them using a unique ID and find people who are stepping outside of ROI boundaries and adjust the count appropriately. To make sure the system is reliable and efficient, we fine-tune its performance using the metrics obtained from the testing dataset. The integrated system combines the people counting module, object tracking module, and trained YOLO model. To improvise the system to make it more efficient by assuring the entire system is thoroughly tested and validated with real surveillance footage and verifying its accuracy, robustness, and real-time performance in a range of environments and crowd situations.

5 Materials and Methodology

5.1 Data Set Description

To ensure the proposed system meets specific requirements, we meticulously annotated and prepared a custom dataset comprising 3,000 images of real-time classroom environments. The dataset preparation process involves resizing, normalizing, and augmenting the data images. Around 2100 images are designated for the training set, 600 for the validation set, and 300 for the testing set from a dataset comprising 3000 custom images.

5.2 Custom Training Methodology of YOLO-P Model

The annotated dataset is employed to fine-tune the YOLOv8 model for individual detection and localization within video frames. Hyperparameters of the model are adjusted in the training phase to minimize both class prediction accuracy and localization loss, which measures the precision of bounding box predictions. These components are consolidated by the loss function, ensuring comprehensive model optimization. Various data augmentation techniques are implemented during training to enhance the dataset and boost the model's generalization capabilities. These strategies include contrast and brightness adjustments, random cropping, and horizontal flipping.

5.3 Object Detection Model Enabled Classroom Monitoring

The plan involves installing 2 surveillance cameras in classrooms to monitor the environment from both sides to detect and count the persons and the ceiling fan accurately. A custom-trained YOLOv8 model for object detection will be trained using real-time classroom environment images to distinguish between humans and electrical ceiling fans. The model will then count the number of fans and human heads to determine the quadrant zones. These zones will be created using a region segmentation image processing technique based on the available fans and the classroom's capacity, as described in Eq. 1. A threshold for each zone will be calculated to activate the relay system, which will in turn activate the required number of fans in each region in a round-robin fashion, as specified in Eq. 2 (Fig. 1).

$$\text{Number of Regions}(R_n) = \text{Total number of fans} \quad (1)$$

$$\text{Region Threshold } (R_t) = \frac{\text{Capacity of the classroom}}{\text{Total number of regions}} \quad (2)$$

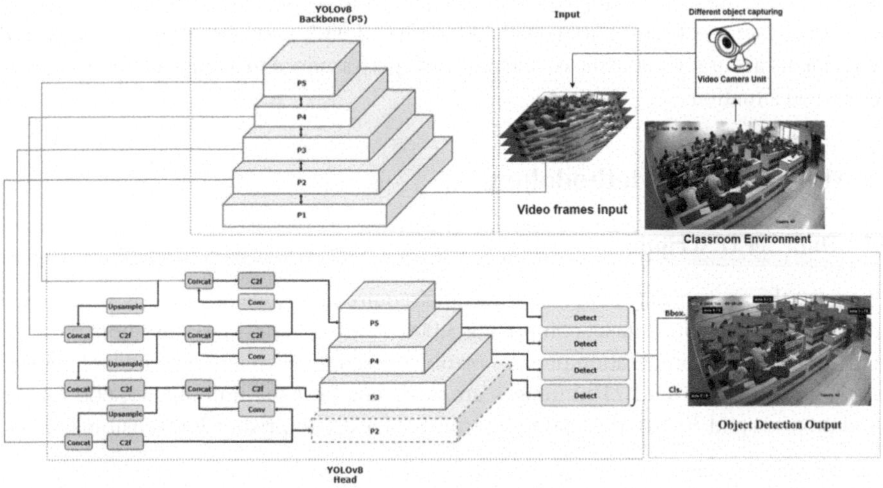

Fig. 1. Development of custom YOLO-v8 model for object classification, person counting, and threshold Calculation.

Algorithm 1 Quadrant-based Person Enumeration and Fan Activation

Initialize $\mathbf{F}_{count}$ and $\mathbf{P}_{count}$ to zero
DetectPersonsAndFans(Frame)
    $\mathbf{P}_{det}$, $\mathbf{F}_{det}$ ← YOLO-P.detect(Frame)
    $\mathbf{F}_{count}$ ← number of $\mathbf{F}_{det}$
Perform ROI Region Segmentation(Frame, $\mathbf{F}_{det}$)
    for each $\mathbf{F}_{det}$ **do**
        Draw ROI zone for $\mathbf{F}_{det}$
    end for
$\mathbf{P}_{count}$ in ROI Zones(Frame, $\mathbf{P}_{det}$, ROI Zones)
    for each ROI zone **do**
    $\mathbf{P}_{count}$ in ROI Zones(Frame, $\mathbf{P}_{det}$, ROI Zones)
        $\mathbf{P}_{count}$ within the zone ← number of $\mathbf{P}_{det}$ within the zone
    end for
AverageFanCount ← $\frac{\sum_{i=1}^{n} \text{FanCounts}_i}{n}$ ▷ Calculate average fan count

function THRESHOLD($\mathbf{R}_{Threshold}$)
    $\mathbf{ROI}_{threshold} \leftarrow \left\lceil \frac{\text{Class capacity}}{\text{no of ROI regions}} \right\rceil$
    Calculate the threshold value based on the $\mathbf{P}_{count}$ in each ROI zone
function ActivateFans($\mathbf{ROI}_{threshold}$)
    F_{act} = true
    return F_{act} for relay channel Fan Activation.

5.4 Implementation of Relay Channel

A multi-channel relay system is connected to the ESP8266 Node MCU module, serving as the client device to receive human count data from the YOLOv8 model, which is deployed in the Raspberry Pi 4 unit through the MQTT server- client protocol. These relay channels are linked to individual fan systems, each designated as a zone/region. The fans are activated and deactivated based on the quadrant threshold derived from the headcount in each quadrant zone, aiming to conserve energy. The YOLOv8 model continually monitors the classroom environment, and the number of heads detected determines the activation of specific zones/regions. For example, in a class with an overall strength of 60 and 6 available fans, there will be 4 regions, each with a threshold of 10. If the detected head count is 10 or fewer, one fan will be activated; if it exceeds 10, another fan will be activated by the multi-channel relay circuit.

5.5 Region-Based Monitoring and Threshold-Based Triggering

The Smart Classroom is segmented into ROI zones and each zone is assigned a unique sequential identifier, as illustrated in Fig. 3. These zones' thresholds control the activation of fans in their respective regions based on headcounts provided by the YOLO model. As headcounts fluctuate, other zones (Q1, Q2, Q3, Q4...Qn) are sequentially triggered. While this round-robin method is effective for smaller classrooms, it may pose challenges in larger settings like seminar halls or auditoriums. To address this, a crowd-based triggering approach is implemented for larger spaces where the threshold value determines the maximum headcount in the area, leading to the activation of the corresponding electrical fan system. Subsequently, the next maximum count in each remaining zone is activated. For instance, in Fig. 4, if quadrant zone Q2 reaches a headcount of fifteen, its relay channel is activated first, followed by the successful triggering of the Q4 channel with the next maximum count (Fig. 2).

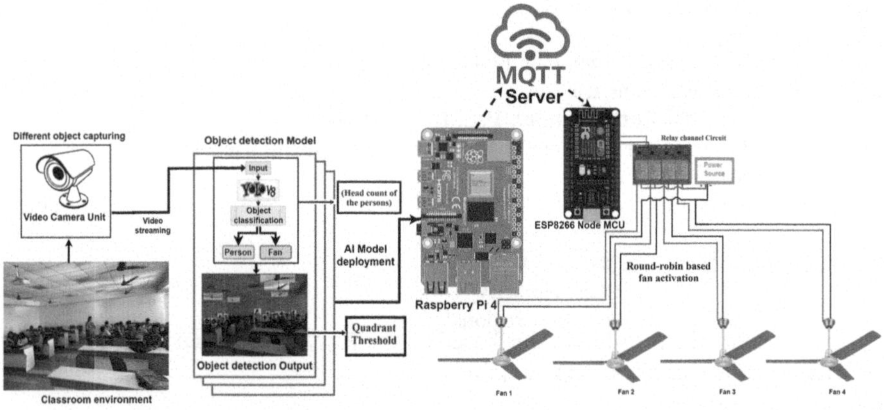

Fig. 2. Object detection-based relay channel quadrant triggering.

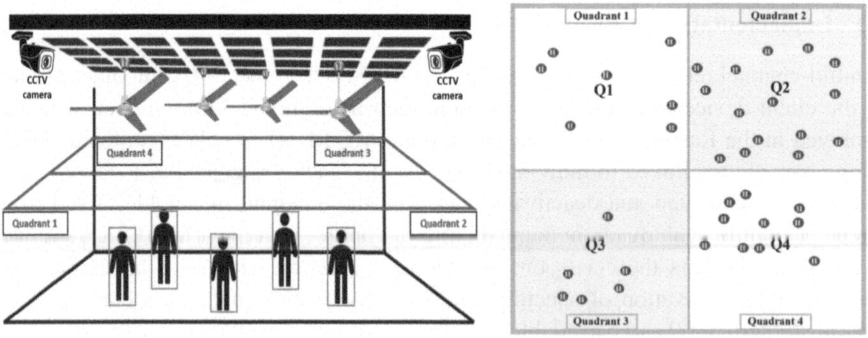

Fig. 3. Regions-based monitoring and person count

5.6 Occupant Enumeration Computation

i **Object localization Box computation:** Bounding box encoding is used by YOLO to symbolize the expected bounding container coordinates, which commonly consist of the size and vicinity of anchor containers.

$$C_x = \frac{x - A_x}{A_{\text{width}}} \tag{3}$$

$$C_y = \frac{y - A_y}{A_{\text{height}}} \tag{4}$$

$$C_w = \log\left(\frac{w}{A_{\text{width}}}\right) \tag{5}$$

$$C_h = \log\left(\frac{h}{A_{\text{height}}}\right) \tag{6}$$

The predicted or expected bounding box's center coordinates are denoted by (Cx, Cy), with its width and height represented by (Cw, Ch). The anchor box's center coordinates are indicated by (Ax, Ay).

ii **Loss Function computation:** During the training phase, YOLO combines localization and class losses, improving its model's overall performance. Class loss assesses the precision of expected class probabilities, while localization loss measures the accuracy of expected or predicted bounding box coordinates.

Localization Loss:

$$\mathcal{L}_{\text{loc}} = \boldsymbol{\lambda}_{\text{coord}} \sum_{i=0}^{S^2} \sum_{i=0}^{B} 1_{ij}^{\text{obj}} \left[(x_i - \hat{x}_i)^2 + (y_i - \hat{y}_i)^2 + (w_i - \hat{w}_i)^2 + \left(h_i - \hat{h}_i\right)^2 \right] \tag{7}$$

λ_{coord} modulates the impact of localization loss. 'S' and 'B' represent grid dimensions and bounding boxes per grid cell. The indicator function 1^{obj} detects objects in cells. x_i, y_i, w_i, and h_i are predicted bounding box coordinates, while x^i, y^i, w^i, and h^i are true values.

Classification Loss

$$\mathcal{L}_{\text{cls}} = \sum_i \left[(p_{e_i} - p_{t_i})^2 \right] \tag{8}$$

"*Lcls* represents the classification loss, quantifying the model's classification performance. It sums the squared differences between predicted (pe_i) and true class probabilities (p_{ti}) for all elements *i*.

iii **Loss function weight computation:** To achieve a balanced equilibrium in the contribution of individual components to the overall loss, YOLO assigns weights to the localization loss and the classification loss. Below are the mathematical formulations for combining these loss components using weights:

Total Loss:

$$L_{total} = (\boldsymbol{\lambda}_{coord} * L_{loc} + L_{cls} + \boldsymbol{\lambda}_{noobj} * L_{noobj}) \tag{9}$$

L_{total}, combines the localization (L_{loc}), classification (L_{cls}), and no-object confidence (L_{noobj}) losses. λ_{coord} and λ_{noobj} adjust the impact of localization and no-object confidence losses, respectively.

6 Results and Discussion

Our YOLO-derived human enumeration method demonstrated exceptional efficacy in accurately identifying and localizing individuals within the CCTV images. The method's average recall and precision over our assessment dataset were 0.88 and 0.95, respectively, showing how well it attempted to understand humans in various environmental scenarios. The method's average accuracy was calculated to be 0.90, indicating its accuracy at classifying entities as human beings.

The people-counting part of the CCTV footage was executed remarkably well, counting the diverse range of humans entering and leaving a designated ROI. We discovered that the mean absolute counting error of the handiest 1.4 individuals in line with the frame was obtained by comparing the counts produced by the algorithm with the manual counts accomplished with the assistance of human operators. This demonstrates the system's ability to fairly accurately calculate crowd density and track people's movements within its identified areas.

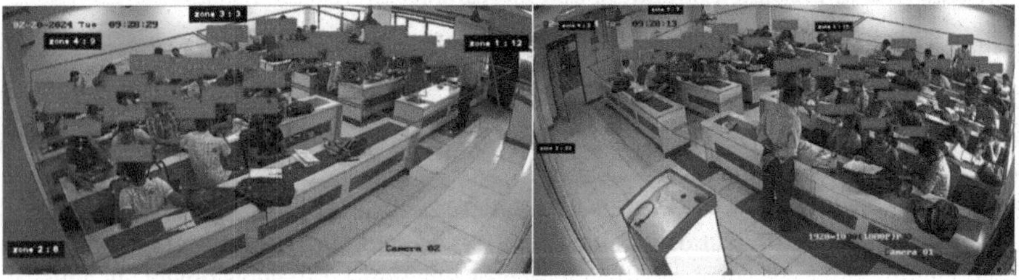

Fig. 4. Person counting in ROI quadrant zones

Figure 4 validates the effectiveness of the human enumeration system and is provided alongside. The bounding boxes overlay on the CCTV frames demonstrate how accurately the YOLO model detects and tracks individuals. The version is fed these images, and for each set of values extracted from the component table, the prediction accuracy and F1-rating are calculated. To determine the high cost of high-quality-tuning the version, a range analysis is performed on each of the seven elements, focusing on the row with the highest accuracy. Because of limitations in displaying accuracy metrics for each stage, Table 1 only shows a portion of the image.

6.1 Comparison of Various Person Enumeration Approaches

Advanced deep learning models used in object detection including Resnet-50 and Densenet-121 were trained and validated using equal datasets and parameters the outcomes were compared with the custom-trained yolov8 model and the evaluation of the training and validation curve results are given below. The scatter plot comparison in Fig. 6 depicts the performance of ResNet-50, DenseNet-121, and YOLOv8 deep learning models. This graphical representation visually tracks the models' convergence during training, emphasizing YOLOv8's superior performance over ResNet-50 and DenseNet-121 across training and validation periods. The plot in Fig. 5 highlights these models' distinct learning capacities and efficiencies.

Table 1. Metrics of accuracy within the initial seven levels of custom-trained YOLOv8 model shows improved accuracy while fine-tuning using transfer learning.

S. No.	Precision	Accuracy	F1-Score	AUC Score
1	0.85 ± 0.020	0.80 ± 0.018	0.832 ± 0.013	0.852
2	0.81 ± 0.202	0.85 ± 0.020	0.812 ± 0.015	0.833
3	0.88 ± 0.039	0.88 ± 0.028	0.835 ± 0.023	0.855
4	0.82 ± 0.032	0.90 ± 0.030	0.840 ± 0.020	0.859
5	0.86 ± 0.011	0.87 ± 0.026	0.833 ± 0.017	0.845
6	**0.89 ± 0.040**	**0.92 ± 0.032**	**0.858 ± 0.029**	**0.882**
7	0.88 ± 0.022	0.91 ± 0.029	0.842 ± 0.025	0.869

6.2 Deliberation of YOLO-P Evaluation Metrics

The results demonstrate the effectiveness of our YOLO-based real-time crowd management technique. The YOLO-P version's outstanding recall and accuracy metrics allow for accurate crowd counting and reliable individual identification and localization. The system maintains low counting discrepancies in challenging conditions characterized by varying crowd densities and barriers, demonstrating resilience. The following plot in Fig. 5 are the performance metrics of the YOLO- P model.

Accuracy Computation:

$$A = \frac{\tau_p + \tau_n}{\tau_p + \tau_n + f_p + f_n} \tag{10}$$

Precision Computation:

$$\rho = \frac{\tau_p}{\tau_p + f_p} \tag{11}$$

Recall:

$$R = \frac{\tau_p}{\tau_p + f_n} \tag{12}$$

F1-Score:

$$F1 = 2 * \frac{\rho * R}{\rho + R} \tag{13}$$

YOLOv8 outperforms ResNet-50 and DenseNet-121 across accuracy, loss, AUC, precision, and F1 score metrics. Its superior performance is evident in higher accuracy, lower loss, and elevated AUC values. Additionally, YOLOv8 demonstrates superior precision and F1 score, indicating robust object detection capabilities. Visualization through a scatter plot affirms YOLOv8's consistent superiority, solidifying its status as the optimal choice for precise and efficient object detection tasks. Here A represents the accuracy, ρ represents the precision, and R represents the recall of a classification model, where τ_p and τ_n represent true positives and true negatives, and f_p and f_n represent false positives and false negatives, respectively.

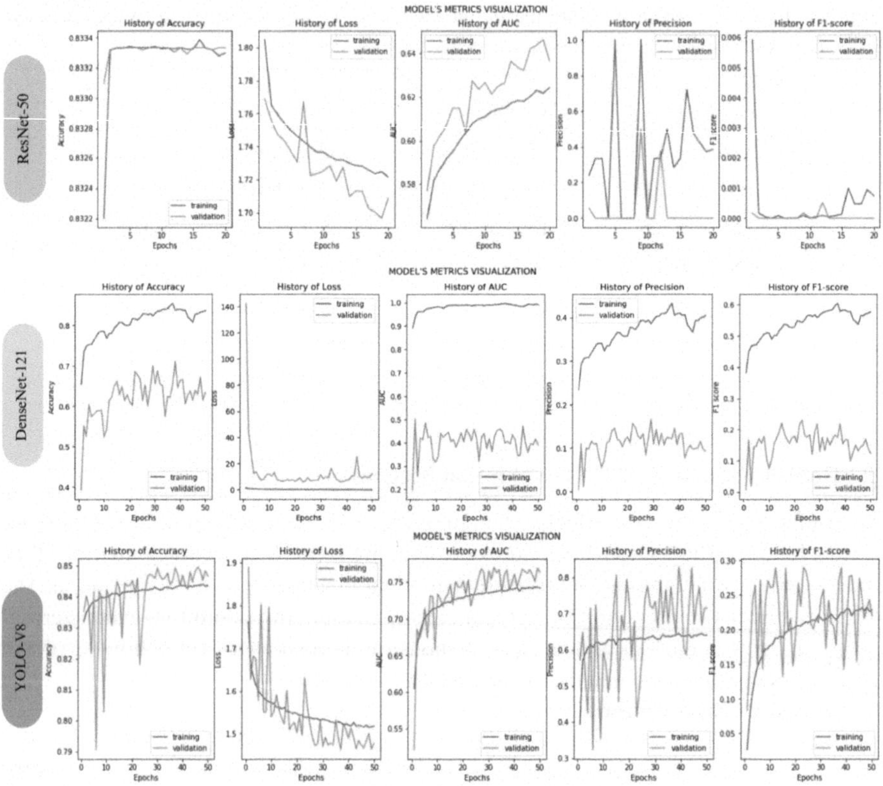

Fig. 5. Deep learning evaluation results comparison

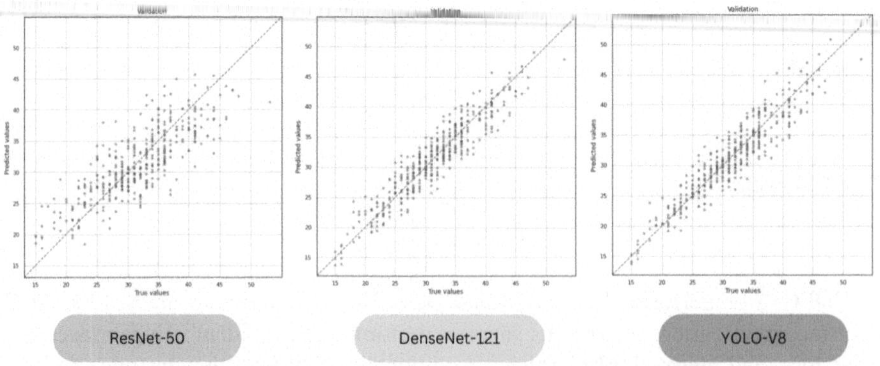

Fig. 6. Scatter plot comparison of precision of different deep learning models

7 Conclusion

In our research project, we developed our sophisticated algorithm based on YOLO object detection architecture for person enumeration. This system demonstrated its utility in real-world situations such as crowd-based energy management, security surveillance, and retail analytics by precisely identifying and counting persons in CCTV images. Our system accurately detected people in a variety of indoor and outdoor environments and remembered costs by skill- fully utilizing deep learning techniques and the YOLO version. This improvement accelerated the counting module's monitoring technique and made it easier to observe people as they entered and exited designated regions of interest (ROIs) within the CCTV feed.

Our counting method demonstrated excellent accuracy of 92.3% and occasional error rates following rigorous testing across multiple datasets. It aided inefficient crowd manipulation and analysis by leveraging real-time population updates and accurately estimating crowd density. Even though the normal machine's overall performance was strong, there were issues when the view was obstructed. These drawbacks are common to object recognition techniques; however, they may be mitigated with additional research and inventions such as incorporating multi-digicam fusion to improve accuracy in difficult settings. By implementing this system we can reduce undesirable wastage of electrical energy and even predict the future energy utilization pattern.

References

1. Sirisha, U., Praveen, S.P., Srinivasu, P.N., et al.: Statistical analysis of design aspects of various YOLO-based deep learning models for object detection. Int J Comput Intell Syst **16**, 126 (2023). https://doi.org/10.1007/s44196-023-00302-w
2. Gong, V.X., Daamen, W., Bozzon, A., et al.: Counting people in the crowd using social media images for crowd management in city events. Transportation **48**, 3085–3119 (2021). https://doi.org/10.1007/s11116-020-10159-z
3. Dong, L., Zhang, H., Yang, K., Zhou, D., Shi, J., Ma, J.: Crowd counting by using top-k relations: a mixed ground-truth CNN framework. IEEE Trans. Consum. Electron. **68**(3), 307–316 (2022). https://doi.org/10.1109/TCE.2022.3190384
4. Gündüz, M.Ş, Işık, G.: A new YOLO-based method for real-time crowd detection from video and performance analysis of YOLO models. J. Real-Time Image Proc. **20**(5), 2022 (2023). https://doi.org/10.1007/s11554-023-01276-w
5. Khel, M.H.K., et al.: Realtime Crowd monitoring—estimating count, speed and direction of people using hybridized YOLOv4. IEEE Access **11**, 56368–56379 (2023). https://doi.org/10.1109/ACCESS.2023.3272481
6. Zheng, S., Wu, J., Duan, S., et al.: An improved crowd counting method based on YOLOv3. Mobile Netw Appl (2022). https://doi.org/10.1007/s11036-022-02082-7
7. Wei, Y., Liu, L., Fu, X., et al.: Crowded pose-guided multi-task learning for instance-level human parsing. Mach. Vis. Appl. **34**, 46 (2023). https://doi.org/10.1007/s00138-023-01392-4
8. Le, V.H.: Deep learning-based for human segmentation and tracking, 3D human pose estimation and action recognition on monocular video of MADS dataset. Multimed Tools Appl **82**, 20771–20818 (2023). https://doi.org/10.1007/s11042-022-13921-w
9. Yen, M.-H., Lin, B.-S., Kuo, Y.-L., Lee, I.-J., Lin, B.-S.: Adaptive indoor people-counting system based on edge AI computing. IEEE Trans. Emerging Topics Comput. Intell. **8**(1), 255–263 (2024). https://doi.org/10.1109/TETCI.2023.3300172

10. Khan, S.D., Basalamah, S.: Scale and density invariant head detection deep model for crowd counting in pedestrian crowds. Vis. Comput. **37**, 2127–2137 (2021). https://doi.org/10.1007/s00371-020-01974-7
11. Thakur, N., Nagrath, P., Jain, R., et al.: Autonomous pedestrian detection for crowd surveillance using deep learning framework. Soft. Comput. **27**, 9383–9399 (2023). https://doi.org/10.1007/s00500-023-08289-4
12. Li, B., Zhang, Y., Xu, H., et al.: CCST: crowd counting with swin transformer. Vis. Comput. **39**, 2671–2682 (2023). https://doi.org/10.1007/s00371-022-02485-3
13. Talaat, F.M., ZainEldin, H.: An improved fire detection approach based on YOLO-v8 for smart cities. Neural Comput. Applic. **35**, 20939–20954 (2023). https://doi.org/10.1007/s00521-023-08809-1
14. Song, Y., Xie, Z., Wang, X., Zou, Y.: MS-YOLO: object detection based on YOLOv5 Optimized fusion millimeter-wave radar and machine vision. IEEE Sensors J. **22**(15), 15435–15447, (2022). https://doi.org/10.1109/JSEN.2022.3167251
15. Li, S., Liu, S., Cai, Z., et al.: TC-YOLOv5: rapid detection of floating debris on rasp- berry Pi 4B. J. Real-Time Image Proc. **20**, 17 (2023). https://doi.org/10.1007/s11554-023-01265-z
16. Mammeri, S., Amroune, M., Haouam, M.Y., et al.: Early detection and diagnosis of lung cancer using YOLO v7, and transfer learning. Multimed Tools Appl **83**, 30965–30980 (2024). https://doi.org/10.1007/s11042-023-16864-y
17. Zhu, H., Sun, L., Qin, W., et al.: AG-YOLO: Attention-guided network for real-time object detection. Multimed Tools Appl **83**, 28197–28213 (2024). https://doi.org/10.1007/s11042-023-16568-3
18. Chaturvedi, P., Lavingia, K., Raval, G.: Detection of traffic rule violation in University campus using deep learning model. Int. J. Syst. Assur. Eng. Manag. **14**, 2527–2545 (2023). https://doi.org/10.1007/s13198-023-02107-8
19. Li, X., He, M., Liu, Y., et al.: SPCS: a spatial pyramid convolutional shuffle mod- ule for YOLO to detect occluded object. Complex Intell. Syst. **9**, 301–315 (2023). https://doi.org/10.1007/s40747-022-00786-7
20. Wang, K., Wang, Y., Ren, R., Zou, H, Shao, Z.: Transformer-based feature aggregation and stitching network for crowd counting, IEEE Access **11** pp. 124833–124844, 2023. https://doi.org/10.1109/ACCESS.2023.3329985
21. Chow, T.E., Yip, P.S.F., Wong, KP.: An integrated framework of mobile crowd estimation for the 2019, July 1st rally in Hong Kong. Multimed Tools Appl. **82**, 43349–43366 (2023). https://doi.org/10.1007/s11042-023-15417-7
22. Massa, L., Barbosa, A., Oliveira, K., et al.: LRCN-RetailNet: A recurrent neural net- work architecture for accurate people counting. Multimed Tools Appl **80**, 5517–5537 (2021). https://doi.org/10.1007/s11042-020-09971-7
23. Collini, E., Palesi, L.A.I., Nesi, P., et al.: Flexible thermal camera solution for Smart city people detection and counting. Multimed Tools Appl **83**, 20457–20485 (2024). https://doi.org/10.1007/s11042-023-16374-x
24. Liu, D., Wang, G., Zhai, G.: Multi-scale dilated convolution of feature Fu- sion Network for Crowd counting. Multimed Tools Appl **81**, 37939–37952 (2022). https://doi.org/10.1007/s11042-022-13130-5
25. Zhou, F., Zhao, H., Zhang, Y., et al.: COMAL: compositional multi-scale feature enhanced learning for crowd counting. Multimed Tools Appl **81**, 20541–20560 (2022). https://doi.org/10.1007/s11042-022-12249-9
26. Wu, D., Fan, Z., Cui, M.: Average up-sample network for crowd counting. Appl. Intell. **52**, 1376–1388 (2022). https://doi.org/10.1007/s10489-021-02470-8
27. Kadhim, T.A., Hariri, W., Smaoui Zghal, N., et al.: A face recognition application for Alzheimer's patients using ESP32-CAM and Raspberry Pi. J. Real-Time Image Proc. **20**, 100 (2023). https://doi.org/10.1007/s11554-023-01357-w

28. Prabhu, B.V.B., Lakshmi, R., Ankitha, R., et al.: RescueNet: YOLO-based object detection model for detection and counting of flood survivors. Model. Earth Syst. Environ. **8**, 4509–4516 (2022). https://doi.org/10.1007/s40808-022-01414-6

Indian Sign Language Recognition in Complex Backgrounds: A Shifted Window Attention Based Approach with Swin Transformers

B. V. Poornima[2(✉)], S. Srinath[1], S. Rashmi[3], and R. Rakshitha[1]

[1] JSS Science and Technology University, Mysuru, India
[2] Sahyadri College of Engineering & Management, Mangaluru, India
Poornimabv.85@gmail.com
[3] RV University, Bangalore, India

Abstract. Gesture recognition is a pivotal area of research, especially in the domain of sign language recognition, where precise recognition of gestures is crucial for effective communication. In this study, a novel approach for Indian sign language gesture recognition is introduced, leveraging the shifted window transformers (SWIN) architecture. SWIN Transformers, a recent advancement in computer vision, offer a scalable and efficient solution for capturing spatial dependencies in images. This research work provides a detailed overview of the SWIN architecture and its suitability for gesture recognition tasks, emphasizing its ability to handle long-range dependencies efficiently. A standard ISL dataset is utilized which comprises of diverse hand gestures, with 36 classes comprising of alphabets and digits. Thorough experiments demonstrate the effectiveness of the SWIN-based approach in achieving state-of-the-art results in gesture recognition. This study contributes to the advancement of gesture recognition research, particularly in the context of Indian scenario, by showcasing the capabilities of transformer-based architectures in handling spatial recognition tasks effectively by achieving a classification accuracy of 99.3%

Keywords: Sign language recognition (SLR) · Indian sign language (ISL) · Complex background · Transformers · Shifted window (SWIN) transformers

1 Introduction

In today's digital world, effective and precise communication is essential. However, there is a significant gap between the needs of spoken language and the needs of sign language users, especially the deaf and hearing-impaired communities. This research seeks to bridge this gap by leveraging the power of artificial intelligence to improve communication. This study primarily focuses on ISL [1]. The study uses advanced technique, which includes attention based model such as shifted window transformer or SWIN transformers. Proposed work has achieved good accuracy in recognizing ISL gestures, using a large ISL dataset which includes alphabets and digits in complex background. Swin transformers introduced by Liu et al. [2] represents a significant development in

J. Kakarla et al. (Eds.): CVIP 2024, CCIS 2473, pp. 58–71, 2026.
https://doi.org/10.1007/978-3-031-93688-3_5

vision transformers architecture. They depart from the conventional approach of processing images with patches of fixed size and instead use a hierarchical and multi-scale processing mechanism. Swin transformers utilize the properties of transformers [3] to capture both spatial and temporal information that are necessary for precise gesture recognition. This is done by dynamically shifting focus and adapting to crucial regions in the input data.

They offer a strong framework with the ability to precisely recognize and categorize static hand gestures and filter out background noise by utilizing the advantages of transformers. By showcasing the efficacy of swin transformers in image classification, this research diversifies the application of transformer architectures beyond their traditional strong hold in natural language processing. This expansion underscores the versatility and relevance of transformers across various domains, including computer vision tasks, thereby enriching the landscape of transformer-based methodologies.

2 Literature Review

Rao et al. [4] introduced a deep CNN architecture specifically designed for SLR. Their approach utilized a dataset comprising 200 gestures across five different backgrounds, achieving an impressive accuracy rate of 92.88% for recognizing ISL gestures. Sharma et al. [5] developed a transfer learning-based deep neural network framework aimed at recognizing 35 different ISL symbols. Their approach utilized the MobileNetV2 model, pre-trained on ImageNet, to facilitate efficient feature extraction. Notably, they aimed to develop a web-based system in the future capable of swiftly decoding ISL signals. A CNN model designed for Arabic sign language is presented by Zakariah et al. [6]. By leveraging data augmentation techniques, they augmented their dataset, increasing it from 32,000 to 160,000 images. This augmentation enabled the consideration of various brightness and angular scenarios, enhancing the robustness of the model. A fully linked dense layer is added to the training process of the EfficientNetB4 approach. In their study, Mannan et al. [7] introduced a Hypertuned DeepCNN tailored specifically for American Static SLR. In order to increase the quantity of learning data samples, the authors used data augmentation techniques. Their proposed architecture adheres to a conventional CNN framework, incorporating hyper parameter tuning to optimize model performance. Impressively, their hyper tuned model achieved an accuracy of 99.67% within just 20 epochs. This research underscores the efficacy of their approach in accurately recognizing American static sign language gestures, showcasing its potential for practical deployment. Specifically focused on static Indian signs, the work [8] offers the transformer encoder as a possible technique for SLR. The authors demonstrate the efficacy of a vision transformer in comparison to conventional convolutional architectures by using it to do this task. By using a transformer block with four self-attention layers and a multilayer perceptron network, the suggested solution splits the images into positional embedding patches. Trial outcomes show that the suggested method outperforms current convolutional architectures in terms of efficiency. Notably, the methodology achieves a remarkable accuracy of 99.29% with only a minimal number of training epochs. This highlights the efficiency and effectiveness of the vision transformer-based approach in static SLR, offering promising implications for practical deployment in real-world scenarios. Dosovitskiy et al. [9] created a revolutionary transformer model called vision transformer (ViT) by taking advantage of the self-attention mechanism that transformers naturally have. ViT is proficient in processing image patches, in contrast to conventional transformers that handle words. Notably, ViT demonstrated better test accuracy across seven different datasets, outperforming sophisticated CNN architectures like EfficientNet and ResNet.

In the study [10], a self-created ISL dataset comprising 72 words is utilized. A novel vision transformer model is proposed, comprising only two transformer layers. Preprocessing methods includes skin segmentation on the images based on morphological operations and conversion from YCbCr. The model remarkably attained an exceptional 99.56% test accuracy. Rajan and Rajendran [11] proposed an ensemble-based CNN model for Hand Gesture Recognition (HGR) that leverages both color and depth information from a finger spelling dataset to achieve a remarkable 99.93% accuracy in identifying American sign language alphabets. Wu et al. [12] developed a double channel CNN (DC-CNN) model that first preprocesses raw images to extract hand gesture and hand edge features, which are then processed through two separate CNN channels for classification. The results demonstrate that the suggested DC-CNN achieved accuracy of 98.02% and 97.29% on the NAO Camera hand posture database and the Jochen Triesch database, respectively. No images with complicated backgrounds have been used to test the suggested DC-CNN model.

According to the literature, earlier research works have primarily used deep CNN models, transfer learning methods such as MobileNetV2, Efficient Net and hyper tuned CNN architectures. However, more recent developments in computer vision have brought transformers, which were first proposed for tasks related to natural language processing. Transformers, as opposed to CNNs, use attention methods to preserve more information for segmentation and classification tasks by enabling interactions across patches in an image. However, CNN based models often suffer from limitations in capturing long range dependencies and global context information. Additionally, transformers, while promising, entail higher computational costs compared to CNN models due to their attention mechanism and typically require more resources for training and inference. Despite these drawbacks, transformers offer significant potential for improving performance in tasks requiring fine-grained understanding of spatial relationships and context within images, such as SLR. In vision transformers, the self-attention mechanism's computational complexity grows quadratically with the input image size, making them less efficient for processing high-resolution images.

To address these drawbacks, the proposed research focuses on shifted window transformers, which aim to overcome scalability issues and enhance the capability to capture spatial dependencies, thereby improving performance in SLR tasks.

3 Materials and Methods

This section presents the methodologies adapted for SLR in diverse background. This section starts with the understanding of the application of swin transformers according to the current literature.

3.1 Understanding Swin Transformers

Shifted window transformers adopt a localized processing approach, where the given input image is partitioned into overlapping windows, with each window being processed separately. This approach allows shifted window transformers to capture fine-grained spatial dependencies more efficiently, particularly in scenarios where objects of interest may be distributed across different regions of the image. The localized processing approach of swin transformers makes them particularly suitable for SLR in complex backgrounds. By dividing the input image into overlapping windows and processing each window independently, shifted window transformers can effectively isolate and analyze the signer's hand gestures regardless of the complexity of the background.

3.2 The Recent Research Work Using Swin Transformers

In their recent study, researchers proposed a novel method for automating blood cell classification using shifting window vision transformers (SW-ViT), as detailed in [13]. Initially, the SW-ViT architecture is pre-trained on the ImageNet dataset and subsequently fine-tuned using blood cell images to enhance its classification capabilities. The study leveraged two transfer learning techniques: one focused on optimizing the linear output layer while freezing other parameters, and another aimed at overall optimization of the SW-ViT architecture. Evaluation is conducted using the publicly available BCCD_Dataset (Blood Cell Count and Detection). Authors in [14] introduced SwinIR, a robust baseline model for image restoration built upon the swin transformer architecture. Shallow feature extraction, deep feature extraction, and high-quality image reconstruction are the three primary parts of SwinIR. Notably, several residual swin transformer blocks (RSTB) are incorporated into the deep feature extraction module. A residual connection connects each of the several swin transformer layers that make up a RSTB, which makes it possible to preserve important image details and extract features efficiently throughout the restoration process. In [15], despite the inherent dataset imbalance, with 80% of samples showing no presence of aneurysm and 20% showing its presence, and developed without explicit annotations, the effectiveness of Transformer-based deep learning architectures is showcased (specifically MACSSwin-T and vidMACSSwin-T) in detecting aneurysms and accurately classifying MACS frames accordingly. Over the past few years, there has been a surge in research focusing on transformer-based models, which have demonstrated notable performance. Despite their successes, trans formers still face challenges in effectively detecting small objects and accurately segmenting edge details. In a recent contribution by the authors in [16], enhancements to the swin transformer have been proposed to overcome existing limitations. Specifically, they introduced the local perception swin transformer (LPSW) as a novel backbone. The LPSW aims to improve the network's ability to perceive local features more effectively, thereby enhancing overall accuracy in various tasks. The research work in [17] introduces a novel methodology inspired by the design principles of the High-resolution network (HRNet). Instead of conventional convolutional layers, transformer blocks are employed within the architecture. Notably, the approach facilitates the continual exchange of information across various resolution feature maps generated by transformer blocks. This innovative network configuration, termed the High-resolution swin transformer network combines the structural robustness of HRNet with the transformative capabilities of swin transformers. In the study detailed in [18], researchers employ a swin transformer model to handle both RGB and depth information within a multimodal recognition framework. The research introduces a process where body node information is first extracted and fused with the original RGB image using the MediaPipe framework. This combined data is then fed into the swin transformer network for training. The purpose of the work [19] is to monitor and conserve coastal wetlands inside the Saint John municipal pilot site in New Brunswick, Canada. The authors looked into the possibility of advanced transformers, specifically the swin transformer, in conjunction with a 3D CNN model and a customized version of the VGG-16 CNN network. The study [20] evaluates how well the swin transformer model classified and segmented lung cancer. According to their results, the pre-trained Swin-B model outperformed ViT by 2.529% and achieved an amazing top-1 accuracy of 82.26% in the classification challenge.

SwinMR, a novel method for fast MRI reconstruction based on the Swin transformer method, is presented in the study [21]. The input module (IM), the feature extraction module (FEM), and the output module (OM) made up the three primary modules of the architecture. While the FEM was built with a cascade of residual swin transformer blocks (RSTBs) next to 2D convolutional layers, the IM and OM were built with 2D convolutional layers. There were several swin transformer layers (STLs) in each RSTB. Interestingly, unlike the original transformer architecture, which used multi-head self-attention (MSA) throughout the full picture space, the shifted windows multi-head self-attention (W-MSA/SW-MSA) mechanism of STL operated within shifted windows. In [22], researchers tackle weather forecasting using a video transformer network known as the video swin-transformer (VST) model. This novel approach includes a dedicated augmentation strategy tailored for video data. Notably, the method integrates gradual spatial reduction in the encoder and employs cross-attention mechanisms in the decoder to improve forecasting accuracy. These enhancements collectively empower the model to effectively predict weather patterns based on video inputs.

Observation

The provided survey highlights the diverse applications of swin transformer models across various domains:

- Blood cell classification: SW-ViT is used for automated blood cell classification, showcasing superior performance in classification accuracy.
- Image restoration: SwinIR is introduced as a robust baseline model for image restoration, incorporating residual swin transformer blocks for effective feature extraction and high-quality image reconstruction.
- Medical image analysis: MACSSwin-T and vidMACSSwin-T are proposed for detecting aneurysms in medical images, achieving high accuracy even with imbalanced datasets and no explicit annotations.
- Enhanced transformers: Several enhancements to swin transformers are proposed, including Local Perception Swin (LPSW) for better small object detection and high-resolution swin transformer network (HRSTNet) for improved image processing tasks.

- Multimodal sign language recognition: Swin transformers are utilized for sign language recognition in complex scenes by processing depth and RGB information and fusing results using statistical data fusion methods.
- Environmental monitoring: Swin transformers are explored for conserving and monitoring coastal wetlands, integrating with CNNs and 3D CNNs for effective analysis of satellite and LiDAR data.
- Medical imaging: Swin transformers are assessed for lung cancer classification and MRI reconstruction, showcasing enhanced performance compared to alternative methods.
- Weather forecasting: A novel video swin-transformer (VST) model is proposed for spatiotemporal weather forecasting, addressing challenges such as computational complexity and data requirements.
- Efficient lung cancer image classification and segmentation: Swin transformers are applied for both classifying and segmenting lung cancer images, demonstrating improved accuracy compared to alternative methods
- MRI Reconstruction: SwinMR, a novel approach based on swin transformers, is introduced for rapid MRI reconstruction, showcasing effectiveness through its architecture comprising input, feature extraction, and output modules.

Despite the widespread success of swin transformers across these domains, there remains a gap in their application for ISL recognition in complex background datasets. This study aims to fill this gap by focusing on applying swin transformers specifically for ISL recognition, aiming for robust performance in challenging environments.

3.3 Proposed Method

The proposed shifted window transformer for ISL gesture classification called as SW-ISL employs a unique shifted window-based self-attention mechanism. This innovation allows for enhanced scalability to high-resolution images without experiencing a quadratic surge in computation.

Steps in SWIN Transformers

Image Patching: The input image undergoes division into non-overlapping patches, where each patch functions as a token. Figure 1 shows the window based patch creation. It can be observed that the patches within each window will be processed locally, making it computationally more efficient. Figure 2 represents the overall displayed window for the given image. Figure 3 represents few samples of the patches created for the given input image.

Patch Embeddings: A lower-dimensional vector representation is linearly embedded with each patch. These embeddings function as the swin transformer's input tokens.

Stage Partitioning: SWIN introduces a hierarchical structure. It divides the tokens into multiple stages or levels. Each stage contains a subset of tokens.

Stage Blocks: Within each stage, there are multiple stage blocks. Each stage block contains a series of operations, including:

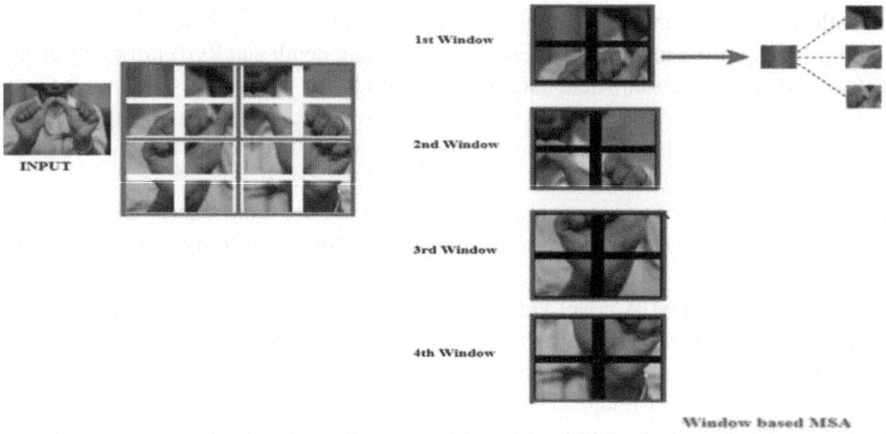

Fig. 1. Window based self-attention approach

Fig. 2. Shape of the output window for the given Image

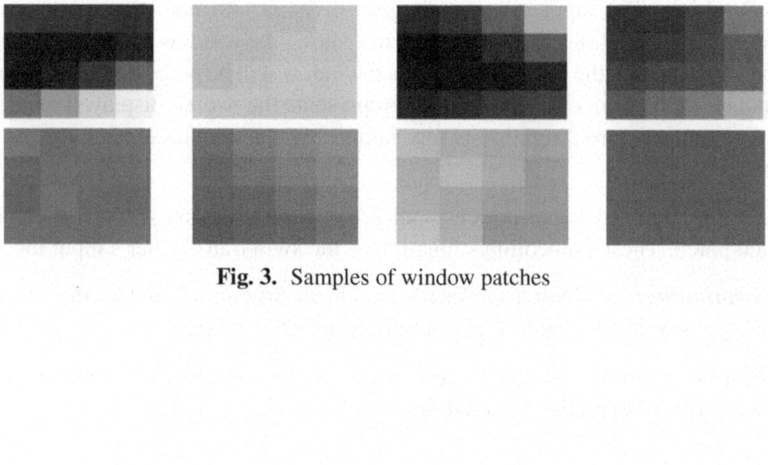

Fig. 3. Samples of window patches

1. Shifted window self-attention: This is a key innovation in SWIN. It restricts attention to a local window of tokens within the same stage, making it computationally more efficient.
2. Local token mixing: Tokens within the same stage can interact through local token mixing, helping capture local relationships effectively.
3. Layer normalization and feedforward networks: These are standard components in transformers used to enhance the representation of tokens.

Token Migration: After processing tokens within a stage, some tokens migrate to the next stage. This migration allows for information flow across different stages and helps capture global context.

Hierarchical Processing: The hierarchical structure and token migration continue through multiple stages, allowing for the gradual aggregation of information from local to global context.

Classification Head: A classification head is often added at the end of the swin transformer in applications like object identification or image classification in order to generate predictions based on the learned features.

Overview of the Proposed Architecture

Patch Splitting Module: The swin transformer segments an input RGB image into non-overlapping patches, representing a distinct fragment of the image.

Patch Feature Representation: The number of color channels and the patch size determine the feature dimension of each patch. In this instance, assuming RGB images, a patch size of N × N yields a feature dimension of N × N × 3.

Layer of Linear Embedding: This phase basically converts the raw pixel values into a higher-dimension space represented by 'C'.

Swin Transformer Blocks (Stage 1): These patch tokens are subjected to many transformer blocks. These blocks, also known as swin transformer blocks, keep track of the amount of tokens (H/N × W/N), where H and W stand for the image's height and width, respectively. The patches are processed in their original spatial order at this stage.

Patch Merging Layers: Patch merging layers are integrated into the architecture to create a hierarchical representation and reduce the number of tokens as the network depth increases. In the initial patch merging layer, typically arranged in pairs, features from adjacent patches are concatenated within the first patch merging layer. The concatenated features' dimensionality is then decreased by applying a linear layer. This yields an output dimension of 2C by effectively down sampling the resolution by a factor of 2×2 = 4.

Swin Transformer Blocks (Stages 2, 3, and 4): Each patch merging step is followed by the application of swin transformer blocks. These blocks keep the features at a specific resolution while continuing to change them. Feature transformation and patch merging are repeated several times, with decreasing output resolutions at each iteration [H/(N * 2) × W/(N * 2)], [H/(N * 4) × W/(N * 4)], and [H/(N * 8) × W/(N * 8)]. The suggested model of the shifted window transformer is shown in Fig. 4.

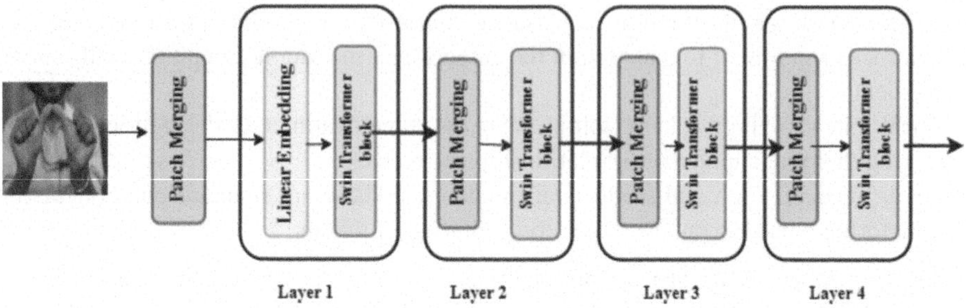

Fig. 4. Proposed SWIN architecture for ISL recognition

4 Experiments and Results

4.1 Dataset Used

The proposed experiment utilizes a publicly available standard ISL dataset, which has been captured across diverse backgrounds, representing complex and non-uniform environments. This dataset is accessible on GitHub at https://github.com/sajanraj/Indian-Sign-Language-Recognition. It comprises of ISL gestures, including 26 ISL alphabets and 10 ISL digits ranging from 0 to 9. There are 450 images in each class. Every image in the collection is 288 by 288 pixels in size. Table 1 provides a comprehensive overview of the dataset details.

Table 1. Samples of the dataset with its details

Dataset repository	Dataset volume	Classes	Resolution
Github	16200	36	288*288

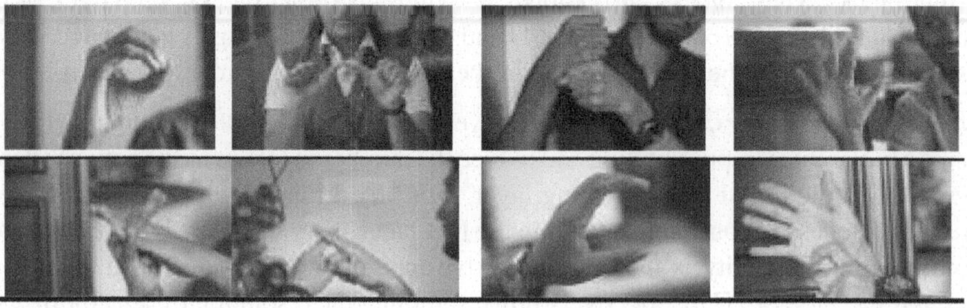

4.2 Experimental Setup

In this study, the model is implemented using PyTorch and all training sessions are conducted on a high-performance computing platform. Cross-entropy loss is employed as the loss function, and the Adam optimizer is utilized. The training session is executed for

100 epochs, with a batch size set to 32. The input image is divided into 4 × 4 patch, with the number of patches in the entire image calculated as, H/4 * W/4. Each patch of the input image is treated as a "token," Since each patch contains RGB values, the feature dimension for each patch is calculated as, for example if patch size is 4 * 4 then it is calculated as 4 × 4 × 3, resulting in 48 features per patch. An embedding layer is employed to transform the raw-valued features into a user-defined dimension, represented as C. Initially, these blocks process the entire image with a consistent number of tokens (H/4 * W/4), referred to as "Stage 1", alongside linear embedding. To establish a hierarchical representation, token numbers progressively decrease as the network deepens through patch merging layers. The first patch merging layer aggregates features from each group of neighboring 2 × 2 patches, followed by a linear layer applied to the concatenated 4C-dimensional features. This process downsamples resolution by a factor of 2 × 2, reducing token count by a factor of 4 and yielding an output dimension of 2C. Swin transformer blocks continue this transformation in "Stage 2", maintaining a resolution of H/8 x W/8. This iterative process continues through "Stage 3" and "Stage 4", further decreasing resolution and enhancing feature abstraction. By the end of "Stage 4", output resolutions are H/16 × W/16 and H/32 × W/32, respectively. Together, these stages produce a hierarchical representation of the input image, facilitating effective extraction of both local and global features by the model. The proposed architecture is based on Tiny Swin (SWIN-T). In stage 1, the model is configured with 96 hidden layers and 2 blocks, followed by 2 blocks in stage 2, 6 blocks in stage 3, and 2 blocks in stage 4. To regularize the model and prevent overfitting, a dropout rate of 0.03 is applied. The attention mechanism utilized 8 attention heads, with each head operating on an embedding dimension of 64. Additionally, the model employed a multi-layer perceptron (MLP) with 256 units. Furthermore, we experimented with a modified configuration where we employed smaller patch sizes of 2 × 2, keeping the same number of attention heads, dropout rates, embedding dimension and MLP layer size. In this configuration, we adjusted the window size and window shift size to 1.

4.3 Results

The experiments are conducted using Keras version 2.2.4 and TensorFlow version 2.12 on Google Colab. To ensure the generalizability of the SWIN transformer model, a systematic approach is employed to partition the dataset. The dataset is split into 80% for training and validation, 20% for testing. For effective model training and hyperparameter tuning, the total training images are further divided into 70% for training and 10% for validation. The proposed architecture has given a better performance when tested on complex ISL gestures. It has given the overall accuracy of 99.34%. Figures 5a and 5b shows the model accuracy and the loss plots respectively. Table 2 shows the class wise accuracy obtained by the proposed model.

Table 3 shows the comparative analysis of the proposed methodology with existing SLR models.

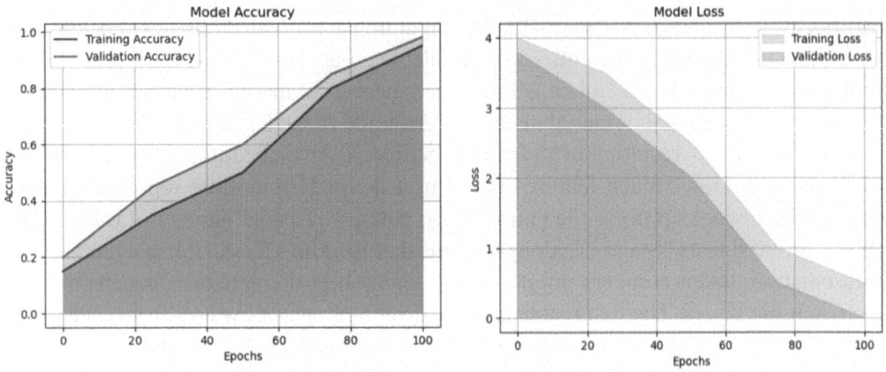

(a) (b)

Fig. 5. **a**. Model accuracy. **b.** Model loss

Table 2. Class wise recognition rate

Class (A-Z) & (0–9)	Recognition rate (%)	Class (A-Z) & (0–9)	Recognition rate (%)
A	99	S	99
B	99	T	100
C	99	U	100
D	100	V	100
E	100	W	99
F	99	X	99
G	99	Y	100
H	100	Z	99
I	100	0	97
J	99	1	100
K	99	2	99
L	100	3	100
M	100	4	99
N	100	5	100
O	99	6	100
P	99	7	100
Q	99	8	99
R	99	9	99

Table 3. Proposed system Vs. Existing approaches

Reference	Classes	Architecture	Accuracy
Nojood M. Alharthi et al. [23]	32	ViT, SWIN, Transfer learning	98%
Sunanda das et al. [24]	46	Deep transfer learning with RF classifier	94.5%
Deep R Kothadiya et al. [25]	36	Ensemble renset50 + self-attention model	98.20%
Chunkeat et al. [26]	36	ViT	99.73%
Proposed	**36**	**Swin model for diverse background**	**99.34%**

5 Conclusion

In summary, the proposed work presents a pioneering approach to Indian sign language gesture recognition by leveraging the shifted window transformers architecture. This novel methodology employs a four-stage SWIN transformer model, which effectively captures spatial relationships within the gestures. Experiment is conducted on a dataset comprising 36 static classes in diverse background, demonstrating the robustness of the proposed method. Notably, SWIN-based approach achieved an impressive accuracy of 99.3%. It is worth noting that the proposed model outperforms traditional models such as convolutional neural networks. Notably, the study breaks new ground by demonstrating the effectiveness of the SWIN transformer architecture in ISL gesture recognition, a domain where this architecture has not been previously explored, as highlighted by existing surveys in the field. In essence, the work not only sets a new benchmark in ISL gesture recognition but also underscores the potential of transformer-based architectures in addressing complex visual recognition tasks across diverse domains.

References

1. Kumbhar, S., Landge, A., Kulkarni, A., Solanki, D., Kurtadikar, V., Karad, V.: Indian sign language recognition system. Int. J. Innov. Sci. Res. Technol. **6**(6) (2021). Accessed 20 Dec 2022. https://about.almentor.net/about/the-deaf-and-mute/
2. Liu, Z., et al.: Swin transformer: hierarchical vision transformer using shifted windows. In: Proceedings IEEE International Conference on Computer Vision, ICCV, pp. 9992–10002 (2021). https://doi.org/10.1109/ICCV48922.2021.00986
3. Bi, J., Zhu, Z., Meng, Q.: Transformer in computer vision. In: 2021 IEEE International Conference on Computer Science, Electronic Information Engineering and Intelligent Control Technology, CEI 2021, pp. 178–188 (2021). https://doi.org/10.1109/CEI52496.2021.9574462
4. Rao, G.A., Syamala, K., Kishore, P., Sastry, A.: Deep convolutional neural networks for sign language recognition. In: 2018 Conference on Signal Processing and Communication Engineering Systems, SPACES, pp. 194–197. IEEE (2018)

5. Sharma, C.M., Tomar, K., Mishra, R.K., Chariar, V.M.: Indian sign language recognition using fine-tuned deep transfer learning model. In: Proceedings of International Conference on Innovations in Computer and Information Science, ICICIS, pp. 62–67 (2021)
6. Zakariah, M., Alotaibi, Y.A., Koundal, D., Guo, Y., Elahi, M.M.: Sign language recognition for Arabic alphabets using transfer learning technique. Comput. Intell. Neurosci. **2022**, 1–15 (2022)
7. Mannan, A., Abbasi, A., Javed, A.R., Ahsan, A., Gadekallu, T.R., Xin, Q.: Hypertuned deep convolutional neural network for sign language recognition. Comput. Intell. Neurosci. **2022**, 1–10 (2022)
8. Kothadiya, D.R., Bhatt, C.M., Saba, T., Rehman, A., Bahaj, S.A.: Signformer: deepvision transformer for sign language recognition (2023)
9. Dosovitskiy, L.B., et al.: An image is worth 16x16 words: transformers for image recognition at scale (2021)
10. Agarwal, A., Sreemathy, R., Turuk, M., Jagdale, J., Kumar, V.: Indian sign language recognition using skin segmentation and vision transformer. In: 2023 IEEE 20th Council International Conference INDICON 2023, pp. 857–862 (2023). https://doi.org/10.1109/INDICON59947.2023.10440818
11. Rajan, R.G., Rajendran, P.S.: Gesture recognition of RGB-D and RGB static images using ensemble-based CNN architecture. In: 2021 5th International Conference on Intelligent Computing and Control Systems (ICICCS), pp. 1579–1584. https://doi.org/10.1109/ICICCS51141.2021.9432163
12. Wu, X.Y.: A hand gesture recognition algorithm based on DC-CNN. Multimed Tools Appl. **79**(13), 9193–9205 (2020). https://doi.org/10.1007/s11042-019-7193-4
13. Chen, S., Lu, S., Wang, S., Ni, Y., Zhang, Y.: Shifted window vision transformer for blood cell classification. Electronics **12**(11), 1–14 (2023). https://doi.org/10.3390/elec-tronics12112442
14. Liang, J., Cao, J., Sun, G., Zhang, K., Van Gool, L., Timofte, R.: SwinIR: image restoration using swin transformer. In: Proceedings IEEE International Conference on Computer Vision, vol. 2021, pp. 1833–1844 (2021)
15. Zhou, J., Muirhead, W., Williams, S.C., Stoyanov, D., Marcus, H.J., Mazomenos, E.B.: Shifted-windows transformers for the detection of cerebral aneurysms in microsurgery. Int. J. Comput. Assist. Radiol. Surg. **18**(6), 1033–1041 (2023). https://doi.org/10.1007/s11548-023-02871-9
16. Xu, X., et al.: An improved swin transformer-based model for remote sensing object detection and instance segmentation. Remote Sens. **13**(23) (2021). https://doi.org/10.3390/rs13234779
17. Wei, C., Ren, S., Guo, K., Hu, H., Liang, J.: High-resolution swin transformer for automatic medical image segmentation. Sensors **23**, 3420 (2023). https://doi.org/10.3390/s23073420
18. Gao, Y., Li, Y., Liu, B., Tian, Y., Zhu, M., Luo, J.: Modal fusion sign language recognition based on swin transformer architecture. In: 2023 8th International Conference on Image and Vision Computing, ICIVC 2023, pp. 107–113 (2023). https://doi.org/10.1109/ICIVC58118.2023.10270259
19. Jamali, A., Mahdianpari, M.: Swin transformer and deep convolutional neural networks for coastal wetland classification using Sentinel-1, Sentinel-2, and LiDAR data. Remote Sens. **14**(2) (2022). https://doi.org/10.3390/rs14020359
20. Sun, R., Pang, Y., Li, W.: Efficient lung cancer image classification and segmentation algorithm based on an improved swin transformer. Electronics **12**(4) (2023). https://doi.org/10.3390/electronics12041024
21. Huang, J., et al.: Swin transformer for fast MRI. Neurocomputing **493**, 281–304 (2022). https://doi.org/10.1016/j.neucom.2022.04.051
22. Bojesomo, A., Almarzouqi, H., Liatsis, P.: A novel transformer network with shifted window cross-attention for spatiotemporal weather forecasting. IEEE J. Sel. Top. Appl. Earth Obs. Remote Sens. **17**, 45–55 (2024). https://doi.org/10.1109/JSTARS.2023.3323729

23. Alharthi, N.M., Alzahrani, S.M.: Vision transformers and transfer learning approaches for Arabic sign language recognition. Appl. Sci. **13**(21), 11625 (2023). https://doi.org/10.3390/app132111625
24. Das, S., Imtiaz, M.S., Neom, N.H., Siddique, N., Wang, H.: A hybrid approach for Bangla sign language recognition using deep transfer learning model with random forest classifier. Expert Syst. Appl. **213**(PB), 118914 (2023). https://doi.org/10.1016/j.eswa.2022.118914
25. Kothadiya, D.R., Bhatt, C.M., Rehman, A., Alamri, F.S., Saba, T.: SignExplainer: an explainable AI-enabled framework for sign language recognition with ensemble learning. IEEE Access **11**, 47410–47419 (2023). https://doi.org/10.1109/ACCESS.2023.3274851
26. Tan, C.K., Lim, K.M., Chang, R.K.Y., Lee, C.P., Alqahtani, A.: HGR-ViT: hand gesture recognition with vision transformer. Sensors **23**(12), 1–20 (2023). https://doi.org/10.3390/s23125555

ViziAssist: Visual Assistance for Visually Impaired Drivers

Kanishk Arya[1(✉)], Meenakshi Sumeet Arya[2], Vedant Deshmukh[1], and Ketaki Dabade[1]

[1] School of Computer Engineering and Technology, MIT-World Peace University, Pune, India
kanishkarya2811.mitwpu@gmail.com

[2] Institute of Transportation, Iowa State University, Ames, USA

Abstract. Visually impaired individuals face significant challenges in navigating the world, and driving, a crucial aspect of independent living, becomes particularly daunting. While autonomous vehicle technology holds promise, its widespread adoption and affordability for all remain distant realities. Addressing this pressing need, we present ViziAssist, an innovative visual assistance system specifically designed to empower visually impaired drivers. Utilizing an NVIDIA Jetson Nano at its core and leveraging the power of the YOLOv7 object detection model, ViziAssist offers real-time object detection and classification capabilities tailored for road scenarios. This paper details the system's architecture, the training methodology employing transfer learning on a custom dataset of Indian roads, and the implementation of an intuitive visual output mechanism using strategically placed LEDs. Rigorous testing procedures, encompassing both indoor and on-field evaluations, were conducted to assess the system's performance. ViziAssist achieved an impressive mean Average Precision (mAP) of 0.681, demonstrating its efficacy in real-time object detection. We achieved particularly high precision scores for crucial object classes like autorickshaws (0.799) and buses (0.8), highlighting the system's reliability in identifying potential hazards on Indian roads.

Keywords: Object Detection · Transfer Learning · Assistive Technology · Autonomous Vehicles · Driver Assistance Systems · Smart Transport Systems

1 Introduction

Vision Impairment is a serious problem in most parts of the world, including India, where about 40 million people are visually impaired [1]. Driving poses challenges for those with low vision due to the absence of smart navigation tools in many vehicles, highlighting a market need for a product enabling visually impaired individuals to drive independently, irrespective of vehicle ownership.

In the past few decades, the artificial intelligence (AI) industry has undergone remarkable growth, fostering the creation of innovative products and services,

J. Kakarla et al. (Eds.): CVIP 2024, CCIS 2473, pp. 72–85, 2026.
https://doi.org/10.1007/978-3-031-93688-3_6

including the Internet of Things (IoT), social media, and intelligent transportation systems (ITS) [2].

Smart transport systems, one of the pillars of the modern world, have also benefited from AI. According to World Health Organization (WHO) statistics, road accidents are an important social problem worldwide, killing an estimated 1.2 million people and injuring about 50 million each year [3].

Utilizing advanced driver assistance systems (ADAS) as a solution, major car manufacturers are incorporating these affordable and evolving technologies to mitigate human errors, a significant factor in most car accidents. Notable projects such as Tesla Autopilot and Google Car Waymo [4] exemplify ongoing advancements in this field.

This paper introduces ViziAssist, an innovative product employing an intelligent attachment device equipped with an onboard NVIDIA GPU and powered by the YOLOv7 [5] deep neural network. The system uses a camera to swiftly detect obstacles in real-time, enhancing safety for visually impaired individuals operating vehicles. Positioned as a valuable asset in automotive industry automation, ViziAssist signifies a notable advancement with its advanced processing capabilities and machine learning techniques.

2 Related Work

The development of assistive technologies for visually impaired individuals has garnered significant research interest, with notable advancements in areas such as navigation aids, object recognition systems, and driving assistance solutions.

Navigation aids for the visually impaired commonly employ GPS technology coupled with tactile feedback or audio cues to guide users through unfamiliar environments [6]. However, these systems often lack the granularity and real-time responsiveness required for safe driving.

Object recognition systems, often based on computer vision and deep learning techniques, have shown promise in assisting visually impaired individuals in identifying objects in their surroundings [7]. These systems typically rely on smartphone cameras or wearable devices, limiting their applicability in driving scenarios where a wider field of view and faster processing speeds are essential.

In the realm of driving assistance for the visually impaired, researchers have explored various approaches, including haptic feedback systems integrated into steering wheels and audio-based object detection systems. However, these solutions often suffer from limitations such as driver distraction, limited object classification capabilities, or the requirement for specialized vehicle modifications.

ViziAssist distinguishes itself from existing solutions by focusing on providing real-time object detection and classification specifically tailored for the challenges faced by visually impaired drivers. Its integration of a powerful edge computing platform like the NVIDIA Jetson Nano enables on-device processing without relying on external infrastructure, ensuring low latency and real-time responsiveness. Additionally, the use of a custom dataset representing Indian road conditions and the implementation of an intuitive visual output mechanism using LEDs cater specifically to the needs of visually impaired drivers in India, enhancing the system's practical relevance and usability.

3 System Architecture

3.1 NVIDIA Jetson Nano GPU

The NVIDIA Jetson Nano is a specialized single-core computer designed for AI and deep learning tasks, boasting a compact and energy-efficient design for complex calculations, such as real-time image and video processing. Built on the Maxwell GPU architecture, it houses a quad-core ARM Cortex-A57 CPU, 4 GB LPDDR4 RAM, and a 128-core NVIDIA Maxwell GPU with 1 TFLOPS processing capacity. With a 40-pin expansion header, three USB 3.0 ports, and a Gigabit Ethernet port, the device offers versatility in connectivity. [8]. The internal architecture of the GPU is referenced in Fig. 1.

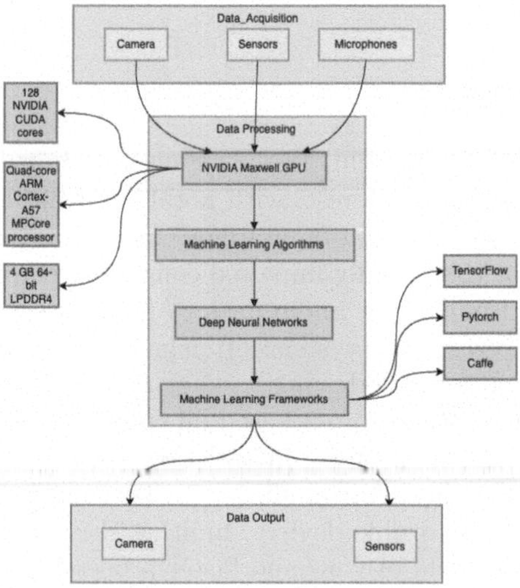

Fig. 1. Jetson Nano Architecture

The NVIDIA Jetson Nano is a high-performance computer tailored for AI and deep learning applications. Compatible with CUDA, cuDNN, TensorRT, and OpenCV, it supports various operating systems, including Ubuntu, Linux for Tegra, and Jetpack. This versatile device excels in real-time data processing, making it well-suited for applications like object detection, facial recognition, and autonomous vehicles.

3.2 YOLOv7

Object detection in computer vision, a crucial task, has seen advancements through models like YOLO (You Only Look Once) [9]. YOLOv7 [5] emerges as a notable evolution, combining the strengths of its predecessors for enhanced accuracy and efficiency. As the successor to YOLOv6 [10], YOLOv7 achieves state-of-the-art performance in both speed and accuracy on object detection benchmarks. Known for its efficiency, YOLOv7 is well-suited for real-time applications. The architecture, depicted in Fig. 2, comprises three main stages.

- **The Backbone**: Extracts the features from input images, utilizing a lightweight and efficient CNN architecture designed for object detection.
- **The Neck**: Acts as a bridge between the backbone and the head, performing operations to preserve accuracy while minimizing computational complexity, crucial for achieving overall efficiency.
- **The Head**: Predicts object bounding boxes and their classes in the image, utilizing a multi-layer perceptron (MLP) connected to the output of the neck component.

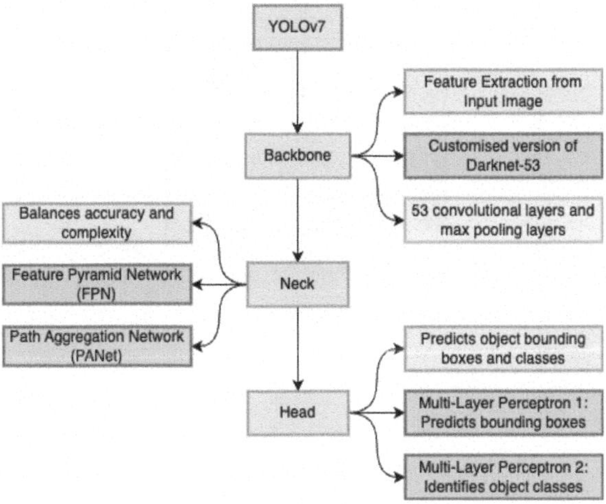

Fig. 2. YOLOv7 Architecture

The YOLOv7 architecture enhances object detection accuracy by addressing varied object sizes and preserving contextual information. Its backbone is a customized version of Darknet-53, featuring 53 convolutional layers and max pooling layers for feature extraction and downsampling.

The neck incorporates the Feature Pyramid Network (FPN) [11] and the Path Aggregation Network (PANet) [12], utilizing pyramid operations and attention mechanisms to amalgamate features and improve learning capabilities.

The head employs two Multi-Layer Perceptrons (MLPs): the first predicts object bounding boxes, and the second identifies object classes.

4 Implementation

The ViziAssist system architecture incorporates essential components for visual assistance to visually impaired drivers. At its core is the NVIDIA Jetson Nano, integrated with a Full HD Raspberry Pi camera module featuring the Sony IMX219PQ CMOS image sensor. This camera, capable of 30 fps at 1080p, interfaces with the Jetson Nano through a CSI ribbon cable. The Jetson Nano utilizes its high-performance GPU and CPU to process the YOLOv7 model for real-time object detection and classification, enabling frame-by-frame inference from the live video feed captured by the camera. The overall system architecture is as displayed below in Fig. 3.

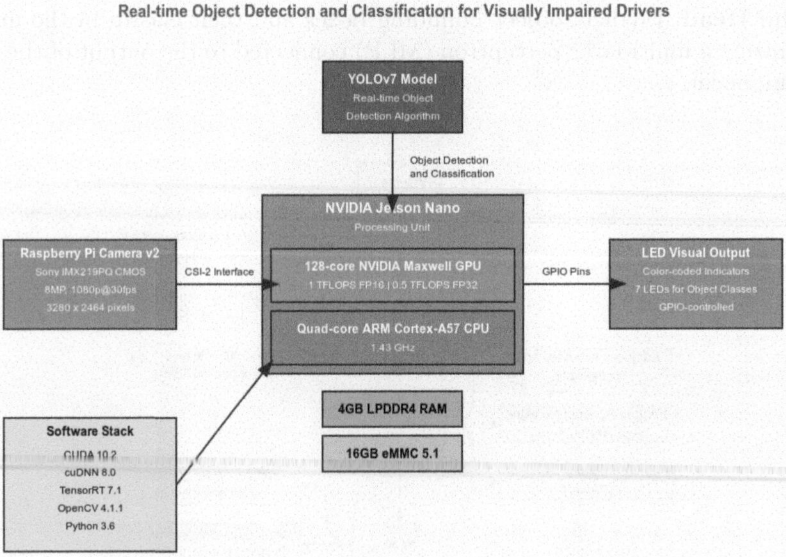

Fig. 3. ViziAssist System Architecture

The modified detection script on the Jetson Nano utilizes a YOLOv7 model, focusing on classes like car, person, motorcycle, truck, autorickshaw, rider, and bus through Transfer Learning. Replacing MS COCO classes with custom road-related classes optimizes performance and resource utilization. The system architecture incorporates GPIO pins linked to LEDs (pins 11, 16, 29, 31, 32, 33, 37) for visual output. The Jetson Nano communicates with LEDs to provide visual cues based on object detection results.

4.1 Model Training Through Transfer Learning

Transfer learning involves leveraging knowledge from a pre-trained model and applying it to a new task. In our case, we modified the YOLOv7 model for ViziAssist by adjusting the detection script initially pre-trained on 80 MS COCO classes and fine-tuning it on a custom dataset subset of the IDD dataset [13]. The process for the same can be viewed in Fig. 4. This dataset includes seven classes relevant to ViziAssist: buses, motorcycles, cars, pedestrians, trucks, autorickshaws, and riders. The object split is outlined below and depicted in Fig. 5. Detailed classwise distribution is presented in Table 1.

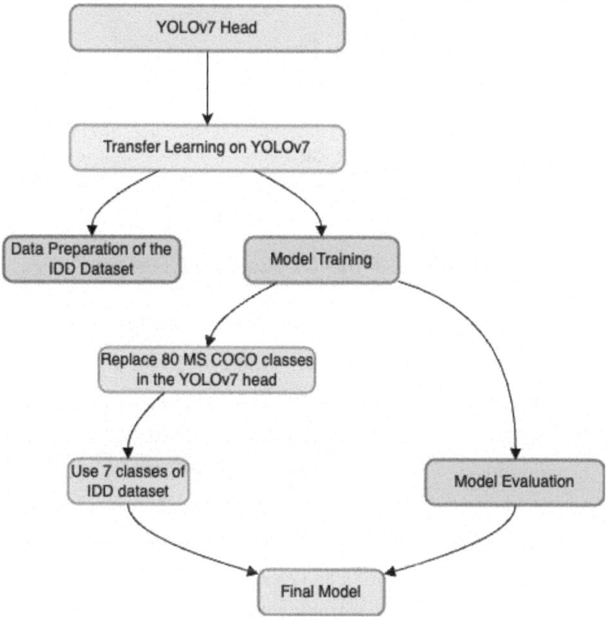

Fig. 4. Transfer Learning Process

The weights of the pre-trained model were updated during this process, optimizing it for our requirements.

The fine-tuned model maintains its adaptability while being customized for the specific requirements of the ViziAssist application, improving real-time identification and classification of relevant objects.

The training of the model was done on a GeForce GTX 1080 Ti GPU so as to facilitate for faster training time. The inference and testing was done on the Jetson Nano GPU. The inference on the GPUs are as displayed in Table 2.

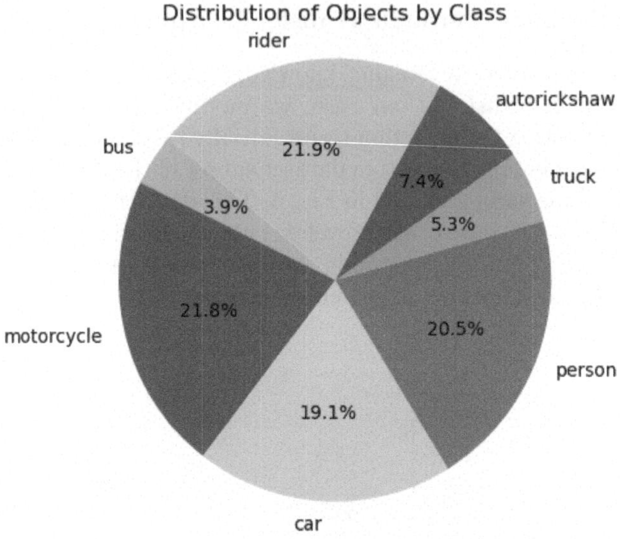

Fig. 5. IDD Dataset

Table 1. Object Counts by Class

Class	Test	Train	Val	Total Objects
bus	1354	4033	1346	6733
motorcycle	7155	23349	7587	38191
car	6679	19076	7615	33470
person	5454	26194	4171	35719
truck	1629	5290	2333	9252
autorickshaw	2641	7833	2471	12945
rider	7156	23132	7952	38240
Total	32068	108907	33475	175450

Table 2. Analysis of Inference on Different GPUs

GPU	Batch	Image Size	Inference Time (ms)
GeForce GTX 1080 Ti	32	640	20.0
Jetson Nano	8	416	247.1
Jetson Nano	8	640	547.4

4.2 Object Detection and Classification

In ViziAssist's object detection and classification pipeline, each frame from the camera module undergoes processing using the modified detection script, utilizing the YOLOv7 model. During inference, the model identifies regions of interest

Fig. 6. Object Detection and Classification on ViziAssist

and outputs bounding boxes, class labels, and confidence scores, corresponding to the detected objects' precise locations within the frame. To cater to visually impaired drivers' needs, the focus is on seven relevant road classes: buses, motorcycles, cars, pedestrians, trucks, autorickshaws, and riders. Filtering out irrelevant classes prioritizes the detection of objects crucial for road safety in this context. A test image of the detection in action can be viewed in Fig. 6.

4.3 Visual Output

ViziAssist employs LEDs strategically positioned in the driver's field of view, each corresponding to specific object classes for quick identification. LEDs illuminate or flash based on detected objects, enhancing situational awareness for visually impaired drivers. The combination of the pretrained YOLOv7 model and modified detection script enables real-time, accurate object detection, focusing on driving-relevant classes. Figure 7 illustrates the visual output mechanism, offering timely and crucial assistance. By associating LEDs with distinct object classes, ViziAssist enhances navigation safety for visually impaired drivers

The visual output component of ViziAssist is carefully designed to be non-distracting and easily comprehensible. Optimized LED positioning and brightness ensure clear visibility without obstructing the driver's line of sight or causing discomfort. By integrating the powerful object detection capabilities of the YOLOv7 model with this visual output mechanism, it provides a user-friendly and effective solution for visually impaired drivers, enhancing their ability to navigate the road with improved safety and confidence.

Fig. 7. ViziAssist Deployment

5 Testing and Refinement

A comprehensive testing and evaluation of ViziAssist, a system of performance metrics were employed as below:

- Detection Accuracy $= \frac{\text{Number of Correctly Detected Objects}}{\text{Total Number of Objects}}$
- Precision $= \frac{\text{True Positives}}{\text{True Positives + False Positives}}$
- Recall $= \frac{\text{True Positives}}{\text{True Positives + False Negatives}}$
- (Mean Average Precision (mAP)) - Calculated using Intersection over Union (IoU) thresholds, which measure the overlap between predicted and ground truth bounding boxes. This method incorporates various IoU thresholds to evaluate detection accuracy across different levels of localization precision.

To evaluate the performance and functionality of ViziAssist, a robust testing methodology was implemented. This included stages such as Raspberry Pi camera integration, indoor testing using an existing dataset of Indian roads, on-field testing integrated with an actual vehicle, result analysis, latency assessment, prototype stabilization, achieving real-time low-latency output with improved accuracy, and enhancing user experience through color coding and LED indicators. These thorough testing procedures aimed to assess the effectiveness, reliability, and usability of ViziAssist in real-world scenarios, offering valuable insights to refine the system and optimize its performance. By following this systematic approach, specified in Fig. 8, the testing methodology ensured a thorough assessment of ViziAssist's object detection and visual assistance capabilities for visually impaired drivers.

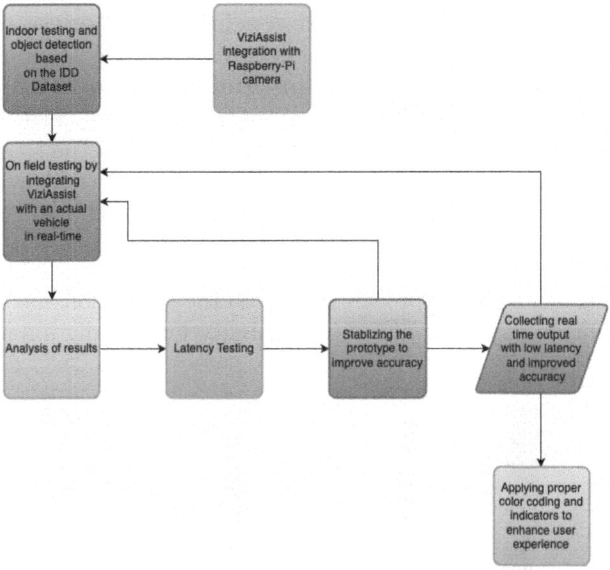

Fig. 8. ViziAssist Inference Flowchart

- **Integration with Raspberry Pi Camera**: The first step in the testing process involved integrating ViziAssist with a Raspberry Pi camera module ensuring seamless capture of live video footage for object detection and classification. The Raspberry Pi camera module was connected to the Jetson Nano, allowing for real-time analysis of the road environment.
- **Indoor Testing**: Image classification performance of the system was evaluated through indoor testing using a diverse dataset of Indian roads. ViziAssist analyzed each image, providing visual output through connected LEDs, and its classification accuracy was assessed by comparing results to ground truth labels.
- **On-Field Testing by Integrating ViziAssist with an Actual Vehicle**: To evaluate real-world performance, on-field testing integrated the system with an actual vehicle. Operating within the vehicle, ViziAssist utilized the Raspberry Pi camera module for real-time object detection and classification, offering visual assistance to the driver through LED cues. The testing assessed the device's reliability, accuracy, and responsiveness across diverse road conditions, including varying traffic densities, lighting, and weather scenarios.
- **Latency Testing**: The system underwent latency testing to measure the real-time response between the live video feed and LED visual cue generation, ensuring timely and accurate assistance to the driver with minimal delay.
- **Stabilizing Prototype to Improve Accuracy**: Following testing, the prototype underwent stabilization efforts, refining object detection algorithms, fine-tuning model parameters, and optimizing the system configuration. Iter-

ative improvements were implemented to reduce false positives/negatives and enhance overall accuracy in object detection and classification in Fig. 9.
- **Applying Proper Color Coding and Indicators to LED to Enhance User Experience (UX)**: To improve user experience, ViziAssist applied color coding and indicators to the LEDs, assigning distinct colors to each class for easy interpretation. Brightness and flashing patterns were fine-tuned to convey proximity and urgency of detected objects, enhancing the overall clarity and comprehensibility of visual cues.

This comprehensive testing approach facilitated the evaluation and refinement of ViziAssist, ensuring its effectiveness and usability for visually impaired drivers.

Fig. 9. ViziAssist Prototype

6 Results

The YOLOv7 model was extensively evaluated for object detection and classification to assist drivers with low vision. Using a dataset of 1724 diverse images, each with corresponding labels, covering various road scenarios, insights were gained into the model's accuracy in spotting and categorizing objects, crucial for enhancing visual assistance for drivers with limited vision. The graphs depicting training and validation results are shown in Fig. 10.

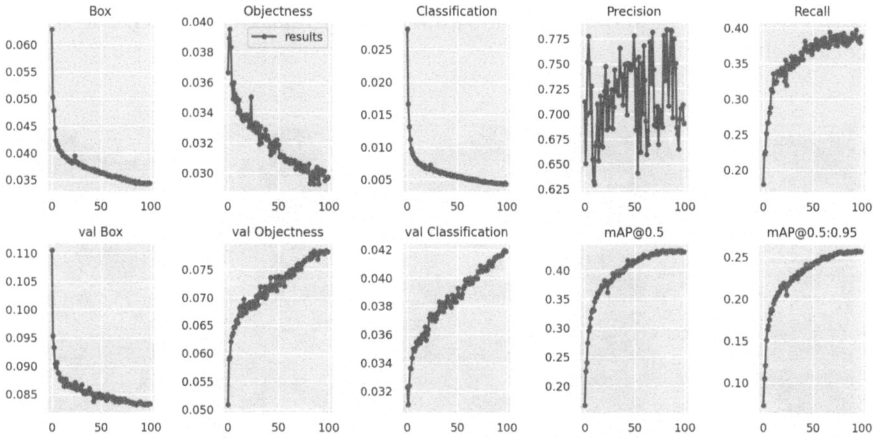

Fig. 10. Training Results

The YOLOv7 model, adapted for ViziAssist, demonstrated strong performance in object detection and classification across various road scenarios. Key findings include:

- Overall mean Average Precision (mAP@0.5) of 0.681
- Highest precision scores for buses (0.8) and autorickshaws (0.799)
- Strong performance for cars (0.799 precision) and motorcycles (0.785 precision)
- Lower, but still notable, precision for pedestrians (0.726) and trucks (0.681)

Table 3 presents detailed class-wise performance metrics.

Table 3. Class-wise Performance Metrics

Class	Precision	Recall	mAP@0.5	mAP@0.5:0.95
Buses	0.8	0.659	0.741	0.517
Motorcycles	0.785	0.657	0.709	0.401
Cars	0.799	0.653	0.713	0.47
Pedestrians	0.726	0.521	0.582	0.31
Trucks	0.681	0.591	0.615	0.409
Autorickshaws	0.799	0.725	0.782	0.531
Riders	0.754	0.57	0.623	0.334
Total mAP			0.681	0.424

ViziAssist excels in object detection, achieving high precision scores, notably 0.799 for Autorickshaws and 0.8 for Buses. With an overall mean Average Precision of 0.681, it stands out as a reliable solution for enhancing road awareness and safety. Figure 11 shows a small sample size of images on which the testing was carried out.

Fig. 11. Testing Results

7 Conclusion

In conclusion, ViziAssist, integrating the NVIDIA Jetson Nano and YOLOv7 model, holds significant promise for enhancing the safety and independence of visually impaired drivers. Through real-time object detection and classification, the device provides reliable visual cues in varied driving conditions. Rigorous testing affirms its reliability and responsiveness. The transfer learning approach, optimized latency, and user experience enhancements ensure accurate and timely detection. ViziAssist aspires to empower visually impaired drivers, with potential for further advancements. Overall, it stands as a promising solution, poised to positively impact the lives of those with visual impairments by enabling safer and independent navigation on the road.

References

1. Mannava, S., Borah, R.R., Shamanna, B.: Current estimates of the economic burden of blindness and visual impairment in India: a cost of illness study. Indian J. Ophthalmol. **70**(6), 2141 (2022)
2. Arya, K., Arya, M.S.: A review of the applications and future scope of artificial intelligence in smart transport. In: ICT Infrastructure and Computing: Proceedings of ICT4SD 2022, pp. 97–103 (2022)

3. Peden, M.M.: World Report on Road Traffic Injury Prevention. World Health Organization (2004)
4. Ingle, S., Phute, M.: Tesla autopilot: semi autonomous driving, an uptick for future autonomy. Int. Res. J. Eng. Technol. **3**(9), 369–372 (2016)
5. Wang, C.-Y., Bochkovskiy, A., Liao, H.-Y.M.: Yolov7: trainable bag-of-freebies sets new state-of-the-art for real-time object detectors. In: Proceedings of the IEEE/CVF Conference on Computer Vision and Pattern Recognition, pp. 7464–7475 (2023)
6. Mulder, M., Abbink, D.A., Boer, E.R.: Sharing control with haptics: seamless driver support from manual to automatic control. Hum. Factors **54**(5), 786–798 (2012)
7. Peng, E., Peursum, P., Li, L., Venkatesh, S.: A smartphone-based obstacle sensor for the visually impaired. In: Ubiquitous Intelligence and Computing: 7th International Conference, UIC: Xi'an, China, 26–29 October 2010. Proceedings 7, pp. 590–604. Springer (2010)
8. Cass, S.: Nvidia makes it easy to embed AI: the Jetson nano packs a lot of machine-learning power into DIY projects-[hands on]. IEEE Spectr. **57**(7), 14–16 (2020)
9. Redmon, J., Divvala, S., Girshick, R., Farhadi, A.: You only look once: unified, real-time object detection. In: Proceedings of the IEEE Conference on Computer Vision and Pattern Recognition, pp. 779–788 (2016)
10. Li, C., et al.: Yolov6: a single-stage object detection framework for industrial applications, *arXiv preprint* arXiv:2209.02976 (2022)
11. Lin, T.-Y., Dollár, P., Girshick, R., He, K., Hariharan, B., Belongie, S.: Feature pyramid networks for object detection. In: Proceedings of the IEEE Conference on Computer Vision and Pattern Recognition, pp. 2117–2125 (2017)
12. Wang, K., Liew, J.H., Zou, Y., Zhou, D., Feng, J.: PANet: few-shot image semantic segmentation with prototype alignment. In: proceedings of the IEEE/CVF International Conference on Computer Vision, pp. 9197–9206 (2019)
13. Varma, G., Subramanian, A., Namboodiri, A., Chandraker, M., Jawahar, C.: IDD: a dataset for exploring problems of autonomous navigation in unconstrained environments. In: 2019 IEEE Winter Conference on Applications of Computer Vision (WACV), pp. 1743–1751. IEEE (2019)

Improved Watermarking Approach Empowered by Deep Learning for Copyright Protection of Digital Images

Rajat Sood, Jyoti Rani(✉), and Ashima Anand

CSED, Thapar Institute of Engineering and Technology, Patiala, Punjab, India
{rsood_be21,jrani60_phd20,ashima.anand}@thapar.edu

Abstract. In recent times, there has been a significant surge in the need to create, distribute, and preserve vast quantities of digital images captured by smart devices and sensors. This gives rise to several problems, such as unauthorized access and deceptive utilization of these images, as well as other security considerations. Nevertheless, the inherent digital aspect of these images renders them readily accessible, modifiable, or susceptible to misuse. To mitigate these issues, watermarking solutions are introduced, basically the process of embedding a unique design or identifier into a digital cover and then removing it later. This is done to address conflicts related to ownership and copyright violations that may arise with media data.

The exponential development of deep neural networks has facilitated the rapid growth of research on deep learning-based watermarking techniques. Deep-learning methods are highly advantageous in watermarking because of their precision, exceptional outcomes, and robust learning capability. This study presents a unified architecture for watermarking based on deep learning to achieve high invisibility and resilience. The cover image is subsampled during the preparation stage. To accomplish watermark embedding, the single encoder utilizes normalizing flow, which essentially merges the secret image with the subsampled cover image. A parallel decoder has been implemented to enhance watermark extraction's imperceptibility and capability. The suggested architecture has been proven to achieve superior watermark robustness and imperceptibility after extensive experimentation. Our approach attains a pixel error rate below 0.1% in the face of several attacks, including Speckle noise, Sharpen noise, Gaussian noise, Alphadropout, and Blur attack. In addition, the suggested approach also demonstrates significant robustness as compared to existing works.

Keywords: Watermarking · Deep learning · Copyright Protection · Encoder · Decoder · Subsampling

J. Kakarla et al. (Eds.): CVIP 2024, CCIS 2473, pp. 86–97, 2026.
https://doi.org/10.1007/978-3-031-93688-3_7

1 Introduction

In the current era of large-scale data, digital images are gaining significance across multiple disciplines due to their potential uses in medicine, online social networks, forensic analysis, visual arts, education, and other areas. Several internet platforms have received massive daily image uploads [14,20]. Sharing and uploading images in large numbers shows diversity but also increases security and information leakage risks. These images might contain sensitive and confidential information regarding the individual. On the contrary, illicit dissemination of these confidential images could lead to far more severe adverse consequences, including violations of privacy and copyright and breaches of confidentiality [10]. The importance of ensuring the security of digital images cannot be emphasized. Currently, watermarking techniques have a significant function in safeguarding digital images. Image watermarking conceals copyright indications within cover images, rendering them indiscernible and resilient [15,21].

Digital watermarking algorithms protect copyright and privacy, making research crucial. Traditional digital image watermarking algorithms are spatial and frequency domain. Spatial domain watermarking modifies pixels to incorporate the watermark. Later research found that frequency domain watermarking methods, including DCT, DWT, and DWT-DCT, are more resistant than pixel domain methods [4,10,19]. The transform domain system is more robust and flexible than the spatial domain strategy [5,6]. Classical watermarking systems are less protected from attacks and have limited applicability. The efficient and resilient watermarking approach for digital images requires more study [7]. Traditional watermarking techniques are less robust since they use manual shallow feature extraction and poorly use the host image. A growing number of individuals are dedicating attention to deep learning-based watermarking for various popular applications [1,9,13,14,18], and it has recently significantly contributed to the security of visual content. Deep learning approaches are immensely advantageous in watermarking because of their robust learning capability and exact outcomes. Significant benefits related to watermarking based on deep learning include the following:

- **Accurate determination of the Embedding Position:-** The ideal embedding location for hiding the watermark inside the cover image can be precisely located with the help of deep learning-based watermarking. These models can detect regions that can be seamlessly watermarked without affecting the perceptibility.
- **Balance between Robustness and Imperceptibility:-** Watermarking based on deep learning enables the determination of the most effective embedding intensity, which achieves an acceptable balance between durability and undetectability. Through the examination of extensive datasets and the manipulation of parameters, it possesses the capability to effectively optimize the embedding procedure in such a way as to preserve the watermark's imperceptibility to the human eye while also protecting it against potential assaults or distortions.

- **Efficient Simulation of Attacks:-** Deep learning-based watermarking enables the simulation of various attacks to evaluate the efficacy of watermark extraction methods. It can simulate practical situations, including the introduction of noise or compression, to assess the resilience of the embedded watermark and subsequently enhance extraction techniques.
- **Improved Error and Noise Reduction:-** Deep learning-based watermarking facilitates the reduction of errors and noise when extracting watermarks. It can improve the accuracy of extracted watermarks by minimizing distortions that occur throughout the embedding and extraction procedures.

Inspired by the current achievements in deep learning [3], a 3-network model is designed to retain the high clarity of the watermarked images. Furthermore, an extractor network is constructed using a Gaussian noise network that eliminates noise variations from the potentially compromised watermarked image before extraction. This enhances the resilience of the watermarking system. Firstly, the cover image is processed by subsampling, creating four subsampled blocks. To conceal the secret image, the subsampled block with the highest entropy is utilized as the cover image. Further, three components are used to complete the watermarking embedding and extracting process: the Preparation network, Hiding network, and Reveal network. The preparation network performs preprocessing on the secret image by extracting its distinct features and getting it for merging with the original cover image. The Hiding network utilizes the secret and cover image in simultaneously altering both to incorporate the hidden information while preserving the authentic aspect of the cover image. The reveal network functions exclusively using the produced watermarked image, extracting the concealed secret information for reconstruction. During the training process, the cover reconstruction loss is utilized to compare the cover image with the encoded image. In contrast, the secret reconstruction loss compares the secret and the extracted secret image.

The subsequent part of the research is structured as follows: Sect. 2 reviews recent literature on our work. The concept underlying our scheme is clarified in Sect. 3, while the results and comparative analysis are presented in Sect. 4. References are provided in Sect. 6 after a summary of the work in Sect. 5.

2 Litereture Review

This section summarizes recent research in deep learning-based watermarking. Initial research focused on improving watermarked images with features extracted from deep-learning models.

A method was introduced in Ref. [8] for utilizing a DNN to include and retrieve a watermark from a digital hologram. The whole process for watermarking digital holograms consisted of three sub-networks. To enhance the resilience of watermarking, a simulated attack is incorporated within the DNN. The DNN for watermarking can achieve invisibility and robustness by incorporating attack simulation and holographic reconstruction into the network. It presented a network training approach that utilizes holograms and restoration. Debolina et al. developed an autoencoder CNN-based watermarking technique using deep learning to maximize resilience and watermark invisibility [11]. A two-network model encompasses embedding and extraction to assess the method comprehensively. The embedding network employs convolutional autoencoders, while the extraction model finds the concealed mark in watermarked data using block-level transposed convolution and the rectified linear unit algorithm. It must assess the performance of color images, improve their resilience and security, and detect possible weaknesses in preparation for subsequent analysis. A higher-dimensional space is created via transpose convolution to blend the original and watermark images [12]. A module called an up-sampler increases dimension. After embedding copyright information, a down-sampler component ensured the blended image had the exact dimensions as the original. The down-sampler also restores some embedding-related changes. A specialized sub-network extracts encoded information to detect watermarking in digital artwork.

The author presented a novel single encoder and two decoders watermarking designs to balance invisibility and resilience [20]. In particular, the single encoder embeds watermarks using normalizing flow to merge them with cover images. It presents a parallel dual-decoder for watermark retrieval to improve visibility and robustness. Reference [21] suggested a JPEG compression-resistant training approach to maintain watermark storage in the lower frequency range for decoding. It can enhance the training process by promoting a noise layer combination. Furthermore, the suggested technique is also resilient to other prevalent network disturbances. This method should be improved to effectively counteract various types of noise and investigate a means of integrating the watermark into the overall characteristics of the image to address intricate noise seen in real-world scenarios. Image denoising using autoencoder-based deep learning is proposed by Ref. [2]. It learns noise from training images and removes it from new images. Research findings demonstrate that the suggested PSNR model outperforms traditional approaches. Himanshu proposed a deep learning-based ocean image data hiding method. Before insertion in the original image, the hidden mark is compressed via downsampling [17]. Next, a CNN was inserted and compressed markings were recovered from the ocean image. Finally, a GAN-based reconstruction network reconstructs a superior mark image. In future, it can be enhanced by using blockchain-based encryption to safeguard the transfer of information and provide copyright protection.

3 Proposed Methodology

This section presents a deep-learning method for concealing a hidden image behind a single cover image, allowing for its recovery with minimal loss in quality. The summary of proposed framework is presented in Fig. 1. Initially, subsampling is applied on the cover image of size 128×128, generating four non-overlapping subsampled image sizes of 64×64 each i.e., $img1$, $img2$, $img3$, and $img4$. The secret image S hidden inside the $img1$ should also be 64×64 pixels. The proposed watermarking methodology has three stages: the Preparation Network, the Hiding Network (Encoder), and the Reveal Network. The specific procedures for

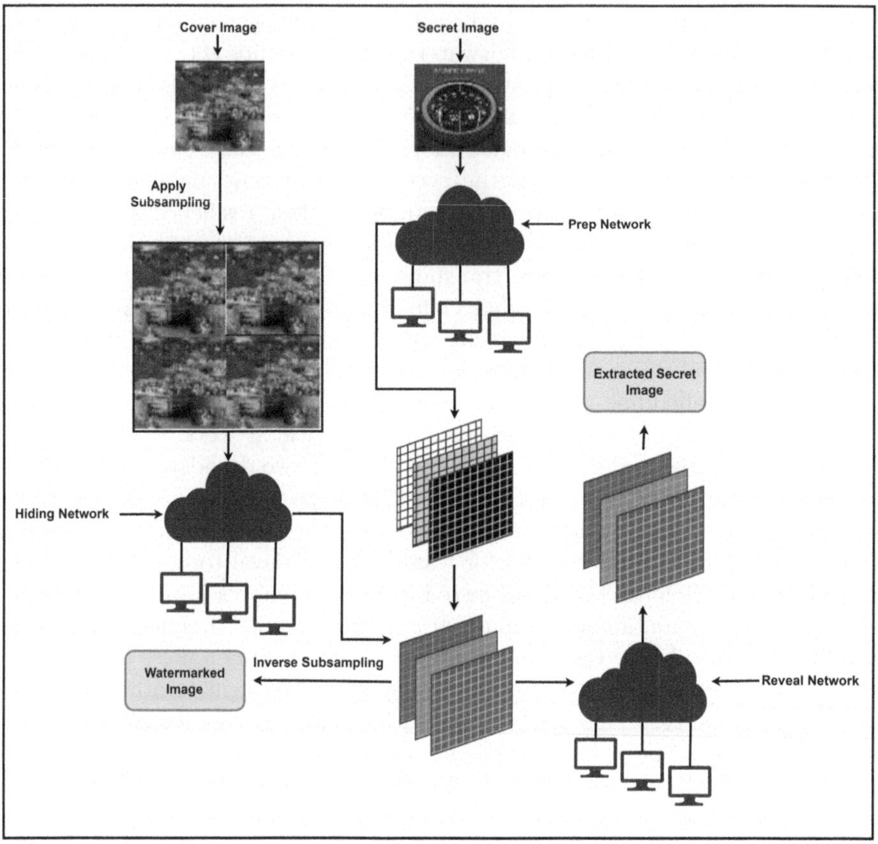

Fig. 1. Flowchart of Deep learning-based proposed method

incorporating the concealed image are detailed in Algorithm 1. Figure 2 shows the simplified structures of the embedding and extraction networks that have been proposed. The fundamental structure of each of the stages is as follows:

1. **Preparation Network:** Each of the preparation networks consists of the aggregation of 2 layers. There are three different convolution layers in each layer. Each of these three convolution layers has 50, 10, and 5 channels. The kernel sizes for these layers are 3, 4, and 5. Along both directions, the stride length always stays the same. Each convolution layer gets the right padding to ensure the output image remains the same size. Each convolution layer is followed with a ReLU activation.
2. **Hiding Network:** The hiding network combines or consolidates five layers. Each of these layers consists of three distinct convolution layers. The convolution layers in the hidden network share a basic structure similar to the convolution layers in the preparation network.

Algorithm 1: Embedding process using deep learning

Input : Cover Image (CI), Secret Image (SI)
Output: Watermarked Image (WI), extracted secret image(ext_SI)

// Step:1 Use dataset for pre-processing
$Resize(CI) 128 \times 128$;
$Resize(SI) 64 \times 64$;
// Step:2 Apply Subsampling on CI of size 128×128
for *p in range(64)* **do**
  for *q in range(64)* **do**
    for *r in range(3)* **do**
      $img1[p, q, r] \leftarrow G1[2 * p, 2 * q, r]$
      $img2[p, q, r] \leftarrow G1[2 * p, 2 * q + 1, r]$
      $img3[p, q, r] \leftarrow G1[2 * p + 1, 2 * q, r]$
      $img4[p, q, r] \leftarrow G1[2 * p + 1, 2 * q + 1, r]$
    end for
  end for
end for
// Step:3 Use Encoder for preparation network
$x3, x4, x5 \leftarrow Encoder(conv\_layers = 3, channels = 50, 10, 5, Kernelsize = 3, 4, 5, Strides = (1, 1), padding\_type =' same', activation =' RELU')(SI)$;
// Step:4 concatenate $x3$,$x4$,$x5$ layers
$x \leftarrow Concat([x3, x4, x5])$;
// Step:5 Apply the step 3 on Layer 2 and again concatenate three layers
$x \leftarrow Concat([\text{img1}, x])$;
// Step:6 For hiding Network, the step 3 1 is applied in Layer 3,4,5,6,7 and then concatenates output of these three layers
$x \leftarrow Concat([x3, x4, x5])$;
// Step:7 After concatenation, apply final convolution layer to generate watermarked image
$WI\_img1 = Conv2D(3, (3, 3), Strides = (1, 1), padding\_type =' same', activation =' RELU', name =' output\_C')(x)$;
// Step:8 After concatenation,apply inverse subsampling for getting a complete watermarked image(WI of size 128×128
$WI \leftarrow inverse(WI\_img1, img2, img3, img4)$;
// Step:9 After getting the watermarked image, Apply a Decoder for extracting the secret image.
$ext\_SI \leftarrow Conv2D(3, (3, 3), strides = (1, 1), padding =' same', activation =' tanh', name =' output\_S')(x)$;
// Step:10. Calculate:
PSNR (CI, WI);
SSIM (CI, WI);
C_pixelerror(CI, WI);
S_pixelerror(S, ext_SI);
NC (S, ext_SI);

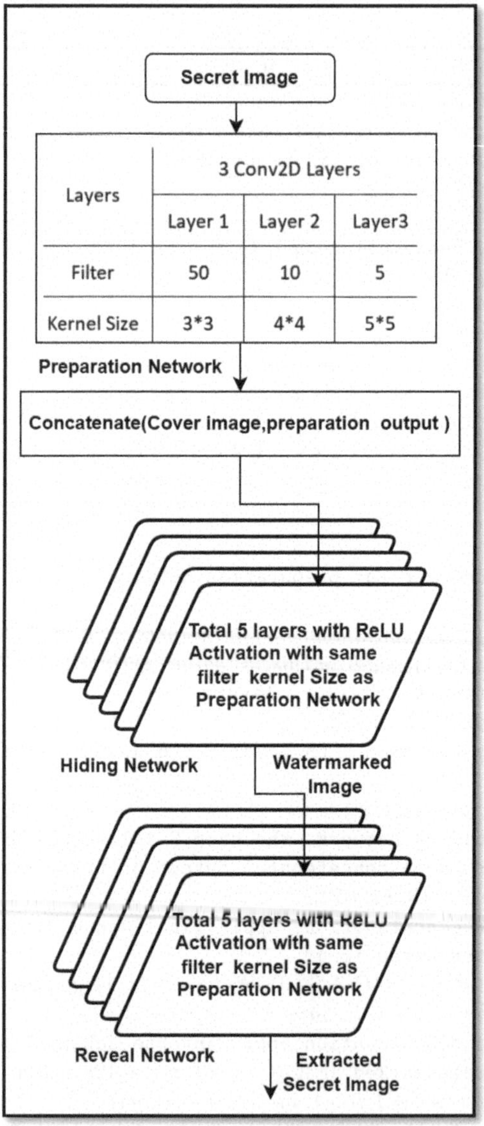

Fig. 2. Layers in the proposed deep learning-based watermarking method

3. **Reveal Network:** Every reveal network possesses a fundamental structure comparable to a hidden network, employing five convolution layers that are shaped similarly.

The training details of the proposed model are given below:

1. The Adam optimizer is used with a learning rate of 0.001 and a custom scheduler.
2. The model completed training for 400 epochs using a batch size of 32.
3. To ensure that weights are modified just once, it is necessary to freeze the network weights before incorporating them into the complete model.
4. Noise of various types, each with a standard deviation of 0.01, is separately added to the output of the encoder before it is transmitted via the decoder..
5. The mean sum of squared error has been utilized to calculate the loss of the decoder.

The main motive of the proposed work is to be able to encode information about the secret image into the $img1$, generating the first subsampled watermarked image WI_img1 that closely resembles cover image $img1$, while still being able to decode information from WI_img1 to generate the extracted secret image, which should resemble secret image as closely as possible.

In the proposed work, the Reveal Network's loss function differs from the loss function for the Preparation and Hiding Networks. To correctly implement the updates for the weights in the networks, we create stacked Keras models, one for the Preparation and Hiding Network (which share the same loss function) and another for the Reveal Network.

4 Results and Comparative Analysis

This section evaluates the effectiveness of the proposed method using various performance metrics, such as PSNR, SSIM, and NC. PSNR and SSIM are utilized to ensure robustness and imperceptibility [1,16]. In contrast, the NC score is commonly utilized to evaluate the performance of resilience. The deep learning-based image watermarking model is trained and evaluated using the tiny imagenet dataset from kaggle, which consists of 10000 images. The cover images used in the model have a size of 128 × 128 pixels. All of the experiments are carried out using Python. To apply watermarks, a collection of 50% images of the dataset used as cover images and remaining secret images measuring 64 × 64 in size are selected and uniformly distributed for usage on the cover images. The comparison of the cover and watermarked images is calculated using PSNR and SSIM. Pixel error C shows the difference between the cover and the watermarked image. Pixel error S shows the difference between secret and extracted secret images. Best pixel error is always nearest to 0.

Table 1 shows results of different evaluation parameters using different iterations range 100 to 400. After applying 400 iterations, the results obtained demonstrate superior imperceptibility and robustness. The PSNR and NC values are 81.12 dB and 0.9920. The pixel error of Secret and Cover is 14.43933 and 11.431194. So, it is noticed that it gives good results of pixel error loss when

Table 1. Results on different iterations

Epochs	Pixel error S	Pixel error C	NC	PSNR (dB)	SSIM
100	13.2436	12.1441	0.955	80.59	1
200	13.6500	5.5665	0.9740	87.37	1
300	14.38705	12.4134	0.9799	79.12	1
400	14.43933	11.4311	0.9920	81.12	1

we increase the no. of iterations, as given in the Table 1. It also provides better robustness i.e., 0.9920.

An average of 15 images in 400 iterations gives the best results, as given in Table 2. A greater NC value indicates a stronger correlation between the secret and extracted secret image. The highest PSNR and NC values are 85.86 dB and 0.9948. The average NC value between the secret and the extracted secret image is 0.9881. The efficacy of the suggested watermarking technique is further evaluated by experimentation with several image processing techniques, including salt and pepper attack, Gaussian noise, Speckle noise, sharpen attack, blur attack, and alpha dropout attack.

Further, Table 3 displays the NC values obtained using the above-mentioned attacks, demonstrating the technique's superior resilience. The highest NC value

Table 2. Results of performance parameters on 400 epochs

Images	PSNR	SSIM	NC	Pixel error S	Pixel error C
I1	83.62	1	0.9920	17.2995	8.5747
I2	85.06	1	0.9856	18.5365	7.2644
I3	80.37	1	0.9876	22.8350	12.4565
I4	83.06	1	0.9927	13.4486	9.1451
I5	85.86	1	0.9948	13.1541	6.6216
I6	81.42	1	0.9919	15.4136	11.0471
I7	83.39	1	0.9906	15.7485	8.8077
I8	82.69	1	0.9905	16.6377	9.5387
I9	81.2	1	0.9936	18.0079	11.3263
I10	81.77	1	0.9858	14.4134	10.6073
I11	83.87	1	0.9785	18.5060	8.3250
I12	80.5	1	0.9780	15.6411	12.2759
I13	83.23	1	0.9805	14.0869	8.9688
I14	83.92	1	0.9879	15.9953	8.2830
I15	81.12	1	0.9921	14.4393	11.4312
Average	**82.74**	**1**	**0.9881**	**16.2776**	**9.6449**

Table 3. Results of different evaluation parameters using different attack

Attack type	Intensity	NC	Pixel error S	Pixel error C	PSNR
Speckle Attack	0.01	0.984201	15.8901	12.9607	85.26
Gaussian Attack	0.01	0.975813	15.79044	9.856343	82.41
Dropout	0.01	0.943259	15.65595	5.011182	88.28
blur	0.1	0.967521	22.10361	13.488	79.6
Alphadropout	0.01	0.967521	22.10361	13.488	79.68
Sharpen Attack	0.5	0.975822	13.57774	12.34744	80.45
Median Attack	0.1	0.950763	23.15916	20.17429	76.19
Salt and Pepper Attack	0.05	0.955072	11.9028	5.064375	88.19

Table 4. Comparative analysis of different performance parameters with existing work

Parameters	Ref. [11]	Ref. [16]	Ref. [17]	Proposed work
PSNR (dB)	31.34	41.1 dB	49.35	85.86
SSIM	0.994	0.992	.99	1
NC	0.9937	0.9982	.999	0.9948

Table 5. Comparative analysis of different attacks with existing work

Attack (Intensity = 0.01)	Ref. [11]	Ref. [16]	Ref. [17]	Proposed work
Speckle Attack	0.9727	0.9783	0.978	0.9842
Gaussian Attack	0.9356	0.9172	0.969	0.9758
Salt and Pepper Attack	0.9694	0.9702	0.978	0.9913
Median Attack	0.92	/	0.974	0.9686688

is obtained for speckle noise which is 0.984201. The experimental results demonstrate that the proposed work successfully embedded the mark in an undetectable way and effectively extracted it even when subjected to attacks. Furthermore, compared to similar studies, the proposed research demonstrates superior performance in imperceptibility and robustness.

Furthermore, the suggested approach is comprehensively evaluated by comparing it to several existing methodologies, as depicted in the Table 4 and 5, achieved superior performance in imperceptibility and robustness. The algorithm's invisibility performance is contrasted with other work in the Table 4. The proposed study exhibits a better level of imperceptibility compared to prior methods [11,16,17]. The PSNR and NC value of the proposed work is 85.86 dB and 1. In the case of NC, the proposed NC value is lower than the [16,17] but higher than the Ref. [11] as given in Table 5. In the case of robustness, the proposed work gives the best NC value in all cases except median noise. Value of median noise in case of Ref. [17] is higher than the proposed NC value.

5 Conclusion

Deep learning has significantly improved image processing and is currently utilized in data concealment, offering a robust watermarking technology with outstanding performance. This work presents a deep-learning model employed in watermarking techniques. The framework aims to improve the resistance to attacks while maintaining high imperceptibility. Digital image copyright can be prevented using a deep learning-based watermarking technology presented in this article. Firstly, subsampling is used to preprocess the image. After that, A three-network model, which includes preparation, hiding, and reveal networks, is used for embedding and extraction. The Preparation Network converts the secret image to combine it with the cover image. The process of the Hiding Network transforms the combined image into an encoded cover. The Reveal Network retrieves the concealed image from the encoded cover. This model thoroughly examines the algorithm's performance. The hidden mark is gathered by implementing a rectified linear unit algorithm to the retrieved features of the watermarked and cover images. Our suggested method is resistant to effective attacks and keeps marked images at a reasonable level, according to the experimental results. Using the embedding and extractor networks ensures that the proposed technique is imperceptible and efficiently protects the hidden image from attackers. Overall, the proposed strategy ensures a high level of invisibility and robustness and enhances performance significantly, with improvements in robustness and invisibility compared to alternative approaches.

References

1. Anand, A., Bedi, J., Aggarwal, A., Khan, M.A., Rida, I.: Authenticating and securing healthcare records: a deep learning-based zero watermarking approach. Image Vis. Comput., 104975 (2024)
2. Bajaj, K., Singh, D.K., Ansari, M.A.: Autoencoders based deep learner for image denoising. Procedia Comput. Sci. **171**, 1535–1541 (2020)
3. Das, A., Wahi, J.S., Anand, M., Rana, Y.: Multi-image steganography using deep neural networks. arXiv preprint arXiv:2101.00350 (2021)
4. Garcia-Nonoal, Z., Mata-Mendoza, D., Cedillo-Hernandez, M., Nakano-Miyatake, M.: Secure management of retinal imaging based on deep learning, zero-watermarking and reversible data hiding. Vis. Comput. **40**(1), 245–260 (2024)
5. Ge, S., Xia, Z., Fei, J., Tong, Y., Weng, J., Li, M.: A robust document image watermarking scheme using deep neural network. Multimed. Tools Appl. **82**(25), 38589–38612 (2023)
6. Gu, W., Chang, C.C., Bai, Y., Fan, Y., Tao, L., Li, L.: Anti-screenshot watermarking algorithm for archival image based on deep learning model. Entropy **25**(2), 288 (2023)

7. Ingaleshwar, S., Dharwadkar, N.V.: Water chaotic fruit fly optimization-based deep convolutional neural network for image watermarking using wavelet transform. Multimedia Tools Appl. **82**(14), 21957–21981 (2023)
8. Kang, J.W., et al.: Digital hologram watermarking based on multiple deep neural networks training reconstruction and attack. Sensors **21**(15), 4977 (2021)
9. Lee, E., Piao, Z., Sim, D., Seo, Y.H.: Deep neural network-based robust hologram watermarking using guided attack module. Expert Syst. Appl., 123486 (2024)
10. Lee, J.E., et al.: Digital image watermarking processor based on deep learning. Electronics **10**(10), 1183 (2021)
11. Mahapatra, D., Amrit, P., Singh, O.P., Singh, A.K., Agrawal, A.K.: Autoencoder-convolutional neural network-based embedding and extraction model for image watermarking. J. Electron. Imaging **32**(2), 021604–021604 (2023)
12. Ming, Y., Ding, W., Cao, Z., Lin, C.T.: A general approach for using deep neural network for digital watermarking. arXiv preprint arXiv:2003.12428 (2020)
13. Radha Kumari, R., Vijaya Kumar, V., Rama Naidu, K.: Deep learning-based image watermarking technique with hybrid DWT-SVD. Imag. Sci. J., 1–17 (2023)
14. Singh, H.K., Singh, A.K.: Comprehensive review of watermarking techniques in deep-learning environments. J. Electron. Imaging **32**(3), 031804–031804 (2023)
15. Singh, H.K., Singh, A.K.: Using deep learning to embed dual marks with encryption through 3d chaotic map. IEEE Trans. Consum. Electron. (2023)
16. Singh, H.K., Singh, A.K.: Digital image watermarking using deep learning. Multimedia Tools Appl. **83**(1), 2979–2994 (2024)
17. Singh, H.K., Singh, K.N., Singh, A.K.: Secure transmission of ocean images using deep learning-based data hiding. Expert Syst., e13469
18. Sinhal, R., Ansari, I.A.: Machine learning based multipurpose medical image watermarking. Neural Comput. Appl. **35**(31), 23041–23062 (2023)
19. Wang, C., et al.: Wavelet-FCWAN: fast and covert watermarking attack network in wavelet domain. J. Vis. Commun. Image Represent. **95**, 103875 (2023)
20. Xiang, Y., Wang, H., Yang, L., He, M., Zhang, F.: SEDD: robust blind image watermarking with single encoder and dual decoders. Comput. J., bxae014 (2024)
21. Zhang, W., Chen, R., Wang, B.: A robust watermarking algorithm against jpeg compression based on multiscale autoencoder. IET Image Proc. **18**(2), 455–469 (2024)

Multi-spectral Sensing to Detect Patterned/Textured Iris Contact Lens Attacks Using Deep Iris Features

Raghavendra Ramachandra[1(✉)], Sushma Venkatesh[2], and Gaurav Jaswal[3]

[1] Norwegian University of Science and Technology (NTNU), Trondheim, Norway
raghavendra.ramachandra@ntnu.no
[2] AiBA AS, Gjøvik, Norway
[3] Technology Innovation Hub, Indian Institute of Technology, Mandi, India

Abstract. Iris recognition systems are widely deployed in various access control applications such as highly secured border control. Recent studies have demonstrated the vulnerability of iris sensors to various types of Presentation Attack Instruments (PAI) that include, including print attacks, prosthetic eyes, and textured contact lenses. Among these PAI, textured/patterned or color cosmetic contact lenses can be used to conceal the identity and thus can be a potential threat to iris recognition systems. In this study, we propose a novel approach to detect textured contact lens attacks by leveraging complementary information from a Multi-Spectral (MS) iris capture device. The method combines deep features extracted from AlexNet and ResNet50 through a fusion framework. The proposed approach utilizes a specialized MS iris capture device capable of capturing iris images across five distinct spectral wavelengths: 800 nm, 830 nm, 850 nm, 870 nm, and 980 nm. We then employed the proposed algorithm to extract the deep features using AlexNet and ResNet50 across five different spectral bands that are combined at the comparison score level to accurately detect textured contact lens attacks on iris recognition systems. To achieve this, we present a new dataset focused on presentation attacks, collected using a MS iris capture device and featuring two types of textured contact lenses. The new dataset comprises 2800 artefact samples corresponding to two different types of contact lenses and 1200 bona fide samples captured in five different spectral bands. Experimental evaluation demonstrates the outstanding performance of texture-based features on multi-spectral iris samples in detecting both known and unknown contact lens iris attacks.

Keywords: Biometrics · Multi-spectral · Spoofing · Presentation attacks · Iris recognition

1 Introduction

The iris is a widely used biometric trait known for its high accuracy in recognition, making it a preferred choice for large-scale biometric applications, including

J. Kakarla et al. (Eds.): CVIP 2024, CCIS 2473, pp. 98–111, 2026.
https://doi.org/10.1007/978-3-031-93688-3_8

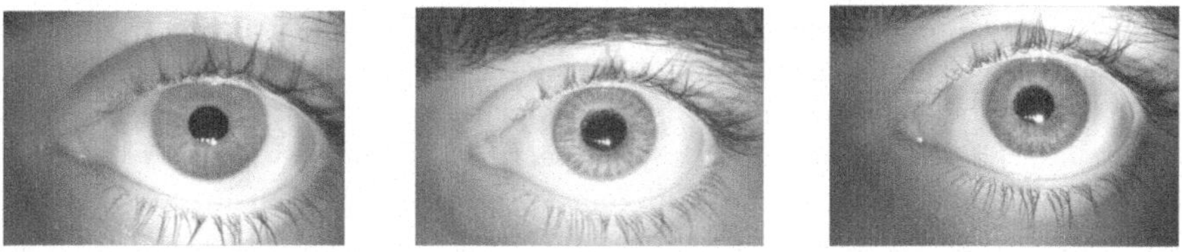

Fig. 1. Iris image captured at 800 nm (a) Bona fide (b) Contact lens-1: Blue (c) Contact lens-2: Green (Color figure online)

national ID programs like Aadhaar in several countries. With the growing popularity of iris recognition systems, there is a high degree of concern regarding covert and subverted attacks that include a variety of direct attacks or presentation attacks. The primary goal of a presentation attack is to either impersonate the identity of a legitimate subject by presenting the artefact or to conceal the identity of the presenting subject to evade the iris recognition system. Previous studies have highlighted the threat posed to iris recognition systems by textured contact lenses and reported a decline in performance when individuals are enrolled without textured contact lenses but later verified while wearing them [24]. The low comparison scores from genuine attempts with a textured lens can be misused to attack iris recognition systems by malignant actors. Therefore, textured contact lenses, among other Presentation Attack Instruments (PAI), are considered a severe threat because they can be easily used to conceal the identity given both the low cost and wide off-the-shelf availability.

The iris textured contact lens detection approaches widely available today can be categorized in five main groups: (1) *Texture based detection* [3,6,10,24], [17], [2,7,11,12,23,25] (2) *Image quality based detection* [4] (3) *Deep learning based detection* [5,18,19,22] (4) *Meta information based detection (i.e., 3D information based)* [1,8] (5) *Multi-spectral imaging based detection* [13,16,20,21]. Each approach has its merits and drawbacks. Among the various texture-based feature extraction methods, the use of Local Binary Pattern (LBP) and Binarized Statistical Image Features (BSIF) have been widely studied, and it was indicated in [2] that the use of BSIF-based texture features can outperform the LBP features when the same type (manufacturer, textured/patterned, and color) of the contact lens is used to train and test the model. This was also confirmed by [17] and [12]. Image-quality-based approaches measure statistical features (for example, BRISQUE and JPEG quality) that reflect the quality of the image captured, which is further used to detect the textured contact lens. However, recent works base end-to-end detection on advances in deep learning approaches. To this end, approaches based on pre-trained CNNs [5] and task-tuned architectures have been proposed [18,19]. Deep-learning-based lens detection approaches have also demonstrated good performance when trained and tested with the same type of textured contact lens. The use of 3D information to detect contact lenses was proposed in [1] which uses photometric stereo features. Gathering the strengths of various features, most recent works have employed multiple features to improve the reliability of the textured contact lens detection [14,23].

However, few studies have been reported on multi-spectral imaging approaches. The first work using multi-spectral iris information was based on Purkinje images [13] where two different spectral bands, 760 nm and 880 nm, were employed to construct four different Purkinje images, which in turn were used to detect presentation attacks on the iris recognition system. Experiments reported on a small database with different types of artefacts, such as 3D artificial eye and 3D patterned contact lens, indicated reasonable performance. However, it is important to note that higher-order Purkinje reflections can be difficult to detect, such as in the case of contact lenses; therefore, this approach [13] is challenged by contact lens presentation attacks [1]. In addition, the use of gradient image features on multi-spectral images captured in four different spectral bands (780 nm, 810 nm, 850 nm, and 900 nm) is presented in [16]. Gradient features were used to construct a fused image from all four spectral bands. Experiments on print attacks on small datasets have demonstrated a reliable performance in artefact detection. The reflectivity of the iris-sclera region was analyzed using two different spectral bands corresponding to 750 nm and 850 nm introduced in [20] to detect various iris artefacts. The experimental results reported on a small dataset comprising both printed and textured contact lens artefacts showed a good performance in detecting different types of iris artefacts. However, the performance reported in [20] is related to the segmentation of a particular iris-sclera region, and obtaining an incorrect area may result in undetected attacks.

Recently, a multi-spectral iris capture device was employed to detect prosthetic eyeballs with a variety of materials [21]. However, we note that the use of prosthetic eyeballs as a presentation attack in real-life applications is minimal, as the texture pattern printed on the glass eye can hardly resemble and mimic the texture of the legitimate subject. Furthermore, the applicability of these attacks is limited if an attacker wants to target a person with brown eyes, that is, with high melanin pigment density.

Based on the aforementioned state-of-the-art approaches, it can be noted that: (1) the majority of the work reported in the literature is on the NIR spectra iris data captured using commercial iris recognition sensors. (2) The state-of-the-art algorithms demonstrated the best performance when trained and tested on the same type of contact lens. This fact is also justified in the recent work on 3D iris features using photometric stereo analysis [1]. *However, to the best of our knowledge, there is no work reported on the cross-textured contact lens detection using multi-spectral iris recognition.* (3) Even though there exists many contact lens dataset captured in the NIR spectrum, *there exists no publicly available dataset for the multi-spectral contact lens detection.* (4) The majority of existing approaches in both NIR and multi-spectral imaging have used multiple algorithms, such as the sclera, iris, and eye regions. The use of multiple regions demands the accurate segmentation in case multiple regions are employed to achieve the robust performance. *This work aims to address the limitations mentioned above.*

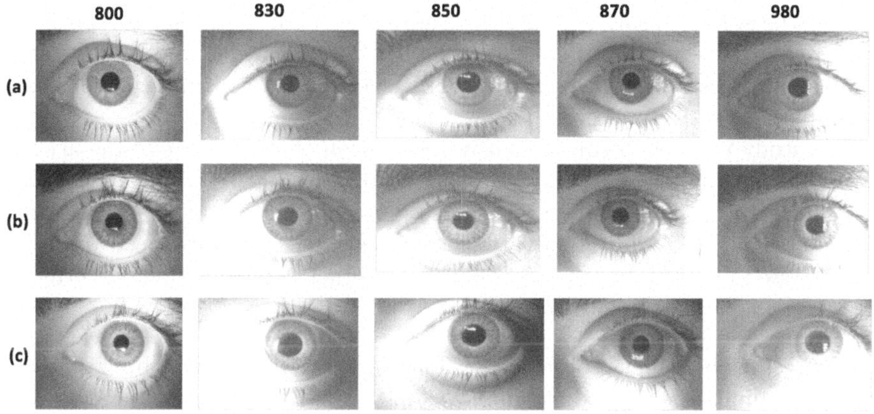

Fig. 2. Example of the multi-spectral iris images captured using the custom built sensor used in this work (a) Bona fide (b) Contact lens-1: Blue (c) Contact lens-2: Green (Color figure online)

Motivated by these factors, we investigated the problem of textured contact lens detection without the explicit need for multiple regions. With this motivation lies another aim of providing a generalizable contact lens attack detection methodology under attacks from unknown textured contact lenses from the scalability aspect, such that future attacks from contact lenses of different make and manufacturing can be mitigated. Therefore, we explore and propose the use of state-of-the-art iris features coupled with multi-spectral imaging abilities. Owing to the unavailability of a commercial-grade multi-spectral iris sensor, we employed a custom-built multi-spectral iris capture device at par with the capabilities of a fully operational commercial sensor.[1]. The (MS iris device captures iris images across five spectral bands (800 nm, 830 nm, 850 nm, 870 nm, and 980 nm), making it compatible with various state-of-the-art iris feature extraction and comparison techniques. As an inherent advantage of our approach, the explicit need to rely on additional/meta-information from other regions was overcome. Finally, we also proposed a novel algorithm that can combine the deep features extracted from an existing convolutional neural network (CNN) using AlexNet and ResNet50 architecture extracted using five different spectral bands. The key contributions of this work are listed as:

- Presents a novel approach to detect the textured contact lens based on combining the off-the-shelf deep CNN features extracted using AlexNet and ResNet50. Figure 1 shows example of the iris images captured using MS iris sensor operating at 800nm.
- Presents a new multi-spectral textured contact lens dataset captured using the custom multi-spectral iris capture device together with the real iris patterns

[1] The device meets the criteria of commercial grade sensor, except for the form-factor of the device which is currently restricted to development mode.

from the same sensor. The dataset consists of bona fide images, two types of contact lenses with different colors with 1200 bona fide and 2800 artefact image samples representing five different spectral bands totaling 4000 image samples.

- This study presents a comprehensive evaluation of seven state-of-the-art feature extraction methods, encompassing both hand-crafted and deep learning-based features. The proposed method's performance is benchmarked against these techniques. Additionally, the attack resistance of multi-spectral sensors is assessed for both known and unknown contact lens detection, adhering to ISO/IEC JTC1 SC37 30107-3 standards [9].

The rest of the paper is organized as follows: Section 2 presents brief information on the multi-spectral sensor employed in this work and the textured contact lens detection framework; Sect. 3 presents the details of the new dataset and the evaluation protocols; Sect. 4 presents the experimental results; and Sect. 5 concludes the work with a brief list of potential future works.

2 Multi-spectral Iris Capture Device

In this section, we provide brief information on the custom-built multi-spectral iris capture device employed in this work. The primary advantage of MS imaging is that it can record the emittance and reflection of light rays from the target (bona fide or artefact) at multiple spectral bands. Because each target (bona fide or artefact) has different characteristics (reflection and emittance) at different spectral bands, the use of a MS sensor can successfully characterize this information, which can contribute to detecting the artefact (or bona fide). *The NIR spectral range (or spectral bands) is selected to accommodate both iris recognition and presentation attack potential of the custom sensor.* Despite some studies in the visible spectrum band, it should be noted that visible spectral iris imaging is not preferred in operational scenarios because of challenges in processing heavily pigmented irises. The lighting units are built using LEDs and controlled using the ARDUINO board, which is programmed to switch the LEDs in a fully automatic manner. Further, all five lighting units were arranged in a ring structure above the camera with a diffuser to achieve uniform illumination in the eye region to mitigate any unwanted reflection. The sensor is based on a high-resolution camera DMK 33UX250 with an IMX250LLR CMOS sensor that has an excellent spectral response in the band spanning–1000 nm. Furthermore, the camera was fitted with a lens with a focal length of 8 mm and an IR pass filter with a cut-off of 700 nm. The accommodated capturing distance was approximately 10–15 cm from the camera, inspired by commercial sensors, and the capture response time was 3 secounds for all five spectral images.

Figure 2 shows an example of the bona fide, contact lens-1 and contract lens-2 images over a natural iris pattern captured using the custom multi-spectral iris capture sensor employed in this work. Notably, there is a clear qualitative distinction between bona fide irises and those with contact lenses. These results highlight the efficacy of the multi-spectral iris recognition framework in identifying contact lenses.

3 Multi-spectral Textured Contact-Lens/iris Data Collection

This section outlines the data collection procedures and the performance evaluation framework used in this study. The MS iris dataset was collected using a custom-built sensor in an indoor scenario with standard lighting conditions. The collected dataset is composed of images corresponding to the bona fide and two different types of textured contact lenses (contact lens-1: is of color Brilliant Blue and Contact lens-2: is of color Gemstone Green from two different manufacturers). Figure 3 illustrates both contact lenses captured in the visible-spectrum RGB camera, which can illustrate the variation of the pattern. This fact is also demonstrated in Fig. 5 (b) and (c), where the variation in the texture patterns is prominent between the textured contact lenses used in this work. Both the bona fide and contact lens iris images were captured in a similar environment following the same protocol. Each data subject (bona fide/contact lens artefact) was allowed to interact with the sensor with human supervision to ensure proper data capture. The custom sensor can capture one eye at a time; thus, each data subject is asked to present the left and right eyes independently of the sensor. Furthermore, eyeglasses (or spectacles) are not included in either bona fide or contact lens data capture to ensure data capture quality.

The developed dataset comprises 4000 image samples collected from five different spectral bands representing both bona fide and two types of contact lenses. Both types of contact lenses were equally represented in the dataset, with each having 1400 samples. However, the number of bona fide samples corresponded to 1200 samples collected using 85 unique iris samples in multiple sessions. The majority of the dataset corresponds to male data subjects representing Asian ethnicity and a small percentage of Caucasian and African ethnicities.

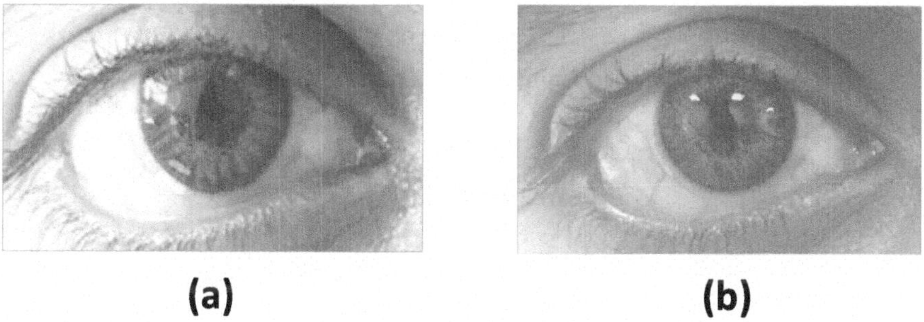

Fig. 3. Example of the contact lens captured in visible spectrum for illustration (a) Contact lens-1: Blue (b) Contact lens-2: Green (Color figure online)

Table 1. Statistics of the newly collected multi-spectral iris dataset

Type	Training set	Development set	Testing set
Bona fide	100 X 5 = 500	50 X 5 = 250	90 X 5 = 450
Contact lens 1	100 X 5 = 500	50 X 5 = 250	130 X 5 = 650
Contact lens 2	100 X 5 = 500	50 X 5 = 250	130 X 5 = 650
Total: 4000 image samples			

3.1 Evaluation Protocol

We developed a performance evaluation protocol to effectively benchmark textured contact lens detection. The entire dataset was divided into three independent groups: Training, Development and Testing. The data distribution for these three sets was based on unique iris samples, and there was no overlap between the three data groups. Table 1 shows the statistics of the data samples distributed across three independent groups. The training subset is used only to train the linear SVM employed in this work, the development subset is used to compute the decision threshold, and the testing set is solely used to report the performance of the proposed approach.

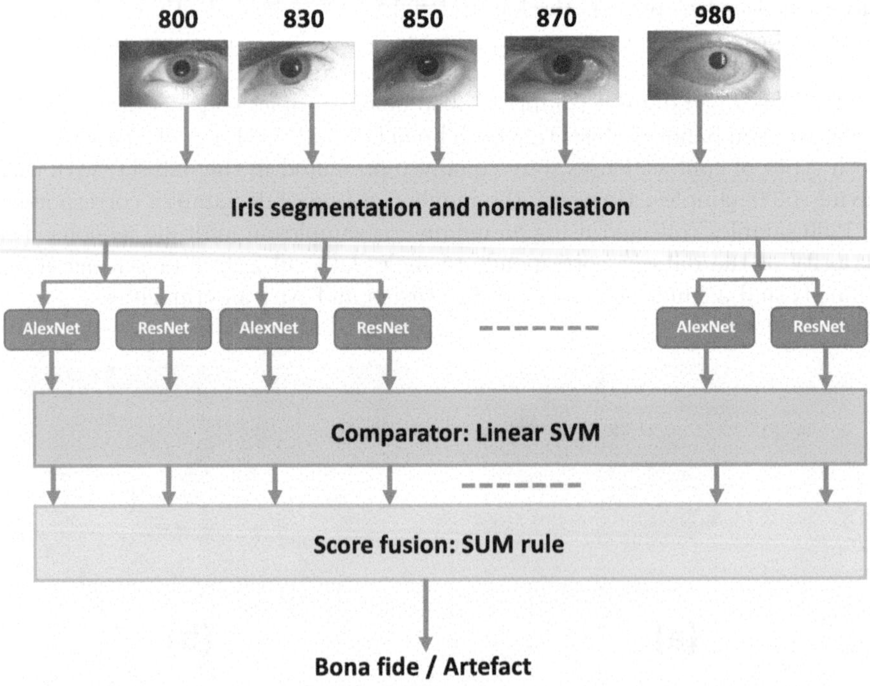

Fig. 4. Block diagram of the proposed contact lens detection framework

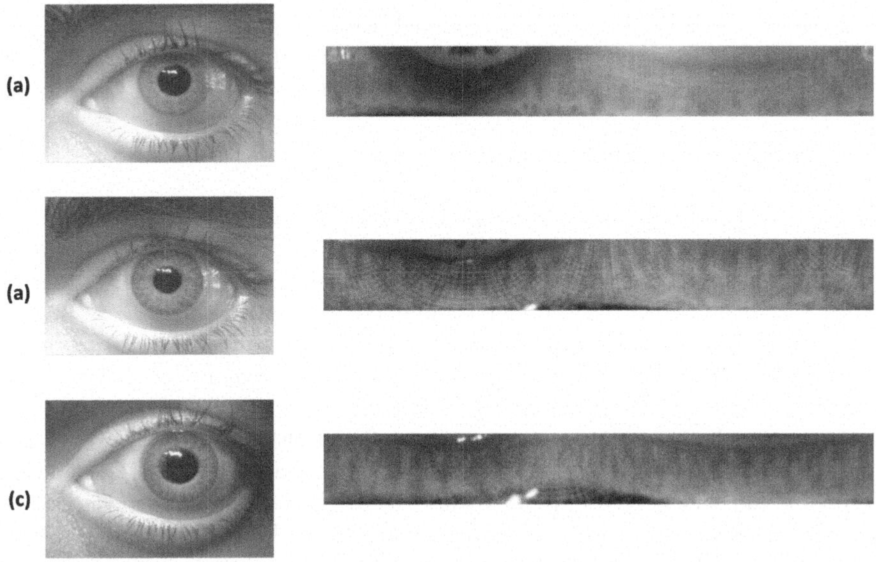

Fig. 5. Example of the iris segmentation and normalisation on the iris image captured at 850 nm (a) Bona fide (b) Contact lens-1: Blue (c) Contact lens-2: Green (Color figure online)

3.2 Proposed Technique for Textured Contact Lens Detection Framework

Figure 4 shows a block diagram of the contact-lens detection framework based on MS iris images. The proposed framework can be structured into four operational building blocks: iris segmentation and normalization, feature extraction, comparator (or classifier), and comparison score-level fusion. Given the MS iris image I_s, $\forall s = 1, 2, 3, 4, 5$, the first step is to segment the iris region. For this purpose, we utilized the open-source OSIRIS v4.1 software [15] to segment and normalize each spectral iris image. The segmented and normalized iris image corresponding to I_s in N_s $\forall s = 1, 2, 3, 4, 5$ has a size of 512×64. Figure 5 illustrates the results of the iris segmentation and normalization using OSIRIS. For illustration, we used the iris image from the 850 nm spectrum, and it can be noticed that the dotted patterns of the contact lens are enhanced. The normalized images were further processed using the proposed feature extraction scheme to extract discriminant features for robust contact lens detection. The proposed feature-extraction scheme is based on an off-the-shelf CNN architecture based on AlexNet and ResNet50. These two networks were selected by considering their individual performance in detecting textured contact lenses. The last fully connected layer from AlexNet and ResNet50 was used to extract the features of the MS iris images independently. Next, the features were compared using a linear Support Vector Machine (SVM) to obtain comparison scores. Finally, the comparison scores obtained corresponding to the individual spectral bands using AlexNet and ResNet50 were combined using a simple SUM rule to obtain a single fused score. The final decision is made by comparing the fused score with the preset threshold to determine the artefact or bona fide.

4 Experiments and Results

This section reports the quantitative performance of multi-spectral textured contact lens detection on a newly collected dataset. To this extent, we evaluated seven different texture features based on hand-crafted and deep CNNs. Performance was evaluated using the metrics defined by IS0/IEC 30107-3 [9]: *bona fide Presentation Classification Error Rate (BPCER) and Attack Presentation Classification Error Rate (APCER).* We report the performance of the proposed method by reporting the value of BPCER while fixing the APCER to 1% 5% and 10% according to the recommendations of ISO/IEC 30107-3 [9].

Quantitative performance was evaluated using the performance evaluation protocol defined in Sect. 3.1. In this work, *we used the development dataset to compute the value of the threshold* corresponding to the BPCER at three different values of APCER, namely 1%, 5% and 10%. These computed values were used to set the threshold and compute the BPCER by comparing the comparison scores obtained by the testing set. Thus, the determined threshold was applied only to the testing set to report the final performance.

In this work, we present two different experiments. *Experiment 1*: This experiment evaluates the performance of the proposed approach and seven different state-of-the-art algorithms when it is trained and tested with the same type of PAI species (for example, training and testing with contact lens-1: Blue). *Experiment 2*: This experiment evaluates the performance of the proposed scheme and also seven different state-of-the-art algorithms when it is trained with one type of PAI species and tested with another type of PAI species (for example, training with contact lens-1: Blue and testing with Contact lens-2: Green). This experiment determines the efficacy of the proposed approach when the unknown PAI species is presented. In the following section, we discuss the quantitative results of these two experiments.

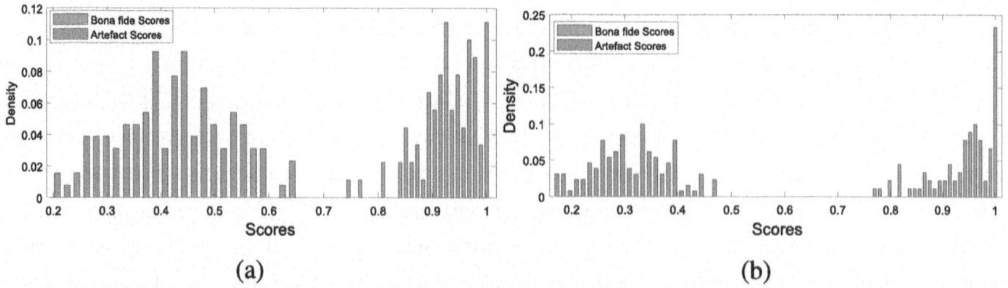

Fig. 6. Distribution of bona fide and artefact scores from Proposed Method (a) Contact lens-1: Blue (b) Contact lens-2: Green (Color figure online)

4.1 Experiment 1

Tables 2 and 3 show the performance of seven different feature extraction schemes to detect contact lens-1: Blue and Contact lens-2: green, respectively. The following are the important observations: (1) It should be noted that the use of texture features using LBP, BSIF, AlexNet, ResNet50, and the proposed method shows a very high performance with D-EER = 0% and BPCER = 0% when APCER is set to 1%, 5% and 10%. This outstanding performance can be attributed to the discriminatory texture information captured in multiple spectral bands. (2) Spectral Signature (SS) features indicate degraded performance, which may be attributed to (i) the variation of the light source and (ii) the limited availability of the spectral bands. However, this is one of the existing methods used in [20] for contact lens detection, which also reports sensitivity to image quality. (3) The GLCM features employed in this study were based on four features: contrast, homogeneity, energy, and correlation. These features are similar to those used by [16] for detecting contact lenses. However, the obtained results show degraded performance owing to the direct influence of variations in image quality. (4) Based on the obtained performance, the detection accuracy of all feature extraction methods (except BSIF-SVM and the proposed method) is slightly reduced on Contact lens-2 and thus is more challenging to detect. A possible reason for this is the density of the textured pattern, which is lower in contact lens 2 than in Contact lens 1 (refer to Fig. 5). (5) The proposed method resulted in outstanding performance for both types of contact lenses. Figure 6 shows the distribution of the proposed method scores for both types of lenses from the testing set, which indicates the separation of the bona fide and artefact scores.

Table 2. Performance of different feature extraction techniques on Contact lens-1: Blue

Algorithms	Development set	Testing set			
	D-EER (%)	D-EER (%)	BPCER @ APCER =		
			1%	5%	10%
BRISQUE-SVM	14-51	13.2	22.22	11.14	7.77
GLCM-SVM	37.12	42.29	97.77	97.77	96.67
BSIF-SVM	0	0	0	0	0
SS-SVM	32.19	36.79	91.14	82.22	73.33
LBP-SVM	0	0	0	0	0
AlexNet Features	0	0	0	0	0
ResNet50 Features	0	0	0	0	0
Proposed Method	**0**	**0**	**0**	**0**	**0**

4.2 Experiment 2

Tables 4 and 5 show the quantitative performance of the proposed method, together with seven different state-of-the-art schemes for detecting unknown

Table 3. Performance of different feature extraction techniques on Contact lens-2: Green

Algorithms	Development set	Testing set			
	D-EER (%)	D-EER (%)	BPCER @ APCER =		
			1%	5%	10%
BRISQUE-SVM	46 .23	43.25	93.33	85.55	75.55
GLCM-SVM	32.65	37.73	100	92.55	86.67
BSIF-SVM	0	0	0	0	0
SS-SVM	32.15	30.9	84.44	70	60
LBP-SVM	0	0	0	0	0
AlexNet Features	0	0	0	0	0
ResNet50 Features	0	0	0	0	0
Proposed Method	**0**	**0**	**0**	**0**	**0**

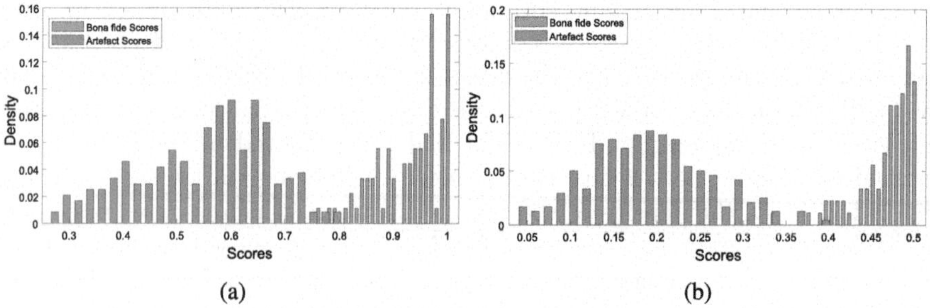

Fig. 7. Distribution of bona fide and artefact scores from Proposed Method (a) Trained with Contact lens-1: Blue and tested with Contact lens-2: Green (b) Trained with Contact lens-2: Green and tested with Contact lens-1: Blue (Color figure online)

contact lenses. It can be noted that the performances of all state-of-the-art algorithms were slightly degraded. Similar to an earlier observation, the proposed method shows the best performance, which can be attributed to the discriminative texture features captured in different spectral bands. The proposed method exhibits the best performance in both (training and testing with different types of contact lenses) experimental protocols with BPCER = 0% when APCER = 5% and 10%. Figure 7 shows the distribution of bona fide and artefact scores corresponding to the testing set. It can be observed that the scores slightly overlap, indicating a BPCER = 1% when APCER = 1% in both cases (training and testing with different types of contact lenses) investigated in this study. The obtained results not only justify the detection of the unknown textured contact lens that can be attributed to the custom multi-spectral iris capture device together with the proposed PAD algorithm.

Table 4. Performance of different feature extraction techniques when: trained with Contact lens-1: Blue and tested with Contact lens-2: Green

Algorithms	Development set	Testing set			
	D-EER (%)	D-EER (%)	BPCER @ APCER =		
			1%	5%	10%
BRISQUE-SVM	34.54	46.72	96.67	100	88.88
GLCM-SVM	36.24	43.27	90	90	85.55
BSIF-SVM	0	1.87	2.40	0	0
SS-SVM	32.12	26.67	91.14	82.22	73.33
LBP-SVM	0	1.87	2.11	0	0
AlexNet Features	0	1.48	1.2	1.2	0
ResNet50 Features	0	2.36	13.12	0	0
Proposed Method	**0**	**1.18**	**1.0**	**0**	**0**

Table 5. Performance of different feature extraction techniques when: trained with Contact lens-2: Green and tested with Contact lens-1: Blue

Algorithms	Development set	Testing set			
	D-EER (%)	D-EER (%)	BPCER @ APCER =		
			1%	5%	10%
BRISQUE-SVM	50.00	36.72	94.44	93.33	92.22
GLCM-SVM	32.65	42.18	100	94.44	86.67
BSIF-SVM	0	1.62	1.41	0	0
SS-SVM	32.22	40.09	84.44	71.14	60
LBP-SVM	0	3.09	5.82	1.4	0
AlexNet Features	0	2.15	3.94	0	0
ResNet50 Features	0	3.33	3.84	3.84	0
Proposed Method	**0**	**1.02**	**1.0**	**0**	**0**

5 Conclusion

Reliable detection of presentation attacks on an iris recognition system is essential for maintaining and improving the robustness of the system in a wide range of secure applications. In this work, we have proposed an approach based on exploiting multi-spectral information together with a novel approach combining deep features to reliably detect textured contact lens attacks on the iris recognition system. To this extent, we used a custom-built multi-spectral iris sensor that captures the iris image in five spectral bands. The proposed method utilizes deep features extracted from multi-spectral images, which are independently classified on each spectral band using a linear SVM. The final decision is obtained by aggregating the comparison scores from all five spectral bands through a sum rule. This work also introduces a multi-spectral contact lens dataset captured using two different types of contact lenses. Extensive experiments were carried out using seven different types of feature extraction techniques to effectively evaluate the efficacy of multispectral information in detecting both known and unknown contact lenses. The results obtained indicate the outstanding performance of the BSIF texture features computed on multispectral information to detect known and unknown contact lens presentation attacks with BPCER = 0% when APCER = 5% and 10%.

References

1. Czajka, A., Fang, Z., Bowyer, K.W.: Iris presentation attack detection based on photometric stereo features. In: IEEE Winter Conference on Applications of Computer Vision (WACV), pp. 1–8 (2019)
2. Doyle, J.S., Bowyer, K.W.: Robust detection of textured contact lenses in iris recognition using BSIF. IEEE Access **3**, 1672–1683 (2015)
3. Doyle, J.S., Flynn, P.J., Bowyer, K.W.: Automated classification of contact lens type in iris images. In: International Conference on Biometrics (ICB), pp. 1–6. IEEE (2013)
4. Galbally, J., Marcel, S., Fierrez, J.: Image quality assessment for fake biometric detection: application to iris, fingerprint, and face recognition. IEEE Trans. Image Process. **23**(2), 710–724 (2014)
5. Gautam, G., Mukhopadhyay, S.: Contact lens detection using transfer learning with deep representations. In: 2018 International Joint Conference on Neural Networks, IJCNN 2018, Rio de Janeiro, Brazil, July 8-13, 2018, pp. 1–8 (2018)
6. Gragnaniello, D., Poggi, G., Sansone, C., Verdoliva, L.: Using iris and sclera for detection and classification of contact lenses. Pattern Recogn. Letter **82**(P2), 251–257 (2016)
7. He, X., An, S., Shi, P.: Statistical texture analysis-based approach for fake iris detection using support vector machines. In: Lee, S.-W., Li, S.Z. (eds.) ICB 2007. LNCS, vol. 4642, pp. 540–546. Springer, Heidelberg (2007). https://doi.org/10.1007/978-3-540-74549-5_57
8. Hughes, K., Bowyer, K.W.: Detection of contact-lens-based iris biometric spoofs using stereo imaging. In: 46th Hawaii International Conference on System Sciences, pp. 1763–1772 (Jan 2013)
9. ISO/IEC JTC1 SC37 Biometrics: ISO/IEC 30107-3. Information Technology - Biometric presentation attack detection - Part 3: Testing and Reporting. International Organization for Standardization (2017)
10. J.Daugman: iris recognition and anti-spoofing countermeasures. In: 7th International Biometrics Conference (2004)
11. Kohli, N., Yadav, D., Vatsa, M., Singh, R.: Revisiting iris recognition with color cosmetic contact lenses. In: 2013 International Conference on Biometrics (ICB), pp. 1–7 (2013)
12. Komulainen, J., Hadid, A., Pietikäinen, M.: Generalized textured contact lens detection by extracting BSIF description from cartesian iris images. In: Biometrics (IJCB), 2014 IEEE International Joint Conference on, pp. 1–7. IEEE (2014)
13. Lee, E.C., Park, K.R., Kim, J.: Fake iris detection by using Purkinje image. In: Zhang, D., Jain, A.K. (eds.) ICB 2006. LNCS, vol. 3832, pp. 397–403. Springer, Heidelberg (2005). https://doi.org/10.1007/11608288_53
14. Mandalapu, H., Ramachandra, R., Busch, C.: Image quality and texture-based features for reliable textured contact lens detection. In: 14th International Conference on Signal Image Technology and Internet Based Systems (SITIS), Gran Canaria, Spain. pp. 1–9 (2018)

15. Othman, N., Dorizzi, B., Garcia-Salicetti, S.: Osiris: an open source iris recognition software. Pattern Recogn. Lett. **82**, 124–131 (2016)
16. Park, J.H., Kang, M.G.: Iris recognition against counterfeit attack using gradient based fusion of multi-spectral images. In: Li, S.Z., Sun, Z., Tan, T., Pankanti, S., Chollet, G., Zhang, D. (eds.) Advances in Biometric Person Authentication (2005)
17. Raghavendra, R., Raja, K.B., Busch, C.: Ensemble of statistically independent filters for robust contact lens detection in iris images. In: Proceedings of Indian Conference on Computer Vision Graphics and Image Processing, pp. 24:1–24:7. ICVGIP '14 (2014)
18. Raghavendra, R., Raja, K.B., Busch, C.: Contlensnet: robust iris contact lens detection using deep convolutional neural networks. In: 2017 IEEE Winter Conference on Applications of Computer Vision (WACV), pp. 1160–1167 (2017)
19. Silva, P., Luz, E., Baeta, R., Pedrini, H., Falcao, A.X., Menotti, D.: An approach to iris contact lens detection based on deep image representations. In: 28th SIBGRAPI Conference on Graphics, Patterns and Images, pp. 157–164 (2015)
20. Lee, S.J., Park, K.R., Lee, Y.J., Bae, K., Kim, J.: Multifeature-based fake iris detection method. Optical Eng. **46**, 127204 (2007)https://doi.org/10.1117/1.2815719
21. Venkatesh, S., Raghavendra, R., Raja, K., Busch, C.: A new multi-spectral iris acquisition sensor for biometric verification and presentation attack detection. In: IEEE Winter Conference on Applications of Computer Vision workshops (WACV), pp. 1–8, year=2019
22. Wei, Z., Qiu, X., Sun, Z., Tan, T.: Counterfeit iris detection based on texture analysis. In: 19th International Conference on Pattern Recognition, pp. 1–4 (2008)
23. Yadav, D., Kohli, N., Agarwal, A., Vatsa, M., Singh, R., Noore, A.: Fusion of handcrafted and deep learning features for large-scale multiple iris presentation attack detection. In: Proceedings of the IEEE Conference on Computer Vision and Pattern Recognition Workshops, pp. 572–579 (2018)
24. Yadav, D., Kohli, N., Doyle, J.S., Singh, R., Vatsa, M., Bowyer, K.W.: Unraveling the effect of textured contact lenses on iris recognition. IEEE Trans. Inf. Forensics Secur. **9**(5), 851–862 (2014)
25. Zhang, H., Sun, Z., Tan, T.: Contact lens detection based on weighted LBP. In: 20th International Conference on Pattern Recognition (ICPR), pp. 4279–4282 (2010)

SemUV: Deep Learning Based Semantic Manipulation Over UV Texture Map of Virtual Human Heads

Anirban Mukherjee(✉), Venkat Suprabath Bitra, Vignesh Bondugula, Tarun Reddy Tallapureddy, and Dinesh Babu Jayagopi

International Institute of Information Technology Bangalore, Bangalore, India
anirban.mukherjee@iiitb.ac.in

Abstract. Designing and manipulating virtual human heads is essential across various applications, including AR, VR, gaming, human-computer interaction and VFX. Traditional graphic-based approaches require manual effort and resources to achieve accurate representation of human heads. While modern deep learning techniques can generate and edit highly photorealistic images of faces, their focus remains predominantly on 2D facial images. This limitation makes them less suitable for 3D applications. Recognizing the vital role of editing within the UV texture space as a key component in the 3D graphics pipeline, our work focuses on this aspect to benefit graphic designers by providing enhanced control and precision in appearance manipulation. Research on existing methods within the UV texture space is limited, complex, and poses challenges. In this paper, we introduce SemUV: a simple and effective approach using the FFHQ-UV dataset for semantic manipulation directly within the UV texture space. We train a StyleGAN model on the publicly available FFHQ-UV dataset, and subsequently train a boundary for interpolation and semantic feature manipulation. Through experiments comparing our method with 2D manipulation technique, we demonstrate its superior ability to preserve identity while effectively modifying semantic features such as age, gender, and facial hair. Our approach is simple, agnostic to other 3D components such as structure, lighting, and rendering, and also enables seamless integration into standard 3D graphics pipelines without demanding extensive domain expertise, time, or resources.

Keywords: Computer Graphics · Computer Vision · Deep Learning · Generative Models · Virtual Humans

1 Introduction

Virtual humans are computer-generated characters designed to appear and behave like real people, created using technologies such as computer graphics, animation, and artificial intelligence. Creating and animating virtual humans is an active area of research due to their use in various application domains such

J. Kakarla et al. (Eds.): CVIP 2024, CCIS 2473, pp. 112–127, 2026.
https://doi.org/10.1007/978-3-031-93688-3_9

as VR, AR, Mixed Reality, Human-Computer Interaction, gaming and entertainment such as VFX and CGI. Designing and editing the facial appearance of the virtual human is a crucial and challenging task, whether the virtual human is based on an existing human, or a generated identity. The appearance comprises of semantic features, i.e. features in the image space having an interpreted meaning, such as age, expression, and facial hair, which need be considered with respect to the context and use-cases while designing and animating virtual human heads.

In traditional 3D graphics, the process of creating such virtual human heads primarily include designing a 3D mesh model, followed by designing a texture map, which is wrapped onto the mesh to give color and material information. These textures such as albedo (representing base color) and normals (representing surface depth) are 2D images, which are mapped onto the mesh using the concept of UV mapping, which helps in specifying how a 3D model's surface will be colored as per the 2D texture image. Therefore, the texture maps lie in the UV coordinates which, although being of 2-dimensions, is different from the XY coordinate of image space where regular images are represented. To design the appearance of a virtual head, graphic designers either paint on the UV space, or directly on the 3D model, which is a challenging and time-consuming task, requires manual effort and expertise in graphics, and difficult to achieve photorealistic results.

Comparatively, generating and editing regular 2D images, as compared to 3D models, has greatly been simplified lately due to the latest advancements in fields of AI such as deep learning and computer vision, where deep neural networks can learn the distribution of these images from thousands of diverse examples in a high dimensional latent space, which allows a user to generate, manipulate and animate photorealistic faces [16,17,25]. Although 2D human images can be edited using some of these approaches, they lack explicit structural information inherent in 3D head objects. The absence of geometry requires the 2D based models to implicitly learn the 3D movements [8]. This leads to structural and temporal inconsistencies and often results in artifacts while talking, performing pose changes and behavioral movements of the virtual heads. Furthermore, creating semantic manipulations in image space could lead to undesirable changes such as modifications in head structure and appearance of unwanted objects, because of the generative models' holistic learning approaches, making it difficult to disentangle specific features implicitly. For instance, while modifying the age of a young person, a generative model might introduce spectacles in the older version of the image (Fig. 6), which, although makes sense from a logical point of view, isn't ideal for 3D modeling purposes (Fig. 1). Such generative models, capable of learning 2D images, could be useful for learning the 2D texture maps, making it bridge the gap between 2D images and 3D computer graphics. However, there is significantly less work done for editing in the texture space for 3D human models. Consequently, our work is a crucial step in advancing the field in this direction. Some works in the lines of reconstructing 3D human heads from 2D images predict the texture maps, along with a 3D mesh. However, most of these approaches do not provide the option for editing semantic features on the texture maps. Moreover, many of these works model only the face area and not the whole head. Some of the works which perform editing in the texture space are trained using inverse rendering approaches which are complicated, dependent on the mesh, and require high computation resources.

Considering the challenges and the limitations of existing approaches, we propose SemUV: a novel method of performing semantic manipulation on the UV texture space of explicitly modelled 3D virtual human heads. We use the dataset provided by FFHQ-UV [1], and train a generative model to learn the distribution of the texture space of 3D heads. Then, we train a boundary using the available labels for disentangling the latent space of the generative model to be able to perform linear interpolation which correspond to semantic feature manipulation in the UV texture space. Our solution is simple to train because of its ability to directly learn from texture maps without relying on the 3D mesh structure, or applying any inverse rendering approach. Given a texture map, our approach is significantly fast because of the simple approach of linear interpolation in the learned latent space, allowing online manipulation of appearances directly in the texture space. Through comprehensive experiments and evaluations, we demonstrate the qualitative and quantitative advantages of SemUV over existing editing approach on the image-space. We discuss the usefulness and the scope of our work in the domains of 3D computer graphics and vision, and explain how SemUV could offer substantial advantages to the broader community. We also discuss the limitations of our approach and propose possible future research directions aimed at filling the existing research gaps and progress the area of 3D virtual human editing.
To summarize, our novel contributions in this work are as follows:

- We propose a simple and novel deep learning based method for supervised semantic manipulation of 3D faces by manipulating their UV texture maps in 2D space.
- We provide a learned UV texture space and present the results of semantic manipulation of age, beard and gender along with stage parameters such as lighting, and pose using UV texture and successfully demonstrated in the realistic 3D faces from various angles.
- We perform a user study to understand the perceived differences between our approach and 2D image based approach, and perform statistical tests to infer insights.
- We discuss how successful semantic manipulation in the texture space will be beneficial in various real life applications such as VR, AR, etc., and will allow a significant reduction in the effort and resource requirements for designers of realistic virtual human.

To the best of our knowledge, our method is the simplest effective solution for controlled semantic manipulation on UV texture space of 3D human heads.

2 Related Works

The topic of generation and manipulation of facial images has been a common area of research in computer vision [14]. Modern generative models such as styleGAN [16] learn the distribution of data, thereby making it possible to generate photorealistic face images with disentangled *styles*. While they provide their method for mapping an image onto the learned latent space, works such as [28] improve the process, allowing more realistic encoding of images to latent space.

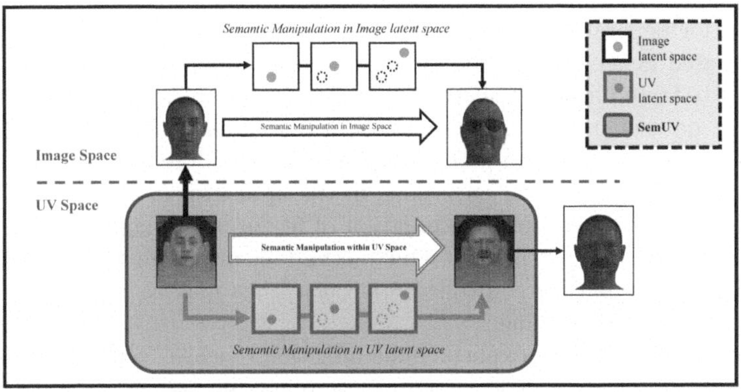

Fig. 1. SemUV vs Image based approach: Our approach works only on the *UV space*, focusing on the face texture, thus preventing unwanted changes possible in the image domain. Moreover, we can see the pathway for performing changes directly in UV space is shorter, thus making the approach simpler and faster.

Apart from generation, manipulation of semantic features is an important area of research. In this regard, the authors of [24] have achieved significant results by disentangling the latent space through learning linear subspaces. This allows step-wise manipulation of features, allowing explicit control of the semantic features. While the 2D facial-image space has greatly benefited from such generative vision models, they lack a 3D geometric representation making them unsuitable for structural deformations, which is inherently present in 3D computer graphics models. Lately, there has been some works which aim at representing heads in 3D using 2D images. Most notably, models such as 3DMM [6] and FLAME [20] are able to generate 3D colored head models, which can be rendered on 2D screen. 3DMM model represent colors using colored vertices, while some of the implementations of FLAME incorporates texture maps along with a 3D mesh. While these works can effectively generate and reconstruct human heads, none of them offer a means to manipulate their texture maps. Similarly, works such as AvatarMe++ [18], StyleUV [19], StyleFaceUV [3] and UV-GAN [5] also have the capability to estimate texture maps. The authors of FFHQ-UV [1] point out some of the challenges of the existing approaches, and propose a state-of-the-art pipeline for creating full head albedo UV maps from images.

They publicly release the dataset, along with labels on the identities, and we use this dataset to train our GAN model, to allow us to perform semantic manipulations on extracted texture maps using this method. While these approaches are targeted towards generating UV maps, manipulating them remains unaddressed in these works.

The authors of [23] learns to estimate 3D shape and texture. However, the pipeline works on both a mesh and a texture level, making it difficult to train a general UV based model for all faces. In contrast, our method focuses solely on the texture space, and is trained using a simpler approach that does not necessitate the use of inverse rendering. Similarly, the authors of [26] have proposed a method for generating and editing faces in 3D. Compared to their diffusion [10] [27] based generative model, our GAN based approach is less data-hungry and easier to train for our use case. This is because of the simpler distribution of FFHQ-UV dataset used in our method, which contrasts with the complex data distributions where diffusion models typically excel. Moreover, while their text driven approach is useful for variations in the appearance, they do not discuss about a step-wise controlled manipulation of features, a crucial concern from a 3D graphic designer's perspective. Our method ensures seamless editing of texture maps in an explicitly controlled approach, thus making it compatible with existing 3D graphics pipeline.

As an alternative to explicit modelling approaches, semantic manipulation has also been studied the realm of implicit modelling methods, such as approaches based on NeRFs [22], which learn the volumetric or geometric information within a neural network. Although there have been methods attempting to disentangle appearance features in this space [11,21], the usage of such implicit models are limited because of a lack of strongly defined explicit structure [8]. Therefore, such implicit models remain inferior as of yet, when compared to explicit 3D models in terms of structural consistency, which is one of the crucial areas of focus in our work.

3 Proposed Work

In our proposed method, we operate within the space of *albedo UV texture maps*, which store the fundamental color information [13] of a virtual human head. Our method involves learning the UV texture feature space using a generative model, subsequently allowing us to perform interpolations in the latent texture space of the model, corresponding to semantic manipulations in the UV texture map. Once the texture map is wrapped onto a head mesh, the rendered results have the changes in the virtual human's head (Fig. 2). To train such as model, first we sample from a labeled dataset [1] with UV albedo texture maps of human faces. Then, we learn the distribution of the texture space using the architecture of StyleGANv2-ada [17]. After this, we train an SVM to learn a boundary for disentangling the latent space of the trained GAN model via subspace projection [24]. This allows linear interpolation in the latent space resulting in precise manipulation of semantics of the face such as facial hair, age and gender without changing other aspects such as identity.

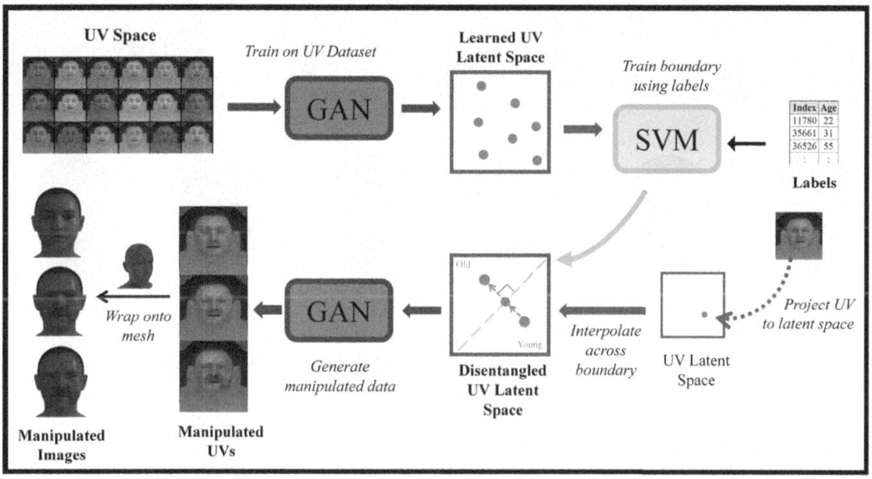

Fig. 2. SemUV Overview: In our approach 1. First we learn the distribution of the UV space using a generative model, in this case StyleGAN. 2. Then, using available labels, we train a linear classifier to learn the decision boundary for the semantic features. 3. Now, given a new UV image, we project it to the UV latent space, and interpolate it in the space across the learned boundary to perform disentangled semantic manipulation. 4. Finally, we take this new latent vector and use our trained GAN to generate the semantically modified UV map, which is wrapped onto the head mesh and rendered for the final output.

3.1 FFHQ-UV Dataset

We have used the FFHQ-UV dataset [1], which is derived from the FFHQ dataset [16], a large-scale face image dataset. FFHQ-UV contains over 50,000 images of 1024 × 1024 resolution of UV albedo maps of human faces. The dataset also has labels corresponding to the images, providing information regarding high-level semantic features such as facial hair, age and gender for each of the images. We use the images for learning the distribution of the image space of these UV texture maps, which we refer to as the UV-space. Then, we use the labels for the semantic features for training our SVM which will be used for performing the desired semantic manipulations.

3.2 Learning the UV Texture Space

To learn the UV space, we train a state-of-the-art generative vision model, commonly used for facial-image generation. StyleGANv2-Ada [15] is a generative adversarial network (GAN) [7] based architecture, whose strengths are a combination of StyleGANv2 [17] and Adaptive Instance Normalization (AdaIN) [12]. Similar to the basic version of StyleGAN [16], the generator produces an intermediate feature map, w, by mapping z through a mapping network, denoted as W. This mapping network learns a non-linear mapping function that projects z to a

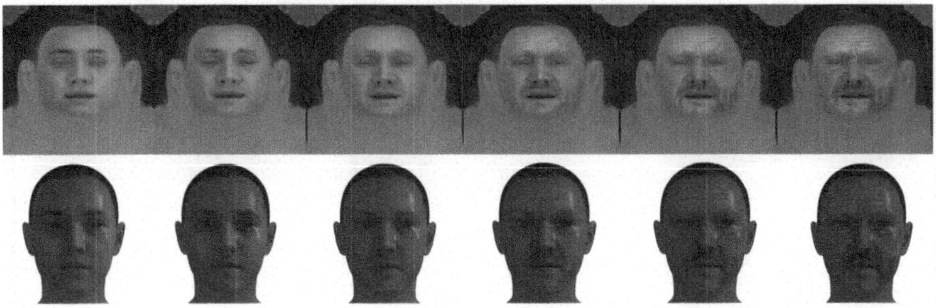

Fig. 3. Outputs of SemUV: Images from *left* to *right* represent increasing age in the (*top*) UV-Texture map and (*bottom*) the final head mesh wrapped with the texture

disentangled latent space, where different dimensions control various attributes of the generated image. The intermediate feature map w is then passed through a series of convolutional layers, each followed by an AdaIN operation, to generate the final synthesized image, $G(z; w)$, possessing the desired style and appearance characteristics. We train the model with our UV texture map dataset on 10000 UV maps from the FFHQ-UV dataset [1], aiming to generate UV maps of albedo textures. This allows the model to learn the distribution of UV maps. Post-training, we can sample points from the latent space and pass them through the model, generating UV maps similar to those of the dataset. When wrapped onto a mesh, these UV maps give rise to the appearance of a realistic human heads.

3.3 Interpolating Semantic Features

GANs learn various semantics in linear subspaces of the latent space, which can be manipulated without retraining the model. Building upon the idea by [24], we train a linear Support Vector Machine (SVM) [4] to classify between the levels of each semantic features within the learned latent space. For our model, we choose the criteria of age, facial hair and gender, as per the available labels from the FFHQ-UV dataset. However, it must be noted that this method can be scaled to any number of semantic features given a labeled dataset. Using the labels, the SVM learns to classify the latent vectors, treating those with highest attribute values in the available labels as positive samples, and those with the lowest values as negative. After training, the coefficients of the SVM are used as the boundary vector for the features. To perform a modification of a semantic in a given image with N steps, we use a projection method proposed in [15] to get the latent vector from the image, and subsequently interpolate N steps in the latent space along the direction orthogonal to the boundary vector. These interpolated steps correspond to incremental manipulation in the semantic features. By ensuring orthogonalization of all the boundaries, we disentangle the interpolation of semantic features. The ability to linearly interpolate with desired number of steps allows precise control over the manipulation, crucial

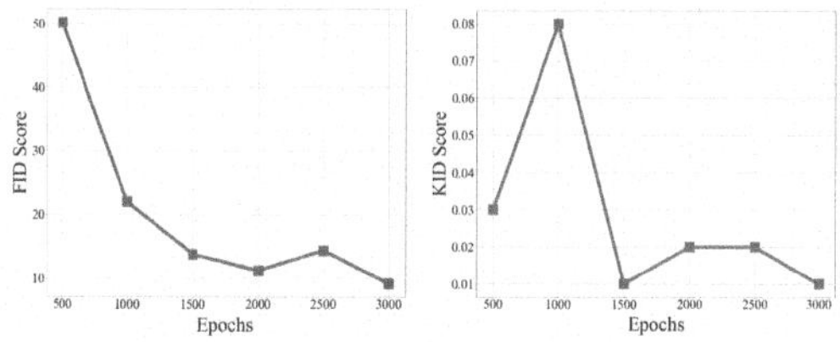

Fig. 4. FID and KID scores over 3000 epochs: Low values of FID and KID scores indicate high-quality of generated samples

for the process of designing and manipulating appearance of 3D human head models.

4 Experiment

We select 10000 UV maps from the FFHQ-UV dataset to train our model. We choose the architecture of [15] since it is the state-of-the-art method for generating images resembling the training data. We train it on the dataset for 3000 epochs on NVIDIA GeForce RTX 2080 Ti. Each epoch was run for 4000 images, following the official PyTorch StyleGAN ADA implementation[1].

Then we use the labels from the dataset to train a SVM, to be able to classify the latent vectors as per the attributes, as mentioned in Sect. 3.3.

5 Results

After training, we have a learned space of UV texture maps. We show the improvements while training the model using Fréchet Inception Distance (FID) score [9] and Kernel Inception Distance (KID) [2] scores across the epochs (Fig. 4), both of which measure the similarity between real and generated samples. Lower values of FID and KID indicate that the generated samples are of high quality, closely resembling the real samples in terms of visual appearance.

5.1 Interpolated Results

To visualize the working of SemUV on head UV texture maps, we sample from the dataset and perform semantic manipulation on 3 the features: age, facial hair, and gender.

After performing the manipulations, we project the texture maps on the 3D mesh provided by the dataset on Blender[2], a 3D graphics engine. Once we have projected the UV map, we have a complete 3D head model which we

[1] https://github.com/NVlabs/stylegan2-ada-pytorch.
[2] https://www.blender.org/.

can view from any direction. Figures 5a, 5b, 5c show the result of the semantic manipulations on the head figure from various angles.

Age: For the change in age in Fig. 5b, going from left to right we observe the features of the face being similar to that of a child, young teen, and a grown man respectively. There is change in the amount of facial hair such as moustache, beard and eyebrows. Also with age, there is an increase of high texture features such as wrinkles.

Gender: For the change in the gender in Fig. 5c, we can observe the difference in face features such as lip shape, eyelid shape and eyebrow shape. Overall, female *(right)* has sharper features and smoother skin. The male *(left)* version had slight facial hair around the mouth area, a feature implicitly learned by the generative model.

Facial Hair: For the change in facial hair in Fig. 5a, we observe the gradual growth of hair as we go from left to right. We note that the growth of hair is same as that of humans, i.e. first slight growth of moustache and beard around the mouth region, followed by more dense beards in the sides of the face.

Overall, we observe that the identity of the figure has been preserved in all the cases, and high level features are visible on the faces. Also, the changes are equally visible from all the angles such as front *(top)*, left *(middle)* and right *(bottom)*, ensuring a structurally consistent editing of semantic features.

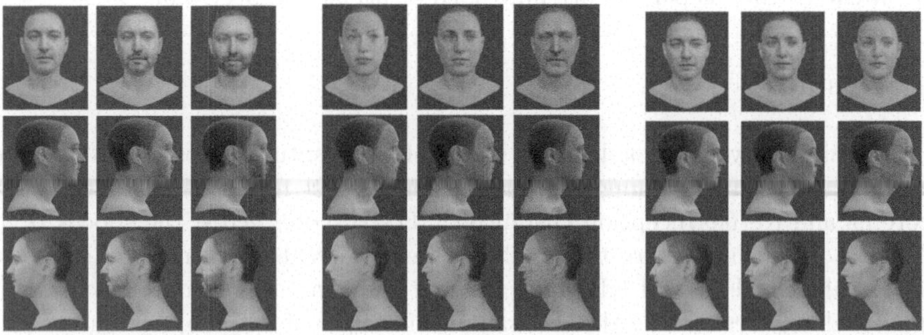

(a) Facial hair (b) Age (c) Gender

Fig. 5. Semantic manipulation results from (top) front, (middle) right and (bottom) left viewpoint. The changes in the features are made from left to right.

5.2 Comparing with Image-Space Manipulations

To evaluate the performance with respect to 2D image based approaches, we select the texture map obtained using the pipeline of FFHQ-UV on a custom image, and manipulate the age of the virtual head.

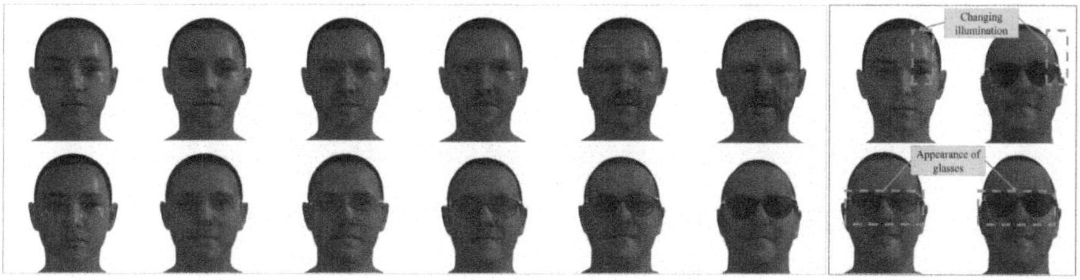

(a) Manipulation of age on UV using SemUV *(top)* and Image based approach *(bottom)* (b) Issues with image based approach

Fig. 6. **(a)** Results of SemUV *(top)* vs Image based approach *(bottom)* **(b)** As we can see, changes in the image space can result in unwanted changes, change in identity, change in illumination, as well as image level artefacts. **SemUV**, is successfully able to add age related features without altering other aspects of appearance.

We choose age attribute in particular because it is a common attribute between the FFHQ-UV labels, and InterFaceGAN [24], which we use as a benchmark for performing semantic manipulation after inverting a given face image using [28]. Gender was another common attribute between the two approaches, however the presence of hair in the image space, and lack of hair on the 3D head could give biased results while user evaluation.

We project the base texture map, along with the manipulated ones on the generic head mesh provided in the official repository of FFHQ-UV. We use Pytorch3D to render the head display with the given mesh and textures, with a field of view of 20°C to approximate the view in face-images datasets. From the base image, we use [28] to get a latent vector, and then interpolate the age feature using the official implementation.

Qualitative Analysis. The outputs obtained through SemUV contain appropriate wrinkles, signifying increasing age, along with some white facial beard. We can see the that on the face of the transformed image, glasses appear across interpolated results.

Computational Comparison. From Fig. 1, we can see that for manipulating a UV texture map using an image based method, there are extra steps for 1. Wrapping the UV map on a head mesh, 2. Rendering a display for the head, giving a head image, and 3. After manipulation, getting the unwrapped UV map of the face using FFHQ-UV pipeline. Considering these steps and ignoring the common tasks of GAN inversion to project into latent space, interpolating in the latent space, and also synthesizing manipulated image from latent space, we record the time taken for a set of 30 images to go through the pipeline (without considering the system operations taken by the CPU). We observe an additional time of *15 min* taken by the image-space pipeline, which is primarily by the step of generating a UV map from a given image. This makes the method of SemUV faster than image based operation, allowing it to scale with multiple images and making it more suitable for real-time appearance editing in graphics based applications.

Table 1. User evaluation results

Question no	Choices for our approach	p-value
Q1	86.67 %	0.000030
Q2	93.34 %	0.000000
Q3	86.67 %	0.000030
Q4	86.67 %	0.000030
Q5	73.34 %	0.008062
Q6	80.00 %	0.000715
Q7	86.67 %	0.000030
Q8	90.00 %	0.000004

User Evaluation. For evaluating the performance of our approach as compared to the image based manipulations, a set of subjects were asked 8 questions as follows:
Q1. Which sequence (left to right) is better at showing increasing age?
Q2. Which sequence (left to right) is better at ensuring ONLY age is changed and no other aspect of appearance is changed?
Q3. Which sequence (left to right) better ensures lighting/illumination is maintained?
Q4. & Q5. In which pair of images does the identity and facial structure of the left image match the most with that of the right image? (without considering age change)
Q6. & Q7. In which pair of images does the expression of the left image match the most with that of the right image?
Q8. Out of the given sequences A and B, in which one does the changes in head pose seem most smooth and structurally consistent?

For Q1, Q2, Q3, participants were shown Fig. 6 (a), i.e. two sequences of manipulation of age, one using SemUV, and the other using image based approach. For Q4 and Q6, participants were shown the left-most and right-most images of Fig. 6 (a), i.e. pairs of images before and after manipulation of features. For Q5 and Q7, we performed an additional task of removing the glasses using [24] once again on the obtained final image, as we can see in Fig. 7 (b). The idea was to see whether the aspects of identity and emotion are preserved after removing the glasses which, even though requires an additional step, would let us know how our approach compares without the addition of unwanted glasses. Finally, for Q8, participants were shown Fig. 7 (a), i.e. two sequences of images with changing pose, the bottom one being changed using image based manipulation, and top ones being changed simply by changing the camera angle during rendering.

To determine if it performed significantly better than chance, we performed one-sided binomial tests at a 5 % significance level ($\alpha = 0.05$) for each question, with N = 30 trials and K successes where K is the number of participants who preferred the results of our approach. Our null hypothesis (H0) is that *our approach is not significantly better than chance*, while our alternative hypothesis (H1) is that *our approach is preferred more often*.

There were 30 participants (18 male and 12 female) for the survey. The mean age of the participants is 26.93, with a standard deviation of 5.02. From Table 1 we can see that there is a significant observation that our approach is able to perform age manipulation better *(Q1)*, by ensuring no other aspect of appearance is changed *(Q2)* and maintaining lighting and illumination *(Q3)*. Our approach also ensures that the identity *(Q4 and Q5)* and expressions *(Q6 and Q7)* are maintained better by our approach. Interestingly, this holds true even after manually removing the glasses *(Q5 and Q7)* which appeared while manipulating the age. Also, due to the inherent 3D nature of our approach, we see that head changes in pose is smooth and consistent *(Q8)* in our approach. While this is a default advantage of any 3D approach, the result indicates that using image based pose changes could result in inconsistencies in the head, leading to unwanted outputs both in the image space, and also UV maps derived from them.

To ensure uniform and spatially consistent appearance manipulation across the whole head surface, our approach proves effective due to its operation over the complete head albedo space.

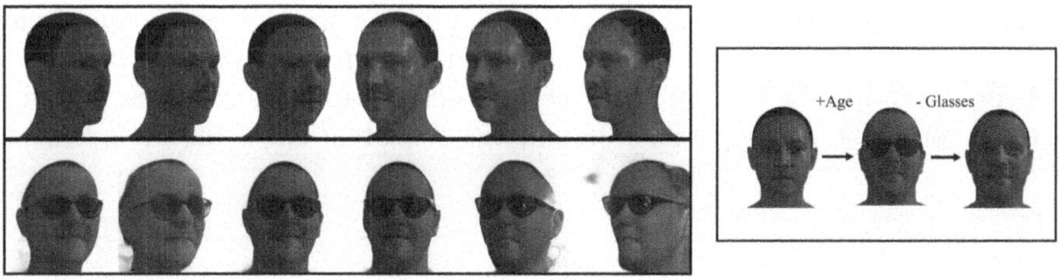

(a) **Pose changes** ***(left to right)*** **on results of SemUV** ***(top)*** **and image based approach** ***(bottom)***

(b) Manual removal of glasses from manipulated head image

Fig. 7. (a) Pose changes *(from left to right)* on results of SemUV and image based approach (b) Removing glasses using [24]

6 Discussion

In this section, we look into the key insights regarding the importance of SemUV, based on our conducted experiments. We examine the limitations of our approach and explore potential future research directions aimed at enhancing our method and expanding the range of successful semantic manipulations of virtual heads in UV space.

6.1 Significance of SemUV

Having a model capable of performing manipulations directly in UV space presents a significant advantage for designers operating in the realm of 3D graphics. While transformations generated by models operating in the 2D image space, such as increasing hair length while changing gender from male to female or adding glasses when increasing age, may seem logically valid, they are not suitable for the process of graphic designing processes, where such elements are typically modelled separately. Moreover, employing image-based approaches for UV editing is time taking due considering the additional steps of conversions between UV and image space. Also, these additional steps can generate unwanted changes in semantic aspects of appearance, including identity, and result in artifacts and structural inconsistencies. In contrast, manipulating in UV space allows the generative model to focus exclusively on the high resolution (1024×1024) texture for head area, and be agnostic to other physical aspects such as structure, lighting and viewing direction. These advantages make SemUV significantly valuable in the area of virtual head modelling using 3D computer graphics.

6.2 Limitations

While our approach is successfully able to perform manipulations in the semantic aspects, there are challenges in disentangling certain features in the latent space where the labels are noisy. In Fig. 3, we see that although there was no facial hair in the initial image, the aged version has added slight patches of white hair. Such challenges could be tackled by using more labelled examples, as well as modified methods for non-linear separation boundaries for latent space disentanglement.

6.3 Future Scope

Some future research directions could explore various realistic face UV datasets. With a dataset of high quality and diverse representations of texture maps, more photorealistic images could be created which will result in even more realistic faces that will be perceptually indifferent from real faces, reaching the photorealistic quality of modern state-of-the-art generative models for 2D face images. This will further reduce the gap between 2D and 3D face manipulations. Apart from the quality of the images in the dataset, there could also be more sets of labels and attributes which correspond to other high level semantic features. These labels could be used for training our proposed pipeline so that there is even more control for variations in the human heads. Another possible future direction for the dataset could be to include normal maps, which include information about the depth of images. Representing details in skin requires depth information along with color. To accurately change features such as age, such details and textures in skin needs to be represented. Allowing the model to learn the normal maps along with albedo maps could enable better semantic manipulations and much higher quality of rendering of the human faces. Considering that these virtual humans are made keeping in mind a diverse range of demographics, the ability to perform manipulations of features such as race and gender will be helpful in introducing diversity in the virtual humans.

7 Conclusion

In this work, we have proposed SemUV: a novel, simple and effective deep learning based method for performing semantic manipulation of 3D human faces in UV texture maps. Leveraging a learned UV texture space from state-of-the-art high resolution dataset, we have successfully demonstrated manipulations of semantic features such as age, beard, and gender. We have conducted a user study to explore the perceived differences between our approach and traditional 2D image-based methods, supported by statistical tests to infer valuable insights for our method. Furthermore, we have highlighted the potential real-life applications of successful semantic manipulation in the texture space, including VR and AR. By enabling more efficient and resource-effective design processes for realistic virtual humans, our approach promises to significantly benefit 3D graphic designers across various domains. This work contributes a promising solution to the ongoing challenges in 3D face manipulation, offering both practical applications and valuable insights for future research advancements in the field of virtual head modelling.

Acknowledgment. This project was funded by MINRO center at IIITB.

References

1. Bai, H., Kang, D., Zhang, H., Pan, J., Bao, L.: FFHQ-UV: Normalized facial UV-texture dataset for 3D face reconstruction. In: IEEE Conference on Computer Vision and Pattern Recognition (June 2023)
2. Bińkowski, M., Sutherland, D.J., Arbel, M., Gretton, A.: Demystifying mmd gans. arXiv preprint arXiv:1801.01401 (2018)
3. Chung, W.C., Zhu, J., Shen, I.C., Wu, Y.T., Chuang, Y.Y.: Stylefaceuv: a 3d face UV map generator for view-consistent face image synthesis. In: BMVC, p. 89 (2022)
4. Cristianini, N., Shawe-Taylor, J.: An introduction to support vector machines and other kernel-based learning methods. Cambridge university press (2000)
5. Deng, J., Cheng, S., Xue, N., Zhou, Y., Zafeiriou, S.: UV-GAN: Adversarial facial UV map completion for pose-invariant face recognition. In: Proceedings of the IEEE Conference on Computer Vision and Pattern Recognition, pp. 7093–7102 (2018)
6. Egger, B., et al.: 3D morphable face models–past, present, and future. ACM Trans. Graph. (ToG) **39**(5), 1–38 (2020)
7. Goodfellow, I., et al.: Generative adversarial nets. Adv. Neural Inform. Process. Syst. **27** (2014)
8. Grassal, P.W., Prinzler, M., Leistner, T., Rother, C., Nießner, M., Thies, J.: Neural head avatars from monocular RGB videos. In: Proceedings of the IEEE/CVF Conference on Computer Vision and Pattern Recognition, pp. 18653–18664 (2022)

9. Heusel, M., Ramsauer, H., Unterthiner, T., Nessler, B., Hochreiter, S.: GANs trained by a two time-scale update rule converge to a local nash equilibrium. Adv. Neural Inform. Process. Syst. **30** (2017)
10. Ho, J., Jain, A., Abbeel, P.: Denoising diffusion probabilistic models. Adv. Neural. Inf. Process. Syst. **33**, 6840–6851 (2020)
11. Hong, Y., Peng, B., Xiao, H., Liu, L., Zhang, J.: Headnerf: A real-time nerf-based parametric head model. In: Proceedings of the IEEE/CVF Conference on Computer Vision and Pattern Recognition, pp. 20374–20384 (2022)
12. Huang, X., Belongie, S.: Arbitrary style transfer in real-time with adaptive instance normalization. In: Proceedings of the IEEE International Conference on Computer Vision, pp. 1501–1510 (2017)
13. Hughes, J.F.: Computer graphics: principles and practice. Pearson Education (2014)
14. Kammoun, A., Slama, R., Tabia, H., Ouni, T., Abid, M.: Generative adversarial networks for face generation: a survey. ACM Comput. Surv. **55**(5), 1–37 (2022)
15. Karras, T., Aittala, M., Hellsten, J., Laine, S., Lehtinen, J., Aila, T.: Training generative adversarial networks with limited data. Adv. Neural. Inf. Process. Syst. **33**, 12104–12114 (2020)
16. Karras, T., Laine, S., Aila, T.: A style-based generator architecture for generative adversarial networks. In: Proceedings of the IEEE/CVF Conference on Computer Vision and Pattern Recognition, pp. 4401–4410 (2019)
17. Karras, T., Laine, S., Aittala, M., Hellsten, J., Lehtinen, J., Aila, T.: Analyzing and improving the image quality of stylegan. In: Proceedings of the IEEE/CVF Conference on Computer Vision and Pattern Recognition, pp. 8110–8119 (2020)
18. Lattas, A., Moschoglou, S., Ploumpis, S., Gecer, B., Ghosh, A., Zafeiriou, S.: Avatarme++: facial shape and BRDF inference with photorealistic rendering-aware GANs. IEEE Trans. Pattern Anal. Mach. Intell. **44**(12), 9269–9284 (2021)
19. Lee, M., Cho, W., Kim, M., Inouye, D., Kwak, N.: Styleuv: Diverse and high-fidelity UV map generative model. arXiv preprint arXiv:2011.12893 (2020)
20. Li, T., Bolkart, T., Black, M.J., Li, H., Romero, J.: Learning a model of facial shape and expression from 4D scans. ACM Trans. Graph. **36**(6), 1–194 (2017)
21. Ma, L., Li, X., Liao, J., Wang, X., Zhang, Q., Wang, J., Sander, P.V.: Neural parameterization for dynamic human head editing. ACM Trans. Graph. (TOG) **41**(6), 1–15 (2022)
22. Mildenhall, B., Srinivasan, P.P., Tancik, M., Barron, J.T., Ramamoorthi, R., Ng, R.: NERF: representing scenes as neural radiance fields for view synthesis. Commun. ACM **65**(1), 99–106 (2021)
23. Rai, A., et al.: Towards realistic generative 3d face models. In: Proceedings of the IEEE/CVF Winter Conference on Applications of Computer Vision, pp. 3738–3748 (2024)
24. Shen, Y., Yang, C., Tang, X., Zhou, B.: Interfacegan: interpreting the disentangled face representation learned by GANs. IEEE Trans. Pattern Anal. Mach. Intell. **44**(4), 2004–2018 (2020)
25. Shi, Y., Yang, X., Wan, Y., Shen, X.: Semanticstylegan: Learning compositional generative priors for controllable image synthesis and editing. In: Proceedings of the IEEE/CVF Conference on Computer Vision and Pattern Recognition, pp. 11254–11264 (2022)
26. Wu, Y., et al.: Text-guided 3D face synthesis–from generation to editing. arXiv preprint arXiv:2312.00375 (2023)

27. Zhang, L., Rao, A., Agrawala, M.: Adding conditional control to text-to-image diffusion models. In: Proceedings of the IEEE/CVF International Conference on Computer Vision, pp. 3836–3847 (2023)
28. Zhu, J., Shen, Y., Zhao, D., Zhou, B.: In-domain GAN inversion for real image editing. In: European Conference on Computer Vision, pp. 592–608. Springer (2020)

Correlation-Based Tracking Cum Recognition Pipeline for Road Signs

Farah Jamal Ansari[1(✉)], Sumeet Agarwal[2], and M. Hanmandlu[3]

[1] Indian Institute of Technology, Delhi, India
eez208423@ee.iitd.ac.in

[2] Yardi School of Artificial Intelligence, Indian Institute of Technology, Delhi, India
sumeet@iitd.ac.in

[3] Department of Electrical Engineering, Indian Institute of Technology, Delhi, India
mhmandlu@ee.iitd.ac.in

Abstract. Road signs provide the necessary information to the drivers and help protect them from the potential hazards on the roads. Hence, a pipeline involving detection, tracking, and recognition of road signs is an integral component of the Advanced Driver Assistance System (ADAS). A tracker helps to follow the detected object in real time. This paper presents a novel correlation-based approach for the localization of road signs while encountering unassociated tracks during tracking. The detection is necessary for the first time, but if in the subsequent frames, an unassociated track is found, then correlation is proposed as the remedial step to estimate the location of the road sign. The correlation along with the neighborhood restriction is attempted to associate the road signs and also help reduce the identity switches. Compared to deep learning-based association techniques, correlation-based tracking is computationally less expensive and can be exploited for real-time tasks. Lastly, the recognition module is included in the proposed pipeline to reduce the false positives and the experimental results validate the effectiveness of this pipeline.

Keywords: Correlation · YOLOv5 · Multi object road sign tracking

1 Introduction

Road signs are placed on the sides of the road to inform a driver of the road conditions that lie ahead. For this, we present a new approach for tracking the detected road sign in every frame of a video sequence. This tracker can serve as a component of the ADAS, which continuously informs the driver of the approaching road signs and helps him/her to make decisions on time. Its main task is to inform the driver of a road sign as soon as it is visible, but a subsidiary task can be to manage the inventory of road signs.

We will now throw light on the need for tracking road signs. For environmental reasons, a detector may not be able to capture a road sign in the desired frame. This information is passed onto the tracker through association and in

J. Kakarla et al. (Eds.): CVIP 2024, CCIS 2473, pp. 128–143, 2026.
https://doi.org/10.1007/978-3-031-93688-3_10

this scenario, the tracker captures the road sign using correlation. The tracker also helps reduce false positives as they lack temporal consistency. No analysis of the detected road sign is possible if it is not tracked.

As a vehicle encounters several road signs in a single frame, we need to track more than one at a time. Therefore, the detection-based Multi-Object Tracking (MOT) framework is proposed here with the sole purpose of tracking multiple road signs to maintain a separate trajectory for each road sign over a time frame. The first task is to associate a newly detected road sign in the current frame with an already existing track. In case of multiple tracks, only one is associated with. The most common technique is Intersection over Union (IoU). In case, a road sign is tracked from a far away location, IoU fails to associate the road sign due to its small size at that location, then recourse is taken to the correlation coefficient to associate the road signs with the given tracks.

Another challenge in MOT is the problem of identity switches, which occurs when a wrong track is associated with a road sign. In addition, there are many more difficult conditions such as occlusion, poor illumination, or the possibility of a road sign entering or leaving the scene in a given frame. The correlation based tracker developed in this paper can locate signs with the help of association techniques, if the detector fails to do so on account of the problems posed by illumination, weather or orientation. The tracking framework is as shown in Fig. 1.

We will now outline the steps involved in tracking.

1. *Detection*: In this step, the road signs in a frame are localized using a suitable object detector. Thereafter a track is created corresponding to each detected road sign.
2. *Data Association*: If some tracks are already present in a scene, then they are associated with the detected road signs termed measurements in the current frame.
3. *Creation & Deletion of Tracks*: A new track is created if the measurement in the current frame fails to be associated with any of the existing tracks. And, a track is deleted if it is not detected consecutively in a given number of frames.

We now review some related work on detection, recognition, and tracking in the literature.

Detection: Integral channel features(ICF) are coined in [9] to detect the road signs in German traffic sign detection benchmark (GTSDB) [5] and [11] compares the performance of ICF with that of the Aggregate Channel Features (ACF) on the US road signs. Performance of various detectors such as region-based Fully Convolutional Network (R-FCN), Faster RCNN (FRCNN), Single Shot Detectors (SSD), and You only look once (YOLOv2) is compared in [1] for the detection of road signs from the GTSDB dataset. FRCNN is employed in [3] for the detection of road signs in images belonging to the GTSDB and the Turkey dataset. Using the deep learning techniques, road signs of different sizes are detected in [4].

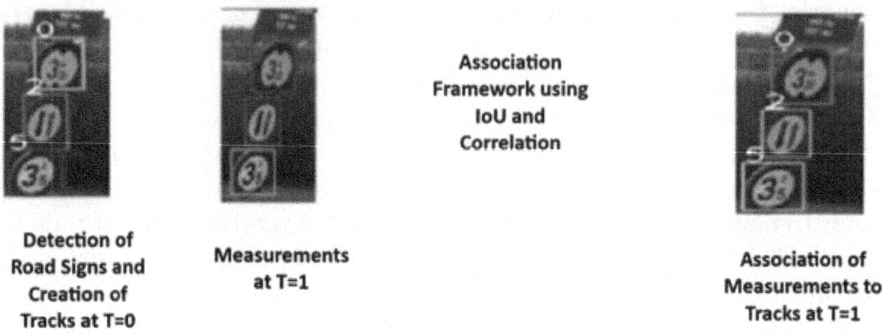

Fig. 1. MOT Framework for road signs.

Recognition: A multi-scale two stage CNN architecture is proposed in [12] to classify the road signs in German traffic sign recognition benchmark(GTSRB) [14]. YOLOv3 along with the customised CNN is used for both the detection and recognition of the road signs in [2].

Tracking: The trends and challenges involved in the detection, recognition, and tracking of road signs are discussed in [17]. However, tracking the performance of the predictive filters is found better than that of the adaptive filters in [8]. In [16], the 3D tracking is developed for the temporal integration along with the detection and recognition of the road signs. The particle filters and sensor information are utilized for the 3D object tracking of the road signs in [10]. In [13], YOLO architecture is modified to improve the detection of the small road signs, and the Deep sort method is invoked for tracking. A combination of the Region Growth Detector (RGD), ThunderNet and LSTM is proposed for the detection of the road signs in [18] followed by the Kalman Filter for the state estimation along with the color histogram for the association.

2 The Proposed Detection, Tracking, Recognition Cum Pipeline

Figure 2 shows the flow of the proposed pipeline. The detection of the road signs is done using the YOLOv5 [6] as it is fast and accurate. The next phase is the correlation coefficient-based tracking framework in which the association phase aids in detecting the lost tracks that are later localized using the correlation coefficient. The last phase is recognition, which not only categorizes the road signs but also employs the rejection threshold to reduce the false positives. As we have used the CURE-TSD dataset [15] for the implementation of the proposed tracking framework, a brief outline of this dataset is given here. This contains 49 real-world sequences each having 300 frames. These sequences are taken from the CURE-TSD dataset, as the ground truth is missing from the Belgium sequences. The number of real-world sequences is divided into 34 for the training set and the remaining for the test set. The steps in the Detection-based Tracking framework using the principle of MOT are explained below:

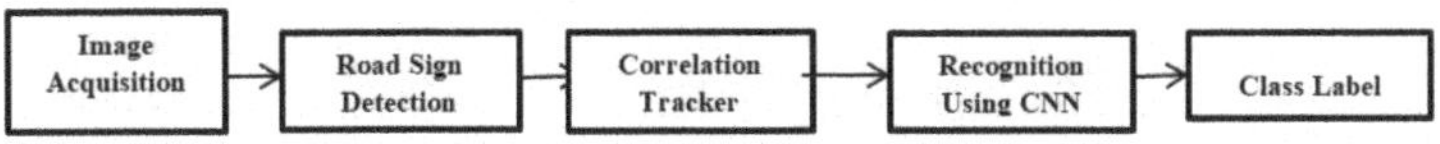

Fig. 2. Block diagram of the proposed Pipeline

1. *Detection*: In this, a track is created for each road sign detected in a frame.
2. *Association*: As shown in Fig. 1, detections in the current frame are known as measurements and those in the past frames are referred to as tracks. In this step, each measurement is associated with a track. For association, several metrics like Intersection over union (IoU), Euclidean distance, histogram matching, or deep association can be employed, though we have used IoU and correlation in this work. For finding the association, a M X N cost matrix, C[i,j] is used where M denotes the number of tracks and N denotes the number of measurements in the current frame. A C[i, j] is formed between the ith track and j^{th} measurement as follows:

$$C[i,j] = 1 - IoU(t_i, m_j) \tag{1}$$

where IoU is given by

$$IoU = \frac{Area\_of\_Intersection}{Area\_of\_Union}$$

In the above, $Area\_of\_Intersection$ is the area common to the track and a measurement, and $Area\_of\_Union$ is the area covered by merging the track and the measurement. A minimum threshold of 0.05 is specified on the value of IoU for a track to be assigned to a measurement. In some cases, tracks cannot be associated with the measurement on the basis of IoU due to the small size of a road sign across frames, thus vouching for the correlation coefficient for association. The Pearson coefficient computes the similarity between the remaining unassociated tracks and a measurement through the correlation of their pixels. The degree of correlation between a track and a measurement is expressed as follows:

$$r = \frac{\sum_{x=1}^{n}(det_x - det').(tr_x - tr')}{\sqrt{\sum_{x=1}^{n}(det_x - det')^2.\sum_{x=1}^{n}(tr_x - tr')^2)}} \tag{2}$$

where r varying from 0 to 1 indicates the similarity between a track and a measurement, n is the pixel count, det_x and tr_x are the respective pixel intensity values or gray levels for the given measurement, and a track, det' and tr' are the respective means of the gray levels corresponding to the measurement and track respectively. By 5-fold cross-validation, it is found that the best F-score is obtained if r is taken to be $>=$ 0.9. The unassociated tracks that were not associated using IoU are matched with one of the remaining unassociated measurements using the correlation coefficient and the Hungarian algorithm. The neighborhood constraint taken as the Euclidean distance, is exercised over and above the correlation coefficient to avoid the identity switches as two similar road signs belonging to different tracks are likely to associate with each other to form a track. It is given by:

$$d = \sqrt{(xT - xM)^2 + (yT - yM)^2} \tag{3}$$

where xT,yT and xM,yM denote the top leftmost pixel coordinates of the track and measurement respectively. If this value is above 20 pixels found by the 5-fold cross-validation, then it is said that the measurement is not associated with the given track thereby avoiding the id switching as shown in Fig. 3.

3. *Estimation of tracks*: As the detector is fairly efficient, tracking is employed only to form the sequence of the road signs from one frame to another. In case, the detector fails to locate a road sign, then using the correlation coefficient the road sign is predicted based on its similarity with the track.
4. *Detection using correlation*: If the track is not able to associate with a measurement then the route is declared to be broken. This might be due to two reasons: the first one, the track has left the scene, and the second one, the detector is unable to detect the road signs on account of the varying environmental conditions. In such cases, the sign is located using the correlation coefficient as demonstrated in Fig. 4. Upon searching for the associated measurement in the current frame, the track is searched in the adjoining region of the track located in the previous frame. The detected road sign, cropped from the previous frame is taken as the reference image, and it is moved from top to bottom and left to right across the search area in the current frame. The window having the maximum normalized correlation coefficient with the reference image is said to be the measurement in the current frame. The normalized correlation coefficient is calculated as follows:

$$r(x,y) = \frac{\sum_{x',y'}(R'(x',y').S(x+x',y+y')}{\sqrt{\sum_{x',y'}((R'(x',y')^2).\sum_{x',y'}(S(x+x',y+y')^2)}} \tag{4}$$

where R denotes the tracked road sign and S is the search area where the measurement is searched by sliding the window across it. R' and S' are formed by subtracting the respective gray-level means from R and S, respectively. x and y are the coordinates of the pixels of the top leftmost point of the sliding window. Note that x+x' and y+y' are the pixel coordinates to be correlated with those of the template image or the tracked road sign. To reduce the effect of illumination, the mean is subtracted from the pixel intensities as follows. $R'(x',y') = R(x',y') - 1/(w.h).\sum_{i,j} R(i,j)$ and $S'(x+x',y+y') = S(x+x',y+y') - 1/(w.h).\sum_{i,j} S(x+i,y+j)$.
where w is the width of the tracked road sign, h is the height and (w.h) is the number of pixels in the tracked road sign. The window having the highest correlation coefficient (r) greater than the specified threshold represents the matched track or measurement. The optimal threshold value of r is found to be 0.9 by the 5-fold cross-validation.

5. *Deletion of a track*: An 'Age' variable is initialized when the detector fails to detect a track in a frame for the first time and it is incremented if the tracked road sign is consecutively not detected in the subsequent frames. As soon as the measurement is detected in a frame, the 'Age' variable is set to zero again. A track is deleted if its 'Age' variable surpasses a certain threshold, found to be 2 after the 5-fold cross validation.
6. *Deletion of tracks using the non maximum suppression (NMS)*: Sometimes a track and a measurement don't associate with each other even after being associated using correlation-coefficient. Therefore two tracks are formed for the same road sign. This is because the tracker finds a new match for the lost track based on the correlation coefficient and also creates a new track for the unassociated measurement. Therefore if these two tracks overlap by more than 50%, they are considered the same, then the measurement found by correlation coefficient is discarded and the new track is merged with the old track and its track id is retained. This action not only avoids the creation of a new track id but also reduces the false positives.
7. *Recognition*: The output of the tracker is the input to the recognition phase, that assigns a correct class to the tracked road sign and also removes the false alarms raised at the detection and tracking phases. For this purpose, the CNN architecture in [12] is chosen as shown in Fig. 5. At this phase, the rejection threshold is introduced to reject the false alarms as no separate class is assigned for the false positives during training. The rejection threshold is defined such that if the highest probability score of a road sign is below a certain threshold (rejection threshold), it is rejected as a non-road sign.
   The CURE dataset used for classification is not publicly available, so the initial training is done on the BelgiumTSC [16] dataset having 62 classes, but the training is carried out only on 14 classes available in the CURE-TSD dataset. The model is again fine-tuned for the cropped images extracted from the CURE-TSD training set, that is split up to facilitate the 5-fold cross-validation. After hyper parameter tuning, the following settings are made for the tracking framework: Age $=2$, correlation coefficient for association $>=$ 0.9, correlation coefficient for detection $>= 0.9$, and association distance in pixels $<= 20$.
   The recognition model is cross-validated for the specified values of epochs, the learning rate, and the rejection threshold. Their best values are selected as 150, 0.01 and 0.8 respectively. Similarly, the cross-validation is conducted on the pipeline without tracking, and their respective values are 150, 0.01 and 0.7. With these values, the pipeline is tested on the test sequences for both with and without the tracking scenarios.

2.1 Reduction of the False Positives While Tracking

To accomplish this, a track is considered valid only if it appears in the subsequent frames. Imposition of this constraint leads to a considerable drop in the false positives as can be observed in Table 1. Figure 6a depicts the detection phase

Fig. 3. Example of id switching

Fig. 4. Parking sign captured by the correlation based tracking not detected by YOLOv5

on account of the occurrence of a false positive and a true positive whereas in Fig. 6b, the false positive is removed after tracking but as can be observed from Table 1 that the recall also falls down. This is due to the assumption that a track is considered valid only when it is confirmed.

2.2 Improvement of the Recognition Performance

In this, various techniques are investigated to improve the performance of the tracking pipeline during the recognition phase. The CNN model is trained and tested on the images of different sizes, and finally, the selected ensemble model

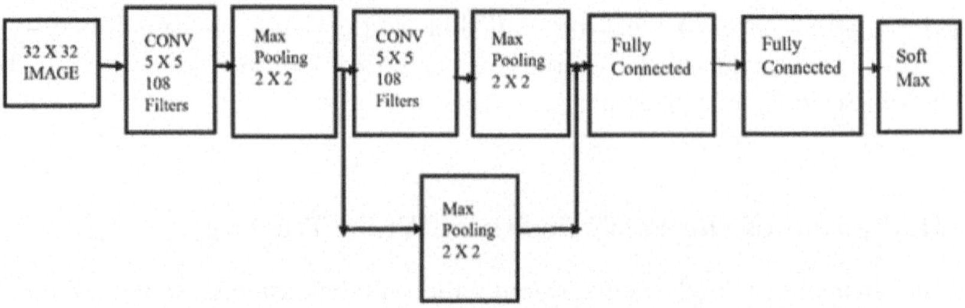

Fig. 5. The Block diagram of the adapted CNN model.

(a) Occurrence of a false positive prior tracking

(b) Removal of the false positive post tracking

Fig. 6. Removal of the false positives due to tracking

yields the best test accuracy. If the test road signs have sizes larger than 256 pixels, we use the model trained on the images with the input size of 32 X 32 and if the test images have sizes smaller than or equal to 256 pixels, we use the model trained on the input images of size 16 X 16. Using an ensemble model to classify the road signs, we see an improvement in both the F score and the recall.

Next, the histogram equalization is used as a pre-processing step for both the training and test sets, to boost the F-score further. As seen in Fig. 7, the histogram equalization considerably improves the contrast of an image.

(a) Input Images

(b) Histogram Equalized images

Fig. 7. Enhancement of Images using the histogram equalization

Lastly, the currently used recognition model is replaced with a pre-trained model that incorporates the transfer learning to increase the performance. Out of several pre-trained models tried the best performance is achieved with VGG16. The architecture is displayed in Fig. 8.

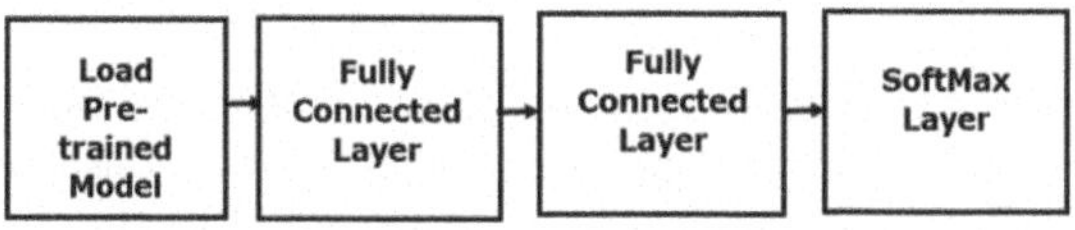

Fig. 8. Transfer learning architecture for recognition

Next, an alternative approach is presented in which the motion equations are utilized to locate a road sign. If in any frame, a detector is unable to locate a road sign, then it is done so using the motion equations described below:

3 Formulation of Motion Equations for the Detection of the Road Signs

If a road sign is not located by the YOLOv5 detector, the correlation-based approach discussed above is then used for its localization. For comparison, a state-space model is presented to localize a road sign in the current frame based on its position in the previous frame, using a transition matrix. The state space model is expressed as:

$$\hat{x}_t = F * \hat{x}_{t-1} + B * u_{t-1} \tag{5}$$

where $\hat{x}_t$ and $\hat{x}_{t-1}$ denote the locations of a road sign in the current and the previous frames respectively. The movement of the system state from one frame to another is represented by the state transition matrix, and F.$B * u_{t-1}$ is the noise to be filtered. Assuming the state to have a constant velocity, the state transition matrix [7] is written as:

$$F = \begin{bmatrix} 1 & dt & 0 & 0 & 0 & 0 & 0 & 0 \\ 0 & 1 & 0 & 0 & 0 & 0 & 0 & 0 \\ 0 & 0 & 1 & dt & 0 & 0 & 0 & 0 \\ 0 & 0 & 0 & 1 & 0 & 0 & 0 & 0 \\ 0 & 0 & 0 & 0 & 1 & dt & 0 & 0 \\ 0 & 0 & 0 & 0 & 0 & 1 & 0 & 0 \\ 0 & 0 & 0 & 0 & 0 & 0 & 1 & dt \\ 0 & 0 & 0 & 0 & 0 & 0 & 0 & 1 \end{bmatrix} \tag{6}$$

$dt = 1$ is kept to one, that is, the transition from one frame to another.

$$\hat{x}_{t-1} = [up, up\_dot, left, left\_dot, down, down\_dot, right, right\_dot] \tag{7}$$

where up, left, down, right denote the leftmost and bottom most pixel coordinates of the tracked road sign in the previous frame and up_dot, left_dot, down_dot, right_dot are the respective velocities. The velocities are computed on the basis of the displacement made by the tracked road sign in the previous frames. A track is created whenever a new road sign enters the scene, but it becomes valid only if it matches some road sign in the subsequent frames. But if it is not matched in the consecutive frames, the 'Age' variable is initialized. When this variable attains a certain limit, the track is deleted. As long as the road sign is associated to a measurement, the velocities are updated. Sometimes the track and the measurement get associated in the consecutive frames but sometimes, they don't, and therefore the 'Age' variable aids in calculating the velocity in such situations. The velocities are computed as follows:

$$up\_dot = (\hat{y}_m[up] - \hat{y}_n[up])/(Age_t + 1) \tag{8}$$

$$left\_dot = (\hat{x}_m[left] - \hat{x}_n[left])/(Age_t + 1) \tag{9}$$

$$down\_dot = (\hat{y}_m[down] - \hat{y}_n[down])/(Age_t + 1) \tag{10}$$

$$right\_dot = (\hat{x}_m[right] - \hat{x}_n[right])/(Age_t + 1) \tag{11}$$

where t denotes a track with m as the current frame and n as the previous frame and $\hat{x}_m$,$\hat{y}_m$ $\hat{x}_n$,$\hat{y}_n$ are the coordinates of the tracked road signs in the respective frames. As observed from Fig. 9, tracking by the motion equations is able to detect an occluded sign which the YOLOv5 detector couldn't, but it leads to more false positives than those due to the correlation-based approach. The reason is that although the motion equations estimate a road sign very accurately, they have no means to affirm whether it has left the scene or not.

Fig. 9. An occluded road sign localized by the tracking based on the motion equations

4 The Results of Implementation of the Pipeline

Table 1 compares the various techniques used for tracking. It is found that the tracking using the correlation coefficient leads to a significant increase in the recall, but the false positives also increase as they are also correlated in the subsequent frames. Their number keeps on increasing till the track doesn't expire. A track is said to be valid if it is matched with the measurements in the subsequent frames so a valid track assures the reduction of the false positives but at the cost of the reduced recall. It is also shown that if the YOLOv5 detector fails to detect a road sign in any one of the frames, then it can also be detected using the motion equations instead of the correlation coefficient-based approach. It is seen from Fig. 9 that an occluded sign is also detected by this approach. A comparison of this approach is made with that in [7] where tracking and association are performed using Kalman filter and IoU respectively. It is found that although it captures a lot of signs, both recall and precision are lesser than those of the baseline tracking. The proposed approach is also compared with that in [19] where the tracking is implemented using the Kalman filter and a deep association metric is used for the association. The approach in [19] originally implemented on the pedestrian dataset is adopted by us to track the road signs. But we see from the results, that the approach of [19] is unable to track the road signs accurately. Table 2 compares the detection, tracking cum recognition results. It is easily observed that the results are better after tracking. Here, the pipeline makes use of the baseline tracking only. It is seen that in both the tracking and non-tracking scenarios there is a fall in the recall after recognition. The main reason for this is the small size of the road signs because of which they are classified into the wrong category. Figure 10 depicts the numbers of both the false positives and negatives arising in the pipeline due to the varying sizes of the road signs. The first plot in the figure shows the number of false positives arising due to the several factors mentioned on the x-axis. The rest of the plots show the number of false positives (non-road signs classified into signs), false negatives, and the misclassified road signs based on the sizes of the road signs. It can be seen that the false positives occur due to the similar color distribution as that of the road signs and also many of them are very small in size. To improve the performance of the recognition module, an ensemble model is employed to recognize the road signs with an increase in the recall and F-score. In addition to this, we have also tested the histogram equalization on both the training and the test sets. These two approaches show an improvement in the F-Score. Lastly, VGG16 is used for the classification thereby facilitating a considerable improvement in the recall of the pipeline. The confusion matrices for all the models are shown in Fig. 11 where 0 to 13 rows and columns are meant for the road signs, but the 14th row is reserved for the false positives. The CURE-TSD dataset was created to take part in the Video and Image Processing (VIP) Cup 2017 competition with the theme titled, "Traffic Sign Detection under Challenging Conditions" [15]. The recognition results are compared in Table 2 with those of the two teams that fared well in the VIP Cup 2017. The better performing team bagged the first rank on the road sign detection task implemented using U-Net. The other team undertook tracking to improve the detection cum recognition results. Both the teams use the CNN models for classification. It is seen that the U-Net team outshines in performance than that of our correlation-based tracking framework whereas the other team is far behind. It may be noted that we have not attempted the challenging conditions as they are not in our scope of research work but we have performed our comparison on the normal circumstances that the teams have also undertaken in addition to the challenging ones. Finally, Tables 3 and 4 analyze the performance of the pipeline based on the varying road sizes. It is observed that the false negatives decrease if the smaller sized road signs are removed from the ground truth and also if they are neither tracked nor detected.

Table 1. Comparison of Tracking with Detection results

Method	Recall	Precision	F-Score
Without Tracking	0.4256	0.755	0.544
With correlation Tracking (baseline)	0.452	0.719	0.554
Baseline but with matching	0.3983	0.766	0.524
Tracking based on motion equations	0.3974	0.720	0.512
Tracking using Kalman filter [7] & IoU	0.3287	0.62	0.430
Tracking using deep sort employing deep association [19]	0.079	0.207	0.114

Table 2. Comparison of Recognition results with and without Tracking

Method	Recall	Precision	F-Score
Without Tracking	0.370	0.749	0.495
With Tracking (Baseline)	0.382	0.745	0.505
Baseline Tracking (Ensemble)	0.400	0.694	0.508
Baseline Tracking (Ensemble&histogram equalization)	0.399	0.722	0.515
Baseline Tracking with pretrained model	0.432	0.702	0.535
Detection using U-Net [15]	0.490	0.700	0.576
Detection using FRCNN and Lucas-Kanade for tracking [15]	0.390	0.575	0.500

Table 3. F-score evaluation based on sizes during tracking

Input Size in pixels	Total Signs in Ground truth	Recall	Precision	F-Score
All	3334	0.452	0.7186	0.554
>= 100	3038	0.470	0.704	0.565
>= 200	2269	0.530	0.730	0.620
>= 300	1906	0.570	0.780	0.660
>= 500	1434	0.640	0.789	0.709

Table 4. F-score evaluation based on sizes of road signs at the recognition phase with tracking

Input Size in pixels	Total Signs in Ground truth	Recall	Precision	F-Score
All	3334	0.382	0.745	0.505
>= 100	3038	0.424	0.723	0.535
>= 200	2269	0.497	0.755	0.599
>= 300	1906	0.535	0.802	0.642
>= 500	1434	0.617	0.836	0.710

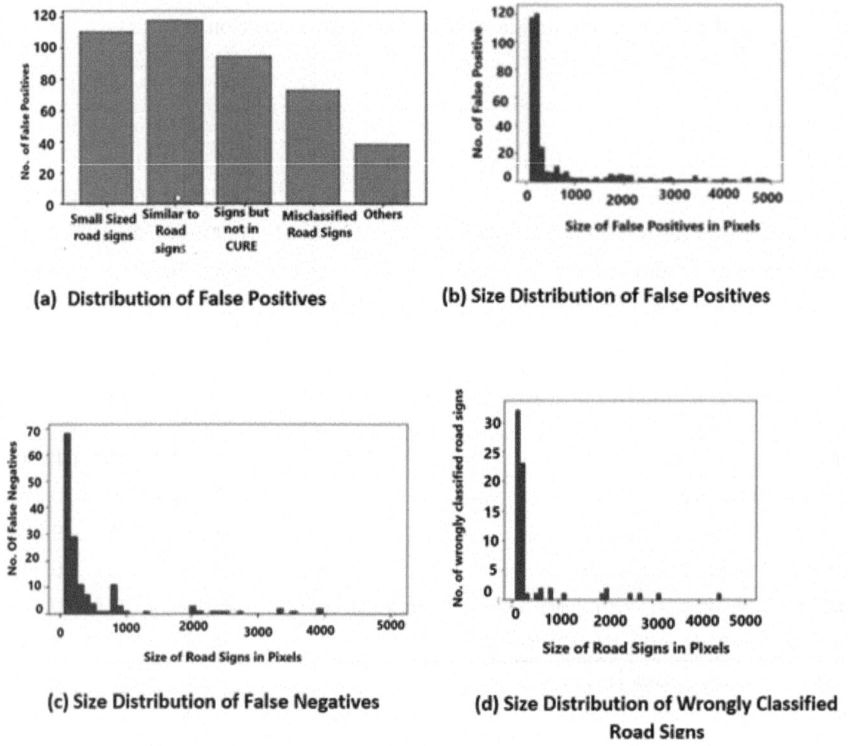

Fig. 10. Error Classification of the tracking cum recognition Pipeline

Some **contributions** made on the correlation based tracking framework are now elaborated . A detection based correlation tracker is developed. We invariably use the YOLOv5 as a detector but if it is unable to detect for some reason, then the same is localized using correlation. For association, in addition to IoU, correlation is also used. To reduce the identity switches, the neighborhood criterion is availed. The investigation of localization of the road signs using the motion equations is also examined as an alternative to the correlation. The recognition performance is enhanced by employing an ensemble model along with the histogram equalization. The use of transfer learning has helped to improve the F score. Lastly, a size analysis of the road signs is made and it is found that the bigger road signs yield a better performance.

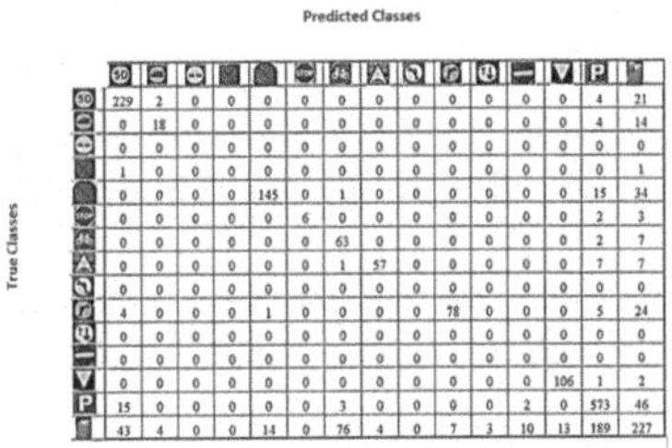

(a) Confusion Matrix of the tracking cum recognition pipeline (baseline)

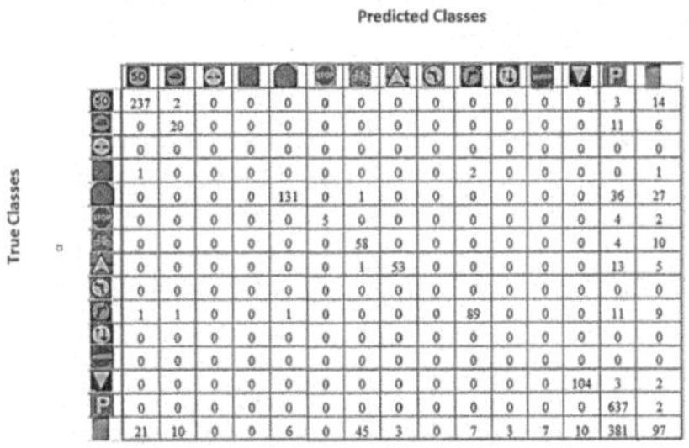

(b) Confusion Matrix of the tracking cum recognition pipeline (baseline) using ensemble model

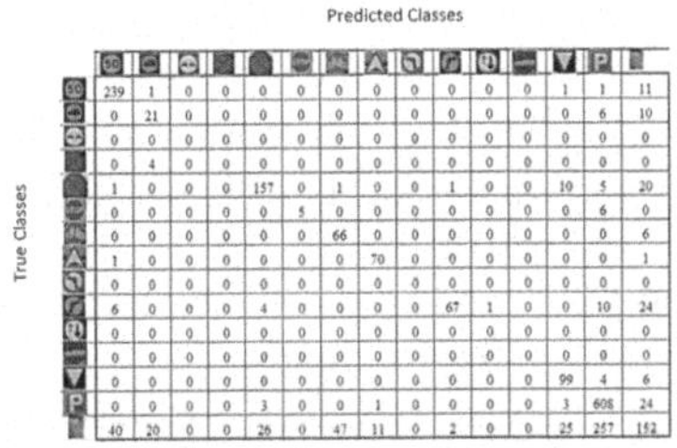

(c) Confusion Matrix of tracking cum recognition pipeline (baseline) using ensemble model with histogram equalization

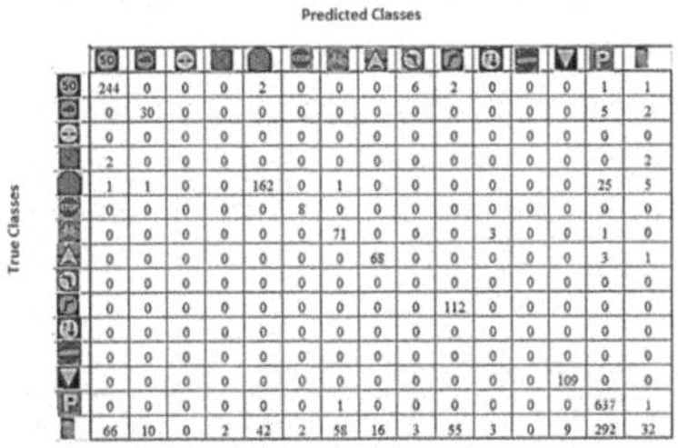

(d) Confusion Matrix of the tracking cum recognition pipeline with pre-trained model

Fig. 11. Confusion matrix

5 Conclusions

In this work, a detection-based MOT framework is developed for the road signs. The correlation coefficient comes to our rescue when the YOLOv5 fails to detect. IoU, correlation coefficient, and the Hungarian Algorithm are used for associating tracks with measurements. An alternate tracking framework is proposed where instead of the correlation coefficient, the state-space model governed by the motion equations is used to detect the lost tracks. However, its performance is found to be inferior to that of the correlation coefficient-based tracking. The false positives are reduced if we come across a measurement in the subsequent frames captured from the valid track. A comparison of the correlation-based tracker with those in [7,19] shows its performance to be superior. An ensemble model and the histogram equalization are used to improve the overall recognition accuracy. Lastly, the VGG pre-trained model helps improve the recognition results. The incorporation of the correlation coefficient aids in improving the capability of the detector and the utility of the pre-trained model whereas the pre-processing techniques help in improving the recognition accuracy. Our future work is to merge the correlation-based tracking framework with the state space model governed by the motion equations.

References

1. Arcos-Garcia, A., Alvarez-Garcia, J.A., Soria-Morillo, L.M.: Evaluation of deep neural networks for traffic sign detection systems. Neurocomputing **316**, 332–344 (2018)
2. Dhawan, K., RK, N.: Identification of traffic signs for advanced driving assistance systems in smart cities using deep learning. Multimed Tools Appl. **82**(17), 26465–26480 (2023)
3. Güney, E., Bayılmış, C.: An implementation of traffic signs and road objects detection using faster R-CNN. Sakarya Univ. J. Comput. Inform. Sci. **5**(2), 216–224 (2022)
4. Hasegawa, R., Iwamoto, Y., Chen, Y.W.: Robust Japanese road sign detection and recognition in complex scenes using convolutional neural networks. J. Image Graph. **8**(3), 59–66 (2020)
5. Houben, S., Stallkamp, J., Salmen, J., Schlipsing, M., Igel, C.: Detection of traffic signs in real-world images: The German traffic sign detection benchmark. In: In International Joint Conference On Neural Networks (2013)
6. Jocher, G., et al.: ultralytics/yolov5: v3.1 - Bug Fixes and Performance Improvements (Oct 2020). https://doi.org/10.5281/zenodo.4154370, https://doi.org/10.5281/zenodo.4154370
7. kyleguan: Vehicle-detection-and-tracking (Nov 8, 2019). https://github.com/kcg2015/Vehicle-Detection-and-Tracking
8. Lafuente-Arroyo, S., Maldonado-Bascon, S., Gil-Jimenez, P., Gomez-Moreno, H., Lopez-Ferreras, F.: Road sign tracking with a predictive filter solution. In: IECON 2006-32nd Annual Conference on IEEE Industrial Electronics, pp. 3314–3319. IEEE (2006)
9. Mathias, M., Timofte, R., Benenson, R., Van Gool, L.: Traffic sign recognition—how far are we from the solution? In: Neural Networks (IJCNN), The 2013 International Joint Conference on, pp. 1–8. IEEE (2013)
10. Meuter, M., Kummert, A., Muller-Schneiders, S.: 3D traffic sign tracking using a particle filter. In: 2008 11th International IEEE Conference on Intelligent Transportation Systems, pp. 168–173. IEEE (2008)
11. Møgelmose, A., Liu, D., Trivedi, M.M.: Detection of us traffic signs. IEEE Trans. Intell. Transp. Syst. **16**(6), 3116–3125 (2015)
12. Sermanet P, L.Y.: Traffic sign recognition with multi-scale convolutional networks. In: Neural Networks (IJCNN), The 2011 International Joint Conference on, pp. 2809–2813 (2011)
13. Song, S., Li, Y., Huang, Q., Li, G.: A new real-time detection and tracking method in videos for small target traffic signs. Appl. Sci. **11**(7), 3061 (2021)
14. Stallkamp, J., Schlipsing, M., Salmen, J., Igel, C.: Man vs. computer: Benchmarking machine learning algorithms for traffic sign recognition. Neural networks **32**, 323–332 (2012)
15. Temel, D., Alshawi, T., Chen, M.H., AlRegib, G.: Challenging environments for traffic sign detection: Reliability assessment under inclement conditions. arXiv preprint arXiv:1902.06857 (2019)
16. Timofte, R., Prisacariu, V.A., Gool, L.V., Reid, I.: Combining traffic sign detection with 3d tracking towards better driver assistance. In: Emerging topics in computer vision and its applications, pp. 425–446. World Scientific (2012)
17. Wali, S.B., et al.: Vision-based traffic sign detection and recognition systems: current trends and challenges. Sensors **19**(9), 2093 (2019)

18. Wang, C., Xie, X., Liao, C.: An adaptive fusion model based on kalman filtering and LSTM for fast tracking of road signs. In: 2020 25th International Conference on Pattern Recognition (ICPR), pp. 1414–1421. IEEE (2021)
19. Wojke, N., Bewley, A., Paulus, D.: Simple online and realtime tracking with a deep association metric. In: 2017 IEEE International Conference on Image Processing (ICIP), pp. 3645–3649. IEEE (2017)

Believable AI: Teaching Classifiers to Know What They Don't Know

Lakshmi Annamalai[1(✉)], Sreedevi Priyanka[1], Faheema AGJ[1], Subrata Rakshit[1], Kaushik Thakkar[2], Pradeep Kumar Gautham[1], and Desiraju Padma[1]

[1] Defence Research and Development Organization, Kanpur, India
{lakshmi.cair,sreedevip.cair,faheema.cair,dgtm.hqr,pradeep.cair, padma.cair}@gov.in
[2] IIT, Kanpur, India
kaushikt22@iitk.ac.in

Abstract. Knowing whether a COTS-AI model is believable for use in a deployment context is crucial. The main concerns are whether actual input distribution matches what was used for training, whether there are some error-prone regions of input space where the AI is prone to fail. Significantly less attention has been given to address such lacuna in deployment scenarios. To fill this gap, we propose a first-of-its-kind novel solution known as Believable AI. This is the first paper to provide a theoretically strong algorithmic solution that will enable the COTS-AI buyer to (i) characterize inputs for which the model should be believed, (ii) certify its usage as believable given the risk tolerance in a given context and (iii) provide evidence based on above characterization for believing the model's output. The proposed solution is based on a statistical analysis of the model performance on labeled inputs and inter-sample distances. We show with a wide variety of network architectures and publicly available datasets how buyers of COTS-AI can benefit from these measures, how designer/developers of AI can make claims about their products without revealing design or complete data related IPR, and how a regulatory compliance mechanism can be built to make COTS-AI products believable to use.

Keywords: Believable AI · Neural Network · Classifier

1 Introduction

In the past decade, AI technologies have become ubiquitous in various high-risk domains such as medical diagnosis, national security, natural disaster control, and law enforcement and are becoming the most sought out solution in all fields. As AI systems begin to get utilized in critical applications, the challenge of these systems shifts from high-performing model development to believable model deployment and its correct use.

The COTS-AI model may achieve very high scores in the research and development environment, but the performance may not be the same when exposed to real-life data at the field. When these COTS-AI systems are deployed in the real

J. Kakarla et al. (Eds.): CVIP 2024, CCIS 2473, pp. 144–158, 2026.
https://doi.org/10.1007/978-3-031-93688-3_11

world, there are scenarios where they fail miserably, resulting in erroneous predictions with very high confidence [16]. It will thereby cause significant negative impact if they don't work as they are intended to. Hence, before the COTS-AI system is brought on board, where it has to make important decisions based on real-life data, the buyer should have a clear strategy to certify whether it will achieve the claims made by the AI designer/developer in his data space.

Furthermore, once deployed, the model is susceptible to degradation, subject to data drift and concept drift. The model might have been trained using biased data, thereby giving it no room to cope with future data. In such situations, AI systems become erroneous with very high confidence, which is pretty dangerous, especially when the AI decisions influence safety-critical applications such as medical diagnosis, military applications, automated driving, *etc.*, where human life is at stake. Hence, it is crucial to make the AI models self-aware and develop the ability to comprehend what they don't know. This will abstain the application from making a decision just based on the AI models and help the buyer to decide when to seek for human intervention and when to ask the designer/developer for model updates.

Despite the widespread use of COTS-AI systems, there has been no standard algorithmic regulatory scrutiny procedure for effective and correct utilization of the same. The buyers do not have a strategy to identify the AI systems that do not perform as per designer/developer's claims and calibrate the input space over which the given AI system is prone to fail. Moreover, the knowledge in deep learning AI systems is so entangled that straightforward quantification is not trivial. An alternative way will be to use the classifier's confidence, such as softmax probability, but it has been strongly proved that the classifier's own score miserably fails to identify error-prone regions; in other words, a classifier cannot provide a certificate for its own believability [16,22].

Faced with these issues, the question that we asked about how to enable buyers to gauge whether the COTS-AI system is believable to use, motivated us to propose a first-of-its-kind interpretable and mathematically grounded algorithm, which we refer to as Believable AI. Believable AI is derived based on labeled space analysis and distance measures. The theory on which the proposed Believable AI algorithms are built does neither have any underlying assumption regarding the decision contour of the classifier nor the architecture of the AI model.

Aligning the inter-sample distance metric computation to the representation used by the model would certainly produce the best results. However, even in the situations of noncooperative AI designer/developer where the buyer may be denied access to training feature space or training data samples, the method can still be implemented with buyer-defined metrics and buyer-selected labeled data. To that extent, the proposed solution is model design agnostic. The proposed solution will also benefit the designer/developer to validate his claims on the buyer's dataset without revealing his data or architecture-related IPR.

2 Literature Review

As the proposed work is first-of-a-kind work, we have looked into related areas of research which are uncertainty prediction, confidence estimation, epistemic alaetropic uncertainty [8,19] and open space recognition [2,3,5–7]. We have given a detailed survey on the uncertainty prediction and confidence score estimation domains.

2.1 Uncertainity Prediction

The majority of the uncertainty prediction work in literature is based on Bayesian formulation. The computational complexity of Bayesian formulation has led to the discovery of a multitude of simplified algorithms such as Laplace approximation, Markov Chain Monte Carlo methods, variational Bayesian methods, assumed density filtering, expectation propagation, Langevin diffusion methods, Hamiltonian methods, *etc.*. Ensemble techniques [21] have also been actively considered for uncertainty estimation. [13] proposed a probabilistic interpretation of dropout, which allowed them to obtain a measure called uncertainty measure from existing deep networks. The model has to be run multiple times to estimate the mean and variance of the set of predictions. [14] provided Monte Carlo (MC) dropout score, where the uncertainty of the given data point is assessed by running the network in forward pass multiple times and by estimating the variance of the response of the neuron corresponding to the most probable class. Despite the simplified methods, uncertainty estimation methods are still computationally intractable as compared to confidence score estimation methods.

2.2 Confidence Score Estimation

Confidence score estimation methods allow us to quantify classifier errors. Confidence score estimation can be categorized into the following types of techniques, i) soft-max based [16,22,23], ii) models that are trained explicitly to detect wrongly classified examples [23], iii) Mahalanobis distance measure in feature space [22,25], iv) models that are trained to output error estimates [12], v) models that generate energy score [15,24].

Given an example, [17] distinguishes it as correctly or erroneously classified sample, by retrieving the soft-max probability of the classification layer. [27] proposed an end-to-end convolutional framework for simultaneous classification and confidence score estimation by projecting soft-max probability onto a single score via a smaller mapping network. [11] and [1] utilize another network to predict the confidence score of the base network, which once again comes with the trust issues of deep networks. Furthermore, it requires modifying the training procedure of the base network. [26] proposed a framework known as RED (Residual-based Error Detection) which estimates a confidence score based on maximum class probability by predicting the distribution of the residual. This involves the computation of kernel-based covariance, which is computationally complex. All the above-mentioned confidence score estimation methods are solely based on soft-max probability, which, when viewed in isolation, will lead to errors. The former might display perfect scores even when the model has high uncertainty [9,13].

[10] and [20] proposed an embedding based scheme to estimate confidence score. [10] estimate a semantic embedding via the Semantic Autoencoder Technique (SAE). Semantic distance is estimated with cosine similarity between the test data point and nearest neighbor training data points. The main disadvantage of this method is the mandatory requirement for domain knowledge. [20] proceeds in two steps: a pre-processing step and a trust score estimation step. Trust score is estimated as the ratio between the distance of the test point from the nearest α-high-density-set of class other than the predicted class to that of the distance from α-high-density-set of predicted class. Scaling becomes a major issue for high-dimensional data.

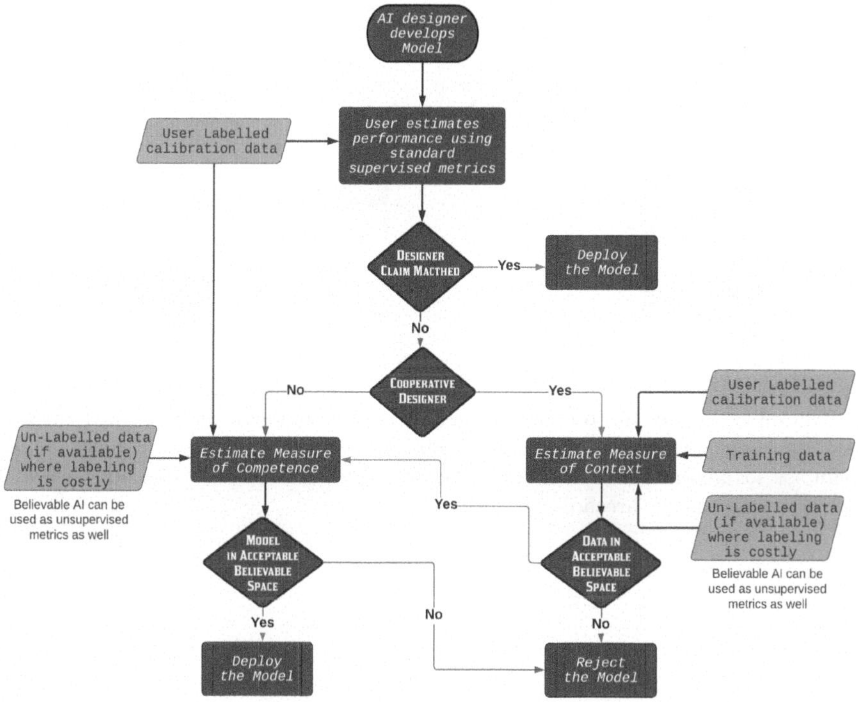

Fig. 1. Believable AI pipeline (Pre-Deployment): The pipeline explains the utility of the proposed Believable AI pre-deployment, especially in the scenarios where the buyer data space is different from that of the designer/developer's data space. The performance of the COTS-AI model on buyer's data space is calibrated as believable (Ω_b) and non-believable (Ω_{nb}). If the Ω_b is below the application-specific acceptable threshold, the model could be deployed.

3 Proposed Solution

Given a supervised multi-class classification network $\varphi(x)$ with predicted class label output $y^p \in R^c$ (c is the number of classes), where the input x and the corresponding label y are random variables drawn from the joint distribution $P(x,y) = P(x/y)P(x)$, we present Believable AI. The technological difference between model development and model deployment stages makes this quantification process a very challenging task. In what follows, we provide theoretical insight into Believable AI measures, followed by its application to model deployment and monitoring.

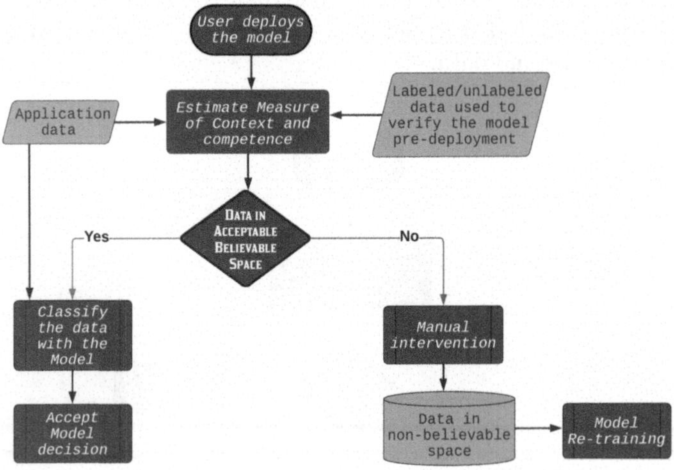

Fig. 2. Believable AI pipeline (Post-Deployment): The pipeline explains the utility of the Believable AI pipeline post-deployment. Post-deployment, as and when the data flows, Believable AI finds out whether the data belongs to believable space. If not, he can ask for manual intervention and go for model updates once the non-believable space grows beyond a threshold.

3.1 Believable AI Measures

In this section, we provide the technical background of the proposed measures, Measure of Context (`MoCn`) and Measure of Competence (`MoCp`). We also argue its theoretical soundness in calibrating the believable space of the given classifier.

Measure of Context (`MoCn`.) The `MoCn` measure considers the task of deciding whether or not a sample is from the distribution on which the model has been trained earlier. Let Ω_{in} and Ω_{out} be the respective spaces occupied by samples drawn from training distribution P_x^{in} and the distribution P_x^{out} which is quite different from that of P_x^{in}. Given the data is drawn from the mixed distribution $P_x^{in \times out}$, `MoCn` is built to distinguish data points sampled from Ω_{in} from those sampled from Ω_{out}.

Given a data sample, `MoCn` (Algorithm. 1) is defined as the inverse of the average distance from the given data sample to its K (application-specific) nearest training data. Samples with high `MoCn` $\geq \alpha_t$ are in Ω_{in} space of the classifier.

We also provide an algorithm to estimate data dependant α_t (Algorithm. 2) given as $\alpha^m \pm \delta\alpha^v$, where α^m and α^v are the mean and variance of the average distance from each of the n training samples to its K nearest neighbors and δ is application dependent scaling factor.

Algorithm 1. Estimation of Measure of Context

Parameters: K
Input: Test data: $\mathbf{x}$, Feature Extractor: $\varphi_f(\mathbf{x})$,
Training data features: $\mathbf{f}_1, \ldots, \mathbf{f}_n$
Extract embedding $\mathbf{f} \leftarrow \varphi_f(\mathbf{x})$
Find K data points $\{\mathbf{f}_k : \|\mathbf{f}_i - \mathbf{f}_k\|_2 \leq \|\mathbf{f}_i - \mathbf{f}_j\|_2, j \in n \text{ and } \forall j \neq k\}$
$B_{AI_1} \leftarrow \frac{1}{K}\sum_k d(\mathbf{f}, \mathbf{f}_k)$
Return `MoCn`$\leftarrow \frac{1}{B_{AI_1}}$

Algorithm 2. Estimation of α^m and α^v

Parameters: K
Input: Training data $\mathbf{X} \leftarrow (x_1, ...\mathbf{x}_n)$,
Classifier feature extractor $\varphi_f(\mathbf{x})$,
$\mathbf{f}_1, \mathbf{f}_2 \ldots, \mathbf{f}_n \leftarrow \varphi_f(\mathbf{x}_1), \varphi_f(\mathbf{x}_2), \ldots, \varphi_f(\mathbf{x}_n)$.
for $i = 1$ **to** n **do**
Find K data points $\{\mathbf{f}_k : \|\mathbf{f}_i - \mathbf{f}_k\|_2 \leq \|\mathbf{f}_i - f_j\|_2, j \in n \text{ and } \forall j \neq k\}$
$\mu_i \leftarrow \frac{1}{K}\sum_k d(\mathbf{f}_i, \mathbf{f}_k)$
end for
Return α^m and α^v as mean and variance of $\mu_i, i \in n$

Measure of Competence (`MoCp`.) The input space of any classifier can be categorized into two complementary spaces, Ω_{rc} and Ω_{wc}. Ω_{rc} satisfies the criteria that any data point $x \in \Omega_{rc}$ is in the correct-classfication region. Correct-classification region obeys the property that the true class of the data point is similar to that of the classifier predicted class. The sample points of Ω_{wc} will be in the mis-classfication region.

Based on the above argument, we provide a measure known as `MoCp` (Algorithm 3) to quantify its belongingness to Ω_{rc} and Ω_{wc}. `MoCp` of the given test sample is defined as the number of samples in *c-class-set*. *c-class-set* is the set of K training samples near to test sample whose true label is similar to the class c predicted by the classifier. Data points with high `MoCp` $\geq \beta$ belong to the well-learnt region of classifier (Ω_r).

Similar to the methodology followed in `MoCn`, we provide an algorithm (Algorithm 4) to estimate β as $\beta^m + \delta * \beta^v$ from the given dataset. β^m and β^v are rspectively the mean and variance of the *c-class-set* of training samples.

Algorithm 3. Estimation of Measure of Competence

Parameters: K
Input: Test data $\mathbf{x}$, $\mathbf{f}_1, \ldots, \mathbf{f}_n$,
predicted class $y_1^+ \ldots y_n^+$, True class $y_1 \ldots y_n$
Find K data points $\{f_k : \|\mathbf{f}_i - \mathbf{f}_k\|_2 \leq \|\mathbf{f}_i - \mathbf{f}_j\|_2, j \in n \text{ and } \forall j \neq k\}$
MoCp$\leftarrow \frac{1}{K} \sum_k I(y_k^+ == y_k)$
Return MoCp

Algorithm 4. Estimation of β^m and β^v

Parameters: K
Input: Training data $(\mathbf{X}, \mathbf{Y}) \leftarrow (\mathbf{x}_1, y_1) \ldots (\mathbf{x}_n, y_n)$,
$(y_1^+, \ldots, y_n^+)$: Soft-max labels of $\mathbf{X}$, $\varphi_f(\mathbf{x})$
$\mathbf{f}_1, \mathbf{f}_2 \ldots, \mathbf{f}_n \leftarrow \varphi_f(\mathbf{x}_1), \varphi_f(\mathbf{x}_2), \ldots, \varphi_f(\mathbf{x}_n)$.
for $i = 1$ **to** n **do**
Find K data points $\{\mathbf{f}_k : \|\mathbf{f}_i - \mathbf{f}_k\|_2 \leq \|\mathbf{f}_i - \mathbf{f}_j\|_2, j \in n \text{ and } \forall j \neq k\}$
$\mu_i \leftarrow \frac{1}{K} \sum_k I(y_k^+ == y_k)$
end for
Return β^m and β^v as mean and variance of μ_i

3.2 Believable AI Pipeline

This section brings out the pipeline through which buyerss and designer/developers of COTS-AI can get benefited from Believable AI in deploying and continuously monitoring the model, as shown in Figs. 1 and 2.

Pre-deployment. The buyer generally verifies the model pre-deployment with supervised metrics such as accuracy, recall, precision, *etc.*. In cases where the buyer data is different from that of training data, the model will get rejected completely. The proposed Believable AI techniques, MoCn and MoCp, enables the buyer to characterize the input space of the model into believable ($\Omega_b \in \Omega_{in} \cap \Omega_{rc}$) and non-believable ($\Omega_{nb} \in \Omega_{out} \cup \Omega_{wc}$) spaces (Fig. 1). Pre-deployment, given the risk tolerance in the given application, the buyer may assess $|\Omega_b| >> |\Omega_{nb}|$ and decide accordingly to deploy the model. If the Ω_b is well below the defined acceptable threshold, the buyer can decide to deploy the model. He can devise a strategy to be followed for the data that falls under non-believable space.

Post-deployment. The model performance might start degrading over a period of time owing to the evolution of data. Model monitoring is of paramount importance to enforce model adaptation at appropriate times as well as to decide when human intervention is required. Hence, post-deployment, the model performance needs to be monitored for $p(x)$ (Data drift) and $p(y/x)$ (concept drift) shifts. Data drift can result in shifting of real-world dataset features away from those of training data features or might make it fall in the Ω_{wc} space of the classifier. The former is estimated through MoCn, and the latter is quantified with the help of MoCp. Concept shift occurs when the relation between input and output learned by the model starts drifting due to various reasons. This is estimated via MoCp.

Additional Benefits. As explained below, Believable AI aids the buyer in these extreme scenarios as well: i) a noncooperative designer/developer who is not ready to expose any flavor of data or model to the buyer. In such scenarios, the buyer needs to collate his own calibration dataset and get Ω_b and Ω_{nb} characterization of the calibration data space. With the calibration dataset as the baseline, he will be able to assess the believability of the AI system pre and post-deployment and make decisions accordingly and ii) Believable AI can also be used as unsupervised metrics to assess the model.

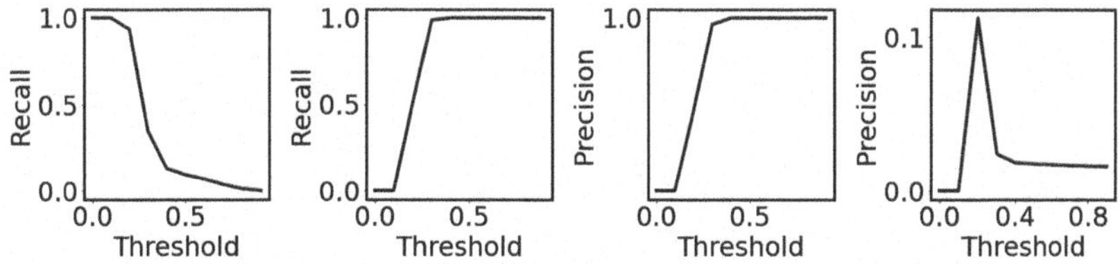

(a) MNIST

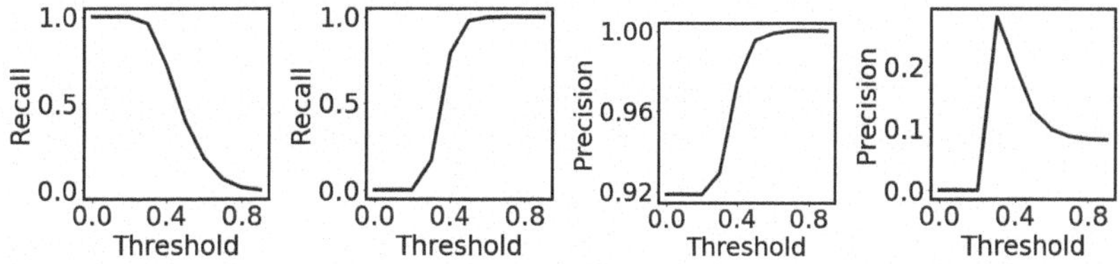

(b) CIFAR-10

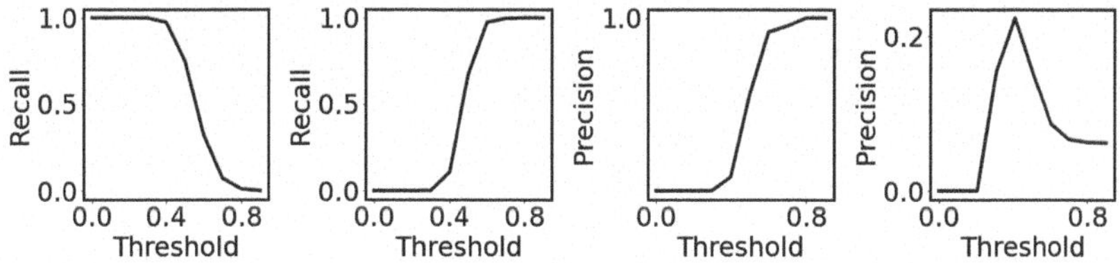

(c) SVHN

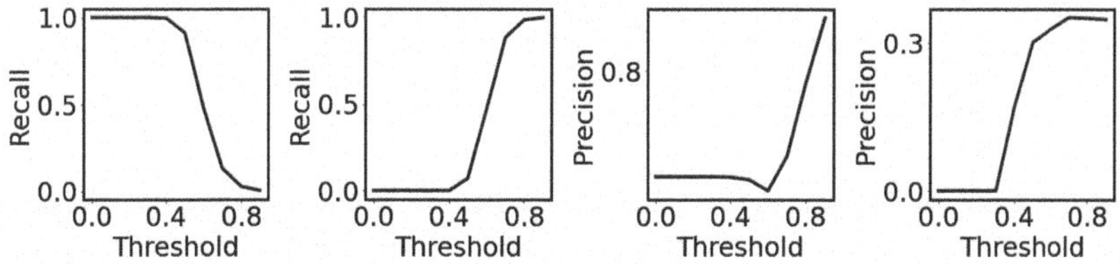

(d) CIFAR-100

Fig. 3. Ablation study for `MoCn`: Recall and precision of `MoCn` ($\Omega_{in}, \Omega_{out}$) in detecting believable (Col 1 and Col 3) vs. non-believable (Col 2 and Col 4) samples. The samples whose Believable AI measure is below the threshold given in the x axis are considered as non-believable samples and vice versa.

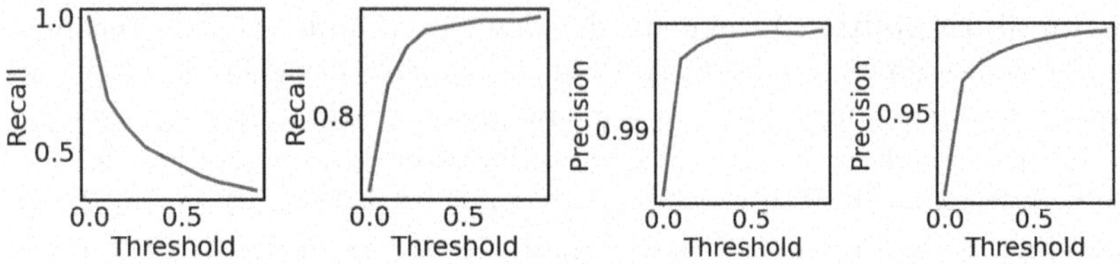

(a) MNIST

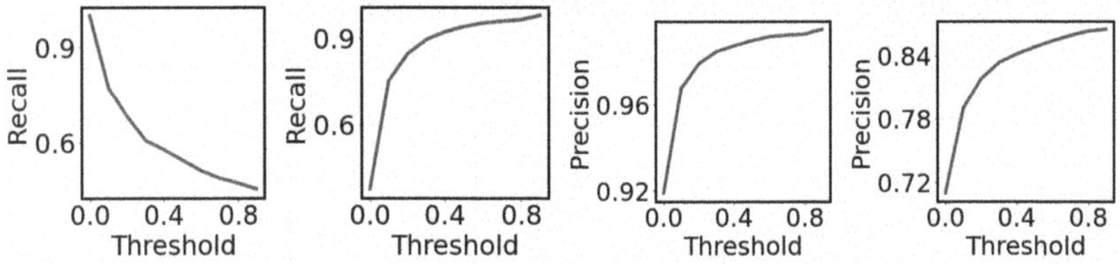

(b) CIFAR-10

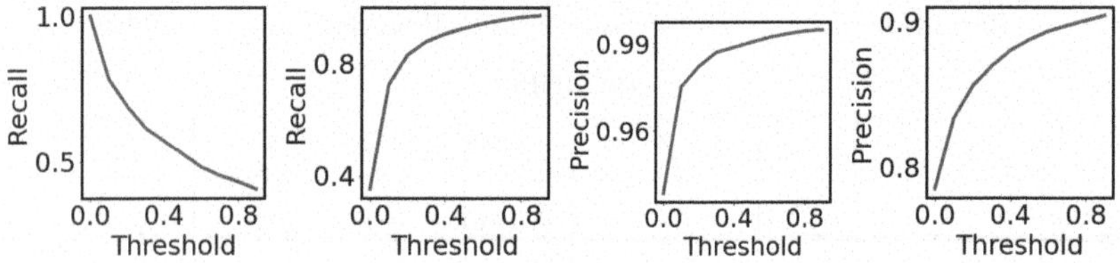

(c) SVHN

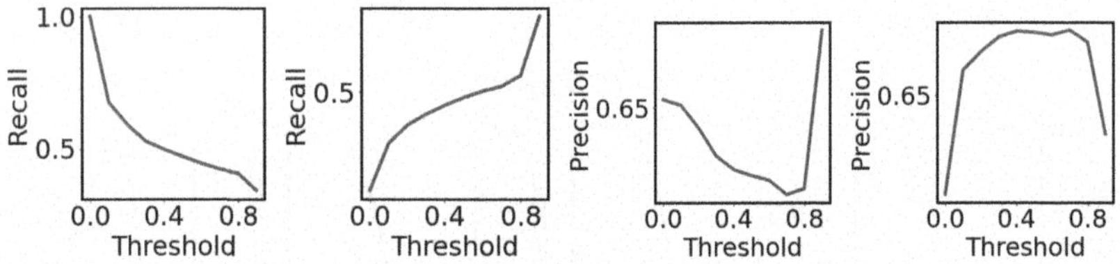

(d) CIFAR-100

Fig. 4. Ablation study for `MoCp`: Recall and precision of `MoCp` (Ω_{rc}, Ω_{wc}) in detecting believable (Col 1 and Col 3) vs. non-believable (Col 2 and Col 4) samples.

4 Experiments and Results

In this section, we describe the wide range of empirical experiments conducted across i) different datasets, ii) different classifiers, ii) different representations to validate that the proposed scores can efficiently detect the believable vs non-believable space of classifiers. Additionally, we have induced data and concept drift in test samples to verify the performance of the `MoCn` and `MoCp`.

We performed these experiments using deep CNN, such as custom network, ResNet-18, and ResNet-50, on four different state-of-the-art datasets, MNIST, CIFAR-10, SVHN, and CIFAR-100. MNIST is a 10 class digit recognition dataset with 60000 and 10000 train and test samples, respectively. CIFAR-10 is drawn

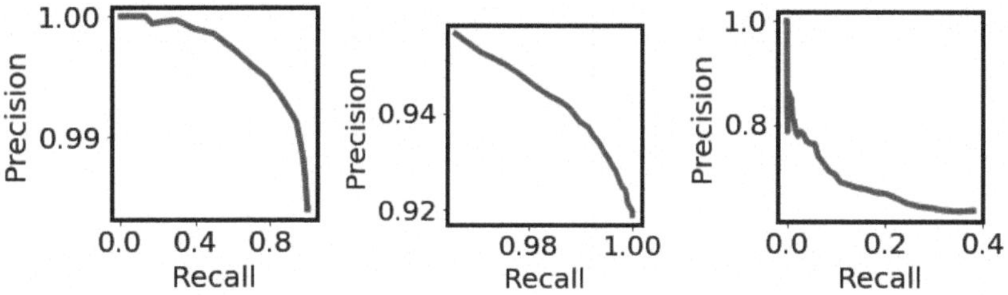

(a) Measure of Context

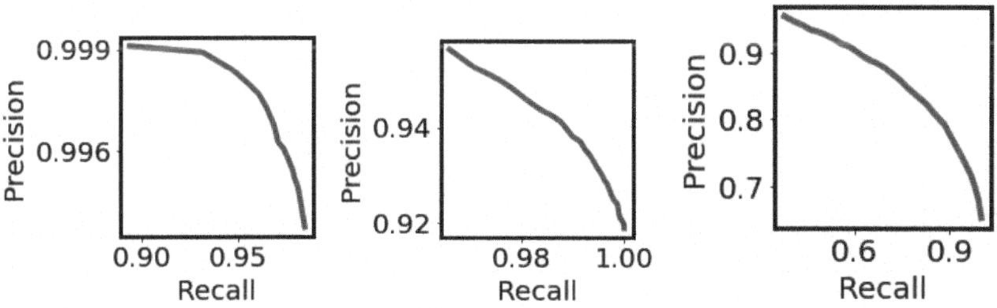

(b) Measure of Competence

Fig. 5. Ablation study (recall vs precision): Plot shows the recall vs precision averaged across believable and non-believable samples. `MoCn` and `MoCp` were able to achieve good recall for high precision.

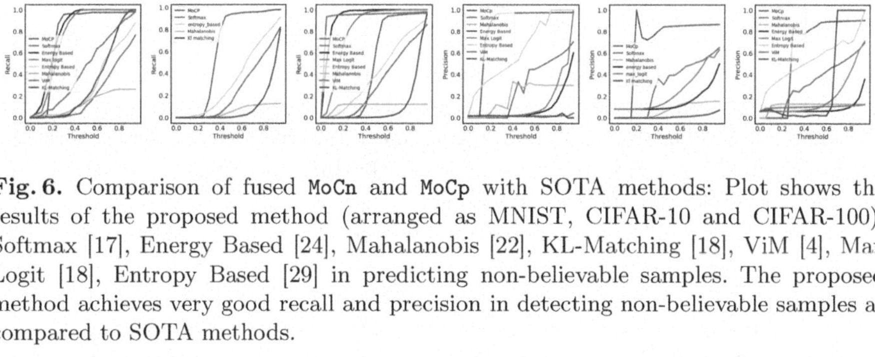

Fig. 6. Comparison of fused `MoCn` and `MoCp` with SOTA methods: Plot shows the results of the proposed method (arranged as MNIST, CIFAR-10 and CIFAR-100), Softmax [17], Energy Based [24], Mahalanobis [22], KL-Matching [18], ViM [4], Max Logit [18], Entropy Based [29] in predicting non-believable samples. The proposed method achieves very good recall and precision in detecting non-believable samples as compared to SOTA methods.

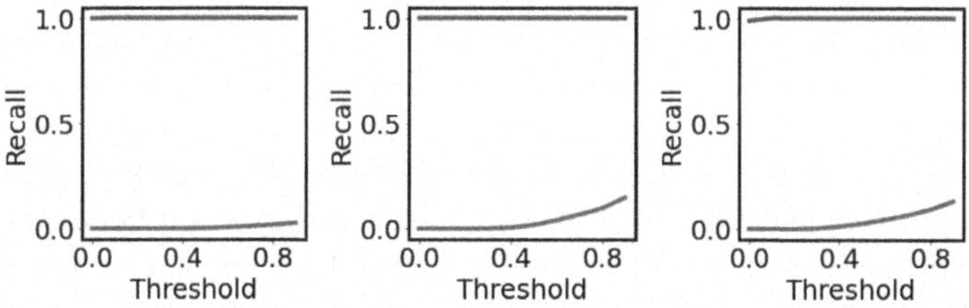

Fig. 7. Concept Drift: Comparison of `MoCp` (brown) with models' own confidence (green) on MNIST, CIFAR-10, and SVHN. y axis shows the recall in identifying the non-believable samples. When there is concept drift, the models' own confidence terribly fails in predicting the non-believable samples.

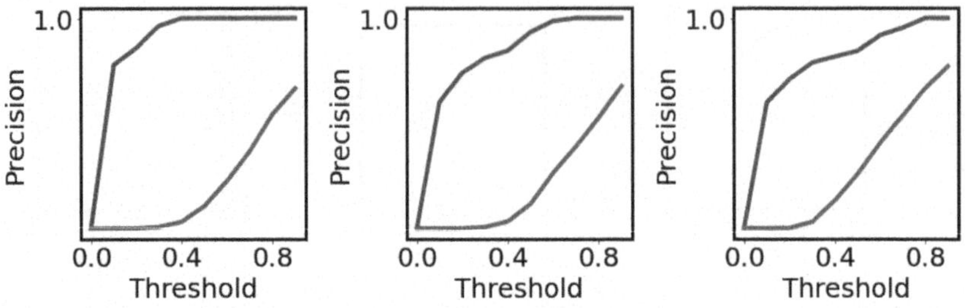

(a) Detect believable samples

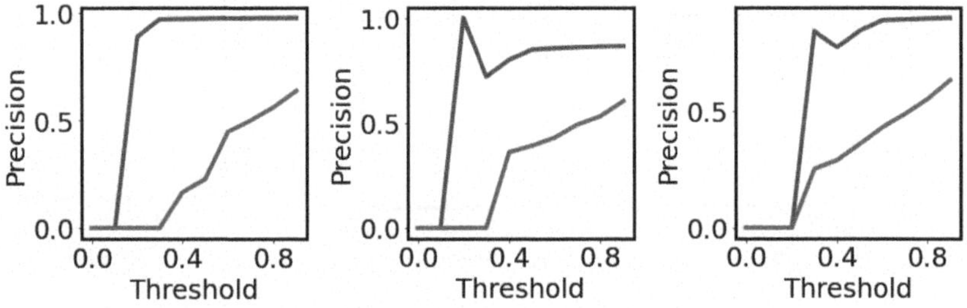

(b) Detect non-believable sample

Fig. 8. Data drift: Comparison of Believable AI measure (`MoCn` (brown) ∩ `MoCp`) with model's own confidence (green) when there is drift in $p(x)$. It could be seen that the proposed measure is much more efficient than the model's own confidence in categorizing the test sample space as believable vs. non-believable. (Color figure online)

from color images of size 32 × 32 and 10 classes with 50000 training samples and 10000 test samples. SVHN is a dataset with images of house number of size 32 × 32 with 10 classes, 73257 training images, and 26032 test images. CIFAR-100 includes 32 × 32 sized color images of 100 different classes with train and test split of 50000 and 10000 respectively.

An ideal Believable AI measure should categorize all the samples into two classes believable (correctly classified samples) and non-believable (mis-classified samples). Hence, we measure the quality of the proposed method with the following metrics: recall, precision and an information theory based measure known as Measure of Information (MOI) [28]. Recall is estimated as the ratio of True positive with respect to the sum of true positive and false negative, whereas precision is the ratio of true positive with respect to the sum of true positive and false positive. True positive and true negative are the believable and non-believable sample points which are correctly identified by the proposed measure. False positive and false negative are non-believable and believable samples misidentified by the proposed measure as believable and non-believable respectively. MOI, $I(y; y_p) = H(y) - H(y/y_p)$, measures the information gain delivered by the classifier as the mutual information between true label (y) and predicted label (y_p), where $H(y)$ and $H(y/y_p)$ are entropy of true label and average conditional entropy of P_{y/y_p} respectively. MOI provides an immune evaluation criteria towards biased classes and outliers.

4.1 Base Architecture and Training Configurations

This section gives details on the base network architecture and the training configuration adopted for each dataset.

MNIST. We adopt a custom three-layer convolutional DNN with the following configuration: a convolution layer with 8 channels and 3×3 kernel, followed by a MaxPooling layer with stride 2, a dense layer with 128 hidden nodes and ReLu activation and a classifier layer with 10 hidden nodes and softmax activation. The network has been trained for 10 epochs with a batch size of 128 to give train and test accuracy of 99.56% and 98.4%, recall and precision of 98.4% and 98.4%. Minimization of categorical cross-entropy loss has been carried out with Adam optimizer with a learning rate of 0.001.

CIFAR-10. For CIFAR-10, we trained a ResNet-18 model with weights initialized from the Glorot distribution. The optimizer used is a stochastic gradient descent optimizer with categorical cross-entropy loss and an initial learning rate of 0.1, which follows cosine decay. While trained for 38 epochs with standard augmentation techniques and weight decay, it yielded train and test accuracy of 97.93% and 91.70%, recall and precision of 91.8% and 91.9%. Early stopping has been applied to avoid overfitting.

SVHN. The network architecture on which the SVHN dataset was trained consists of the following layers: Two blocks, with each block consisting of two convolution layers with 32 and 64 channels, respectively (3×3 kernel), a Maxpooling layer with stride 2, followed by two dense layers of 512 and 128 nodes and a classification layer of 10 nodes with softmax activation. The layers were augmented in between with Batch normalization layers and dropout layers. The network was trained to 94.45% and 93.81% train and test accuracy respectively for 20 epochs with a Stochastic Gradient optimizer with a learning rate of 0.01, momentum of 0.9 and categorical cross-entropy loss.

CIFAR-100. Experiments on CIFAR-100 have been done with ResNet-50 with the following additional layers: a GlobalAveragePooling layer, a dense layer with 512 nodes, and a softmax classifier layer with 100 nodes. The base network was initialized with weights pre-trained on the ImageNet dataset. Images are resized to $224 \times 224 \times 3$ to match the pre-trained ResNet-50 configuration. The added last layers of the network have been initialized with weights drawn from Glorot distribution and trained for 50 epochs with stochastic gradient descent optimizer, which has been initialized with a learning rate of 0.001 and momentum of 0.9. ResNet-50 with the given training configurations yielded train and test accuracy of 83% and 66%, recall and precision of 66.1% and 65.2% respectively.

Hyperparameters. The two hyperparameters for Believable AI are δ and K. In all the experiments, we have considered k as 50. The value of k has been chosen empirically. As far as δ is concerned, the thresholds α and β have been swept across different values from 0 to 1.

4.2 Performance for Cooperative Designer/Developer

In this section, we show the performance of the proposed measure when the designer/developer is cooperative to share the data on which the model has been trained and also allow the buyer to extract features from the given layer of the model. We analyze the measures with respect to their efficiency in detecting believable and non-believable samples.

Ablation Study. In this section, we furnish the results of the experiments conducted to understand the behavior of individual measures. The performance of individual measures in terms of recall and precision of believable and non-believable samples vs. threshold have been provided in Figs. 3 and 4. Based on the application, the threshold of tolerance of recall and precision of believable vs. non-believable samples can be chosen by the user. Additionally, recall vs. precision plots are provided in Fig. 5. The recall and precision shown in Fig. 5 are estimated as average of the performance of believable and non-believable samples.

`MoCn` and `MoCp`, as expected, were able to identify most of the non-believable samples without compromising on the identification of believable samples. We were able to retrieve most of the believable and non-believable samples (Fig. 5) with good precision. This qualifies the above-mentioned two measures as trustable.

Comparison with SOTA. The performance has been compared with various State-of-the-art methods (Fig. 6) in detecting non-believable samples in terms of recall and precision. The experiments clearly bring out that the proposed measure surpasses the model's own confidence in detecting Ω_b vs. Ω_{nb}. For MNIST, the proposed measure performs better than other methods in terms of recall except for energy-based [24] and max-logit [18]. However, precision of the proposed method is far higher than the above mentioned methods. For, CIFAR-10, our measure perfoms better than all the other methods in terms of both recall and precision. When it comes to SVHN, though ViM [4], energy-based [24] and Max-logit [18] gives good results for lower threshold, their precision is far below than the propsoed method.

Comparison with Model's Own Confidence as Concept Drifts. In Fig. 7, we show the performance of `MoCp` as the relation between x and $y = f(x)$ changes over time. To simulate this, the labels of samples in the test set have been manually jittered. As an example, in the MNIST dataset, a few test samples belonging to class 0 have been labeled as class 5 and vice versa. As the concept drift will be identified only by `MoCp`, not `MoCn`, the results are shown for the former alone, which brings out the performance superiority of `MoCp` over model's own confidence.

Comparison with Model's Own Confidence as Data Drifts When there is a difference between $p(x)$ of the data on which the model is trained and on which the model will be operating in a buyer deployment scenario, the model predictions will start becoming unbelievable. A drift in $p(x)$ may happen due to various reasons. In order to simulate the same, we have corrupted the test features with random noise drawn from Gaussian distribution with ($\mu = 0, \sigma = 0.001$). Figure 8 furnishes the results of the proposed measures in terms of their efficiency in how precisely it is able to identify the believable and non-believable samples as compared to the model's confidence.

In addition to this, we have conducted experiments where the data drift is simulated by drawing samples from a completely different data distribution. As compared to the base network precision of 53.06%, 51.9% and 43.91%, Believable AI boosted the former to around $\sim$ 85% (MNIST), $\sim$ 65% (CIFAR-10) and $\sim$ 55% (CIFAR-100) for a recall of around $\sim$ 98.4%, $\sim$ 91.87% and $\sim$ 65.26%.

5 Conclusion

In this paper, we have provided a new measure known as Believable AI measure, which provides a simple and effective way to judge how far the model provided by the designer/developer is believable for deployment and to what extent the predictions made by the model can be believed. The proposed measure enables trust-worthy deployment of the model by identifying the error prone regions of the model in the space of calibration data. Additionally, the proposed method is computationally inexpensive and can be applied to any existing state-of-the-art network without incurring any modification to the network. Empirical results across different architectures, datasets and different representations of data show that our method consistently outperforms classifiers own confidence in identyfying believable and non-believable samples even in the adverse condition of the designer/developer being non-cooperative. Additionally, Believable AI displays superior recall and precision as against state-of-the-art methods. The proposed first-of-its-kind technique has immense potential and practical implications in the AI domain. Note that the proposed measure has been validated in the context of classifiers alone. However, as part of future work, we will be extending its benefit to other domains of AI.

References

1. Aigrain, J., Detyniecki, M.: Detecting adversarial examples and other misclassifications in neural networks by intro-spection. ArXiv, abs/1905.09186 (2019)
2. et al, B.: Towards open set deep networks. CVPR (2016)
3. et al, B.: Learning and the unknown: surveying steps toward open world recognition. In: AAAI (2019)
4. et al, H.W.: VIM: out-of-distribution with virtual-logit matching. In: IEEE Conference on Computer Vision and Pattern Recognition (CVPR) (2022)
5. et al, S.: Probability models for open set recognition. TPAMI **36**(11), 2317–2324 (2013)
6. et al, S.: Towards open set recognition. TPAMI **35**(7), 72–1757 (2014)
7. et al, Y.: Classification-reconstruction learning for open-set recognition. In: CVPR (2019)
8. Amersfoort, V., L, S., Teh, Y, G.: Uncertainty estimation using a single deep deterministic neural network. PMLR **119**, 9690–9700 (2020)
9. Bendale, A., Boult, T.E.: Towards open set deep networks. In: Proceedings of the 2016 IEEE Conference on Computer Vision and Pattern Recognition, pp. 1563–1572 (2016)

10. Thomas, B., et. al.: Leveraging semantic embeddings for safety-critical applications. In: IEEE/CVF Conference on Computer Vision and Pattern Recognition Workshops (2019)
11. Corbiere, C., Thome, N., BarHen, A., Cord, M., Pérez, P.: Addressing failure prediction by learning model confidence. Adv. Neural Inf. Process. Syst. **32** (2019)
12. DeVries, T., Taylor, G.W.: Learning confidence for out-of-distribution detection in neural networks. arXiv preprint arXiv:1802.04865 (2018)
13. Gal, Y., Ghahramani, Z.: Dropout as a Bayesian approximation: representing model uncertainty in deep learning. Proceedings of the 33rd International Conference on Machine Learning, ICML pp. 1050–1059 (2016)
14. Geifman, Yonatan, ElYaniv, R.: Selective classification for deep neural networks. Neural Info. Process. Syst. **30** (2017)
15. Grathwohl, W., Wang, K.C., Jacobsen, J.H., Duvenaud, D., Swersky, K., Norouzi, M.: Your classifier is secretly an energy-based model and you should treat it like one. In: International Conference on Learning Representations (ICLR) (2020)
16. Guo, C., Pleiss, G., Sun, Y., Weinberger, K.Q.: On calibration of modern neural networks. In: International Conference on Machine Learning (ICML) (2017)
17. Hendrycks, D., Gimpel, K.: A baseline for detecting misclassified out of distribution examples in neural networks. ICLR (2017)
18. Hendrycks, D., Mazeika, M., Dietterich, T.: Deep anomaly detection with outlier exposure. In: International Conference on Learning Representations (ICLR) (2019)
19. Mukhoti, J., Kirsch, A., van Amersfoort, J., Torr, P.H., Gal, Y.: Deterministic neural networks with appropriate inductive biases capture epistemic and aleatoric uncertainty. arXiv:2102.11582 (2021)
20. Jiang, H., Kim, B., Guan, M.Y.: To trust or not to trust a classifier. Neural Info. Process. Syst. **31** (2018)
21. Lakshminarayanan, B., Pritzel, A., Blundell, C.: Simple and scalable predictive uncertainty estimation using deep ensembles. In: International Conference on Neural Information Processing Systems (NIPS) (2017)
22. Lee, K., Lee, K., Lee, H., Shin, J.: A simple unified framework for detecting out-of-distribution samples and adversarial attacks. In: International Conference on Neural Information Processing Systems (NIPS) (2018)
23. Liang, S., Li, Y., Srikant: enhancing the reliability of out-of-distribution image detection in neural networks. In: International Conference on Learning Representations (ICLR) (2018)
24. Liu, W., Wang, X., Owens, J.D., Li, Y.: Energy-based out-of-distribution detection. In: International Conference on Neural Information Processing Systems (NIPS) (2020)
25. Nalisnick, E., Matsukawa, A., Teh, Y.W., Gorur, D., Lakshminarayanan, B.: Do deep generative models know what they don't know.In: International Conference on Learning Representations (ICLR) (2019)
26. Qiu, X., Miikkulainen, R.: Detecting misclassification errors in neural networks with a gaussian process model. In: AAAI Conference on Artificial Intelligence (2022)
27. Wan, S., Wu, T.Y., W.H.W., Lee, C.Y.: ConfNet: Predict with confidence. In: ICASSP (2018)
28. Sindhwani, V., Rakshit, S., Dheodhare, D., et. al.: Feature selection in MLPS and SVMS based on maximum output information. IEEE Trans. Neural Netw. **15**(4), 937–948 (2004)
29. Vemuri, N.: Scoring Confidence in Neural Networks. Technical Report, University of California (2020)

CUNIT-GAN: Constraining Latent Space for Unsupervised Multi-domain Image-to-Image Translation via Generative Adversarial Network

Krishanu Saini[1], Anikeit Sethi[1], Rituraj Singh[1(✉)], Aruna Tiwari[1], Sumeet Saurav[2], and Sanjay Singh[2]

[1] Computer Science and Engineering, Indian Institute of Technology, Indore 452020, Madhya Pradesh, India
phd2001201002@iiti.ac.in
[2] Intelligent System Groups, CSIR-CEERI, Pilani 333031, Rajasthan, India

Abstract. Image-to-image translation has gained significant interest due to the success of deep learning models that enforce cycle consistency constraints. However, the recent studies are particularly limited to a subset of domains with significant constraints on style or texture variations. Also, these models show limited performance in multi-domain settings where one image is translated to numerous domains. We propose a Constrained Unsupervised Image-to-Image Generative Adversarial Network (CUNIT-GAN) to address the above problems. It consists of an asymmetric Auto-encoder (AE) based Generator network and a dual-purpose Discriminator network that detects real and fake samples and classifies the input image. This study focuses on enhancing the explainability and representation power of the multidomain latent space through our novel latent contrastive loss, which leads to the clustering of class-level feature embeddings and decoupling of latent space. The effectiveness of CUNIT-GAN is demonstrated through a comprehensive qualitative and quantitative analysis conducted on benchmark multi-domain image datasets.

Keywords: Image-to-Image Translation · Generative Adversarial Networks · Contrastive Learning

1 Introduction

A typical requirement in image processing, computer graphics, and computer vision is transforming an input image to a target domain by utilizing a variety of feature representations such as gradient field, edge detection or edge map [16], and other high-frequency features [40,45]. The main challenge of transforming "Image-to-Image" (I2I) is to create a new image from an input image, aiming to alter the appearance but retain the underlying semantic value. I2I has several important applications like image synthesis [30,31], image segmentation [39],

J. Kakarla et al. (Eds.): CVIP 2024, CCIS 2473, pp. 159–174, 2026.
https://doi.org/10.1007/978-3-031-93688-3_12

conditional data augmentation [2], image super-resolution [17,22], and image colourization [43].

I2I requires learning a translation mapping between source and target domains with unpaired samples. As with existing methods [8], these mappings can be divided into two subsets: Strong and weakly constrained. The constraint represents the amount of content of the source image to be preserved. For example, Colourization [21], Image enhancement [27], and style transfer [3,9,10] can be solved by strongly constrained techniques such that the final outcome shares similar structural information with the input. However, object-to-object translation [15,23] belongs to weakly constrained settings as the generated outcome may belong to an entirely different domain as shown in Fig. 1.

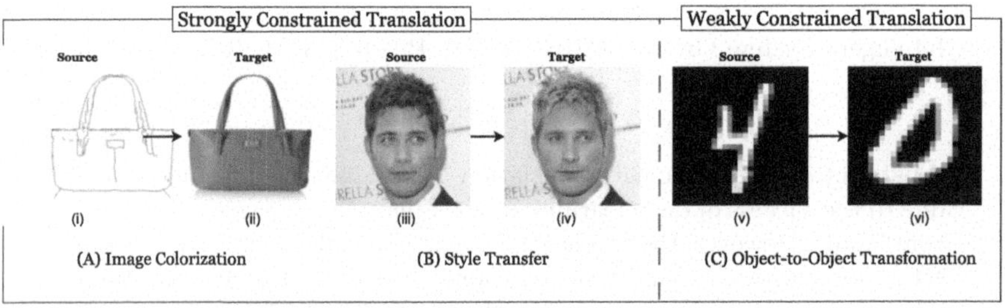

Fig. 1. I2I strongly constrained and weakly constrained translation. The following figures show various I2I techniques: Figure (A) Image colorization, (B) Style transfer, and (C) Object-toobject transformation, from left to right respectively

There is a fundamental ambiguity in the definition of the style and content of an image because of their complex interrelation. Gatys et al. [9] define the content as the spatial arrangement, layout, and structure of the image. They also define the style as textures, color, and other domain relevant features. For example, in CelebA, hair color is considered as style, whereas face structure is considered as content.

Recently proposed models such as StarGAN-v1 [3], Pix2Pix [16], SuperStarGAN [18] are based on style transfer between semantically similar images, such as human faces. These belong to the category of strongly-constrained translation. Such models failed to provide adequate translation capacity for datasets with high structural variance, such as Sketches [7]. In light of the above-mentioned challenge, latent disentanglement [23] aims to segregate generative factors(GF) [14] within the latent space. We denote this problem as fundamental to the task for I2I because of its wide usage in graphics, forensics, and animation tasks.

In order to handle the high structural variance, we propose CUNIT-GAN for weakly constrained I2I translation. It is a robust and unified model designed for multi-domain unpaired GAN-based translation addressing the need for scalability and space-efficiency. We concatenate our input image with a one-hot vector representing each domain. This allows us to modify the latent space for translation from the source domain to the target domain. Here, the variation in our latent space decides the variation in the generated content. Also, we imposed a constraint on latent space and imposed a Contrastive loss (triplet loss) during training which takes advantage of the latent dissimilarity and allows a robust style and content transfer. In addition, our constraint technique allows the latent space to be very sensitive to content changes. Thus, a minor change in latent space results in the successful translation of an image from one domain into an image of a different domain.

Overall, our main contributions are as follows:

1. We proposed an asymmetric AE-based Generator with dilated residual blocks to increase the receptive field for multi-domain translation and a Discriminator with a dual nature, which determines real/fake images along with its domain classification.
2. We introduce the Latent Contrastive Loss to enhance multidomain weakly constrained image-to-image translation. This loss facilitates class-level clustering and feature embedding disentanglement.
3. Additionally, we conduct a comprehensive analysis of the latent space, showcasing the improvement in weakly constrained translation. We also illustrate the impact of this enhancement on both qualitative and quantitative performance metrics of our model.

The rest of the paper is organized as follows: We discuss related work in Sect. 2. The proposed approach with the architecture of our CUNIT-GAN model is described in Sect. 3. The results with SOTA comparison are described in Sect. 4 and finally, we conclude our work in Sect. 5.

Fig. 2. Images from the CelebA dataset translated into different domains using CUNIT-GAN (right). The images show the conversion of the style of celebrity faces into chosen classes (brown hair, Pale skin, Moustache, and Glasses) and their comparison with existing models (left).

2 Related Work

Generative adversarial networks (GANs) [11] shows commendable results in computer vision task such as image translation [3,4] and super-resolution [18]. Isola et al. [16] proposed a pix2pix model, which utilizes paired images from source and target domains as input to a GAN model. However, pix2pix has limitations in generating truly novel outputs beyond the training data. To address this, Zhu et al. [45] proposed cycle-GAN, an unpaired image-to-image translation method that enforces cycle consistency between translations. Cycle-GAN suffers from imbalanced content distortion in translated images due to domain compatibility constraints.

In the context of multi-domain translation, Choi et al. [3] introduced StarGAN-v1, the first model capable of translating one domain into multiple desired domains using a single model. Multi-domain I2I translation models can be computationally heavy and inefficient [12]. To alleviate this, Kumar et al. [20] proposed a parameter-efficient approach using dilated convolutions in a stack of residual blocks. Recent advancements have focused on disentangling style and content, such as MUNIT [15] and SCS-UIT [25], which decompose images into domain-invariant content codes and domain-specific style codes. Additionally, leveraging high-level vision tasks like key point detection [38], bounding box detection [34], and semantic segmentation [33,37] has been explored for translation purposes.

To combine the source and target styles, Lee et al. [23] proposed the DRIT model, which utilizes cross-domain mapping and attribute vector swapping between the images. Building upon this work, Park et al. [29] proposed Contrastive Unpaired Translation (CUT), which incorporates conditional patchwise contrastive loss in a GAN architecture. Thus, it helps to establish relationships between images and domains, enabling more effective image translation. Further, in order to enhance the diversity and quality of the synthesized images, Zhao et al. [44] proposed EGSDE architecture based on GAN, which only learns the domain-independent features and removes the domain-specific features.

3 CUNIT-GAN

In this section, we will discuss the proposed CUNIT-GAN architecture and its training objective functions for the I2I translation task.

3.1 Multi-domain I2I Translation

Let $\mathcal{D} = d_1, d_2, ..., d_n$ be the set of n possible domains in the dataset, and let $\mathcal{X}_i$ be the set of images belonging to d_i. Our goal is to take any arbitrary image X and target domain $d_{trg} \in \mathcal{D}$ to learn the generation of images resembling the target set $\mathcal{X}_{trg}$. We use a single Generator network, which takes input as the source image along with a target-specific one-hot vector (c_{cls}). This type of conditioning, adopted from Choi et al. [3], allows CUNIT-GAN to utilize the

(X, c_{cls}) information jointly. Thus, emphasizing the style transfer while ensuring some similarity to the source content. The proposed CUNIT-GAN is an adversarially trained model comprising the Generator network G and the Discriminator network D.

3.2 Network Architecture

Our proposed CUNIT-GAN model for I2I translation is based on SOTA deep-learning models like Unet [32], cGAN [16], CycleGAN [45], and StarGAN v1 [3]. The different components and their roles are explained below:

Generator: The network architecture of G is present in supplementary material. It adopts an asymmetric Encoder-Decoder architecture following a StarGAN-v1 [3] architecture, which allows us to combine domain information and the source image X. The encoder down-samples this combined information into a latent space using additional residual blocks to mix the source and target domain information. We adopt the dilated-residual block [20] with a dilation factor of 2; this effectively allows the network to double its receptive field and capture information from a wider area. Further, the decoder up-samples this hybrid image into a relevant output image $G(X, c_{cls})$ reflecting a domain-specific style and content code c_{cls}. We use instance normalization [6,36] to inject c_{cls} into G. We observe that this technique removes the necessity of explicitly providing target image Y to G and allows G to synthesize images of all domains.

Discriminator: The network architecture of the D is present in supplementary material. Our D adopts the Markovian patch discriminator, which assumes that each block of the image represents a Markov random field (MRF) [16]. Our D is an extended version of the MRF in the form of a multitask discriminator [24,28]. It determines whether the input image is real or fake, along with its domain classification. Thus, our proposed D consists of dual output branches $D : X \rightarrow D_{real}, D_{cls}$. Here, D_{real} is the real or fake, and D_{cls} is the classification score of the input image.

3.3 Style and Content Injection

Instance Normalization (IN) is recently adopted for style transfer [3]. IN is applied across all channels in every training sample, which allows the model to inject the target domain information into the translated image. To perform IN for a single instance x_t, we require the mean and variance as shown in Eq. 1.

$$\begin{aligned} y_{tijk} &= \frac{x_{tijk} - \mu_{ti}}{\sqrt{\sigma_{ti}^2 + \epsilon}}, \quad \mu_{ti} = \frac{1}{HW} \sum_{l=1}^{W} \sum_{m=1}^{H} x_{tilm}, \\ \sigma_{ti}^2 &= \frac{1}{HW} \sum_{l=1}^{W} \sum_{m=1}^{H} (x_{tilm} - mu_{ti})^2 \end{aligned} \tag{1}$$

where, x_{tijk} denotes an element, where k and j represent the spatial dimensions $(H \times W)$, and i is the feature channel.

3.4 Training Objectives

CUNIT-GAN takes an image X and target domain d_{trg} as an input. First, the stylizing function creates the required one-hot vector c_{cls} and performs pixel-wise concatenation of this information with input image X, which we refer to as I. The encoder converts I into a latent space z. Then, the decoder utilizes these low-dimensional features to generate the target image X_{new} resembling the target domain. In the next section, we will discuss the loss functions to train our model (Fig. 3).

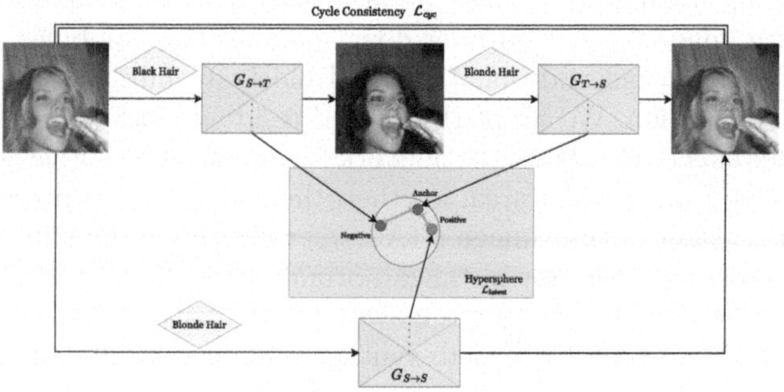

Fig. 3. The training pipeline of CUNIT-GAN shows the Cycle consistency framework that converts $S \rightarrow T$ (left), $T \rightarrow S$ (right), and $S \rightarrow S$ (bottom). The Latent Contrastive loss is introduced in the cycle consistency framework which ensures class-level clustering and decoupling of latent space.

Adversarial Training. CUNIT-GAN is trained using $G+D$ min-max game. G learns to generate quality outputs that can fool D, and D learns to distinguish real from fake samples and classify their domains. The adversarial training is summarized in Eq. 2.

$$\begin{aligned}\mathcal{L}_{adv} = &-\frac{1}{2}\mathbb{E}_{\boldsymbol{x}\sim p_{\text{data}}} \log D_{real}(\boldsymbol{x}) - \frac{1}{2}\mathbb{E}_{\boldsymbol{z}} \log(1 - D_{real}(G(\boldsymbol{z}))) \\ &- \alpha_{grad}\mathbb{E}_{\hat{x}}\left[(\|\nabla_{\hat{x}} D_{real}(\hat{x})\|_2 - 1)^2\right]\end{aligned} \quad (2)$$

where D_{real} denotes the real/fake outcome of the discriminator and α_{grad} is the coefficient of gradient penalty loss which is used to prevent mode collapse. In this case, x is sampled from real dataset p_{data}, and z is the input expected by the generator. We have taken $\alpha_{grad} = 10$ in our experiments.

Classification Loss. CUNIT-GAN transforms an input image X into the specified target domain d_{trg}. In order to fulfill this need, we extend the D model with an additional classifier layer and utilize this domain classification loss to optimize the G and D networks. The domain classification loss for G and D are defined in Eq. 3.

$$\begin{aligned} \mathcal{L}_{cls}^{real} &= \mathbb{E}_{x,d_{src}}[-logD_{cls}(d_{src}|x)] \\ \mathcal{L}_{cls}^{fake} &= \mathbb{E}_{x,d_{trg}}[-logD_{cls}(d_{trg}|G(x,d_{trg}))] \end{aligned} \tag{3}$$

where, D_{cls} is the classification score of domain labels obtained from D. The goal is to minimize this objective in order to make D learn the classification of real image x to its corresponding source domain d_{src}.

Cycle Consistency Loss. The cycle consistency loss encourages G to produce translated images that are consistent with the original image in terms of content and style. The minimization of L_{cls} and L_{adv} together still does not guarantee that the obtained image preserves the content of the original image while only changing the domain-related part in an image. By minimizing this loss, the G can learn to produce more accurate and realistic image translations. The framework involves the translation of the image from domain d_{src} to domain d_{trg} and vice-versa. The cycle-consistency loss is shown in Eq. 4.

$$\mathcal{L}_{cyc} = \mathbb{E}_{x,d_{src},d_{trg}}[||x - G(G(x, d_{src}), d_{trg})||] \tag{4}$$

Latent Space Constraints. Latent space is the low-level representation of the image. Ideally, each variable in latent space gets affected by a set of generative factors (GF) computed following Higgins et al. [14]. These generative factors vary depending on the domain and dataset used. For example, facial images may have GF for Hairstyle, Pose, and Expression, and Sketches may have Position and stroke Thickness as GFs. In a practical scenario, a single latent space cell might map to the multiple generative factors, this leads to latent entanglement, which is unsuitable for Multidomain I2I.

To overcome the above limitation, we introduce the Latent Contrastive loss to exploit the implicit latent dissimilarity between the two-way transformations in the cycle consistency framework. It is implemented using the triplet loss as shown in Eq. 5.

$$\mathcal{L}_{triplet}(a, p, n) = max(0, f(a, p) - f(a, n) + margin) \tag{5}$$

where a, p, n is the anchor, positive and negative samples, and $f(.)$ represents the mean squared distance. This loss function ensures that positive samples are closer than negative samples, thus allowing the clustering of feature embeddings on a domain basis and improving the latent disentanglement.

As shown in Fig. 3, we utilize the cycle consistency framework and define anchor as $z_{t\to s}$, positive as $z_{s\to s}$, and negative as $z_{s\to t}$, where $z_{x\to y}$ represents the latent space of $x \to y$ transformation. The latent space $z_{s\to s}$ is chosen as the positive because it reflects the accurate and homogeneous content space for the domain d_s. Further, to ensure that $z_{t\rightarrow s}$ and $z_{s\rightarrow t}$ do not represent the same hybrid space, we chose $z_{s\rightarrow t}$ as the negative sample. The final loss function is given in Eq. 6.

$$\mathcal{L}_{latent} = \mathcal{L}_{triplet}(a = z_{t\rightarrow s}, p = z_{s\rightarrow s}, n = z_{s\rightarrow t}) + \alpha_{reg}||z_{t\rightarrow s}||^2 \quad (6)$$

The $\mathcal{L}_{latent}$ results in a class-wise cluster in the feature embedding space which is crucial for explaining the latent transfer of multi-domain I2I. Additionally, we observe that target style injection has a limited impact on feature embeddings in latent space. To overcome this limitation, we introduce a regularization term to enhance latent transfer. We fine-tune this loss using α_{reg} to enhance the sensitivity of the target image to the latent space, thereby improving both style and content transfer.

Complete Training Objective. The training of G consists of four parts: an adversarial loss $\mathcal{L}_{adv}$, a cycle consistency loss $\mathcal{L}_{cycle}$, a classification loss $\mathcal{L}_{cls}$, and a latent contrastive loss $\mathcal{L}_{latent}$. The combined loss function is shown in Eq. 7.

$$\mathcal{L}_{gen} = \mathcal{L}_{adv} + \alpha_{cls}\mathcal{L}_{cls}^{fake} + \alpha_{cycle}\mathcal{L}_{cycle} + \alpha_{latent}\mathcal{L}_{latent} \quad (7)$$

The training of D consists of two parts: an adversarial loss $\mathcal{L}_{adv}$, a classification loss for real images $\mathcal{L}_{cls}^{real}$.

$$\mathcal{L}_{disc} = -\mathcal{L}_{adv} + \alpha_{cls}\mathcal{L}_{cls}^{real} \quad (8)$$

where, α are the corresponding weights of the losses, in our case $\alpha_{latent}, \alpha_{reg} = 10$, and all others are set to 40.

4 Experimentation

In this section, we evaluated CUNIT-GAN against some SOTA I2I translation models. To analyze our model, we considered widely used benchmark datasets Celeba-HQ [26] and MNIST [5], and for content transfer, we utilized Sketchy dataset [7]. Celeba-HQ consists of 30,000 high-resolution (1024×1024) face images from the CelebA dataset. Every image has a segmentation mask of face characteristics matching CelebA. The MNIST dataset consists of 60,000 handwritten digits ($0-9$), with each having a resolution of 32×32. The Sketchy dataset consists of hand-drawn images of 250 classes, including animals, fruits, and commodities. In our experiments, we resize the input images to 128×128 resolution, which is then normalized to the range $[-1, 1]$. Further, we randomly select 10 domains and form a one-hot vector to represent them.

4.1 Quantitative Evaluation

We followed the evaluation protocols proposed in previous work [3,15,45]. The Learned Perceptual Image Patch Similarity (LPIPS) [42], Fréchet inception distance (FID) [13], and Inception Score [1] measure is utilized to evaluate the quantitative performance of the model.

The Fréchet Inception Distance (FID) is utilized to compare the dissimilarities in feature representations between real and generated images. In our work, we employed Inception-v3 [35], pre-trained on the ImageNet dataset, to extract feature vectors and calculate the distance between the two distributions. FID was computed using ten thousand actual images from the CelebA dataset and ten thousand generated images.

Additionally, the Learned Perceptual Image Patch Similarity (LPIPS) metric, based on an ImageNet-pre-trained version of AlexNet [19], was used to evaluate the perceptual similarity between pairs of generated and source images. Two thousand pairs of source images and the corresponding generated image features were extracted from AlexNet are compared using mean squared error (MSE). These differences are averaged to calculate LPIPS. A low LPIPS score indicates a higher level of perceptual similarity between the two images, which is unfavorable for translation. The Inception Score (IS) was also employed to assess the generated image diversity and class distribution uniformity. In our evaluation, CUNIT-GAN achieved an FID of 19.97, an LPIPS of 0.54751 ± 0.0020, and an IS of 2.28, outperforming various existing benchmarks (Table 1).

To evaluate the content transfer capability of CUNIT-GAN on the MNIST dataset, we compute the classification accuracy on a pre-trained model. We randomly select 250 real images and translate them to 10 MNIST classes. As shown in Table 2, our proposed CUNIT-GAN obtained an accuracy of 99.40%, outperforming the other benchmark models.

Table 1. Quantitative evaluation on CelebA dataset based on FID, IS and LPIPS.

Methods	FID ↓	IS ↑	LPIPS ↑
MUNIT [15]	31.4	–	0.36 ± 0.0060
DRIT [23]	31.0	–	0.17 ± 0.0080
StarGAN-v1 [3]	30.29	1.54	0.41 ± 0.0012
StarGAN-v2 [4]	**17.14**	2.18	0.45 ± 0.0035
CUT [29]	31.94	–	–
EGSDE [44]	30.61	–	–
Ours	19.97	**2.28**	$\mathbf{0.54 \pm 0.0020}$

Table 2. Quantitative evaluation on MNIST dataset based on classification accuracy (pre-trained model).

Methods	Accuracy (%)
MUNIT [15]	95.90
CycleGAN [45]	96.65
StarGAN-v1 [3]	98.24
Ours	**99.40**

4.2 Latent Space Analysis

To observe the effect of the latent contrastive loss on style and content transfer. We utilize the t-SNE visualization, which plots the high-dimensional latent space into the two-dimensional plane (where PC1 and PC2 are the principal components, Fig. 4) while preserving the local information.

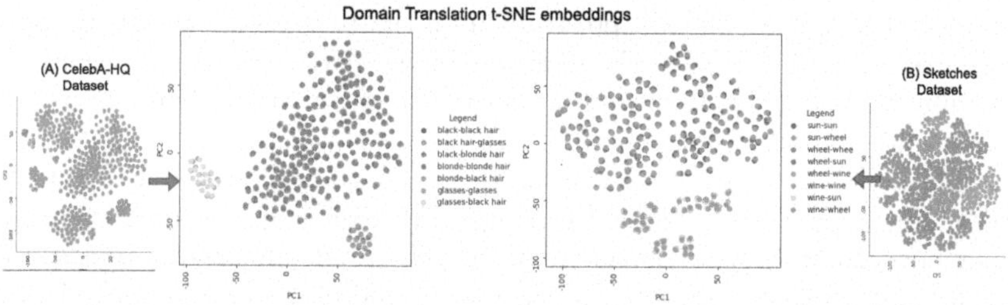

Fig. 4. Visualization of latent space t-SNE mapping for CelebA-HQ and Sketches dataset.

Latent Clustering. The Fig. 4 shows the latent space encodings of intra-class and inter-class I2I translation. There exists a separation between the latent space of different domains. This clustering of domains is the main contribution of our contrastive loss. Moreover, we observe that the embeddings become more decoupled in the Sketches dataset as compared to CelebA. This allows higher content transfer, making our model suitable for weakly constrained translation.

Latent Disentanglement. Multidomain I2I suffers from an implicit problem of latent entanglement (Fig. 5). It is highly dependent on dataset properties and model parameters such as latent space dimension and training conditions. CUNIT-GAN overcomes the issue by utilizing the Latent Contrastive loss and regularization which tunes the feature embeddings according to domain-specific GFs.

4.3 Ablation Study

Latent Dimension. The dimension of the latent vector is a critical factor for controlling the sensitivity of latent variables. From Table 3, we observe that a constricted latent space shows poor FID scores caused by latent entanglement and the inability to represent all the different Generative Factors (GFs). However, the larger latent spaces suffer from redundancy and shallow networks incapable of learning low-level GFs.

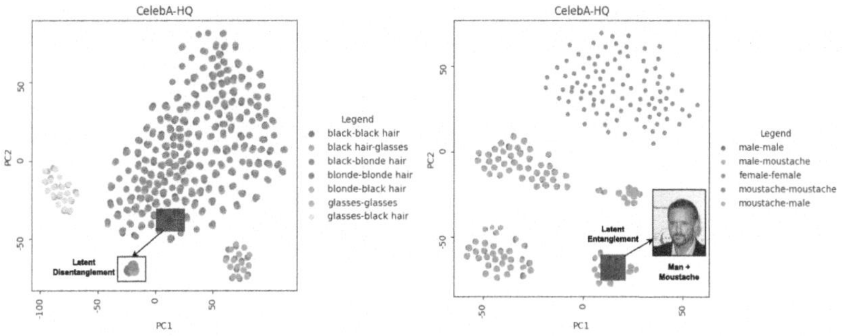

Fig. 5. Visualization of latent disentanglement (left) and latent entanglement (right) for selected CelebA-HQ domains and their translation. Latent entanglement occurs naturally due to implicit relations between features. For example, a person is male and has a mustache. Therefore, latent disentanglement is necessary for multidomain I2I.

Table 3. Comparison of CelebA-HQ FID results on different latent space dimensions.

Dimension	Network Parameters	$FID_{\downarrow}$
$128 \times 2 \times 2$	3.6M	46.50
$256 \times 2 \times 2$	12.6M	30.44
$128 \times 32 \times 32$	2.5M	22.25
$256 \times 32 \times 32$	8.4M	**19.97**
$128 \times 64 \times 64$	2.0M	20.19
$256 \times 64 \times 64$	7.6M	20.32

Latent Contrastive Loss. The latent space t-SNE mappings (Fig. 4) show that the translated latent space $Z_{s \to t}$ does not move too far away from the domain of s in terms of latent value. However, we need to exploit this small yet indispensable change. For this task, we employ L_2 regularisation. Regularisation constrains the value of latent variables, pushing z towards 0. This increases the sensitivity of the latent variable which affects the generated image based on the slight changes in its value.

However, the regularization of latent space increases the possibility of latent entanglement. We employ the Latent Contrastive Loss to address this issue, which conditions the latent space into domain-based clusters. At the latent-space level, this isolates the domain-relevant generating components. This, in turn, gives us greater influence over the representation of generative factors. The evaluation results are presented in Table 4.

4.4 Effect of Dilation

In this section, we will analyze the effect of dilated residual networks for style and content transfer. Dilation allows the network to increase its receptive power

Table 4. Comparison of CelebA-HQ FID results on combinations of Latent Regularization and Latent Contrastive Loss.

Regularization	Other Latent Loss	α_{reg}	$FID_{\downarrow}$
L_2	No Constraint	0	28.28
		1	25.20
		10	24.50
	Lat. Contrastive loss	0	–
	$\alpha_{latent} = 10$	1	21.22
		10	**19.97**

without significantly increasing computational time. The transferred CelebA-HQ images using Dilated Residual networks (DRN) [41] acquire more features of the target class with significant modifications in features such as hairstyle and structure. However, the images suffer from gridding artifacts [41]. To incorporate the receptive power of dilation in our generator model without giving up image quality, we use dilated convolution layers in the bottleneck residual layers. The comparisons of the models on Celeba-HQ are shown in Table 5.

Table 5. Results of Image-to-image translation on CelebA-HQ dataset using different combinations of dilation layers. DRN represents Dilated Residual Networks.

Backbone	Specification	$FID_{\downarrow}$
DRN	DRN-A-18	32.60
	DRN-D-38	28.75
Unet	Residual Bottleneck	20.20
	Dilated Residual Bottleneck	**19.97**

4.5 Qualitative Analysis

Through experimental results, we have shown that our model outperforms the existing SOTA models in terms of FID, IS, and LPIPS metrics. In this section, we will show that our model is capable of generating visually transformed images while maintaining the semantic features of the source image. We also show the superiority of our model in content and style transfer tasks. Figures 2 and 6 show the transformation of images into various target domains in different datasets.

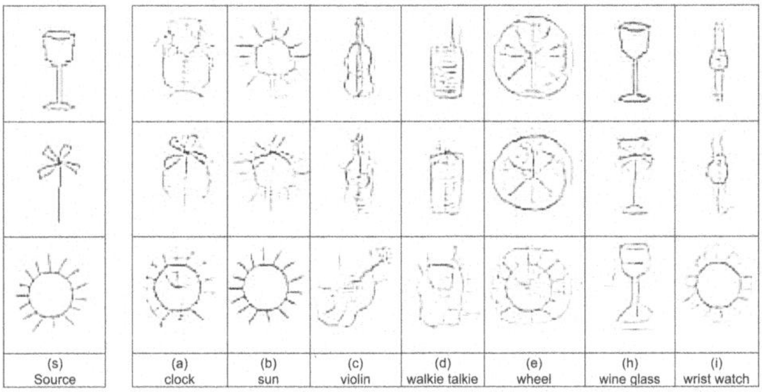

Fig. 6. Qualitative analysis of translation between selected seven domains (Sketches) tested on sketch images.

5 Conclusion

In this paper, we proposed the CUNIT-GAN model for the multi-domain I2I (image-to-image) translation task using a single Generator network and a Discriminator network to determine real/fake image and domain classification showcasing its dual capability. The presented approach not only addresses the challenge of encompassing multiple domain classes using a single Generator network but also yields images with better visual quality and improves translation capabilities. Further, we overcome the problem of weakly constrained translation by introducing constraints on latent space that decouples and clusters the feature embeddings based on classes improves the model's explainability, and produces qualitatively and quantitatively superior translation results as compared to SOTA models. Our work expands the scope of latent space understanding for image synthesis and translation tasks, which can be utilized to transform raw data into more human-understandable visual representations.

References

1. Barratt, S., Sharma, R.: A note on the inception score. arXiv preprint arXiv:1801.01973 (2018)
2. Cao, J., Hou, L., Yang, M.H., He, R., Sun, Z.: Remix: towards image-to-image translation with limited data. In: Proceedings of the IEEE/CVF Conference on Computer Vision and Pattern Recognition, pp. 15018–15027 (2021)
3. Choi, Y., Choi, M., Kim, M., Ha, J.W., Kim, S., Choo, J.: StarGAN: unified generative adversarial networks for multi-domain image-to-image translation. In: Proceedings of the IEEE Conference on Computer Vision and Pattern Recognition, pp. 8789–8797 (2018)
4. Choi, Y., Uh, Y., Yoo, J., Ha, J.W.: StarGAN v2: diverse image synthesis for multiple domains. In: Proceedings of the IEEE/CVF Conference on Computer Vision and Pattern Recognition, pp. 8188–8197 (2020)
5. Deng, L.: The mnist database of handwritten digit images for machine learning research. IEEE Signal Process. Mag. **29**(6), 141–142 (2012)

6. Dumoulin, V., Shlens, J., Kudlur, M.: A learned representation for artistic style. arXiv preprint arXiv:1610.07629 (2016)
7. Eitz, M., Hays, J., Alexa, M.: How do humans sketch objects? ACM Trans. Graph. (Proc. SIGGRAPH) **31**(4), 44:1–44:10 (2012)
8. Fan, W., Chen, J., Ma, J., Hou, J., Yi, S.: Styleflow for content-fixed image to image translation. arXiv preprint arXiv:2207.01909 (2022)
9. Gatys, L.A., Ecker, A.S., Bethge, M.: A neural algorithm of artistic style. arXiv preprint arXiv:1508.06576 (2015)
10. Gatys, L.A., Ecker, A.S., Bethge, M.: Image style transfer using convolutional neural networks. In: Proceedings of the IEEE Conference on Computer Vision and Pattern Recognition, pp. 2414–2423 (2016)
11. Goodfellow, I., et al.: Generative adversarial nets. In: Advances in Neural Information Processing Systems, vol. 27 (2014)
12. Grassucci, E., Sigillo, L., Uncini, A., Comminiello, D.: Hypercomplex image-to-image translation. In: 2022 International Joint Conference on Neural Networks (IJCNN), pp. 1–8. IEEE (2022)
13. Heusel, M., Ramsauer, H., Unterthiner, T., Nessler, B., Hochreiter, S.: GANs trained by a two time-scale update rule converge to a local nash equilibrium. In: Advances in Neural Information Processing Systems, vol. 30 (2017)
14. Higgins, I., et al.: Beta-vae: learning basic visual concepts with a constrained variational framework. In: International Conference on Learning Representations (2017)
15. Huang, X., Liu, M.Y., Belongie, S., Kautz, J.: Multimodal unsupervised image-to-image translation. In: Proceedings of the European Conference on Computer Vision (ECCV), pp. 172–189 (2018)
16. Isola, P., Zhu, J.Y., Zhou, T., Efros, A.A.: Image-to-image translation with conditional adversarial networks. In: Proceedings of the IEEE Conference on Computer Vision and Pattern Recognition, pp. 1125–1134 (2017)
17. Johnson, J., Alahi, A., Fei-Fei, L.: Perceptual losses for real-time style transfer and super-resolution. In: Leibe, B., Matas, J., Sebe, N., Welling, M. (eds.) ECCV 2016. LNCS, vol. 9906, pp. 694–711. Springer, Cham (2016). https://doi.org/10.1007/978-3-319-46475-6_43
18. Ko, K., Yeom, T., Lee, M.: Superstargan: generative adversarial networks for image-to-image translation in large-scale domains. Neural Netw. **162**, 330–339 (2023)
19. Krizhevsky, A., Sutskever, I., Hinton, G.E.: Imagenet classification with deep convolutional neural networks. Commun. ACM **60**(6), 84–90 (2017)
20. Kumar, K., et al.: MelGAN: generative adversarial networks for conditional waveform synthesis. In: Advances in Neural Information Processing Systems, vol. 32 (2019)
21. Kumar, M., Weissenborn, D., Kalchbrenner, N.: Colorization transformer. arXiv preprint arXiv:2102.04432 (2021)
22. Ledig, C., et al.: Photo-realistic single image super-resolution using a generative adversarial network. In: Proceedings of the IEEE Conference on Computer Vision and Pattern Recognition, pp. 4681–4690 (2017)
23. Lee, H.Y., Tseng, H.Y., Huang, J.B., Singh, M., Yang, M.H.: Diverse image-to-image translation via disentangled representations. In: Proceedings of the European Conference on Computer Vision (ECCV), pp. 35–51 (2018)
24. Liu, M.Y., et al.: Few-shot unsupervised image-to-image translation. In: Proceedings of the IEEE/CVF International Conference on Computer Vision, pp. 10551–10560 (2019)

25. Liu, Y., Wang, H., Yue, Y., Lu, F.: Separating content and style for unsupervised image-to-image translation. arXiv preprint arXiv:2110.14404 (2021)
26. Liu, Z., Luo, P., Wang, X., Tang, X.: Deep learning face attributes in the wild. In: Proceedings of International Conference on Computer Vision (ICCV) (2015)
27. Lore, K.G., Akintayo, A., Sarkar, S.: Llnet: a deep autoencoder approach to natural low-light image enhancement. Pattern Recogn. **61**, 650–662 (2017)
28. Mescheder, L., Geiger, A., Nowozin, S.: Which training methods for GANs do actually converge? In: International Conference on Machine Learning, pp. 3481–3490. PMLR (2018)
29. Park, T., Efros, A.A., Zhang, R., Zhu, J.Y.: Contrastive learning for conditional image synthesis. In: ECCV, vol. 2, p. 8 (2020)
30. Park, T., Liu, M.Y., Wang, T.C., Zhu, J.Y.: Semantic image synthesis with spatially-adaptive normalization. In: Proceedings of the IEEE/CVF Conference on Computer Vision and Pattern Recognition, pp. 2337–2346 (2019)
31. Regmi, K., Borji, A.: Cross-view image synthesis using conditional GANs. In: Proceedings of the IEEE Conference on Computer Vision and Pattern Recognition, pp. 3501–3510 (2018)
32. Ronneberger, O., Fischer, P., Brox, T.: U-Net: convolutional networks for biomedical image segmentation. In: Navab, N., Hornegger, J., Wells, W.M., Frangi, A.F. (eds.) MICCAI 2015. LNCS, vol. 9351, pp. 234–241. Springer, Cham (2015). https://doi.org/10.1007/978-3-319-24574-4_28
33. Roy, P., Häni, N., Isler, V.: Semantics-aware image to image translation and domain transfer. arXiv preprint arXiv:1904.02203 **7** (2019)
34. Shen, Z., Huang, M., Shi, J., Xue, X., Huang, T.S.: Towards instance-level image-to-image translation. In: Proceedings of the IEEE/CVF Conference on Computer Vision and Pattern Recognition, pp. 3683–3692 (2019)
35. Szegedy, C., Vanhoucke, V., Ioffe, S., Shlens, J., Wojna, Z.: Rethinking the inception architecture for computer vision. In: Proceedings of the IEEE Conference on Computer Vision and Pattern Recognition, pp. 2818–2826 (2016)
36. Ulyanov, D., Vedaldi, A., Lempitsky, V.: Improved texture networks: maximizing quality and diversity in feed-forward stylization and texture synthesis. In: Proceedings of the IEEE Conference on Computer Vision and Pattern Recognition, pp. 6924–6932 (2017)
37. Wang, Y., Gonzalez-Garcia, A., Herranz, L., van de Weijer, J.: Controlling biases and diversity in diverse image-to-image translation. Comput. Vis. Image Underst. **202**, 103082 (2021)
38. Wu, W., Cao, K., Li, C., Qian, C., Loy, C.C.: Transgaga: geometry-aware unsupervised image-to-image translation. In: Proceedings of the IEEE/CVF Conference on Computer Vision and Pattern Recognition, pp. 8012–8021 (2019)
39. Yang, Q., et al.: MRI cross-modality neuroimage-to-neuroimage translation. arXiv preprint arXiv:1801.06940 (2018)
40. Yang, Y., Soatto, S.: FDA: fourier domain adaptation for semantic segmentation. In: Proceedings of the IEEE/CVF Conference on Computer Vision and Pattern Recognition, pp. 4085–4095 (2020)
41. Yu, F., Koltun, V., Funkhouser, T.: Dilated residual networks. In: Proceedings of the IEEE Conference on Computer Vision and Pattern Recognition, pp. 472–480 (2017)
42. Zhang, R., Isola, P., Efros, A.A., Shechtman, E., Wang, O.: The unreasonable effectiveness of deep features as a perceptual metric. In: Proceedings of the IEEE Conference on Computer Vision and Pattern Recognition, pp. 586–595 (2018)

43. Zhang, R., et al.: Real-time user-guided image colorization with learned deep priors. arXiv preprint arXiv:1705.02999 (2017)
44. Zhao, M., Bao, F., Li, C., Zhu, J.: EGSDE: unpaired image-to-image translation via energy-guided stochastic differential equations. arXiv preprint arXiv:2207.06635 (2022)
45. Zhu, J.Y., Park, T., Isola, P., Efros, A.A.: Unpaired image-to-image translation using cycle-consistent adversarial networks. In: Proceedings of the IEEE International Conference on Computer Vision, pp. 2223–2232 (2017)

YOLOv9++: An Improved YOLOv9 Detector for Plant Biometrics Using Pseudo-labels

Vipin Gautam and Shitala Prasad(✉)

School of Mathematics and Computer Science, Indian Institute of Technology Goa, Ponda, India
{vipin2113106,shitala}@iitgoa.ac.in

Abstract. Agriculture remains crucial to many economies worldwide, yet plant diseases threaten its productivity and sustainability. Early detection and timely treatment are essential for mitigating their impact. Traditional detection methods are labor-intensive and costly, necessitating real-time solutions. Deep learning holds promise, but existing approaches struggle with simultaneous localization and classification. To address this, we propose YOLOv9++, an enhanced variant of YOLOv9 integrated with Convolutional Block Attention Module (CBAM). Our model significantly improves accuracy and efficiency in plant leaf disease detection. We introduce a large-scale leaf disease detection dataset called PlantVillage-LD2 inspired by the PlantVillage dataset. YOLOv9++ achieves competitive performance, surpassing the baseline YOLOv9, achieving a mAP:50 of 93.7% on the PlantVillage detection dataset. Moreover, on the PlantDoc dataset, YOLOv9++ achieves an mAP:50 of 61.7%, surpassing other detection algorithms. Our findings highlight the practicality of YOLOv9++ for real-time plant disease detection, fostering sustainable agricultural practices globally.

Keywords: Deep Learning · Leaf Disease Detection · Plant Pathology · Semi-Supervised · YOLO

1 Introduction

Agriculture plays a significant role in the global economy, serving as the primary provider of food, livelihoods, and jobs. In India, similar to numerous low- and middle-income nations, where a substantial portion of the population engages in farming, agriculture constitutes 18% of the nation's earnings and plays a pivotal role in bolstering the employment rate to 53% [1]. Given the critical role agriculture plays in sustaining economies and livelihoods, safeguarding crops from diseases becomes paramount. Plant diseases can devastate harvests, leading to food shortages, economic instability, and social unrest. Therefore, prioritizing

J. Kakarla et al. (Eds.): CVIP 2024, CCIS 2473, pp. 175–189, 2026.
https://doi.org/10.1007/978-3-031-93688-3_13

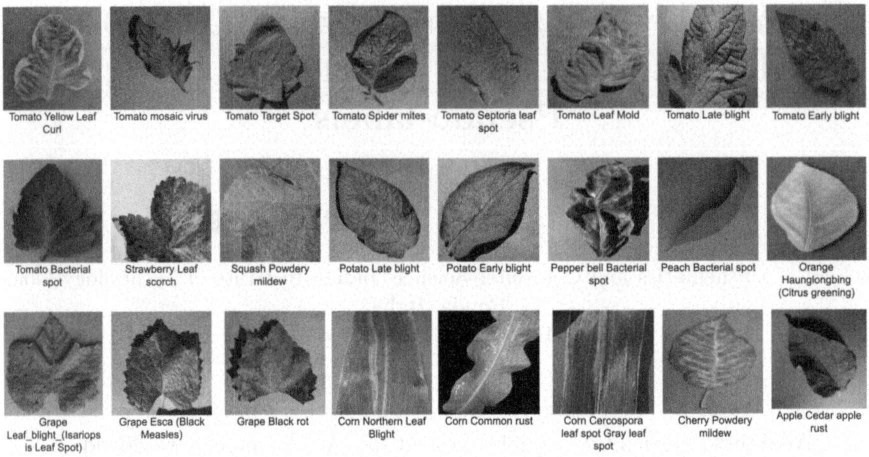

Fig. 1. Samples from the PlantDoc dataset, depicting a variety of challenges, underscoring real-world complexities in detection tasks.

the identification of illnesses affecting plants and affected leaves is essential to safeguarding global food security and promoting sustainable agricultural development. The major obstacle agriculture faces is accurately identifying the symptoms of major crop diseases [2,3]. Early detection of plant diseases has the potential to enhance decision-making within the agricultural sector. Typically, plants showing signs of infection display visible discolorations on their fruits, stems, flowers, or leaves. These infections tend to manifest unique patterns, facilitating the diagnosis of abnormalities. Effective identification of plant diseases necessitates specialized expertise and sufficient manpower.

Generally, two approaches are employed: manual examination by trained experts or farmers and automated systems utilizing advanced technologies. The traditional approach involves manual examination by trained experts. This method relies heavily on human observation and expertise to identify symptoms and patterns indicative of disease. However, the manual inspection is tedious and demanding, requiring significant manpower and sometimes misleading [4]. The impact of misleading diagnosis could result in potentially incorrect treatment plans, leading to ineffective management of plant diseases and further agricultural losses. In contrast, automated systems offer the potential for faster and more efficient disease diagnosis. These systems employ advanced technologies like machine learning algorithms and computer vision to automatically analyze plant images and identify signs of disease. By leveraging large datasets and sophisticated algorithms, automated systems can potentially identify diseases with high accuracy and speed.

Deep learning and computer vision techniques have emerged as powerful tools not only for common tasks [5,6] but also for plant leaf disease detection [7], revolutionizing the field with their ability to automate and enhance the process. These methods leverage neural networks, particularly convolutional neural networks (CNNs), to extract detailed features from images of plant leaves and classify them based on disease symptoms. By training on large datasets containing labeled images of healthy and diseased plants, CNNs can learn to recognize subtle patterns and variations indicative of different diseases. This capability enables highly accurate and efficient disease detection, even in complex agricultural environments with varying lighting conditions and background clutter. Figure 2 illustrates the simultaneous handling of recognition and localization in plant leaf disease detection.

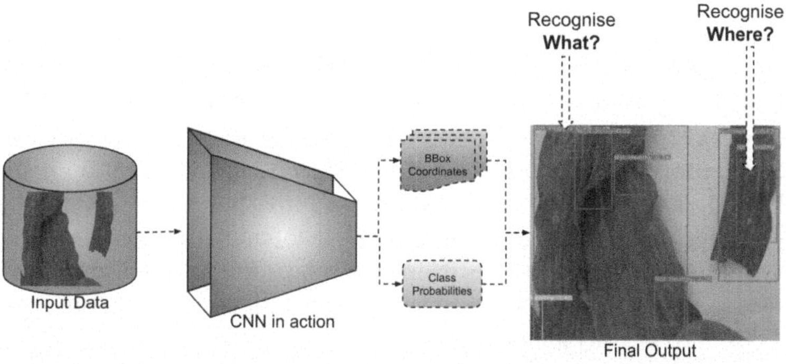

Fig. 2. Simultaneous handling of recognition and localization of plant leaf disease detection: CNN detects both the class (what) and location (where) of the defects in the plant image.

While numerous deep learning approaches employ novel architectures for detecting plant diseases [8,9], various challenges persist in phytopathology research. These challenges include the biological and physical diversity of crops, as well as the wide array of pests and diseases. Figure 1 visually illustrates different types of plant diseases, further emphasizing the complexity of phytopathology research and the need for robust methodologies to tackle them. Additionally, the unavailability of large-scale leaf disease detection datasets further complicates the development and evaluation of robust and generalizable detection models. We believe that there's a notable gap in the literature regarding the simultaneous handling of localization and classification in plant leaf disease detection. Therefore, the major contributions are mentioned below in threefolds:

- For the first time, to the best of our knowledge, we propose YOLOv9++ that incorporates CBAM [10] on the low-level extracted features of the backbone to boost plant biometric performance.
- We introduce a large-scale Plant leaf disease detection dataset based on the PlantVillage dataset [11], named the PlantVillage-LD2 dataset. The URL for the dataset is: https://www.kaggle.com/dsv/9054050.
- Competitive analysis of the proposed YOLOv9++ against the state-of-the-art (SOTA) detection methods, demonstrating improvements in accuracy and efficiency.

The rest of the paper is structured as follows: Background section provides a comprehensive overview of related work in the field of plant leaf disease detection. Subsequently, the Methodology section discusses the development process of YOLOv9++, CBAM, and the pseudo-label generation algorithm. Following this, we discuss the datasets and evaluation criteria. In the experiments section, we detail the evaluation of our proposed method, encompassing both quantitative and qualitative analyses. Finally, the paper concludes with a summary.

2 Background

In the field of agricultural sustainability, plant leaf disease detection plays a crucial role. Numerous approaches have been developed to address this critical issue, highlighting its significance in ensuring global food security [12–15].

In the work [16] authors addressed the issue of detecting plant diseases using digital image processing techniques coupled with a backpropagation neural network (BPNN). The authors detailed various approaches for detecting plant diseases by analyzing leaf images. They applied Otsu's thresholding along with boundary and spot detection algorithms to isolate the infected areas on leaves. Subsequently, they extracted diverse features including color, texture, morphology, and edges to classify plant diseases.

In a study [17] Peyman Moghadam et al. showcased the application of hyperspectral imaging in detecting plant diseases. Their research employed visible, near-infrared (VNIR), and short-wave infrared (SWIR) spectrums. They applied the k-means clustering algorithm to segment leaves based on their spectral properties. Additionally, they introduced a novel grid removal algorithm to successfully eliminate grids from hyperspectral images. In another study [18], CNNs were employed to classify diseases in maize plants, augmented by histogram techniques to evaluate the model's efficacy. Subsequently, in [19], the authors focused on identifying tomato leaf diseases using well-known CNN architectures like AlexNet, GoogLeNet, and ResNet. In the work [20], authors utilized LeNet architecture for detecting diseases in banana leaves and evaluated using metrics such as classification accuracy and F1-score in both Color and Gray Scale modes. Another work [21] explored the efficacy of five CNN architectures, including AlexNet, AlexNetOWTbn, GoogLeNet, Overfeat, and VGG, with VGG exhibiting superior performance. Similarly, in the study [22] authors delved into the recognition of eight different plant diseases, employing classifiers like Support Vector Machines (SVM), Extreme Learning Machine (ELM), and K-Nearest Neighbor (KNN) in conjunction with modern deep learning models such as GoogLeNet, ResNet-50, ResNet-101, Inception-v3, InceptionResNetv2, and SqueezeNet. Comparative analysis revealed ResNet-50 coupled with an SVM classifier as the optimal configuration, showcasing superior sensitivity, specificity, and F1-score metrics. Other research has investigated visualization-based methods. For example, in the study by Brahimi et al. [23], authors introduced the use of saliency maps to visualize symptoms of plant diseases, and presented a new method for identifying affected regions. Likewise, Sladojevic et al. [9] utilized the CaffeNet CNN architecture to differentiate between 13 distinct types of plant diseases, achieving an impressive classification accuracy of 96.30%. This surpassed traditional methods such as Support Vector Machines (SVM) and involved the application of various filters to accurately pinpoint areas of disease. Similarly, [2] utilized the AlexNet and GoogLeNet CNN architectures, leveraging the publicly available PlantVillage dataset [11] to further explore plant disease classification techniques. In [24], researchers utilized a modified LeNet model for olive plant disease detection. They employed segmentation and edge maps to identify diseases within the plants. Another study [25] focused on detecting four cucumber diseases and compared the accuracy of various models including Random Forest, Support Vector Machines, and AlexNet. Additionally, they utilized image segmentation techniques to observe disease symptoms in the plants. Deep learning models incorporating detectors were also utilized in [26], where diseases in plants were identified along with their corresponding confidence scores.

3 Methodology

In this section we first discuss YOLOv9++, highlighting architectural aspects, along with modified CBAM and then we discuss the pseudo-label generation algorithm for dataset creation.

3.1 YOLOv9++

YOLO [27] models are well known for their speed and state-of-the-art performance in object detection. Building upon this, we extend YOLOv9 [28] in the domain of plant leaf disease detection. More specifically, we propose YOLOv9++. YOLOv9++ not only inherits the strengths of YOLOv9 but also integrates novel enhancements, particularly through the integration of the CBAM [10], to further refine its detection capabilities.

YOLOv9 uses Generalized Efficient Layer Aggregation Network (GELAN) and Programmable Gradient Information (PGI) to improve the extraction of features. PGI, functioning as an auxiliary supervision framework, is intended to manage the flow of gradients through different semantic levels, thereby augmenting the model's detection capabilities. PGI is composed of three main components: the main branch, the auxiliary reversible branch, and multi-level auxiliary information. As the depth of the network expands, there's a potential for a bottleneck in information, resulting in loss function that might not produce gradients that are helpful. In such instances, reversible functions are used by the auxiliary reversible branch to preserve information integrity and reduce information loss. To enhance the efficiency of information integration and propagation, YOLOv9 introduced a novel lightweight network architecture called the Generalized Efficient Layer Aggregation Network (GELAN). It combines components from ELAN and CSPNet to efficiently fuse features, and enhance better interaction between layers.

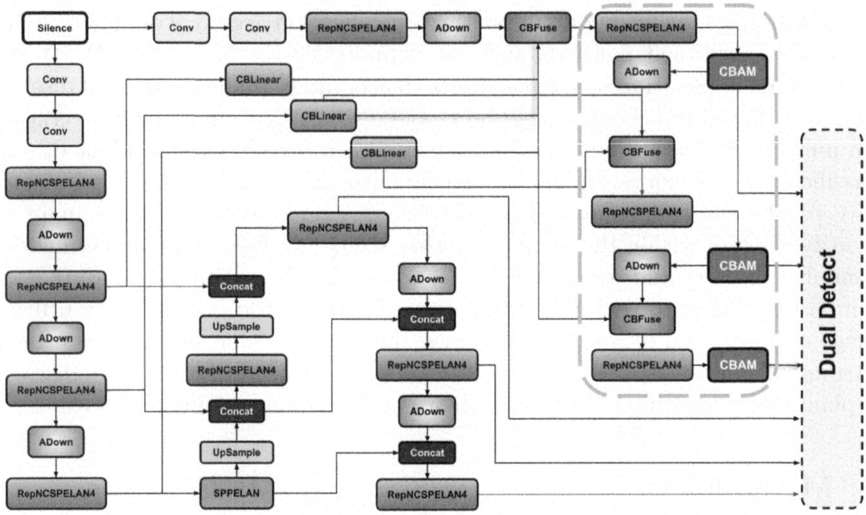

Fig. 3. The complete architecture of YOLOv9++.

In the context of plant leaf disease detection, these advancements translate to more accurate and efficient detection of diseased areas on leaves. The enhanced feature extraction capability enabled by PGI and the efficient information integration facilitated by GELAN contribute to a more robust and effective detection system, ultimately aiding in the early identification and management of plant diseases. The complete network architecture of YOLOv9++ is shown in Fig. 3.

Convolutional Block Attention Module (CBAM). To further enhance the YOLOv9's capabilities for leaf disease detection, we integrate the CBAM [10] following RepNCSPELAN4 and just before the detector's head as highlighted in Fig. 3. CBAM operates by selectively enhancing the informative features within the input data through a combination of channel-wise attention module (CAM) and spatial attention module (SAM) as shown in Fig. 4. CAM utilizes global average pooling (GAP) operation to determine channel weights, guiding the network to prioritize channels crucial for disease detection. This is followed by SAM, which further refines feature maps by accentuating significant spatial regions while suppressing irrelevant ones. As a result, the integration of CBAM improves the model's performance in identifying and categorizing leaf diseases accurately.

3.2 Pseudo Labeling

For plant leaf disease detection, the availability of large-scale labeled detection datasets remains a significant challenge. This natural limitation hinders the development of robust detection models. In response to this challenge, inspired

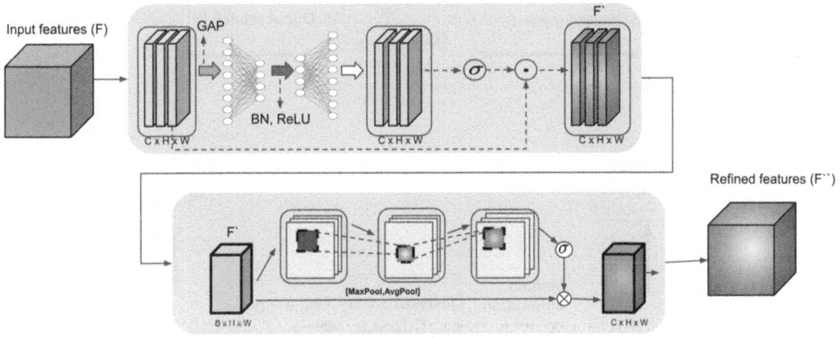

Fig. 4. Visualization of the CBAM module: Channel-wise Attention module (CAM) followed by Spatial Attention module (SAM) for enhanced CNN feature representation.

by [29], we turn to the pseudo-labeling approach to create PlantVillage-LD2 dataset. The pseudo-labeling algorithm is an iterative approach designed to effectively expand the size of the dataset. Initially, the algorithm starts with a limited amount of labeled data L^d to train a detection model D^m in a training (cycle t). Subsequently, the trained model is employed to infer on unlabeled data U^d, resulting in the identification of low-confidence L_c^d and high-confidence H_c^d subsets within the dataset based on a confidence threshold θ, where $\theta = 0.95$. L_c^d is then manually checked for stability and is labeled using dataset labeling tools, and the resulting labeled data, along with H_c^d, is merged with the original labeled dataset. This iterative process continues, progressively augmenting the labeled dataset until it reaches completeness. The complete flow of the algorithm is indicated in Fig. 5.

4 Implementation and Datasets

The hardware configuration includes two Intel Xeon Gold 6248 processors, each with 20 cores running at 2.5 GHz, along with an NVIDIA DGX 1 $\times$ A100 GPU. We optimized the proposed model using Stochastic Gradient Descent (SGD), setting the initial learning rate (lr) at 0.01, a momentum factor of 0.937, and a weight decay of 0.0005. The training process involved feeding batches of data with size 16 to the model for 300 rounds, utilizing network input dimensions of 640×640.

4.1 Evaluation Criterion

For evaluation, we employed standard performance metrics, including precision (P), recall (R), and mean average precision (mAP). The mAP is calculated by averaging the average precision (AP) values for each category, which are obtained from the Precision-Recall (PR) curve. Precision and Recall are determined using

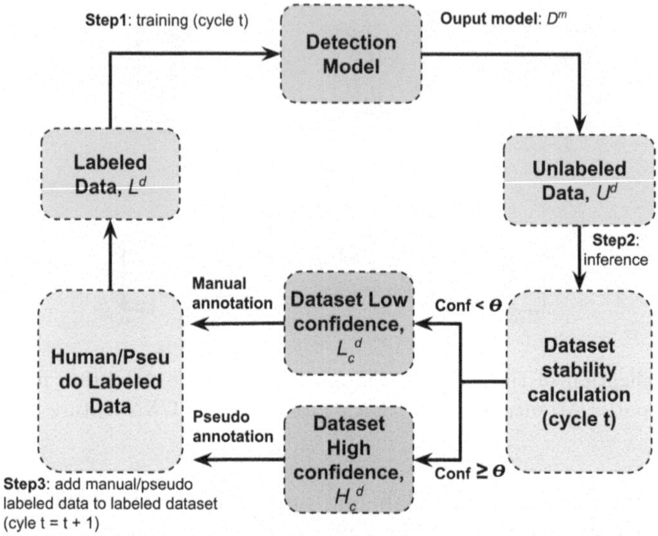

Fig. 5. Pseudo-Label generation algorithm

the formulas below:

$$P = \frac{TP}{TP + FP}, \quad R = \frac{TP}{TP + FN} \tag{1}$$

where FP is false positives, TP is true positives, and FN is false negatives.

4.2 Datasets Description

For evaluation, we employed two widely used benchmark datasets for Plant Leaf Disease Detection: the PlantDoc dataset [30] and the proposed PlantVillage-LD2 dataset. These datasets are highly regarded and pose substantial challenges in the field of plant pathology.

PlantDoc Dataset. The PlantDoc dataset [30] comprises 2589 images featuring more than 13 plant species and 29 classes. It's divided into a training set consisting of 1882 images, a validation set with 470 images, and a test set containing 237 images. During preprocessing, the images underwent uniform resizing to 640 × 640 pixels following auto-orientation. Figure 1 shows the sample images of the PlantDoc dataset.

PlantVillage-LD2 Dataset. In the absence of a large-scale dataset for plant leaf disease detection, we propose PlantVillage-LD2 dataset specifically curated to bridge the gap of large-scale detection datasets. The dataset generation process is indicated in Fig. 5. The dataset comprises 36 classes, as outlined in Fig. 6.

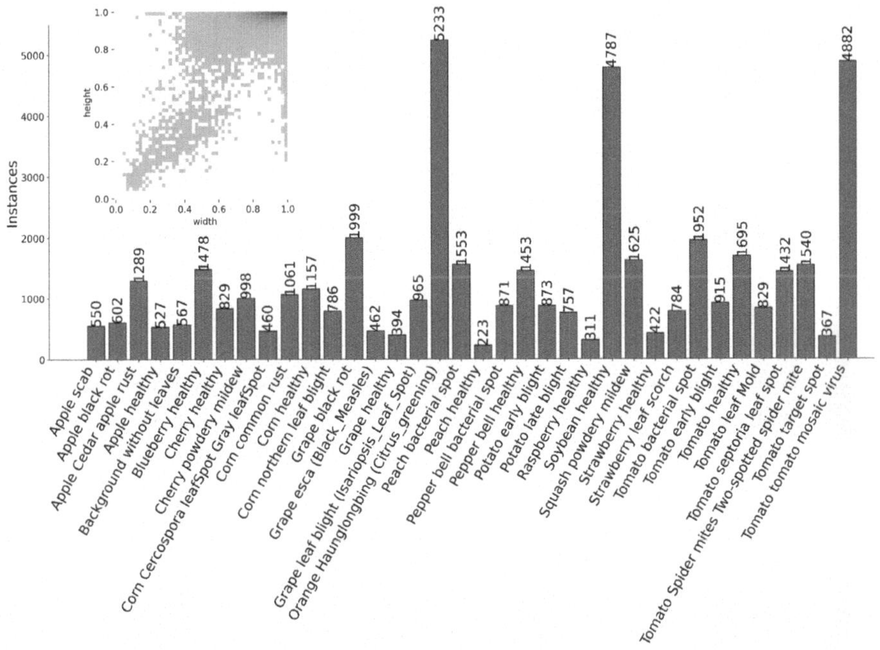

Fig. 6. Statistics of PlantVillage-LD2 dataset

It consists of 46628 samples, with 60% allocated for training (27,978 samples), roughly 20% for validation (9,325 samples), and another 20% for testing (9,325 samples). We believe that this dataset will serve as a foundation for initializing detection models in the field of plant pathology.

5 Experimental Results

This section details the comprehensive evaluation of YOLOv9++ on the aforementioned datasets. We thoroughly analyze the findings, covering both quantitative and qualitative aspects. Furthermore, a comparative analysis is conducted, contrasting the proposed model's efficacy against the SOTA object detection methods.

5.1 Benchmarking Against State-of-the-Art Methods

In response to the lack of research work done in leaf disease detection, we compare the performance of YOLOv9++ against the current SOTA models within the YOLO family and other widely-used architectures, using the PlantDoc dataset. This comparative analysis aims to address the critical need for advancements in this field and to provide insights into the efficacy of YOLOv9++ for improving object detection accuracy in plant pathology applications.

Table 1. State-of-the-art comparison of YOLO family models and benchmarks from the PlantDoc dataset.

Model	P	R	mAP:50
YOLOv5s [31]	0.517	0.606	0.577
YOLOv5m [31]	0.471	0.864	0.588
YOLOv5l [31]	0.657	0.546	0.594
YOLOv6s [32]	0.538	0.6	0.572
YOLOv6m [32]	0.566	0.65	0.613
YOLOv7Tiny [33]	0.522	0.603	0.592
YOLOv7 [33]	0.667	0.575	0.614
YOLOv8s [34]	0.517	0.566	0.558
YOLOv8m [34]	0.595	0.51	0.585
YOLOv9-c [28]	0.608	0.598	0.606
YOLOv9-e [28]	0.59	0.506	0.542
MobileNet* (COCO) [30]	-	-	0.328
MobileNet* (COCO+PVD) [30]	-	-	0.224
Faster-rcnn-inception-resnet* (iNaturalist) [30]	-	-	0.361
Faster-rcnn-inception-resnet* (COCO) [30]	-	-	0.389
YOLOv9++ [Proposed]	0.596	0.599	**0.617**

Note: '*' indicates the model utilizes pre-trained weights, while the other models are trained from scratch.

Table 1 presents a comparison of state-of-the-art object detection models. Results indicate that the proposed YOLOv9++ achieves the highest mAP:50 score of 0.617 (higher is better), and its precision (P), and recall (R) values of 0.596 and 0.599, respectively, are competitive with other models. YOLOv9++ also demonstrates a notable improvement of 1.1% over the baseline YOLOv9-c model. Additionally, YOLOv9++ outperforms other benchmarked models such as MobileNet and Faster-rcnn-inception-resnet in terms of mAP:50 by a large margin, underscoring its effectiveness in plant disease detection tasks. We also provide a detailed class-wise comparison against the proposed YOLOv9++ and baseline YOLOv9-c in Fig. 7.

Overall, YOLOv9++ demonstrates robust performance even without relying on pre-trained weights, distinguishing it as a promising solution for plant disease localization and classification tasks.

5.2 Evaluation on PlantVillage-LD2 Dataset

We also analyzed the performance of YOLOv9++ on the PlantVillage-LD2 dataset against the baseline model, YOLOv9-c. The proposed YOLOv9++ outperforms the baseline on all three metrics, achieving a significant improvement in mAP:50 as shown in Table 2. More specifically, YOLOv9++ achieves a precision of 0.905, compared to the baseline YOLOv9-c's precision of 0.774. recall

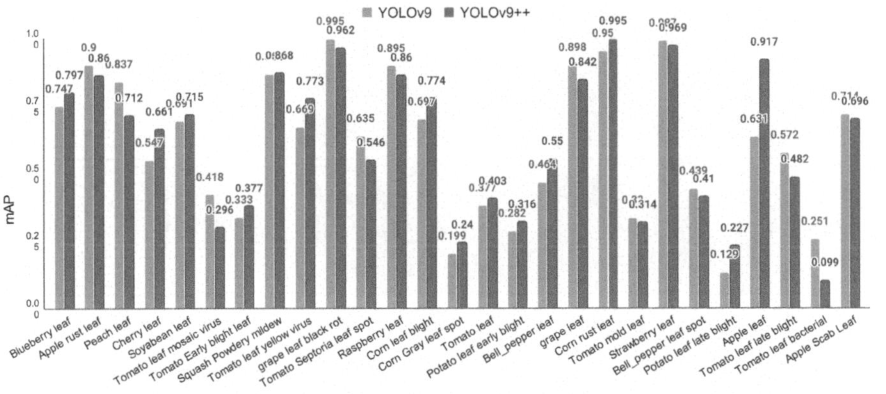

Fig. 7. Visualization of Class-wise mAP:50 comparison for YOLOv9++ against baseline YOLOv9 on PlantDoc Dataset: Each bar represents the Class-wise mAP:50 for different classes. X-axis denotes classes, while Y-axis shows the corresponding class mAP:50 scores.

Table 2. Comparison of Precision, Recall, and mAP:50 for baseline YOLOv9 and proposed YOLOv9++.

Model	P	R	mAP:50
YOLOv9-c	0.774	0.823	0.86
YOLOv9++ [Proposed]	**0.905**	**0.923**	**0.937**

metric for YOLOv9++ is 0.923, whereas YOLOv9-c achieves a recall of 0.823. This signifies that YOLOv9++ successfully detects a higher proportion of actual leaves present in the dataset compared to the baseline model. In other words, YOLOv9++ misses fewer leaves compared to YOLOv9-c.

Our analysis suggests that the integration of the CBAM directly contributes to YOLOv9++'s superior performance. By strategically focusing the model's attention on relevant leaf regions within the images, CBAM enables more accurate leaf detection and reduces confusion with background elements.

5.3 Qualitative Study

We also undertook a qualitative analysis to contrast the detection capabilities of our proposed YOLOv9++ against the baseline YOLOv9-c model, as illustrated in Fig. 8. In particular, (a) depicts the bounding boxes representing ground truth instances, (b) illustrates the detection outcomes from baseline YOLOv9-c, and (c) represents bounding box detections generated by our proposed YOLOv9++. The visual results strongly highlight the superior performance of YOLOv9++ in accurately localizing and identifying leaf disease instances, even amidst background complexities. In contrast, detection results from YOLOv9-c (b) demonstrate shortcomings, where certain instances are either missed or misidentified.

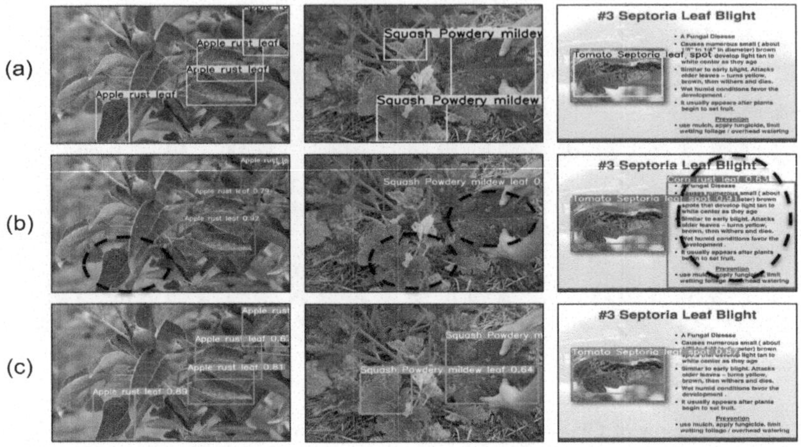

Fig. 8. Visual comparison of detection performance on the PlantDoc Dataset: (a) Ground truth labels, (b) Detection using the baseline YOLOv9-c, and (c) Detection results with YOLOv9++.

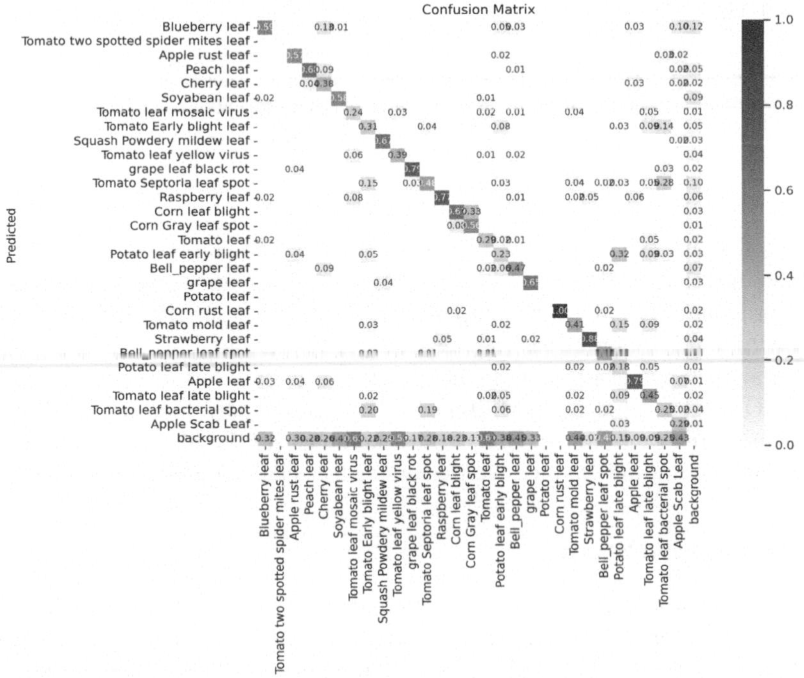

Fig. 9. Confusion matrix generated through the proposed YOLOv9++.

Furthermore, to provide a comprehensive understanding of the proposed YOLOv9++ model's performance, we present the confusion matrix shown in

Fig. 10. Visual results obtained from our proposed detection model, YOLOv9++, showcasing its efficacy in identifying a range of plant leaf diseases.

Fig. 9. This matrix outlines the model's performance across the 29 classes within the PlantDoc dataset, revealing both prediction accuracy and associations between predictions. Rows represent true labels, columns denote predicted categories, and diagonal elements indicate correct detection rates. Impressively, our model achieved high accuracy across all categories, as evidenced by the matrix. A more comprehensive visual output of YOLOv9++'s detection capabilities is shown in Fig. 10.

6 Conclusion and Future Work

In this paper, we presented YOLOv9++, an enhanced version of the YOLOv9 that integrates the Convolutional Block Attention Module (CBAM). YOLOv9++ significantly enhances both the accuracy and efficiency of detecting plant leaf diseases. Additionally, we present a large-scale leaf detection dataset inspired by PlantVillage, called PlantVillage-LD2 dataset. YOLOv9++ outperforms SOTA methods on benchmark datasets, achieving the highest mAP:50 of 0.617 on the PlantDoc dataset and a mAP:50 of 0.937 on the PlantVillage leaf disease detection dataset. These results highlight the effectiveness and practicality of YOLOv9++ in real-time plant disease detection. Future work could focus on optimizing YOLOv9++ for cross-domain adaptation and integrating it with precision agriculture systems.

References

1. Alston, J.M., Pardey, P.G.: Agriculture in the global economy. J. Econ. Perspect. **28**(1), 121–146 (2014)
2. Mohanty, S.P., Hughes, D.P., Salathé, M.: Using deep learning for image-based plant disease detection. Front. Plant Sci. **7**, 215232 (2016)
3. Prasad, S., Peddoju, S.K., Ghosh, D.: AgroMobile: a cloud-based framework for agriculturists on mobile platform. IJAST **59**, 41–52 (2013)
4. Dawod, R.G., Dobre, C.: Upper and lower leaf side detection with machine learning methods. Sensors **22**(7), 2696 (2022)
5. Prasad, S., Singh, V.K., Sapre, A.: Handwriting analysis based on segmentation method for prediction of human personality using support vector machine. IJCA **8**(12), 25–29 (2010)
6. Chai, T., Li, J., Prasad, S., Qi, L., Zhang, Z.: Shape-driven lightweight CNN for finger-vein biometrics. J. Inf. Secur. Appl. **67**, 103211 (2022)
7. Nagaraju, M., Chawla, P.: Systematic review of deep learning techniques in plant disease detection. Int. J. Syst. Assur. Eng. Manag. **11**(3), 547–560 (2020). https://doi.org/10.1007/s13198-020-00972-1
8. Alirezazadeh, P., Schirrmann, M., Stolzenburg, F.: Improving deep learning-based plant disease classification with attention mechanism. Gesunde Pflanzen **75**(1), 49–59 (2023)
9. Sladojevic, S., Arsenovic, M., Anderla, A., Culibrk, D., Stefanovic, D.: Deep neural networks based recognition of plant diseases by leaf image classification. Comput. Intell. Neurosci. **2016** (2016)
10. Woo, S., Park, J., Lee, J.-Y., Kweon, I.S.: CBAM: convolutional block attention module (2018)
11. Hughes, D.P., Salathe, M.: An open access repository of images on plant health to enable the development of mobile disease diagnostics (2016)
12. Prasad, S., Peddoju, S.K., Ghosh, D.: Multi-resolution mobile vision system for plant leaf disease diagnosis. Sig. Image Video Process. **10**(2), 379–388 (2016)
13. Prasad, S., Sateesh Kumar, P., Ghosh, D.: An efficient low vision plant leaf shape identification system for smart phones. Multimedia Tools Appl. **76**, 6915–6939 (2017)
14. Prasad, S., Peddoju, S.K., Ghosh, D.: Mobile mixed reality based damage level estimation of diseased plant leaf. In: IEEE International Conference on Next Generation Mobile Apps, Services and Technologies, pp. 72–77 (2014)
15. Prasad, S., Kumar, P., Hazra, R., Kumar, A.: Plant leaf disease detection using Gabor wavelet transform. In: Panigrahi, B.K., Das, S., Suganthan, P.N., Nanda, P.K. (eds.) SEMCCO 2012. LNCS, vol. 7677, pp. 372–379. Springer, Heidelberg (2012). https://doi.org/10.1007/978-3-642-35380-2_44
16. Khirade, S.D., Patil, A.B.: Plant disease detection using image processing. In: International Conference on Computing Communication Control and Automation, pp. 768–771. IEEE (2015)
17. Moghadam, P., Ward, D., Goan, E., Jayawardena, S., Sikka, P., Hernandez, E.: Plant disease detection using hyperspectral imaging. In: International Conference on Digital Image Computing: Techniques and Applications, pp. 1–8. IEEE (2017)
18. Sibiya, M., Sumbwanyambe, M.: A computational procedure for the recognition and classification of maize leaf diseases out of healthy leaves using convolutional neural networks. AgriEngineering **1**(1), 119–131 (2019)

19. Zhang, K., Wu, Q., Liu, A., Meng, X., et al.: Can deep learning identify tomato leaf disease? Adv. Multimedia **2018** (2018)
20. Amara, J., Bouaziz, B., Algergawy, A.: A deep learning-based approach for banana leaf diseases classification (2017)
21. Ferentinos, K.P.: Deep learning models for plant disease detection and diagnosis. Comput. Electron. Agricult. **145**, 311–318 (2018)
22. Türkoğlu, M., Hanbay, D.: Plant disease and pest detection using deep learning-based features. Turk. J. Electr. Eng. Comput. Sci. **27**(3), 1636–1651 (2019)
23. Brahimi, M., Arsenovic, M., Laraba, S., Sladojevic, S., Boukhalfa, K., Moussaoui, A.: Deep learning for plant diseases: detection and saliency map visualisation. In: Human and Machine Learning: Visible, Explainable, Trustworthy and Transparent, pp. 93–117 (2018)
24. Cruz, A.C., Luvisi, A., De Bellis, L., Ampatzidis, Y.: Vision-based plant disease detection system using transfer and deep learning. In: 2017 ASABE Annual International Meeting, p. 1. American Society of Agricultural and Biological Engineers (2017)
25. Ma, J., Keming, D., Zheng, F., Zhang, L., Gong, Z., Sun, Z.: A recognition method for cucumber diseases using leaf symptom images based on deep convolutional neural network. Comput. Electron. Agric. **154**, 18–24 (2018)
26. Fuentes, A., Yoon, S., Kim, S.C., Park, D.S.: A robust deep-learning-based detector for real-time tomato plant diseases and pests recognition. Sensors **17**(9), 2022 (2017)
27. Terven, J., Cordova-Esparza, D.: A comprehensive review of YOLO architectures in computer vision: from YOLOv1 to YOLOv8 and YOLO-NAS. arXiv preprint arXiv:2304.00501 (2023)
28. Wang, C.-Y., Liao, H.-Y.M.: YOLOv9: learning what you want to learn using programmable gradient information (2024)
29. Prasad, S., Li, Y., Lin, D., Sheng, D.: maskedFaceNet: a progressive semi-supervised masked face detector. In: Proceedings of the IEEE/CVF Winter Conference on Applications of Computer Vision, pp. 3389–3398 (2021)
30. Singh, D., Jain, N., Jain, P., Kayal, P., Kumawat, S., Batra, N.: PlantDoc: a dataset for visual plant disease detection. In: Proceedings of the 7th ACM IKDD CoDS and 25th COMAD, CoDS COMAD 2020, pp. 249–253. Association for Computing Machinery, New York, NY, USA (2020)
31. Jocher, G., et al.: ultralytics/YOLOv5: v7.0 - YOLOv5 SOTA Realtime Instance Segmentation, November 2022
32. Li, C., et al.: YOLOv6: a single-stage object detection framework for industrial applications (2022)
33. Wang, C.-Y., Bochkovskiy, A., Liao, H.-Y.M.: YOLOv7: trainable bag-of-freebies sets new state-of-the-art for real-time object detectors. In: Proceedings of the IEEE/CVF Conference on Computer Vision and Pattern Recognition (CVPR) (2023)
34. Jocher, G., Chaurasia, A., Qiu, J.: Ultralytics YOLO, January 2023

A Transfer Learning Approach for Emotion Recognition Integrated with Cognitive Evaluation in Virtual Learning

Jeena A. Thankachan[1(✉)] and Bama Srinivasan[2]

[1] Department of Artificial Intelligence and Data Science, Sri Sairam Engineering College, Chennai 600 044, Tamil Nadu, India
jeena.ai@sairam.edu.in

[2] Department of Information Science and Technology, College of Engineering, Anna University, Chennai 600 025, Tamil Nadu, India
bama@auist.net

Abstract. The paper focuses on the deep learning based model selection for the emotion recognition of a learner. The emotion is recognized through the facial images captured by the proctor module in a Virtual Learning Environment (VLE). A facial emotion recognition (FER) model is developed on the FER2013 dataset using transfer learning techniques. The purpose of the FER model is to propose an emotional construct in addition to cognitive constructs for the multi-modal evaluation of the learners performance in a virtual learning task. The work presented in this paper includes two main parts: first, propose a mathematical model for cognitive evaluation and second, selection of a deep learning model for emotion recognition. The proposed work assess the multi-modal performance in terms of memory, visual processing, processing speed, attention score and emotion. The proposed system provides relevant information about learners' emotional health and the cognitive elements that need further support, which helps learners' improve cognitively and emotionally.

Keywords: Multi-modal evaluation · Cognition · Emotion · Virtual Learning Environment (VLE)

1 Introduction

Recent advancements in technology and the rise of virtual learning environments (VLEs) have significantly transformed the educational landscape. Learning Management Systems (LMS) now serve as essential platforms for delivering content and facilitating interactive learning. However, traditional evaluation methods for these systems often rely heavily on quantitative metrics such as completion rates and test scores, which fail to capture the comprehensive nature of the learning experience.

J. Kakarla et al. (Eds.): CVIP 2024, CCIS 2473, pp. 190–203, 2026.
https://doi.org/10.1007/978-3-031-93688-3_14

To address this limitation, there is a growing need to customize LMS platforms to better accommodate the diverse needs of learners. This involves integrating features that assess not only academic performance but also emotional and cognitive states. Understanding and evaluating these aspects can lead to more personalized and engaging learning experiences.

This paper proposes a novel strategy for customizing LMS platforms through emotion and cognition-based evaluation. The objectives of this paper include:

- First, a proposed multi-modal system design that includes a FER module and a cognition evaluation module for a customized LMS.
- Second, FER model selection for the emotion recognition of the images obtained from the proctor module in LMS.
- Third, a proposed mathematical framework for the assessment of cognition and emotion of a learner from the data extracted with the LMS.

The structure of the paper includes a review of the research background, a detailed system overview, and an examination of algorithms, implementation, results, and analysis.

2 Research Background and State of the Art

Emotions play a vital role in learning, significantly affecting cognitive processes and academic performance. The integration of technology in education, through Intelligent Tutoring Systems (ITSs) and Learning Management Systems (LMSs), has opened new possibilities for enhancing the learning experience. This section reviews research on the impact of emotions in education and underscores the need for adaptive e-learning systems that address learners' emotional states. It also examines recent advancements in emotion recognition technologies, including convolutional neural networks (CNNs) and hybrid intelligent systems, in the context of e-learning.

2.1 Research Background

Learners' emotional states frequently change throughout the learning process, requiring regular assessment to address these fluctuations. The growing use of computer-based educational technologies like Intelligent Tutoring Systems (ITSs) [6,21] and Learning Management Systems (LMSs) [7] reflects an interest in monitoring these emotions, which impact cognition and learning performance [18]. Students experiencing anxiety or depression often struggle with learning and processing information [7], highlighting the need for educational systems that consider emotional influences [9].

Recent research emphasizes the importance of integrating emotion into educational technology. Wang et al. advocated for incorporating cognitive, emotive, and social factors to improve teaching effectiveness [25], and a model developed in 2001 linked emotion with different learning phases [12]. Tyng et al. highlighted the effect of emotions on learning and memory through neuroimaging, suggesting emotional considerations in educational design [24].

However, some adaptive e-learning systems focus solely on location, time, and preferences without addressing emotions. For example, an adaptive mobile learning environment was proposed in 2009 [14], and ontologies for personalized e-learning based on preferences were suggested in 2011 [1].

2.2 State of the Art

Recent research in e-learning systems has explored various methods for detecting emotional states. For instance, a hybrid intelligent system combining convolutional neural networks (CNNs) and fuzzy systems for facial expression detection was proposed in 2020 [15], and a multimodal emotion recognition system using face and voice modules was developed in 2016 [4]. However, these methods may not be practical where face and voice recognition devices are unavailable. Advancements in emotion recognition include CNNs trained on databases such as CK+, JAFFE, NVIE, FER2013, and Cohn-Kanade (CK+) [8,11,19,20]. Hybrid systems combining computer vision and machine learning, such as k-Nearest Neighbors (kNN) and Support Vector Machines (SVM), have provided real-time feedback to educators [3]. Transfer learning with models like VGG16 has improved emotion recognition accuracy in educational settings [19]. Deep learning models like Inception-V3, VGG19, and ResNet-50 have been used for real-time engagement detection [8], and continuous image frame analysis with CNNs captures complex emotions more accurately than single-image methods [16]. Multitask cascaded convolutional networks (MTCNN) and Temporal Relational Networks (TRN) have been employed for effective emotion classification and recognizing changes in facial expressions [13,17]. Efficient CNN models have also achieved high accuracy in emotion, age, and gender recognition [11]. Despite these advancements, practical, accessible methods for influencing emotional states in e-learning remain limited. This study addresses this gap by proposing a framework usable on any device.

3 Proposed System Design

This section presents the proposed system design that aims to analyse a learner's cognitive and emotional health through an LMS. As shown in Fig. 1, the system consists of four interconnected modules: LMS Module, FER module, Cognitive evaluation module and the Data Analytics Module, where each serve a distinct purpose.

The work flow of the proposed system design in experimental set up consists of the following steps:

- Student at the user end access LMS, the Moodle
- Student is instructed to go through learning material and attend a quiz through LMS

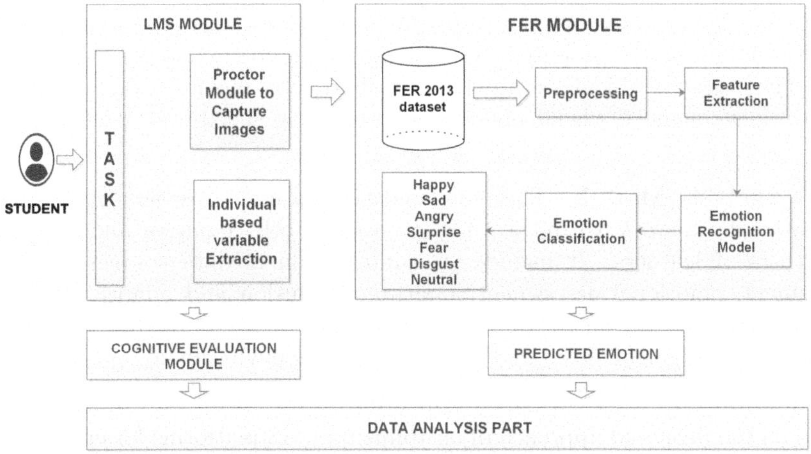

Fig. 1. Proposed System Design

- Moodle tracks and records the performance variables, while the student attends the quiz
- Similarly, the proctor plugin captures the image, while the student attends the quiz
- The captured images are fed to a FER model, to predict the learner emotion
- The extracted performance data is fed to the cognitive evaluation module to evaluate the strength of the cognitive abilities
- The relation between cognitive performance metrics and the respective emotion is analysed in the data analysis part

LMS Module: In our work, Moodle has been used as the LMS platform for the extraction of individual variables to analyze the proposed system. Moodle allows educators to upload and organize learning materials, that fosters easy access for learners. Its quiz module supports various question types, automatic grading, and customizable settings.

Moodle also offers a feature of proctoring module that provides a secure and controlled environment for online assessments. In our proposed work, webcam monitoring feature of the proctoring module has been used for monitoring and capture the image of the learner. Moodle facilitates the flexible features for learning materials and quizzes to track progress and performance in online courses.

FER Module: In VLE, where face-to-face interaction is limited, facial emotion recognition can enhance engagement and communication between educators and learners. In this module, emotion is obtained from images captured by the proctoring module. This feature leverages image analysis techniques to detect and interpret emotions displayed by users during online assessments or learning activities. The emotion recognition system assigns weights to each detected emotion based on its significance in assessing learners' engagement, stress levels, or understanding of the content.

Cognitive Evaluation Module: In this module the strength of the learners' cognitive abilities are computed from the data extracted while performance of a task. The cognitive abilities evaluated are: short term memory, long term memory, working memory, visual processing, processing speed and attention score [5].

Data Analysis Module: The data analysis module serves as a multi-modal evaluation framework within a VLE, to assess both cognitive and emotional constructs of learners'. It includes the integration of data sources, cognitive assessment, emotional assessment, multi-modal fusion and adaptive feedback for continuous improvement. Therefore, the data analysis module contributes towards a more personalized and effective learning environment.

Applications of the Proposed Approach

Based on the proposed approach of customizing LMS platforms for emotion and cognition-based evaluation, the following applications are possible:

- Personalized Learning Pathways: Adaptive content and dynamic difficulty adjustments based on learners' emotional and cognitive states.
- Enhanced Student Support: Real-time emotion-aware feedback and personalized interventions.
- Improved Engagement: Gamification and interactive experiences tailored to emotional and cognitive needs.
- Data-Driven Insights: Learner analytics and predictive analytics for performance.
- Enhanced Assessments: Emotionally informed and adaptive assessments.
- Support for Diverse Learning Styles: Customized experiences and cognitive load management.
- Research and Development: Innovative evaluation methods and longitudinal studies.

4 Extraction of Attributes from LMS Platform

In an LMS, a learner will be provided with a learning material followed by an assessment like Quiz, puzzles, conceptual games etc. The platform facilitates the tools that track and report the learner progress and engagement with learning material, as shown in Fig. 2.

An assessment on the LMS platform using a quiz is performed. The Quiz performance results are saved in the csv format. The csv file is then analysed to evaluate the performance of the learner with respect to the extracted variables. Some of the key variables that can be obtained from the progress track of Moodle quizzes include: score/grade, number of attempts, time spent on the quiz, completion status, and interaction patterns, as shown in Fig. 3.

A plugin is used for proctoring the quiz, as shown in Fig. 4. The proctoring plugin captures some images during the test. The best of the captured images of

Download table data as | Comma separated values (.csv) | Download

	First name / Surname	Email address	State	Started on	Completed	Time taken	Grade/1	Q. 1 /1
	Student2 Student2 Review attempt	student2@annauniv.edu	Finished	26 May 2023 3:09 PM	26 May 2023 3:27 PM	18 mins 37 secs	1	✓ 1
	Student3 Student3 Review attempt	student3@annauniv.edu	Finished	26 May 2023 3:48 PM	26 May 2023 4:33 PM	44 mins 3 secs	1	✓ 1
	Student4 Student4 Review attempt	student4@annauniv.edu	Finished	26 May 2023 4:03 PM	26 May 2023 4:24 PM	21 mins 18 secs	1	✓ 1
	Student1 Student1 Review attempt	student1@annauniv.edu	Finished	27 May 2023 3:03 PM	27 May 2023 3:19 PM	16 mins 26 secs	1	✓ 1
	Student5 Student5 Review attempt	student5@annauniv.edu	Finished	27 May 2023 4:23 PM	27 May 2023 4:36 PM	13 mins 15 secs	1	✓ 1
	Student6 Student6 Review attempt	student6@annauniv.edu	Finished	27 May 2023 8:09 PM	27 May 2023 8:31 PM	22 mins 1 sec	1	✓ 1

Fig. 2. A snippet of Data Extraction with Learning material in Moodle

a learner is the input to the facial emotion recognition (FER) model. The image is then analysed with the FER Model to evaluate the emotion, E, of the learner.

The variables extracted from an LMS platform like Moodle are: completion status, time taken on learning material and quiz, score or grade, and emotion.

5 A Mathematical Framework for Multimodal Evaluation of a Learner

This paper proposes a mathematical framework to evaluate cognitive and emotional constructs of a learner based on data from an LMS. In response to the global shift to remote learning due to the COVID-19 pandemic, virtual learning environments (VLEs), including learning management systems (LMS) and online collaboration platforms, became increasingly prominent. Extensive research is now focused on developing mathematical models of learner cognition to enable more personalized learning experiences [22,23].

5.1 Memory

Short-Term Memory (STM): STM involves temporary information storage. It can be measured as:

$$\text{Accuracy}_{\text{STM}} = \frac{\text{Number of correctly recalled items}}{\text{Total number of items presented}} \times 100\% \tag{1}$$

Working Memory (WM): WM refers to the temporary storage and manipulation of information. It is assessed by the accuracy of responses in tasks requiring information manipulation.

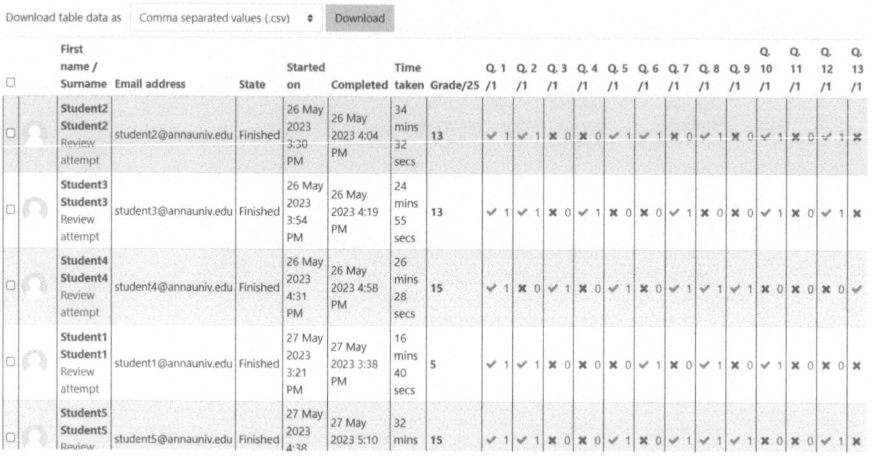

Download table data as Comma separated values (.csv) Download

First name / Surname	Email address	State	Started on	Completed	Time taken	Grade/25	Q. 1 /1	Q. 2 /1	Q. 3 /1	Q. 4 /1	Q. 5 /1	Q. 6 /1	Q. 7 /1	Q. 8 /1	Q. 9 /1	Q. 10 /1	Q. 11 /1	Q. 12 /1	Q. 13 /1
Student2 Student2 Review attempt	student2@annauniv.edu	Finished	26 May 2023 3:30 PM	26 May 2023 4:04 PM	34 mins 32 secs	13	✓ 1	✓ 1	✗ 0	✗ 0	✓ 1	✓ 1	✗ 0	✓ 1	✗ 0	✓ 1	✗ 0	✓ 1	✗
Student3 Student3 Review attempt	student3@annauniv.edu	Finished	26 May 2023 3:54 PM	26 May 2023 4:19 PM	24 mins 55 secs	13	✓ 1	✓ 1	✗ 0	✓ 1	✗ 0	✗ 0	✓ 1	✗ 0	✗ 0	✓ 1	✗ 0	✓ 1	✗
Student4 Student4 Review attempt	student4@annauniv.edu	Finished	26 May 2023 4:31 PM	26 May 2023 4:58 PM	26 mins 28 secs	15	✓ 1	✗ 0	✓ 1	✗ 0	✓ 1	✗ 0	✓ 1	✓ 1	✓ 1	✗ 0	✗ 0	✗ 0	✓
Student1 Student1 Review attempt	student1@annauniv.edu	Finished	27 May 2023 3:21 PM	27 May 2023 3:38 PM	16 mins 40 secs	5	✓ 1	✓ 1	✗ 0	✗ 0	✗ 0	✓ 1	✗ 0	✓ 1	✗ 0	✓ 1	✗ 0	✗ 0	✗
Student5 Student5 Review	student5@annauniv.edu	Finished	27 May 2023 4:38	27 May 2023 5:10	32 mins	15	✓ 1	✓ 1	✗ 0	✗ 0	✓ 1	✗ 0	✓ 1	✓ 1	✓ 1	✗ 0	✗ 0	✓ 1	✗

Fig. 3. A snippet of Data Extraction from Quiz in Moodle

Long-Term Memory (LTM): LTM involves storing information over long periods. Accuracy is measured as:

$$\text{Accuracy}_{\text{LTM}} = \frac{\text{Number of correctly recalled items after delay}}{\text{Total number of items presented initially}} \times 100\% \quad (2)$$

5.2 Visual Processing (VP)

Visual processing involves perceiving, storing, and retrieving visual information. Accuracy is assessed by comparing responses to the original content. Speed of visual processing is calculated as:

$$\text{VP}_{\text{time}} = \frac{\text{Total time taken to navigate and comprehend content}}{\text{Total number of stimuli presented}} \quad (3)$$

5.3 Processing Speed (PS)

Processing speed refers to the rate of task completion. It is measured by:

$$\text{Task Completion Rate (PS)} = \frac{1}{\text{Time taken for the task}} \quad (4)$$

5.4 Attention Score (AS)

The attention score reflects focus and engagement, combining processing speed, short-term memory, and task completion status:

$$AS = \frac{PS + STM + CS}{3} \quad (5)$$

Here, CS denotes completion status (1 for completed tasks, 0 for non-completed tasks).

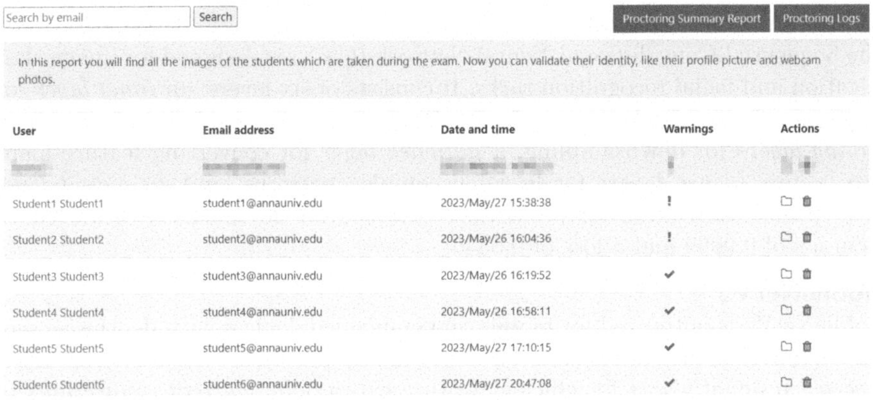

Fig. 4. A snippet of Data Extraction from Proctoring Module in Moodle

5.5 Emotion (E)

In a virtual learning platform, where learners may feel isolated or detached from instructors and peers, managing emotions becomes particularly important. Emotions are assigned weights based on their impact, as shown Table 1:

Table 1. Weightage Assigned to Different Emotions

Emotion (E)	Anger	Disgust	Fear	Happiness	Sadness	Surprise	Neutral
Weight	0.2	0.1	0.3	0.4	0.2	0.1	0

5.6 Multimodal Computational Score (Y)

The Multimodal Computational Score integrates cognitive and affective data:

$$Y = \beta_1[\text{Accuracy}_{\text{STM}}] + \beta_2[\text{Accuracy}_{\text{LTM}}] + \beta_3[\text{VP}_{\text{time}}] + \beta_4[\text{PS}] + \beta_5[AS] + \beta_6[E] \quad (6)$$

Here, $\beta_1, \beta_2, \beta_3, \beta_4, \beta_5, \beta_6$ are coefficients reflecting the importance of each variable in calculating Y. This approach combines cognitive and emotional aspects to provide a comprehensive assessment of learner performance.

6 Fine Tuned FER Model Selection

The deep learning CNNs, have significant contribution to develop the models for FER. In the proposed work, we explore the FER with a benchmark dataset and three different deep learning model architectures: Sequential, MobileNetV2 and VGG16, as discussed below:

Sequential CNN Model

The Sequential Convolutional Neural Network (CNN) is designed for image classification and facial recognition tasks. It consists of six layers: an *input layer* for image input, *convolutional layers* with ReLU activation for feature extraction, *pooling layers* for downsampling, a *flattened layer* for converting feature maps into vectors, *dense layers* for learning complex patterns, and an *output layer* with softmax activation for predictions. Trained for 20 epochs, it achieved an accuracy of 0.9899 and a loss of 0.0346.

MobileNetV2

MobileNetV2 is optimized for mobile and embedded devices with depthwise separable convolutions. It features an *input layer*, an *initial convolutional layer*, *inverted residual blocks* for efficient feature extraction, *shortcut connections* to enhance gradient flow, a *final convolutional layer*, *global average pooling*, and a *fully connected layer* for classification. After 20 epochs, it reached an accuracy of 0.9922 and a loss of 0.0282.

VGG-16

The VGG-16 model has 16 weight layers, including 13 convolutional layers and 3 fully connected layers. It starts with an *input layer*, followed by convolutional layers with ReLU activation, max-pooling layers for dimensionality reduction, and fully connected layers with dropout for regularization. The final layer uses softmax for multi-class classification. Trained on the dataset, it achieved an accuracy of 0.9427 and a loss of 0.1436.

Choosing the model depends on application needs: the Sequential model offers flexibility but may require more resources; MobileNetV2 is efficient for constrained devices; VGG16 provides high accuracy but needs more computational power.

7 Results

In this section, the results of the study on emotion recognition using various deep learning models are presented. The section begins by description of the dataset, followed by the explanation of the models selected for this task, including a sequential CNN model and two pre-trained models: VGG16 and MobileNetV2. Next, a comparative analysis of the proposed method against state-of-the-art methods is presented, highlighting the performance of different techniques based on accuracy metrics.

Table 2. Distribution of Emotion Class within the Dataset

	anger	disgust	fear	happiness	sadness	surprise	neutral
train	3995	436	4097	7215	4830	3171	4965
test	958	111	1024	1774	1247	831	1233

Table 3. Analysis of pre-trained CNN models for Emotion Recognition

	Sequential	MobilenetV2	VGG16
Training accuracy	0.6950	0.8818	0.9728
Training loss	0.8217	0.3465	0.5569
Validation accuracy	61.38	61.67	0.9022
Validation loss	1.0324	1.6659	1.4281
Learning rate	5.0000×10^{-5}	4.0000×10^{-5}	2.5000×10^{-5}

7.1 Dataset

In this work, *FER2013* , a widely used benchmark dataset is used. It consists of 35,887 grayscale images with 48×48 pixels.

The dataset includes 28,709 samples in the training set, 3,589 samples in the testing set, and an additional 3,589 samples in the validation test set. The dataset is categorised into seven emotional classes: anger, disgust, fear, happiness, sadness, surprise, and neutral. The distribution of each category within the dataset is as shown in the Table 2.

7.2 Model Selection for Emotion Recognition

In this paper a sequential CNN model and two pre-trained models, VGG16 and MobileNetV2, are used to select the most appropriate model for the study.

Transfer learning leverages the learned features and representations from a pre-trained model to overcome the limitations of limited labeled data and reduce training time and resources. This approach allows us to adapt the model to the specific task by fine-tuning the model's parameters or adding additional layers, thereby improving the accuracy and performance of the facial emotion recognition model.

Loading the Pre-trained Model: We start by loading the pre-trained VGG-16 model, including its layers and weights. The VGG-16 model, originally designed for ImageNet classification, provides rich feature representations from a large-scale dataset.

Modifying the Model: The last fully connected layer of VGG-16, which is designed for ImageNet classification, is removed. This allows us to replace it with our own classification layer for emotion recognition. A new fully connected layer is added to take the output of the previous layer and map it to the number of emotion categories we want to classify.

Freezing Pre-trained Layers: The weights of the pre-trained layers are frozen to prevent them from being updated during training. This helps retain the learned feature representations from VGG-16.

Compiling the Model: The model is compiled by specifying the loss function as "categorical cross-entropy" and the optimizer as "Adam".

Training the Model: The model is trained using the labeled dataset with a batch size of 64 and a learning rate of 0.0001. In training on FER2013, the official training, validation, and test sets as established by ICML (International Conference on Machine Learning) are adhered to. This split ensures a sufficient amount of data for both training the model and evaluating its performance on unseen data. The number of epochs is initially set to 100. However, due to early stopping, the training process stopped at 57 epochs.

Table 3 shows the results of the comparative analysis of these models. As seen from the table, VGG16 shows a better results with respect to its training and validation accuracy. Henceforth, VGG16 is selected as the main design model for the emotion detection of the images from proctoring module.

Saving the Trained Model: The trained and the selected model is saved for future use, where it can be employed to predict the emotion of the learner.

7.3 Comparison with State-of-the-Art Methods

In this section, the proposed method is compared with state-of-the-art methods in emotion recognition. Table 4 provides a summary of the different techniques and their respective performance metric, accuracy.

Table 4. Comparison of State-of-the-Art Methods in Emotion Recognition

Author & Year	Method	Accuracy
Bahreini et al., 2016 [4]	Face and voice modules	0.72
Agrawal and Mittal, 2019 [2]	CNN - various kernel sizes and filters	0.65
Megahed et al., 2020 [15]	CNNs, fuzzy systems	0.67
Swada Gupta et al., 2023 [8]	Inception-V3, VGG19, and ResNet-50	0.89, 0.901, 0.923
Sharma et al., 2019 [19]	Transfer learning, VGG16	0.90
Mukhopadhyay et al., 2020 [16]	Continuous frame analysis with CNN	0.65
Li et al., 2021 [13]	Multitask cascaded CNN, Temporal Relational Networks (TRN)	0.66
Pise et al., 2022 [17]	Multi-scale Temporal Relational Network (TRN)	0.927
Khaireddin et al., 2021 [10]	VGGNet	0.732
Proposed work	VGG16	0.972

The comparison reveals that the proposed method achieves competitive accuracy compared to existing methods. Specifically, advanced deep learning models such as Inception-V3, VGG19, and ResNet-50 demonstrate good performance in emotion recognition tasks. This comparison highlights the effectiveness of modern deep learning techniques and sets a benchmark for evaluating the emotion of an individual.

7.4 Performance Evaluation of the Selected Deep Learning Model

The VGG16 model demonstrates comparatively good performance in classifying the emotion recognition data. The performance of the model is evaluated, and the results are summarized in Table 5.

Table 5. Evaluation Metrics for the Task Performance

Metrics	Training Data	Validation Data
Loss	0.331	1.428
Accuracy	0.977	0.902
Precision	0.931	0.666
Recall	0.907	0.633
AUC	0.994	0.902
F1 Score	0.919	0.651

Figure 5 presents the visualization of the performance metrics for the VGG16 model. Both training and validation losses are relatively low, indicating effective learning without significant overfitting. The model achieves high accuracy on both the training and validation sets, demonstrating its ability to classify most samples correctly.

However, while precision is high on the training set, it decreases on the validation set, suggesting an increase in the false positive rate. Similarly, recall is higher on the training set, indicating better capture of true positives during training. The model exhibits high AUC scores on both sets, reflecting strong discrimination between positive and negative samples. The F1 score is high on the training set but decreases on the validation set, suggesting a trade-off between precision and recall.

Overall, the VGG16 model performs well; however, the disparities in performance between the training and validation sets indicate overfitting. To address this, hyperparameter tuning may be applied to improve the model's generalization.

8 Discussions

The paper discusses the selection of a deep learning-based model for emotion recognition in a learner's cognitive and emotional constructs through a Virtual Learning Environment (VLE). The model is developed using transfer learning techniques and is used to evaluate the learner's performance in a virtual learning task. The study includes two main parts: a mathematical model for cognitive evaluation and a deep learning model for emotion recognition. The proposed system would be used in future to assess a learner's multi-modal performance in terms of memory, visual processing, processing speed, attention score, and emotion. In such scenario, the system provides information about learners' emotional health and the cognitive elements that need further support. The paper proposes a novel strategy to customize LMS platforms for emotion and cognition-based evaluation, that enhances the effectiveness of online education. The objectives include a multi-modal system design, FER model selection, and a mathematical framework for assessing cognition and emotion from data extracted with the LMS.

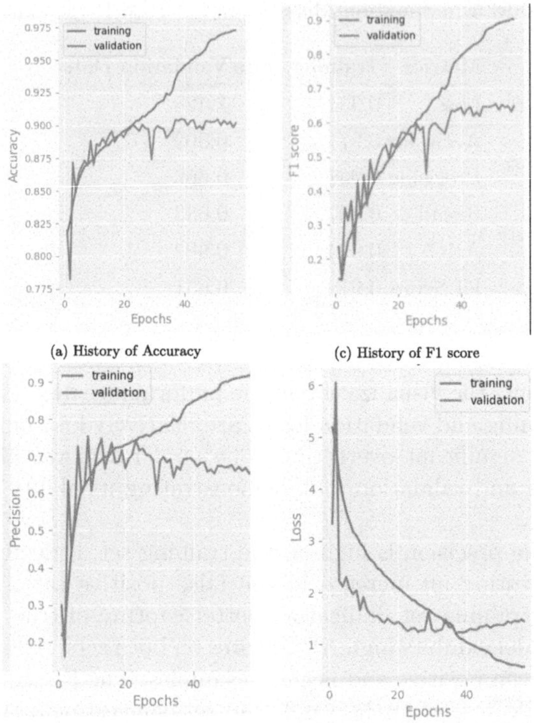

(a) History of Accuracy

(c) History of F1 score

(b) History of Precision

(d) History of Loss

Fig. 5. Visualization of Performance Metrics for VGG16

References

1. Acampora, G., Gaeta, M., Loia, V.: Hierarchical optimization of personalized experiences for e-learning systems through evolutionary models. Neural Comput. Appl. **20**, 641–657 (2011)
2. Agrawal, A., Mittal, N.: Using CNN for facial expression recognition: a study of the effects of kernel size and number of filters on accuracy. Vis. Comput. **36**(2), 405–412 (2020)
3. Ayvaz, U., Gürüler, H., Devrim, M.O.: Use of facial emotion recognition in e-learning systems (2017)
4. Bahreini, K., Nadolski, R., Westera, W.: Towards multimodal emotion recognition in e-learning environments. Interact. Learn. Environ. **24**(3), 590–605 (2016)
5. Caemmerer, J.M., Keith, T.Z., Reynolds, M.R.: Beyond individual intelligence tests: application of Cattell-Horn-Carroll theory. Intelligence **79**, 101433 (2020)
6. Chen, C.M.: Intelligent web-based learning system with personalized learning path guidance. Comput. Educ. **51**(2), 787–814 (2008)
7. Darejeh, A., Mashayekh, S., Marcus, N.: Cognitive-based methods to facilitate learning of software applications via e-learning systems. Cogent Educ. **9**(1), 2082085 (2022)

8. Gupta, S., Kumar, P., Tekchandani, R.K.: Facial emotion recognition based real-time learner engagement detection system in online learning context using deep learning models. Multimedia Tools Appl. **82**(8), 11365–11394 (2023)
9. Imani, M., Montazer, G.A.: A survey of emotion recognition methods with emphasis on e-learning environments. J. Netw. Comput. Appl. **147**, 102423 (2019)
10. Khaireddin, Y., Chen, Z.: Facial emotion recognition: state of the art performance on FER2013. arXiv preprint arXiv:2105.03588 (2021)
11. Khattak, A., Asghar, M.Z., Ali, M., Batool, U.: An efficient deep learning technique for facial emotion recognition. Multimedia Tools Appl. **81**(2), 1649–1683 (2022)
12. Kort, B., Reilly, R., Picard, R.W.: External representation of learning process and domain knowledge: affective state as a determinate of its structure and function. In: Workshop on Artificial Intelligence in Education (AI-ED 2001), San Antonio, May 2001, pp. 64–69 (2001)
13. Li, X., Yue, R., Jia, W., Wang, H., Zheng, Y.: Recognizing students' emotions based on facial expression analysis. In: 2021 11th International Conference on Information Technology in Medicine and Education (ITME), pp. 96–100. IEEE (2021)
14. Martin, E., Carro, R.M.: Supporting the development of mobile adaptive learning environments: a case study. IEEE Trans. Learn. Technol. **2**(1), 23–36 (2009)
15. Megahed, M., Mohammed, A.: Modeling adaptive e-learning environment using facial expressions and fuzzy logic. Expert Syst. Appl. **157**, 113460 (2020)
16. Mukhopadhyay, M., Pal, S., Nayyar, A., Pramanik, P.K.D., Dasgupta, N., Choudhury, P.: Facial emotion detection to assess learner's state of mind in an online learning system. In: Proceedings of the 2020 5th International Conference on Intelligent Information Technology, pp. 107–115 (2020)
17. Pise, A., Vadapalli, H., Sanders, I.: Facial emotion recognition using temporal relational network: an application to e-learning. Multimedia Tools Appl. **81**(19), 26633–26653 (2022)
18. Seli, P., Wammes, J.D., Risko, E.F., Smilek, D.: On the relation between motivation and retention in educational contexts: the role of intentional and unintentional mind wandering. Psychon. Bull. Rev. **23**, 1280–1287 (2016)
19. Sharma, A., Mansotra, V.: Deep learning based student emotion recognition from facial expressions in classrooms. Int. J. Eng. Adv. Technol. **8**(6), 4691–4699 (2019)
20. Sun, A., Li, Y.-J., Huang, Y.-M., Li, Q.: Using facial expression to detect emotion in E-learning system: a deep learning method. In: Huang, T.-C., Lau, R., Huang, Y.-M., Spaniol, M., Yuen, C.-H. (eds.) SETE 2017. LNCS, vol. 10676, pp. 446–455. Springer, Cham (2017). https://doi.org/10.1007/978-3-319-71084-6_52
21. Teo, C.B., Gay, R.K.L.: A knowledge-driven model to personalize e-learning. J. Educ. Resources Comput. (JERIC) **6**(1), 3–es (2006)
22. Thankachan, J.A., Srinivasan, B.: A machine learning approach to analyze and predict the factors in education system: case study of India. In: Kumar, S., Purohit, S.D., Hiranwal, S., Prasad, M. (eds.) Proceedings of International Conference on Communication and Computational Technologies. AIS, pp. 619–634. Springer, Singapore (2021). https://doi.org/10.1007/978-981-16-3246-4_48
23. Thankachan, J.A., Srinivasan, B.: A mathematical formulation of learner cognition for personalised learning experiences. Cogn. Syst. Res. **88**, 101283 (2024)
24. Tyng, C.M., Amin, H.U., Saad, M.N., Malik, A.S.: The influences of emotion on learning and memory. Front. Psychol., 1454 (2017)
25. Wang, M., Kang, M.: Cybergogy for engaged learning: a framework for creating learner engagement through information and communication technology. Engaged Learn. Emerging Technol., 225–253 (2006)

Can Defence Mechanisms Restore Interpretability in an Adversarial Setting?

Naveen Radhakrishnan[1], Snofy D. Dunston[1], and V. Mary Anita Rajam[2(✉)]

[1] Department of Computer Science and Engineering, College of Engineering Guindy, Anna University, Chennai, India

[2] Centre for Cyber Security, Department of Computer Science and Engineering, College of Engineering Guindy, Anna University, Chennai, India

anitav@annauniv.edu

Abstract. In this study, we center our focus on how interpretability works in the presence and absence of defence mechanisms for adversarial attacks. We scrutinise the susceptibility of medical image classification models to adversarial attacks, specifically honing in on the Adversarial Imperceptible Patch Attack. By employing the GradientSHAP method, we delve into the vulnerabilities of the VGG16 model trained on SARS-CoV-2 CT-scan and Malaria Cell Image datasets, seeking to understand how it responds to adversarial perturbations. Additionally, we explore defensive mechanisms such as adversarial training and denoise filtering to mitigate the impact of these attacks. We study how interpretability using GradientSHAP varies after the attack and how it varies again after the defence mechanisms are employed. Our work deepens stakeholder understanding of AI diagnostic risks, strengthens model resilience, and promotes confidence in healthcare integration.

Keywords: GradientSHAP · Convolutional Neural Network · Projected Gradient Descent · Adversarial Imperceptible Patch Attack · Adversarial Training · Denoising Filters

1 Introduction

Traditional medical image diagnosis relies on manual processes, prone to human error. However, the emergence of Deep Learning has offered a robust solution for visual analysis, effectively managing vast data volumes. Incorporating automated systems driven by artificial intelligence enhances diagnostic precision and workflow efficiency. Among the prominent architectures for medical image analysis, Convolutional Neural Networks (CNNs) stand out. Architectures such as VGG [1], EfficientNet [2], and ResNet [3] have revolutionised tasks like lesion detection [4], tumor classification [5], and organ segmentation [6], significantly advancing the field.

However, these CNN architectures are vulnerable to adversarial attacks [7], which are deliberate alterations to input data designed to deceive models into

J. Kakarla et al. (Eds.): CVIP 2024, CCIS 2473, pp. 204–219, 2026.
https://doi.org/10.1007/978-3-031-93688-3_15

incorrect predictions. While imperceptible to humans, these perturbations significantly impact performance. Various attack methods include optimisation-based attacks like Projected Gradient Descent (PGD) [8], gradient-based approaches like the Fast Gradient Sign Method (FGSM) [9], and iterative techniques such as the Iterative Least-Likely Class method. Other methods include Carlini and Wagner (C&W) attack [11] and Deep Fool [10]. Another form of attack involves targeting only specific patches within an image. Adversarial patch attacks like Adversarial Imperceptible Patch Attack (AIPA) [12] and Threatening Patch Attack (TPA) [13] manipulate small areas of an image to mislead classification models, potentially undermining their performance without human detection.

To thwart adversarial attacks, various defence mechanisms exist. These include adversarial training [14], which involves training models with adversarial examples to improve robustness; use of denoising filters [15], which preprocess input data to remove adversarial perturbations before model inference; gradient masking [16], which conceals gradient information to prevent attackers from crafting effective adversarial examples; ensemble methods [18], which combine predictions from multiple models to enhance resilience against adversarial inputs; and defensive distillation [17], a method of training models to be less sensitive to small changes in input data.

Interpretability techniques in machine learning aim to provide insights into how models make predictions, enhancing transparency and trustworthiness. These techniques include feature attribution methods, such as gradient-based methods like Integrated Gradients [19] and perturbation-based methods like LIME [20], which assign importance scores to input features. Model-specific interpretation approaches, such as decision tree visualisation for tree-based models, and global interpretation techniques like SHAP (SHapley Additive exPlanations) [21], offer broader insights into model behavior. These techniques enable practitioners to understand model decisions, identify biases, and debug erroneous predictions, fostering better decision-making and model improvement.

However, interpretability of neural networks also have been found to be inconsistent in the presence of adversarial attacks [12]. This motivates us to study how interpretability works before and after adversarial attacks, and before and after employing defence mechanisms for adversarial attacks. In this work, we study the interpretability plots generated using GradientSHAP before adversarial attack, after attack and after employing defence mechanisms. We employ a patch attack, AIPA, which uses PGD on VGG model trained on the SARS-CoV-2 CT-scan dataset and the Malaria Cell Image dataset. We use adversarial training and denoising filter (Gaussian filter) as defense mechanisms.

Our research findings indicate that the AIPA attack interchanges the interpretation of positive and negative samples. This challenge can be seen to be mitigated through the implementation of adversarial training and denoising filters, ensuring that post-defence interpretations align with those prior to the attack.

To summarise, these are our key contributions:

1. Conduct a thorough analysis of the performance of AIPA attacks on the VGG16 model trained using both the SARS-CoV-2 CT-scan dataset and the Malaria Cell Image dataset.
2. Implement defensive strategies, specifically adversarial training and denoising filters, to mitigate the impact of these attacks.
3. Gain insights into model interpretability by assessing it before and after the attack, post-denoising, and post-adversarial training using the GradientSHAP method.

The rest of the paper is organised as follows: Sect. 2 explains the methodology used in the current work, Sect. 3 describes the experimental setup, Sect. 4 handles with results and discussions, and Sect. 5 deals with the conclusion.

2 Materials and Methods

In this section, we briefly describe the models and methods used in this study.

2.1 Adversarial Attacks Studied

Project Gradient Descent iteratively adjusts input data within an L_P Norm ball, striving to identify the nearest boundary. By confining the perturbations within a predefined range, PGD aims to maximise the model's loss function while minimising noticeable alterations to the input.

Adversarial Imperceptible Patch Attack utilises a small patch of noise, selecting its size and position in insignificant areas like image borders. The process is as follows: adversarial noise is initially generated using PGD attack across the entire image. Subsequently, a smaller rectangular patch is extracted from the resulting noisy image. This extracted noise patch is then added to the original image, synthesizing the AIPA image.

2.2 Deep Neural Network (DNN) Classifier Used

The experimental DNN model is based on a modified VGG16 architecture pre-trained on ImageNet, where layers 20 to 31 of the original 31 layers are trainable. Customized fully connected layers follow this modification: 25088 input features to 2048 hidden units, a dropout layer with dropout probability of 0.60, and a final layer with 2048 input units and 2 outputs using Sigmoid activation.

2.3 Interpretability

In this study, interpretability method GradientSHAP (SHapley Additive exPlanations) is explored using the Captum library [22], specifically designed for understanding neural network decisions. GradientSHAP assesses how changes in input features impact the model's output. GradientSHAP considers a range of points between a baseline input and the actual input, representing various feature combinations. It then computes the average of these gradients, weighted by Shapley values, indicating each feature's incremental contribution to the model's prediction.

2.4 Defence Mechanisms Studied

Adversarial Training. During adversarial training, the DNN model specified in Sect. 2.2 is exposed to both the original and perturbed samples (using AIPA), forcing it to learn to make accurate predictions while also being resilient to small changes in the input data. By repeatedly training on perturbed examples, the model becomes more adept at generalising to unseen data and more resistant to adversarial attacks during inference.

Denoising Filter. This involves preprocessing input data to remove adversarial perturbations before feeding it into the model for inference. By applying denoising filters, such as Gaussian filter, median filter, or wavelet transforms, perturbations introduced by adversaries can be effectively suppressed, while preserving the original features of the input data. The denoising filter operates as follows: augment the unperturbed training dataset with a Gaussian filter. The standard deviation of the Gaussian blur varies randomly across training samples; for instance, some images may be maximally blurred while others remain unblurred. Once the model training is completed, it encounters the testing set. Before model inference, the images are preprocessed by a Gaussian filter with a fixed standard deviation, and then predictions are made.

2.5 Dataset Description

SARS-CoV-2 CT-Scan Dataset. The dataset of SARS-CoV-2 CT-scan [23] comprises 2,481 images, with a near equal distribution of COVID-positive and COVID-negative images. For this study, we split the dataset in the ratio of 80:20, a training set containing 1,984 images and a test set containing 497 images, with an even distribution of images across the two classes in each set. Figure 1 represents negative and positive covid lungs. In COVID-positive lungs, distinct features such as a ground glass pattern, a gray, foggy region on the lungs, and thickening of interlobular and intralobular lines are observable [24]. Conversely, in COVID-negative lungs, the ground glass pattern is absent, and the interlobular and intralobular lines appear thinner.

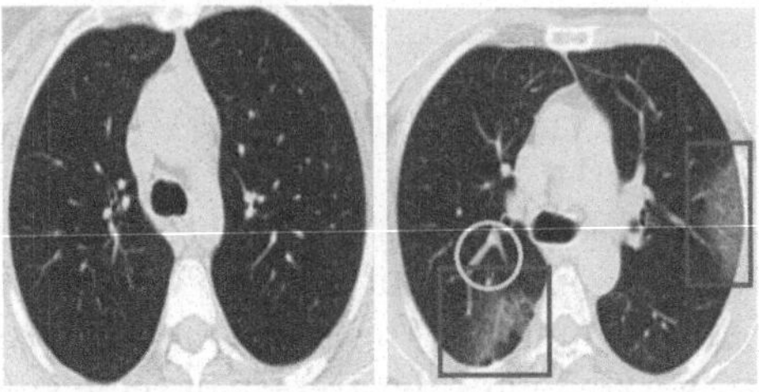

Fig. 1. The left image is COVID-negative, while the right image is COVID-positive. The red boxes highlight the ground glass pattern and yellow circle highlights the thickening of interlobular and intralobular lines, which are common COVID-positive symptoms. (Color figure online)

Malarial Cell Image Dataset. The dataset of Malarial Cell Images [25] comprises 27,558 cell images, with an equal distribution of parasitised and uninfected cells. Parasitised samples contain Plasmodium falciparum, while uninfected cells do not contain Plasmodium but may include staining artifacts or impurities. In our study, we split the dataset in the ratio of 75:25, a training set containing 20,668 images and a test set containing 6,890 images, with an even distribution of images across the two classes in each set. Figure 2 represents both uninfected and parasitised Malaria samples.

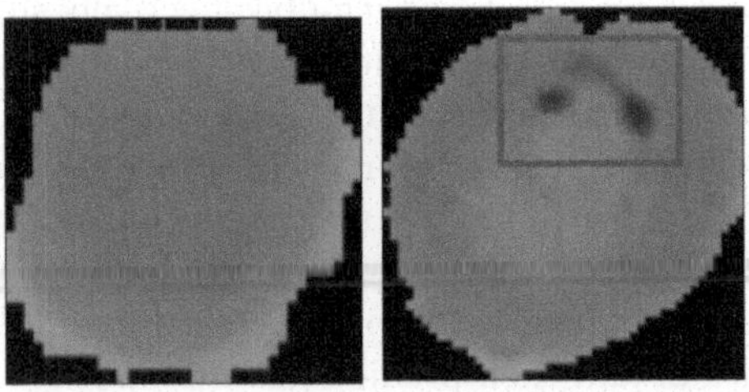

Fig. 2. The left image is uninfected, while the right image is parasitised. The red box highlights the infection. (Color figure online)

3 Experimental Setup

3.1 Training Details

The modified VGG16 model comprises 20 to 31 trainable layers, with a CrossEntropy loss function. Stochastic Gradient Descent (SGD) is utilised as the optimisation algorithm with a learning rate of 0.001 and a momentum value of 0.9. A learning rate scheduler is implemented with a step size of 7 and a decay factor (gamma) of 0.1. Training is conducted over 15 epochs with a batch size of 64.

3.2 Attack Details

The underlying attack used for this study is PGD, the criterion utilised for optimisation is Cross Entropy. The process involves a specified number of steps, with 10 steps allocated for addressing SARS-CoV-2 CT-scan dataset and 30 steps for tackling Malarial Cell Image dataset. Each step is taken with a fixed step size of 0.01. Additionally, two distinct epsilon values are employed, with 0.01 designated for SARS-CoV-2 CT-scan dataset and 0.015 for Malaria Cell Image dataset. The epsilon norm utilised is L_∞, indicating the maximum absolute value among the components of the vector, while the step norm also follows L_∞, implying that the maximum absolute value among the step components determines the step size.

In AIPA, we extract a portion of the PGD noise from the bottom and right sides. For the SARS-CoV-2 CT-scan dataset, we select a bottom strip that is 24 pixels high from the bottom edge and extends across the entire width of the image. For the right-hand strip, we choose a strip that is 24 pixels wide from the right edge and spans the entire height of the image. However, for the Malaria dataset, these dimensions are changed to 34 pixels due to the presence of a black border around the cell.

3.3 Interpretation Details

We use GradientSHAP for interpretations, we pass the input image and the predictions given by the model for that image. We also set the number of samples used to approximate the integral when computing the Shapley values to 50, the standard deviation for the noise added to the input samples during the estimation process to 0.0001, for stabilising the computation. For the baseline distribution, we set the range to be between black grayscale and the original image.

3.4 Defence Mechanism Details

Adversarial training follows a straightforward process: first, the dataset is divided into training and testing sets. Then, for each image in the training set, an AIPA image is generated and added back into the training set, effectively doubling its size. Once this augmentation step is completed, the model is trained using the expanded training set. For the denoising filter, we employ the Gaussian Filter provided by PyTorch's torchvision library, specifically GaussianBlur, with a kernel size of 5×5. During training, the sigma parameter is randomly selected from a range of values between 0.0001 and 2.0. We found these values for sigma to give the best result. This variation in sigma values introduces diverse levels of blur to the images, enhancing the model's robustness. In contrast, during testing, the sigma value is fixed at 1.0. This ensures consistent blurring applied to the test images, facilitating fair evaluation of the model's performance.

4 Results and Discussion

4.1 Performance Evaluation

In this study, the performance evaluation metrics include classification accuracy, precision, recall, and F1-score. These metrics rely on the values of True Positive (TP), True Negative (TN), False Positive (FP), and False Negative (FN) for calculation purposes.

In the SARS-CoV-2 CT-scan dataset, True positive denotes an image correctly classified as "COVID-positive" when the true label is also "COVID-positive". True negative signifies an image correctly classified as "COVID-negative" when the true label is also "COVID-negative".

In the malaria dataset, True positive signifies an image correctly classified as "Parasitised" when the true label is also "Parasitised". True negative denotes an image correctly classified as "Uninfected" when the true label is also "Uninfected".

Table 1. Performance for SARS-CoV-2 CT-scan Dataset

	TP	TN	FP	FN	Precision	Recall	F1-Score	Accuracy
Before AIPA Attack	242	228	14	13	95%	95%	95%	95%
After AIPA Attack	132	159	124	82	59%	59%	58%	59%
After Adversarial Training	501	475	11	7	98%	98%	98%	98%
After Filtering	235	210	21	31	90%	90%	90%	90%

4.2 SARS CoV 2 CT Scan Dataset

Table 1 presents the performance metrics before and after the AIPA attack, post-adversarial training, and post-filtering. It is evident that AIPA significantly reduces the accuracy from 95% to 59%. Adversarial training makes the model more robust and also improves the overall performance to 98%. Although Gaussian filtering provides good improvement, it is not as effective as adversarial training. Notably, the time required for adversarial training is nearly double that of Gaussian filtering. Additionally, false positives in the after-attack metrics indicate the model's tendency to incorrectly predict a COVID-negative sample as COVID-positive.

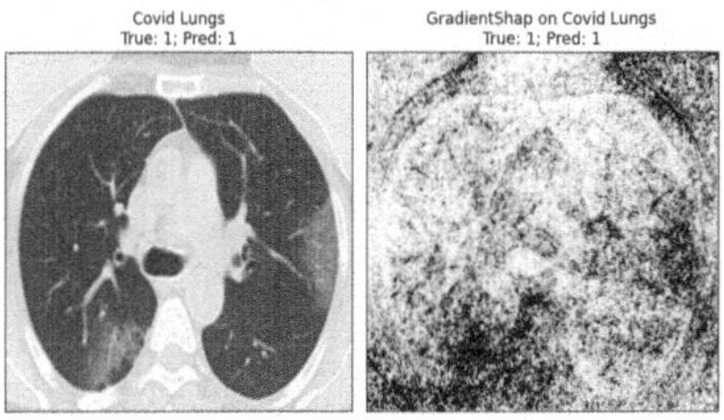

Fig. 3. COVID-positive lungs and its GrandientSHAP

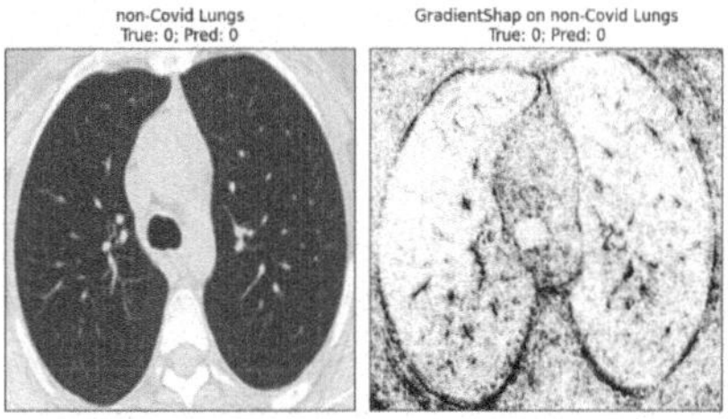

Fig. 4. COVID-negative lungs and its GrandientSHAP

Before Attack: Figure 3 illustrates lung images affected by COVID-19. The GradientShap visualisation reveals the model's focus, denoted by black points, primarily on the ground glass pattern present within the lungs. Additionally, it is evident that the lung boundaries lack clarity, with black points forming a large, dispersed cluster within the lung area. In contrast, Fig. 4 showcases lung image unaffected by COVID-19, where the lung boundaries are clearly defined and darker. Few dark points are observed within the majority of lungs, suggesting minimal attention. These findings suggest that the model emphasises the surrounding areas and borders of the lungs more prominently in COVID-negative cases.

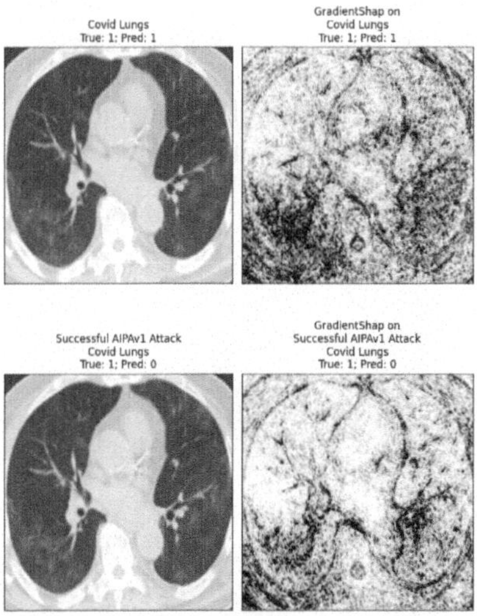

Fig. 5. Successful attack on COVID-positive lungs

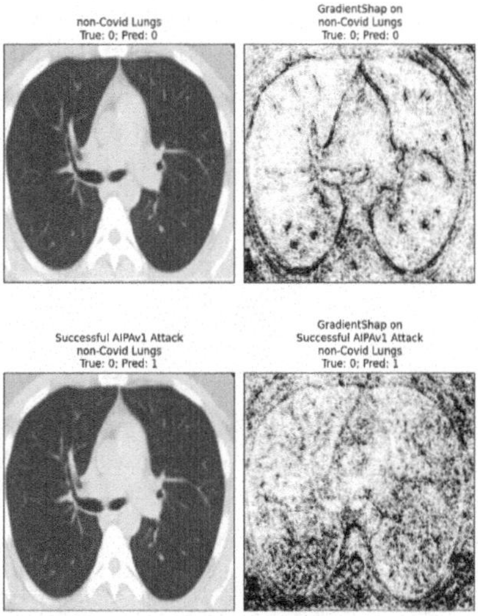

Fig. 6. Successful attack on COVID-negative lungs

After Attack: Figure 5 depicts a successful AIPA attack on COVID-positive lungs, where the first row represents the original image along with its GradientSHAP plot, and the second row represents the perturbed image and its GradientSHAP plot. Comparing the images we can infer that the presence of dark points within lungs have decreased significantly, and the borders of the lungs are very distinct after the attack. These after attack features are similar to COVID-negative lung features.

Figure 6 depicts a successful AIPA attack on COVID-negative lungs, where the first row represents the original image along with its GradientSHAP plot, and the second row represents the perturbed image and its GradientSHAP plot. Comparing the images we can infer that the presence of dark points within lungs have increased significantly, and the borders of the lungs are diminishing after the attack. These after attack features are similar to COVID-positive lung features.

Adversarial Training: In Fig. 7, the top row represents adversarial trained model interpretation on unperturbed COVID-positive lungs and bottom row represents adversarial trained model interpretation on perturbed COVID-positive lungs. We can notice that the interpretations are quite similar, except that the perturbed's SHAP image contains fewer black points than the unperturbed SHAP image. In Fig. 8, the top row represents adversarial trained model interpretation on unperturbed COVID-negative lungs and bottom row represents adversarial trained model interpretation on perturbed COVID-negative lungs. We can notice that the interpretations are quite similar, except that the perturbed's SHAP image contains more dark spots than the unperturbed SHAP image.

Comparing both images, we also notice that the model now becomes very selective in choosing what contributes to the predictions. This can be inferred by the amount of black points present in the GradientSHAP plots. The model with adversarial training works well although this process doubles the training time, and the overhead time required to generate adversarial samples for training.

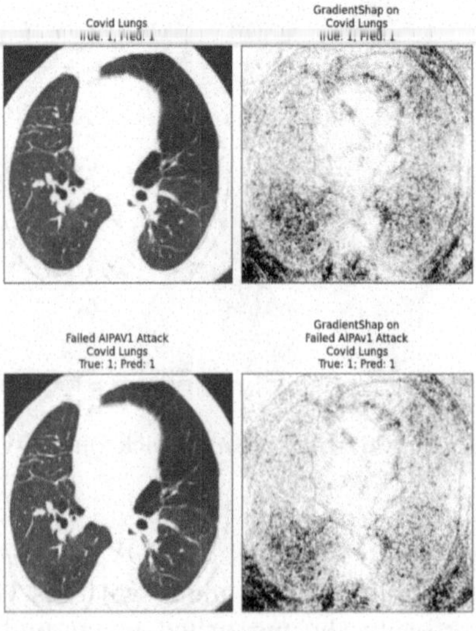

Fig. 7. Adversarial trained model predictions on COVID-positive lungs

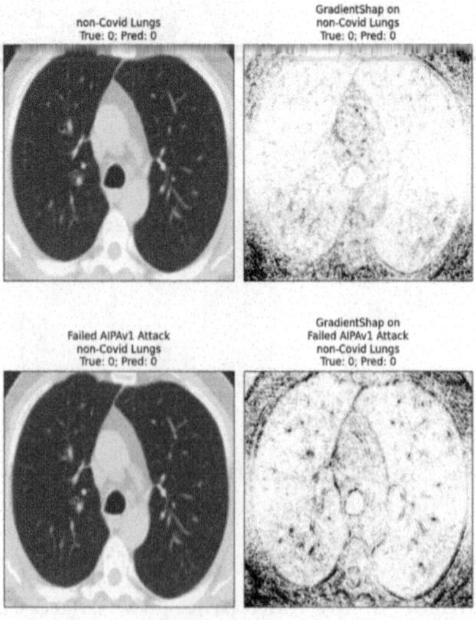

Fig. 8. Adversarial trained model predictions on COVID-negative lungs

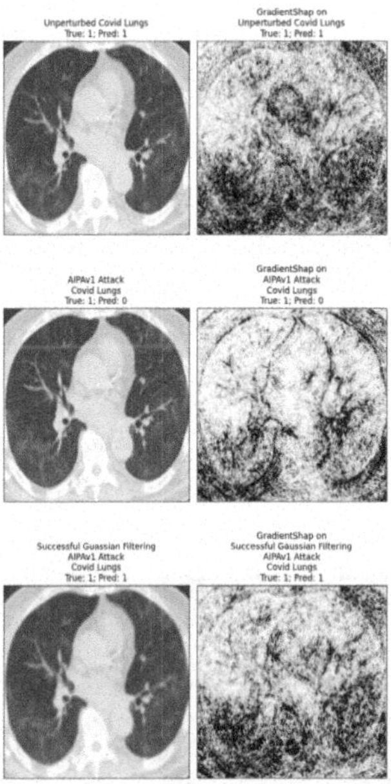

Fig. 9. Gaussian filtered predictions on COVID-positive lungs

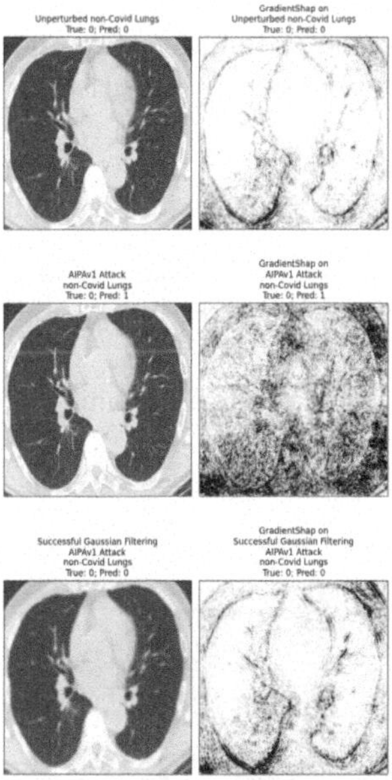

Fig. 10. Gaussian filtered predictions on COVID-negative lungs

Denoising Filters: Figure 9 represents Gaussian filters on COVID-positive lungs, the first row represents the original image, the second row represents the attacked image, and the third row represents Gaussian filtered image. We can see that the Gaussian filter is trying to revert the changes made by the attack. The attack tries to reduce the focus from the lungs and create strong boundaries, but this is nullified by the Gaussian filter in the third row. Figure 10, represents Gaussian filters on COVID-negative lungs, the first row represents the original image, the second row represents the attacked image, and the third row represents Gaussian filtered image. We can see that the Gaussian filter is trying to revert the changes made by the attack. The attack tries to bring in attention to the lungs and diminish the boundaries, but this is counteracted by the Gaussian filter in the third row.

4.3 Malaria Cell Image Dataset

Table 2 displays the performance metrics both pre and post-attack, following adversarial training, and after filtering. The AIPA technique notably diminishes the accuracy from 96% to 63%. However, the model's robustness significantly improves with adversarial training, elevating overall performance to 98%. Despite providing considerable enhancement, Gaussian filtering falls short compared to adversarial training. Remarkably, the time invested for adversarial training is nearly double that of Gaussian filtering. Moreover, false positives in the post-attack metrics underscore the model's tendency to erroneously classify uninfected samples as parasitised.

Table 2. Performance for Malaria Cell Image Dataset

	TP	TN	FP	FN	Precision	Recall	F1-Score	Accuracy
Before AIPA Attack	3316	3311	100	163	96%	96%	96%	96%
After AIPA Attack	1461	2866	1955	608	65%	63%	61%	63%
After Adversarial Training	6756	6739	76	214	98%	98%	98%	98%
After Filtering	3067	3219	349	255	91%	91%	91%	91%

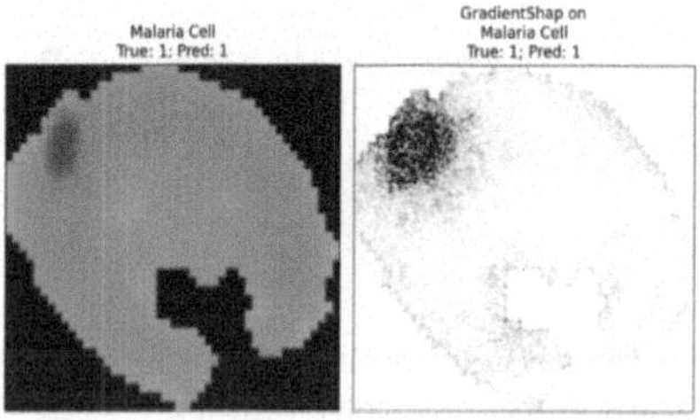

Fig. 11. Parasitised cell and its GradientSHAP

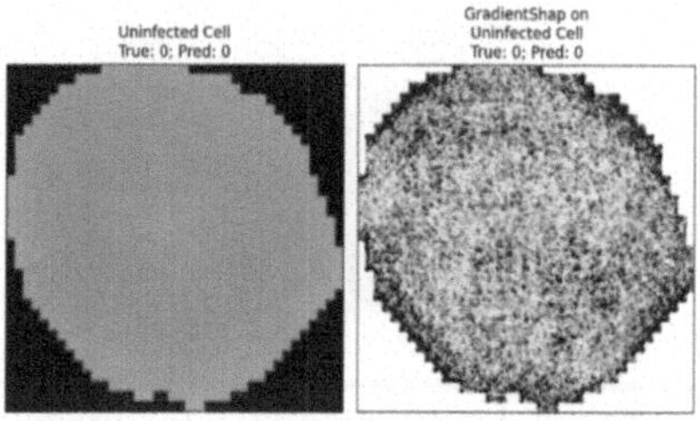

Fig. 12. Uninfected cell and its GradientSHAP

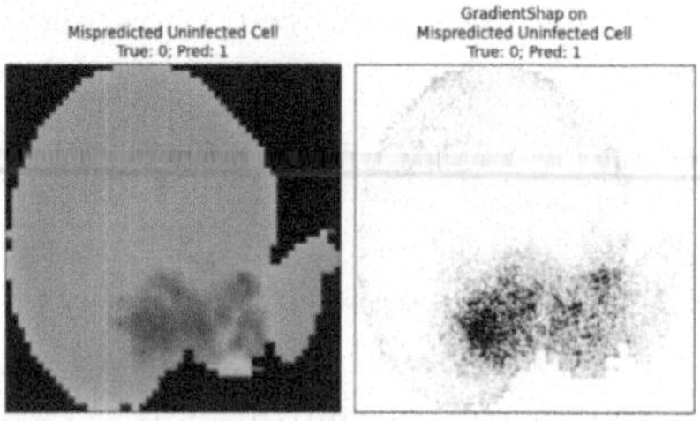

Fig. 13. Uninfected outlier and its GradientSHAP

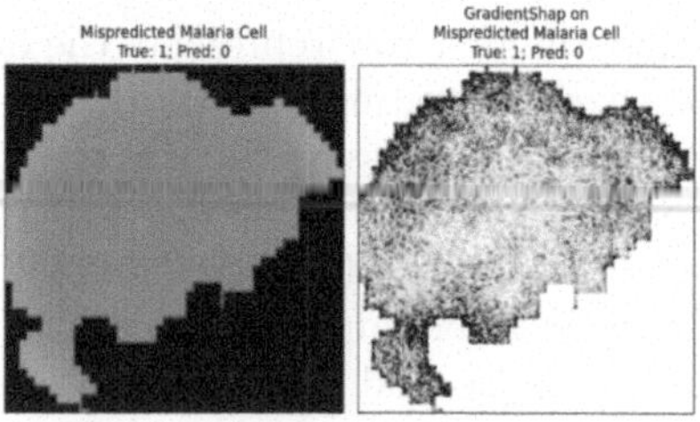

Fig. 14. Parasitised outlier and its GradientSHAP

Before Attack: Figure 11 illustrates a parasitised cell characterised by a dark spot. Conversely, the uninfected cell depicted in Fig. 12 lacks such a spot, with gradients dispersed throughout the cell instead of concentrated in one area. The dataset inherently contains outlier-like images that resemble the mispredicted class, making classification challenging. Despite the presence of a dark patch in Fig. 13, the true label indicates it as malaria uninfected. Similarly, in Fig. 14, there is no spot or patch, yet the true label indicates it as parasitised.

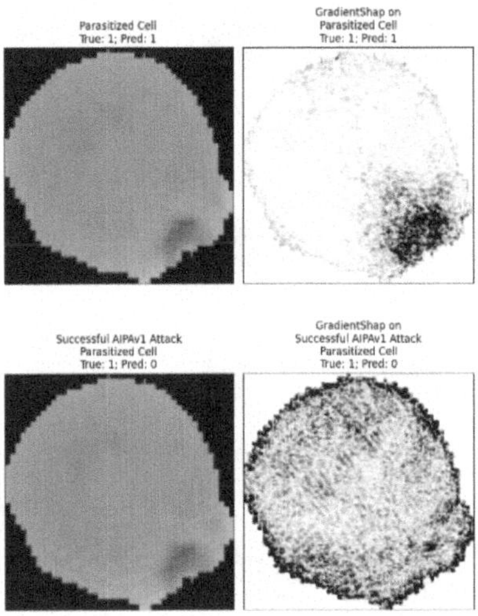

Fig. 15. Successful attack on parasitised cell and its GradientSHAP

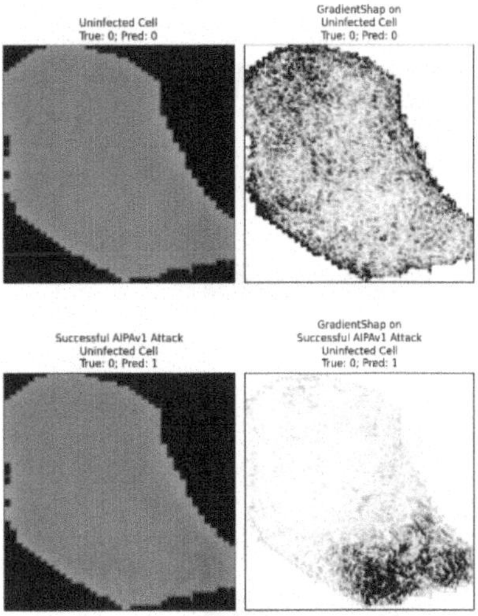

Fig. 16. Successful attack on uninfected cell and its GradientSHAP

After Attack: Figure 15 represents a parasitised case, the first row represents the original image and the second row represents the perturbed image. After the attack the model no longer focuses on the dark spot, but rather focuses on the entire cell. Figure 16 represents uninfected case, the first row represents the original image and the second row represents the perturbed image. After the attack the model no longer focuses on the entire cell, but rather focuses on the bottom right region of the cell. The attack transfers the attention from the dark spot to the entire cell in case of infected cell, or transfer the attention from the entire cell to one spot/region for uninfected cell.

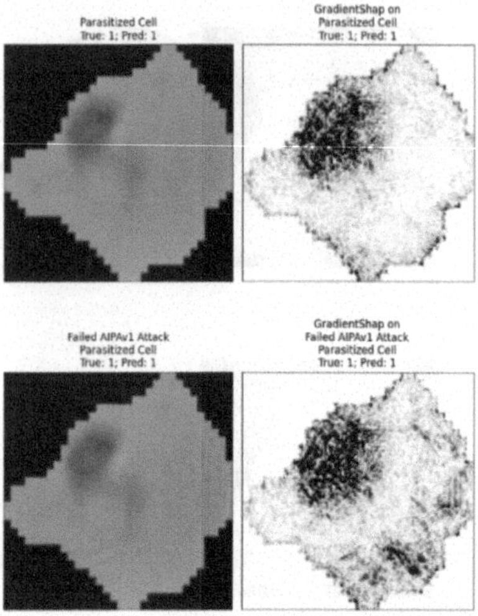

Fig. 17. Adversarial trained model prediction on parasitised cell

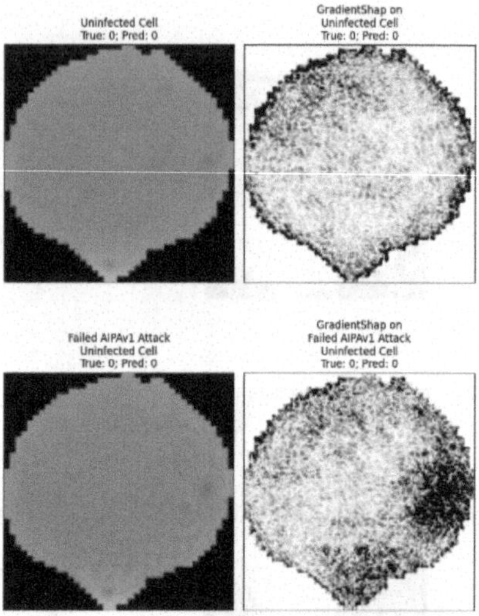

Fig. 18. Adversarial trained model prediction on uninfected cell

Adversarial Training: Figure 17 takes a parasitised case, the first row represents adversarial trained model interpretation on the original image, and second represents adversarial trained model interpretation on the perturbed image. We can infer that noise added tries to redistribute the attention, but fails. Although we can see some residue in the bottom right corner of the cell. Figure 18 takes an uninfected case, the first row represents adversarial trained model interpretation on the original image, and the second represents adversarial trained model interpretation on the perturbed image. Here we can see that noise tries to bring in the attention to the bottom of the cell, but the adversarial trained model gracefully ignores it.

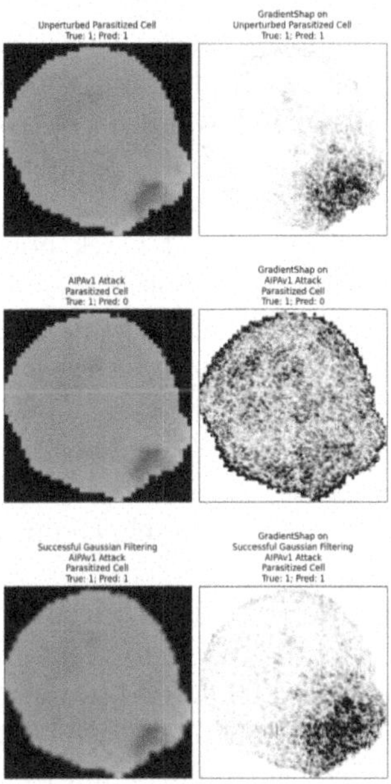

Fig. 19. Gaussian filtered predictions on parasitised cell

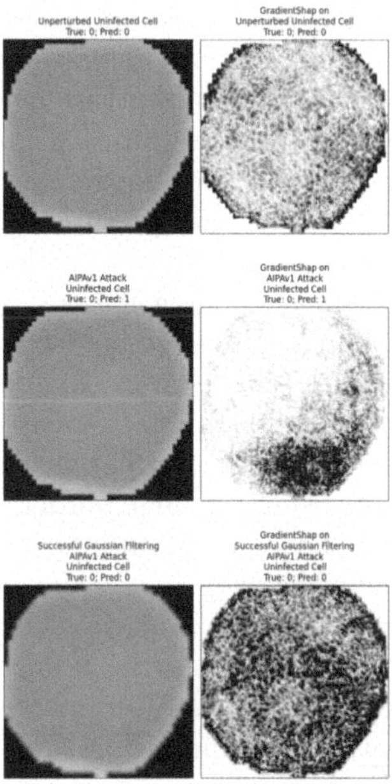

Fig. 20. Gaussian filtered predictions on uninfected cell

Denoising Filters: Figure 19 depicts an infected case, the first row represents the original image, the second row represents the attacked image, and the third row represents the Gaussian filtered image. We can see that the Gaussian filter is trying to revert the changes made by the attack. The attack tries to take away the attention from the dark patch and redistributes to the entire cell, but this is counteracted by the Gaussian filter as seen in the third row. The Gaussian filter successfully nullifies the distribution of black points caused by the attack to only focus on the dark spot. Figure 20 depicts an uninfected cell, the first row represents the original image, the second row represents the attacked image, and the third row represents Gaussian filtered image. We can see that the Gaussian filter is trying to revert the changes made by the attack. The attack tries to bring attention to the bottom of the cell, but this is counteracted by the Gaussian filter as seen in the third row. The Gaussian filter successfully redistributes the black points from the cluster caused by the attack.

5 Conclusions

The AIPA attack, though simple, is highly effective in deceiving the model. Even a small patch of imperceptible perturbation suffices to make consistent misprediction by the model. Adversarial training enhances model performance surpassing pre-attack metrics but comes with a trade off of higher time complexity. Conversely, denoising filters effectively restore model performance, although it does not exceed pre-attack metrics. Notably, the model's training time remains unaffected since the filtering process mimics a single convolution operation on the image, and does not require generating adversarial training samples.

In terms of interpretability for the SARS-CoV-2 CT-scan dataset, observations suggest that the model tends to predict clusters of black points over COVID-infected lung regions, alongside delineating dark boundaries for uninfected lungs. However, following the attack, the model shifts focus away from COVID-infected regions, highlighting lung boundaries for infected cases, and lung regions for uninfected cases. Adversarial training helps the model become selective, directing attention solely to lung regions in COVID-positive cases, while focusing on lung borders for COVID-negative cases. Employing denoising filter helps maintain interpretations akin to those pre-attack, confirming the efficacy of filtering.

Regarding the Malaria Cell Image dataset, interpretations unveil clustering around dark patches within infected cells, with no black points present elsewhere in the cell. Conversely, uninfected cells are uniformly highlighted by dark points. Post-attack interpretations for malaria-infected cells mirror those of uninfected cells, and vice versa. Adversarial training and denoising efforts aim to mitigate the impact of the attack by reversing its effects, as indicated by the similarity to the pre-attack interpretation.

Acknowledgements. This work was supported under the POWER Grant scheme by the Science and Engineering Research Board (SERB), Department of Science and Technology, Government of India [SPG/2021/000813].

References

1. Simonyan, K., Zisserman, A.: Very deep convolutional networks for large-scale image recognition. arXiv preprint arXiv:1409.1556 (2014)
2. Tan, M., Le, Q.: EfficientNet: rethinking model scaling for convolutional neural networks. In: International Conference on Machine Learning, pp. 6105–6114. PMLR (2019)
3. He, K., Zhang, X., Ren, S., Sun, J.: Deep residual learning for image recognition. In: Proceedings of the IEEE Conference on Computer Vision and Pattern Recognition, pp. 770–778 (2016)
4. Adegun, A., Viriri, S.: Deep learning techniques for skin lesion analysis and melanoma cancer detection: a survey of state-of-the-art. Artif. Intell. Rev. **54**(2), 811–841 (2021)
5. Amin, J., Sharif, M., Haldorai, A., Yasmin, M., Nayak, R.S.: Brain tumor detection and classification using machine learning: a comprehensive survey. Complex Intell. Syst. **8**(4), 3161–3183 (2022)
6. Fu, Y., Lei, Y., Wang, T., Curran, W.J., Liu, T., Yang, X.: A review of deep learning based methods for medical image multi-organ segmentation. Physica Med. **85**, 107–122 (2021)

7. Bajaj, A., Vishwakarma, D.K.: A state-of-the-art review on adversarial machine learning in image classification. Multimedia Tools Appl. **83**(3), 9351–9416 (2024)
8. Madry, A., Makelov, A., Schmidt, L., Tsipras, D., Vladu, A.: Towards deep learning models resistant to adversarial attacks. arXiv preprint arXiv:1706.06083 (2017)
9. Goodfellow, I.J., Shlens, J., Szegedy, C.: Explaining and harnessing adversarial examples. arXiv preprint arXiv:1412.6572 (2014)
10. Moosavi-Dezfooli, S.-M., Fawzi, A., Frossard, P.: DeepFool: a simple and accurate method to fool deep neural networks. In: Proceedings of the IEEE Conference on Computer Vision and Pattern Recognition, pp. 2574–2582 (2016)
11. Carlini, N., Wagner, D.: Towards evaluating the robustness of neural networks. In: 2017 IEEE Symposium on Security and Privacy (SP), pp. 39–57. IEEE (2017)
12. Dunston, S.D., Rajam, V.M.A.: AIPA: an adversarial imperceptible patch attack on medical datasets and its interpretability. Comput. Secur. **136**, 103574 (2024)
13. Sun, X., Cheng, G., Pei, L., Li, H., Han, J.: Threatening patch attacks on object detection in optical remote sensing images. IEEE Trans. Geosci. Remote Sens. (2023)
14. Bai, T., Luo, J., Zhao, J., Wen, B., Wang, Q.: Recent advances in adversarial training for adversarial robustness. arXiv preprint arXiv:2102.01356 (2021)
15. Mafi, M., Martin, H., Cabrerizo, M., Andrian, J., Barreto, A., Adjouadi, M.: A comprehensive survey on impulse and Gaussian denoising filters for digital images. Signal Process. **157**, 236–260 (2019)
16. Athalye, A., Carlini, N., Wagner, D.: Obfuscated gradients give a false sense of security: circumventing defence to adversarial examples. In: International Conference on Machine Learning, pp. 274–283. PMLR (2018)
17. Papernot, N., McDaniel, P., Wu, X., Jha, S., Swami, A.: Distillation as a defence to adversarial perturbations against deep neural networks. In: 2016 IEEE Symposium on Security and Privacy (SP), pp. 582–597. IEEE (2016)
18. Tramèr, F., Kurakin, A., Papernot, N., Goodfellow, I., Boneh, D., McDaniel, P.: Ensemble adversarial training: attacks and defences. arXiv preprint arXiv:1705.07204 (2017)
19. Sundararajan, M., Taly, A., Yan, Q.: Axiomatic attribution for deep networks. In: International Conference on Machine Learning, pp. 3319–3328. PMLR (2017)
20. Ribeiro, M.T., Singh, S., Guestrin, C.: "Why should I trust You?" Explaining the predictions of any classifier. In: Proceedings of the 22nd ACM SIGKDD International Conference on Knowledge Discovery and Data Mining, pp. 1135–1144 (2016)
21. Lundberg, S.M., Lee, S.-I.: A unified approach to interpreting model predictions. In: Advances in Neural Information Processing Systems, vol. 30 (2017)
22. Kokhlikyan, N., et al.: Captum: a unified and generic model interpretability library for PyTorch. arXiv preprint arXiv:2009.07896 (2020)
23. Soares, E., Angelov, P., Biaso, S., Froes, M.H., Abe, D.K.: SARS-CoV-2 CT-scan dataset: a large dataset of real patients CT scans for SARS-CoV-2 identification. MedRxiv (2020)
24. Zhou, S., Wang, Y., Zhu, T., Xia, L.: CT features of coronavirus disease 2019 (COVID-19) pneumonia in 62 patients in Wuhan, China. Am. J. Roentgenol. **214**(6), 1287–1294 (2020)
25. Rajaraman, S., et al.: Pre-trained convolutional neural networks as feature extractors toward improved malaria parasite detection in thin blood smear images. PeerJ **6**, e4568 (2018)

Autonomous Non-Intrusive Inspection for Risk Detection in Cargo Containers Using Deep Learning

Ramesh Moorthy[1(✉)], Bhanu Jain[1], and Prashant Gidde[2]

[1] National Customs Targeting Center (NCTC), Mumbai, India
{mramesh.irs,bjain.90}@gov.in
[2] Tata Consultancy Services, Mumbai, India
prashant.gidde@tcs.com

Abstract. With global trade highly increasing, Non-Intrusive Inspection (NII) of containerised cargo using X-ray scanners has been identified as one of the important areas of the World Customs Organization (WCO) SAFE Framework of Standards. The framework aims to promote the secure movement of goods through international trade supply chains. Non-Intrusive inspection systems, such as X-ray instruments, have become integral in imaging the contents of cargo containers, serving as a primary tool for identifying potential threats, contraband and mis-declared items. These scanned images are analyzed alongside shipping manifest data to efficiently target containers for thorough physical examination. Considering the bottlenecks in manual analysis of scanned images, AI based Image analysis for automated risk detection is emerging as critical area in Non-intrusive inspection (NII). With paradigm shift and rapid advancements in AI based Image analytics from Image classification towards Object detection algorithms, this paper explores the potential of deep learning to enhance NII by employing cutting edge object detection algorithms for automated threat detection. This paper evaluates the performance of four SOTA deep learning architectures Faster R-CNN, Retina-Net, YOLOv5, and YOLOv7 on a custom Scanned X-ray Image dataset of NCTC (National Customs Targeting Centre) of Indian Customs. Our findings demonstrate the superiority of YOLOv7, achieving a mean Average Precision (mAP) of 0.9144, highlighting its effectiveness in object detection within X-ray images of containerised cargo. Beyond mAP, the paper demonstrates the importance of considering factors like higher inference speed and computational efficiency for real-world deployments. Additionally, this research contributes to the advancement of concept of Autonomous image analytics based Risk management framework for Customs administrations and signifies the pivotal role of AI and open source algorithms in bolstering border security.

Keywords: Non-Intrusive Inspection (NII) · X-ray imaging · YOLOv7

J. Kakarla et al. (Eds.): CVIP 2024, CCIS 2473, pp. 220–233, 2026.
https://doi.org/10.1007/978-3-031-93688-3_16

1 Introduction

1.1 Background

Non-Intrusive Inspection (NII) using X-ray scanners of containerized cargo is one of the essential area within the WCO's SAFE Framework of Standards [18], emphasizing the need for robust and effective cargo inspection methods without physical opening of the containers. NII involves the utilization of advanced radio wave based Imaging technologies to inspect cargo inside container without physically opening or disturbing them. This can be done using a variety of methods, including X-ray imaging [5,6,12], gamma ray imaging, infrasound imaging, radar imaging, and magnetic imaging. Here we will focus on the use of NII for inspecting shipping containers using X-ray Imaging. Customs administrations worldwide face the challenge of detecting and preventing smuggling activities, as smugglers constantly devise new methods to conceal contraband and restricted items. The increased use of tariff and non-tariff barriers further emphasizes the need for effective cargo inspection to safeguard national security and revenue.

1.2 Need for Automated Detection

Customs administrations have their own specific objects/commodities of interest that are prone to smuggling across their borders in containerized cargo. These objects can range from illicit drugs, restricted commodities like cigarettes or any other commodities that require high regulatory compliance or high incident duty rates by the country. Detecting these objects manually poses significant challenges due to the vast volume of cargo passing through ports and limited human resources and their learning capabilities. Furthermore, smugglers continuously adapt their techniques, making it imperative to have advanced and automated solutions to detect concealed contraband items accurately.

1.3 Use of AI in NII

Traditionally, NII relies on X-ray scanners and human analysts to identify threats and contraband. However, this approach is slow and susceptible to human error. Recent developments in Artificial Intelligence (AI) and image analytics have opened up new opportunities for improving NII systems to address the above said limitations of human based Image analysis. There has been continuous research on the use of Machine learning and Artificial intelligence in developing Computer vision models and algorithms for automated risk identification in X-ray of cargo and integration with Image analysis systems at Port. Once the AI algorithms have analysed the images, they are matched manually with the declared bill details for the shipping container. This helps to ensure that the cargo is what it is supposed to be and that there are no threats present. If the AI algorithms detect any threats, they send a notification to the port where the shipping container is located [13].

1.4 SOTA Algorithms in Image Analytics and Object Detection

Of late, the field of Computer vision and AI based Image analytics saw the emergence of cutting edge algorithms on Object detection with high precision and speed which are being harnessed and applied by various industries and markets. Customs administrations and related market stakeholders dealing with NII has started to research and develop their own customised models for Image analytics using these open source AI libraries and Computer vision algorithms in the area of Automated risk detection in Non-Intrusive Inspection. However development of Deep learning models requires vast data of X-ray images which is a challenge in this area as the scanned images of cargo are not readily available for research purposes. Moreover the research has more focussed on images of baggage cargo with little emphasis on containerised cargo. Related works revealed that research has not taken for large number of category/classes of objects/products for evaluation of performance of their AI algorithms reflecting the real-time scenario. In this paper, we propose the application of the state-of-the-art object detection algorithm, YOLO (You Only Look Once), in the analysis of X-ray images of containerized cargo. The motivation behind the research paper is on the YOLO's real-time performance and high accuracy and its potential for automating the detection of risky commodities concealed within containers. By training the YOLOv7 model on a diverse dataset of different commodities found in containerized cargo, we aim to achieve accurate and efficient risk detection in real-time. The World Customs Organization (WCO) published its non-binding view on supply chain security in its SAFE framework. In this framework, the WCO proposed technical standards to enhance security without impeding international trade. Technological advances and smart policies are required to facilitate inspection and achieve integrated security. The European Union emphasizes public-private collaboration to enhance its supply chain security [14–16]. The use of AI techniques is making NII more accurate and efficient, and it is helping to keep our borders secure.

2 Literature

Although a vision-based approach powered by deep learning algorithms seems to be the most impeccable approach for X-ray screening system, the works done so far are majorly pertaining to low energy X-ray systems involving small cargo like baggage. It is pertinent to mention that there are a few works in the literature dealing with high energy, containerised cargo X-ray systems which are done on synthetically generated datasets. This is mainly attributed to the lack of adequate number of scanned images of containerised cargo X-ray data available in the literature which will be required for performing deep learning experiments. This paper focuses completely on application of latest deep learning vision-based approach on high energy, containerised cargo and actual scanned images dataset which will be unique and value adding to research in that area.

Viriyasaranon et al. present the detection of prohibited items in complex X-ray cargo and Baggage security using a Deep learning approach [4]. The author developed the MFA-net model to identify the four different types of knives within cargo containers. They generated synthetic data for knife detection. Moreover this research is on low energy baggage scanned images and not on containerised cargo which is the scope of this paper. Liu, Jian, et al. proposed text-driven framework that utilizes Generative Adversarial Networks (GANs) to synthesize X-ray security inspection images, addressing challenges such as overlap and background disorder [8]. The framework comprises a conditional GAN for generating prohibited item images, a pix-to-pix GAN for converting them into X-ray format, and a high-definition pix-to-pixel GAN for background synthesis. Evaluation using YOLO-v5 shows significant performance enhancements: a 4.6% increase in mAP (0.5) and a 15.9% increase in mAP (0.5–0.95). These results highlight the effectiveness of the proposed method in improving object detection during X-ray security screening, particularly through dataset augmentation and enhanced algorithm performance. Visser, Wicher, et al. proposed the integration of X-ray technology for cargo scanning at customs sites worldwide, aiming to enhance inspection efficiency and effectiveness [9]. Funded by the European 7th Framework Program, the "Automated Comparison of X-ray Images for Cargo Scanning (ACXIS)" project reviews current inspection procedures, identifies risks, and proposes an automated solution. Automated target recognition (ATR) functions analyse X-ray images to detect prohibited items like cigarettes, weapons, and drugs, facilitating information exchange between customs administrations. A manufacturer-independent format is used for image storage, and machine learning techniques are employed for ATR functions. Additionally, a computer-based training software is developed to improve the X-ray image interpretation skills of customs officers, validated through studies involving Dutch and Swiss Customs administrations. This approach doesn't use any deep learning methods but other image comparison techniques in containerised cargo images.

Che et al. presents an attempt to classify commodities in containers using HS (Harmonized System) codes, which is challenging due to the large number and hierarchical structure of HS categories [10]. The proposed ensemble model incorporates fine-grained image categorization, data analysis on cargo manifests, and a human-in-the-loop paradigm. Deep learning is employed to train a triplet network for image categorization, while analysis of cargo manifests helps filter out unreasonable predictions. Human intelligence is integrated to justify the resulting HS codes through the human-in-the-loop approach. Additionally, a semantic tree of HS codes is constructed to balance specificity and accuracy. This paper demonstrated a validation of prediction out of image analytics against the declared text information of the cargo for an automated image inspection and validation system, which is further enhanced as Autonomous Image analytics based Risk management framework in this paper. Jaccard, Nicolas, et al. present the development of a deep learning framework for classifying X-ray cargo images based on their content. The framework utilizes convolutional neural networks (CNNs), which have shown superior performance in various machine learning and vision tasks [11]. CNNs have not been extensively applied to X-ray cargo image classification previously. Due to the multiplicative nature of X-ray transmission image formation, realistic training images can be generated economically. The framework aims to automate object detection in X-ray cargo images, thereby enhancing inspection efficiency. While the focus is on cargo containers, the framework is expected to generalize to other X-ray image types, potentially aiding in the development of specialized software packages for inspection workflow automation. The paper used image classification algorithm but not any object detection architecture, which are capable of both classification and localisation which is the state-of-the-art algorithm as on date. Galvez, Reagan L. et al. proposed an automated approach for detecting threat objects in X-ray images using a YOLO-based object detector [17]. The study evaluated the performance of two training methods transfer learning and training from scratch using an IEDXray dataset containing scanned X-ray images of improvised explosive device (IED) replicas. Training from scratch achieved higher mean average precision (mAP) scores across different image sizes: 45.89% for 416 × 416, 51.48% for 608 × 608, and 52.40% for multi-scale images. In contrast, transfer learning resulted in lower mAP scores, with 29.54% for single scale and 29.17% for multi-scale images.

Galvez, Reagan L., et al. proposed an exploration of various object detection techniques such as Faster R-CNN, SSD, and R-FCN, along with different feature extractors including ResNet, MobileNet, Inception, and Inception-ResNet, all based on convolutional neural networks (CNN) [19]. The study utilized a novel IEDXray dataset to detect components of improvised explosive devices(IEDs). Due to limited X-ray data availability for training the entire network from scratch, transfer learning with data augmentation was employed. Evaluation results demonstrated significant performance, with individual detection achieving an average precision (AP) of 99.08% in mortar detection and a mean average precision (mAP) of 77.29% across three IED components.

The critical challenge of AI based X-ray inspection system is limited availability of X-ray image dataset of good quality Image. Many literature mentioned above used a synthetically generated dataset [8,11] for evaluation of performance of their algorithms. Previously, there has been few works on use of YOLOv3 on the X-ray images of baggage scanners [17]. However, recently YOLOv7 surpasses all known object detectors in both speed and accuracy in the range from 5 FPS to 120 FPS and has the highest accuracy 56.8% AP among all known real-time object detectors [3]. In this contribution, we will a present a approach with precise focus on use of cutting edge object detection algorithms with special focus to YOLOv7 on containerised cargo with the actual scanned image datasets.

3 Dataset and Ground-Truth Preparation

The dataset comprises a collection of scanned X-ray images of cargo containers obtained from a Drivethrough Scanner of 6 MeV X-ray energy source. Scanned container X-ray images pose several challenges when it comes to applying AI techniques for analysis and interpretation. Container X-ray images are cluttered and complex, containing a mix of materials, shapes, and densities. These X-ray images are stored in the widely-used JPEG format. Depicting various types of containers, namely 20 ft, 40 ft, and 42 ft containers, the scanned X-ray images offer a unique perspective for each container size in the dataset. The images exhibit consistent specifications, with varying height and width, providing a standardized aspect ratio for analysis. Additionally, the images possess a resolution of 96 dots per inch (dpi) and a bit depth of 24. One important feature of this research paper is that the dataset used is actual scanned images of containerized cargo and does not involve any generation of synthetic dataset. This dataset holds value in advancing research and development efforts related to container item inspection, security screening, and other relevant domains. The Fig. 1 illustrates the distribution of the dataset concerning different instances of classes. The scanned images are annotated with product labels using the publicly available open-source tool LabelImg.

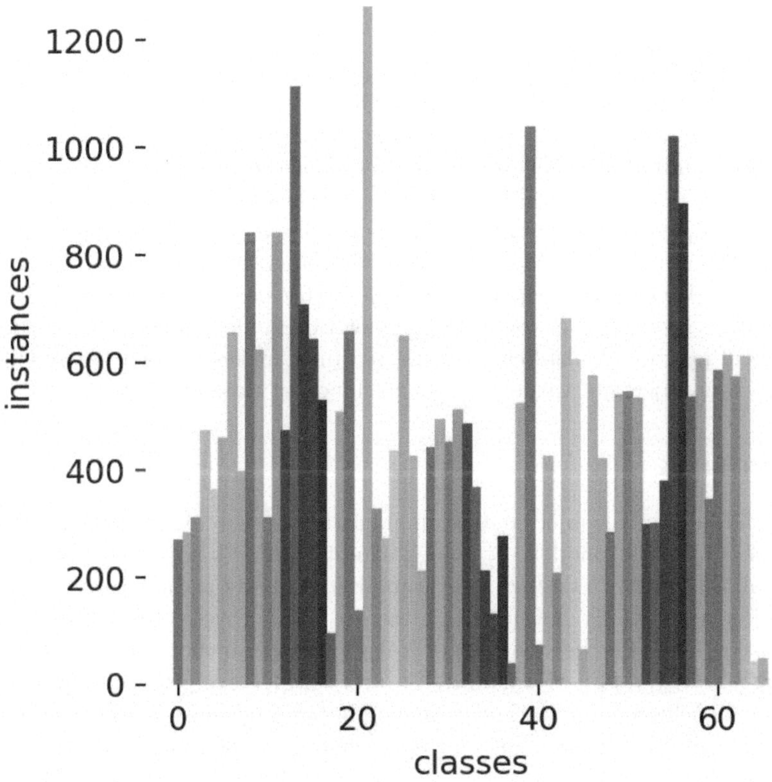

Fig. 1. Distribution of the dataset concerning different instances of class.

4 Methodology

In this work, four different state-of-the-art deep learning-inspired architectures have been used for object detection.

4.1 Faster R-CNN

The Faster R-CNN algorithm is widely used in computer vision for object detection [1]. It is a two-stage object detection algorithm designed to enhance both speed and accuracy. To achieve this goal, it introduces a Regional Proposal Network (RPN) that shares convolutional layers with the object detection process. The key components of Faster R-CNN include the Region Proposal Network, Shared Convolution Layers, and Region of Interest. By enabling end-to-end training, Faster R-CNN achieves improved performance and faster inference times.

4.2 Retina-Net

Retina-Net is a single-stage detection algorithm designed to address the challenge of detecting objects at multiple scales and handling objects with varying sizes [2]. It can handle the problem of class imbalance in object detection. The key feature in Retina-Net is focal loss, which helps the model focus more on hard-to-classify examples during training. This improvement aids in detecting smaller or more challenging objects that might otherwise be overwhelmed by the presence of abundant background regions. The key features of Retina-Net include Focal loss, Feature Pyramid Network, and Anchor Boxes. The combination of Retina-Net's focal loss and Multi-Scale feature pyramid makes it particularly effective for detecting objects of varying sizes and handling class imbalance.

4.3 YOLOv5

YOLOv5 is a popular object detection algorithm and architecture that is part of the YOLO family of models. It gained attention for its improved performance, speed, and accuracy. YOLOv5 uses a modified YOLO architecture with different backbone networks and neck architecture to improve feature extraction and information flow. The key features of Yolov5 include anchor generation, scaling, training strategy, and performance. With its competitive performance on object detection benchmarks, Yolov5 offers a good balance between accuracy and speed, making it suitable for real-time and resource-constrained applications.

4.4 YOLOv7

YOLOv7, a real-time object detection algorithm, is currently revolutionizing the computer vision industry with its incredible features [3]. Trained solely on the MS COCO dataset from scratch, Yolov7 doesn't rely on any pre-trained weights. One of its remarkable aspects is the incorporation of Extended Efficient Layer

Aggregation Networks (E-ELAN). E-ELAN utilizes expand, shuffle, and merge cardinality techniques to continuously enhance the network's learning ability without disrupting the original gradient path. Additionally, Yolov7 implements model scaling for concatenation-based models. The primary goal of model scaling is to adjust certain attributes of the model and generate models of varying scales to cater to different inference speed requirements.

5 Results

The NCTC Scanned X-ray Image dataset comprises 4065 scanned X-ray images in JPEG format, divided into 66 distinct classes of sensitive risky commodities of interest to Indian Customs administration involving prohibition, restriction for import, high duty incidence or special regulatory compliance. Out of these, 3256 scanned X-ray images are allocated for training purposes, while the remaining data is employed for validation.

In this section, we delve into the various experiments conducted on the NCTC Scanned X-ray Image Dataset. All experiments were executed within a PyTorch environment, utilizing a single GEFORCE RTX 4070 Ti GPU with CUDA 11.6 Environment. The mean Average Precision (mAP) of the Evaluation Metrics is used. In our study, we focused on evaluating the performance of various object detection algorithms on scanned X-ray image data. We conducted training and evaluation on four distinct algorithms: Faster R-CNN, which utilized a pre-trained ResNet-50 model with a two-stage approach and an image size of 1333×800; Retina-Net, with a ResNet-50 backbone and an image size of 1333×800; YOLOv5, employing a pre-trained model with an image size of 1280×1280 and utilizing the SGD optimizer; and YOLOv7, implementing a transfer learning approach with an image size of 1280×1280 and also utilizing the SGD optimizer. For Faster R-CNN and Retina-Net, SGD optimization was applied with a batch size of 3, resulting in mAP values of 0.8640 and 0.8620, respectively. YOLOv5, achieving a mAP of 0.8597. Notably, YOLOv7, trained under similar conditions to YOLOv5, emerged as the top performer with an impressive mAP of 0.9144. This underscores its superiority in effectively detecting objects within the X-ray images. These outcomes strongly highlight the effectiveness of YOLOv7 for this specific task. Dataset, while Faster R-CNN and Retina-Net demonstrated comparable performance. Notably, YOLOv5 yielded a slightly lower mAP in this context. It's important to note that although mAP serves as a valuable metric, other factors, such as computational efficiency and application-specific requirements, should also guide the selection of the object detection algorithm. Table 1 presents the performance metrics of the proposed object detection model on the NCTC custom dataset. The Fig. 2 shows the Confusion Matrix graph generated using the YOLOv7 model, and Fig. 3 shows the Precision-Recall metric Graph, while Fig. 4 displays the training graph of the YOLOv7 model with the NCTC CUSTOM Dataset.

The below two cases presented in Fig. 5, and Fig. 6 show the real-time identification of concealed/misdeclared sensitive commodities, i.e., Cigarettes and betelnuts in containerized cargo.

Table 1. Performance metric of proposed object detection model on NCTC custom dataset.

Architecture	mAP (0.5)	mAP(0.5–0.9)	Inference Time(ms)
YOLOv7	0.9144	0.7691	15.6
YOLOv5	0.8598	0.7136	46.9
Faster R-CNN	0.8610	0.6980	325.7
Retina-Net	0.8620	0.7070	306.8

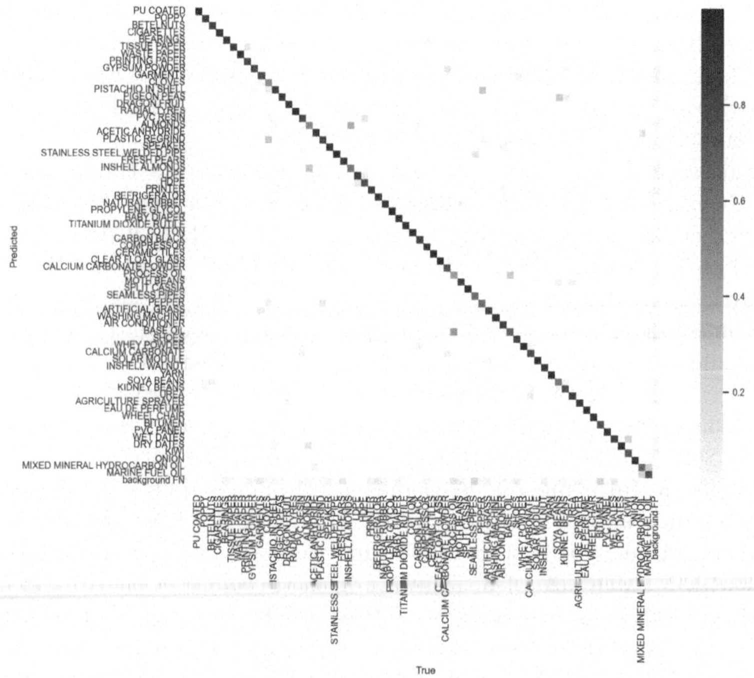

Fig. 2. Confusion Matrix graph using YOLOv7.

5.1 Realtime Performance of Trained YOLOv7 Model

The developed object detection algorithm based on YOLOv7 has been integrated as one of the AI models in the NII Autonomous Risk Detection Application developed by NCTC, to evaluate the performance in real-time on the actual scanned images received as input from the scanners in the port. Figure 7 screenshot of one instance where the output image was labeled with the description '12X20DV FCL/FCL CY/CY CONTAINERS STC GYPSUM POWDER (PLASTER)' and our developed YOLOv7 model correctly predicted it as 'GYPSUM POWDER' with a high confidence score. The predicted description and confidence score are displayed on the output image within the application.

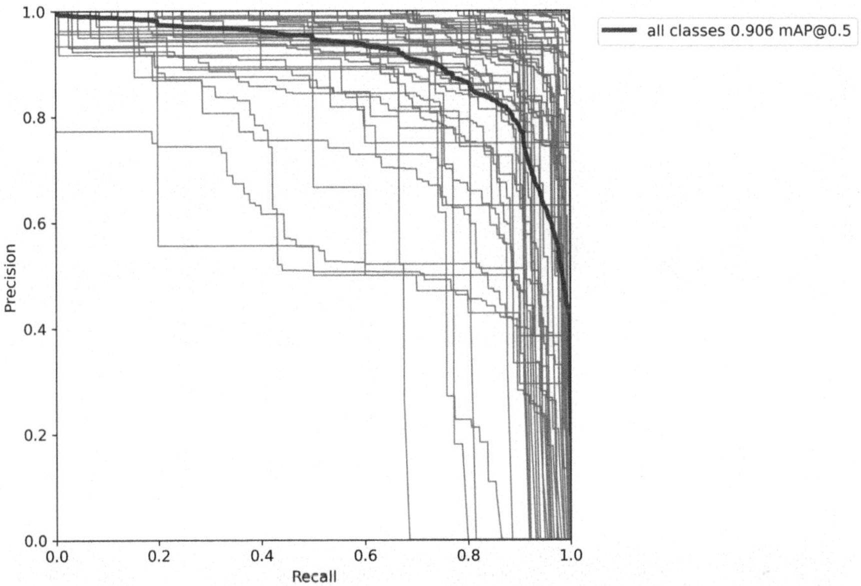

Fig. 3. Precision-Recall metric Graph using YOLOv7.

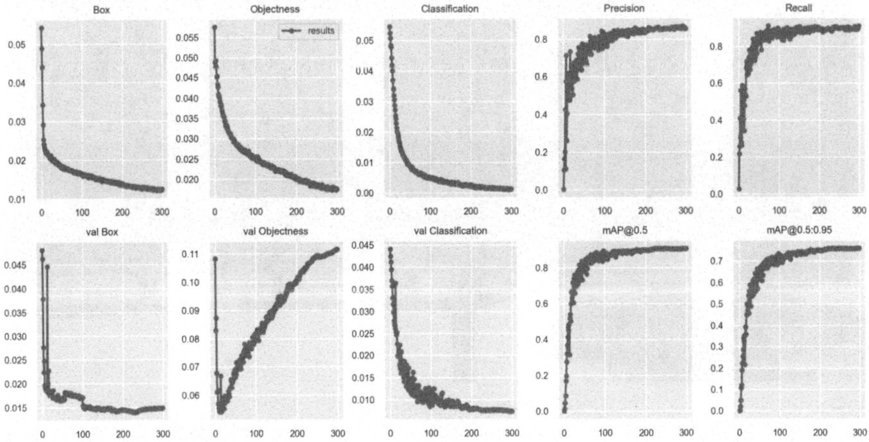

Fig. 4. Results after training the YOLOv7 model using NCTC CUSTOM Dataset.

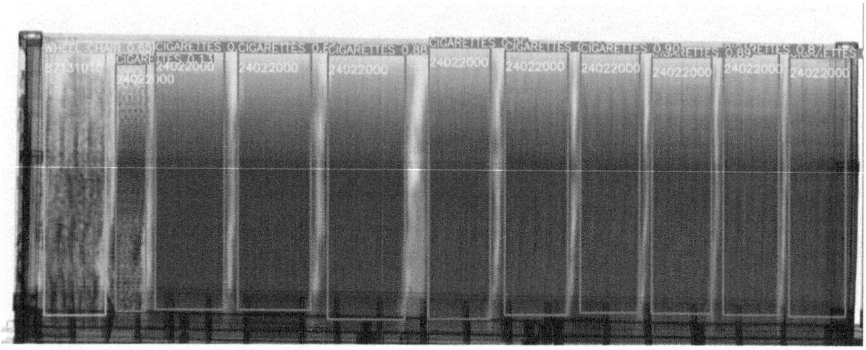

Fig. 5. Prediction of Scanned X-ray Image: Automated Detection of concealment of Contraband Cigarette using Product Detection Model.

Fig. 6. Prediction of Scanned X-ray Image: Identification of Betel Nut, falsely declared as Calcium carbonate to avoid high customs duty, using Product Detection Model.

6 Discussion

The presented results exemplify the real-time identification of concealed or misdeclared sensitive commodities, such as cigarettes and betel nut, within containerized cargo using the trained YOLOv7 object detection algorithm. Leveraging advanced product detection models, including YOLOv7, these instances showcase the capability to accurately detect and classify items, even when disguised to avoid customs duties or regulatory scrutiny. Integration of such algo-

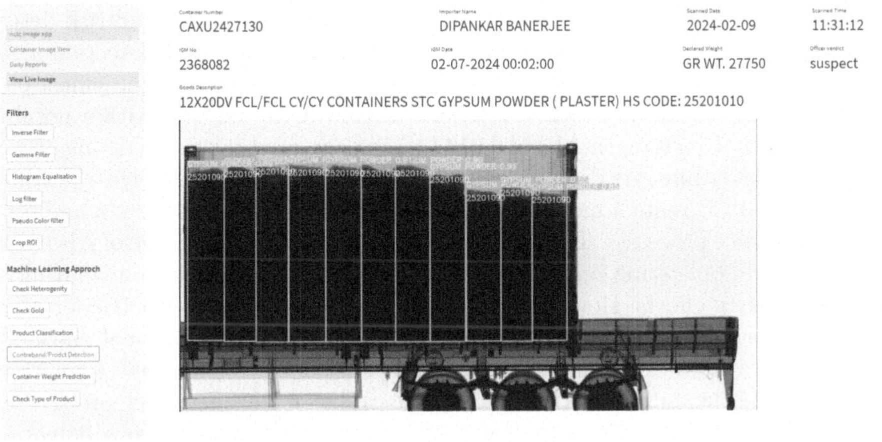

Fig. 7. Realtime Evaluation of YOLOv7 based AI Product Detection Model.

rithms into Non-Intrusive Inspection (NII) systems by any customs administration in their systems will enable swift evaluation of scanned images received from port scanners. The seamless identification of misrepresented cargo, as demonstrated in the screenshots, underscores the efficacy of AI-driven solutions in bolstering cargo security and regulatory compliance.

6.1 From Automated to Autonomous NII

With the rapid advancement of AI-based algorithms, computer vision, and image analytics for automated risk detection, the trajectory is shifting towards more autonomous NII architectures. These architectures encompass centralized AI solutions capable of processing all scanned images alongside manifest declarations using Natural Language Processing (NLP) validation AI algorithms to generate and synthesizing risk insights from both sources, patterns, anomalies, and potential risks within the shipping process can be discerned with greater accuracy. By leveraging AI to discern risky cargo effectively, these systems reduce reliance on manual intervention, streamlining processes for faster clearance and handling of high traffic volumes. Moving towards AI-based validations signifies a paradigm shift towards enhanced efficiency, accuracy, and regulatory compliance in cargo inspection and clearance procedures.

7 Conclusion

By harnessing advanced State-of-the-art Object detection algorithms like YOLOv7 in the area of Non-intrusive inspection of containerized cargo, NII systems can achieve high accuracy in real-time object detection from X-ray cargo scans, which can significantly improve efficiency, security, and risk detection capabilities in customs operations. The evaluation of object detection algorithms on the NCTC Scanned X-ray Image dataset highlights the efficacy of YOLOv7 in accurately identifying objects within X-ray images, with a notable mean Average Precision (mAP) of 0.9144 when compared to other existing object detection algorithms. As deep learning technologies continue to evolve, they offer the potential to create a more autonomous NII framework, further streamlining cargo clearance processes. These findings underscore the significance of AI-driven approaches in bolstering cargo inspection capabilities, ultimately contributing to border security efforts. However, while mAP serves as a crucial metric for algorithm performance evaluation, considerations such as computational efficiency and specific application requirements should also guide algorithm selection. Moving forward, the future work may explore transfer learning with pre-trained models on even larger X-ray image datasets to potentially improve detection accuracy. It may also include investigating explainable AI techniques to enhance trust and understanding in the model's decision-making process. In a futuristic perspective, further research and development in NII technologies, coupled with ongoing advancements in AI algorithms, towards more autonomous and intelligent NII risk management architecture encompassing multiple AI models to predict the image based risks and cross compare with declared data to discern the truly few risky container shipments for the purview of officer for further examination. By developing such autonomous and self-intelligent architectures for NII effectively, authorities can strengthen their ability to combat smuggling and ensure the safe and secure transportation of goods across borders.

Acknowledgements. The authors would like to thank Member (Compliance Management), CBIC and Director General, Directorate General of Analytics and Risk Management (DGARM) and Principal Additional Director General, National Customs Targeting Center (NCTC), for supporting the research under Central Board of Indirect taxes and Customs (CBIC).

References

1. Ren, S., et al.: Faster R-CNN: towards real-time object detection with region proposal networks. In: Advances in Neural Information Processing Systems, vol. 28 (2015)
2. Lin, T.-Y., et al.: Focal loss for dense object detection. In: Proceedings of the IEEE International Conference on Computer Vision (2017)
3. Wang, C.-Y., Bochkovskiy, A., Liao, H.-Y.M.: YOLOv7: trainable bag-of-freebies sets new state-of-the-art for real-time object detectors. In: Proceedings of the IEEE/CVF Conference on Computer Vision and Pattern Recognition (2023)
4. Viriyasaranon, T., Chae, S.-H., Choi, J.-H.: MFA-net: object detection for complex X-ray cargo and baggage security imagery. PLoS ONE **17**(9), e0272961 (2022)
5. Duan, X., et al.: X-ray cargo container inspection system with few-view projection imaging. Nucl. Instrum. Methods Phys. Res., Sect. A **598**(2), 439–444 (2009)

6. Lim, C.H., et al.: Advanced container inspection system based on dual-angle X-ray imaging method. J. Instrum. **16**(08), P08037 (2021)
7. Chang, C.L., He, M., Nguyen, M.H.: Computational model for automatic cargo container inspection systems. In: 2010 IEEE International Conference on Technologies for Homeland Security (HST). IEEE (2010)
8. Liu, J., Lin, T.H.: A framework for the synthesis of X-ray security inspection images based on generative adversarial networks. IEEE Access (2023)
9. Visser, W., et al.: Automated comparison of X-ray images for cargo scanning. In: 2016 IEEE International Carnahan Conference on Security Technology (ICCST). IEEE (2016)
10. Che, J., Xing, Y., Zhang, L.: A comprehensive solution for deep-learning based cargo inspection to discriminate goods in containers. In: Proceedings of the IEEE Conference on Computer Vision and Pattern Recognition Workshops (2018)
11. Jaccard, N., et al.: Using deep learning on X-ray images to detect threats. In: Proceedings Cranfield Defence and Security Doctoral Symposium (2015)
12. Akçay, S., et al.: Transfer learning using convolutional neural networks for object classification within X-ray baggage security imagery. In: 2016 IEEE International Conference on Image Processing (ICIP). IEEE (2016)
13. Drug of abuse: Economic and Social Consequences of Drug Abuse and Illicit Trafficking (1998)
14. Bliss, J.: US backs off all cargo scanning goal with inspections at 4%. Bloomberg LP **13** (2012)
15. Ireland, R.: The WCO SAFE framework of standards: avoiding excess in global supply chain security policy. Glob. Trade Customs J. **4**(11/12) (2009)
16. EOS: A European approach for integrated supply chain security (2009)
17. Galvez, R.L., et al.: YOLO-based threat object detection in X-ray images. In: 2019 IEEE 11th International Conference on Humanoid, Nanotechnology, Information Technology, Communication and Control, Environment, and Management (HNICEM). IEEE (2019)
18. SAFE Framework of Standards -World Customs Organisation
19. Galvez, R.L., et al.: Object detection in X-ray images using transfer learning with data augmentation. Int. J. Adv. Sci. Eng. Inf. Technol. **9**(6), 2147 (2019)

Enhancing Accuracy in Indic Handwritten Text Recognition

Evani Lalitha(✉), Ajoy Mondal, and C. V. Jawahar

CVIT, International Institute of Information Technology, Hyderabad, India
lalitha.e@research.iiit.ac.in, {ajoy.mondal,jawahar}@iiit.ac.in

Abstract. Handwritten Text Recognition (HTR) presents a significant challenge in computer vision due to various factors such as individual writing styles, noise, blur, and other imperfections in the text. This challenge is further exacerbated when dealing with languages using Indian scripts, which are characterized by complex character structures, extensive character inventories, and specific cultural nuances. In this study, we address these challenges by focusing on enhancing handwritten text recognition for ten Indic languages: *Hindi, Bengali, Telugu, Tamil, Gujarati, Gurumukhi, Oriya, Kannada, Malayalam, and Urdu*. We aim to improve recognition accuracy by leveraging the Permuted Autoregressive Sequence Model (PARSeq), an extension of the transformer-based model. Our results demonstrate the superiority of the PARSeq model over existing approaches, particularly in achieving state-of-the-art performance across most languages. Additionally, we investigate the efficacy of transfer learning from printed text to handwritten text, revealing its potential to enhance recognition performance. The trained models and code are publicly available at https://github.com/LalithaEvani/Indic-HTR-CVIP-2024.

Keywords: Indic handwritten text · transfer learning · recognizer · transformer · pre-train · PARSeq

1 Introduction

Handwritten Text Recognition (HTR) is a sub-domain in Optical Character Recognition (OCR), which focuses on automatically converting handwritten text into digital text, mimicking the capabilities of human readers. Recognizing Handwritten text is one of the important and challenging problems in computer vision. One of the main challenges of HTR is the uniqueness of the writing. In most cases, text written by one writer is unique to the others. Hence, the ability to recognize the same text written by different writers is complex, and it is even utilized in forensic handwriting analysis to identify the person based on the handwriting. The uniqueness in handwriting style is also used in graphology which attempts to assess a person's personality through handwriting. One such application is to identify the profession of a person via handwriting [15]. This characteristic

J. Kakarla et al. (Eds.): CVIP 2024, CCIS 2473, pp. 234–248, 2026.
https://doi.org/10.1007/978-3-031-93688-3_17

makes developing models that generalize well across different styles challenging. Other challenges include noise, blur, smudges, incomplete characters, variation in the density of the ink, the orientation of characters, and scaling of characters.

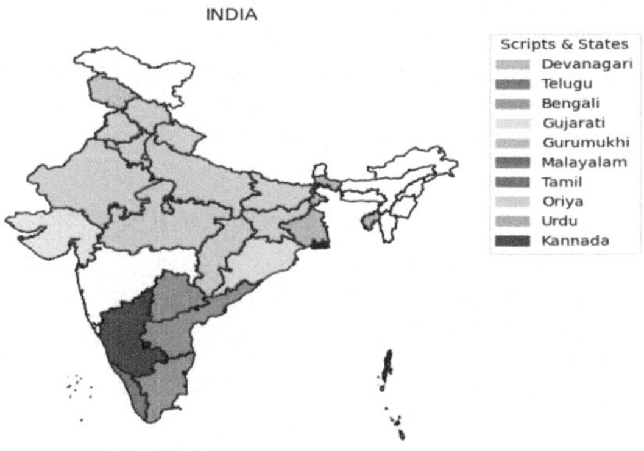

Fig. 1. India map representing the ten scripts dominantly used in several states.

There have been numerous attempts at recognizing handwritten text, and with the evolution of deep learning, the accuracy of the recognizers drastically increased [1,7,9]. Language plays a crucial role in handwriting recognition, as recognizers are typically designed to be language-specific. Therefore, a recognizer must be trained specifically for the language it is intended to recognize. Generating handwritten data manually imposes limitations on the data collection process, affecting the ability to enhance accuracy. In modern deep learning models, selecting suitable models is as critical as gathering sufficient data.

Handwritten text recognizers are primarily seen in prevalent languages such as English [12,17,23], Chinese [22,29,30], Arabic [13,19], and Japanese [18,21]. The ability to build recognizers on languages other than these is essential because, if not, thousands of languages spoken worldwide are at risk of slowly becoming extinct. Indic languages, prevalent in the Indian subcontinent, originate mainly from the Brahmi script and encompass hundreds of dialects. The reliance on training data hinders building effective recognizers for these languages; thus, the scarcity of extensive datasets is a significant drawback. Furthermore, research and development efforts focusing on Indic languages are relatively limited. These languages present unique complexities compared to scripts like Latin, including intricate character structures and a more extensive character inventory, intensifying recognition challenges. Handling diacritics and ligatures, variations in writing styles, and cultural nuances further complicate recognizer development, making achieving accurate results daunting.

Building upon prior research in handwritten text recognition for Indic languages, this paper focuses on enhancing recognizers for ten of the 22 major languages recognized under the "8th schedule" of the Indian constitution. These languages include *Hindi, Bengali, Telugu, Tamil, Gujarati, Gurumukhi, Oriya,*

Kannada, Malayalam, and Urdu. Figure 1 illustrates the states where these scripts are predominantly used. This paper aims to enhance the accuracy of handwritten text recognition in Indic languages using a transformer-based model extension known as the Permuted Auto-regressive Sequence Model (PARSeq), proposed by Darwin *et al.* [4]. The PARSeq models are trained on handwritten text data in Indic languages and compared with previous results, highlighting the novelty of the transformer-based approach compared to CNN and RNN-based methods utilized in previous studies.

We summarise contributions as follows:

- Implement a transformer-based model using PARSeq [4] to enhance recognition accuracy for Indic handwritten text.
- Showcase the models state-of-the-art performance across most languages by comparing our method with prior approaches (refer Table 2).
- Highlighting the effectiveness of transfer learning by investigating its impact from printed to handwritten text (refer Table 4).

2 Related Work

In the context of Indic scripts, handwritten text recognition typically employs three main methods. The first method involves segmentation, where characters within a word image are segmented, and individual characters are recognized using isolated symbol classifiers like Support Vector Machine (SVM) [3] or Artificial Neural Network (ANN) [2,16]. For instance, Roy *et al.* [24] segmented Indic language word images into three zones (lower, middle, and upper) with the utilization of morphological operations, shape matching and other such image processing techniques. Support Vector Machines were then applied to recognize the upper and lower zones, while Hidden Markov Models were employed for the middle zone. At last, the results that were obtained from three zones were combined.

The second method is developing recognizers using methods that are segmentation-free, which focus on recognizing the entire word or obtaining a holistic representation [14,26,27]. For example, Shaw *et al.* [27] used histogram of chain-code directions to extract features from word images, by by scanning the image strips from left to right using a sliding window. To recognize Devanagari handwritten words, a continuous density Hidden Markov Model (HMM) was proposed. Another study done by Shaw *et al.* [26], introduced a novel approach for holistic recognition of offline handwritten word images by combining two feature vectors. However, these methods are limited in their ability to recognize a diverse lexicon due to their reliance on predefined lexicons.

The third category of methods involves sequence modeling, where the handwritten text recognition task is transformed into a sequence-to-sequence prediction task, where both the input and output are treated as sequences of vectors. This approach is commonly addressed using Recurrent Neural Networks

(RNN) [11,25]. Sequence-to-sequence models are designed to optimize the likelihood of generating the output label based on the input feature sequence [1,7,8]. It overcomes the limitations of previous methods by eliminating the need for explicit symbol segmentation and allowing for the recognition of variable-length lexicons. For example, Garain *et al.* [9] proposed a recognizer that uses Bidirectional Long-Short-Term Memory (BLSTM) with a Connectionist Temporal Classification (CTC) layer to recognize Bengali handwritten words without constraints offline. Adak *et al.* [1] developed a Bengali handwritten text recognizer using a Convolutional Neural Network (CNN) integrated with LSTM and a CTC layer. Dutta *et al.* [7,8] constructed handwritten text recognizers for Devanagari, Bengali, and Telugu languages using a CNN-RNN hybrid model trained end-to-end. Santoshini *et al.* [10] built a recognizer consisting of a Spatial Tranformer Network in addiction to the hybrid CNN-RNN and CTC layer for eight Indic scripts, including Urdu, Bengali, Tamil, Gujarati, Malayalam, Gurumukhi, Kannada, and Odia. Additionally, various data augmentations were employed to enhance the recognizer's accuracy.

As deep learning continues to evolve, the adoption of transformer architectures [28], has become increasingly prominent which was initially designed for natural language processing (NLP) tasks. Unlike previous methods, these architectures capture relationships among various elements of a sequence by leveraging self-attention mechanisms. As a result of transformers being a success in NLP, they were extended into the vision domain, resulting in the development of Vision Transformers [5]. These models eliminate the need for CNNs and RNNs by segmenting the images into a sequence of patches, which are then processed by the transformer. One notable extension of the transformer architecture is PARSeq [4], initially developed for Scene Text Recognition (STR). This paper uses the PARSeq model to enhance handwritten text recognizers for Indic languages.

3 Methodology

In this study, we employ PARSeq, a Permuted auto-regressive Sequence Model based on transformer architecture. Initially designed for Scene Text Recognition, PARSeq is adept at recognizing text from cropped regions within a scene. Leveraging its permutation capability and transformer extension, we apply PARSeq to recognize handwritten text in Indic languages.

PARSeq comprises an encoder and a decoder, the encoder comprising 12 layers and the decoder featuring a single layer, the architecture of which is shown in Fig. 2. This configuration is chosen for computational efficiency. The Encoder is ViT Encoder. ViT implements transformers on images. But in PARSeq all the output tokens z of the encoder are given as input to the decoder. Here x is the input image, H and W are height and width of the image, respectively, divided into $p_w \times p_h$ patches, while d_{model} being the dimension.

$$\mathbf{z} = \text{Enc}(x) \in \mathbb{R}^{\frac{WH}{p_w p_h} \times d_{\text{model}}} \tag{1}$$

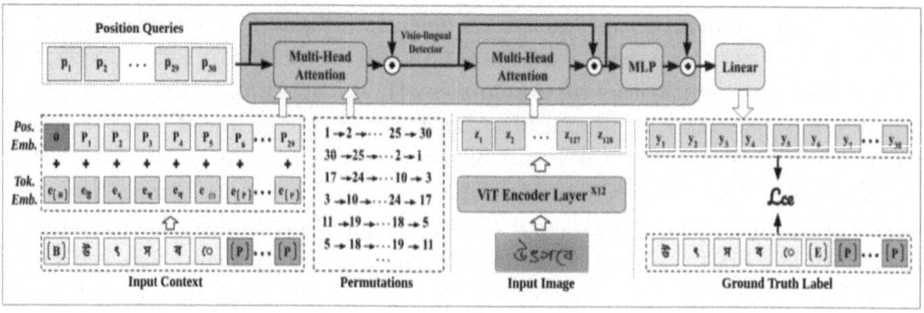

Fig. 2. PARSeq architecture. [P], [B], and [E], are padding tokens, *beginning-of-sequence* (BOS), and *end-of-sequence* (EOS), respectively. $\mathcal{L}_{ce}$ is the cross-entropy loss.

There are two MHA modules, they are used for context-position attention and image-position attention respectively. The context-position attention is given by:

$$\mathbf{h_c} = \mathbf{p} + \text{MHA}(\mathbf{p}, \mathbf{c}, \mathbf{c}, \mathbf{m}) \in \mathbb{R}^{(T+1)\times d_{\text{model}}}, \tag{2}$$

where $\mathbf{p} \in \mathbb{R}^{(T+1)\times d_{\text{model}}}$ are the position tokens, T is the context length, $\mathbf{c} \in \mathbb{R}^{(T+1)\times d_{\text{model}}}$ are the context embeddings with positional information, and $\mathbf{m} \in \mathbb{R}^{(T+1)\times(T+1)}$ is the optional attention mask.

The image-position attention is given by:

$$\mathbf{h_i} = \mathbf{h_c} + \text{MHA}(\mathbf{h_c}, \mathbf{z}, \mathbf{z}) \in \mathbb{R}^{(T+1)\times d_{\text{model}}} \tag{3}$$

The output logits are given by:

$$\mathbf{y} = \text{Linear}(\mathbf{h}_{\text{dec}}) \in \mathbb{R}^{(T+1)\times(S+1)}, \tag{4}$$

where S is the size of the character set used for training, and h_{dec} is the last decoder hidden state.

The decoder function is given by:

$$\mathbf{y} = \text{Dec}(\mathbf{z}, \mathbf{p}, \mathbf{c}, \mathbf{m}) \in \mathbb{R}^{(T+1)\times(S+1)}. \tag{5}$$

The main feature of PARSeq is permutation language modeling, which trains the model on all Tfactorization of the likelihood, where T is the number of tokens in the output sequence. Considering the standard Vision Transformers, it is nothing but a particular case of PLM where one of the permutations $[1, 2, \ldots, T]$ is used. It can be stated as:

$$\log p(\mathbf{y}|\mathbf{x}) = \mathbb{E}\mathbf{z} \sim \mathcal{Z}_T \left[\sum_{t=1}^{T} \log p_\theta(y_{z_t}|\mathbf{y}_{\mathbf{z}<t}, \mathbf{x}) \right]. \tag{6}$$

Due to computational requirements, the model is only trained on some T factorization but K of the T permutations. This K is chosen so that the first half of the permutations are left-to-right randomly sampled permutations, and the other half are right-to-left permutations, which is the flipped version of the former. The loss thus calculated is given by:

$$\mathcal{L} = \frac{1}{K} \sum_{k=1}^{K} \mathcal{L}_{\mathrm{ce}}(\mathbf{y}_k, \hat{\mathbf{y}}), \tag{7}$$

where $\hat{\mathbf{y}}$ is the ground truth label and $\mathbf{y}_k = \mathrm{Dec}(\mathbf{z}, \mathbf{p}, \mathbf{c}, \mathbf{m_k})$.

As mentioned in the previous section, the previous works focussed on CNN based models to improve the accuracy of the recognizers. Transformer based approaches are latest advancements in the deep learning domain. PARSeq is especially chosen because of its permutation capabilities. It is capable of context-free and context-aware decoding, and iterative refinement. It combines various decoding schemes into a single model and leverages the parallel computation capabilities of Transformers. It also uses attention extensively, demonstrating the robustness on vertical and rotated text in images[1].

4 Experiments and Results

4.1 Implementation Details

All PARSeq models were trained on four Nvidia GeForce GTX 1080 Ti GPUs for approximately 160,000 iterations, employing a batch size of 254. Pre-training utilized a 1-cycle learning rate scheduler, while training employed the SWA scheduler with the Adam optimizer. Consistent with the original PARSeq model, a permutation count of $K = 6$, a patch size of 8×4, a drop out rate of 0.1 and a learning rate of 7e−4, were employed for the entire pre-training and most of the training. For some of the languages, namely, Bengali, Gujarati, Kannada, Oriya, and Malayalam fine-tuning was done at a permutation count of $K = 14$, dropout rate of 0.4 and a learning rate of 7e−6. The maximum label length across all languages was set to 35, chosen based on the dataset to accommodate significant words during future inference. The character set included language-specific characters, special symbols, and digits, with the number of characters used for training varying depending on the language.

4.2 Training/Testing Details

Training is conducted through two approaches. The first approach involves training all languages on the *IIIT-INDIC-HW-WORDS* dataset, utilizing the 1-cycle learning rate scheduler during initial training and the SWA scheduler a few iterations before training completion. The second approach employs transfer learning, where the model undergoes initial pre-training on a printed dataset for all languages, followed by training on the *IIIT-INDIC-HW-WORDS* dataset. Three optimal model checkpoints, determined by achieving the minimum validation loss, were saved and tested on the test set of *IIIT-INDIC-HW-WORDS* dataset across all languages.

[1] For more information on PARSeq, please refer [4].

4.3 Dataset

We used *IIIT-INDIC-HW-WORDS* dataset for experimental purposes. It includes handwritten word level images of ten languages—*Hindi, Bengali, Telugu, Tamil, Kannada, Gurumukhi, Gujarati, Oriya, Malayalam and Urdu.* Table 1 shows the statistics of this dataset, and Fig. 3 shows a few sample word level images from this dataset.

Table 1. Shows the statistics of *IIIT-INDIC-HW-WORDS* dataset used in this experiment.

Script	#Writers	#Word Instances	Lexicon Size	#Train Instances	#Val Instances	#Test Instances
Devanagari	12	95K	11,030	69,853	12,708	12,869
Telugu	11	120K	12,945	80,637	19,980	17,898
Bengali	24	113K	11,295	82,554	12,947	17,574
Gujarati	17	116K	10,963	82,563	17,643	16,490
Gurumukhi	22	112K	11,093	81,042	13,627	17,947
Kannada	11	103K	11,766	73,517	13,752	15,730
Odia	10	101K	13,314	73,400	11,217	16,850
Malayalam	27	116K	13,401	85,270	11,878	19,635
Tamil	16	103K	13,292	75,736	11,597	16,184
Urdu	8	100K	11,936	71,207	13,906	15,517

4.4 Evaluation Metrics

The performance of the model is assessed with the help of Word Error Rate (WER), which calculates the ratio of incorrectly classified words to the total number of words. A word is considered correct if all its characters are predicted accurately; otherwise, it is deemed incorrect. We also used Character Error Rate (CER), which calculates the error at the character level. In general, Error Rate (ER) is the ratio of the total number of errors to the total number of predictions.

$$\mathrm{ER} = \frac{\mathrm{S + D + I}}{\mathrm{N}} \tag{8}$$

where S indicates the number of substitutions, D indicates the number of deletions, I indicates the number of insertions and N the number of instances in reference text. In the case of CER, the Eq. (8) is applied at the character level, while in the case of WER, it is used on the word level.

Fig. 3. Some sample word images from the dataset used in this experiment.

4.5 Results Analysis

Quantitative Results: We compare the results obtained using PARSeq with previous works [6,10,20], as presented in Table 2. When contrasting with Dutta *et al.* [6], it's evident that for Hindi, our achieved WER is substantially lower at 6.93 compared to previous 26.22, indicating significant improvement without the use of a lexicon. Similarly, for Telugu, our WER of 10.37 surpasses the previous 23.98. In comparison with Santoshini *et al.* [10], for the remaining eight

Table 2. Presents WER and CER comparisons across different languages. ↓ denotes that better performance is represented by a smaller value.

Language	CRNN [6,10]		Mondal *et al.* [20]		Ours	
	WER↓	CER↓	WER↓	CER↓	WER↓	CER↓
Hindi	26.22	3.17	9.06	**1.98**	**6.93**	2.93
Telugu	23.98	3.18	12.11	**2.15**	**10.37**	2.50
Bengali	15.71	4.85	**12.34**	**2.35**	16.35	4.17
Gujarati	18.59	2.39	**9.21**	**1.19**	12.04	2.74
Gurumukhi	18.37	3.42	**10.77**	**2.1**	11.92	3.24
Kannada	7.65	1.79	8.57	**1.01**	**6.55**	1.13
Odia	19.19	3	**12.32**	**1.32**	14.86	3.38
Malayalam	10.23	1.92	9.37	1.12	**5.97**	**0.98**
Tamil	**7.82**	1.92	9.18	**1.25**	8.02	1.43
Urdu	24.11	5.07	18.76	**3.89**	**17.81**	5.51

languages, our results show higher WER values in Gurumukhi, Gujarati, and Urdu, with differences exceeding 6% from the previous WER. Additionally, our WER is higher by more than 4% for Malayalam and Odia, and more then 1% for Kannada. However, there is minimal change in WER for Tamil and Bengali. Overall, as the WER decreases compared to [6,10], it suggests that transformer based models outperform CNN-RNN based models. In the case of CER, when compared with Dutta *et al.* [6] and Santoshini *et al.* [10], it can be seen that our CER is lower for most of the languages with the lowest being in Malayalam and Tamil.

Furthermore, comparing the results with Mondal *et al.* [20], the PARSeq model demonstrates satisfactory performance in Hindi, Telugu, Malayalam, Kannada, Tamil, and Urdu. However, for Gurumukhi, the WER is slightly higher for PARSeq. Significant differences in WER are observed in the Bengali, Gujarati, and Odia languages. In the case of CER, our CER is higher for most of the languages or similar otherwise. One of the reasons for a low CER in [20] could be that, there is an additional module, called semantic module, which predicts the semantic information which is then given as additional input to the decoder, thus leveraging the accuracy of predicting the characters.

Qualitative Analysis: Figure 4 depicts the qualitative outcomes achieved through PARSeq across the ten Indic languages. The accurate predictions are displayed in the initial three columns, while the subsequent two columns showcase incorrect predictions. Wrongly recognized characters within the words are highlighted in red for clarity.

Another comparison is made between the CNN-RNN model [6,10,20] and PARSeq model across the ten Indic languages as shown in Fig. 5. The first column contains words that are correctly predicted by both the CNN-RNN model and the PARSeq model; the second column includes words that the CNN-RNN model

Fig. 4. Shows selected samples showcasing qualitative results obtained using PARSeq across ten Indic languages. Text highlighted in blue refers to the Ground truth and text highlighted in red refers to text recognized incorrectly. (Color figure online)

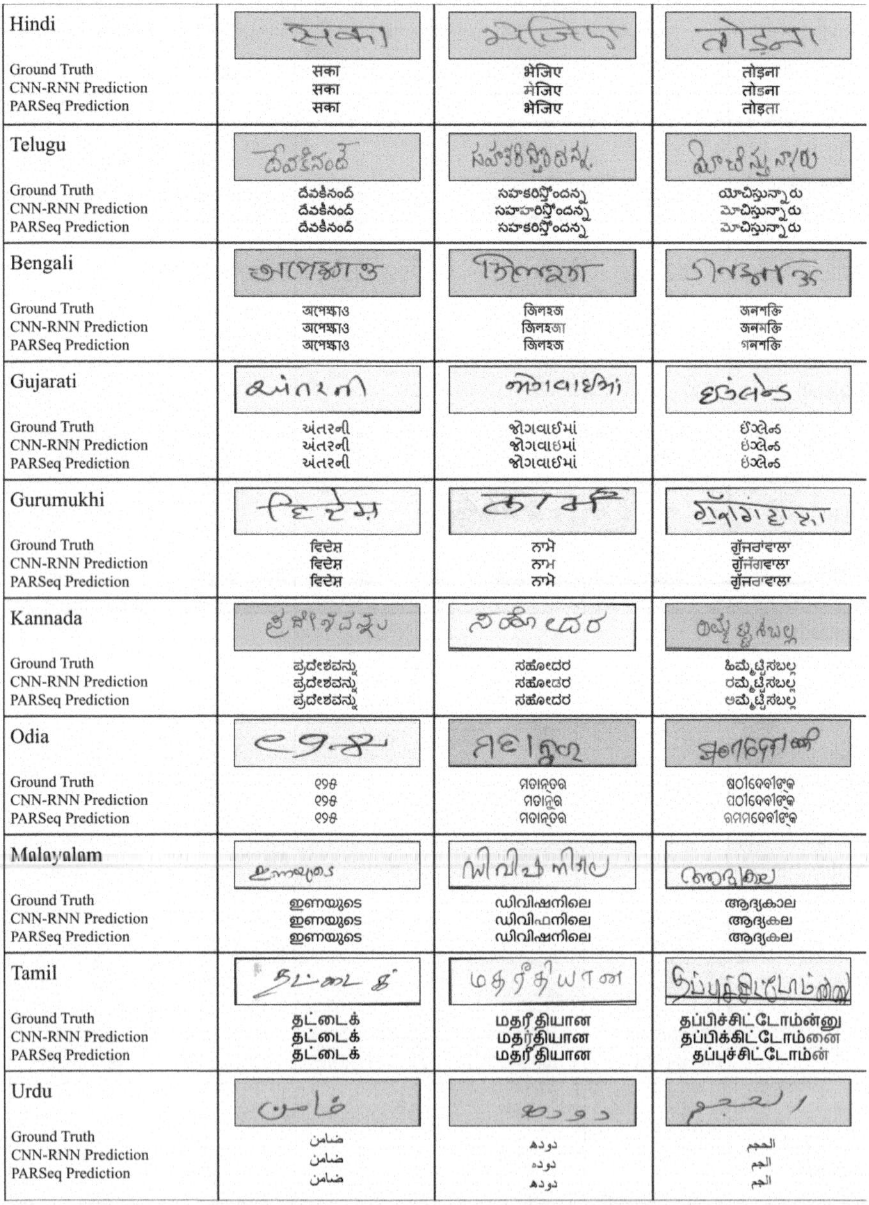

Fig. 5. Shows qualitative comparison between CNN-RNN [20] model and PARSeq model across ten Indic languages. Text highlighted in blue refers to the Ground truth and text highlighted in red refers to text recognized incorreclty. (Color figure online)

wrongly predicts and correctly predicted by the PARSeq model, and the last column contains the words that both models wrongly predict. PARSeq could predict words across languages that the CNN-RNN model could not predict correctly. In the case of wrong predictions, both the models wrongly predicted almost the same character across languages.

Table 3. Presents post-OCR results across ten Indic languages. ↓ denotes that better performance is represented by a smaller value.

Language	Recall 1↓		Recall 2↓		Recall 3↓		Recall 4↓		Recall 5↓	
	WER	CER	WER	CER	WER	CER	WER	CER	WER	CER
Hindi	4.14	2.03	3.06	1.59	2.52	1.34	2.16	1.15	1.93	1.05
Telugu	2.84	1.54	1.68	1.05	1.31	0.86	1.13	0.76	1.04	0.07
Bengali	7.77	3.66	5.6	2.8	4.6	2.32	4.06	2.08	3.68	1.83
Gujarati	4.41	1.92	2.52	1.26	1.87	0.97	1.55	0.83	1.38	0.74
Gurumukhi	6.76	2.87	4.07	2.06	3.61	1.6	3.04	1.38	2.67	1.21
Kannada	1.64	0.61	0.87	0.41	0.71	0.33	0.49	0.25	0.39	0.21
Odia	6.08	2.62	3.61	1.78	2.72	1.43	2.32	1.26	2.08	1.34
Malayalam	1.29	0.54	0.71	0.36	0.53	0.29	0.44	0.24	0.35	0.2
Tamil	1.6	0.78	0.96	0.54	0.8	0.47	0.66	0.41	0.56	0.37
Urdu	14.75	5.98	11.98	4.79	10.34	4.12	9.04	3.64	8.01	3.29

Post-OCR Error Correction: As the name suggests, Post-OCR Error Correction is implemented after obtaining predictions from the model. Errors in these predictions are identified and corrected using several methods. A lexicon is created by concatenating the training, validation, and test datasets. The edit distance between the predicted words and the lexicon is then calculated to identify the top five words with the least edit distances, which are considered potentially correct words. For Recall 1, the final word chosen is the word which has the least edit distance, and the CER (Character Error Rate) and WER (Word Error Rate) are calculated. For Recall 2, the top two words are considered potential correct words, and the one with the least edit distance to the ground truth is used to calculate CER and WER. This process is repeated for Recall 3, Recall 4, and Recall 5. Our paper applies this post-OCR error correction method to all ten languages considered, with the CER and WER results presented in Table 3. For each language, CER and WER are calculated up to Recall 5.

Ablation Study: An experiment was conducted to assess the impact of transfer learning on model training. In this experiment, the PARSeq model underwent training in two distinct approaches, both with the same hyperparameters. Initially, it was trained on handwritten data from the *IIIT-INDIC-HW-WORDS* dataset. At the same time, the latter method involved applying transfer learning

Table 4. Highlights the impact of transfer learning on the performance of the recognizer. Bold value indicates the best results.

Language	Word Error Rate (WER)↓	
	Trained model	(Pre-trained + Trained) model
Bengali	23.69	**19.08**
Gujarati	17.69	**12.32**
Gurumukhi	14.63	**11.92**
Kannada	11.59	**7.28**
Odia	21.03	**16.78**
Malayalam	10.49	**5.97**
Tamil	9.82	**8.02**

by pre-training the model on printed data before training it on handwritten data. Table 4 illustrates the comparison of results obtained for select languages. For Bengali, Gujarati, Kannada, Odia and Malayalam the WER achieved by the pre-trained model is significantly lower than that of the model without pre-training, with the difference exceeding 4%. Similarly, for Gurumukhi, the WER is reduced by 3% and for Tamil, it reduced by 2%. Thus, it can be inferred that leveraging learned representations from printed data as a starting point for training on handwritten data can substantially enhance the recognizer's performance.

5 Conclusions

This study focuses on enhancing handwritten text recognition by employing the Permutated Autoregressive Sequence Model (PARSeq), an extension of transformer-based models. Trained on the *IIIT-INDIC-HW-WORDS* dataset, PARSeq produces models for ten major Indic languages. Comparative analysis with existing approaches demonstrates state-of-the-art performance across most languages. Post-OCR error correction showcases the advantage of using lexicon in correcting the predicted words, which can significantly improve the accuracy across all languages. Additionally, the study investigates the impact of transfer learning by pre-training models on printed data before training them on handwritten data. The findings suggest that models trained with transfer learning exhibit superior performance compared to those trained solely on handwritten data.

Acknowledgments. This work is supported by MeitY, Government of India, through the NLTM-Bhashini project.

References

1. Adak, C., Chaudhuri, B.B., Blumenstein, M.: Offline cursive Bengali word recognition using CNNs with a recurrent model. In: 2016 15th International Conference on Frontiers in Handwriting Recognition (ICFHR), pp. 429–434. IEEE (2016)
2. Alonso-Weber, J.M., Sesmero, M., Sanchis, A.: Combining additive input noise annealing and pattern transformations for improved handwritten character recognition. Expert Syst. Appl. **41**(18), 8180–8188 (2014)
3. Arora, S., Bhattacharjee, D., Nasipuri, M., Malik, L., Kundu, M., Basu, D.K.: Performance comparison of SVM and ANN for handwritten Devnagari character recognition. arXiv preprint arXiv:1006.5902 (2010)
4. Bautista, D., Atienza, R.: Scene text recognition with permuted autoregressive sequence models. In: European Conference on Computer Vision, pp. 178–196. Springer (2022)
5. Dosovitskiy, A., et al.: An image is worth 16x16 words: transformers for image recognition at scale. arXiv preprint arXiv:2010.11929 (2020)
6. Dutta, K., Krishnan, P., Mathew, M., Jawahar, C.: Offline handwriting recognition on Devanagari using a new benchmark dataset. In: 2018 13th IAPR International Workshop on Document Analysis Systems (DAS), pp. 25–30. IEEE (2018)
7. Dutta, K., Krishnan, P., Mathew, M., Jawahar, C.: Towards accurate handwritten word recognition for Hindi and Bangla. In: Computer Vision, Pattern Recognition, Image Processing, and Graphics: 6th National Conference, NCVPRIPG 2017, Mandi, India, 16–19 December 2017, Revised Selected Papers 6, pp. 470–480. Springer (2018)
8. Dutta, K., Krishnan, P., Mathew, M., Jawahar, C.: Towards spotting and recognition of handwritten words in Indic scripts. In: 2018 16th International Conference on Frontiers in Handwriting Recognition (ICFHR), pp. 32–37. IEEE (2018)
9. Garain, U., Mioulet, L., Chaudhuri, B.B., Chatelain, C., Paquet, T.: Unconstrained Bengali handwriting recognition with recurrent models. In: 2015 13th International Conference on Document Analysis and Recognition (ICDAR), pp. 1056–1060. IEEE (2015)
10. Gongidi, S., Jawahar, C.V.: IIIT-INDIC-HW-WORDS: a dataset for Indic handwritten text recognition. In: Lladós, J., Lopresti, D., Uchida, S. (eds.) ICDAR 2021. LNCS, vol. 12824, pp. 444–459. Springer, Cham (2021). https://doi.org/10.1007/978-3-030-86337-1_30
11. Graves, A., Liwicki, M., Fernández, S., Bertolami, R., Bunke, H., Schmidhuber, J.: A novel connectionist system for unconstrained handwriting recognition. IEEE Trans. Pattern Anal. Mach. Intell. **31**(5), 855–868 (2008)
12. Graves, A., Schmidhuber, J.: Offline handwriting recognition with multidimensional recurrent neural networks. In: Advances in Neural Information Processing Systems, vol. 21 (2008)
13. Jemni, S.K., Ammar, S., Kessentini, Y.: Domain and writer adaptation of offline Arabic handwriting recognition using deep neural networks. Neural Comput. Appl. **34**(3), 2055–2071 (2022)
14. Kaur, H., Kumar, M.: On the recognition of offline handwritten word using holistic approach and AdaBoost methodology. Multimedia Tools Appl. **80**(7), 11155–11175 (2021)
15. Kumar, P., Gupta, M., Gupta, M., Sharma, A.: Profession identification using handwritten text images. In: Nain, N., Vipparthi, S.K., Raman, B. (eds.) CVIP 2019. CCIS, vol. 1148, pp. 25–35. Springer, Singapore (2020). https://doi.org/10.1007/978-981-15-4018-9_3

16. Labani, M., Moradi, P., Ahmadizar, F., Jalili, M.: A novel multivariate filter method for feature selection in text classification problems. Eng. Appl. Artif. Intell. **70**, 25–37 (2018)
17. Li, M., et al.: TrOCR: transformer-based optical character recognition with pre-trained models. In: Proceedings of the AAAI Conference on Artificial Intelligence, vol. 37, pp. 13094–13102 (2023)
18. Ly, N.T., Nguyen, C.T., Nakagawa, M.: Training an end-to-end model for offline handwritten Japanese text recognition by generated synthetic patterns. In: 2018 16th International Conference on Frontiers in Handwriting Recognition (ICFHR), pp. 74–79. IEEE (2018)
19. Maalej, R., Kherallah, M.: Improving the DBLSTM for on-line Arabic handwriting recognition. Multimedia Tools Appl. **79**, 17969–17990 (2020)
20. Mondal, A., Jawahar, C.: Enhancing Indic handwritten text recognition using global semantic information. In: International Conference on Frontiers in Handwriting Recognition, pp. 360–374. Springer (2022)
21. Nguyen, K.C., Nguyen, C.T., Nakagawa, M.: A semantic segmentation-based method for handwritten Japanese text recognition. In: 2020 17th International Conference on Frontiers in Handwriting Recognition (ICFHR), pp. 127–132. IEEE (2020)
22. Peng, D., et al.: Recognition of handwritten Chinese text by segmentation: a segment-annotation-free approach. IEEE Trans. Multimedia (2022)
23. Pham, V., Bluche, T., Kermorvant, C., Louradour, J.: Dropout improves recurrent neural networks for handwriting recognition. In: 2014 14th International Conference on Frontiers in Handwriting Recognition, pp. 285–290. IEEE (2014)
24. Roy, P.P., Bhunia, A.K., Das, A., Dey, P., Pal, U.: Hmm-based Indic handwritten word recognition using zone segmentation. Pattern Recogn. **60**, 1057–1075 (2016)
25. Sankaran, N., Neelappa, A., Jawahar, C.: Devanagari text recognition: a transcription based formulation. In: 2013 12th International Conference on Document Analysis and Recognition, pp. 678–682. IEEE (2013)
26. Shaw, B., Bhattacharya, U., Parui, S.K.: Combination of features for efficient recognition of offline handwritten Devanagari words. In: 2014 14th International Conference on Frontiers in Handwriting Recognition, pp. 240–245. IEEE (2014)
27. Shaw, B., Parui, S.K., Shridhar, M.: Offline handwritten Devanagari word recognition: a holistic approach based on directional chain code feature and HMM. In: 2008 International Conference on Information Technology, pp. 203–208. IEEE (2008)
28. Vaswani, A., et al.: Attention is all You need. In: Advances in Neural Information Processing Systems, vol. 30 (2017)
29. Wu, Y.C., Yin, F., Chen, Z., Liu, C.L.: Handwritten Chinese text recognition using separable multi-dimensional recurrent neural network. In: 2017 14th IAPR International Conference on Document Analysis and Recognition (ICDAR), vol. 1, pp. 79–84. IEEE (2017)
30. Xie, Z., Sun, Z., Jin, L., Feng, Z., Zhang, S.: Fully convolutional recurrent network for handwritten Chinese text recognition. In: 2016 23rd International Conference on Pattern Recognition (ICPR), pp. 4011–4016. IEEE (2016)

Deep Feature Extraction and Feature Map Explainability for Landmark Localization in Cephalometric Radiographs

S. Rashmi[2(✉)], S. Srinath[1], R. Rakshitha[1], and B. V. Poornima[3]

[1] JSS Science and Technology University, Mysuru, India
[2] RV University, Bangalore, India
rashmibe.nayak@gmail.com
[3] Sahyadri College of Engineering & Management, Mangaluru, India

Abstract. The localization of landmarks plays a critical role in medical image analysis, particularly in tasks like cephalometry which involves the radiographic examination of the human cranium. This paper proposes a method for identifying anatomical points in cephalometric images using pre-trained models to address the challenge of insufficient data, a major obstacle in medical image training. A patch classification model is developed utilizing deep feature maps extracted from renowned pre-trained models such as VGGNet16, ResNet50, InceptionNetV3, and DenseNet121, trained on the ImageNet dataset with the exclusion of the last dense layers. These feature maps are then classified using the Light Gradient Boosting Machine algorithm. Landmark coordinates are extracted from patches that get the highest probability value in patch classification for containing the desired anatomical point. Experimental evaluation conducted on a dataset comprising 300 cephalometric images for 19 anatomical landmarks demonstrates average identification accuracies of 81.78%, 78.43%, 68.11%, and 77.50% for VGG16, ResNet50, InceptionNetV3, and DenseNet121, respectively. Additionally, the gradient-based explainability method is employed on the most effective VGGnet16 feature-extracting model to discern the image attributes extracted from patches, using ImageNet training weights, which are particularly conducive to prioritizing landmark localization.

Keywords: Cephalometric Radiographs · Landmark Annotation · Pre-trained Models · Feature Extraction · Deep Features

1 Introduction

Cephalometry constitutes a vital aspect of the medical field, focusing on the study of the human cranium. Among various diagnostic tools employed in this domain, lateral cephalometric images stand out, aiding orthodontists in analyzing dental and skeletal relationships within the human skull through a method known as cephalometric analysis. This analysis comprises a two-stage process: firstly, the precise localization of anatomical landmark points, followed by the measurement of diagnostically significant

J. Kakarla et al. (Eds.): CVIP 2024, CCIS 2473, pp. 249–263, 2026.
https://doi.org/10.1007/978-3-031-93688-3_18

linear and angular parameters between these points. These measurements are crucial for determining the classification of skeletal structures or for devising further treatment plans, such as orthodontic surgeries. The initial phase of this process heavily influences the quality and reliability of cephalometric analysis [1]. The gold standard followed for landmark identification is manual annotation by skilled professionals. However, this method has inherent limitations, including its time-consuming nature and susceptibility to subjective interpretation [2, 3]. Consequently, there is a growing emphasis on automating landmark detection tasks to alleviate the burden on professionals, enhance accuracy, and streamline analysis timelines. The automation of this process holds promise for improving practitioner efficiency and productivity, thereby advancing the standard of care in orthodontic practice.

In the era of Artificial Intelligence (AI), the automation of landmark identification has undergone various methodologies [4–6]. The progression of automation techniques began with rudimentary methods and has now evolved into sophisticated machine learning (ML) and deep learning (DL) technologies. With the swift advancements in neural networks, the availability of huge training data, and resources, and the prevailing trend of convolutional-based AI, the focus has shifted towards transfer learning approaches, leveraging vast datasets for model training [7, 8]. Typically, deep learning models necessitate extensive datasets for effective training. To tackle this challenge, benchmark datasets such as ImageNet, encompassing 1000 classes covering a wide array of real-world classification data, have been established. Complex deep learning architectures are trained on such datasets to attain generalized results for classification tasks. These learnings can then be repurposed or adapted for similar or disparate problem domains, particularly in scenarios where data availability poses a challenge, as observed in medical imaging.

The primary advantages of transfer learning approaches lie in their ability to construct accurate models with reduced time and computational resources [9]. Four distinct strategies have been devised for reusing pre-trained models: Firstly, for similar datasets of small size, straightforward reuse of pre-trained models involves adapting the final layer to suit the specific problem requirements. Secondly, for large similar datasets, the model architecture is trained from scratch, incorporating the weights acquired from the pretraining task. However, this strategy necessitates careful fine-tuning of other hyperparameters such as learning rates. Thirdly, for completely different small-sized datasets, feature extraction from pre-trained models is performed by freezing the initial layers, followed by feature finetuning by training a major part of convolutional-based layers of the model to achieve the desired output. Lastly, for entirely different large-sized datasets, the model architecture is reused, and the model is trained from scratch using various weight initialization methods. These avenues of research have opened up opportunities for reusing bulk dataset-trained models to mimic state-of-the-art results. Building upon this concept, the idea of leveraging the knowledge gained from benchmark dataset training on various models is applied to the problem of landmark localization. In the proposed work, the third strategy of reusing pre-trained models is employed. Despite the landmark annotation task revolving around the localization of specific points, the approach is tackled from a classification perspective, transitioning to a landmark regression task. The fusion of transfer learning and classical machine learning methods is employed to classify patches as either containing the landmark or not. This work contributes by addressing the challenge of landmark annotation through a classification-based approach, achieved through the development of an area of interest extraction framework followed by patch classification techniques. The principal contributions of the presented work are outlined as follows:

1. The integration of widely recognized pre-trained models such as VGG16, ResNet50, InceptionV3, and DenseNet221 to extract features from patches to classify the patch containing landmarks.
2. A comparative performance evaluation and analysis is conducted to evaluate patch classification efficiency for precise landmark identification across 19 considered landmarks, employing various pre-trained models for feature extraction and Light Gradient Boosting Machine (LGBM).
3. Elucidation of suitability for feature extraction purposes and bolstering the rationale behind its utilization in the study using model explainability.

2 Related Work

The methodologies employed for landmark annotation exhibit a temporal progression, categorized based on chronological periods or prevailing trends. Initially, the landscape was dominated by pure image processing techniques, which heavily relied on the quality of radiographic images. Methods such as edge and contour detection, pattern matching, shape descriptors, statistical models, and histogram transformation operations formed the cornerstone of this era [10–13]. These algorithms laid the groundwork for the subsequent wave of machine learning-based approaches. With the advent of benchmark datasets, traditional machine learning methodologies, particularly those based on forest algorithms, were explored in conjunction with various feature extraction techniques to ascertain landmark positions [14–18]. A pivotal milestone in the evolution of landmark annotation methodologies occurred around the year 2019, marking a significant surge in detection accuracy. This coincided with the emergence of convolutional-based architectures [19, 20], which revolutionized performance benchmarks in a myriad of tasks. Consequently, these advanced methodologies experienced heightened adoption to address the challenges posed by landmark annotation tasks, tailored to suit specific annotation requirements. Noteworthy challenges such as ISBI 2014 [21], and MCCAI 2023 [22] have catalyzed substantial research outcomes in the realm of cephalometric analysis. Several recent contributions within the field, pertinent to our research, warrant discussion and will be elaborated upon below.

Arik et al. [20] demonstrated a detection rate of 72.87% utilizing a combination of Convolutional Neural Network (CNN) and shape model-based systems for identifying landmark locations within raw image patches. Qian et al. [23] achieved an average detection accuracy of 77.45% by employing multi-task loss and multiscale training strategies alongside the ResNet50 model. Dai et al. [24] proposed an image input to image output framework incorporating generative autoencoder and decoder networks, supplemented by regression voting, resulting in an 80% detection rate. Lee et al. introduced a [25] convolutional neural network (BCNN) architecture, employing 38 models to regress 19 landmark coordinates, achieving an 82.11% detection accuracy. Reaching a step ahead of the landmark annotation task in cephalometric analysis, Yu et al. [26] proposed a direct skeletal structure classification model utilizing a modified DenseNet, enhancing performance through transfer learning and data augmentation techniques. Song et al. [27] utilized a pre-trained ResNet50 model with an added fully connected layer for direct regression of coordinates from the region of interest patches, reporting a detection accuracy of 80.2%. Recently, Neeraja et al. [28] introduced a convolutional model integrated with a Squeeze and Excitation attention block for landmark position classification and prediction, yielding an average detection accuracy of 84.3% on benchmark datasets. In the course of our research, our group conducted extensive experimentation on various feature learning approaches, culminating in the identification of context and feature level combinations for patch classification, resulting in a peak detection accuracy of 75.84% [29].

Thus far, the exploration of methods in landmark annotation has primarily consisted of two distinct categories: non-deep learning methods and deep learning methods, each with various sub-categorizations. However, there has been no reported experimentation involving a hybrid approach combining deep learning and non-deep learning algorithms for landmark annotation, specifically utilizing pre-trained models for feature extraction purposes. While the primary objective of employing deep learning convolutional architectures is to circumvent the complexities associated with feature extraction and engineering, commonly observed in traditional machine learning methods, there exist a few reported works that demonstrate the efficacy of leveraging deep feature extractions within non-deep learning frameworks to achieve commendable results.

3 Methodology

3.1 Dataset

In this study, we utilized a custom dataset gathered from JSS Dental College and Hospital, Mysore. The dataset comprises 300 high-resolution lateral cephalometric radiographs, each boasting a resolution of 1340×1938 pixels with a pixel resolution of 0.127 mm. These radiographs were meticulously annotated with 19 of the most frequently employed anatomical landmarks by three experienced professionals affiliated with JSS Dental College and Hospital. The radiographs selected for the dataset were obtained from patients who underwent treatment over the past decade, thereby encompassing a wide age range from 5 to 60 years old. The ethical clearance was obtained from the Institutional Ethical Clearance Board before conducting the study. Of the 300 images in our dataset, 200 were allocated for training purposes, while the remaining 100 images were reserved for testing. An example of the landmark annotation can be observed in Fig. 1, providing a visual representation of the 19 annotated landmarks.

3.2 Method

The proposed methodology is illustrated in Fig. 2 below, depicting a flowchart comprising four main steps. The first step involves an area of interest extraction, followed by classification data generation, feature extraction, and finally, patch classification, culminating in the extraction of coordinates from the correct patch.

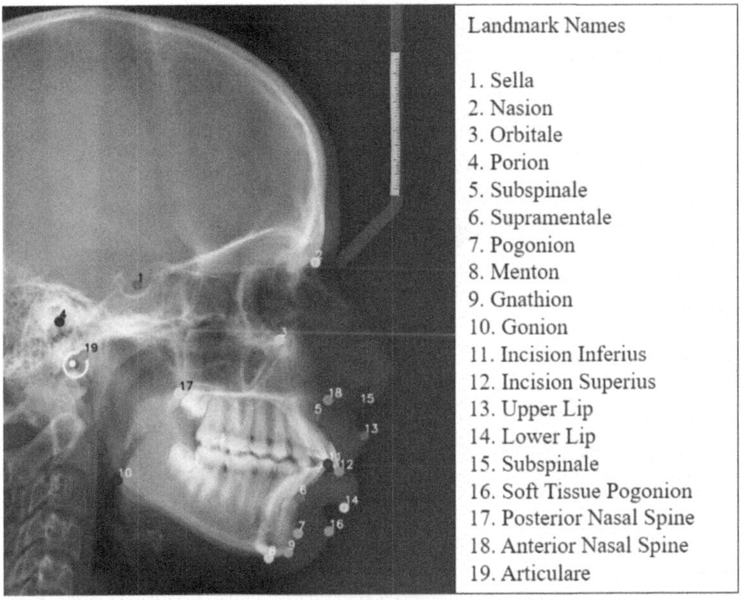

Fig. 1. Sample Cephalometric radiograph with annotations.

Area of Interest Extraction. We followed multimodal architecture to identify individual landmarks. Each landmark identification requires a specific region of interest identification within the cephalometric structure. To accomplish this, a normalized correlation-based template matching approach is employed. A source template is created by averaging patches of size 300 × 300 pixels from all training images, cropped around the ground truth landmarks for all 19 landmarks. After generating the average template, Contrast Limited Adaptive Histogram Equalization (CLAHE), a variant of adaptive histogram equalization, is applied to the templates to mitigate noise introduced during the averaging process. These templates serve as the source template for scanning the entire radiograph images to identify the matching center point of the pattern. The normalized correlation coefficient is utilized to assess the match score at each pixel position, facilitating the identification of the area of interest.

Patch Extraction. After identifying the maximum probability match between the source template and the target image, a localized area centered around this match is extracted, satisfying the maximum correlation match value. Within this thresholded region, random points are generated, and patches of size 256 × 256 pixels are extracted around these points, thus forming the training dataset.

Classification Data Generation. Patches containing the landmark precisely at the center region are assigned a class value of 1, while the remainder is assigned a value of 0. The ground truth labels for the patches are generated by computing the distance between the ground truth landmark and the center of each patch. To maintain an acceptable error range of 2 mm between the ground truth and predicted values, a threshold of 15 pixels is utilized, ensuring a maximum distance value of 1.9 mm. Patches falling within this threshold are labeled as class 1, while those outside are labeled as class 0.

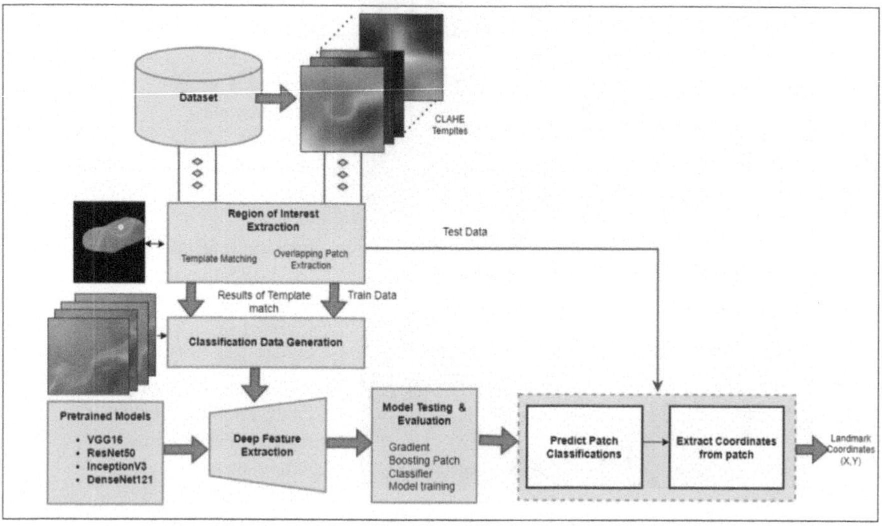

Fig. 2. Flow chart of the proposed work.

In this work, pre-trained models were leveraged to extract feature maps, aiming to alleviate two notable shortcomings evident in prior literature. Firstly, past studies have often fine-tuned the final layers of pre-trained models to directly predict landmark coordinates. However, since these models are predominantly trained on expansive datasets for classification tasks, repurposing them for regression may result in slight inaccuracies. Secondly, the datasets utilized to train these models typically exhibit significantly distinct target classes and features compared to radiographic images. Directly utilizing these features by flattening the final layer and adding a few more layers to further finetune it, requires resources. To circumvent these challenges, we implemented a methodology wherein feature maps were extracted from the final non-dense layers of each pre-trained model. Subsequently, an LGBM [30] model, reliant on gradients, was trained using these feature maps. Furthermore, a comprehensive analysis was conducted on the feature maps generated by the pre-trained model and the LGBM algorithm. This comparative examination sheds light on the efficacy of our approach and offers valuable insights into the disparities observed in the feature maps.

The selection of the renowned benchmark pre-trained models, namely VGG16, ResNet50, InceptionV3, and DenseNet121, for feature extraction comparison, is underpinned by their architectural diversity, performance, accessibility, and widespread availability. These models have been extensively trained on the ImageNet dataset, a pivotal benchmark in computer vision tasks. VGG16 is esteemed for its architectural simplicity, characterized by a deeper structure. In contrast, ResNet50 introduces innovative residual connections to effectively address the challenge of vanishing gradient problems. InceptionV3 leverages inception modules, optimizing feature extraction efficiency, while

DenseNet121 harnesses densely connected layers to promote feature reuse and mitigate vanishing gradient issues. Each model offers distinct advantages and complexities, making them well-suited for diverse tasks in computer vision. Below, we provide a succinct overview of these models to elucidate their architectural intricacies and functionalities.

1. VGG16: Developed by Simonyan and Zisserman [31] of the Visual Geometry Group in the year 2014, VGG16 is characterized by a series of convolutional, pooling, and fully connected layers, culminating in a total of 16 layers within its architecture. Its straightforward design and depth have made it a popular choice for image classification tasks. Moreover, the feature extraction capabilities of VGG16 have been widely utilized in various computer vision applications, owing to its ability to learn rich representations of visual data. The hierarchical structure of convolutional layers in VGG16 enables it to capture intricate patterns and features present in images, facilitating robust feature extraction for subsequent tasks. The feature map contains 32,768 values after reshaping the VGG16 feature extraction output.
2. ResNet50: To address the challenge of the exploding gradient problem encountered in architectures like VGG16, ResNet50 variants were introduced by He et al. [32] in 2015. By incorporating residual connections into a 50-layer convolutional neural network architecture, ResNet50 enables more efficient training of deep networks. These residual connections allow the network to learn residual functions, making it easier to optimize and train very deep architectures. This innovation significantly improves the stability and convergence of the training process, facilitating the extraction of rich and informative features from input images. As a result, ResNet50 has become a popular choice for feature extraction tasks in various computer vision applications. The feature map from ResNet50 contains 131,072 values after reshaping.
3. InceptionV3: Introduced by Google Research [33] in 2015, as an evolution of the original Inception architecture, InceptionV3 incorporates auxiliary classifiers connected to intermediate layers of the network, which assist in injecting additional gradients during training, thereby addressing the vanishing gradient problem and enhancing training stability. Additionally, InceptionV3 having 47 layers of deep architecture, employs advanced convolutional techniques and factorization methods to efficiently extract features from input images. The feature map from InceptionV3 contains 131,072 values after reshaping.
4. DenseNet121: Proposed in 2017 by Huang et al. [34], DenseNet121 is distinguished by its unique characteristic of dense layer connections, where each layer is directly linked to all others in a feedforward manner. This architecture incorporates dense layers and transition layers strategically designed to alleviate challenges related to feature and gradient propagation across the network. The dense connectivity within DenseNet121 facilitates efficient feature extraction and representation learning from input images, resulting in enhanced performance outcomes. The DenseNet121 gives a feature map of 50,179 values after reshaping.

Classification and Coordinates Generation. The extracted features from benchmark models are subsequently employed to train the LGBM model, enabling it to capture the intrinsic features learned from these models. The LGBM classifier model is trained with parameters such as learning rate of 0.05 and a boosting type of 'gbdt' and the objective function value set to 'binary'. Although LGBM is conventionally trained for classification tasks, it outputs probabilities for classification. The patch with the highest probability of being classified as a class 1 patch is identified as the patch containing the actual landmark. The coordinates of the patch center are then added to the patch coordinate values to derive the final landmarks for the specific landmark of interest.

4 Results and Discussion

The experiments were conducted within the Google Colab environment. The size of the training data varied for each landmark depending on the extracted area of interest. For result evaluation, a set of 100 test images was utilized across all landmarks. Commonly used metrics in landmark annotation tasks, such as the success detection rate (SDR) within the precision range of 2 mm, 2.5 mm, 3 mm, and 4 mm, are employed for result analysis. The SDR quantifies the ratio of detected landmarks within specified precision thresholds compared to actual landmarks. The mean radial error (MRE) between predicted and ground truth values is also computed. Furthermore, Figs. 3, 4, 5 and 6 depict the variations in SDR for all 19 landmarks at precision thresholds of 2 mm, 2.5 mm, 3 mm, and 4 mm, respectively with the x-axis showing the landmark numbers and the y-axis showing the SDR in percentage values.

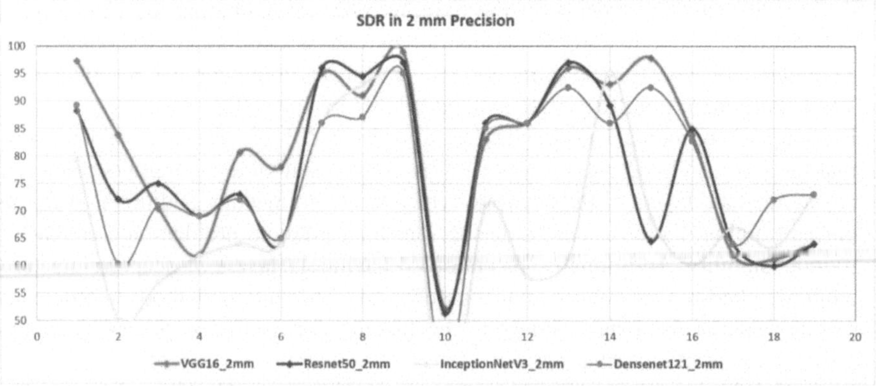

Fig. 3. Detection rate within 2 mm for all feature extraction methods.

Based on the depicted plots, it is evident that the VGG16 model consistently surpasses all other models across all precision ranges. The straightforward design of VGG16, comprised of a sequence of convolutional and pooling layers, offers a simplicity in architecture that stands in contrast to the more intricate structures of other feature extractors. This simplicity appears to facilitate the extraction of patch discriminative features crucial for accurately classifying candidate patches of the landmark. In contrast, the complexity inherent in models like ResNet50, InceptionV3, and DenseNet121 seems to adversely affect their classification performance. As the feature map progresses through the layers of these complex architectures, it appears to lose its ability to provide a discriminative representation, as evidenced by the results obtained. Specifically, DenseNet121 and

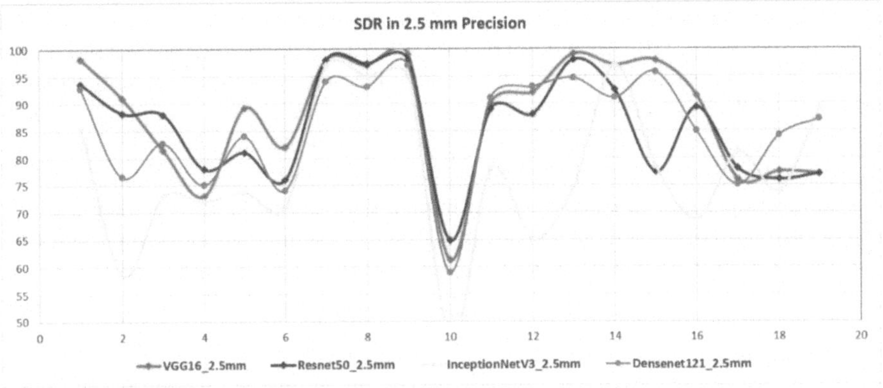

Fig. 4. Detection rate within 2.5 mm for all feature extraction methods.

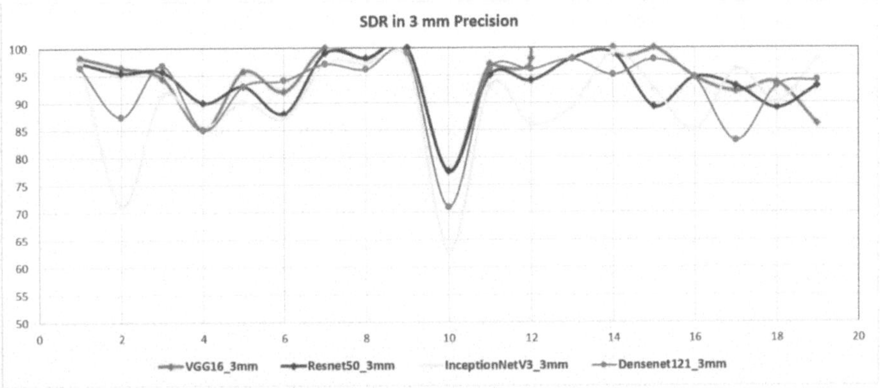

Fig. 5. Detection rate within 3 mm for all feature extraction methods.

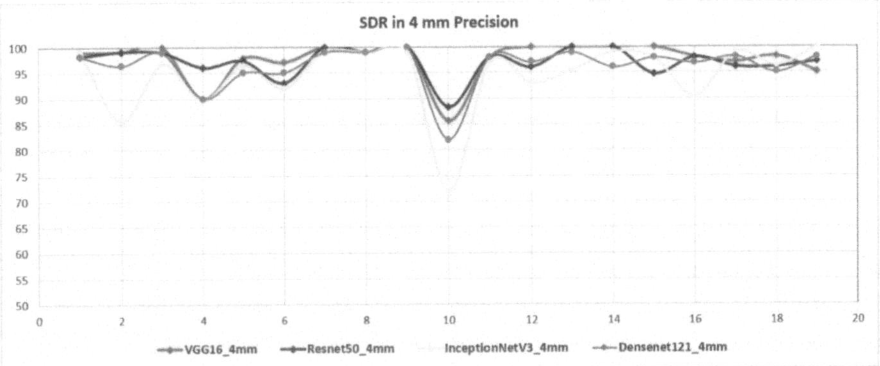

Fig. 6. Detection rate within 4 mm for all feature extraction methods.

ResNet50 demonstrate comparable performances of average SDR values of 78.43% and 77.50% respectively. While InceptionV3 struggles to extract sufficiently discriminative features from the patches to effectively identify landmarks resulting in SDR value of 68.11%. This observation underscores the importance of architectural simplicity in facilitating the extraction of discriminative features crucial for accurate landmark classification. In addition, we conducted an ablation study on all aforementioned models, where we examined their performance by either including or excluding the last dense layers, and also by modifying the target classes in the pre-trained models. However, the results were considerably lower, ranging between 40% to 65%, and were not consistent across the landmarks compared to the performance achieved using the LGBM model. This finding underscores the efficacy of non-deep learning classifiers when coupled with deep feature extraction methods. A comprehensive table highlighting the best-performing results obtained with the VGG16 model is presented for reference and comparison in Table 1.

Table 1. Best performing VGG16 feature extraction and classification results.

No.	Landmark Name	MRE (mm)	SDR (mm)	SDR (%)			
				2 mm	2.5 mm	3 mm	4 mm
1	Sella	1.14	1.12	97.29	98.19	98.19	99
2	Nasion	1.65	1.02	83.78	90.99	96.39	99.09
3	Orbitale	1.91	1.1	70.37	81.48	94.44	100
4	Porion	2.58	2.11	62	73	85	90
5	Subspinale	1.8	1.12	80.64	89.24	95.69	97.84
6	Supramentale	1.9	1.7	78	82	92	97
7	Pogonion	1.08	0.72	95	98	100	100
8	Gnathion	1.66	3.8	91	97	98	99
9	Menton	1.04	0.57	99	99	100	100
10	Gonion	2.95	1.89	52.25	61.23	77.47	85.58
11	Lower Incisor	1.71	1.2	83	90	97	98
12	Upper Incisor	1.45	0.91	86	92	98	100
13	Upper Lip	1.06	0.57	96	99	100	100
14	Lower Lip	1.24	0.73	93	97	100	100
15	Nasion	1.23	0.67	97.8	97.8	100	100
16	Soft Pogonion	1.64	1.66	83.87	91.39	94.62	98
17	PNS	2.21	1.22	62	76	92	97
18	ANS	2.1	1.2	61.2	77.4	93.6	98.1
19	Articulare	2.39	2.09	64	77	86	95
	Average	**1.72**	**1.33**	**81.78**	**88.37**	**95.13**	**97.70**

The results were also compared with our previous work on various hand-crafted feature extraction methods for the same dataset [29], as shown in Table 2. Exhaustive experimentation with gradient features in four different contextual combinations identified HOG as the best performer for local handcrafted feature extraction. However, the results in the table below indicate that most deep feature extraction methods outperform the handcrafted gradient-based techniques. This suggests that employing transfer learning feature extraction, even with smaller datasets, can yield remarkable results for landmark annotation.

Table 2. Performing comparison of hand-crafted features vs. deep features for landmark annotation.

Type	Method	MRE (mm)	SD (mm)	SDR (%)
Hand-crafted features	Raw pixel as a feature map	2.73	1.61	68.11
	Gradient magnitude as a feature map	2.21	1.88	65
	Gradient direction as a feature map	1.88	2.73	73.37
	HOG as a feature map	1.61	1.38	75.87
Deep features	**VGG16**	**1.72**	**1.33**	**81.78**
	ResNet50	1.8	1.34	78.43
	InceptionNetV3	2.25	1.94	68.11
	DenseNet121	1.93	1.96	77.50

Feature Map Explainability: Feature map explainability refers to the interpretability of the learned representations of input data generated by a neural network's convolutional layers. To substantiate the efficacy of our proposed methodology and to understand the feature maps training using LGBM, an in-depth examination of the explainability aspects is conducted. Specifically, we investigated the interpretability of the VGG16 feature extraction gradients that serve as feature input to the LGBM model to get the patch classification results. To visualize the feature maps on patch images, we employed Gradient-weighted Class Activation Mapping (Grad-CAM). The visualization of the explainability results using the VGG16 feature map on individual patch images is shown in Fig. 7.

This visualization technique allowed us to discern the importance of different image regions or features generated by the model, which predominantly influenced the classification outcomes. In most of the landmark patches, contours generated by skeletal structures and soft tissue structures contribute to the feature map. In the context of explainability, for landmark features 13, 14, and 15 related to soft tissue identification, the feature map fails to adequately distinguish the surrounding features near the landmarks. The GradCAM analysis reveals that the current method primarily extracts edge and contour features around landmark points, rather than capturing the finer and more specific features relevant to individual landmarks. However, accurate classification heavily relies on the relative positions of hard tissues, achieving high rates of 93%, 96%, and 97.8% for landmarks 13, 14, and 15 respectively which complicates the model explainability. This limitation could significantly impact the applicability and reliability of the methodology, particularly in the rigorous context of medical image processing.

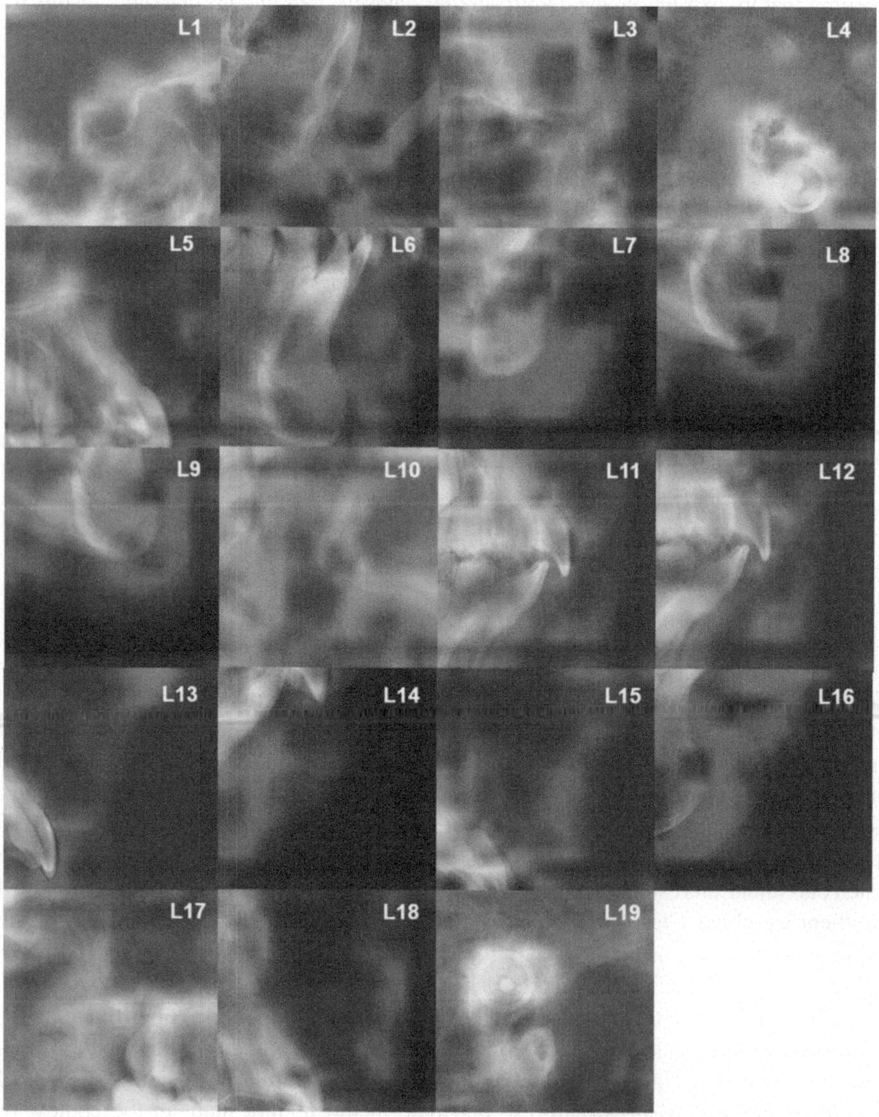

Fig. 7. Grad-CAM results on individual landmark patches for the VGG16 feature map.

5 Conclusion

The proposed methodology introduces a novel approach for identifying cephalometric anatomical landmarks through patch classification using deep feature extraction techniques. Experiments were conducted using various pre-trained transfer learning models—VGG16, ResNet50, InceptionV3, and DenseNet121—leveraging their ImageNet weights to extract feature maps from candidate landmark patches. Among these models, VGG16 achieved the highest average landmark detection metric of 1.72 mm MRE with a success detection rate of 81.78%. This performance surpasses our previous work with hand-crafted feature extraction methods, demonstrating the potential of deep feature extraction for landmark annotation tasks.

Furthermore, the methodology provided insights into patch explainability, highlighting regions within images crucial for accurate classification. Understanding these visual patterns is critical, especially given deviations in feature generation weights from the problem context. The use of pre-trained models streamlines feature extraction, enhancing efficiency compared to traditional machine learning techniques. Moving forward, we aim to further enhance our methodology by focusing on extracting deep features specifically tailored to our dataset, rather than solely relying on pre-trained weights for these architectures.

References

1. Junaid, N., et al.: Development, application, and performance of artificial intelligence in cephalometric landmark identification and diagnosis: a systematic review. Healthcare **10**(12), 2454 (2022). https://doi.org/10.3390/healthcare10122454
2. Kamoen, A.: The clinical significance of error measurement in the interpretation of treatment results. Eur. J. Orthod. **23**(5), 569–578 (2001). https://doi.org/10.1093/ejo/23.5.569
3. da Silveira, H.L.D., Silveira, H.E.D.: Reproducibility of cephalometric measurements made by three radiology clinics. Angle Orthod. **76**(3), 394–399 (2006). https://doi.org/10.1043/0003-3219(2006)076[0394:ROCMMB]2.0.CO;2
4. Johnston, B., de Chazal, P.: A review of image-based automatic facial landmark identification techniques. EURASIP J. Image Video Process **2018**(1), 86 (2018). https://doi.org/10.1186/s13640-018-0324-4
5. Vandaele, R., et al.: Landmark detection in 2D bioimages for geometric morphometrics: a multi-resolution tree-based approach. Sci. Rep. **8**(1), 538 (2018). https://doi.org/10.1038/s41598-017-18993-5
6. Bier, B., et al.: Learning to detect anatomical landmarks of the pelvis in X-rays from arbitrary views. Int. J. Comput. Assist. Radiol. Surg. **14**(9), 1463–1473 (2019). https://doi.org/10.1007/s11548-019-01975-5
7. Hosna, A., Merry, E., Gyalmo, J., Alom, Z., Aung, Z., Azim, M.A.: Transfer learning: a friendly introduction. J. Big Data **9**(1), 102 (2022). https://doi.org/10.1186/s40537-022-00652-w
8. Pan, S.J., Yang, Q.: A survey on transfer learning. IEEE Trans. Knowl. Data Eng. **22**(10), 1345–1359 (2010). https://doi.org/10.1109/TKDE.2009.191
9. Yosinski, J., Clune, J., Bengio, Y., Lipson, H.: How transferable are features in deep neural networks? In: Proceedings of the 27th International Conference on Neural Information Processing Systems - Volume 2, NIPS 2014, Cambridge, MA, USA, pp. 3320–3328. MIT Press (2014)

10. Chakrabartty, S., Yagi, M., Shibata, T., Cauwenberghs, G.: Robust cephalometric landmark identification using support vector machines. In: 2003 International Conference on Multimedia and Expo, ICME 2003. Proceedings (Cat. No. 03TH8698), pp. III–429. IEEE (2003). https://doi.org/10.1109/ICME.2003.1221340
11. Rueda, S., Alcañiz, M.: An approach for the automatic cephalometric landmark detection using mathematical morphology and active appearance models, pp. 159–166 (2006). https://doi.org/10.1007/11866565_20
12. Kafieh, R., Mehri, A., Sadri, S.: Automatic landmark detection in cephalometry using a modified active shape model with sub-image matching. In: 2007 International Conference on Machine Vision, pp. 73–78. IEEE, December 2007. https://doi.org/10.1109/ICMV.2007.4469276
13. Vucinic, P., Trpovski, Z., Scepan, I.: Automatic landmarking of cephalograms using active appearance models. Eur. J. Orthod. **32**(3), 233–241 (2010). https://doi.org/10.1093/ejo/cjp099
14. Pouyan, A.A., Farshbaf, M.: Cephalometric landmarks localization based on histograms of oriented gradients. In: 2010 International Conference on Signal and Image Processing, pp. 1–6. IEEE, December 2010. https://doi.org/10.1109/ICSIP.2010.5697431
15. Ibragimov, B., Likar, B., Pernuš, F., Vrtovec, T.: Automatic cephalometric X-ray landmark detection by applying game theory and random forests. In: ISBI International Symposium on Biomedical Imaging, Automatic Cephalometric X-Ray Landmark Detection Challenge (2014)
16. Mirzaalian, H., Hamarneh, G.: Automatic globally-optimal pictorial structures with random decision forest based likelihoods for cephalometric X-ray landmark detection, pp. 1–12, December 2014. https://www.researchgate.net/publication/268789845_Automatic_Globally-Optimal_Pictorial_Structures_with_Random_Decision_Forest_Based_Likelihoods_For_Cephalometric_X-Ray_Landmark_Detection. Accessed 20 Dec 2022
17. Kaur, A., Singh, C.: Automatic cephalometric landmark detection using Zernike moments and template matching. Sig. Image Video Process **9**(1), 117–132 (2015). https://doi.org/10.1007/s11760-013-0432-7
18. Lindner, C., Cootes, T.: Fully automatic cephalometric evaluation using random forest regression-voting, December 2015
19. Lee, H., Park, M., Kim, J.: Cephalometric landmark detection in dental x-ray images using convolutional neural networks. In: Armato, S.G., Petrick, N.A. (eds.) Medical Imaging 2017: Computer-Aided Diagnosis, p. 101341W, March 2017. https://doi.org/10.1117/12.2255870
20. Arık, S.Ö., Ibragimov, B., Xing, L.: Fully automated quantitative cephalometry using convolutional neural networks. J. Med. Imaging (Bellingham) **4**(1), 014501 (2017). https://doi.org/10.1117/1.JMI.4.1.014501
21. Lindner, C., Wang, C.-W., Huang, C.-T., Li, C.-H., Chang, S.-W., Cootes, T.F.: Fully automatic system for accurate localisation and analysis of cephalometric landmarks in lateral cephalograms. Sci. Rep. **6** (2016). https://doi.org/10.1038/srep33581
22. Cephalometric Landmark Detection in Lateral X-ray Images 2023. https://cl-detection2023.grand-challenge.org/
23. Qian, J., Cheng, M., Tao, Y., Lin, J., Lin, H.: CephaNet: an improved faster R-CNN for cephalometric landmark detection. In: 2019 IEEE 16th International Symposium on Biomedical Imaging (ISBI 2019), pp. 868–871. IEEE, April 2019. https://doi.org/10.1109/ISBI.2019.8759437
24. Dai, X., Zhao, H., Liu, T., Cao, D., Xie, L.: Locating anatomical landmarks on 2D lateral cephalograms through adversarial encoder-decoder networks. IEEE Access **7**, 132738–132747 (2019). https://doi.org/10.1109/ACCESS.2019.2940623
25. Lee, J.H., Yu, H.J., Kim, M.J., Kim, J.W., Choi, J.: Automated cephalometric landmark detection with confidence regions using Bayesian convolutional neural networks. BMC Oral Health **20**(1) (2020). https://doi.org/10.1186/s12903-020-01256-7

26. Yu, H.J., Cho, S.R., Kim, M.J., Kim, W.H., Kim, J.W., Choi, J.: Automated skeletal classification with lateral cephalometry based on artificial intelligence. J. Dent. Res. **99**(3), 249–256 (2020). https://doi.org/10.1177/0022034520901715
27. Song, Y., Qiao, X., Iwamoto, Y., Chen, Y.-W.: Automatic cephalometric landmark detection on X-ray images using a deep-learning method. Appl. Sci. (Switzerland) **10**(7) (2020). https://doi.org/10.3390/app10072547
28. Neeraja, R., Jani Anbarasi, L.: CephXNet: a deep convolutional squeeze-and-excitation model for landmark prediction on lateral cephalograms. IEEE Access **11**, 90780–90800 (2023). https://doi.org/10.1109/ACCESS.2023.3307636
29. Murthy, P.M., Deshmukh, S.: Landmark annotation through feature combinations: a comparative study on cephalometric images with in-depth analysis of model's explainability. Dentomaxillofacial Radiol. (2023). https://doi.org/10.1093/dmfr/twad011
30. Ke, G., et al.: LightGBM: a highly efficient gradient boosting decision tree. In: Guyon, I., et al. (eds.) Advances in Neural Information Processing Systems. Curran Associates, Inc. (2017). https://proceedings.neurips.cc/paper/2017/file/6449f44a102fde848669bdd9eb6b76fa-Paper.pdf
31. Simonyan, K., Zisserman, A.: Very deep convolutional networks for large-scale image recognition. arXiv:1409.1556, April 2014
32. He, K., Zhang, X., Ren, S., Sun, J.: Deep residual learning for image recognition. In: 2016 IEEE Conference on Computer Vision and Pattern Recognition (CVPR), pp. 770–778. IEEE, June 2016. https://doi.org/10.1109/CVPR.2016.90
33. Szegedy, C., Vanhoucke, V., Ioffe, S., Shlens, J., Wojna, Z.: Rethinking the inception architecture for computer vision. In: 2016 IEEE Conference on Computer Vision and Pattern Recognition (CVPR), pp. 2818–2826. IEEE, June 2016. https://doi.org/10.1109/CVPR.2016.308
34. Huang, G., Liu, Z., Van Der Maaten, L., Weinberger, K.Q.: Densely connected convolutional networks. In: 2017 IEEE Conference on Computer Vision and Pattern Recognition (CVPR), pp. 2261–2269. IEEE, July 2017. https://doi.org/10.1109/CVPR.2017.243

A Novel Hierarchical Pipeline for Fine-Grained Punch Recognition in Uncontrolled Setting

Vipul Baghel[1], Sagar Deep Deb[2], Rithihas Nagisetti[3], Babji Srinivasan[2], and Ravi Hegde[1](✉)

[1] Department of Electrical Engineering, Indian Institute of Technology Gandhinagar, Gandhinagar, Gujarat, India
{baghelvipul,hegder}@iitgn.ac.in

[2] Department of Applied Mechanics, Indian Institute of Technology Madras, Chennai, Tamil Nadu, India
babji.srinivasan@iitm.ac.in

[3] Department of Electronics and Communication Engineering, Indian Institute of Technology Kharagpur, Kharagpur, West Bengal, India

Abstract. Human Action Recognition (HAR) is one of the most emerging topics in the field of Computer Vision. It finds utilization in a wide range of applications like athletics, healthcare, security, sports performance, etc. In sports, HAR can be used to monitor athletes' movements to facilitate skill development and decision-making training. However, in case of highly dynamic sports like boxing, automatic HAR becomes more difficult. Variations in lighting conditions, background, camera perspectives, and rapid movements collectively compound the complexity in automatic HAR and its performance further worsens with the involvement of uncontrolled environment videos. This manuscript proposes a hierarchical pipeline for robust sports activity recognition. For this purpose, a novel regression-based detection is introduced using a Dual Stream Spatio Temporal Transformer, and a 3D Convolutional Neural Network (CNN) is used for fine-grained classification. The approach commences with regression-based detection to identify punch instances within unedited boxing video streams. Subsequently, a fine-grained classification module is employed to categorize detected punches into six basic punch types: jabs, cross, lead, and rear hooks, or lead and rear uppercuts. This hierarchical architecture enables efficient and accurate punch recognition in diverse real-world wild settings. Experimental results on various unedited YouTube videos show the effectiveness of our proposed approach. The proposed approach achieves an overall mean detection accuracy of 96.09% and a mean classification accuracy of 88.25% on test videos.

Keywords: Sports Activity Recognition · Regression · Classification · Spatio-temporal Transformer

J. Kakarla et al. (Eds.): CVIP 2024, CCIS 2473, pp. 264–278, 2026.
https://doi.org/10.1007/978-3-031-93688-3_19

1 Introduction

Human Activity Recognition (HAR) is one of the major research domains in Computer Vision. It finds application in various fields of research like healthcare, anomaly detection, sports analytics, human-computer interaction, etc. [2,9]. HAR in sports makes it easier to analyze games tactically and physically and evaluate athletes' performances for the coaches and the sports world at large [12]. Despite this growing need, there is limited research on combat sports like boxing. In settings where sports are competitive, like boxing, the post-match analysis of the number of different kinds of punches attempted provides a valuable source of information.

Initially, statistics in various combat sports like boxing were generated by human annotators. It required hours of human efforts to minutely segment the punches for its analysis [14]. Various sporting arrangements also used Inertial Measurement Unit (IMU) based sensors, which consist of gyroscopes and accelerometers, for punch classification. IMU sensors come with various disadvantages, like wearing them during boxing training or matches may disrupt an athlete's focus or comfort and sometimes lead to various injuries [6].

With Vision-based approaches, actions can be detected automatically, thus reducing human intervention. But many visual-based approaches use depth cameras, which are costly and thus are not effective for historical videos [6,24,32]. Thus, there is a need for the development of an accurate punch classifier pipeline suitable for *in-the-wild* settings to understand the total number of punches a boxer attempts during a bout. This will also provide a base for the future development of punch analyzers. The following are the major contributions:

- A hierarchical-based approach for punch classification from unedited videos is proposed. The two-step approach involves detecting the fixed-length punch clips from the input video and, finally, classifying the detected punch clip into one of the six basic punch categories.
- Considered the task of punch detection as a regression problem rather than classification, which allows us to quantify the partial actions. Employing a sigmoid activation function in the final layer restricts the output probabilities within the interval [0, 1], wherein a value of 1 denotes the inception of a punch.
- Demonstrated the utility of the proposed methodology on different unedited videos collected from YouTube. Distinct sets of train and test videos featuring different subjects were selected to underscore the generalizability of the proposed approach.

2 Related Work

Human motions can be represented as sequences of poses, encapsulating spatio-temporal data. Human Action Recognition (HAR) is a vibrant and rapidly evolving field with diverse applications, from enhancing human-computer interactions to bolstering security systems. The computational interpretation of such data offers extensive benefits across diverse domains like surveillance [4] [13], Human-Computer Interaction [20], sports analytics [28] [17], and medicine [7,33]. In this section, we delve into two pivotal approaches: vision-based and sensor-based methods, each representing a substantial body of research and innovation.

Several studies [3,14,27,30] have showcased the utility of Human Action Recognition (HAR) in individual and team sports, facilitating player training and fair assessment. Even with simple MLP models, accurate kinematic data can lead to decent action recognition accuracy regardless of the players' proficiency levels [14]. In recent years, the advancements in deep learning techniques within computer vision have notably enhanced video-based sports HAR [30], providing satisfactory outcomes applicable to various individual and team sports, thereby augmenting player training and evaluation protocols. Deep learning models surpass traditional machine learning approaches [3] due to their capacity to capture intricate data patterns through extensive parameterization. However, the sensitivity of deep learning models to dataset characteristics, especially with small dataset sizes, remains a challenge.

2.1 Sensor-Based HAR

In sensor-based HAR, sensors capturing the kinematics of specific body parts during actions are utilized. For example, in boxing, Inertial Measurement Unit (IMU) sensors placed at key body locations such as wrists, elbows, and shoulders provide precise 3D kinematic data, including linear and angular velocities and accelerations. This results in multiple time series data, which can be classified using various techniques such as Convolutional Neural Networks (CNNs) [11], Long Short-Term Memory networks (LSTMs) [21], statistical embeddings like Multiview Cauchy Estimator Feature Embedding (MCEFE) [8], and Physic-aware adversarial networks [23], among other deep learning approaches [16,29], on accelerometer data for action classification.

Although sensor-based methods achieve satisfactory accuracy, obtaining on-body sensor data during combat sports presents challenges due to potential damage during bouts. Furthermore, collecting data during official matches is often impractical due to restrictions on using add-ons to equipment during matches, making on-body sensor-based evaluation during matches unfeasible.

2.2 Vision-Based HAR

Visual data is categorized into two domains based on their dimensionality, i.e., 2D and 3D (with depth) images. 2D imagery is straightforward to capture using any low-end camera system. However, they exhibit an intrinsic self-occlusion problem, resulting in the corrupted or missing pose estimation. 3D imagery is captured with multiple camera systems or Time-of-Flight (ToF) based cameras. It can capture RGB videos and depth information during motion despite occlusions. However, sophisticated and expensive vision sensors are required to obtain 3D images or videos that include ground truth depth information.

Vision-based human action recognition involves analyzing sequences of images and capturing subjects in various activities. This approach categorizes based on how images are processed:

RGB Image-Based Action Recognition. Several studies, such as Mohith et al. [22] and Abdul et al. [1], harnessed trajectory descriptors from optical flow to classify general human actions. However, these approaches demanded substantial computational resources, limiting their real-time applicability. On the other hand, Yi et al. [32] adopted dense-trajectory descriptors, correlation, and weighted trajectory encoding as features extracted from 2D visual data, achieving accurate human action classification. Stefański et al. [26] labeled a 50 FPS video of an Olympic match, employing clash detection to remove frames with significant player distance. Their CNN model classified actions into the head, corpus, and block categories, lacking fine-grained boxing punch classification and sequential context.

Skeleton-Based Action Recognition. Skeleton-based Human Action Recognition (HAR) has emerged as a more promising approach, focusing on human landmarks as perceptible cues for action understanding. Luo et al. [18] introduced a time-series modeling of HAR by integrating Pose Estimation with Long Short-Term Memory (LSTM) networks. Silva et al. [24] proposed a rapid human action recognition method using visual question-answering techniques, processing a 2D image frame in a mere 190 milliseconds. Their approach involved an ensemble of Bayesian, Multinomial, Complement, and Gaussian classifiers. These classifiers were applied to same-side and cross-side Euclidean distances between selected joints and knee, elbow, and shoulder joint angles. Additionally, relative keypoint coordinates concerning the nose, assumed to be a static point during the action, were incorporated as features. Yang et al. [31] employed graph convolutional neural networks during boxing actions, addressing frame coarseness with Neville interpolation. Conversely, Hudovernik et al. [10] used Vision Transformers in Jiu-jitsu videos, applying rule-based algorithms for automated scoring but facing challenges with covariate shifts across different fighting styles. Researchers like Shujah et al. [25] have also explored various human pose kinematic features for pose information encoding. One of the most active research topics in Artificial intelligence and Computer Vision is Mixed Reality, which allows humans to interact with real-world and computer-generated environments. It automates fitness and sports training in virtual, augmented, or mixed reality. Makarov and Petrov [19] developed a prototype of a Shadow Boxing simulator for automated control and gamification processes.

Recent works predominantly focus on general and weak human action classification with existing large datasets using proprietary controlled datasets. For fine-grained, highly dynamic action recognition, such as sports activity, highly accurate and 3-dimensional data is required, which can be achieved with the help of sensors. However, sensor-based methods are not applicable in real-time gameplay. Since vision-based are non-invasive, they can be used for sports activity recognition. Fine-grained action recognition requires accurate 3D poses, but it requires complex and expensive video acquisition systems. Classifying fine-grained sports action using 2D pose sequences is intrinsically challenging due to high self-occlusion and monocular view. To the best of our knowledge, sensor-based and vision-based methods employed controlled environment datasets captured with constrained settings, which are not generalized for real-time or historical videos. In-the-wild videos with a monocular view make the task of fine-grained analytics extremely formidable. We aim to design a multi-stage deep learning-based pipeline to tackle this problem of fine-grained sports activity recognition on monocular view videos in the wild setting. For this task, various types of boxing punch recognition is taken as a showcase example.

3 Methodology

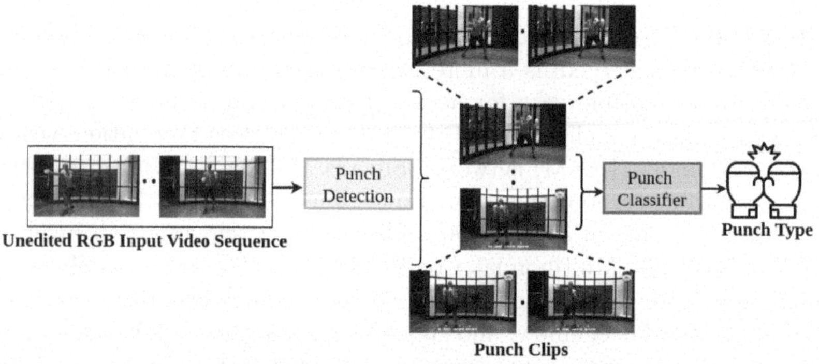

Fig. 1. The overall pipeline of the proposed methodology. The unedited input video is passed through the detection model, which returns fixed-length punch clips. The 2D poses of the punch clips are passed through the classification model for final classification.

3.1 Overview

The end-to-end pipeline for fine-grained boxing punch recognition is shown in Fig. 1. It takes an unedited RGB video of variable duration as input. Eventually, it provides the starting and ending frame numbers of detected punches and the punch class. The proposed pipeline is a deep learning-based hierarchical approach consisting of a deep learning-based detection module followed by a classification module. Firstly, the input video sequence is partitioned into multiple clips of fixed frame length and fed to the detection module. The module detects clips belonging to the punching activity, and the remaining clips are discarded. Punching activity is highly dynamic, varies from person to person, and depends on fps and view angle. Therefore, direct binary classification of the clips into a punch and no punch would result in misleading and imprecise punch detection with respect to the frame number. To resolve this problem of accurate and precise detection of high-speed activity, i.e., punching in our case, we encouraged the problem statement as a regression task instead of classification. In this regression task, the probability of exhibiting a punch in the clip is computed using a deep-learning model. For model training purposes, all the clips are assigned with punch probability as target values instead of binary labeling. Here, we introduce the concept of two types of matching in action recognition problems, i.e., hard matching and soft matching. In hard matching, a pose sequence can have only two probability values as targets: 0 or 1. Meanwhile, in soft matching, a pose sequence is assigned with a target value equal to the probability of finding a particular action. This concept of soft matching enables partial action recognition and helps generalize feature representation learning. During the training process, our task is to learn the probability of having a punch within the input pose sequence. Learning confidence scores as probability empowers discriminative latent space representation to distinguish between a complete start-to-end punch and no punch adequately.

All these selected candidate clips are processed through a classifier module to find the specific or fine-grained type of punches. The proposed algorithm considers six basic punch categories: Jab, Cross, Lead Hook, Lead Uppercut, Rear Hook, and Rear Uppercut.

3.2 Network Architecture

Detector. As shown in Fig. 2, the Punch Detector module takes fixed-length (F frames) clips in RGB format as input and provides the frame numbers of detected punches as output. It first extracts 2D poses in each frame using AlphaPose [5]. AlphaPose outputs 17 key body joints in COCO. Since punching depends on the body's extremities, 12 joints out of 17 joints are selected for the feature extraction stage. These critical 12 joints include shoulders, elbows, wrists, hips, knees, and ankles. Hereafter, 2D pose sequences are fed to a deep learning-based punch probability estimator. The backbone of the punch probability estimator is the Dual Stream Spatio-Temporal Transformer (DSTformer) [34], which allows motion encoding to capture dynamic features among skeleton keypoints. Initially, it encodes spatial and temporal features separately in a latent space and combines them to get spatiotemporal feature representation using the adaptive feature fusion technique. These features are converted into k-dimensional embeddings using a Fully Connected (FC) layer. An MLP-based regression head followed by a sigmoid layer is attached to the backbone to find the punch probability. To restrict probability values from 0 to 1, the sigmoid function layer is used to get the final output. To supervise this regression task of estimating the probability, Huber loss is employed, a combination of Mean Square Error (MSE) and Mean Absolute Error (MAE) 1.

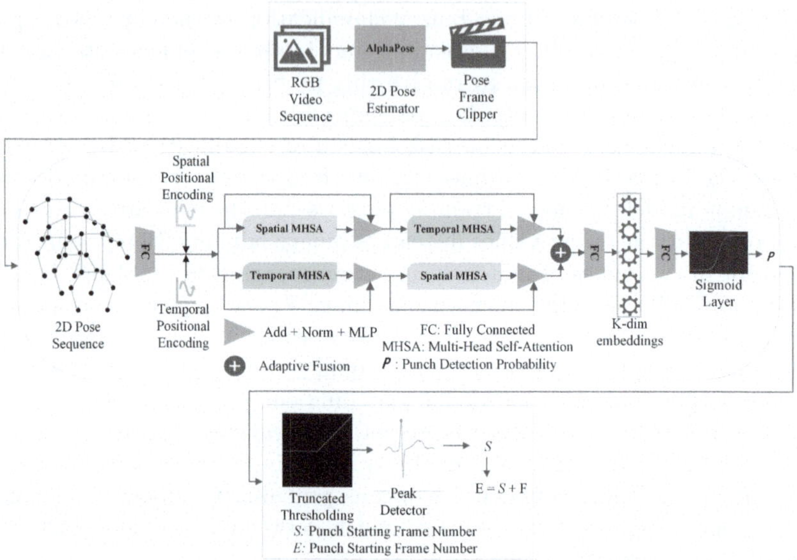

Fig. 2. The end-to-end Punch Detection module. The module is divided into three sub-modules: The upper one is the Pose Estimator, the Middle one is the Probability Estimator, and the lower one is the Peak Detector. Out of them, the probability estimator sub-module (middle) is trainable.

$$L_\delta(y, f(x)) = \begin{cases} \frac{1}{2}(y - f(x))^2 & \text{if } |y - f(x)| \leq \delta \\ \delta(|y - f(x)| - \frac{1}{2}\delta) & \text{otherwise} \end{cases} \tag{1}$$

All the clipped pose sequences of an input video are fed to the punch probability estimator in time sequential format to obtain the probabilities as time series data. This output time series probability data undergoes truncated threshold operation to remove local maxima. The thresholded probability score as time series data is smoothened using a Savitzky-Golay filter with a window size 7 and a polynomial order of 4. The filter's input-output relationship equation is 2, where x_{k+i} represents the data points within the window centered at x_k and c_i are the coefficients of the polynomials that best fit the data points using the least squares method 3. Afterward, a gradient-based zero-crossing detector is applied to find the peaks or maxima throughout time series data. These peaks correspond to the clipped pose sequences, with the highest probability of detecting punches throughout the video.

$$y_k = \sum_{i=-3}^{3} c_i \cdot x_{k+i} \tag{2}$$

$$\mathbf{C} = \left(\mathbf{X}^T \cdot \mathbf{X}\right)^{-1} \cdot \mathbf{X}^T \cdot \mathbf{Y} \tag{3}$$

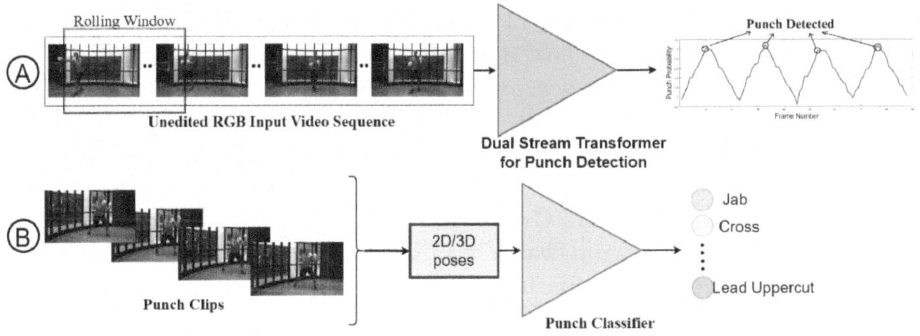

Fig. 3. (A) Punch detection algorithm (B) Classification algorithm.

Classifier. The classifier model is attached after the detector to classify the punches detected into six basic punch categories: Jab, Cross, Lead Uppercut, Rear Uppercut, Lead Hook, and Rear Hook, as shown in Fig. 3. A 3D Convolutional Neural Network (3D-CNN) is used as a classification module. As the previous subsection explains, a 3D-CNN is strategically selected to capture the spatiotemporal features from the 2D or 3D punch sequences detected using the detector. The 2D poses from the punch sequences are extracted using Alphapose, whereas the 3D poses are extracted using the MotionBert model. The classification module has three convolutional layers, each using kernels of size $3 \times 3 \times 3$. The first layer consists of 32 kernels, and in subsequent layers, the number of kernels is increased by a factor of 2 to learn hierarchical representations of input data. The early layers typically learn low-level features, while deeper layers learn more abstract and complex features [15]. By increasing the number of kernels in deeper layers, the classifier can capture more diverse and abstract features, allowing it to learn richer representations of the poses. ReLU activation function follows each convolutional layer. The final dense layer has a sigmoid activation function to squash the output values to the range [0, 1], making it interpretable as probabilities.

4 Experiments

4.1 Dataset Description

The proposed pipeline takes an unedited RGB video of variable duration as input. Eventually, it provides the starting and ending frame numbers of detected punches and the punch class. As mentioned in the methodology section, the hierarchical-based approach detects the punch clips followed by their fine-grained boxing punch type classification. All the unedited videos considered for training and testing are collected from YouTube and are publicly available thus, no ethical clearance is taken for our experiments. The detector and the classifier are trained on https://www.youtube.com/watch?v=KidSVNv0WcY&t=212s (Subject 1, Video 1). The video (S11) is 15 min and 40 s long and consists of almost 415 punches. Subsequently, four videos of the same and different subjects are selected for further experiments to see how the model adapts to unknown subjects. The video collected from https://www.youtube.com/watch?v=rIk9fylC0Rk is of the same subject named S12 (Subject 1, video 2). The video https://www.youtube.com/watch?v=wB8GhqtKLdk&list=LL&index=3&t=11s is the second video from the test set and is named S21 (Subject 2, video 1). Similarly, https://www.youtube.com/watch?v=o9qPlLLGv6k&list=LL&index=4&t=156s is named S31 and https://www.youtube.com/watch?v=aXaKD-jSiDQ&t=257s is named S41. Further, the dataset preparation for the detector and classifier is explained in more detail below.

Detector. The video stream is manually annotated for training purposes with exact starting and ending frame numbers of punches, irrespective of their types. Afterward, the video is partitioned into multiple clips of definite length frames (F = 11) with a rolling window of size 1. Let's assume there are N punches annotated from the training video, L = P_1, P_2,..., P_{N-1},P_N, where P_i represents the set of frames from starting to ending of the punch i. C_t is the clip partitioned at time instant t. Each clip is assigned with a confidence score P_{C_t} governed by the Eq. 4.

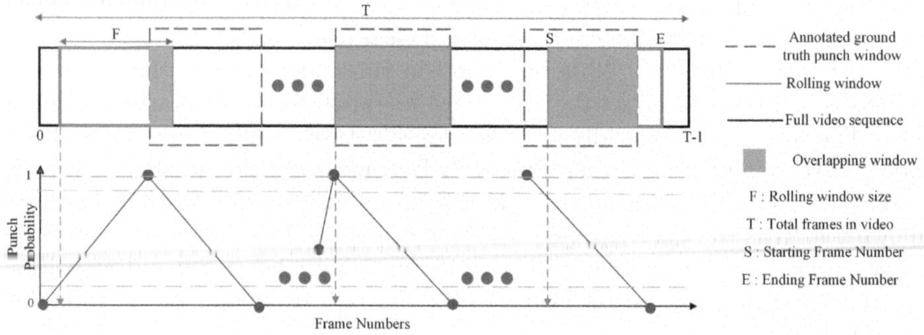

Fig. 4. Labelling formulation of the training dataset to compute probability score of each video clip

$$P_{C_t} = \frac{\sum_{i=1}^{N} |C_t \cap P_i|}{F} \tag{4}$$

Figure 4 shows that red-colored windows represent manually annotated starting and ending frame numbers, whereas colored windows correspond to the fixed-length clips. Clips are marked at the starting frame number, and the corresponding confidence values are arranged in the series graph below. There are a total 21305 number of clipped video sequences labeled with confidence scores for the training.

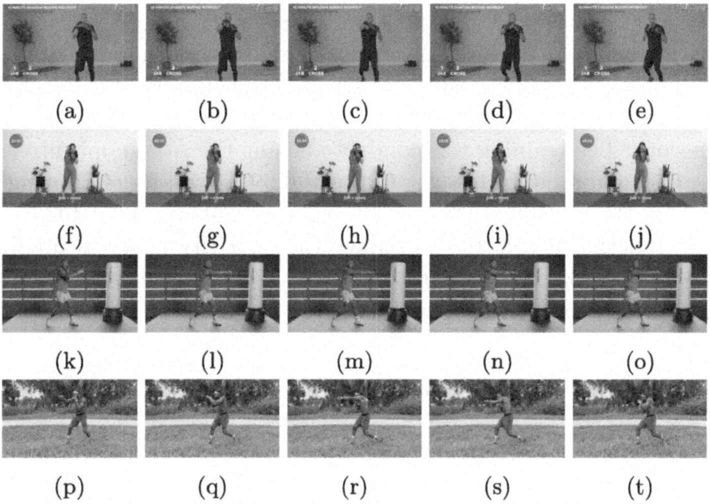

Fig. 5. (a)-(e) S11 (f)-(j) S21 (k)-(o) S31 (p)-(t), and S41 showing *Cross*.

Classifier. The video denoted as S11 was considered for training. Subsequently, the punches identified by the detector in the first stage were subject to manual categorization into six basic punch types, thereby constituting the training dataset. The ground truth was decided based on what the boxing trainer in the video said. However, in S11, various punch categories like lead hook, rear hook, lead uppercut, and rear uppercut were underrepresented. So, a few clips belonging to the underrepresented class from S12 were also considered for training. This is done to have a balanced dataset so that the final classifier is not biased towards a particular class. S21, S31, and S41 are considered for testing. All subjects' visuals are shown in Fig. 5. Notably, since all video materials used for our experiments consist of boxing training sessions, thus the ground truth annotations were derived from the spoken directives provided by the respective trainers.

4.2 Training Details

Detector. The detector module's deep learning model has a spatio-temporal transformer backbone. This backbone and the regression head are end-to-end trained on a single subject video. The spatiotemporal backbone is trained with depth N = 5, number of heads = 8, and feature and embedding dimension = 128. Input spatial and temporal feature dimensions are J = 12 and T = 11, respectively. The Adam optimizer is employed for training with a batch size 4028 for 300 epochs. The initial learning rate is 0.0001 with an exponential decay factor of 0.99 per epoch.

Classifier. The 3D (CNN) architecture for classification tasks consists of 595,110 trainable parameters. In the case of AlphaPose, the model's input dimensions are defined as $11 \times 12 \times 2$, where 11 signifies the number of frames within the input clips, while 12 denotes the 2D pose coordinates derived from the AlphaPose framework. The training was conducted using the Adam optimizer; a batch size is set to 16, and an initial learning rate of 0.001 is considered during training sessions. Given the classification task's categorical nature, the categorical cross-entropy loss function is selected to reduce the disparity between predicted and actual class labels. The training process is iteratively executed for 100 epochs to refine the model's final performance.

5 Results and Discussion

5.1 Detector

During the inferencing, all the test video sequences are fed to the detector in RGB format. The detector outputs the probability of exhibiting punches throughout each video as time series data. This time series data is passed through the truncated detector with threshold value *lamba*, followed by the Savitzky-Golay filter. The zero-crossing peak detection technique is applied to find the starting frame numbers of the detected punches. The detection accuracy is calculated by the formula given by the Eq. 5. The equation states that if any frame between the starting and ending frames of the detected punch lies between the starting and ending frames of ground truth punches, in a causal sense, it would taken as positive and vice-versa. The number of detected punches varies with threshold value λ, so average accuracy is calculated over different values of λs, i.e., 0.1, 0.2, 0.3, 0.4, 0.5, 0.6, 0.7, 0.8, and 0.9. The mean accuracy over all the test video subjects is found to be 96.09%.

$$Accuracy = \frac{\sum_{\lambda \in Thr} \frac{\sum_{P_i \in detP} I(P_i \cap P_j \geq 0, P_j \in L \cap \lambda)}{|L|}}{|Thr|} \tag{5}$$

The limitation of the detector is the threshold value, which is adjustable but depends on the view angle and subject. It is applied to avoid false detection and introduce high-frequency components for better peak detection.

5.2 Classifier

The clips containing the punches as detected by the detector in the first stage, are presented to the classifier for final classification. The punch clips are classified into six basic punches: Cross, Jab, Lead Hook, Lead Uppercut, Rear Hook, and Rear Uppercut. The 2D poses from the punch clips are extracted using AlphaPose [5]. 12 important joints out of 17 joints that are necessary for determining the type of punches are selected for final classification. The final performance of the 3D-CNN-based classifier is given in Table 1. For S11, as mentioned in the section Dataset Description, both the detection and classification models are

Table 1. Detection and Classification performance of the proposed models over various subjects.

Metric	S11	S21	S31	S41
Subject	S11	S21	S31	S41
Length	15.40	11.26	5.03	11.45
Detection Accuracy (%)	100	90.65	100	97.61
Total Punches	116/125	74/81	29/34	134/160
Cross	23/23	16/17	6/6	51/58
Jab	23/24	17/17	8/8	34/38
Lead Hook	16/21	24/24	2/3	20/23
Lead Uppercut	19/19	4/8	6/6	9/16
Rear Hook	8/10	13/15	3/7	9/10
Rear Uppercut	27/28	0/0	4/4	11/15
Classification Accuracy (%)	92.79	91.36	85.29	83.75

trained using the clips extracted from S11. The results corresponding to S11 are presented using a 70–30 split, where 70% are used for training, and the rest 30% are used for testing. The Precision, Recall, and F1 score performance metrics are given in Table 2.

(a) (b) (c) (d) (e)

Fig. 6. Rear Hook Punch of S31 misclassified as Cross.

For S21, the model achieved an accuracy of 91.35%. In the case of S31, the proposed 3D-CNN achieved an accuracy of 85.29%. As shown in Table 2, the model achieved 100% precision, recall, and f1-score corresponding to Lead and Rear Uppercut. In the case of S31, 29 punches out of 34 detected punches are classified accurately. All Cross, Jab, Lead, and Rear Uppercut punches are correctly classified. As shown in Table 2, the precision, recall, and F1 score corresponding to class Rear Hook is comparatively poor. This is because most of the rear punches are misclassified as cross. Few frames from one of the rear hook punch mis-classified as cross is shown in Fig. 6. And finally, in case of S41, the model accurately classified 134 punches out of 160 punches detected. The most misclassification was reported in the Lead and Rear Uppercut category.

Since this study of fine-grained action recognition is performed on a novel YouTube video dataset (manually labelled), there is no state-of-the-art methodology that exist to be compared against the proposed work.

Table 2. Subject-wise performance metrics.

Subject	Performance Metrices	Types of punches					
		Cross	Jab	Lead Hook	Lead Uppercut	Rear Hook	Rear Uppercut
S11	Precision	0.82	0.96	0.93	1.00	1.00	1.00
	Recall	1.00	0.96	0.96	1.00	0.73	1.00
	F1 Score	0.90	0.96	0.95	1.00	0.84	1.00
S21	Precision	0.94	0.71	0.96	1.00	1.00	-
	Recall	0.94	1.00	1.00	0.67	0.50	-
	F1 Score	0.94	0.83	0.98	0.80	0.67	-
S31	Precision	0.60	0.89	1.00	1.00	1.00	1.00
	Recall	1.00	1.00	0.67	1.00	0.43	1.00
	F1 Score	0.75	0.94	0.80	1.00	0.60	1.00
S41	Precision	0.91	0.97	0.83	1.00	0.38	0.92
	Recall	0.88	0.89	0.87	0.56	0.90	0.73
	F1 Score	0.89	0.93	0.85	0.72	0.58	0.81

6 Conclusion

This paper presents a novel hierarchical framework tailored for robust sports activity recognition task. The proposed approach uses a fusion of regression-based detection employing a Dual Stream Spatio-Temporal Transformer followed by a fine-grained classification network powered by a 3D Convolutional Neural Network (CNN) for punch recognition from unedited boxing videos. Through rigorous experimentation on YouTube footage, the methodology achieves remarkable mean detection and classification accuracies of 96.09% and 88.25%, respectively, underscoring its robustness across diverse real-world scenarios. Beyond its immediate applications in sports performance analysis and athlete training, the research paves the way for broader implications, including real-time event monitoring and enhanced decision-making training for athletes. One of the major drawbacks of the proposed approach is that both the detector and the classifier are trained and tested using videos of frontal viewpoints only. In future, we aim to mitigate the drawback in case of boxing and make the pipeline view-invariant.

References

1. Abdul-Azim, H.A., Hemayed, E.E.: Human action recognition using trajectory-based representation. Egypt. Inf. J. **16**(2), 187–198 (2015)
2. Arshad, M.H., Bilal, M., Gani, A.: Human activity recognition: review, taxonomy and open challenges. Sensors **22**(17), 6463 (2022)

3. Cuperman, R., Jansen, K.M., Ciszewski, M.G.: An end-to-end deep learning pipeline for football activity recognition based on wearable acceleration sensors. Sensors **22**(4), 1347 (2022)
4. Elharrouss, O., Almaadeed, N., Al-Maadeed, S., Bouridane, A., Beghdadi, A.: A combined multiple action recognition and summarization for surveillance video sequences. Appl. Intell. **51**, 690–712 (2021)
5. Fang, H.S., et al.: Alphapose: whole-body regional multi-person pose estimation and tracking in real-time. IEEE Trans. Pattern Anal. Mach. Intell. (2022)
6. Gatt, I.: Effects of bandaging techniques and shot types on wrist motion in boxing. Ph.D. thesis, Sheffield Hallam University (2023)
7. Giannakeris, P., et al.: Fusion of multimodal sensor data for effective human action recognition in the service of medical platforms. In: International Conference on Multimedia Modeling, pp. 367–378. Springer (2021)
8. Guo, Y., Tao, D., Liu, W., Cheng, J.: Multiview cauchy estimator feature embedding for depth and inertial sensor-based human action recognition. IEEE Trans. Syst. Man Cybern. Syst. **47**(4), 617–627 (2016)
9. Gupta, S.: Deep learning based human activity recognition (har) using wearable sensor data. Int. J. Inf. Manag. Data Insights **1**(2), 100046 (2021)
10. Hudovernik, V., Skocaj, D.: Video-based detection of combat positions and automatic scoring in jiu-jitsu. In: Proceedings of the 5th International ACM Workshop on Multimedia Content Analysis in Sports, pp. 55–63 (2022)
11. Jayakumar, B., Govindarajan, N.: Multi-sensor fusion based optimized deep convolutional neural network for boxing punch activity recognition. In: Proceedings of the Institution of Mechanical Engineers, Part P: Journal of Sports Engineering and Technology, p. 17543371241237085 (2024)
12. Kasiri, S., Fookes, C., Sridharan, S., Morgan, S.: Fine-grained action recognition of boxing punches from depth imagery. Comput. Vis. Image Underst. **159**, 143–153 (2017)
13. Khan, M.A., et al.: Human action recognition using fusion of multiview and deep features: an application to video surveillance. Multimedia Tools Appl. **83**(5), 14885–14911 (2024)
14. Khasanshin, I.: Application of an artificial neural network to automate the measurement of kinematic characteristics of punches in boxing. Appl. Sci. **11**(3), 1223 (2021)
15. Krizhevsky, A., Sutskever, I., Hinton, G.E.: Imagenet classification with deep convolutional neural networks. Commun. ACM **60**(6), 84–90 (2017)
16. Labintsev, A., Khasanshin, I., Balashov, D., Bocharov, M., Bublikov, K.: Recognition punches in karate using acceleration sensors and convolution neural networks. IEEE Access **9**, 138106–138119 (2021)
17. Li, Y., Chen, L., He, R., Wang, Z., Wu, G., Wang, L.: Multisports: a multi-person video dataset of spatio-temporally localized sports actions. In: Proceedings of the IEEE/CVF International Conference on Computer Vision, pp. 13536–13545 (2021)
18. Luo, Y., et al.: Lstm pose machines. In: Proceedings of the IEEE Conference on Computer Vision and Pattern Recognition, pp. 5207–5215 (2018)
19. Makarov, I., Petrov, S.: On the impact of computer vision algorithms on sport training automation: proof of concept for shadow boxing virtual instructor (2021)
20. Malibari, A.A., et al.: Quantum water strider algorithm with hybrid-deep-learning-based activity recognition for human-computer interaction. Appl. Sci. **12**(14), 6848 (2022)

21. Mekruksavanich, S., Jitpattanakul, A.: Lstm networks using smartphone data for sensor-based human activity recognition in smart homes. Sensors **21**(5), 1636 (2021)
22. Mohith, S.S., Vijay, S., Sanjana, V., Krupa, N.: Trajectory based human action recognition using centre symmetric local binary pattern descriptors. In: 2020 IEEE 17th India Council International Conference (INDICON), pp. 1–6. IEEE (2020)
23. Ni, J., Tang, H., Ngu, A.H., Liu, G., Yan, Y.: Physical-aware cross-modal adversarial network for wearable sensor-based human action recognition. arXiv preprint arXiv:2307.03638 (2023)
24. dos S Silva, F.H., et al.: A novel feature extractor for human action recognition in visual question answering. Pattern Recogn. Lett. **147**, 41–47 (2021)
25. Shujah Islam, M.: Computer vision-based approach for skeleton-based action recognition, sahc, pp. 1–12. Signal, Image and Video Processing (2023)
26. Stefański, P., Jach, T., Kozak, J.: Classification of punches in olympic boxing using static rgb cameras. In: International Conference on Computational Collective Intelligence, pp. 540–551. Springer (2023)
27. Stoeve, M., Schuldhaus, D., Gamp, A., Zwick, C., Eskofier, B.M.: From the laboratory to the field: Imu-based shot and pass detection in football training and game scenarios using deep learning. Sensors **21**(9), 3071 (2021)
28. Wang, X., Guo, Y.: The deep learning-based human action recognition system for competitive sports. J. Imaging Sci. Technol. 1–16 (2024)
29. Worsey, M.T., Espinosa, H.G., Shepherd, J.B., Thiel, D.V.: An evaluation of wearable inertial sensor configuration and supervised machine learning models for automatic punch classification in boxing. IoT **1**(2), 360–381 (2020)
30. Wu, F., et al.: A survey on video action recognition in sports: datasets, methods and applications. IEEE Trans. Multimedia (2022)
31. Yang, Q., Xia, S.: Boxnet: fine-grained action classification in boxing. In: 2023 35th Chinese Control and Decision Conference (CCDC), pp. 3520–3525. IEEE (2023)
32. Yi, Y., Li, A., Zhou, X.: Human action recognition based on action relevance weighted encoding. Sig. Process. Image Commun. **80**, 115640 (2020)
33. Zhang, Y., Guo, Q.: A human action recognition algorithm in dynamic scene of emergency rescue. In: 2021 IEEE 4th International Conference on Computer and Communication Engineering Technology (CCET), pp. 12–16. IEEE (2021)
34. Zhu, W., Ma, X., Liu, Z., Liu, L., Wu, W., Wang, Y.: Motionbert: a unified perspective on learning human motion representations. In: Proceedings of the IEEE/CVF International Conference on Computer Vision, pp. 15085–15099 (2023)

Projection-Based Perceptual Visual Quality Estimation of Point Clouds

Apoorva Goswami, Pramit Mazumdar(✉), and Kamal Kishor Jha

Indian Institute of Information Technology Vadodara, Gujarat, India
{202262003,pramit.mazumdar,kamal}@iiitvadodara.ac.in

Abstract. The recent advancement of 3D sensing technologies has led to immense collection of voluminous and complex point clouds. Evidently, we are witnessing multiple developments related to assessing the voluminous point cloud data. The no-reference quality assessment is challenging but is widely accepted as a suitable quality estimator as it does not require the pristine stimuli. The no-reference quality metrics when applied directly to the point cloud fails to consider features that are close to the human visual system. Incidentally, visual quality is always driven by how scenes are perceived by the observer. Hence, there is a need to devise a novel quality estimation model which does not require the references, and exploits the perceptual features from the distorted point clouds. In this work, we propose a projection-based no-reference point cloud quality estimation model (PB-PCQA). The applied projection approach considers all possible viewing angles for a given distorted point cloud. Further, the model also extracted feature maps which are close to the human visual system from each 2D projection of the point cloud. In addition to this, a set of statistical parameters are extracted from each of the feature maps for estimating the distribution of the feature values. The proposed model is evaluated on benchmark SJTU-PCQA dataset and is compared with recent state-of-the-art metrics.

Keywords: Point clouds · Quality Metric · Projection · Feature extraction · Statistical parameters · Regressor

1 Introduction

Point clouds serve as the backbone of many applications across diverse domains, ranging from autonomous navigation [30] to augmented reality [2]. Consequently, ensuring the fidelity and reliability of these data structures is paramount for the success of such systems.

In recent years, the proliferation of 3D sensing technologies has led to an explosion in the volume and complexity of point cloud data. This surge in data necessitates robust quality assessment methods to guarantee the accuracy and usability of point cloud representations [3,14,37].

Full-reference methods compare distorted point clouds with their pristine counterparts, relying on access to high-quality reference data. While effective,

J. Kakarla et al. (Eds.): CVIP 2024, CCIS 2473, pp. 279–292, 2026.
https://doi.org/10.1007/978-3-031-93688-3_20

these methods may not always be feasible due to the unavailability or impracticality of obtaining reference data in real-world scenarios.

To address this, no-reference methods offer a pragmatic solution by estimating point cloud quality without direct access to the reference data. These techniques leverage various features and statistical properties inherent in the point cloud itself, enabling assessment in scenarios where reference data is scarce or non-existent [25,34].

There has been enough effort in the literature towards quality estimation of point clouds. Deep learning techniques, in particular, have gained prominence due to their ability to automatically learn complex representations from data [7]. By harnessing Convolution Neural Networks (CNN) and other advanced architectures, researchers have achieved remarkable success in predicting point cloud quality with high accuracy [15].

Furthermore, the integration of geometric and perceptual features has enriched the array of quality assessment metrics. These metrics capture not only geometric fidelity, but also perceptual aspects such as visual saliency and structural coherence, aligning more closely with human perception [9]. However, the perceptual quality assessment task is still a challenge since the visual acuity changes among subjects are not constant and varies on basis of different parameters. This work focuses on developing a projection-based no-reference visual quality assessment model for the distorted point clouds, denoted as PB-PCQA. The approach combines geometry-based and low-level image-based features for quality estimation. The following section summarizes the related state-of-the-art approaches along with their limitations and contributions of this work.

2 Literature Survey

This section is divided in three approaches, traditional no-reference quality assessment for point clouds, quality assessment using saliency maps, and projection-based quality assessment of point clouds.

2.1 No-reference Quality Assessment

Liu et al. introduced LS-PCQA [15], a dataset with 104 reference point clouds and 22,000 distorted samples, addressing Full-reference (FR) point cloud quality assessment (PCQA). They propose ResSCNN, a novel no-reference metric based on sparse convolutional neural networks (CNN), outperforming existing NR-PCQA metrics and some FR metrics. LS-PCQA enhances generalization ability for learning-based NR-PCQA metrics.

Smitskamp et al. [27] evaluate full-reference features for no-reference quality assessment of point cloud contents, suggesting their potential for predicting point cloud quality without a reference.

Zhou et al. [38] propose PointPCA+, an extension of PointPCA, enhancing descriptor richness and achieving high predictive performance against subjective ground truth scores.

Chetouani et al. [3] propose a FR approach for quality estimation of point clouds. Shan et al. [25] propose GPA-Net, a novel no-reference PCQA metric tailored for irregular point cloud structures. Utilizing GPAConv, a graph convolution kernel, GPA-Net captures structure and texture perturbations effectively. Its multitask framework integrates quality regression, and distortion type, with a coordinate normalization module for ensuring invariance. Experimental results demonstrate GPA-Net's superiority over existing PCQA metrics and some full-reference metrics, highlighting its efficacy in assessing point cloud quality.

2.2 Saliency-Based Quality Assessment

Zhang et al. [35] proposed a NR metric for 3D point clouds. It uses entropy and natural scene statistics, and subsequently employing support vector regression [1]. In [36], a method for constructing saliency maps for 3D point clouds is introduced, assessing point importance for model prediction loss. The authors demonstrate scoring point contribution by gradient of loss under a scaled spherical-coordinate system, enabling standardized point-dropping processes and verifying efficacy in characterizing saliency. Extensive evaluations across PointNet [22], PointNet++ [23], and DGCNN [28] confirm the accuracy and generality of the proposed method.

Laazoufi and El Hassouni [9] introduced a saliency-based no-reference quality assessment method for 3D point cloud quality assessment. By computing 3D visual saliency maps and employing a threshold-based filter, salient points are selected and used to extract geometrical and perceptual attributes. Statistical properties form a feature vector, utilized for quality score prediction via support vector regression. Experimental validation on an open dataset demonstrates superior correlation with average opinion scores, showcasing the method's effectiveness.

2.3 Projection-Based Quality Assessment

Zhou et al. [37] proposed a reduced reference point cloud quality assessment (RR-CAP). The reference and distorted point clouds are initially projected using the six perpendicular projection approach [33] which considers the Human Visual System (HVS). The projections are downsampled and subsequently, a DCT-based saliency estimation approach is employed to extract the respective saliency maps. Further, content-based similarity and statistical similarity between the reference saliency map and the distorted saliency map is combined to obtain the estimated visual quality score.

Liu et al. [14] propose PQA-Net, a no-reference point cloud quality assessment method for efficient quality metrics in communication systems. It integrates a multi-view-based joint feature extraction and fusion (MVFEF) module, distortion type identification (DTI), and quality vector prediction (QVP) module. By leveraging distortion type labels for pre-training, the network effectively evaluates point cloud quality. Experimental results on the Waterloo Point Cloud dataset show PQA-Net's competitive performance, advancing NR quality estimation for point clouds.

Yang et al. [34] introduce IT-PCQA, which leverages deep neural networks and unsupervised adversarial domain adaptation to bridge 2D and 3D perception. IT-PCQA utilizes a hierarchical feature encoder and conditional-discriminative network to minimize domain discrepancy. Experimental results demonstrate its superiority over traditional metrics, suggesting its feasibility in assessing specific media content without subjective evaluations.

2.4 Limitations of Existing Approaches

Current methods for assessing point cloud quality encounter several challenges. Reduced-reference techniques depend heavily on pristine reference data, limiting their applicability in real-world scenarios. Some methods rely on subjective human assessments or costly testing procedures, introducing variability and expense. Generalization issues also plague certain approaches, reducing effectiveness across diverse datasets. Moreover, deep learning-based methods face hurdles due to complexity and computational demands, requiring substantial expertise and resources.

- The novel projection-based approach is employed for generating projections which covers all possible visual exploration angles. This also simplifies visualization and interpretation of point cloud data. 2D projections allow extraction of low-level features which are close to HVS and are difficult to extracted directly from a point cloud.
- The extracted feature maps are used for extracting various statistical parameters. Such parameters indicate the variability and distribution of feature maps.
- The proposed model is experimented on SJTU dataset and compared with both baseline and existing state-of-the-art quality metrics using standard evaluation metrics.

3 Proposed Methodology

The workflow of the proposed Projection-based Point Cloud Quality Assessment (PB-PCQA) model is presented in Fig. 1. The PB-PCQA approach is divided into four modules; point cloud projection, feature extraction, statistical parameters, and the regressor model.

3.1 Point Cloud Projection

Following a similar approach as mentioned in [37], a novel projection methodology is adapted in this work. Projection-based approaches offer several advantages in data analysis, including point cloud analysis. Firstly, they facilitate dimensionality reduction by projecting high-dimensional data onto lower-dimensional

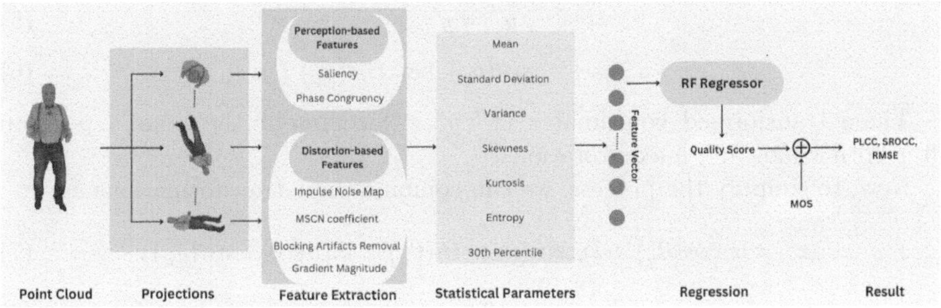

Fig. 1. The framework of the proposed PB-PCQA.

spaces, simplifying visualization and interpretation. Secondly, these methods enable enhanced feature extraction by capturing multiple perspectives through projections from different angles. Thirdly, projection-based approaches are compatible with existing techniques in fields such as computer vision and image analysis. Fourthly, the process reduces data complexity while retaining essential information, thus, enabling faster processing times and lower resource requirements. Additionally, projections provide enhanced visualization capabilities, aiding in exploratory data analysis and pattern recognition. Overall, projection-based approaches offer a versatile framework for data analysis, with advantages including dimensionality reduction, enhanced feature extraction, compatibility with existing techniques, improved computational efficiency, and enhanced visualization capabilities. The points of a distorted point cloud were studied from various angles along the sides. Readings were taken from 0 to 180° with respect to the x-axis, with steps of 30°, and from 0 to 330° with respect to the y-axis, also in steps of 30°. In this way, a total of 84 different views were obtained from a single distorted point cloud. Each projection depicted the point cloud from a distinct angle, contributing to a better analysis of the perceived quality. The 84 unique projected angle views depicted a 360° exploration of a point cloud structure. Features from different angles were observed by moving the viewpoint around the point cloud. In this manner, the point cloud data could be studied extensively, allowing for a deeper understanding of its composition and characteristics.

Let, the original coordinates of any point in a point cloud is denoted as (x, y, and z). Further, rotation operation around the x-axis by an angle θ_x, the coordinates are modified as follows,

$$x' = x \tag{1}$$

$$y' = y.cos(\theta_x) - z.sin(\theta_x) \tag{2}$$

$$z' = y.sin(\theta_x) - z.cos(\theta_x) \tag{3}$$

Similarly, after rotation around the y-axis by an angle θ_y, the coordinates are modified as follow:

$$x'' = x'.cos(\theta_y) + z'.sin(\theta_y) \tag{4}$$

$$y'' = y' \quad (5)$$

$$z'' = -x'.sin(\theta_y) + z'.cos(\theta_y) \quad (6)$$

These transformed coordinates (x'', y'', z'') represent the point's position after both x-axis and y-axis rotations.

Now, to simplify the process, we can combine these transformations as,

$$x'' = x.cos(\theta_y) + (y.sin(\theta_x).sin(\theta_y) - z.cos(\theta_x).sin(\theta_y)) \quad (7)$$

$$y'' = y.cos(\theta_x) - z.sin(\theta_x) \quad (8)$$

$$z'' = -x.sin(\theta_y) + (y.sin(\theta_x).cos(\theta_y) + z.cos(\theta_x).cos(\theta_y)) \quad (9)$$

These equations provide a simplified representation for generating projections of a point cloud based on the rotation angles θ_x and θ_y. Each combination of θ_x and θ_y generates a unique projection of the point cloud.

3.2 Feature Extraction

The proposed PB-PCQA typically converts a point clouds into 2D projections or images. Further, the feature extraction module selectively extracts two perception-based and four distortion-based image features.

Perception-Based Features

Saliency. A fsidered as the perception-based feature. It is used to identify the region which is most significant to the human visual system [16]. Since the model PB-PCQA is based on projections, hence saliency is used as an important feature to incorporate the visual attention model [4,17,29]. In this work, the gradient method is used to obtain the saliency maps [24,26]

$$S = \frac{\partial f}{\partial I} \quad (10)$$

where:
S represents the saliency map
f denotes the model's output score
I denotes the input image

With the help of the gradient, the most important region of the projection is determined. When the gradient is high, it indicates that such image pixels are very important for human perception.

Further, Guassian smoothing operation is performed on the obtained saliency maps. This operation aids in reducing noise and producing more coherent visualizations of important regions within the images. The smoothing process typically entails averaging or blurring neighboring pixel values to create a smoother transition between adjacent regions.

Figure 2(b) represents a sample gradient-based saliency map smoothed using Gaussian kernel. The generated saliency maps are normalized for augmenting with the other low-level image features.

Phase Congruency. Phase congruency computation involves analyzing each image file to identify significant features [6]. Initially, if an image contains an alpha channel, it is removed to ensure consistency. Subsequently, the image is converted to grayscale. Phase congruency is computed using the Prewitt filter, aiding in identifying regions where phase congruency is high, indicating prominent features or edges (refer sample image in Fig. 2(c)).

Distortion-Based Features

Impulse Noise Map. It is generated by initially converting the input colored image to grayscale. Then, a median filter with a specified kernel size is applied to the grayscale image to eliminate impulse noise [5]. The difference between the original grayscale image and the median-filtered image is computed to obtain the impulse noise map Fig. 2(d). Each pixel in the impulse noise map represents the magnitude of impulse noise. Higher impulse indicate a stronger presence of impulse noise, while lower values indicate less noise or noise-free regions.

MSCN Coefficient. The MSCN coefficients are a crucial image-based feature that indicates the contrast variations across different regions of images, aiding in the visualization of texture and structural details. MSCN has been widely used as an indicator towards estimating the level of distortion in a given image [10,18,19]. Initially, the colored images are converted to grayscale. Subsequently, Gaussian blur is applied to estimate the average brightness and color dispersion within these regions. This process involves subtracting the average brightness surrounding each pixel from its own brightness and then dividing by the variance of brightness in that vicinity. This ensures that the coefficients accurately represent the contrast variations across different areas of the image. The Fig. 2(e) indicates MSCN coefficient extracted from a sample point cloud projection.

Blocking Artifacts. Existing literature identified the blocking artifact in images as an important indicator for visual quality assessment [21]. Following the same approach, the proposed PB-PCQA first identifies the regions in a point cloud projection with blocking artifact and subsequently, extracts pixel properties at those regions as features for the quality assessment mode. Firstly, the image is converted to grayscale, subsequently, a Discrete Cosine Transform (DCT) is applied to the grayscale image, aiding in the analysis of its frequency components. The average of these DCT coefficients are computed to assess the presence of blocking artifacts in the image [21]. This metric serves as a reference to identify regions affected by the artifacts. Following this, the inverse DCT is employed to reconstruct the filtered image, aiming to diminish the presence of blocking artifacts. The goal of this filtering procedure is to mitigate the impact of these artifacts while preserving the overall image quality. The resulting output includes the filtered image and the calculated blocking artifact removal

(a) Sample Projection

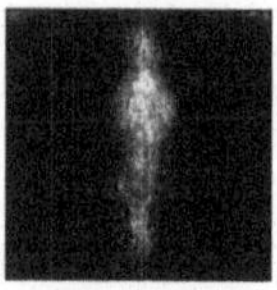

(b) Saliency

(c) Phase Congruency

(d) Impulse Noise Map

(e) MSCN coefficient

(f) Blocking Artifacts Removal

(g) Gradient Magnitude

Fig. 2. Perception-based and Distortion-based Feature maps extracted from a sample point cloud projection.

feature, providing insights into the effectiveness of the artifact removal process. Figure 2(f) represents a sample point cloud projection with the blocking artifact as a feature.

Gradient Magnitude. The methodology begins with initial preprocessing steps aimed at preparing an input image for edge detection purposes. This involves converting the image to grayscale. Following grayscale conversion, edge detection is carried out using the Sobel operator, which calculates gradients along both the horizontal and vertical directions of the image [31]. These gradients are then utilized to determine the magnitude of edges in the image. Normalization of the gradient magnitude ensures that the values are appropriately scaled for visualization. A sample gradient magnitude extracted image is represented in Fig. 2(g).

3.3 Statistical Parameters

A total of seven statistical parameters are extracted from each of the six image-based features maps mentioned in Sect. 3.2. The statistical parameters in general indicate distribution and variability among the different low-level features extracted from each image [12,13].

Mean. The average intensity of the pixel values on a grayscale feature map.

Standard Deviation. The dispersion or spread of pixel intensities around the mean value. Indicates the amount of variation or deviation from the average intensity value in the feature map.

Variance. Variance quantifies the average squared deviation of the pixel values from the mean intensity. Provides information on the overall distribution of pixel intensities and their spread within the feature map.

Third Central Moment (Skewness). The asymmetry of the distribution of pixel intensities around the mean value [12]. A positive skewness signifies a distribution skewed to the right, whereas a negative skewness signifies a skew to the left.

Fourth Central Moment (Kurtosis). Kurtosis characterizes the distribution of pixel intensities relative to a normal distribution within the feature map [12]. Higher Kurtosis values indicate sharper peaks and heavier tails compared to a normal distribution.

Entropy. Entropy quantifies the amount of uncertainty or disorder in the distribution of pixel intensities in the feature map [12,16]. It measures the average information content or unpredictability of pixel intensities.

30th Percentile. The 30th percentile represents the pixel intensity value below which 30% of the data points fall. It provides insight into the lower range of pixel intensities in the image and is useful for assessing the distribution of low-intensity features [32].

x_{30} is such that 30% of the data points are less than or equal to x_{30}

These features highlight various aspects of the images, making them beneficial for tasks like image classification, segmentation, and analysis.

3.4 Regressor Model

In the proposed, PB-PCQA the Random Forest Regressor (RFR) is employed as the regressor. RFR can efficiently handle large datasets with high-dimensional features [8]. We employ min-max normalization as a preprocessing step to scale the features. This ensures that each feature contributes equally to the RFR model's learning process and prevents features with larger scales from dominating those with smaller scales during training. After normalization, the quality score of the feature vector is predicted.

4 Experimental Evaluation

4.1 Experimental Setup

The benchmark SJTU-PCQA database [33] consists of nine point clouds, with seven types of distortions at six levels. A total of 294 distorted point clouds are used for training the PB-PCQA and the rest 84 distorted point clouds are used for testing the model.

4.2 Evaluation Metric

We employ the three widely used evaluation metrics namely; Pearson Linear Correlation Coefficient (PLCC), Spearman Rank Correlation Coefficient (SRCC), and Root Mean Squared Error (RMSE). An ideal model should achieve high PLCC and SRCC values close to 1, indicating strong correlations between predicted and actual quality scores. Additionally, a low RMSE value indicates accurate prediction performance.

4.3 Regressor Selection

We conducted an ablation study on the regressor model with the best performance for the proposed PB-PCQA. Here we employ the Support Vector Regressor (SVR) [1,11], Linear Regression (LR), and RFR. Linear regression (LR) is an effective method for modeling the connection between a dependent variable and one or more independent variables by fitting a linear equation to observed data. It considers a linear relationship between the input features and the target variable. RFR is an ensemble learning method that constructs a multitude of decision trees during training. The final prediction is made by averaging the predictions of all trees in the forest, resulting in robust performance. RFR is proven to be a good regression approach for high-dimensional data with complex relationships.

Table 1. Performance of different Regressing approaches on the proposed PB-PCQA.

Method	Train/Test	PLCC	SRCC	RMSE
SVR	8/1	0.892	0.953	0.128
LR	8/1	0.915	0.927	0.201
RFR	8/1	0.864	0.842	0.159
SVR	7/2	0.741	0.747	**0.171**
LR	7/2	0.738	0.725	0.403
RFR	**7/2**	**0.742**	**0.762**	0.220

The regressing approaches were tested on two different setting. First, eight point clouds (336 distorted point clouds out of 378 in dataset) were used for training and subsequently, the rest 42 for testing. Second, seven point clouds (294 distorted point clouds out of 378 in dataset) were used for training and subsequently, the rest 84 for testing. The same evaluation metrics were used, which are selected for evaluating the proposed model with the existing state-of-the-art approaches. The obtained results are depicted in Table 1. It can be observed that the RFR provides better correlation between actual and predicted Mean Opinion Score (MOS). Whereas, SVR provides a better RMSE for the second experimental setting. However, it can be noted here that although the 8:1 (train/test) split provides better result, instead we consider the 7:2 (train/test) split in this work to remove any chances of overfitting the model. Cross-validation is another approach which could also be used in this regard.

4.4 Performance Comparisons

For assessing the effectiveness of, PB-PCQA we considered two baseline 2D image quality metrics, NIQE [20] and BRISQUE [19]. Further, we compare with no-reference point cloud quality metrics such as IT-PCQA [34], PQA-Net [14], ResCNN [15], GPA-Net [25], NR-3DQA [35]. For comparison, we also considered quality metrics which are projection-based similar to this work, and also the standard point cloud based approach. The observed results on SJTU-PCQA dataset is mentioned in Table 2.

Table 2. Comparison table between the proposed PB-PCQA and the state-of-the-art no-reference point cloud quality metrics on SJTU-PCQA database.

Reference	Type	Method	SJTU-PCQA Database		
			PLCC	SRCC	RMSE
NR	Model Based	NR-3DQA [35]	0.738	0.714	1.769
		GPA-Net [25]	0.598	0.582	–
		ResCNN [15]	0.598	0.619	–
	Projection Based	IT-PCQA [34]	0.580	0.630	–
		NIQE [20]	0.376	0.221	2.267
		PQA-Net [14]	0.477	0.486	–
		BRISQUE [19]	0.224	0.205	2.243
		PB-PCQA	**0.742**	**0.762**	**0.220**

It can be observed that the traditional image-based metrics exhibit limited effectiveness in assessing quality of point clouds. Secondly, the projection-based approaches are capable of extracting significant low-level features which have a high impact quality. It can be observed from the performance comparison between model-based and projection-based approaches. Projection-based models offer several advantages over the model-based approaches. Firstly, it enables dimensionality reduction, making it easier to visualize and interpret the data while retaining essential features. By projecting point clouds onto 2D or 3D planes from various angles, a broader range of features related to shape, texture, and spatial distribution can be extracted, enhancing the analysis process.

Moreover, projection-based approaches simplify analysis by transforming the data into formats compatible with conventional image processing techniques, thereby leveraging existing tools and methodologies for more efficient processing. Moreover, among the projection-based approaches, the proposed PB-PCQA outperforms the existing quality metrics in the literature. The incorporation of statistical parameters on the extracted six feature maps is probably considering distribution and variability of the extracted features. Saliency map and phase congruency as a perception-based feature improve the overall assessment quality of the proposed model. However, the projection-based approach could be optimized by giving higher weightage to certain projections which have more chance of exploration and rejecting the rest.

5 Conclusion

In this work, a projection-based no-reference point cloud quality assessment metric is proposed. The model consists of four modules; image projections, feature extractor, statistical parameters, and the regressor model. We employed perceptual and distortion-based features in the model, along with seven statistical parameters for each feature map. Finally, a regressor is employed to predict the quality of distorted point clouds. The model is experimented on benchmark SJTU-PCQA dataset and compared with existing state-of-the-art quality metrics. The obtained results showcase the performance improvement on exploiting projection-based approach and combining perceptual and distortion-based features for quality assessment.

Acknowledgements. This work was supported by Science and Engineering Research Board, Department of Science and Technology, Government of India, under project grant CRG/2023/003741.

References

1. Abouelaziz, I., El Hassouni, M., Cherifi, H.: No-reference 3d mesh quality assessment based on dihedral angles model and support vector regression. In: Image and Signal Processing: International Conference, International Conference on Image and Signal Processing, pp. 369–377 (2016)
2. Alexiou, E., Upenik, E., Ebrahimi, T.: Towards subjective quality assessment of point cloud imaging in augmented reality. In: IEEE International Workshop on Multimedia Signal Processing (MMSP), pp. 1–6 (2017)
3. Chetouani, A., Quach, M., Valenzise, G., Dufaux, F.: Deep learning-based quality assessment of 3d point clouds without reference. In: IEEE International Conference on Multimedia & Expo Workshops, pp. 1–6 (2021)
4. Fan, L., He, F., Song, Y., Xu, H., Li, B.: Look inside 3d point cloud deep neural network by patch-wise saliency map. In: Integrated Computer-Aided Engineering (Preprint), pp. 1–16 (2024)
5. Jayaraman, S., Esakkirajan, S., Veerakumar, T.: Digital image processing tmh publication. Year of Publication, pp. 444–542 (2009)

6. Kovesi, P.: Phase congruency detects corners and edges. In: The Australian pattern recognition society conference: DICTA. vol. 2003 (2003)
7. Krizhevsky, A., Sutskever, I., Hinton, G.E.: Imagenet classification with deep convolutional neural networks. Commun. ACM **60**, 84–90 (2017)
8. Kumar, K., Mazumdar, P., Jha, K.K., Lamichhane, K.: A random forest-based no-reference quality metric for ugc videos. In: International Conference on Computer Vision and Image Processing, pp. 554–566. Springer (2022)
9. Laazoufi, A., El Hassouni, M.: Saliency-based point cloud quality assessment method using aware features learning. In: IEEE International Conference on Wireless Networks and Mobile Communications, pp. 1–5 (2022)
10. Lamichhane, K., Carli, M., Battisti, F.: A cnn-based no reference image quality metric exploiting content saliency. Sig. Process. Image Commun. **111**, 116899 (2023)
11. Lamichhane, K., Mazumdar, P., Battisti, F., Carli, M.: A no reference deep learning based model for quality assessment of ugc videos. In: International Conference on Multimedia & Expo Workshops, pp. 1–5. IEEE (2021)
12. Lamichhane, K., Neri, M., Battisti, F., Paudyal, P., Carli, M.: No-reference light field image quality assessment exploiting saliency. IEEE Trans. Broadcast. (2023)
13. Li, D., Jiang, T., Lin, W., Jiang, M.: Which has better visual quality: the clear blue sky or a blurry animal? IEEE Trans. Multimedia **21**(5), 1221–1234 (2018)
14. Liu, Q., et al.: PQA-Net: deep no reference point cloud quality assessment via multi-view projection. IEEE Trans. Circuits Syst. Video Technol. **31**, 4645–4660 (2021)
15. Liu, Y., Yang, Q., Xu, Y., Yang, L.: Point cloud quality assessment: Dataset construction and learning-based no-reference metric. ACM Trans. Multimed. Comput. Commun. Appl. **19**, 1–26 (2023)
16. Mazumdar, P., Battisti, F.: A content-based approach for saliency estimation in 360 images. In: International Conference on Image Processing, pp. 3197–3201. IEEE (2019)
17. Mazumdar, P., Lamichhane, K., Carli, M., Battisti, F.: A feature integrated saliency estimation model for omnidirectional immersive images. Electronics **8**(12), 1538 (2019)
18. Mittal, A., Moorthy, A.K., Bovik, A.C.: Blind/referenceless image spatial quality evaluator. In: IEEE Conference Record of the Forty Fifth Asilomar Conference on Signals, Systems and Computers, pp. 723–727 (2011)
19. Mittal, A., Moorthy, A.K., Bovik, A.C.: No-reference image quality assessment in the spatial domain. IEEE Trans. Image Process. **21**(12), 4695–4708 (2012)
20. Mittal, A., Soundararajan, R., Bovik, A.C.: Making a completely blind image quality analyzer. IEEE Signal Process. Lett. **20**, 209–212 (2012)
21. Palaparthi, R., Srivastava, V.K.: A simple deblocking method for reduction of blocking artifacts. In: IEEE Students' Conference on Electrical, Electronics and Computer Science, pp. 1–4 (2012)
22. Qi, C.R., Su, H., Mo, K., Guibas, L.J.: Pointnet: deep learning on point sets for 3d classification and segmentation. In: IEEE Conference on Computer Vision and Pattern Recognition, pp. 652–660 (2017)
23. Qi, C.R., Yi, L., Su, H., Guibas, L.J.: Pointnet++: deep hierarchical feature learning on point sets in a metric space. In: Advances in Neural Information Processing Systems, vol. 30 (2017)
24. Selvaraju, R.R., Cogswell, M., Das, A., Vedantam, R., Parikh, D., Batra, D.: Grad-cam: visual explanations from deep networks via gradient-based localization. In:

Proceedings of the IEEE International Conference on Computer Vision, pp. 618–626 (2017)
25. Shan, Z., et al.: GPA-net: no-reference point cloud quality assessment with multi-task graph convolutional network. IEEE Trans. Visual. Comput. Graph. (2023)
26. Simonyan, K., Vedaldi, A., Zisserman, A.: Deep inside convolutional networks: visualising image classification models and saliency maps. arXiv preprint arXiv:1312.6034 (2013)
27. Smitskamp, G., Viola, I., Cesar, P.: Evaluation of point cloud features for no-reference visual quality assessment. In: IEEE International Conference on Quality of Multimedia Experience, pp. 147–152 (2023)
28. Wang, Y., Solomon, J.M.: Object dgcnn: 3d object detection using dynamic graphs. Adv. Neural. Inf. Process. Syst. **34**, 20745–20758 (2021)
29. Wang, Z., Zhang, Y., Yang, Q., Xu, Y., Sun, J., Liu, S.: Point cloud quality assessment using 3d saliency maps. In: International Conference on Visual Communications and Image Processing, pp. 1–5. IEEE (2023)
30. Whitty, M., Cossell, S., Dang, K.S., Guivant, J., Katupitiya, J.: Autonomous navigation using a real-time 3d point cloud. In: 2010 Australasian Conference on Robotics and Automation, pp. 1–3 (2010)
31. Xue, W., Zhang, L., Mou, X., Bovik, A.C.: Gradient magnitude similarity deviation: a highly efficient perceptual image quality index. IEEE Trans. Image Process. **23**, 684–695 (2013)
32. Yang, H., Baladandayuthapani, V., Rao, A.U., Morris, J.S.: Quantile function on scalar regression analysis for distributional data. J. Am. Stat. Assoc. (2019)
33. Yang, Q., Chen, H., Ma, Z., Xu, Y., Tang, R., Sun, J.: Predicting the perceptual quality of point cloud: a 3d-to-2d projection-based exploration. IEEE Trans. Multimedia **23**, 3877–3891 (2020)
34. Yang, Q., Liu, Y., Chen, S., Xu, Y., Sun, J.: No-reference point cloud quality assessment via domain adaptation. In: Proceedings of the IEEE/CVF Conference on Computer Vision and Pattern Recognition, pp. 21179–21188 (2022)
35. Zhang, Z., Sun, W., Min, X., Wang, T., Lu, W., Zhai, G.: No-reference quality assessment for 3d colored point cloud and mesh models. IEEE Trans. Circuits Syst. Video Technol. **32**, 7618–7631 (2022)
36. Zheng, T., Chen, C., Yuan, J., Li, B., Ren, K.: Pointcloud saliency maps. In: IEEE/CVF International Conference on Computer Vision, pp. 1598–1606 (2019)
37. Zhou, W., Yue, G., Zhang, R., Qin, Y., Liu, H.: Reduced-reference quality assessment of point clouds via content-oriented saliency projection. IEEE Signal Process. Lett. **30**, 354–358 (2023)
38. Zhou, X., Alexiou, E., Viola, I., Cesar, P.: PointPCA+: extending PointPCA objective quality assessment metric. In: IEEE International Conference on Image Processing Challenges and Workshops, pp. 1–5 (2023)

DAA-Net: Enhanced DuckNet with Reverse Axial Attention for Endoscopy Image Segmentation

Sai Sivakesh, Potluri Pravith, and Prerana Mukherjee(✉)

Jawaharlal Nehru University, New Delhi, India
prerana@jnu.ac.in

Abstract. Medical imaging has emerged as an indispensable tool for diagnosing and treating diseases. Medical imaging facilitates the generation of images of various body parts as needed. The utilisation of medical imaging techniques has yielded improved outcomes in diagnosing diseases. Endoscopy represents a form of medical imaging that enables a doctor to inspect a patient's body visually. Although endoscopy is primarily employed for analyzing digestive tract issues and symptoms, it is occasionally used to treat problems. Analyzing the vast footage captured during Wireless Capsule Endoscopy (WCE) procedures remains time consuming and prone to human error. In this work, we propose a novel approach to improve bleeding detection in WCE footage by integrating Duck module with axial attention mechanisms. DuckNet, known for its robust feature extraction capabilities, is augmented with co-axial attentive mechanism to enhance context understanding, thereby enhancing model performance across various tasks. The architecture integrates U-Net's encoder and decoder formulation with DuckNet's features, culminating in a comprehensive segmentation model. Additionally, we employ a Channel-wise Feature Pyramid (CFP) module for hierarchical feature fusion and Reverse Axial Attention for localized saliency enhancement and enriching localization information and multiscale features. We have exhaustively experimented with our proposed technique on benchmark datasets provided by MISAHUB Auto WCEBleedGEN challenge, CVC-Clinic and the Kvasir-SEG datasets and achieved competitive results.

1 Introduction

In today's world, medical imaging has become an essential tool for diagnosing and treating diseases. Medical imaging helps us to create images of various body parts based on requirements. The use of medical imaging processes has provided better outcomes in terms of diagnosing diseases. Endoscopy is a type of medical imaging that allows a doctor to look inside the inaccessible regions of the gastrointestinal (GI) tract of a patient's body. It is mainly used to analyse digestive tract problems and symptoms thus allowing suitable treatment for various problems. Wireless capsule endoscopy (WCE) is a device that allows gastroenterologists to examine the digestive tract (mainly the small bowel). Unlike traditional

J. Kakarla et al. (Eds.): CVIP 2024, CCIS 2473, pp. 293–307, 2026.
https://doi.org/10.1007/978-3-031-93688-3_21

endoscopic treatments, this device looks at the small bowel without anesthesia, sedation, or air insufflation. The procedure involves patients swallowing a small capsule-shaped pill without discomfort in the presence of clinical experts. The procedure's outcome would be to capture a video of the digestive tract. Experienced health experts then examine the footage to analyse the presence of colon ulcers or bleeding in the digestive tract. The diseases diagnosable using wireless capsule Endoscopy (WCE) procedures include intestinal bleeding, colon polyps or rectal and colon cancer, Crohn's disease, and other inflammatory bowel disease (IBD) types. The footage captured may contain around 57,000–1,00,000 frames and is analysed by an experienced gastroenterologist. It takes approximately 2–3 hours to inspect the captured footage through a frame-by-frame analysis, which is time-consuming and susceptible to human errors.

In this work, we propose a novel end-to-end trainable network by integrating Duck module with reverse axial attention mechanism and Channel-wise Feature Pyramid (CFP) module, thus enhancing segmentation performance. By combining the strengths of DuckNet's [9] robust feature extraction capabilities with co-axial attentive mechanisms for context understanding, we aim to achieve robust segmentation performance. Wireless capsule endoscopy dataset images that have blood can appear similar to healthy tissue, and the images themselves are often noisy and unclear. These challenges make it difficult to accurately identify abnormalities. Kvasir Dataset includes images from multiple classes of gastrointestinal disorders such as polyps, ulcers, and normal tissue. Developing accurate classification models capable of distinguishing between these classes can be challenging due to the subtle visual differences between them. CVC-Clinic Dataset is challenging due to variations in lesion appearance, size, and shape, as well as the presence of artifacts such as shadows and motion blur.

The Context Feature Pyramid (CFP) Module enhances the Feature Pyramid Module (FPM) by integrating advanced contextual mechanisms to capture multi-scale features, aiding bleeding detection in medical images. CFP module aggregates spatially adjacent and semantically similar features, improving the network's ability to distinguish between normal tissue and bleeding regions for accurate diagnosis. DuckBlock, featuring the Res2Net block, enhances multi-scale feature extraction in wireless endoscopy images, capturing intricate structures for precise segmentation and improved diagnostics. It employs separable convolutions to simulate large kernels efficiently, crucial for distinguishing low-contrast regions in WCE images by leveraging a larger receptive field to capture more information effectively. In light of the challenges presented by the datasets, our model showcased remarkable performance by integrating attention mechanism with Duck block, underscoring the effective synergy between them.

2 Related Work

Image segmentation is one of the fundamental aspect in computer vision. The rise of CNNs and the availability of annotated datasets led to advancements in the field. It started with the seminal work of the U-Net model in 2015 by

O, Ronneberge r [1], a convolutional neural network for biomedical segmentation with an encoder-decoder-based architecture. The encoder helps the model extract deep feature maps, and the decoder allows the model to construct a segmentation mask as output. A skip connection at each level between the encoder and decoder aids in propagating the deep features derived by the encoder to the appropriate decoder, thus preventing spatial information loss. It helps in predicting more accurate pixel-level segmentation masks.

U-Net++ [2] is a U-Net-based variant with nested and dense skip connections for efficiently capturing subtle details of objects of interest from images. Oktay et al. proposed the Attention U-Net [3], which pioneered self-attention gating modules to the networks for better extraction of features from local regions.

ResUNet++ [4] is an enhanced iteration of the conventional ResUNet. This upgraded version incorporates an additional layer into the network, featuring elements such as a squeeze-and-excite block, atrous spatial pyramidal pooling (ASPP), and attention block and utilising dice loss as the loss function. The proposed architecture demonstrates superior performance in generating segmentation maps on the Kvasir-SEG and CVC-ClinicDB datasets compared to U-Net and ResUNet.

HarDNet-MSEG [5] was a straightforward encoder-decoder polyp segmentation neural network that incorporated a HarDNet backbone for efficiency and a cascaded partial decoder for optimised feature utilisation. The Receptive Field Block (RFB) [15] module, which strengthened deep features with multi-branch convolutions, and dense aggregation, which enhanced segmentation by effectively fusing multi-scale information, were integral components of the network.

HarDNet-DFUS [6] enhances the vanilla HarDNet-MSEG architecture by introducing HarDBlockV2 and Lawin Transformer-based decoder. The backbone incorporates channel splitting and a new link pattern for improved efficiency, while the decoder leverages Large Window Attention for higher accuracy in non-real-time tasks like foot ulcer segmentation.

FCBFormer [7], a model for polyp segmentation, integrates a Transformer Branch (TB) based on SSFormer [13] and a Fully Convolutional Branch (FCB). TB employs a Pyramidal Vision Transformer v2 (PVTv2) for feature extraction and a modified Progressive Locality Decoder (PLD+). FCB utilises residual blocks and U-Net style skip connections for multi-scale feature fusion.

CaraNet [8] integrates a Res2Net [12] backbone for feature extraction, a parallel partial decoder for high-level feature aggregation, and a channel-wise feature pyramidal module for multi-scale representation. Additionally, it employs an axial reverse attention module to refine feature information and enhance segmentation accuracy. Deep supervision with weighted loss functions is used for training, while attention mechanisms, especially axial reverse attention, play a crucial role in feature refinement and small object segmentation analysis.

The DUCK-Net [9] model presents a novel architecture integrating various convolutional blocks, including Residual, Midscope, Widescope, and Separated blocks, aimed at capturing both low-level and high-level features efficiently. Through parallel utilisation of these blocks, the network adapts dynamically to different feature representations, enhancing its ability to detect intricate patterns. Unlike traditional approaches, DUCK-Net employs a diverse range of simulated kernel sizes, optimising feature extraction while minimising computational overhead. Additionally, the model incorporates a secondary downscaling layer and employs additional feature combination, improving performance and resource efficiency. This architecture modified the traditional U-Net structure and employed parameter tuning for optimal performance.

In contrast to CaraNet [8] which utilizes a ResNet block, we used a multi-path feature extractor in the encoder. We combined the multi-path feature extractor from Duck-net with the CFP module for identifying bleeding regions of various sizes. We used an Axial reverse attention module to further focus on the important features and regions extracted from the CFP and the saliency map of the previous decoder layer. Also instead of regular self-attention we have used axial attention to reduce computational overhead. We employed bilinear upsampling to construct the mask from semantic features. This method contrasts with the DuckNet approach [9], which relies on convolution blocks with padding and dilation.

3 Proposed Methodology

In this work, we propose a novel technique namely *DAANet* that utilizes UNet like framework and fuses Duck block [9] with reverse axial attention mechanism [8], offering a distinctive approach to improve model's performance as shown in Fig. 1. By combining DuckNet's robust feature extraction abilities with co-axial attentive mechanisms for context comprehension, our goal is to attain notable outcomes across diverse tasks. This pioneering fusion not only expands upon the established methodologies but also initiates exploration into novel directions within deep learning research.

Ducknet [9] has already demonstrated in the medical segmentation field that UNet [1] can perform well. To enhance its performance further, we used the Duck Block at the encoder level and combined it with reverse axial attention. The input layer accepts an image with dimensions 224*224*3. The input image is passed through a series of convolutional layers with an increasing number of filters, resulting into feature maps with reduced spatial resolution. Five convolutional layers with kernel size 2×2 and stride of 2 are used for downsampling. This process helps in extracting features at different scales. It comprises multiple duck blocks and is passed to the convolution Block. We merge the output of each convolutional block with the corresponding downsampling layer. These connections aid in maintaining spatial information and gradients throughout the training process.

After merging, the data flows into the Duck block, followed by traversal through the Channel-wise feature pyramidal module (CFP) [8] and subsequently into the Reverse Axial Attention mechanism [8]. Following this, a skip connection is established between the output of the Reverse Axial Attention and the upscaling of the feature map. The upsampling process progressively augments the dimensions of the feature map.

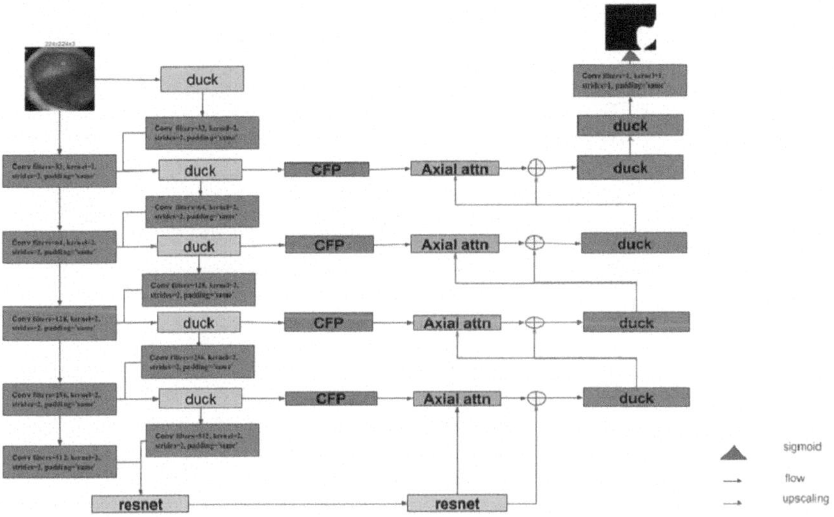

Fig. 1. Proposed model *DAANet* for endoscopy image segmentation.

This process is repeated four times, and in the final step, another UpSampling layer is applied to double its spatial dimensions. The upsampled feature map is merged with the feature map from the initial encoder layer using a skip connection. Subsequently, the combined feature map proceeds to the Duck block. Finally, a convolutional layer with a 1×1 kernel size is applied to refine the feature map. The activation function employed is sigmoid, generating pixel-wise class probabilities for each of the segmentation classes.

3.1 Channel Feature Pyramid Module

The lightweight channel-wise feature pyramid (CFP) module [8] was successfully applied to both natural and medical image segmentation tasks. The architecture of the CFP module, depicted in Fig. 2, comprises a total of K channels, each with its dilation rate rK. In similar lines to [8], we also set K=4, with dilation rates $r1, r2, r3, r4 = 1, 2, 4, 8$, resulting in each channel's dimension being $M/4$. Hierarchical feature fusion (HFF) is then applied to sum the outputs of all channels incrementally.

The overall FP is derived by concatenating these sub-pyramids obtained from hierarchical feature fusion. The final FP comprises four levels of feature stacks, denoted as level $i, i = 1, \ldots, 4$, computed as follows: level1 = outFP1 level2 = level1 + outFP2 level3 = level2 + outFP3 level4 = level3 + outFP4 The final FP is computed by summing up all levels of feature stacks.

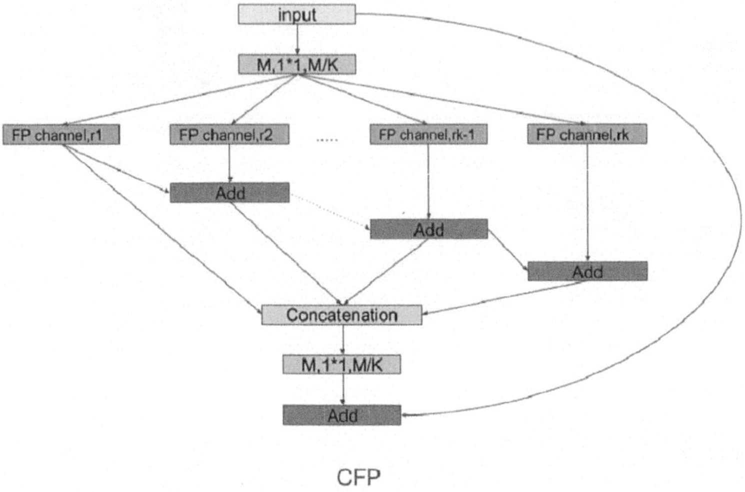

Fig. 2. Channel Feature Pyramid Module as employed in [8].

3.2 Reverse Axial Attention Module

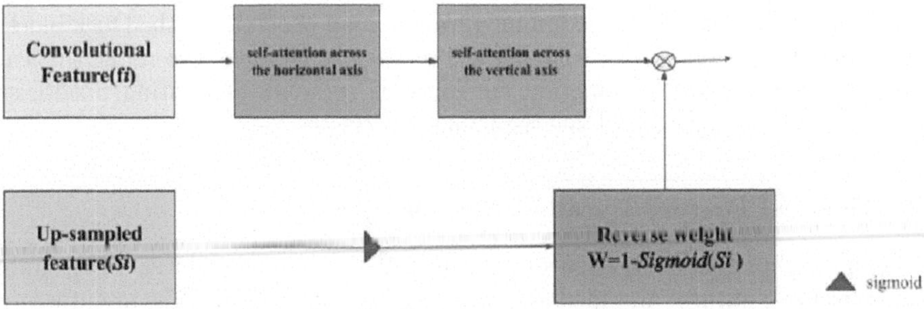

Fig. 3. Architecture of the Reverse Axial Attention block.

We utilize Reverse Axial Attention [8] as shown in Fig. 3, where Axial attention divides 2D attention into two seperable 1D attention blocks along the vertical and horizontal axes. The upscaled feature map undergoes a sigmoid activation function, followed by the computation of the reverse operation as $Ri = 1 - sigmoid(Si)$. The complete axial reverse attention operation merges the results of axial attention and reverse operation through element-wise multiplication.

3.3 Duck Block

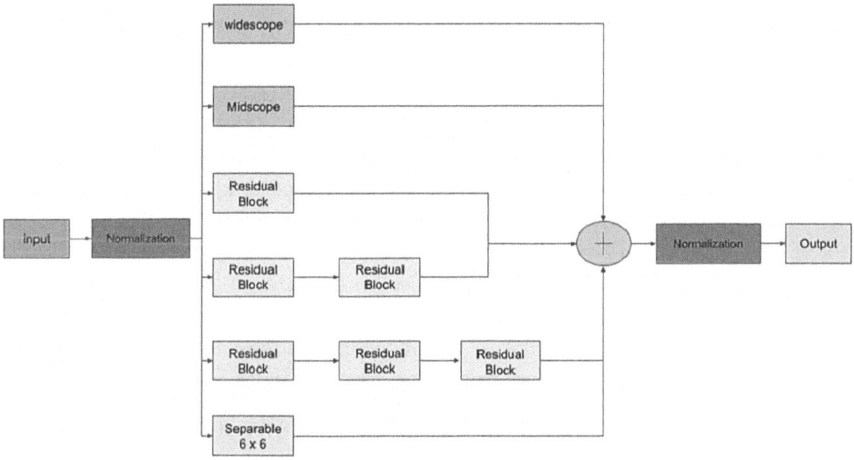

Fig. 4. Duck Block as employed in [9].

We employed the Duck Block from the Duck-Net architecture [9] as shown in 4, which integrates various convolutional blocks in parallel to leverage different behaviors at each step. DUCK block incorporates a wide range of kernel sizes simulated in three different ways, enabling the network to select the most suitable approach dynamically for its current task.

Residual Blocks: These are the foundational components of DUCK block, initially introduced in ResUNet++. They are designed to capture fine details crucial for polyp identification. Parallel combinations of one, two, and three Residual blocks are utilised to extract features effectively.

Midscope and Widescope Blocks: These blocks utilise dilated convolutions to reduce the parameters required for simulating larger kernels while enhancing the network's understanding of higher-level features. Midscope simulates a kernel size of 7×7, while Widescope simulates a kernel size of 15×15. They aim to capture prominent features with minimal attention to detail, compensating for the loss of information caused by dilation.

Separable Block: This block adopts a unique strategy to mimic large kernels by combining 1xN and Nx1 convolutions, effectively replicating the behaviour of an NxN kernel.

4 Experimental Results

4.1 Datasets

We performed experiments on three distinct datasets: WCE-dataset[1], Kvasir [10] and CVC-Clinic [11]. Exhaustive experiments were conducted to demonstrate

[1] https://misahub.in/CVIP/challenge.html.

the effectiveness and versatility of the proposed model across various data sets, ensuring robust performance in diverse scenarios. Figure 5 shows few sample images of the datasets used.

WCE-Dataset: MISAHUB provided the dataset via a challenge called Auto-WCEBleedGEN, where the training dataset contained 2618 bleeding and non-bleeding frames. For testing the developed model, MISAHUB provided a testing dataset of TEST containing 515 with marked areas.

Kvasir Dataset [10]: The Kvasir-SEG [10] provides a dataset for gastrointestinal polyp segmentation containing 1000 polyp images and their corresponding ground truth. The resolution of the images contained in Kvasir-SEG varies from 332×487 to 1920×1072 pixels.

CVC-Clinic Dataset [11]: The CVC-Clinic Dataset [11] was designated the official training database for the MICCAI 2015 Sub-Challenge on Automatic Polyp Detection Challenge in Colonoscopy Videos. The dataset contains 612 polyp images and their corresponding ground truth, with a resolution of 384×288 pixels.

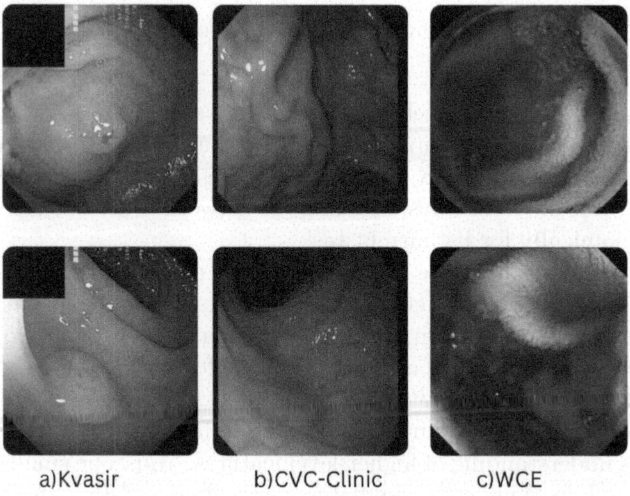

Fig. 5. Sample Images of Datasets.

4.2 Parameter Settings

The segmentation model was configured with specific parameters to optimize its performance. Images were standardized to a size of 224×224 pixels to ensure uniformity in input data. Random number generation was controlled using a seed value of 58800 for reproducibility of results.

For training, a learning rate of 1e–4 was chosen to regulate the update steps during optimization. The model architecture incorporated 16 filters, determining the complexity and capacity of the network to capture features from the input data. Training optimization was achieved through the RMSprop optimizer, a widely used algorithm for efficiently updating model parameters.

The training spanned 300 epochs, with an early stopping mechanism implemented to prevent overfitting. A patience of 50 epochs was set, ensuring that training would cease if no improvement in performance was observed within that window. Additionally, a minimum loss threshold of 0.2 was established to save the model only when its performance surpassed a predefined level.

The model was compiled with a custom Tversky loss function [14], tailored to the specific needs of the segmentation task. Metrics including Intersection over Union (IoU), accuracy, precision and Dice coefficient were employed to evaluate the model's performance.

Implementation was carried out using TensorFlow, a popular framework known for its flexibility and scalability in deep learning applications. The training utilized a T4 GPU, enabling efficient computation of complex neural network operations.

These meticulously chosen parameter settings collectively defined the training environment and architecture configuration, aiming to maximize the model's effectiveness in accurately segmenting target objects within images.

Data Augmentation. In this work, we incorporate data augmentation techniques using the Albumenations library [16], which proved to be instrumental in enhancing the generalization capabilities of our model. This augmentation strategy was so effective that traditional regularization methods like dropout became unnecessary. We improve the model's ability to generalize and perform effectively on unseen data. The augmentation techniques we employ includes: Horizontal and vertical flips. Color jitter, where the brightness factor was uniformly sampled from the range [0.6, 1.6], contrast was set at 0.2, saturation factor at 0.1, and hue factor at 0.01. Affine transforms, incorporating rotations sampled uniformly from [–180°, 180°], horizontal and vertical translations sampled uniformly from [–0.125, 0.125], scaling sampled uniformly from [0.5, 1.5], and shearing sampled uniformly from [–22.5°, 22°]. Among these augmentations, color jitter was exclusively applied to the image, while the remaining transformations were consistently applied to both the image and its corresponding segmentation map.

4.3 Performance Metrics

We validate the model performance on three prominent benchmark datasets Misahub WCE Dataset, Kvasir Dataset, and the CVC-ClinicDB Dataset. The quantitative findings affirm the efficacy of our approach, surpassing established methods such as CARANET, FCB-FORMER, DUCK-NET, SSFormer, unet, and resnet++.

Our model *DAANet* demonstrates competitive performance across various metrics, encompassing Mean Intersection over Union (Miou), Mean Dice (Mdice), accuracy, and precision. In particular the performance on the Kvasir

Dataset is significant, where it achieves a Miou of 0.8991 and a Mdice of 0.9401, outperforming all other compared competing methods. These outcomes highlight the potential of our approach in enhancing polyp segmentation accuracy within colonoscopy videos, thereby playing a pivotal role in the early detection and treatment of colorectal cancer.

The quantitative results of the WCE dataset are obtained after training the model with the WCE dataset. We then evaluate the model using a test dataset provided by Mishub. These test results reflect the superior performance of the model on the Mishub test dataset (Table 1).

Table 1. Quantitative results of WCE Dataset. - denotes the public results were not available.

Model	Miou	Mdice	accuracy	precision
Our Model DAANet(16 filters)	**0.8245**	**0.8673**	**0.933**	0.9137
DUCK-NET (17 filters) [9]	0.652	0.7932	0.901	0.803
CARANET [8]	0.659	0.748	0.862	**0.926**
FCB-FORMER [7]	0.67	0.695	0.756	0.444
SSFormer-S [13]	0.71	0.732	0.719	0.847
Resunet++ [4]	0.368	0.521	0.82	–
unet [1]	0.262	0.54	–	–

The results of the other models are taken from the publicly available results reported on the Kvasir (Table 2) and CVC-ClinicDB (Table 3) datasets.

Table 2. Quantitative results of Kvasir Dataset.

Model	Miou	Mdice
Our Model DAANet (16 filters)	**0.8991**	**0.9401**
FCB-FORMER [7]	0.8903	0.9385
DUCK-NET (17 filters) [9]	0.8769	0.9343
SSFormer [13]	0.8743	0.9261
CARANET [8]	0.865	0.918
Resunet++ [4]	0.7927	0.8133
unet [1]	0.4334	0.7147

Ablation Study. In our ablation study, we conducted a thorough examination of our model's performance by systematically evaluating its components using metrics such as Mean Intersection over Union (mIoU) and Mean Dice Similarity

Table 3. Quantitative results of CVC-ClinicDB Dataset.

Model	Miou	Mdice
Our Model DAANet (16 filters)	**0.91**	0.94
FCB-FORMER [7]	0.902	**0.946**
DUCK-NET(17 filters) [9]	0.8952	0.945
CARANET [8]	0.887	0.936
SSFormer-S [13]	0.8759	0.9268
Resunet++ [4]	0.7962	0.7955
unet [1]	0.4711	0.6419

Coefficient (mDice). Our model incorporates both attention and CFP (Cross Feature Pyramid) modules.

During the study, we analyzed the impact on performance when each module was individually removed, leaving only the attention module or only the CFP module operational. By comparing the resulting mIoU and mDice scores across these different configurations, we gained insights into the significance of each module in contributing to the model's ability to accurately segment or classify objects within our dataset.

This meticulous analysis allowed us to understand the relative importance and effectiveness of the attention and CFP modules within our model architecture as shown in Tables 4, 5 and 6.

Table 4. Ablation Study on WCE Dataset

Model	Miou	Mdice
Our model	**0.8245**	**0.8673**
Our model with CFP module	0.751	0.815
Our model with Attention	0.732	0.803

Table 5. Ablation Study on Kvasir-SEG Dataset

Model	Miou	Mdice
Our model	**0.8991**	**0.9401**
Our model with CFP module	0.868	0.924
Our model with Attention	0.773	0.842

Table 6. Ablation Study on CVC-Clinic Dataset

Model	Miou	Mdice
Our model	**0.91**	**0.946**
Our model with CFP module	0.843	0.895
Our model with Attention	0.837	0.906

4.4 Discussion

Despite the inherent challenges presented by the WCE (Wireless Capsule Endoscopy) dataset, particularly concerning the resemblance in color between blood and specific tissues, as well as the abundance of noise within the images, our predictive models demonstrate remarkable efficacy. Through innovative algo-

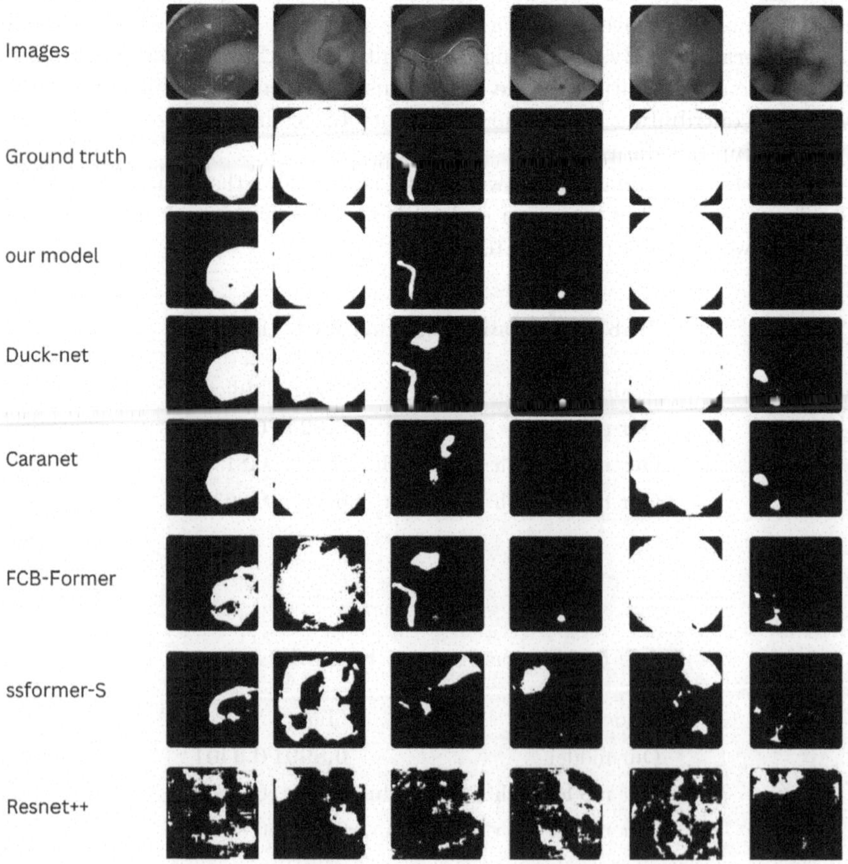

Fig. 6. Qualitative Analysis on WCE Dataset.

rithmic design and robust training methodologies, our models excel in discerning subtle nuances and identifying minute patches within the imagery.

In our qualitative analysis of the Wireless Capsule Endoscopy (WCE) dataset, we conducted a comparative evaluation with state-of-the-art models, including DuckNet, CaraNet, FCBFormer, SSFormer-S and ResNet++ as shown in Fig. 6. Notably, our proposed model demonstrated superior performance across all metrics, outperforming its counterparts. A key observation was the propensity of other models to generate false positives for certain images, highlighting the robustness and accuracy of our model in distinguishing relevant features and minimizing erroneous classifications. This underscores the efficacy of our approach in advancing the state-of-the-art WCE image analysis, offering promising implications for enhanced diagnostic accuracy and patient care in gastrointestinal healthcare settings.

The Class Activation Maps for the WCE Dataset, depicting activation patterns are shown in Fig. 7. These maps offer visual insights into our model's performance on six chosen figures. They enhance explainability of how our model processes and identifies features and provides attention on the blood smeared regions in the GI tract. Owing to the incorporation of the reverse axial attention we are able to restrict to the regions of disease and due to the CFP block we have hierarchical feature fusion.

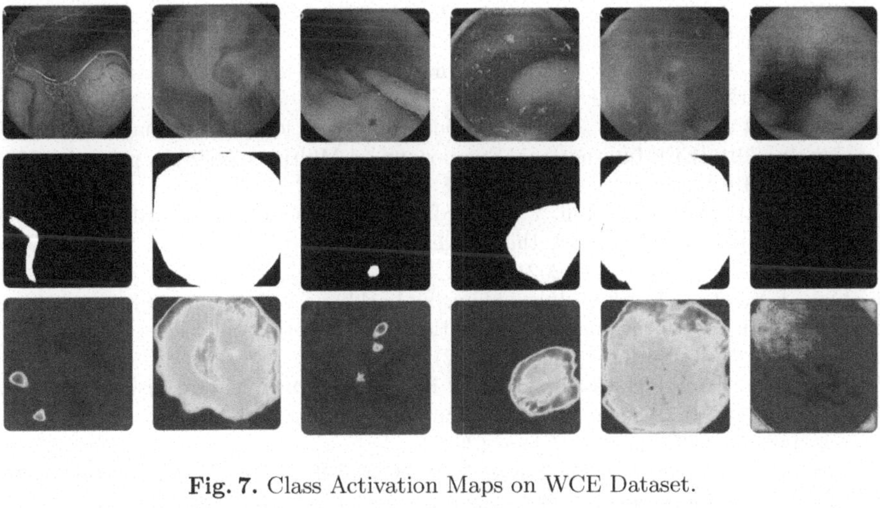

Fig. 7. Class Activation Maps on WCE Dataset.

5 Conclusion

In medical imaging, especially Wireless Capsule Endoscopy (WCE), is indispensable for diagnosing gastrointestinal disorders. However, analyzing WCE footage is time-consuming and prone to errors. To address this, UNet based framework integrating Duck block with reverse axial attention mechanism and channel feature pyramid module enhances segmentation accuracy. Experimental results across various datasets, including WCE, Kvasir, and CVC-ClinicDB, demonstrate superior performance in polyp segmentation. This fusion of robust feature extraction and attentive mechanism marks a significant advancement in medical imaging. Competitive results in Mean Intersection over Union (Miou) and Mean Dice (Mdice) metrics showcase the method's efficacy. This approach holds promise for improving diagnostic accuracy and patient care in gastroenterology. Overall, this work contributes to the evolution of medical imaging technologies for enhanced healthcare outcomes.

References

1. Ronneberger, O., Fischer, P., Brox, T.: U-net: convolutional networks for biomedical image segmentation. In: Medical Image Computing and Computer-Assisted Intervention MICCAI 2015: 18th International Conference, Munich, Germany, 5–9 October 2015, proceedings, Part III 18, pp. 234–241. Springer (2015)
2. Zhou, Z., Rahman Siddiquee, M.M., Tajbakhsh, N. and Liang, J.: Unet++: a nested u-net architecture for medical image segmentation. In: Deep Learning in Medical Image Analysis and Multimodal Learning for Clinical Decision Support: 4th International Workshop, DLMIA 2018, and 8th International Workshop, ML-CDS 2018, Held in Conjunction with MICCAI 2018, Granada, Spain, 20 September 2018, Proceedings 4, pp. 3–11. Springer (2018)
3. Oktay, O., et al.: Attention u-net: learning where to look for the pancreas. arXiv preprint arXiv:1804.03999 (2018)
4. Jha, D., et al.: Resunet++: an advanced architecture for medical image segmentation. In: 2019 IEEE International Symposium on Multimedia (ISM), pp. 225–2255. IEEE (2019)
5. Huang, C.H., Wu, H.Y., Lin, Y.L.: Hardnet-mseg: a simple encoder decoder polyp segmentation neural network that achieves over 0.9 mean dice and 86 fps. arXiv preprint arXiv:2101.07172 (2021)
6. Liao, T.Y., et al.: Hardnet-dfus: enhancing backbone and decoder of hardnet-mseg for diabetic foot ulcer image segmentation. In: Diabetic Foot Ulcers Grand Challenge, pp. 21-30. Springer, Cham (2022)
7. Sanderson, E. and Matuszewski, B.J.: FCN-transformer feature fusion for polyp segmentation. In: Annual Conference on Medical Image Understanding and Analysis, pp. 892–907. Springer, Cham (2022)
8. Lou, A., Guan, S., Ko, H., Loew, M.H.: CaraNet: context axial reverse attention network for segmentation of small medical objects. In: Medical Imaging 2022: Image Processing, vol. 12032, pp. 81–92. SPIE (2022)
9. Dumitru, R.-G., Peteleaza, D., Craciun, C.: Using DUCK-net for polyp image segmentation. Sci. Rep. **13**(1), 9803 (2023)
10. Jha, D., et al.: Kvasir-SEG: a segmented polyp dataset. In: Ro, Y.M., et al. (eds.) MMM 2020. LNCS, vol. 11962, pp. 451–462. Springer, Cham (2020). https://doi.org/10.1007/978-3-030-37734-2_37
11. Bernal, J., et al.: WM-DOVA maps for accurate polyp highlighting in colonoscopy: Validation vs. saliency maps from physicians. Comput. Med. Imaging Graph. **43**, 99–111 (2015)

12. Gao, S., et al.: Res2net: a new multi-scale backbone architecture. IEEE Trans. Pattern Anal. Mach. Intell. (2019)
13. Wang, J., Huang, Q., Tang, F., Meng, J., Su, J., Song, S.: Stepwise feature fusion: local guides global. In: International Conference on Medical Image Computing and Computer-Assisted Intervention, pp. 110–120. Springer, Cham (2022)
14. Salehi, S.S.M., Erdogmus, D., Gholipour, A.: Tversky loss function for image segmentation using 3D fully convolutional deep networks. In: International Workshop on Machine Learning in Medical Imaging, pp. 379–387. Springer, Cham (2017)
15. Liu, S., Huang, D.: Receptive field block net for accurate and fast object detection. In: Proceedings of the European Conference on Computer Vision (ECCV), pp. 385–400 (2018)
16. Buslaev, A., Iglovikov, V.I., Khvedchenya, E., Parinov, A., Druzhinin, M., Kalinin, A.A.: Albumentations: fast and flexible image augmentations. Information **11**(2), 125 (2020)

Enhancing Robotic Interaction and Navigation with Pick and Place Operations and Visual SLAM Techniques

Pravat Kumar Panda[1(✉)], Prashnik Bhattacharya[1], Aadithya Iyer[2], and Deepak Mishra[1]

[1] Department of Avionics, Indian Institute of Space Science and Technology, Thiruvananthapuram 675547, Kerala, India
pravatpanda2001@gmail.com

[2] Department of Mechanical Engineering, Birla Institute of Technology and Science KK Birla Goa Campus, Sancoale 403726, Goa, India

Abstract. In this paper, we introduce a mobile robotic system with a 7-Degrees of Freedom Robotic Arm designed for executing various pick-and-place operations and autonomous navigation within indoor environments. This system integrates vision-based object recognition and localization to facilitate precise grasping actions. A visual simultaneous localization and mapping (SLAM) algorithm is utilized to enable the robot's autonomous navigation in unfamiliar indoor settings. Additionally, we employed the YOLOv3 algorithm which enhances object detection and tracking capabilities, which is crucial for responding to any sudden positional changes in the target object. The process begins with YOLOv3 identifying and locating the object, followed by monitoring the next frame to detect any immediate shifts before the robotic arm's movement to grasp the object. Once the object to be picked up is decided by the Robot, we employ a Countour-based Object boundary detection technique that gives us both, the objects' coordinates in 3D space and the orientation at which the object is placed. Subsequently, a coordinate transformation is performed, converting the coordinates of the target object from the camera's frame of reference to that of the robotic arm's base frame, thereby facilitating accurate grasping operations. Furthermore, the robot is equipped with a human-following algorithm, enabling it to track and transport payloads to a human target efficiently, placing the payload in proximity to the person. Experimental results highlight a significant grasping success rate of 94%, underscoring the system's efficacy in autonomous robotic navigation and pick-and-place operations. This advancement holds substantial promise for enhancing robotic autonomy and operational efficiency in real-world scenarios.

Keywords: Visual SLAM · Robotic arm Grasping · YOLOv3

J. Kakarla et al. (Eds.): CVIP 2024, CCIS 2473, pp. 308–322, 2026.
https://doi.org/10.1007/978-3-031-93688-3_22

1 Introduction

Mobile manipulators [1] represent a critical category in robotics, combining the capabilities of autonomous navigation and operation to potentially replace human guidance to robots in complex environments. A typical mobile rover consists of a robotic arm mounted on a mobile platform. This configuration benefits from the extensive operational range of the mobile platform and the precise manipulative abilities of the robotic arm, further enhanced by integrated vision systems that allow operation in increasingly complex settings as well as in space applications and interplanetary rover missions. For these missions, the development of high-precision algorithms for robotic arms used in sample collection necessitates highly accurate positioning of the end effector's pose. Consequently, conducting research on effective pick-and-place operations for robotic arms is of utmost importance. Our work not only focuses on orienting the end effector relative to objects in space but also involves developing algorithms for pick-and-place operations.

The structure of this document is methodically organized into many sections for clarity and depth of discussion: Sect. 2 elaborates on the literature review and theoretical foundations of Visual SLAM and YOLO, preparing the groundwork for their integration into our system. Section 3 explicates algorithms and methodologies developed to enhance the autonomy of the mobile rover. Section 4 addresses the implementation details of these algorithms. Section 5 delineates the hardware specifications utilized in this project. Section 6 presents empirical results that validate the effectiveness of our proposed solutions. Section 7 concludes the document, summarizing key findings and outlining fields for future research.

2 Literature Review

Path planning is a crucial aspect of autonomous navigation, enabling robots to determine an optimal path from a starting point to a destination. Algorithms such as A* [2], Dijkstra's [3], and Rapidly-exploring Random Trees (RRT) [4] have been extensively studied. More recent approaches incorporate probabilistic methods and machine learning techniques to enhance path planning in dynamic environments [5].

Visual Simultaneous Localization and Mapping (SLAM) [6] is an essential technology in robotics and autonomous systems, providing the means for devices to dynamically understand and navigate their environments. This review aggregates significant findings from contemporary literature, emphasizing the progression and technological advances in the field.

Visual SLAM faces considerable challenges, particularly in dynamic settings where integrating multiple sensor modalities and enhancing feature extraction methods are critical. Recent literature points towards efforts to bolster algorithm robustness and efficiency in complex environments, suggesting a move towards more resilient solutions [7].

There has been a noticeable evolution from traditional frameworks to modern techniques that incorporate deep learning. [8] highlights the evolution from traditional frameworks to modern techniques with deep learning, detailing the shift from monocular to complex RGB-D and stereo-visual SLAM approaches. The integration of deep learning with SLAM has significantly enhanced semantic comprehension and environmental interaction. Recent methodologies use neural networks to refine scene understanding and manage dynamic objects [9].

Furthermore, collaborative visual SLAM has shown great promise in improving mapping accuracy and robustness, particularly in dynamic scenarios. The works of [10] explore multi-agent systems, emphasizing decentralized architectures that enhance scalability and operational efficiency. These developments underscore a vibrant and rapidly advancing field, poised to revolutionize robotic navigation and autonomous systems further.

Among the various algorithms available in the literature for object detection, notable examples include the Histogram of Oriented Gradients (HOG) [11], Deformable Parts Model (DPM), You Only Look Once (YOLO), Region-based Convolutional Neural Networks (R-CNN), Single Shot Multibox Detector (SSD) [12], and Faster R-CNN [13]. While HOG and DPM rely on handcrafted features and are generally faster, they often lack the accuracy of CNN-based methods. These CNN classifiers, although typically slower due to their complex architectures, offer substantially higher accuracy due to their ability to learn discriminative features directly from the data.

In [14], CNNs were used to detect screwdrivers, focusing on the center of mass for pick-and-place operations. A research gap exists in determining object orientation, as bounding boxes fail to align accurately. We developed a contour-based oriented bounding box technique to better capture orientation, improving grasping capabilities and enabling operations in cluttered environments.

YOLO [15] stands out among CNN-based detectors for balancing speed and accuracy by using a single neural network to predict multiple bounding boxes and class probabilities simultaneously. Unlike R-CNN, which first generates bounding boxes and then classifies them, YOLO processes images in real-time. SSD also detects objects in one pass using multiple feature maps at different scales but generally lacks YOLO's accuracy. Faster R-CNN improves on R-CNN with Region Proposal Networks for faster proposals, but is still slower than YOLO due to its two-stage processing.

The direct approach of YOLO not only speeds up the detection process, but also reduces the error rate compared to other detectors that process the parts of the image independently.

Autonomous robotic navigation and pick-and-place operations [16–18] have made significant strides, driven by advancements in algorithms, sensor technologies, and machine learning. However, challenges such as robust navigation in dynamic and unstructured environments, real-time decision-making, and efficient human-robot interaction remain significant research gaps.

3 Methodology

3.1 Navigation Methods

In robotic navigation, two primary approaches are employed: the known trajectory method [19] and the unknown trajectory method. The known trajectory method involves a predefined path that the rover autonomously follows. While this method requires minimal hardware, making it cost-effective, it struggles with adaptability, particularly if there are unforeseen changes along the path which can disrupt the rover's positioning and navigation. On the other hand, the unknown trajectory method leverages advanced computer vision techniques such as Simultaneous Localization and Mapping (SLAM) for navigation. This technique, especially when utilizing Visual SLAM, requires only minimal hardware such as an RGB-D camera [20], yet offers significant accuracy and flexibility in dynamic environments. Our system adopts Visual SLAM, optimizing hardware use while ensuring precise navigation.

3.2 Grasping Methods

Grasping technology in robotics has evolved from manual teaching methods to more sophisticated deep-learning approaches. Manual teaching involves preprogramming specific grasping operations into the robotic system, which, while reliable for repetitive tasks, lacks flexibility. Conversely, deep learning-based grasping methods utilize neural networks to enable robots to learn and improve their grasping capabilities dynamically, adapting to a variety of objects and scenarios.

An integral part of our system's object recognition and grasping capability is the YOLO algorithm. YOLO excels in real-time object detection, crucial for the robotic arm to efficiently identify and manipulate objects. By continuously analyzing visual input to detect and track objects, YOLO enables the robotic system to dynamically adjust its grasping strategy, significantly improving the efficacy and reliability of pick-and-place operations.

Along with this, we developed a Contour-based Object Detection algorithm, which operates as follows:

- **Edge Detection:** Utilizes the Canny Edge Detection Algorithm to identify edges within the visual input for the detected target object with YOLO.
- **Morphological Operations:** Implements erosion and dilation to refine detected edges, enhancing the clarity and usability of the edge map.
- **Contour Detection:** Systematically identifies and delineates contours from the refined edge map, crucial for subsequent object localization.
- **Oriented Bounding Box:** Draws oriented bounding boxes around suitable contours, while with YOLO we were not able to get the orientation details of the object to be picked.
- **Coordinate and Orientation Determination:** Calculates the precise coordinates to which the robotic arm should move to grasp the object, along with the orientation of the object. This facilitates effective and efficient object manipulation.

3.3 Human Searching and Reaching to It

Our mobile manipulator incorporates a Human searching algorithm, which is essential for tasks that require the robot to interact with or assist humans directly.

The robot starts its navigation by rotating in place to detect a human using YOLOv3, which provides a bounding box and depth data at the centroid of the box. This depth information is crucial for measuring the distance to the human, informing the robot's next navigation steps.

After detecting a human, the robot aligns itself to face the person directly, enhancing interaction. It then moves forward until the person is less than 0.6 m away. If the person comes within 0.5 m, the robot automatically reverses to maintain a safe distance, ensuring user-friendly navigation (Fig. 1).

When the human moves laterally, the robot dynamically adjusts its orientation by rotating to maintain a direct line of sight. This adaptability allows the robot to smoothly track the human's movements, ensuring a responsive and robust navigation system.

This algorithm enables the robot to track and follow a human operator or target within its environment. This feature is particularly useful in environments such as warehouses or hospitals where dynamic human interaction is necessary.

4 Implementation

4.1 Visual SLAM

Visual SLAM is integrated to provide real-time localization and mapping capabilities, which are fundamental for the robot's ability to navigate autonomously.

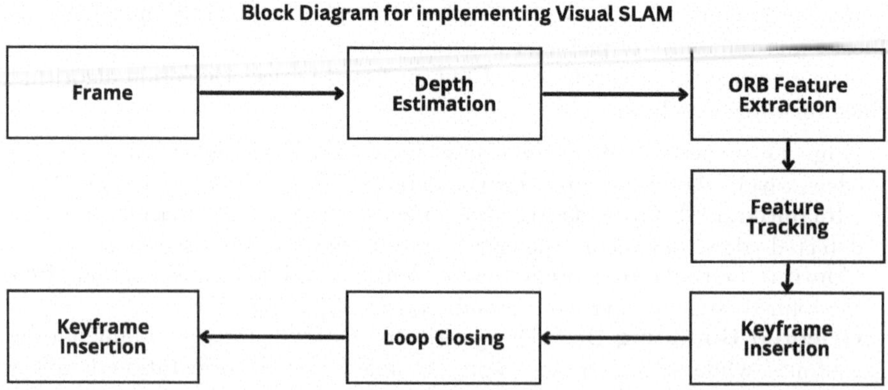

Fig. 1. This schematic illustrates the key stages involved in implementing Visual Simultaneous Localization and Mapping (SLAM).

Depth Estimation. Depth estimation is a pivotal aspect of scene understanding in computer vision and robotics. For our work, we utilized the Intel RealSense D415 camera to estimate the depth map of the scene.

Feature Tracking. Feature tracking is crucial in SLAM for creating a detailed map by establishing correspondences between different views of the scene. Features tracked are chosen for their uniqueness and robustness, helping in recognizing them under varying conditions like changes in lighting or viewpoint.

- **ORB Features:** The ORB algorithm [21], combining the FAST feature detector and BRIEF descriptor, efficiently identifies and encodes corner-like features. Known for its speed and robustness, ORB performs comparably to SIFT and outperforms SURF, while being significantly faster.
- **Feature Matching Process:**
  - **Extraction and Description:** After detecting ORB features, they are encoded into binary descriptors which capture unique aspects of each feature.
  - **Correspondence Search:** Feature matching uses brute force methods in OpenCV to find features with similar descriptors across consecutive frames.
  - **Distance Metrics and Thresholds:** The Hamming distance metric is used to measure dissimilarity between descriptors, with a threshold applied to identify potential matches.
  - **Lowe's Ratio Test:** This test refines matching by comparing the distances of the closest descriptors, eliminating ambiguous matches by ensuring that the ratio between the distances of the two nearest neighbours falls below a set threshold.

Motion Estimation: Motion estimation is crucial for SLAM, enabling the algorithm to understand camera or platform movement through the environment, which is vital for the precision and robustness of Visual SLAM algorithm.

To begin the motion estimation, a depth map is captured for a specific frame. This depth map is crucial as it provides the data necessary to compute the three-dimensional coordinates of key points. These coordinates are calculated using the equations:

$$x = z \cdot \frac{u - cx}{fx} \tag{1}$$

$$y = z \cdot \frac{v - cy}{fy} \tag{2}$$

Here x and y denote the key points' three-dimensional coordinates in the camera's coordinate system. z corresponds to the depth value of the key points, extracted from the depth map. u and v represent the pixel coordinates of the key points in the image. cx and cy refer to the principal point (image centre) along the x and y directions, respectively. fx and fy signify the camera's focal lengths in the x and y directions, respectively (Fig. 3).

After computing the 3-dimensional coordinates, the motion estimation uses the RANSAC [22], as in Fig. 2, to derive rotation and transformation matrices. These matrices capture changes in orientation and translation between frames, crucial for the SLAM system to track and map the environment accurately.

Loop Closing: In Visual SLAM, loop closing [23] is essential for maintaining map coherence and trajectory consistency. It addresses drift—cumulative errors that cause trajectory discrepancies—by reconnecting previously visited areas.

Fig. 2. Feature being tracked across two consecutive frames using RANSAC. This image demonstrates the feature tracking process in Visual SLAM, where key features are identified and their movements are traced between successive frames.

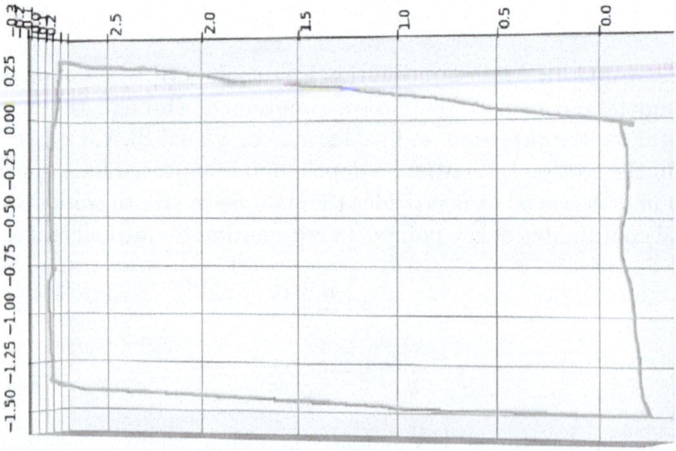

Fig. 3. This plot illustrates the spatial map generated through the Visual SLAM process, highlighting the use of loop closing to correct drift and ensure map coherence and trajectory consistency.

This realignment corrects and prevents significant drift, ensuring the trajectory closely matches the actual path.

Loop closing in Visual SLAM recalibrates coordinates upon detecting a loop to align the current frame with relevant keyframes, correcting accumulated errors. This enhances map integrity and optimizes computational resources. Keyframes are added selectively—only after 20 frames and based on their distinctiveness from prior frames, balancing precision with computational efficiency and reducing memory usage.

4.2 Object Detection

Object detection is crucial for robotic navigation and grasping, enabling intelligent interactions in dynamic environments. It plays a key role in mobile robotics by allowing precise identification and localization of objects like bottles or humans, supporting informed decision-making and adaptive navigation.

We employed the YOLOv3 algorithm for object detection within our system. Upon detecting an object, YOLOv3 delineates the target by enclosing it within a rectangular bounding box. Subsequently, we extract the segment of the image confined by this rectangle and apply our custom Contour-based boundary detection algorithm. This process facilitates the generation of an oriented bounding box, which provides critical information about the object's orientation, essential for the robotic arm to accurately grasp and manipulate the object (Figs. 4 and 5).

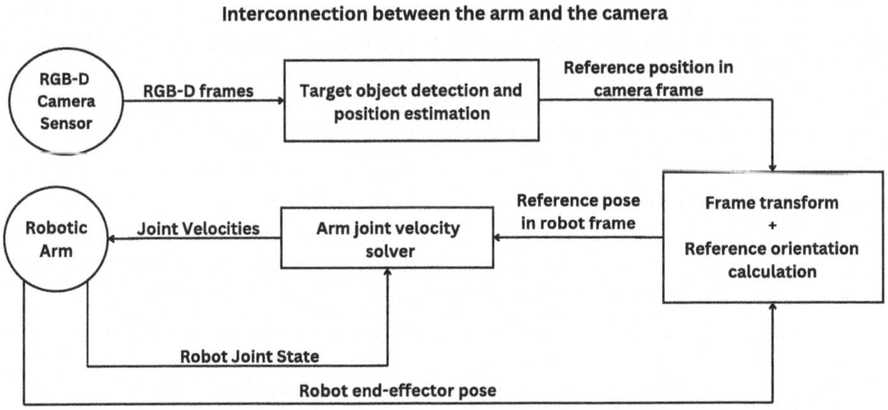

Fig. 4. This diagram outlines the integration of the RGB-D camera sensor and a robotic arm

4.3 Autonomous Rover Manipulation

This phase involved the integration of object recognition, specifically targeting detection and interaction with a designated payload—here, a bottle. Leveraging

Fig. 5. As it can be seen in the given figure bottle has been successfully detected the numbers written in white are the 3D coordinates of the centroid of the bottle in the camera's coordinate frame.

the powerful YOLOv3 algorithm, the robot undertakes a systematic exploration, rotating until a bottle is successfully identified within its visual field.

Upon detecting the bottle, the robot initiates an alignment procedure, dynamically orienting itself to position the bottle squarely in its frontal perspective. This meticulous alignment sets the stage for the subsequent interaction, where the robot transitions into a purposeful forward motion directed towards the bottle. A carefully calibrated proximity threshold, set at less than 450 mm, triggers a halt in the robot's movement to ensure a precise and controlled approach to the target. Further enhancing its interaction capabilities, a contour-based boundary detection technique is employed to extract precise coordinates of the bottle as well as the orientation. Armed with this spatial information, the robot executes a grasping manoeuvre, securing the bottle with precision. This delicate and coordinated operation underscores the robot's dexterity in interacting with its environment (Fig. 6).

With the bottle securely in its grasp, the robot transitions back to a rotational exploration phase, scanning its surroundings for the presence of a human subject. Upon successfully detecting the human, the robot seamlessly integrates the Human Searching Algorithm.

As a culmination of this intricate sequence, once the robot achieves a distance of approximately 0.5 m to 0.6 m from the human subject, it exhibits an additional layer of functionality by placing the bottle in proximity to the human's feet. This deliberate and context-aware action demonstrates the robot's ability to not only navigate and interact with diverse objects but also to discern and respond to the spatial relationships within its environment (Fig. 7).

The block diagram presents an algorithm for a rover's navigation that includes picking up and placing objects. The process begins with the rover searching for the target object by rotating clockwise. If the target is found, the rover

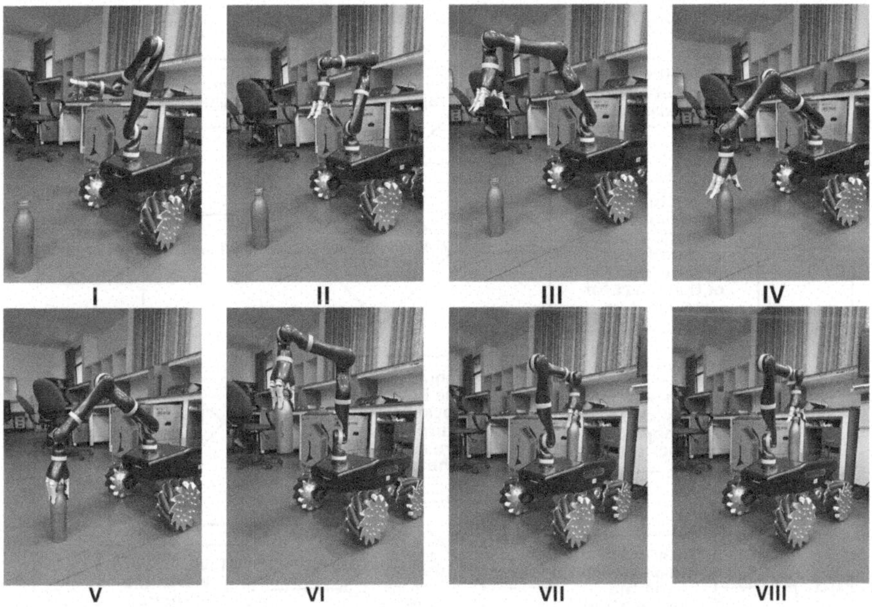

Fig. 6. Illustrates the Perception-based Pick and Place demonstration. (I) Depicts the Home Position of the Robotic Arm. (II) Shows the positioning for the Picking operation. (III) Represents the movement above the target object. (IV) Indicates the descent and preparation for grasping. (V) Displays the grasping of the target object. (VI) Depicts the payload being lifted. (VII) Demonstrates the rotation and placement of the payload on the rover. (VIII) Depicts the ungrasping of the payload.

aligns itself and moves forward towards it. Once within 40 cm of the target, the rover's arm positions itself to pick up the object. After grasping the object, the rover searches for the destination (a human) by rotating clockwise. When the destination is found and the rover is within 0.5 m to 0.6 m, it moves forward, and the arm places the object at the destination, concluding the process.

5 Setup

The hardware configuration comprises a seven degrees-of-freedom (7-DoF) robotic arm integrated into a mobile rover platform equipped with mecanum wheels. The rover's computational capabilities are powered by an onboard Intel Core i7 (9th Generation) processor, embedded within a motherboard that lacks an external GPU. Additionally, an Intel RealSense D415 RGB-D camera is mounted on the rover to facilitate depth and visual data acquisition.

The onboard PC exclusively executes several algorithms: the YOLOv3 algorithm for object detection, SLAM for mapping and navigation, a human searching algorithm, and contour-based object boundary detection and orientation algorithms. Additionally, the PC is equipped with a WiFi module, enabling

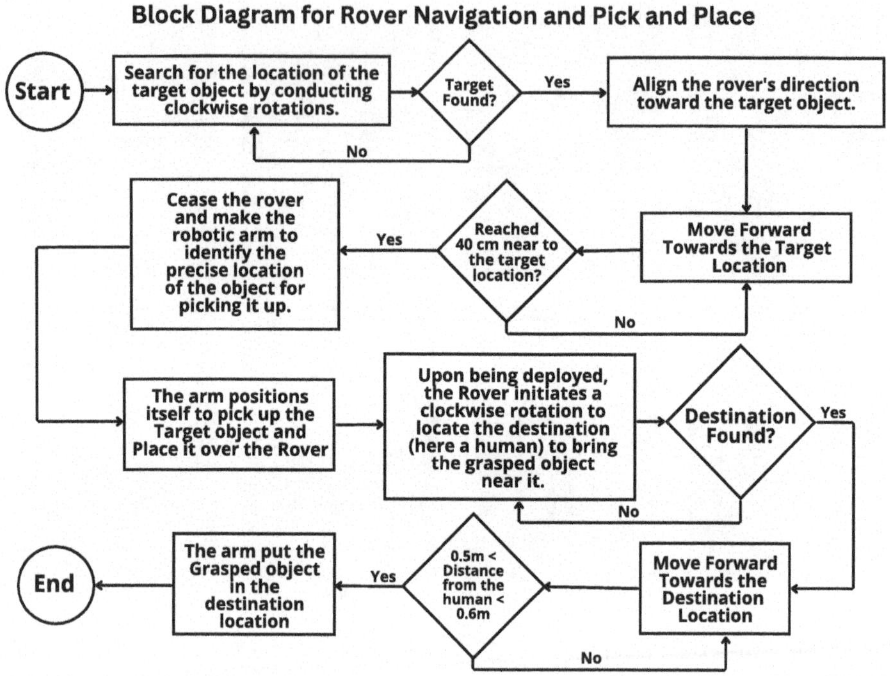

Fig. 7. Autonomous Rover Manipulation Block Diagram. This diagram illustrates the process of rover navigation and object manipulation, detailing the steps from target searching and alignment to object pickup and placement at the destination.

internet connectivity to the motherboard. This setup also facilitates the transmission of camera's feeds to a remote PC via Remote Desktop software, allowing for remote Visualization of the camera feed.

6 Experimental Results

6.1 Mapping and Navigation

In this study, we implement Simultaneous Localization and Mapping (SLAM) to facilitate smooth autonomous navigation within a confined laboratory environment (10 m x 4 m). The objective is to enable the robotic system to navigate efficiently, while simultaneously constructing an accurate map of the surroundings. Our evaluation metric for the Visual SLAM algorithm's effectiveness is its ability to locate both stationary and moving targets with minimal or no collisions. The algorithm is designed to pivot and search for designated objects and humans not initially within the camera's field of view. Upon detection, the system realigns its trajectory towards the target to ensure optimal navigation and object interaction (Fig. 8).

6.2 Object Detection and Localization

The object detection capabilities of our system are assessed using a YOLOv3 model configured with an Intersection Over Union (IOU) threshold of 0.6. The input to the model consists of images with dimensions of 640×480 pixels, processed at a rate of 30 frames per second. The real-time detection results, captured through the onboard Intel Realsense D415 camera, demonstrate the model's robustness in identifying various objects under different lighting conditions. These results are summarized in Table 1, illustrating the system's detection accuracy.

Fig. 8. Object detection using YOLOv3. This image demonstrates the YOLO algorithm's ability to detect multiple objects used in this experiment.

Table 1. Object Detection Results on the objects present in the Lab. SN: Number of times the image was taken, TP: True Positive, FN: False Negative, FP: False Positive. Precision of Detection = $\frac{TP}{TP+FP}$

Target Object	SN	TP	FN	FP	Precision(in %)
Copper Bottle	50	49	0	1	98
Blue Bottle	50	48	1	1	97.95
Hand washer	50	47	2	1	97.91
Cup	50	49	1	0	100
Detergent	50	47	0	3	94
White Bottle	50	49	0	1	98
Total	300	289	4	7	97.63

6.3 Grasping Experiments

The grasping capabilities of the Kinova 7-DoF robotic arm were evaluated through experiments involving multiple object types under varying lighting conditions. The system's camera identifies the object, calculates its coordinates, and employs coordinate transformation to align these with the robot's end-effector frame. The outcomes of these experiments, detailed in Table 2, showcase the precision and adaptability of the grasping mechanism.

Table 2. Result of Grasping Experiment on different objects.

Target Object	Grasping Tried	Successful Grasp	Unsuccessful Grasp	Success(in %)
Copper Bottle	50	47	3	94
Blue Bottle	50	48	2	96
Hand washer	50	45	5	90
Cup	50	47	3	94
Surf Excel	50	46	4	92
White Bottle	50	49	1	98
Total	300	282	18	94

Human Searching. The system's effectiveness in human following is quantified by its ability to detect and track a human target across 1000 frames. Our findings indicate a detection success rate of 98.6%, with the rover successfully identifying the human in 986 frames out of 1000 frames. This high success rate underscores the system's reliability in human detection and following capabilities under dynamic conditions.

7 Conclusion

This study successfully demonstrates the capabilities of an autonomous robotic system within an indoor environment. By leveraging advanced techniques such as Visual SLAM and YOLOv3 for object detection, the system achieves high levels of precision in navigation, object recognition, and human following. Experimental results reveal robust performance across various tasks, including a 98.6% success rate in human searching and significant effectiveness in object detection and grasping under varied lighting conditions. Future prospects include the utilisation of more powerful systems enabling the usage of more recent YOLO versions, faster computation, and an overall increase in task efficiency. Looking forward, enhancing the deep learning models for object detection and exploring adaptive navigation algorithms could further improve the system's efficiency and adaptability in more dynamic and unpredictable environments.

Acknowledgments. This study was conducted using the Robotnik Rover and the Kinova JACO2 7-DoF arm in the CV-VR Lab of the Indian Institute of Space Science and Technology(IIST), Thiruvananthapuram, India.

References

1. Zelinsky, A.: A mobile robot navigation exploration algorithm. IEEE Trans. Robot. Autom. **8**(6), 707–717 (1992)
2. Hart, P.E., Nilsson, N.J., Raphael, B.: A formal basis for the heuristic determination of minimum cost paths. IEEE Trans. Syst. Sci. Cybern. **4**(2), 100–107 (1968). https://doi.org/10.1109/TSSC.1968.300136
3. Wang, H., Yu, Y., Yuan, Q.: Application of dijkstra algorithm in robot path-planning. In: 2011 Second International Conference on Mechanic Automation and Control Engineering, pp. 1067–1069. IEEE (2011). https://doi.org/10.1109/MACE.2011.5987118
4. Kuffner, J.J., LaValle, S.M.: Rrt-connect: an efficient approach to single-query path planning. In: Proceedings 2000 ICRA. Millennium Conference. IEEE International Conference on Robotics and Automation. Symposia Proceedings (Cat. No. 00CH37065), vol. 2, pp. 995–1001. IEEE (2000). https://doi.org/10.1109/ROBOT.2000.844730
5. Mohanan, M.G., Salgaonkar, A.: Probabilistic approach to robot motion planning in dynamic environments. SN Comput. Sci. **1**(3), 1–16 (2020). https://doi.org/10.1007/s42979-020-00185-0
6. Taketomi, T., Uchiyama, H., Ikeda, S.: Visual SLAM algorithms: a survey from 2010 to 2016. IPSJ Trans. Comput. Vis. Appli. **9**(1), 1–11 (2017). https://doi.org/10.1186/s41074-017-0027-2
7. Choi, Y.H., Oh, S.Y.: Grid-based visual slam in complex environments. J. Intell. Rob. Syst. **50**, 241–255 (2007). https://doi.org/10.1007/s10846-007-9163-8
8. Gong, H., Gong, L., Ma, T., Sun, Z., Li, L.: Ahy-slam: toward faster and more accurate visual slam in dynamic scenes using homogenized feature extraction and object detection method. Sensors **23**(9), 4241 (2023). https://doi.org/10.3390/s23094241
9. Qin, Y., Yu, H.: A review of visual slam with dynamic objects. Indust. Robot: Int. J. Robot. Res. Appli. **50**(6), 1000–1010 (2023). https://doi.org/10.1108/IR-07-2023-0162
10. Zou, Q., Sun, Q., Chen, L., Nie, B., Li, Q.: A comparative analysis of lidar slam-based indoor navigation for autonomous vehicles. IEEE Trans. Intell. Transp. Syst. **23**(7), 6907–6921 (2021). https://doi.org/10.1109/TITS.2021.3063477
11. Dalal, N., Triggs, B.: Histograms of oriented gradients for human detection. In: 2005 IEEE Computer Society Conference on Computer Vision and Pattern Recognition (CVPR 2005), vol. 1, pp. 886–893. IEEE (2005). https://doi.org/10.1109/CVPR.2005.177
12. Liu, W., et al.: SSD: single shot multibox detector. In: Leibe, B., Matas, J., Sebe, N., Welling, M. (eds.) ECCV 2016. LNCS, vol. 9905, pp. 21–37. Springer, Cham (2016). https://doi.org/10.1007/978-3-319-46448-0_2
13. Girshick, R.: Fast r-cnn. In: Proceedings of the IEEE International Conference on Computer Vision, pp. 1440–1448 (2015)
14. Perng, J.W., Wang, C.S., Tsai, Y.C., Chang, Y.C.: Robotic arm object detection system. In: 2019 Second International Conference on Artificial Intelligence for Industries (AI4I), pp. 75–78. IEEE (2019). https://doi.org/10.1109/AI4I46381.2019.00026

15. Redmon, J., Farhadi, A.: Yolov3: an incremental improvement. arXiv preprint arXiv:1804.02767 (2018). https://doi.org/10.48550/arXiv.1804.02767
16. Zafar, M.N., Mohanta, J., Sanyal, A.: Design and implementation of an autonomous robot manipulator for pick & place planning. In: IOP Conference series: materials science and Engineering, vol. 691, p. 012008. IOP Publishing (2019). https://doi.org/10.1088/1757-899X/691/1/012008
17. Iriondo, A., Lazkano, E., Susperregi, L., Urain, J., Fernandez, A., Molina, J.: Pick and place operations in logistics using a mobile manipulator controlled with deep reinforcement learning. Appl. Sci. **9**(2), 348 (2019). https://doi.org/10.3390/app9020348
18. Rahmadian, R., Widyartono, M.: Autonomous robotic in agriculture: a review. In: 2020 Third International Conference on Vocational Education and Electrical Engineering (ICVEE), pp. 1–6. IEEE (2020). https://doi.org/10.1109/ICVEE50212.2020.9243253
19. Song, Z., Wu, X., Xu, T., Sun, J., Gao, Q., He, Y.: A new method of agv navigation based on kalman filter and a magnetic nail localization. In: 2016 IEEE International Conference on Robotics and Biomimetics (ROBIO), pp. 952–957. IEEE (2016). https://doi.org/10.1109/ROBIO.2016.7866447
20. Megalingam, R.K., Raj, R.V.R., Akhil, T., Masetti, A., Chowdary, G.N., Naick, V.S.: Integration of vision based robot manipulation using ros for assistive applications. In: 2020 Second International Conference on Inventive Research in Computing Applications (ICIRCA), pp. 163–169. IEEE (2020). https://doi.org/10.1109/ICIRCA48905.2020.9183013
21. Luo, C., Yang, W., Huang, P., Zhou, J.: Overview of image matching based on orb algorithm. In: Journal of Physics: Conference Series, vol. 1237, p. 032020. IOP Publishing (2019). https://doi.org/10.1088/1742-6596/1237/3/032020
22. Chum, O., Matas, J., Kittler, J.: Locally optimized RANSAC. In: Michaelis, B., Krell, G. (eds.) DAGM 2003. LNCS, vol. 2781, pp. 236–243. Springer, Heidelberg (2003). https://doi.org/10.1007/978-3-540-45243-0_31
23. Chen, X., et al.: Overlapnet: loop closing for lidar-based slam. arXiv preprint arXiv:2105.11344 (2021). https://doi.org/10.48550/arXiv.2105.11344

Perceptually Driven Loss Function Modelling for Training GAN to Enhance Underwater Images

Rajarshi Mitra[1(✉)], Samiran Dey[2], and Sanjoy Kumar Saha[1]

[1] Jadavpur University, Kolkata, India
rajmitra13@gmail.com
[2] Indian Association for the Cultivation of Science, Kolkata, India

Abstract. Underwater image enhancement is a subject of significant interest due to its wide-ranging applications across various domains. However, underwater imaging faces numerous challenges including poor visibility, color distortion, and loss of image details. In this paper, we try to resolve these problems using a novel ensemble loss function comprising three new loss terms - gradient loss, contrast loss, and brightness loss. These novel loss functions are specifically designed to address the unique challenges associated with underwater imaging to enhance image quality, instead of using conventional perceptual loss. The proposed methodology is evaluated using the EUVP (Enhanced Underwater Vision Benchmarking) dataset, a widely adopted benchmark dataset in the field of underwater image enhancement. Experimental results demonstrate significant improvements in the enhanced images when incorporating the proposed loss functions alongside the conventional losses. These enhancements include improved fidelity, enhanced colour correctness, and reduced artefacts, leading to an overall enhancement of the visual quality of underwater images. Furthermore, the performance of the proposed approach is compared against existing methods, showcasing its superiority in terms of image quality, fidelity and visual perception. The results affirm the effectiveness and robustness of the proposed methodology in addressing the challenges inherent in underwater image enhancement.

Keywords: Underwater Image Enhancement · Deep learning techniques · Generative Adversarial Network (GAN) · Ensemble loss · EUVP dataset

1 Introduction

Underwater image enhancement serves vital purposes across research, exploration, and practical applications. Improved imagery enhances visibility underwater, aiding observation of structures, organisms, and geological formations, crucial for scientific studies like marine ecosystems and oceanography. In sectors such as underwater archaeology and offshore infrastructure inspection, enhanced

J. Kakarla et al. (Eds.): CVIP 2024, CCIS 2473, pp. 323–337, 2026.
https://doi.org/10.1007/978-3-031-93688-3_23

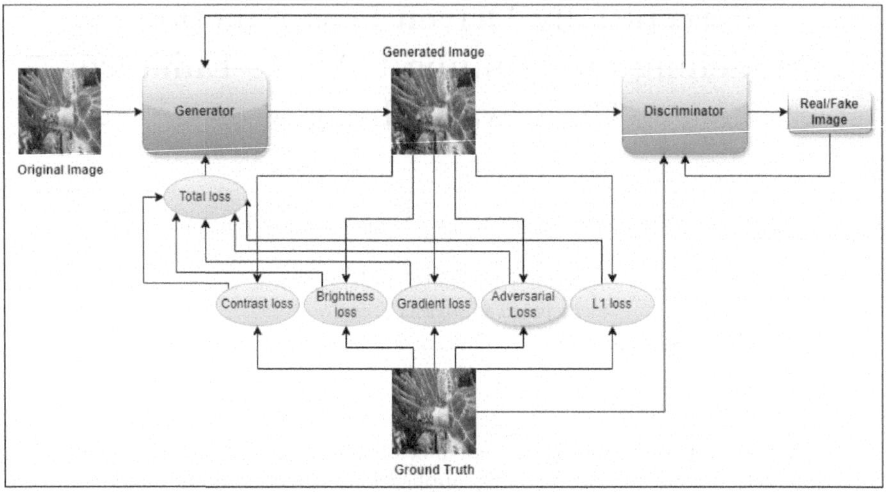

Fig. 1. The input image is processed by the generator to create a generated image. Five losses (Contrast, Brightness, Gradient, Adversarial, and L1) are calculated between the generated and ground truth images and summed into a Total Loss, which is fed back to the generator. The discriminator classifies the generated image as true or false, and this result is also passed to the generator.

images help in decision-making and operations. Security systems benefit from clearer images, ensuring maritime safety. Enhanced images also contribute to education, raising awareness about marine conservation.

In our underwater image enhancement (UIE) research, we utilized paired images from the EUVP dataset, comprising original underwater images and their enhanced versions. These pairs were crucial training data for the pix2pix GAN, consisting of a generator and discriminator network. We introduced three novel loss functions - gradient, contrast, and brightness loss - to improve the pix2pix GAN's performance in addressing underwater imaging challenges. Our goal is to enhance the clarity of underwater images for applications in marine biology, oceanography, and underwater archaeology.

The overview of our proposed methodology is illustrated in Fig. 1. The contributions of the paper include -

1. The use of gradient loss to preserve edges and fine details by aligning gradients between the generated and ground-truth images.
2. The use of brightness loss to minimize the difference in brightness levels between the generated and ground-truth images, as perceived in underwater images.
3. The use of contrast loss to lower the discrepancies in contrast characteristics by enhancing visual clarity and depth perception.
4. The adaptation of pix2pix GAN for underwater image enhancement by integrating our novel ensemble loss function.

In Sect. 2, we survey the extensive research in Underwater Image Enhancement (UIE), analyzing contributions to offer a comprehensive overview of methodologies and advancements done by various scientists. Section 3 details our approach, explaining the architecture of the generator and discriminator networks with illustrative figures. We discuss conventional and ensemble loss functions and their roles in enhancement. Moving to Sect. 4, we present experimental findings, including dataset overview, preprocessing, training process, and qualitative and quantitative assessments of results. We explore hyper-parameter tuning's impact on model performance and conclude with an examination of each loss function's effect on our GAN framework's efficacy.

2 Related Works

Peng et al. [1] tackle poor underwater imaging quality due to light absorption and scattering. They introduce a dataset called LSUI and propose a U-shape Transformer network with multi-scale feature fusion and global feature modelling. They also designed a novel loss function based on RGB, LAB, and LCH colour spaces to enhance contrast and saturation. Extensive experiments confirm state-of-the-art performance, surpassing existing methods.

Islam et al. [2] propose a conditional GAN for real-time underwater image enhancement. Their model, trained through supervised adversarial training, optimizes an objective function to consider global content, colour, local texture, and style information. They introduce the EUVP dataset, facilitating thorough model training and evaluation. Results show enhanced image quality, improving performance in tasks like object detection and human pose estimation, suggesting its suitability to use in visually-guided underwater robot systems.

Fu, Lin, et al. [3] introduce SCNet, enhancing underwater image quality by addressing degradation diversity caused by water. SCNet normalizes across spatial and channel dimensions to learn water type desensitized features. Whitening and standardization decorrelate activations and eliminate channel-wise correlation at each scale of the U-Net architecture for multi-scale representations. Experimental results demonstrate SCNet's effectiveness in enhancing images with diverse water types, achieving competitive improvements in visual quality.

Anwar et al. [4] propose UWCNN, a convolutional neural network for enhancing underwater scenes. UWCNN directly reconstructs clear latent underwater images through end-to-end training, leveraging synthetic underwater image databases. Multiple models are trained for various underwater image formation types. Experimental evaluations demonstrate UWCNN's robust generalization across diverse scenes, outperforming existing methods both qualitatively and quantitatively.

Uplavikar et al. [5] propose a model for enhancing raw underwater images, mitigating challenges from light attenuation and scattering in diverse water types. Their model learns content features while disentangling unwanted nuisances associated with different water types. Leveraging domain-agnostic features, it generates superior underwater images, outperforming previous methods in SSIM and PSNR scores across various water types. Generalization on real-world datasets is effective, and enhanced images improve object detection performance.

Islam et al. [6] propose Deep SESR for simultaneous enhancement and super-resolution in underwater robot vision. Their approach employs a multi-modal objective function to address various image degradation factors, enabling global contrast enhancement and saliency prediction. End-to-end training facilitates fast inference, while the UFO-120 dataset, comprising over 1500 samples, supports large-scale learning. Experimental results demonstrate Deep SESR's superior performance across diverse degradation levels and scenes, with computational feasibility for visually-guided underwater robots.

Chen et al. [7] propose an innovative underwater image enhancement algorithm to enhance visual perception in underwater robots. Leveraging deep learning and image formation models, their method mitigates colour distortion, enhances details, and enriches colours in captured images. Experimental results show superior performance in PSNR and SSIM metrics, along with improved feature key-point matching and faster computation speed compared to existing methods. This advancement holds promise for enhancing visual perception in underwater robotics applications.

Li et al. [8] present Ucolor, an underwater image enhancement network addressing colour casts and low contrast from attenuation and scattering. Ucolor integrates a multi-colour space encoder network for enriched feature representations and employs an attention mechanism for adaptability. A medium transmission-guided decoder prioritizes quality-degraded regions. Combining physical model-based and learning-based approaches, Ucolor significantly enhances visual quality, outperforming state-of-the-art methods in both visual and quantitative assessments.

Peng et al. [9] propose RAUNE-Net to enhance underwater images, tackling challenges like low contrast, high turbidity, blurriness, and colour distortion. Inspired by residual and attention mechanisms, RAUNE-Net integrates residual learning and attention manipulations, yielding promising results. Two datasets are curated for evaluation, where experimental validation demonstrates RAUNE-Net's effectiveness, outperforming eight other methods in objective metrics and offering consistent visual results across diverse underwater images.

Li et al. [10] introduce the Underwater Image Enhancement Benchmark (UIEB), comprising 950 real-world underwater images. This dataset enables comprehensive evaluations of enhancement algorithms, with 890 images having corresponding references and 60 challenging ones. They propose Water-Net, a baseline CNN trained on UIEB, to assess algorithm generalization. Benchmark evaluations and Water-Net highlight performance and limitations, guiding future research in underwater image enhancement.

Mu et al. [11] introduce GUPDM, enhancing underwater images by addressing color distortion and low contrast. GUPDM utilizes a Physical-knowledge-guided Dynamic Model with three components: Atmosphere-based Dynamic

Structure (ADS), Transmission-guided Dynamic Structure (TDS), and Prior-based Multi-scale Structure (PMS). ADS and TDS employ dynamic convolutions for adaptive prior information extraction, while PMS utilizes multi-scale feature extraction with convolution blocks, channel attention blocks, and feature map fusion to improve performance in underwater image enhancement.

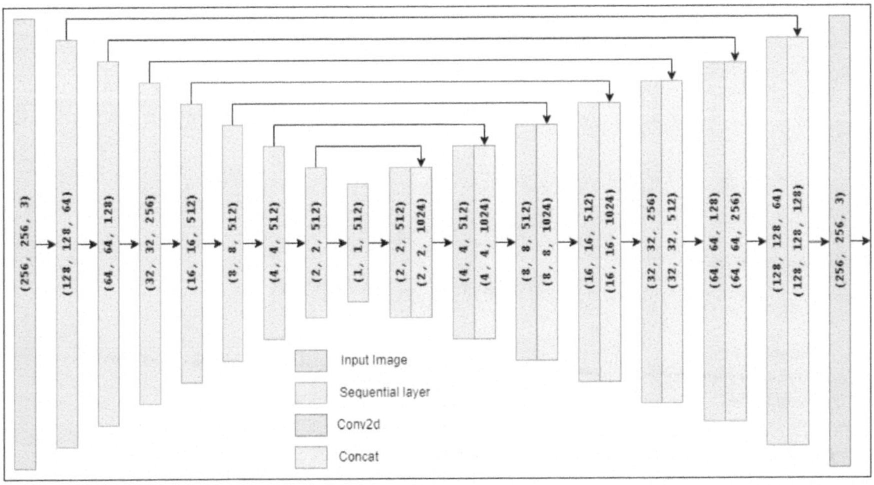

Fig. 2. The above figure illustrates the architecture of the generator used in our model. The model takes 256 × 256 RGB images, uses an encoder with downscale blocks increasing filters from 64 to 512, compresses features into a latent space, then reconstructs images via a decoder mirroring the encoder, using Conv2DTranspose with Tanh activation for output in the range [–1, 1].

3 Methodology

In this section, we will first discuss the architecture of the generator and the discriminator in detail along with illustrative figures. After that, we will dive deep into the individual loss functions and the ensemble loss function along with their equations.

3.1 Architecture

The model's input layer in Fig. 2 expects tensors of shape (256, 256, 3), which are RGB pictures with 256 pixels for height and width. The encoder is made up of downscale blocks that extract hierarchical features, with the number of filters rising from 64 to 512. One downscale block compresses the feature representation into a latent space following encoding. By using upscale blocks that reflect the design of the encoder, the decoder recreates the image from the latent space while preserving spatial relationships. Fine details are preserved from the encoder to the decoder by skip connections. Tanh activation is used in the output layer, a Conv2DTranspose with three filters, to upsample feature maps and create the final image with pixel values in the range [−1, 1].

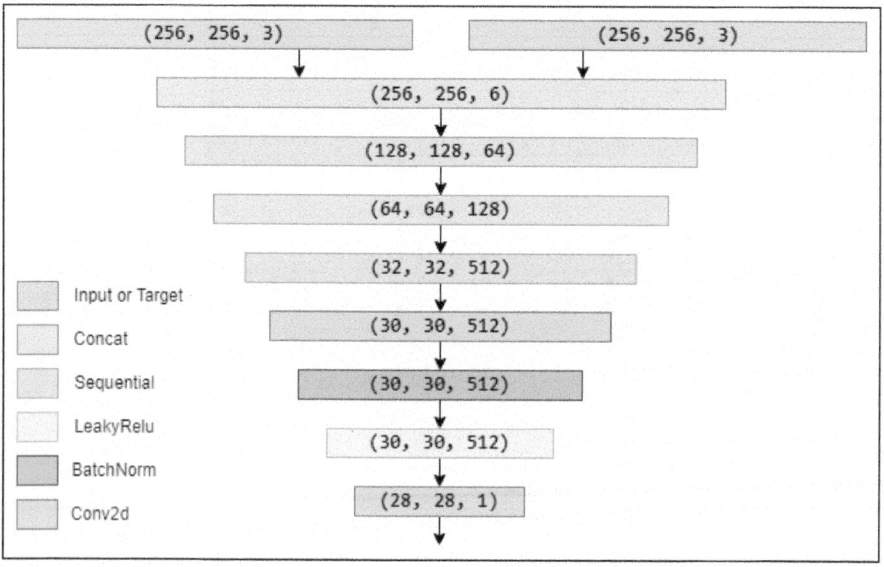

Fig. 3. This figure illustrates how the discriminator works. The discriminator takes image and target inputs of shape (256, 256, 3), concatenates them, passes through downscale blocks with increasing filters, extracts high-level features with a convolutional layer, applies batch normalization and leaky ReLU activation, and outputs the likelihood of real/fake using a single-filter convolutional layer.

In Fig. 3 the discriminator consists of two input layers with the shape (256, 256, 3) for the image and target inputs, which are then combined by concatenation. Using 64, 128 and 512 filters, successive downscale blocks increase feature depth while decreasing spatial dimensions. High-level features are extracted using a convolutional layer with 512 filters and a 3×3 kernel. Batch normalization is then used for activation stabilization. Next, non-linearity is introduced by using a leaky ReLU activation. The final output reflecting the likelihood that the input image-target combination is real or fake is produced by the output layer, a single-filter convolutional layer.

3.2 Loss Function

We implemented an ensemble loss function in our GAN which includes three new losses - gradient, brightness and contrast loss along with the conventional adversarial and L1 losses.

Adversarial Loss: The adversarial loss function, also known as the GAN loss, drives a competitive learning process between the generator and discriminator networks in GANs. It trains the generator to produce synthetic data resembling real data by minimizing the loss, while simultaneously training the discriminator to effectively distinguish between real and synthetic data by maximizing the same loss.

$$L_{\text{adv}} = -\frac{1}{N}\sum_{i=1}^{N}(y_i \log(D(I_{target})) + (1-y_i)\log(1-D(I_{generated}))) \tag{1}$$

L1 Loss: The L1 loss helps to make generated images look more like real ones by penalizing differences in individual pixels. It works alongside the adversarial loss, which focuses on overall similarity, to stabilize training and prevent mode collapse. By adjusting how much importance is given to the L1 loss, we can control how much the generator prioritizes making images realistic versus diverse.

$$L_1 = \frac{1}{wh}\sum_{i=1}^{w}\sum_{j=1}^{h} \mid I_{generated_{ij}} - I_{target_{ij}} \mid \tag{2}$$

Gradient Loss: The gradient loss function preserves edges and fine details by aligning gradients between the generated and ground-truth images and hence is crucial for underwater image enhancement. It encourages the generated image to have similar gradients as the target image, thus reducing artefacts.

$$L_{grad} = \frac{1}{2wh}\sum_{k=1}^{2}\sum_{i=1}^{w}\sum_{j=1}^{h} \mid \nabla I_{generated_{ijk}} - \nabla I_{target_{ijk}} \mid \tag{3}$$

Contrast Difference Loss: The contrast loss quantifies discrepancies in the contrast between the generated and ground-truth images, penalizing deviations to ensure similarity in contrast characteristics. It encourages the generator to produce images with similar contrast levels to the target images, contributing to overall visual quality. The image is divided into $m \times m$ patches and the average difference, in contrast, is computed over all the patches.

$$L_{con} = \frac{1}{n_{patch}}\sum_{i=1}^{n_{patch}} \mid contrast(I_{generated_i}) - contrast(I_{target_i}) \mid \tag{4}$$

Brightness Difference Loss: The brightness loss function minimizes differences in brightness levels between generated and ground-truth images. Its goal is to ensure that the generated outputs closely match the luminosity characteristics of the targets, contributing to the overall perceptual quality and realism of the generated images. The image is divided into $m \times m$ patches and the average difference in brightness is computed over all the patches.

$$L_{br} = \frac{1}{n_{patch}} \sum_{i=1}^{n_{patch}} \mid brightness(I_{generated_i}) - brightness(I_{target_i}) \mid \tag{5}$$

The total loss to train the generator is calculated as,

$$L_{total} = L_{adv} + \lambda_{L1} * L_1 + \lambda_{grad} * L_{grad} + \lambda_{con} * L_{con} + \lambda_{br} * L_{br} \tag{6}$$

The coefficients $\lambda_{L1}, \lambda_{grd}, \lambda_{br}$, and λ_{con} in Eq. 6 control the weightage of each loss function in the training process. The values of the coefficients that are taken are discussed in detail in the Table 2.

Fig. 4. Comparison of Original, Ground Truth, and Predicted Images. The first row consists of the original images, the second row consists of the ground truth or target images, and the third row consists of the predicted images.

4 Results and Experiments

In this section, we'll cover the dataset, preprocessing steps, training method, and results analysis, splitting our discussion into qualitative and quantitative aspects. Additionally, we'll explore coefficient tuning and the effects of different loss functions on the generator's performance.

4.1 Dataset

We've prepared a subset of the EUVP [2] dataset with 2500 paired images for deep learning model training and evaluation for image enhancement. Our preprocessing involves resizing images to (256, 256, 3) using TensorFlow's "tf.image.resize" and normalizing pixel values to a range of 0 to 1. Preprocessed images are stored in NumPy arrays, "images" for ground truth and "masks" for original images. We split the dataset into 80% training and 20% testing, ensuring reproducibility with a random-state parameter set to 42. This sets the stage for training robust models on the EUVP dataset subset.

4.2 Training Details

During generator training, we employed Eq. 6 with coefficients from Table 2 (100 for λ_{L1}, 10 for $\lambda_{gradient}$, 50 for $\lambda_{contrast}$, and 10 for $\lambda_{brightness}$) to enhance image quality. The discriminator relied solely on Eq. 1 to distinguish real and generated images. Our training spanned 960 epochs, allowing iterative refinement of both generator and discriminator parameters. Using the Adam optimizer facilitated efficient learning rate adjustments and momentum optimization throughout training. This extensive process was conducted on an NVIDIA Tesla P100, known for its capabilities in deep learning tasks.

4.3 Result and Analysis

We analyze our results using both qualitative and quantitative methods. Qualitatively, we examine data for patterns, themes, and examples to identify enhancements in image quality, including improved details, colour fidelity, and reduced artefacts. Quantitatively, we measure metrics such as PSNR [19], SSIM [19], LPIPS [20], and FID [21], comparing our model with Uw-HL [13], Mband-EN [14], Res-WGAN [12], Res-GAN [22], LS-GAN [17], Pix2Pix [16], UGAN-P [15], CycleGAN [18], FUnIE-GAN-UP [2], and FUnIE-GAN [2]. This comprehensive approach validates the effectiveness of our method in enhancing image quality.

Table 1. Quantitative comparison for average PSNR and SSIM values between our model and currently existing models. Red denotes the best score, Green denotes the second best score and Blue denotes the third best score. The values of the existing models are taken from the paper [2].

Model	PSNR ↑	SSIM ↑	LPIPS ↓	FID ↓
Uw-HL	18.85	0.7722	–	–
Mband-EN	12.11	0.4565	–	–
Res-WGAN	16.46	0.5762	–	–
Res-GAN	14.75	0.4685	–	–
LS-GAN	17.83	0.6725	–	–
Pix2Pix	20.27	0.7081	–	–
UGAN-P	19.59	0.6685	–	–
CycleGAN	17.14	0.6400	–	–
FUnIE-GAN-UP	21.36	0.8164	-	-
FUnIE-GAN	21.92	0.8876	-	-
ours	24.54	0.8301	0.1101	25.7173

Table 2. Results of hyperparameter tuning of the loss component weights for 100 epochs each. Red denotes the best score, Green denotes the second best and Blue denotes the third best.

λ_{L1}	λ_{grad}	λ_{con}	λ_{br}	PSNR ↑	SSIM ↑	LPIPS ↓	FID ↓
100	5	50	15	23.4818	0.8051	0.1411	33.8159
100	10	5	5	24.1639	0.8261	0.1325	29.9676
100	10	5	10	23.6102	0.8051	0.1483	35.4820
100	10	5	50	23.4842	0.7874	0.1537	36.4361
100	10	10	5	23.7412	0.7947	0.1353	29.0098
100	10	10	10	24.1538	0.8283	0.1269	27.1378
100	10	10	50	23.7621	0.8095	0.1400	29.9546
100	10	50	5	23.6252	0.8101	0.1352	30.8749
100	10	50	10	24.0587	0.8297	0.1307	26.0066
100	10	50	50	23.5317	0.8115	0.1377	32.6069
100	10	75	10	24.0561	0.8292	0.1258	28.3741
100	50	5	5	23.6690	0.8115	0.1331	29.5434
100	50	5	10	23.5424	0.7966	0.1524	35.4284
100	50	5	50	23.2306	0.7825	0.1728	39.5365
100	50	10	5	23.8045	0.8044	0.1332	34.5407
100	50	10	10	24.0122	0.8256	0.1306	31.1802
100	50	10	50	23.6440	0.8056	0.1407	32.4527
100	50	50	5	23.1910	0.7970	0.1823	33.1958
100	50	50	10	23.6674	0.8040	0.1303	30.5419
100	50	50	50	23.6099	0.8226	0.1244	31.0072

Qualitative Analysis. In qualitative analysis, we visually compare three types of images: the inputs (referred to as original), their corresponding ground truth images, and the images our model generates. By comparing them side by side, we aim to see how closely our model's predictions resemble the real images and gain insights into the accuracy of our model. The images are shown in Fig. 4. It is evident that the predicted images closely resemble the ground truth images not only in terms of visual content but also in brightness, colour, and contrast, suggesting a high level of accuracy and fidelity in the model's predictions. To test for the robustness of our model, we have also experimented on another underwater dataset and obtained similar results. The images obtained are similar to their corresponding ground truth.

Quantitative Analysis. In our work, we used Peak Signal-to-Noise Ratio (PSNR) [19], Structural Similarity Index (SSIM) [19], Fréchet Inception Distance (FID) [21], Learned Perceptual Image Patch Similarity (LPIPS) [20] to evaluate our model against others using the same dataset.

PSNR : PSNR measures how much noise is present in the generated image compared to the ground truth image, with higher values indicating better quality.

$$\text{PSNR} = 10 \cdot \log_{10} \left(\frac{\text{MAX}^2}{\text{MSE}} \right) \tag{7}$$

SSIM : SSIM quantifies the structural similarity between two images, considering luminance, contrast, and structure.

$$\text{SSIM}(x, y) = \frac{(2\mu_x\mu_y + C_1)(2\sigma_{xy} + C_2)}{(\mu_x^2 + \mu_y^2 + C_1)(\sigma_x^2 + \sigma_y^2 + C_2)} \tag{8}$$

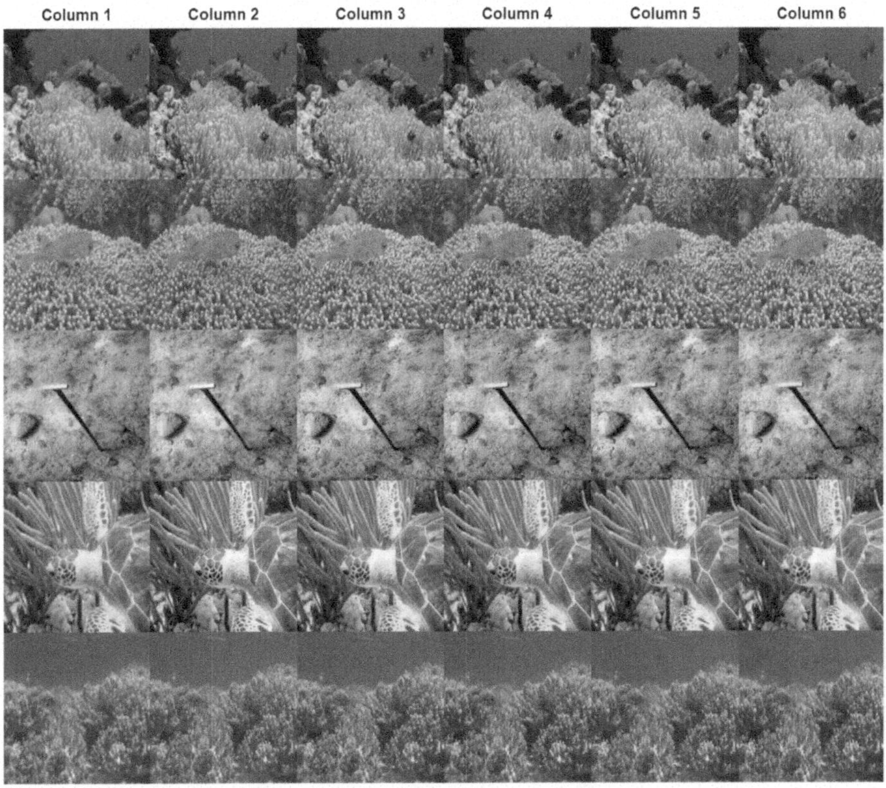

Fig. 5. Qualitative result of ablation on loss function. Column 1 represents the original images, Column 2 represents the ground truth images, Column 3 represents the predicted images generated using L_{adv} and L_1, Column 4 represents the predicted images generated using L_{adv}, L_1 and L_{gradient}, Column 5 represents the predicted images generated using L_{adv}, L_1, L_{grad} and L_{br}, Column 6 represents the predicted images generated using L_{adv}, L_1, L_{grad}, L_{br} and L_{con}.

Table 3. Ablation study on the implementation of loss functions for 400 epochs each.

L_{L1}	L_{adv}	L_{grad}	L_{br}	L_{con}	PSNR ↑	SSIM ↑	LPIPS ↓	FID ↓
✓	✓	×	×	×	23.6613	0.7948	0.1474	33.8219
✓	✓	✓	×	×	23.7215	0.7988	0.1456	32.4273
✓	✓	✓	✓	×	23.7281	0.8080	0.1365	32.4245
✓	✓	✓	✓	✓	19.5719	0.8031	0.2019	34.8391

FID : FID measures the similarity between two sets of feature representations extracted from ground truth and generated images in generative models.

$$\text{FID} = \|\mu_X - \mu_Y\|^2 + \text{Tr}(\Sigma_X + \Sigma_Y - 2(\Sigma_X \Sigma_Y)^{1/2}) \tag{9}$$

LPIPS : LPIPS measures the perceptual similarity between two images, taking into account human perception and visual quality.

$$\text{LPIPS}(x, y) = \frac{1}{N} \sum_{i=1}^{N} \|\phi_i(x) - \phi_i(y)\|_2 \tag{10}$$

Our model outperformed many existing ones with higher PSNR, SSIM, FID and LPIPS scores, and closely matched others, showcasing its competitive efficacy and potential for significant advancements in the field. From Table 1 we can see that our model outperforms all the other models in terms of PSNR value with 24.55, secures the second best score for SSIM with value 0.8301, a FID value of 25.7173 and an LPIPS value of 0.1101.

Albation Study. We determine the coefficients of the components of our ensemble loss function by conducting hyperparameter tuning. By systematically adjusting these coefficients and evaluating their impact on the performance, we aim to optimize the effectiveness of our loss function. The results are shown in Table 2. We took the 100, 10, 50, 10 for λ_{L1}, λ_{grad}, λ_{con}, λ_{br} respectively as this combination generates the best result for SSIM and FID, also the third best result for PSNR.

Table 4. Comparison of our novel perceptually driven loss with the conventional perceptual loss

L_{L1}	L_{adv}	$L_{perceptual}$	L_{grad}	L_{br}	L_{con}	PSNR ↑	SSIM ↑	LPIPS ↓	FID ↓
✓	✓	✓	×	×	×	23.0607	0.7182	0.2595	39.4555
✓	✓	×	✓	✓	✓	24.0587	0.8297	0.1307	26.0066

In our model development, we initially employed the GAN loss alongside the L1 loss as our primary loss. Then, we introduced gradient loss for edge preservation, followed by brightness loss for brightness control, and contrast loss for improving contrast. This gradual integration of additional loss components allowed us to iteratively observe the distinct impacts of each loss on the training and the quality of the generated images. The numerical results are presented in Table 3, providing a quantitative analysis of the outcomes. It is observed that the performance improves consistently on the inclusion of the loss terms one at a time. However, on the inclusion of the contrast difference loss, we find that the performance deteriorated. This is because while performing the particular experiment a patch size of 3 was considered, which happens to be too small a region to effectively discriminate between contrasts of the images. The visual results are depicted in Fig. 5. As evident from Column 4 of Fig. 5, the images are much sharper than Column 3, thus the use of gradient loss helps to achieve greater sharpness. The images in Column 5 have luminescence similar to the ground truth images in Column 2, thus the usage of the brightness difference loss helps to gain a luminescence look alike of the ground-truth images. On the inclusion of the contrast difference loss, the difference in contrast between the ground truth images in Column 2 and the image in Column 6 is reduced. Thus, we conclude that our ensemble loss helps in enhancing underwater images with high fidelity, perceptual quality and structural similarity.

Further, we compare our perceptually driven loss with the conventional perceptual loss. We train the model with the combination of adversarial loss, L1 loss and perceptual loss for 225 epochs. We observe that even after training for 100 epochs our ensemble loss can obtain much better results. The results are provided in Table 4 and Fig. 6. Our loss outperforms in all metrics quantitatively. Also, we obtain images with better perceptual quality and high fidelity to ground truth images. Since the conventional perceptual loss uses the VGG model pre-trained on ImageNet, it is unable to generate appropriate feature vectors for underwater images which have a completely different underlying distribution, and hence does not perform well.

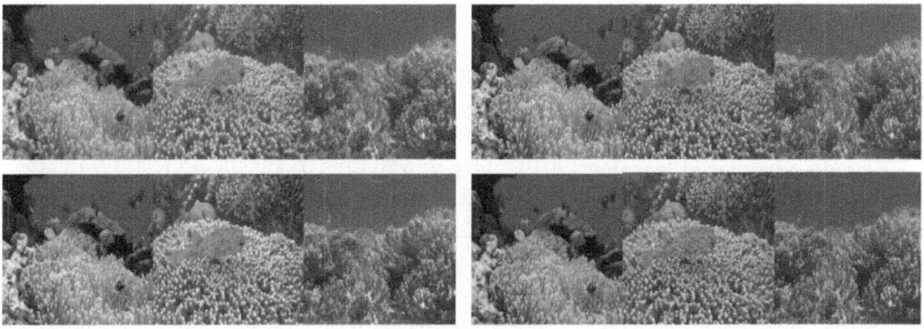

Fig. 6. The top left block represents the input images, the top right block represents the ground truth image, the bottom left represents the images generated using our model of perceptual loss, and the bottom right represents the images generated using conventional perceptual loss.

5 Conclusion

In this paper, we address the challenges of underwater image enhancement by introducing a novel ensemble loss function comprising three new losses: gradient loss, contrast loss, and brightness loss. Through meticulous hyper-parameter tuning, we determine optimal coefficients for each loss, systematically enhancing the performance of the pix2pix GAN framework. Our experimental results demonstrate that our proposed model outperforms the majority of existing approaches, showcasing superior performance. Further, our ensemble loss performs better than the conventional perceptual loss in generating perceptually enhanced underwater images with high fidelity and structural similarity. Moreover, our model achieves comparable results to several state-of-the-art models, further underscoring its efficacy and potential in the domain of underwater images and thus suggesting that the loss function may be applied for enhancement tasks in other domains as well. Overall, our research emphasizes the importance of integrating innovative loss functions and conducting rigorous hyper-parameter optimization to advance the state-of-the-art in model development and achieve remarkable results in challenging tasks.

References

1. Peng, L., Zhu, C., Bian, L.: U-shape transformer for underwater image enhancement. IEEE Trans. Image Process. **32**, 3066–3079 (2023). https://doi.org/10.1109/TIP.2023.3276332
2. Islam, M.J., Xia, Y., Sattar, J.: Fast underwater image enhancement for improved visual perception. IEEE Robot. Autom. Lett. **5**(2), 3227–3234 (2020). Article 9001231. https://doi.org/10.1109/LRA.2020.2974710
3. Fu, Z., Lin, X., Wang, W., Huang, Y., Ding, X.: Underwater image enhancement via learning water type desensitized representations. In: ICASSP 2022 - 2022 IEEE International Conference on Acoustics, Speech and Signal Processing (ICASSP), Singapore, Singapore, pp. 2764–2768 (2022). https://doi.org/10.1109/ICASSP43922.2022.9747758
4. Li, C., Anwar, S., Porikli, F.: Deep underwater image enhancement, pattern recognition, vol. 98, 107038 (2018). ISSN 0031-3203, https://doi.org/10.48550/arXiv.1807.03528
5. Uplavikar, P., Wu, Z., Wang, Z.: All-in-one underwater image enhancement using domain-adversarial learning (2019). https://doi.org/10.48550/arXiv.1905.13342
6. Islam, M.J., Luo, P., Sattar, J.: Simultaneous enhancement and super-resolution of underwater imagery for improved visual perception (2020). https://doi.org/10.48550/arXiv.2002.01155
7. Chen, X., Zhang, P., Quan, L., Yi, C., Lu, C.: Underwater image enhancement based on deep learning and image formation model (2021). https://doi.org/10.48550/arXiv.2101.00991
8. Li, C., Anwar, S., Hou, J., Cong, R., Guo, C., Ren, W.: Underwater image enhancement via medium transmission-guided multi-color space embedding. IEEE Trans. Image Process. **30**, 4985–5000 (2021). https://doi.org/10.1109/TIP.2021.3076367

9. Peng, W., Zhou, C., Hu, R., Cao, J., Liu, Y.: RAUNE-Net: a residual and attention-driven underwater image enhancement method. Depart. Comput. Sci. Technol. (2023). https://doi.org/10.48550/arXiv.2311.00246
10. Li, C., et al.: An underwater image enhancement benchmark dataset and beyond. In: IEEE Transactions on Image Processing 2019 (2019). https://doi.org/10.48550/arXiv.1901.05495
11. Mu, P., Xu, H., Liu, Z., Wang, Z., Chan, S., Bai, C.: A generalized physical-knowledge-guided dynamic model for underwater image enhancement (2023). https://doi.org/10.48550/arXiv.2308.05447
12. Arjovsky, M., Chintala, S., Bottou, L.: Wasserstein generative adversarial networks. In: International Conference on Machine Learning (ICML), pp. 214–223 (2017). https://doi.org/10.48550/arXiv.1701.07875
13. Berman, D., Levy, D., Avidan, S., Treibitz, T.: Underwater single image color restoration using haze-lines and a new quantitative dataset. arXiv preprint arXiv:1811.01343 (2018). https://doi.org/10.48550/arXiv.1811.01343
14. Cho, Y., Jeong, J., Kim, A.: Model-assisted multiband fusion for single image enhancement and applications to robot vision. IEEE Robot. Autom. Lett. (RAL) **3**(4), 2822–2829 (2018). https://doi.org/10.1109/LRA.2018.2843127
15. Fabbri, C., Islam, M.J., Sattar, J.: Enhancing underwater imagery using generative adversarial networks. In: 2018 IEEE International Conference on Robotics and Automation (ICRA), Brisbane, QLD, Australia, pp. 7159–7165 (2018). https://doi.org/10.1109/ICRA.2018.8460552
16. Isola, P., Zhu, J.-Y., Zhou, T., Efros, A.A.: Image-to-Image translation with conditional adversarial networks. In: IEEE Conference on Computer Vision and Pattern Recognition (CVPR), pp. 1125–1134 (2017). https://doi.org/10.48550/arXiv.1611.07004
17. Mao, X., Li, Q., Xie, H., Lau, R.Y., Wang, Z, Paul Smolley, S.: Least squares generative adversarial networks. In: IEEE International Conference on Computer Vision (ICCV), pp. 2794–2802 (2017). https://doi.org/10.48550/arXiv.1611.04076
18. Zhu, J.-Y., Park, T., Isola, P., Efros, A.A.: Unpaired image-to-image translation using cycle-consistent adversarial networks. In: 2017 IEEE International Conference on Computer Vision (ICCV), Venice, Italy, pp. 2242–2251 (2017). https://doi.org/10.1109/ICCV.2017.244
19. Horé, A., Ziou, D.: Image quality metrics: PSNR vs. SSIM. In: 2010 20th International Conference on Pattern Recognition, Istanbul, Turkey, pp. 2366–2369 (2010). https://doi.org/10.1109/ICPR.2010.579
20. Zhang, R., Isola, P., Efros, A.A., Shechtman, E., Wang, O.: The unreasonable effectiveness of deep features as a perceptual metric (2018). https://doi.org/10.48550/arXiv.1801.03924
21. Heusel, M., Ramsauer, H., Unterthiner, T., Nessler, B., Hochreiter, S.: GANs trained by a two time-scale update rule converge to a local nash equilibrium (2017). https://doi.org/10.48550/arXiv.1706.08500
22. Li, J., Liang, X., Wei, Y., Xu, T., Feng, J., Yan, S.: Perceptual generative adversarial networks for small object detection. In: IEEE Conference on Computer Vision and Pattern Recognition (CVPR), pp. 1222–1230 (2017). https://doi.org/10.48550/arXiv.1706.05274

Quantitative Assessment of Class Activation Maps: An Empirical Study on Musculoskeletal Disorders

Gokaramaiah Thota(✉), K. Nagaraju, and Sathya Babu Korra

CSE Department, Indian Institute of Information Technology Design and Manufacturing Kurnool, Jagannathagattu Hill, Kurnool 518 008, Andhra Pradesh, India
{322cs0001,knagaraju,ksb}@iiitk.ac.in
https://iiitk.ac.in/

Abstract. Musculoskeletal Disorders (MSDs) affect 1.7 billion people worldwide, causing pain and mobility issues [22]. Though convolutional neural network (CNN) models can detect MSDs, their opaque nature raise concerns regarding transparency and accountability. The class activation map (CAM) method provides insight into CNN predictions by visually highlighting regions of interest or local discrimination. This assists medical professionals in visualizing the decisions made by the CNN model. CAM utilizes activation maps of a specific convolutional layer, typically the last convolutional layer, along with the predicted class score. CAM's local discrimination effectiveness depends on activation maps and weight computation. Therefore, CAM's ability to local discrimination depends on the dataset and the CNN model. Therefore, it is essential to conduct an empirical study on datasets with popular CNN models used in MSD classification. This is important for ensuring unbiased decision-making in medical imaging. This study quantitatively evaluates various CAMs, including CAM, Grad-CAM, Extended CAM, Smooth Grad-CAM and Score-CAM. Three CNN models, ResNet-50, DenseNet-169, and Inception-v3, were trained on the MURA dataset. The evaluation employs quantitative measures such as average drop, average increase, maximum coherency, and minimum complexity. Average drop coherency complexity (ADCC) is a single metric that compares qualitative measures. Results indicate that Smooth Grad-CAM and Score-CAM outperform in local discrimination regions for predictions. Smooth Grad-CAM outperforms in average drop, average increase, and ADCC for ResNet-50. However, for DenseNet-169 and Inception-v3, Score-CAM excels in ADCC.

Keywords: Class activation map (CAM) · CAM quantitative metrics · Guided Grad-CAM · Local discrimination · Musculoskeletal disorders

1 Introduction

MSDs are a major concern globally and the second-largest cause of disability [1]. Detecting MSDs through radiographs can be time-consuming due to a shortage of

J. Kakarla et al. (Eds.): CVIP 2024, CCIS 2473, pp. 338–352, 2026.
https://doi.org/10.1007/978-3-031-93688-3_24

radiologists, leading to the development of machine learning mechanisms. Deep learning techniques, including CNN models such as ResNet-50 [5], Inception-v3 [23], and DenseNet-169 [6], have effectively classified MSDs. However, their opaque nature raises concerns, as accountability and transparency are crucial for critical functions like medical diagnosis [9]. This lack of explainability may decrease trust in the model's predictions, hindering their adoption for real-world medical decision-making [7]. Approaches for visualizing CNN's final decisions have evolved from visualization of the activations [26] to CAM.

The CNNs are used in deep learning to identify higher-level features during neural network training. These features can be visualized by looking at the weights of the neurons in the CNNs [26]. However, the visualizations don't explain how CNNs make their final decisions. To explain this, gradient-based approaches like activation maximization have been developed to work with neurons that are more receptive to inputs [14]. Even with these methods, CNN's decision-making for individual images is still not fully understood.

One approach to understand CNN predictions is the CAM method [28]. CAM provides valuable insights into neural networks that lead to decisions by highlighting important image regions. CAM techniques are used in various applications, such as action detection [3], pedestrian intention prediction [19] and face spoof detection [4]. The CAMs are classified into gradient-based methods such as CAM [28], Grad-CAM [18], Grad-CAM++ [2], Smooth Grad-CAM [20], and Extended-CAM [8], as well as non-gradient methods like Score-CAM [25], Ablation-CAM [17], and Eigen-CAM [12].

CAM utilize activation maps extracted from a specific convolutional layer, usually the final one, along with the predicted class score. Since these activation maps and class scores are dependent on CNN training with specific dataset, the effectiveness of a CAM can vary based on the dataset and the CNN architecture employed. Consequently, the performance depends on the dataset and the CNN model [27]. CAMs provide local discrimination, making it essential to conduct careful qualitative and quantitative evaluations to avoid biased decisions. An empirical evaluation of CAMs' local discrimination is necessary, especially in fields like medical imaging, where biased decisions can have serious consequences. Thorough evaluation of CAMs offers valuable insights into the model's reasoning process and helps mitigate potential biases in decision-making [24].

The MURA dataset is commonly used to train CNN models to classify musculoskeletal radiographs (X-Ray) [13]. Popular CNN models for this task include ResNet-50, Inception-v3, and DenseNet-169. Empirical evaluations of CAM methods have been conducted on the MURA dataset with the CNN models ResNet-50, Inception-v3, and DenseNet-169 CNN model. The quantitative assessment includes several metrics: the average drop (Eq. 16), the average increase (Eq. 17), the maximum coherency (Eq. 19), and the minimum complexity (Eq. 20). These metrics are aggregated into a composite metric referred to as ADCC in Eq. 21(Average Drop coherency complexity) [15]. An empirical investigation of CAM methods on musculoskeletal disorders is conducted, and involves the following:

- Three CNN models, ResNet-50, DenseNet-169, and Inception-v3, are trained on the MURA dataset-specific elbow and wrist study types.
- These CNN model prediction is interpreted qualitatively by CAM, Grad-CAM, Smooth Grad-CAM, Extended-CAM, and Score-CAM.
- The study also performs a quantitative assessment of CAM visualization using metrics such as average drop, average increase, maximum coherency, minimum complexity, and ADCC.

The paper presents a structured sequence of empirical study findings. It begins by introducing CAM methods in Sect. 2. The next section, Sect. 3, outlines the quantitative measures. Section 4 discusses the dataset, experiments, and results. Finally, Sect. 5 concludes the paper by presenting future works.

2 CAM Methods

CAMs are critical tools for interpreting CNNs' decision-making process. They can determine the portions of an input image that contribute the most to a network's decision. Based on how the weights of the activation maps are obtained, CAMs can be broadly categorized into two types: gradient-based and non-gradient-based CAMs.

Gradient-based CAMs utilize the gradients that pass through the CNN during the backpropagation process. These gradients are analyzed to compute the weights, and class activation mappings are produced. CAM, Grad-CAM (gradient-weighted class activation map), Grad-CAM++, Smooth Grad-CAM, and Extended-CAM are examples of gradient-based CAMs.

The Non-gradient-based CAMs derive weights from CNN model predicted class scores rather than relying on gradients [11]. Examples of non-gradient-based CAMs include Score-CAM, Ablation-CAM, and Eigen-CAM. Although gradient-based CAMs are computationally efficient, they may produce lo-quality CAM local discrimination due to gradient errors during backpropagation [25].

2.1 Class Activation Map

CAM [28] is a technique for generating local discriminate highlights of the pixels in an input image, leading to a specific class prediction. It involves passing the image through a CNN to obtain the activation maps A of the last convolutional layer output. The activation maps A are then flattened into a vector using global average pooling [10], and a classification layer uses these vector values. The CAM visualization includes a linear combination of weights W_k^c of the fully connected layer for class c with scaled activation maps A. This process can be represented mathematically as follows:

$$L_{\mathbf{CAM}}^{c} = \text{ReLU}\left(\sum_{k} W_k^c \cdot A_{ij}^k\right) \tag{1}$$

However, CAM has limitations: It requires retaining the fully connected classification layer weights. Hence, CAM is dependent on the CNN architecture.

2.2 Grad-CAM

Grad-CAM [18] is a popular method used to visualize a CNN's explanation without retraining the weights in the fully connected layer. This technique utilize the gradients that flow during backpropagation from the output layer to the final convolutional layer. The class score Y_c and the activation map A^k used in computing the gradients denoted by $\frac{\partial Y^c}{\partial A^k_{i,j}}$. These gradients are globally averaged and used to compute the weight W^c_k. The visualization map of Grad-CAM is defined as:

$$L^c_{\textbf{Grad-CAM}} = ReLU\left(\sum_k W^c_k A^k\right). \tag{2}$$

However, Grad-CAM has limitations, including resolution and localization accuracy, specificity to the target class, computational intensity, inability to detect objects with less spatial footprint, and fading of some object instances due to different shapes or orientations.

2.3 Grad-CAM++

Grad-CAM++ [2] is an advanced technique that enhances Grad-CAM by computing pixel-wise weights. It provides a more detailed visualization of model predictions by pinpointing exact object locations in images. Grad-CAM++ creates visualization from the linear combination of pixel-wise weights, weights from gradients and action maps from the last convolutional layer of the CNN model. The Grad-CAM++ visualization map highlights areas where the model focuses most. The gradient of the predicted class score Y_c with respect to the activation maps A^k is computed, and pixel-wise weights α^{kc}_{ij} are calculated using the formula:

$$\alpha^{kc}_{ij} = \frac{\frac{\partial^2 Y^c}{(\partial A^k_{i,j})^2}}{2\frac{\partial^2 Y^c}{(\partial A^k_{ij})^2} + \sum_a \sum_b A^k_{ab}\{\frac{\partial^3 Y^c}{(\partial A^k_{ij})^3}\}} \tag{3}$$

Grad-CAM++ then performs a weighted combination of the forward activation maps A^k using the computed importance weights α^c_k:

$$W^c_k = \sum_i \sum_j \alpha^c_{i,j} \text{ReLU}\left(\frac{\partial Y^c}{\partial A^k_{i,j}}\right) \tag{4}$$

$$L^c_{\textbf{Grad-CAM++}} = \sum_k W^c_k A^k. \tag{5}$$

Grad-CAM++ is more resource-intensive due to the computation of higher-order gradients and does not handle noise well.

2.4 Extended-CAM

Extended-CAM [8], or Gaussain-CAM is a variant of Grad-CAM that applies a Gaussian filter to the activation map of the last convolutional layer of a CNN model. This technique helps to smooth out noisy activation maps, making the CAM more accurate, reliable, and robust to noise in the input image. The implementation of Extended-CAM involves computing the Gaussian filter $G(x, y)$ is defined as:

$$G(x, y; \mu, \sigma) = \frac{1}{2\pi\sigma^2} \exp\left(-\frac{(x-\mu_x)^2 + (y-\mu_y)^2}{2\sigma^2}\right) \tag{6}$$

The Gaussian filter $G(x, y)$ is applied to the activation map A^k of the last convolutional layer.

$$\hat{F}^k(x, y) = (F^k * G)(x, y) = \sum_m \sum_n F^k(m, n) G(x-m, y-n) \tag{7}$$

The Grad-CAM method is used to calculate gradients, which are then employed to compute the Extended-CAM using filtered activation maps. The Extended-CAM is subsequently normalized to have a value between 0 and 1, and it is superimposed on the input image.

$$L_c(x, y) = \sum_k W_k^c \hat{F}^k(x, y) \tag{8}$$

2.5 Smooth Grad-CAM

Smooth Grad-CAM [20] is an advanced technique that uses smoothing over image gradients to visualize deep convolutional neural network models. It involves adding Gaussian noise to images and performing Grad-CAM on them, resulting in improved feature visualization. To implement it, add Gaussian noise to an image and perform Grad-CAM on the modified image. It is defined as:

$$x_i = x + N(0, \sigma^2). \tag{9}$$

For each noisy image, the model predicts its class score and obtains the gradient of the class score with respect to the features of the last convolutional layer, i.e., $frac\partial M_c \partial x_i$ The average score obtained for prediction is used to get the average gradient value:

$$\alpha_c = \frac{1}{n} \sum_n \frac{\partial M_c}{\partial x_i}(x_i). \tag{10}$$

Grad-CAM is then applied using the previous average value as the gradient to obtain the final visualization map:

$$L^c_{SmoothGrad-CAM} = Relu(\sum \alpha_c A_c) \tag{11}$$

2.6 Score-CAM

Score-CAM [25] is a non-gradient approach that addresses the limitations of gradient-based methods. Score-CAM provides better visualization maps than Grad-CAM. Given an input image x and a CNN model $f(x)$ with output activation maps A from the last convolutional layer. The action map is normalized. The dot product between the input image x and each activation map A^k is performed. This highlights portions of the image x that correspond to the activation map A^k. The scores S^k are then computed as the difference between the output of the CNN model for these highlighted regions and the output for a baseline input image x. Mathematically, this is written as:

$$S^k = f(x \odot A^k) - f(x_b) \tag{12}$$

It calculates S^k the importance of each kth activation map based on its model prediction scores for the target class c, The coefficient α_c^k represents the normalized importance score for each activation map A^k for the target class c as follows:

$$\alpha_c^k = \frac{\exp(S_c^k)}{\sum_j \exp(S_c^j)} \tag{13}$$

The final visualization is a combination of these weights and activation maps written as:

$$L^c_{\text{Score-CAM}} = \text{ReLU}\left(\sum_k \alpha_c^k A_k\right) \tag{14}$$

This produces a visualization map that highlights the regions of the input image that are most relevant to the target class c.

2.7 Ablation-CAM

Ablation-CAM [17] is a technique used to determine the importance of activation map units with respect to a specific class. This is achieved by systematically ablating (i.e., setting to zero) the activation values in each activation map A^k and observing the effect on the prediction score. By removing individual activation maps A^k and evaluating the prediction score of the CNN model, Ablation-CAM assesses the contribution of each activation map to the prediction for a given class c. Compared to Grad-CAM and Score-CAM, Ablation-CAM is more robust to noise and local artifacts. It provides insights into the impact of each activation map on the model's prediction for a specific class. However, the process requires multiple evaluations of the model with different ablated maps and careful selection of the most informative ablation areas, which can be time-consuming.

2.8 Eigen-CAM

The Eigen-CAM technique [12] uses principal component analysis within convolutional layers to extract important features from an input image x with dimensions size $(i \times j)$. which is then projected onto the combined weight matrix, W^L, of the network's first k layers, yielding the class-activated output, O.

This projection involves matrix multiplication, where $O = W^L I$. Subsequently, SVD is applied to O, decomposing it into its principal components and Eigen-CAM Calculation:

$$L_{\text{Eigen-CAM}} = OV_1 \quad (15)$$

Here, V_1 is the first column of the matrix V^T of SVD. This allows for the discovery of various feature disparities that the model has captured, providing insight into the learning process without the need for category classification, which differs from other CAM methods. It's important to note that Eigen-CAM is not a multi-class local discriminator. The effectiveness of Eigen-CAM can vary depending on the neural network architecture.

3 Quantitative Evaluation Metrics

The quantitative assessment metrics provide crucial insights into the performance of CAM visualization maps [15], which are presented below.

3.1 Average Drop (Lower Value Best)

The metric calculates the average decrease between the model solely relying on the visualization map and the entire image I for the target class c. It can be defined as:

$$\text{Average Drop(I)} = \left(\max\left(0, \frac{y_c - o_c}{y_c}\right)\right) \cdot 100 \quad (16)$$

In which y_c means an output score for class c if the entire input image is used, and o_c gives the output score when the visualization map is applied.

3.2 Average Increase (Higher Value Best)

The average increase counts the number of times the system confidence is greater after using the visualization map compared to analyzing the whole picture. It is calculated as:

$$\text{Average Increase}(I) = \mathbb{K}(y_c < O_c) \cdot 100 \quad (17)$$

where $\mathbb{K}$ is the indicator function. The indicator function counts the number of times the model's confidence y_c is lower than the confidence when using the visualization map o_c.

3.3 Maximum Coherency (Higher Value Best)

The coherence refers to the consistency of the generated visualizations based on the input image. CAM should present informative key factors that explain the CNN prediction while omitting unnecessary ones in a more detailed and accurate manner.

$$CAM_c(I \odot CAM_c(I)) = CAM_c(I). \quad (18)$$

The CAM technique is utilized to emphasize the important sections of an image while disregarding the rest. Afterwards, a coherency score is calculated and normalized between 0 and 1. To calculate the maximum coherency (MC) score, the following formula is applied:

$$\text{MC}(I) = \frac{1}{2}\left(1 + \frac{\text{Cov}(CAM_c(I \circledast CAM_c(I)), CAM_c(I))}{\sigma_{CAM_c}(I \circledast CAM_c(I))\sigma_{CAM_c}(I)}\right) \tag{19}$$

In this equation, the symbol Cov represents the covariance between the convolved CAM and the original CAM. On the other hand, the symbol σ represents the standard deviation of the CAM at a particular position. These statistical measures are used to assess the coherence of the CAM in emphasizing significant regions of an image. A lower score indicates that the visualization map only highlights a few crucial pixels.

3.4 Minimum Complexity (Lower Value Best)

Complexity measures how good a CAM visualization is. It is quantified using the L_1 norm of the CAM, represented as

$$\text{Minimum Complexity(I)} \ = ||CAM_c(I)||. \tag{20}$$

3.5 ADCC: Average Drop Coherency Complexity (Higher Value Best)

This metric combines the average drop, maximum coherency, and minimum complexity (ADCC) to give a comparable single score. It is defined as

$$ADCC(I) = 3\left(\frac{1}{\text{Maximum Coherency}(I)} + \frac{1}{1 - \text{Minimum Complexity}(I)} + \frac{1}{1 - \text{AverageDrop}(I)}\right)^{-1}. \tag{21}$$

4 Experiments and Results

4.1 Dataset and Pre-processing

The musculoskeletal radiographs (MURA) dataset is a valuable resource for research in musculoskeletal imaging, consisting of 40,664 meticulously annotated radiograph images from various study types [16]. The dataset is ideal for accurately classifying MSD in the upper extremity, with a training subset of 37,467 radiographs and a validation subset of 1,667 and 1,530 radiographs, respectively. The MURA dataset is available on the Stanford machine learning group's website [13]. Preparing the radiographs for analysis involves several transformations, including grayscale conversion, precise cropping, contrast-limited adaptive histogram equalization (CLAHE) technique, and resizing to a uniform resolution of 224×224 pixels. These preprocessed images are then used in a CNN architecture.

4.2 CNN Architectures

The convolutional neural networks such as ResNet-50 [5], DenseNet-169 [6], and Inception-v3 [23] that were trained on elbow and wrist radiograph images from the MURA dataset. The models were initialized using transfer learning and pre-trained weights from the imagenet. For binary classification tasks, the models used sigmoid activation at the final output layer, and a global average pooling layer [10] was added after the last convolutional layer. The extracted features were then converted into a vectorized shape to aid in interpreting the class activation maps. The ResNet-50, DenseNet-169 and Inception-v3 are trained on elbow study of the MURA dataset and their training accuracy vs validation accuracy graphs are shown in Fig. 1. In the analysis of elbow studies, the DenseNet-169 model has an accuracy of 76%, the ResNet-50 model has an accuracy of 75%, and the Inception-v3 has an accuracy of 73%. Similarly, for wrist studies, the DenseNet-169 model has an accuracy of 74%, the ResNet-50 model has an accuracy of 77%, and the Inception-v3 has an accuracy of 75%.

4.3 Setup

The PARAM SHAVAK HPC was used to perform an empirical study on the MURA dataset, which has dual-socket Intel Xeon Gold 6226 processors, 96GB DDR4 RAM, two high-speed network ports, 16 PCI-E Gen3 slots for GPUs, and four 4TB SATA or NL-OSAS disks for comprehensive storage. The system supports hardware-based RAID 0 and 1 configurations, with RAID 5 offering redundant storage capabilities. The PARAM SHAVAK HPC can be used for compute-heavy activities like deep learning, scientific simulations, and visualizations with two Nvidia RTX P5000 GPUs.

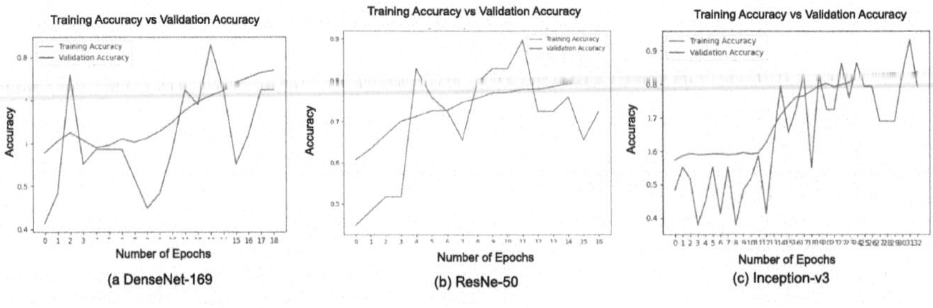

Fig. 1. Various CNN models' training accuracy versus validation accuracy in the MURA dataset's elbow study type.

4.4 Hyperparameters

The CLAHE data pre-processing hyperparameters include setting a clip limit and grid size of 8×8. The CNN model learned at a rate of 0.01 with batches of 8 and trained for 60 epochs with an early stop. The leakyrelu activation function and Adam optimizer are deployed with default values. The architectural framework uses binary cross entropy as its loss function.

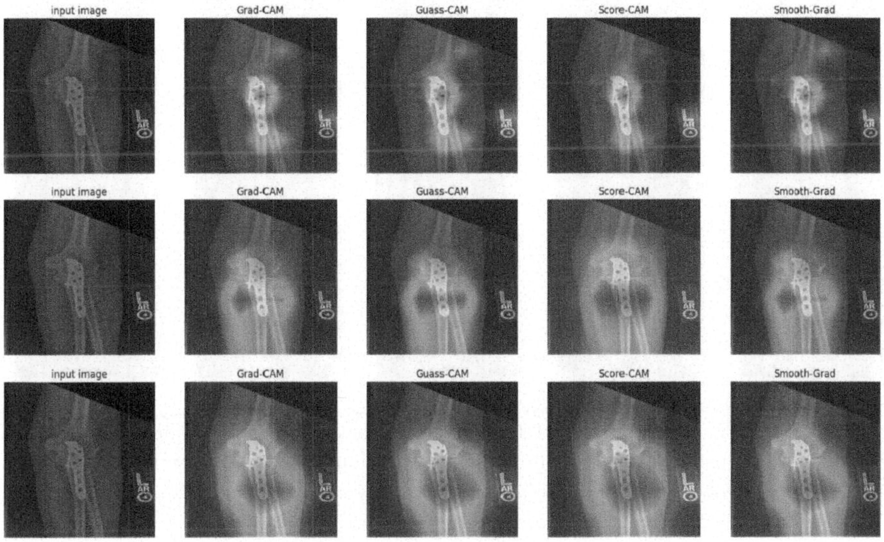

Fig. 2. Qualitative comparison of CAMs visualization: First row shows ResNet-50, second shows DenseNet-169, and third shows Inception-v3 trained on elbow radiographs.

4.5 Experiment-1: Qualitative Assessment

This qualitative assessment of various CAM local discrimination, including CAM, Grad-CAM, Smooth Grad-CAM, Extended-CAM, and Score-CAM, on the MURA dataset. The assessment focused on visual explanations produced by these CAM methods on CNN models trained using elbow and wrist radiograph images from the MURA dataset shown in Fig. 2 and Fig. 3, respectively.

Table 1. Quantitative evaluation of CAMs visualization on Elbow and wrist study type using DenseNet-169

Scenario A: Elbow study type						Scenario B: Wrist study type				
CAM Method	Avg Drop$\downarrow$	Avg Increase$\uparrow$	Coherency$\uparrow$	Complexity$\downarrow$	ADCC$\uparrow$	Avg Drop$\downarrow$	Avg Increase$\uparrow$	Coherency$\uparrow$	Complexity$\downarrow$	ADCC$\uparrow$
CAM	4.627	20	52.197	9.682	73.682	23.621	49.167	68.645	12.270	76.807
Grad-CAM	4.627	20	52.176	9.682	73.682	23.621	49.167	68.645	12.270	76.807
Smooth Grad-CAM	0.713	48	52.197	9.6	74.437	0.545	37.5	68.644	12.269	83.283
Extended-CAM	3.266	28	51.904	10.55	73.559	23.004	49.267	68.931	12.401	77.101
Score-CAM	2.219	26	63.15	2.523	82.5961	18.578	68.3	88.539	6.527	87.528

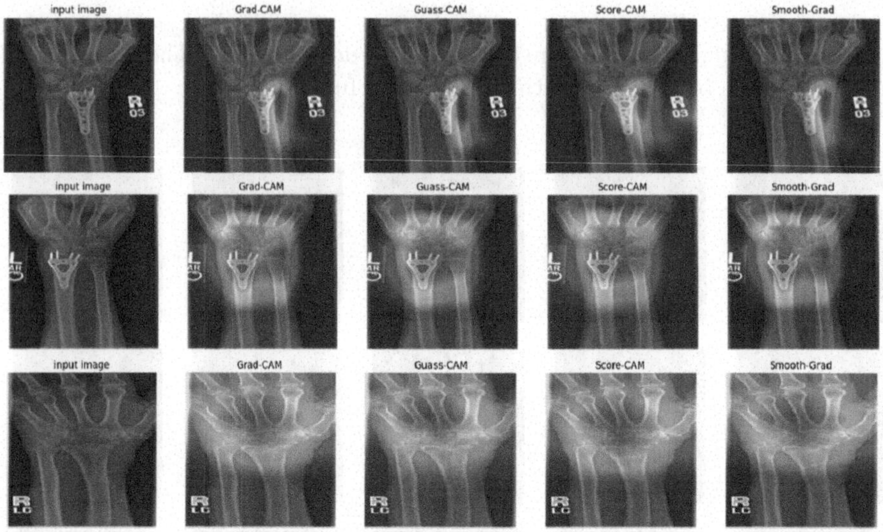

Fig. 3. Qualitative comparison of CAMs visualization: First row shows ResNet-50, second shows DenseNet-169, and third shows Inception-v3 trained on wrist radiographs.

4.6 Experiment-2: Quantitative Evaluation of CAMs Visualization

An empirical evaluation was performed on visual explanations generated by CAM methods with CNN models trained on elbow and wrist radiograph images from the MURA dataset. This assessment involved using images from the validation set, specifically selecting elbow and wrist radiographs for the evaluation. The quantitative assessment results of the CAM methods are displayed in Table 1, Table 2 and Table 3.

The CAM methods were assessed using the DenseNet-169 model for the elbow study type, as detailed in Table 1 of scenario A. In the elbow study, Smooth Grad-CAM shows the lowest average drop (0.713) and highest average increase (48), indicating effective highlighting of decision-making regions. Score-CAM stands out with the highest maximum coherency, lowest minimum complexity, and highest ADCC, offering highly interpretable visualization with lower computational overhead. After thoroughly evaluating various CAM methods on wrist images using the DenseNet-169 model presented in Table 1 of scenario B. Smooth Grad-CAM performs moderately, while Score-CAM is highly interpretable and has a superior correlation with ground truth.

After thoroughly evaluating various CAM methods using the ResNet-50 model on elbow study presented in Table 2 of scenario A. Smooth Grad-CAM was found to have the least average drop with a significant increase in model confidence. Additionally, it maintained a high ADCC, indicating good reliability. On the other hand, Score-CAM stood out with the second-highest maximum coherency and lowest minimum complexity.

Table 2. Quantitative evaluation of CAMs visualization on elbow and wrist study type using ResNet-50

Scenario A: Elbow study type						Scenario A: Wrist study type				
CAM Method	Avg Drop↓	Avg Increase↑	Coherency↑	Complexity↓	ADCC↑	Avg Drop↓	Avg Increase↑	Coherency↑	Complexity↓	ADCC↑
CAM	5.726	28	5.726	5.726	72.808	33.405	10	62.946	5.643	72.287
Grad-CAM	5.726	28	49.814	4.959	72.808	33.405	10	62.946	5.643	72.287
Smooth Grad-CAM	5.04	28	51.815	3.12	74.715	30.322	10	72.956	2.003	78.404
Extended-CAM	5.961	25	49.32	5.638	72.276	32.214	6.6	62.925	5.629	72.743
Score-CAM	5.561	28	46.161	4.509	70.400	34	23.34	73.223	2.557	76.787

Table 2 of scenario B presents the CAMs assessment for wrist images using ResNet-50. Smooth Grad-CAM displayed the highest average increase and coherency with lower complexity compared to other CAM methods for ResNet-50. This makes it the most promising method with a strong correlation to ground truth. Score-CAM also showed good results with a reduced average drop. Overall, Smooth Grad-CAM provides a balanced performance with significant improvement in model confidence and highly interpretable visualizations.

Table 3. Quantitative evaluation of CAMs visualization on elbow and wrist study type using Inception-v3

Scenario A: Elbow study type						Scenario B: Wrist study type				
CAM Method	Avg Drop↓	Avg Increase↑	**Coherency**↑	Complexity↓	ADCC↑	Avg Drop↓	Avg Increase↑	Coherency↑	Complexity↓	ADCC↑
CAM	7.645	28	49.171	16.778	69.474	20.893	34.167	74.46	23.74	76.561
Grad-CAM	7.23	29	50.121	16.521	70.2403	20.893	34.167	74.46	23.77	76.551
Smooth Grad-CAM	0.72	20	53.427	15.67	73.804	1.741	40	75.23	26.74	80.819
Extended-CAM	9.96	28	52.757	18.108	70.968	20.98	34.16	74.17	26.78	75.386
Score-CAM	8.741	30	57.321	5.86	76.87	19	40	77.987	4.819	84.093

In the evaluation of CAM methods using the Inception-v3 model on elbow study as shown in Table 3 of scenario A, Smooth Grad-CAM stands out with the lowest average drop and a reasonable average increase, indicating effective highlighting of decision-making regions while enhancing model confidence. Score-CAM achieves the highest ADCC value of 84.09, indicating a strong correlation with ground truth. Overall, while Smooth Grad-CAM offers a balanced performance, Score-CAM emerges as the most promising method, providing highly interpretable visualizations with superior correlation with ground truth. In evaluating CAM methods using the Inception-v3 model on wrist images as shown in Table 3 of scenario B, both CAM and Grad CAM exhibit similar and consistent behaviour, albeit with higher complexity. Smooth Grad-CAM offers a balanced performance. Score-CAM emerges as the most promising method with a lower average drop, higher average increase, highest coherency, lowest complexity, and strong correlation to ground truth.

4.7 Experiment-3: Coarse Localization Map

The guided backpropagation [21] is used to analyze the contribution of individual pixels towards the CNN prediction. It is accomplished by altering the original backpropagation algorithm. It guarantees that only the positive gradients are sent back, which indicates important features in the input image affecting the prediction. On the other hand, Guided Grad-CAM combines the spatial localization benefits of Grad-CAM with the detailed pixel-level insights of guided backpropagation as in Fig. 4. Grad-CAM produces coarse localization maps by attaching importance to the gradients passing through the final convolutional layer and then using guided backpropagation to achieve high-resolution visualizations. This combination makes it possible to achieve a better and more interpretable representation in the case of medical imaging.

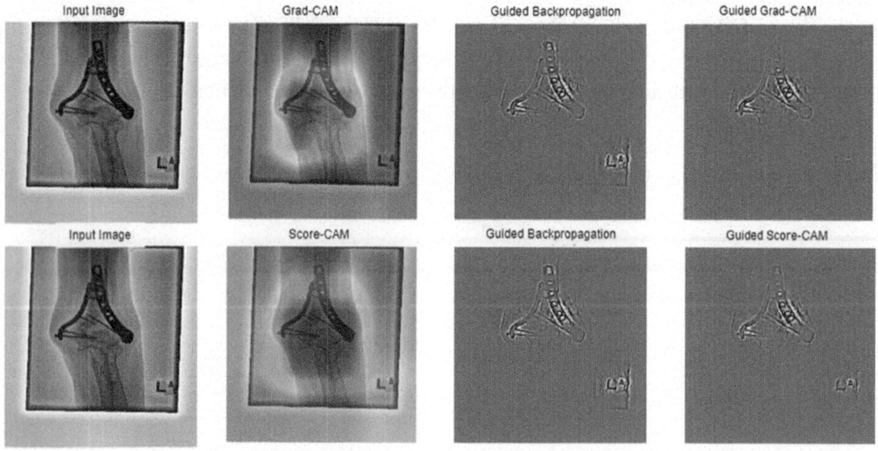

Fig. 4. The first column shows the input image. The second column displays the CAMs visualization (Grad-CAM and Score-CAM). The third column presents the output of guided backpropagation, which displays the prediction's contributing features. The final column shows the combined result of guided backpropagation and CAM visualization.

5 Conclusion and Future Work

Several CAM methods were implemented, including CAM, Grad-CAM, Score-CAM, Extended-CAM, and Smooth Grad-CAM. Their results were compared quantitatively to identify the most effective CAM methods for predicting musculoskeletal abnormalities in radiographs. Based on the analysis of the results, Smooth Grad-CAM and Score-CAM performed better than CAM, Grad-CAM methods, and Extended-CAM. It found that Score-CAM is a promising choice for DenseNet-169 and Inception-v3 models, while Smooth Grad-CAM is best for ResNet-50, offering highly interpretable visualizations and strong correlation with the ground truth. These findings hold significant potential for enhancing decision-making in clinical practice.

Although Score-CAM offers improved visualization, its extensive computational demands pose a challenge. One potential avenue for further development involves optimizing Score-CAM to require fewer computational resources, potentially by combining Score-CAM visualization with a visual transformer for enhanced interpretation.

References

1. Andrews, P., Steultjens, M., Riskowski, J.: Chronic widespread pain prevalence in the general population: a systematic review. Eur. J. Pain **22**(1), 5–18 (2018)
2. Chattopadhay, A., Sarkar, A., Howlader, P., Balasubramanian, V.N.: Grad-cam++: generalized gradient-based visual explanations for deep convolutional networks. In: 2018 IEEE winter conference on applications of computer vision (WACV), pp. 839–847. IEEE (2018)
3. Chaturvedi, K., Dhiman, C., Vishwakarma, D.K.: Fight detection with spatial and channel wise attention-based convlstm model. Expert. Syst. **41**(1), e13474 (2024)
4. Dhiman, C., Antil, A., Anand, A., Gakhar, S.: A deep face spoof detection framework using multi-level elbps and stacked lstms, Signal, Image and Video Processing, pp. 1–14 (2024)
5. He, K., Zhang, X., Ren, S., Sun, J.: Deep residual learning for image recognition. In: Proceedings of the IEEE Conference on Computer Vision and Pattern Recognition, pp. 770–778 (2016)
6. Huang, G., Liu, Z., Van Der Maaten, L., Weinberger, K.Q.: Densely connected convolutional networks. In: Proceedings of the IEEE Conference on Computer Vision and Pattern Recognition, pp. 4700–4708 (2017)
7. Kang, X., Guo, J., Song, B., Cai, B., Sun, H., Zhang, Z.: Interpretability for reliable, efficient, and self-cognitive dnns: From theories to applications. Neurocomputing **545**, 126267 (2023)
8. Kim, B.J., Koo, G., Choi, H., Kim, S.W.: Extending class activation mapping using gaussian receptive field. Comput. Vis. Image Underst. **231**, 103663 (2023)
9. Kim, C., Lee, S., Lee, K.: Tremor feature extraction for enhanced interpretability of vocal disease classification. In: International Conference on Pattern Recognition, pp. 618–633. Springer (2022). https://doi.org/10.1007/978-3-031-37742-6_48
10. Lin, M., Chen, Q., Yan, S.: Network in network. ICLR-2014, arXiv preprint arXiv:1312.4400 (2013)
11. Molnar, C.: Interpretable machine learning. Lulu. com (2020)
12. Muhammad, M.B., Yeasin, M.: Eigen-cam: class activation map using principal components. In: 2020 International Joint Conference on Neural Networks (IJCNN), pp. 1–7. IEEE (2020)
13. Mura (2018). https://stanfordmlgroup.github.io/competitions/mura/ Accessed 8-April-2023
14. Olah, C., Mordvintsev, A., Schubert, L.: Feature visualization. Distill **2**(11), e7 (2017)
15. Poppi, S., Cornia, M., Baraldi, L., Cucchiara, R.: Revisiting the evaluation of class activation mapping for explainability: a novel metric and experimental analysis. In: Proceedings of the IEEE/CVF Conference on Computer Vision and Pattern Recognition., pp. 2299–2304 (2021)

16. Rajpurkar, P., et al.: Large dataset for abnormality detection in musculoskeletal radiographs. In: 1st Conference on Medical Imaging with Deep Learning (MIDL 2018). Amsterdam, The Netherlands (2018)
17. Ramaswamy, H.G.: Ablation-cam: Visual explanations for deep convolutional network via gradient-free localization. In: proceedings of the IEEE/CVF Winter Conference on Applications of Computer Vision, pp. 983–991 (2020)
18. Selvaraju, R.R., Cogswell, M., Das, A., Vedantam, R., Parikh, D., Batra, D.: Grad-cam: Visual explanations from deep networks via gradient-based localization. In: Proceedings of the IEEE International Conference on Computer Vision, pp. 618–626 (2017)
19. Sharma, N., Dhiman, C., Indu, S.: Visual-motion-interaction guided pedestrian intention prediction framework. IEEE Sensors J. (2023)
20. Smilkov, D., Thorat, N., Kim, B., Viégas, F., Wattenberg, M.: Smooth-grad: removing noise by adding noise. In: ICML, 2017 Workshop on Visualization for Deep Learning: arXiv preprint arXiv:1706.03825 (2017)
21. Springenberg, J.T., Dosovitskiy, A., Brox, T., Riedmiller, M.: Striving for simplicity: the all convolutional net. In: ICLR 2015 (2014)
22. Storheim, K., Zwart, J.A.: Musculoskeletal disorders and the global burden of disease study. Ann. Rheum. Dis. **73**(6), 949–950 (2014)
23. Szegedy, C., et al.: Going deeper with convolutions. In: Proceedings of the IEEE Conference on Computer Vision and Pattern Recognition, pp. 1–9 (2015)
24. Van der Velden, B.H., Kuijf, H.J., Gilhuijs, K.G., Viergever, M.A.: Explainable artificial intelligence (xai) in deep learning-based medical image analysis. Med. Image Anal. **70**, 102470 (2022)
25. Wang, H., et al.: Score-cam: score-weighted visual explanations for convolutional neural networks. In: Proceedings of the IEEE/CVF Conference on Computer Vision and Pattern Recognition Workshops, pp. 24–25 (2020)
26. Yosinski, J., Clune, J., Nguyen, A., Fuchs, T., Lipson, H.: Understanding neural networks through deep visualization. In: Deep Learning Workshop, 31st International Conference on Machine Learning, Lille, France-2015, arXiv preprint arXiv:1506.06579 (2015)
27. Zhang, H., Torres, F., Sicre, R., Avrithis, Y., Ayache, S.: Opti-cam: optimizing saliency maps for interpretability. arXiv preprint arXiv:2301.07002 (2023)
28. Zhou, B., Khosla, A., Lapedriza, A., Oliva, A., Torralba, A.: Learning deep features for discriminative localization. In: Proceedings of the IEEE Conference on Computer Vision and Pattern Recognition, pp. 2921–2929 (2016)

Unstructured Outdoor Terrain Segmentation Using SegNav for Safe AGV Navigation

Tanudeep Ganguly, Rapti Chaudhuri(✉), and Suman Deb

National Institute of Technology Agartala, Agartala, India
{rapti.ai,sumandeb.cse}@nita.ac.in
https://www.sumandeb.com/

Abstract. Safe locomotion by AGV (Automated Guided Vehicle) in off-road terrains and unstructured environments requires robust execution of vision-mediated path navigation techniques. Efficient navigation can be obtained from precise surrounding perception and identification of manoeuvrable paths. However, the present well-known end-to-end approaches proved to have a substantial success rate of their performances in well-structured, on-road settings, but on the contrary, it is yet a challenge in complex and amorphous terrains to detect a proper manoeuvrable region for an autonomous point-to-point rescue or service robot. The research work majorly focuses on constructing an efficient perception system proposed as SegNav (Segmentation for Navigation). This is established featuring both semantic and geometric precision accuracy. The architecture of the projected model is constructed relative to reasonable insights of surroundings for obtaining consistent outputs. Feature extraction through group-wise attention defines the navigability of terrains. The assimilation of information is carried out by including multiview RGB inputs. The standardization of the model is established by training and experiment on a benchmarking off-road terrain dataset RUGD to evaluate its performance. It has also been tested on outdoor environmental custom data established from the real-world scenario. The model has also been compared with SOTA methods for benchmarking. SegNav achieves an improvement over mIoU (mean Intersection over Union) by 1.26%, and aAcc (Average Precision Accuracy) of 0.21% on the taken datasets. The findings of the experiment adds notable validation and confidence on AGV self-navigation across off road terrains.

Keywords: SegNav · Off-road navigation · Segmentation · AGV · Machine vision

1 Introduction

Complex terrain is one of the major challenging parts to be covered for executing collision-free AGV navigation. Significant service and rescue robotics domains

J. Kakarla et al. (Eds.): CVIP 2024, CCIS 2473, pp. 353–366, 2026.
https://doi.org/10.1007/978-3-031-93688-3_25

include areas like agricultural sectors, mines, disasters, environmental surveys, etc. These complex areas need to be understood at both semantic and geometric levels to detect drivable regions on unstructured surfaces. Compared to well-structured on-road and indoor navigation, outdoor terrains are algorithmically difficult to traverse by an autonomous vehicle. The absence of proper lane marks or a structured feature of the maneuverable regions makes it difficult to recognize the continuous movable zone. Handling such situations involves the visual perception of the terrain structure, generally resulting from segmentation at the pixel level (semantic segmentation) [1,2]. An extensive literature survey reveals the use of semantic segmentation mostly in on-road navigation systems [3,4]. Terrain navigation constitutes some significant work including [5,6]. Terrain classification works are largely based on vision transformer-mediated multi-modal segmentation (MMseg) or different attention mechanisms generated from various deep neural architectures for their ability of precise object detection and scene understanding. The presented paper uses the concept of a vision transformer for multiscale feature extraction and combines it with a spatial-attention-based segmentation header to extract the environmental information at geometric and semantic levels. For experimenting, some major challenging terrain areas are addressed.

Fig. 1. The performance of the proposed neural architecture, SegNav has been highlighted here. Four major terrain regions are perfectly classified and segmented by SegNav.

Unstructured environment with long vegetation: Maneuverable regions within an unstructured area in a forest where no well-defined guidance for navigation is present.

Partially identifiable zones: Movable zones in between small water bodies or puddles, that create confusion in path detection.

Regions with bifurcated moving zone: Sudden bifurcation in paths, that create confusion in deciding the correct moving area for a while.

Regions with ambiguous movable zone: Terrain containing multiple featured movable areas (bumpy, smooth, rough) covered with vegetation.

Rocky backcountry trail: Unstructured zones with rock shelves along with narrow movable paths are grouped under this category. This paper proposes a novel neural architecture, SegNav which works on the principle of coarse-fine-grained pixelated information extraction with upgraded featured terrain classification ability. SegNav focuses on model size compression through a vision transformer, which also degrades its run-time complexity. The significant contributions of this research work are mentioned below:

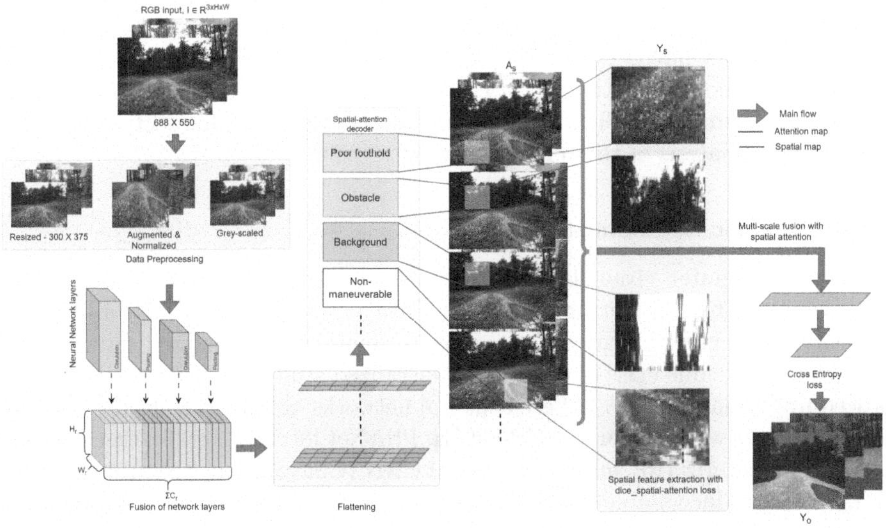

Fig. 2. Architecture of SegNav which works on the principle of Mixvision transformer (a vision transformer technique) and spatial-attention mechanism (A_g, Y_s) to extract block-wise spatial feature and gather pixel-wise high-level information (Y_o) by coarse-fine grain analysis.

- An upgraded neural network model, SegNav is proposed which works on the principle of multiscale feature extraction. The efficiency of the architecture has been confirmed from a benchmarking analysis with different SOTA (State-Of-The-Art) multiscale backbone designs. SegNav outperforms other existing segmentation techniques in terms of mIoU by 90.34% on one of the standard terrain datasets, RUGD.
- Introduction of a unique segmentation decoder head. It has been designed using a spatial attention mechanism that extracts pixel-level information and evaluates the inference accuracy of the model as presented in Fig. 1.

- Demonstration of SegNav is also carried out by deploying it into a customized differential drive platform. It supersedes other existing methods by a 97.92% success rate and a reduction of 0.009% in the false positive rate. The proposed architecture is presented in Fig. 2.

The paper organization is followed by an extensive literature survey in Sect. 2, the collection of methodologies with algorithmic construction of the proposed model in Sect. 3, Experimental and result benchmarking in Sect. 4 and is concluded with result analysis and discussion of future work in this area in Sect. 5.

2 Related Works

The review processes with parameterized visual perception methodologies to extract information from a compound unstructured environment for executing safe mobile robot navigation. This particular study has divided the review process into the following sections: (1) Semantic Segmentation (2) Modeling on well-structured environment (3) Modeling on complex terrain. This section presents an elaborate analysis of the related studies.

2.1 Semantic Segmentation

A part of computer vision is executed through pixel-wise information extraction, which is termed as segmentation. Path segmentation is basically based on semantic level information generation through which clustered data can be extracted from same class of object. A generalized study has been conducted on procedural visual percept. Different neural networks are noted from the existing research works which include OCRNet [7], PSANet [8], PSPNet [9], transformer-based architectures [10], and conventional CNN (Convolutional Neural network) [11], which produce viable outputs in path segmentation but executes expensive computational rate. The quality to execute viable performance led the use of transformer-based techniques in the latest research works for adjusting the perception time and computational cost [10] of the respective model. CNN-based models are noted to be efficient in encoding and decoding the geometric and spatial information from the environment through fine and coarse grained techniques. These result in precise segmentation and information accumulation from a considered complex environment. Compared to neural networks, vision transformers are efficient in computational time and space reduction of the model.

The proposed SegNav is incorporated with the qualitative vision transformer and encoder-decoder based hierarchical spatial-attention mediated CNN architecture to generate feature-map and execute multi-modal segmentation.

2.2 Modeling on Well-Structured Environment

Significant DNN (Deep Neural Networks) models extracted from basic CNN architectures have many-a-times appeared to be unique in accumulating important information from the environment. The primary NN-based segmentation

Table 1. State-of-The-Art comparison of the proposed technique with existing related works

Source Reference	Technique used	Environment	Accuracy	Pros	Cons
Guan et al. [5]	GA-NAV: a segmentation based on Group-wise Attention mechanism	Terrain environments	95.66%	Good model size with fewer parameters which use vision transformer for segmentation	Lack of precise categorical segmentation
Meng et al. [6]	TerrainNet: a segmentation process based on Group-wise Attention mechanism	Complex terrain structures	Approx 50%	Model achieves efficient visual modeling from geometric and semantic data from the environment and high-speed off-road navigation	Lack of precise categorical segmentation and lack of good accuracy in prediction
Alexandre et al. [12]	ELM neural network	Constrained environment	85%	Proved to give comparative movement and analysis through the surface area due to omi-directional wheel.	Minimized overall accuracy of classification
Alex et al. [13]	PointPillars: Fast encoder for object detection	On-road environment	72.6%	Successful extraction of all environment data from KITTI dataset using point cloud mapping.	Proposed algorithm executes overall very low mean average precision and also for each categorical class of instances
Zhu et al. [14]	3D Convolution Network	Large scale driving scene	76.1%	LiDAR segmentation is used for proper depth-wise data collection	Mean Intersection over Union (MIoU) value is low degrading the accuracy of performance.
Chen et al. [15]	Adaptformer: Vision transformer	Congested scenarios in external cross section	60%	Scalable vision recognition using light-weight model.	Accuracy of performance is not up to the mark
Proposed network	SegNav: A segmentation model with spatial attention and Vision transformer	Congested scenarios in external cross section	95.87%	Precise categorical segmentation with very good accuracy and with balanced execution time.	The number of parameters increases the model size slightly

models can provide correct distinction of differently featured maneuverable zones. These NN models are extensively used in the autonomous on-road navigation [14] using various optical sensors and cameras. The application of NN-based networks are highly used in image [15] or point cloud segmentation [14]. Various depth sensors like LiDAR (Light Detection And Ranging) [13] and Intel Realsense 3D depth camera series are responsible for collecting edge-dependent site information. Along with these, simple cameras are also used and are highly encouraged for accomplishing these works in low cost and execute less computational complexity. Visual perception is important in performance upgradation of receiving semantic data from the environment. This process is clearly evident from SimpleBEV (Simple Bird's Eye View) [16] and BEVFormer [17] methods. SegNav is composed of a unique segmentation decoder head that works on the principle of spatial-attention mechanism for extracting semantic as well as geo-spatial features from the objective environment at an increased precision. Simple RGB images are used as input to the model and passed through the vision-transformer based backbone for qualitative feature extraction. Vision transformer not only balances the model execution speed and time but also produce proper detection of various features in complex terrain with convenient model size. A comparative theoretical analysis is presented in Table 1.

2.3 Off-Road Environment Modeling

Performance measure in navigation through uneven terrain structures is computed through different NN and transformer-based methods by both small mobile robots [18–21] and large AGV [22–24]. To tackle the topological challenges in complex terrain, a proper understanding of the terrain semantics is important to make a precise decision about the traversibility. Terrain structural features are inferred using one of the three methods: (a) Proprioceptive-based methods (b) Appearance-based methods and (c) Geometric methods.

Proprioceptive methods [25] depicts robot sensors and ML-mediated techniques for collection of information from frequent domain vibrations of terrains. Extraction of features using SIFT (Scale-Invariant Feature Transform) or SURF (Speeded Up Robust Features) [26] come under Appearance-based methods [18]. Geometric method involve use of various optical sensors for collecting the geometric features of the environment resulting in proper percept [24,27]. This method comprises of range sensor, RGB camera, or different depth sensors such as LiDAR (Light Detection And Ranging) and 3D depth camera. those sensors and cameras generate pixel-wise clear data, accumulated to a 3D point cloud map. Depth sensors are responsible for distinguishing different terrain features like elevation, slope, bump, and roughness. SegNav adapts the qualitative appearance-based criteria in an aggregation of both geometric and semantic information about the considered environment.

3 Proposed Methodological Approach

An upgraded spatial attention-based approach, SegNav is presented in this work for identifying the traversability of terrain regions using multi-modal feature extraction. Terrain environments contain structures like bumps, elevations, slopes, and rough regions which make the system challenging to predict and difficult to accomplish smoothly. The use of MixVision transformer (MiT), sectioned under Vision-transformer (ViT) is incorporated with an encoder-decoder-based hierarchical structure for the collection of geometric and spatial information from the environment. The mechanism proves to be convenient with respect to adjusted model sizes containing fewer parameters and with good execution time. SegNav model consists of MiT as the backbone and spatial-attention mechanized decoder head.

Problem Definition: An RGB input image vector $I \in \mathbb{R}^{3\times H\times W}$, ($\mathbb{R}$ denotes the set of real numbers) is fed into the model with its ground-truth mask value $G \in \mathbb{Z}^{H\times W}$ ($\mathbb{Z}$ is the set of integers, each pixel belonging to S spatial structures). The spatial segmentation generates computed probability maps $M_p$distributed on a pixel of S spatial structure in that input area.

3.1 System Architecture

Vision transformers are noted for having compatible model size and weight, responsible for multi-scale feature extraction.

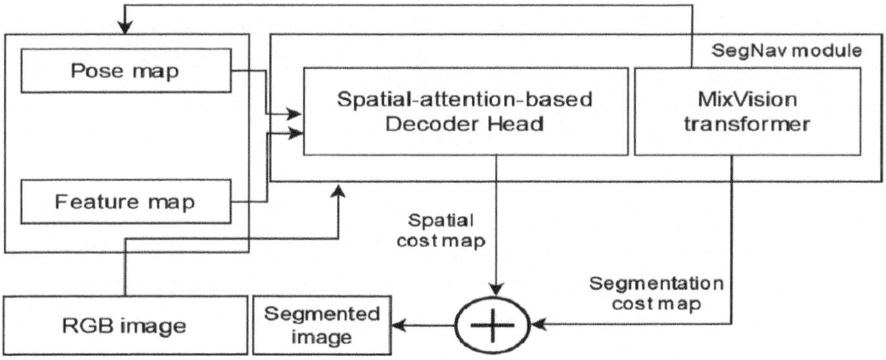

Fig. 3. The proposed architecture of SegNav, showing inter module integration of MixVision transformer backbone and spatial-attention decoder. It is modelled for semantic and spatial-geometric information extraction for better visual percept.

ViTs (Vision Transformers) consist of deep neural networks and are widely in alternative use in place of ResNet. ViTs use Multi-Head Self-Attention (MHSA) technique to extract multi-scale features. MiT (MixVision Transformer) has been specifically derived from ViTs with convenient parameterized modifications and is used as **backbone** of the said model.

The **SegNav decoder head** construct follows with accumulation and application of the attention blocks on feature maps, which are generated from the MixVision transformer backbone of the model. The workflow of the proposed architecture has been clarified visually in different in Fig. 3. The decoder head is designed based on the working principle of encoder-decoder hierarchy and enhanced with a spatial attention mechanism derived from cross-attention. Multi-scale feature extraction is accompanied with linear fusion for and followed by a final layer of segmented predictions. The major functional layers in decoder head consist of the following:

1. **MLP layer**: The Multi-layer perceptron (MLP) executes depth-wise convolutions, linear transformations, along with various activations.
2. **Depth-wise Conv**: DWConv (Depth-wise Convolution) function captures the spatial dependency.
3. **CatKey module**: Catkey (Concatenation Key) processes and fuses various scaled features.
4. **Spatial-attention function**: This implements cross-attention inspired spatial attention mechanism which refines inter-scale features.
5. **Block**: Block concatenates spatial-attention and MLP layers for generating normalized and residual connections.
6. **SegNav Head**: The decoder head comprises of multi-scale feature processing (msfp), application of spatial attention, and final production of predicted results.

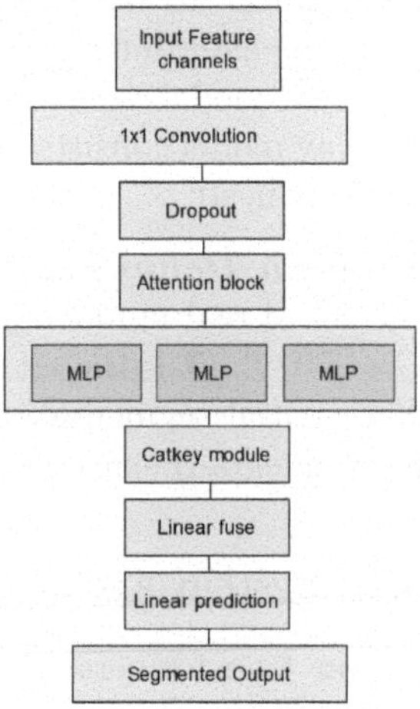

Fig. 4. The interconnected modules of the constructed decoder head of the proposed network SegNav.

Truncated normal distribution or constant initialization process the weight initialization of the network. Application of dropout layer executes a normalized and regularized network structure. Downsampling of the feature maps is performed through average pooling and the input images are passed to GELU (Gaussian error linear unit) activation function which handles the non-linearity in MLP layers. Droppath and padding techniques ensure stochastic depth regularization and spatial-dimension conservation in a respective way. Added advantage in the designed decoder head lies in application of residual connections which is important in preserving the information flow. Schematic of the decoder head construct has been shown in Fig. 4.

Spatial alignment reduces the resolution of the input image which results in degradation of the model performance. Based on the structure of the decoder head, a SA_dice (Spatial Attention dice) loss has been introduced which mitigates the degraded performance. SA_dice loss function is constructed in a matrix format which evaluates the ML models in vision-based segmentation works. It calculates the similarity of two classified binary images - the ground truth mask value and the predicted value (Eq. 1).

$$\textbf{SA\_dice loss} = 2 \times \frac{(s \cap s_{pred})}{(s + s_{pred})} \tag{1}$$

The dice_spatial attention loss signifies the underexposed regions that need further classification.

3.2 Overall Model Loss

Overall model loss has been calculated in the form of a standard segmentation loss, Cross entropy loss. It is represented as in Eq. 2:

$$\textbf{Cross Entropy loss} = -\sum_{h,w}\sum_{s \in S} G_s log(M_{p_s}) \tag{2}$$

h, w are the height and width of the image, S is the spatially represented image, M_{p_s} is probability of output spatial map generation and G_s denotes the ground truth value of the input image.

Apart from this overall loss, some amount of auxiliary loss is also computed where FCN (Fully Connected Network) is used twice using channels {32,32} which reduces training time and regularize the model.

4 Experimental Setup and Result Analysis

A sample experiment of the proposed model network has been carried out on a standard RUGD dataset to validate its respective performance outcome. The visual results of SegNav implementation with respective remarks are done in Table 2. Later on, SegNav was also been tested on test outdoor data and compared extensively (one-to-one) with the performance of one of the latest segmentation algorithms GA-Nav proposed by Guan et al., shown in Table 3. As the comparison is conducted on test outdoor data, no Ground truth masking is included here.

4.1 Implementation of SegNav on Considered Datasets

The benchmarking experiments are carried on RUGD dataset, which has been primarily used for benchmarking and SGD (Stochastic Gradient Descent) is used as an optimizer, with a variable learning rate starting from 0.093 relative to the adapted prediction accuracy policy.

The dataset has been undergone through the process of data augmentation and preprocessing where the original size of 688 × 550 is reduced to 300 × 375 and trained with a batch size of 6 with 2,40,000 iterations. For fitting the outdoor test data in the model, the test images are resized to the needed pixel values

Table 2. Obtained results of categorical segmentation performed by SegNav with Ground Truth mask and respective remarks.

Original image	Ground_Truth (GT)	SegNav results	Remarks
			Segmentation of an unstructured village scene is done here. SegNav correctly segments the regions and differentiates them into rocky (yellow), immovable (red), grey (background), and purple (obstacle).
	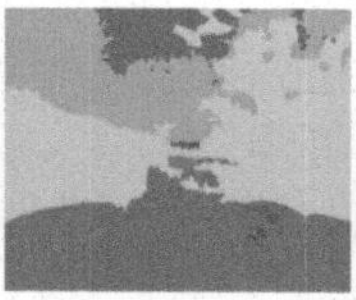		Segmentation of a creek scene is done here. SegNav correctly segments and differentiates the regions into resistive (yellowish-red), immovable (red), grey (background), and purple (obstacle).
			Segmentation of a park scene is done here. SegNav correctly segments and differentiates the regions into smooth (green), immovable (red), grey (background), and purple (obstacle).
			Segmentation of a trail is done here. SegNav correctly segments and differentiates the regions into rocky (yellow), immovable (red), grey (background), and purple (obstacle).

adjusted according to the camera perspective. For RGB image vector I, the prediction label has been pointed to be $P(a, b)$ at (a,b) location, G(a,b) is taken as the ground truth masking label at (a,b), and $\nVdash(A)$ denotes the indicator function for a set of B class labels. Primarily 6 classes are featured for precise segmentation namely, **smooth**, **rocky**, **resistive**, **background**, **obstacle**, and **immovable**. Analysis of SegNav relative to different parameters like Intersection Over Union (IOU), mean IOU, and average pixel accuracy (aAcc) (Eq. 3-5) are accomplished and compared with other benchmarking segmentation models.

$$IOU_c = \frac{\sum_I \sum_{a,b} i(P(a,b) = c \text{ and } G(a,b) = c}{\sum_I \sum_{a,b} i(P(a,b) = c \text{ or } G(a,b) = c} \tag{3}$$

$$MeanIoU(mIoU) = \frac{\sum_c \mathrm{mIoU_c}}{\sum_B} \tag{4}$$

$$aAcc = \frac{\sum_I \sum_{a,b} \nVdash(P(a,b) = G(a,b))}{\sum_I \sum_{a,b}} \tag{5}$$

Table 3. Extensive comparative analysis carried out in some special test scenarios using GA-NAV by Guan et al. and the proposed model SegNav.

Original image	GA-Nav results	SegNav results	Differentiation
			**GA-Nav** accumulates the whole region as the rocky region in a creek. **SegNav** correctly points out the rocky region and also the immovable zone.
			**GA-Nav** points out the whole region as the rocky region in a creek scene. **SegNav** correctly points out the rocky region and the immovable zone.
			**GA-Nav** points to the bushy region as a rocky area. **SegNav** correctly points it as an immovable area.
			**GA-Nav** accumulates the full region as the rocky region. **SegNav** correctly points out the rocky region and the immovable area in a dangerous narrow zone.

Multi-modal segmentation (MMSeg) merged with spatial attention here shows an improvement of 1.26% mIoU on the RUGD dataset. SegNav is extensively compared with some of the latest segmentation techniques with respect to model parameter size, run-time (image/sec), space complexity in terms of inference memory, and GFLOPS (Giga Floating Point Operations Per Second), success rate, and false positive rate. The results are presented in Table 4, which highlights its algorithmic efficiency.

Comparative analysis of SegNav and GA-Nav is done on outdoor test data collected by a customized differential drive robot platform. The potentiality analysis of SegNav is graphically presented in Fig. 5.

5 Conclusion and Future Work

This paper proposes an upgraded learning-based neural network architecture, SegNav which works on the principle of spatial-attention-based vision-transformer. It executes its novelty in robust environment visual percept with precise distinction between different off-road terrain features. The performance accuracy of SegNav is standardized by benchmark comparison with other existing segmentation techniques on the RUGD dataset and test data collected by

Table 4. Parameterized comparisons of SegNav model architecture with other three latest best performing models.

Methods (%)	Parameters (M)	Run-time (image/sec)	GFLOPS	Success rate (%)	False positive rate (%)
Segformer [28]	3.72	72.12	9.29	58	29.09
OCRNet [29]	36.51	20.65	221.47	62	39.12
GA-Nav [5]	6.94	65.53	18.69	71	0.88
SegNav	**8.34**	**21.76**	**13.87**	**97.92**	**0.871**

Table 5. State-of-The-Art comparison of the performance of SegNav with other models in terms of six challenging off-road features.

Methods	Smooth region	Resistive region	Rocky region	Obstacle on path	Back-ground	Immovable region	mIoU	aAcc
OCRNet [29]	66.31	**94.52**	76.22	88.83	79.10	59.10	76.61	93.51
DANet [29]	2.26	81.47	8.70	82.60	74.89	15.17	44.18	88.91
PSPNet [30]	48.67	89.0	70.32	88.10	78.13	29.09	66.98	93.12
DeepLabv3+ [30]	5.97	85.11	51.21	**92.50**	82.52	25.03	55.92	91.53
FastFCN [31]	25.23	90.23	85.96	91.34	74.56	83.34	75.89	93.31
FastSCNN [31]	82.04	92.98	85.49	91.23	75.27	80.56	87.11	94.79
BiseNetv2 [28]	25.07	90.12	90.15	91.92	75.45	82.13	75.32	92.12
SETR [28]	87.89	92.46	85.23	89.64	71.23	70.22	82.76	94.08
Segformer [28]	93.43	93.14	87.45	92.1	78.4	77.45	87.87	94.12
CGNet [5]	40.78	90.23	87.67	87.09	73.29	74.56	76.22	94.98
Segmenter [28]	90.45	92.56	85.67	88.9	68.9	67.89	81.12	93.44
PSANet [5]	34.78	87.9	32.12	87.95	78.45	8.44	54.45	92.0
DPT [5]	1.11	87.3	23.98	87.9	73.5	25.68	49.17	88.88
GA-Nav [5]	95.15	**94.45**	89.83	91.95	76.86	86.25	90.08	95.68
SegNav	**95.9**	89.89	94.68	90.16	**80.99**	**87.45**	**90.34**	**95.89**

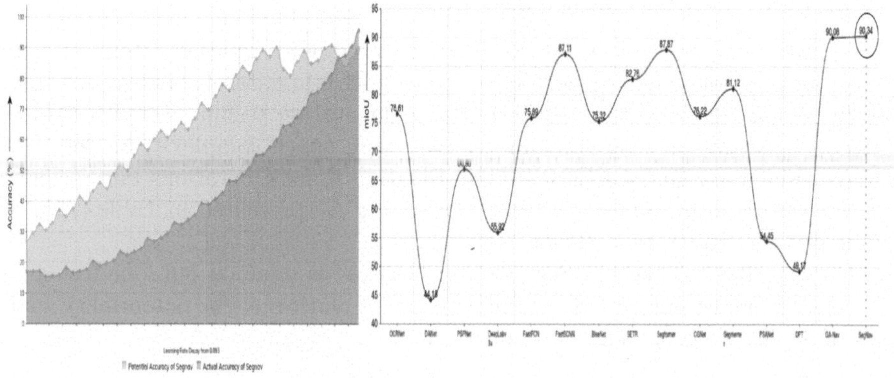

(a) (b)

Fig. 5. (a) SegNav actual performance referred with model potential over increasing iterations (experimented with 2,40,000 iterations) (b) mIoU comparison of different segmentation models (maximum mIoU achieved by SegNav=90.34).

customized differential drive. SegNav proves its efficiency in producing a high success rate of performance. Although the accumulation of pixelated segmentation procedure using neural network architecture increases the model size by approximately 2% which in turn increases space complexity. This limitation of the model is focused and is being tried to be worked upon in the future. Further, the research would also include comparative experimentation of other complex off-road terrain datasets to analyze the required modifications and degradation of the proposed model for retaining global acceptability.

References

1. Hao, S., Zhou, Y., Guo, Y.: A brief survey on semantic segmentation with deep learning. Neurocomputing **406**, 302–321 (2020)
2. Zhao, H., Shi, J., Qi, X., Wang, X., Jia, J.: Pyramid scene parsing network. In: Proceedings of the IEEE Conference on Computer Vision and Pattern Recognition, pp. 2881–2890 (2017)
3. Alhaija, H.A., Mustikovela, S.K., Mescheder, L., Geiger, A., Rother, C.: Augmented reality meets computer vision: efficient data generation for urban driving scenes. Int. J. Comput. Vision **126**, 961–972 (2018)
4. Cordts, M., et al.: The cityscapes dataset for semantic urban scene understanding. In: Proceedings of the IEEE Conference on Computer Vision and Pattern Recognition, pp. 3213–3223(2016)
5. Guan, T., Kothandaraman, D., Chandra, R., Sathyamoorthy, A.J., Weerakoon, K., Manocha, D.: Ga-nav: efficient terrain segmentation for robot navigation in unstructured outdoor environments. IEEE Robot. Autom. Lett. **7**(3), 8138–8145 (2022)
6. Meng, X., et al.: Terrainnet: visual modeling of complex terrain for high-speed, off-road navigation. arXiv preprint, arXiv: 2303.15771 (2023)
7. Chen, X., Liu, Z., Zhou, S., Yu, H., Chen, J., Liu, Y.: Lite-hrnet-ocr: a lightweight high-resolution network and object-contextual representation for road extraction on remote sensing images. In: Fourth International Conference on Geoscience and Remote Sensing Mapping (GRSM 2022), vol. 12551, pp. 330–334. SPIE, (2023)
8. Lin, X., et al.: Intelligent identification of pavement cracks based on psa-net. Front. Environ. Sci. **11**, 1105467 (2023)
9. Pham, T.: Semantic road segmentation using deep learning. In: 2020 Applying New Technology in Green Buildings (ATiGB), pp. 45–48. IEEE (2021)
10. Strudel, R., Garcia, R., Laptev, I., Schmid, C.: Segmenter: transformer for semantic segmentation. In: Proceedings of the IEEE/CVF International Conference on Computer Vision, pp. 7262–7272 (2021)
11. Wei, Y., Zhang, K., Ji, S.: Simultaneous road surface and centerline extraction from large-scale remote sensing images using cnn-based segmentation and tracing. IEEE Trans. Geosci. Remote Sens. **58**(12), 8919–8931 (2020)
12. Vicente, A., Liu, J., Yang, G.-Z.: Surface classification based on vibration on omni-wheel mobile base. In: 2015 IEEE/RSJ International Conference on Intelligent Robots and Systems (IROS), pp. 916–921 (2015)
13. Lang, A.H., Vora, S., Caesar, H., Zhou, L., Yang, J., Beijbom, O.: Pointpillars: fast encoders for object detection from point clouds. In: Proceedings of the IEEE/CVF Conference on Computer Vision and Pattern Recognition, pp. 12697–12705 (2019)
14. Zhu, X., et al.: Cylindrical and asymmetrical 3d convolution networks for lidar segmentation. In: Proceedings of the IEEE/CVF Conference on Computer Vision and Pattern Recognition, pp. 9939–9948 (2021)

15. Chen, S., et al.: Adaptformer: adapting vision transformers for scalable visual recognition. Adv. Neural. Inf. Process. Syst. **35**, 16664–16678 (2022)
16. Harley, A.W., Fang, Z., Li, J., Ambrus, R., Fragkiadaki, K.: Simple-bev: what really matters for multi-sensor bev perception. In: 2023 IEEE International Conference on Robotics and Automation (ICRA), pp. 2759–2765. IEEE (2023)
17. Li, et al.: Bevformer: learning bird's-eye-view representation from multi-camera images via spatiotemporal transformers. In: European Conference on Computer Vision, pp. 1–18. Springer (2022). https://doi.org/10.1007/978-3-031-20077-9_1
18. Matsuzaki, S., Yamazaki, K., Hara, Y., Tsubouchi, T.: Traversable region estimation for mobile robots in an outdoor image. J. Intell. Robotic Syst. **92**, 453–463 (2018)
19. Procopio, M.J., Mulligan, J., Grudic, G.: Learning terrain segmentation with classifier ensembles for autonomous robot navigation in unstructured environments. J. Field Robot. **26**(2), 145–175 (2009)
20. Kahn, G., Abbeel, P., Levine, S.: Badgr: an autonomous self-supervised learning-based navigation system. IEEE Robot. Autom. Lett. **6**(2), 1312–1319 (2021)
21. Pereira, G., et al.: Robot navigation in multi-terrain outdoor environments. Inter. J. Robot. Res. **28**(6), 685–700 (2009)
22. Manduchi, R., Castano, A., Talukder, A., Matthies, L.: Obstacle detection and terrain classification for autonomous off-road navigation. Auton. Robot. **18**, 81–102 (2005)
23. Reina, G., Milella, A., Rouveure, R.: Traversability analysis for off-road vehicles using stereo and radar data. In: 2015 IEEE International Conference on Industrial Technology (ICIT), pp. 540–546. IEEE (2015)
24. Larson, J., Trivedi, M., Bruch, M.: Off-road terrain traversability analysis and hazard avoidance for ugvs. In: IEEE Intelligent Vehicles Symposium, pp. 1–7 (2011)
25. Dupont, E.M., Moore, C.A., Collins, E.G., Coyle, E.: Frequency response method for terrain classification in autonomous ground vehicles. Auton. Robot. **24**, 337–347 (2008)
26. Mistry, D., Banerjee, A.: Comparison of feature detection and matching approaches: sift and surf. GRD Journals-Global Res. Developm. J. Eng. **2**(4), 7–13 (2017)
27. Chaudhuri, R., Deb, S., Das, H.: Geometric representation of obstacles depth in a partially unknown environment for achieving optimized navigation by mobile robots. In: International Conference on Frontiers of Intelligent Computing: Theory and Applications, pp. 429–439. Springer (2022). https://doi.org/10.1007/978-981-19-7524-0_38
28. Wang, J., et al.: Rtformer: efficient design for real-time semantic segmentation with transformer. Adv. Neural. Inf. Process. Syst. **35**, 7423–7436 (2022)
29. Wang, L., Yin, H., Yuan, H.: A maritime target identification algorithm based on improved ocrnet. In: 2022 15th International Symposium on Computational Intelligence and Design (ISCID), pp. 134–138. IEEE (2022)
30. Qian, X., Shu, C., Jin, W., Yunxiang, Yu., Yang, S.: Mfsnet: enhancing semantic segmentation of urban scenes with a multi-scale feature shuffle network. Electronics **13**(1), 12 (2023)
31. Sohail, A., Nawaz, N.A., Shah, A.A., Rasheed, S., Ilyas, S., Ehsan, M.K.: A systematic literature review on machine learning and deep learning methods for semantic segmentation. IEEE Access **10**, 134557–134570 (2022)

Obstacle Detection and Enhanced Safety for Self-driving Automobiles (ODESSA)

Tushar Mahendrakar[1], Suhas D. Yadwad[1(✉)], and Ujwala Patil[2]

[1] School of Electrical and Electronics Engineering, KLE Technological University, Hubbali, India
suhas.yadawad65@gmail.com

[2] School of Electronics and Communication Engineering, KLE Technological University, Hubbali, India
ujwalapatil@kletech.ac.in

Abstract. As autonomous driving technology evolves, ensuring car dependability and safety is crucial. The versatile Quanser Car (Q-car) platform provides an ideal testing ground for driverless vehicles. This research focuses on enhancing self-driving car safety by implementing an effective obstacle detection system. The study aims to improve obstacle recognition in self-driving Q-Cars by integrating depth cameras with MATLAB Simulink. Depth cameras offer advantages over yolo v5, providing vital three-dimensional environmental data essential for accurate obstacle detection and distance measurement. The research explores depth camera usage in driverless cars, detailing their integration into the Q-Car platform via Simulink. Additionally, it investigates how depth cameras can enhance safety features, especially collision avoidance. By leveraging depth cameras and MATLAB Simulink, the project aims to significantly boost autonomous vehicle safety and reliability on the Q-car platform, potentially advancing autonomous driving technology and fostering the development of safer self-driving cars.

Keywords: Quanser Car (Q-Car) · MATLAB/Simulink · Depth Camera

1 Introduction

The development of safe and reliable self-driving cars has become a major focus in the automotive industry. With the potential to revolutionize transportation by providing improved efficiency, convenience, and safety, autonomous vehicles are rapidly gaining traction. However, ensuring the safety of selfdriving vehicles remains a paramount challenge. Accurate obstacle detection and timely decision-making are crucial for safe navigation in dynamic environments. Integrating depth cameras and MATLAB Simulink offers a powerful approach to address these challenges and enhance the safety of the self-driving Quanser-Car [Lawan and Wamdeo, 2017]. Depth cameras provide a significant advantage over traditional cameras by capturing 3D information of the surrounding

J. Kakarla et al. (Eds.): CVIP 2024, CCIS 2473, pp. 367–375, 2026.
https://doi.org/10.1007/978-3-031-93688-3_26

environment [Awano, 2020][Arnold et al., 2019]. This real-time 3D data enables: Accurate distance measurement: Depth cameras measure the distance to objects more precisely than conventional cameras, allowing for better collision avoidance manoeuvres [Zaarane et al., 2020]. Enhanced obstacle detection: Depth information facilitates identifying complex obstacles like pedestrians blending into the background or transparent objects, which might be difficult to detect with traditional cameras [Al-Kaff et al., 2017]. The Self-Driving Car Studio's flagship vehicle, QCar, is a scaled-down, open-architecture model car intended for use in academic instruction and research. Numerous sensors are included in its configuration, such as encoders, LIDAR, depth sensor, IMU, and user-expandable IO. An NVIDIA® JetsonTM TX2 supercomputer, which provides remarkable speed and power efficiency, powers the car [Vincke et al., 2021]. The Intel RealSense D400 depth camera mounted on the Q-Car uses Stereo vision to calculate depth. It has three sensors left imager and right imager capture the scene and sends data to depth processor, which calculate depth value and IR projector uses non-visible IR patterns to improve depth value The integration of depth sensors in autonomous vehicles has revolutionized the field of obstacle detection. This enable the vehicle to perceive its surroundings in three dimensions, capturing detailed information about the distance to objects in its environment [Griffin and Corso, 2021]. In this project, we focus on implementing an obstacle detection system for a Q-car, using MATLAB Simulink [Alandkar and Gengaje, 2016] The objectives are to detect an object, control the speed of the Quanser Car, and stop the Q-car when an object is detected within a specified distance. These tasks aim to enhance the autonomous capabilities of the Q-car, ensuring safe and efficient operation in various environments.

2 Proposed Methodology

The suggested model's system overview is displayed in Fig. 1. With its front facing camera, the depth camera offers a real-time feed of the road and its surroundings. The QCar's onboard computer processes the video feed in order to detect and track obstructions. The Q-Car makes safe and wellinformed navigational and safety judgements using the depth camera data. For motor commands, obstacles are identified and distances are measured. Lane tracking aids in keeping the vehicle travelling along the intended route [Wang et al., 2023]. For best system performance, the motor commands are executed in tandem with the directive orders that are acquired. The above model can perform the following tasks:

Avoid collisions: The QCar can accurately measure the distance to obstacles and take evasive maneuvers to avoid collisions.

Maintain a safe distance: The QCar can use the depth camera data to maintain a safe distance from the vehicle ahead.

Trigger emergency braking: The QCar can trigger emergency braking if an imminent collision is detected.

The depth camera provides a live video feed of the road and surrounding objects. This video feed is processed by the QCar's onboard computer to identify

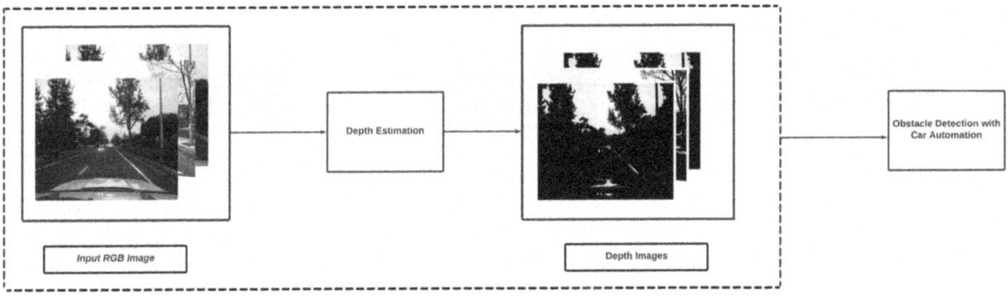

Fig. 1. System Overview

and track obstacles. The QCar's onboard computer is responsible for processing the data from the depth camera and other sensors. It uses this data to make informed decisions about navigation and safety. [Al-Kaff et al., 2017][Zaarane et al., 2020]

2.1 Functional Block Diagram

The functional block diagram in Fig. 2 describes the developed model and the process.

In the first stage, visual data from the surroundings is captured via the Camera Serial Interface (CSI) i.e. RGB Camera along with depth camera is mounted on the Q-car. Maintaining the vehicle's course requires the system to recognise lanes, which is accomplished by processing the visual data that has been gathered. Steering directives are created to manoeuvre the vehicle based on lane detection. In addition to lane detection, the system is also required to record depth data from the Intel RealSense D400 camera mounted on the front bumper of the Q-Car[Vincke et al., 2021], perhaps for determining how far away objects and barriers are. The car can identify things and determine how far away any barriers are from it. In order to modify the vehicle's speed, the system creates speed orders or commands based on the presence of obstacles. The vehicle maintains its present speed if there are no nearby obstacles and the speed is nominal. The model makes a comparison between the detected obstacle distance and the planned stop distance[Zaarane et al., 2020]. The system determines the proper speed and sends throttle commands to maintain or change speed if the stop distance is larger than the obstacle distance. The model instructs the vehicle to stop in order to prevent a collision if an obstacle is identified within the designated stop distance.

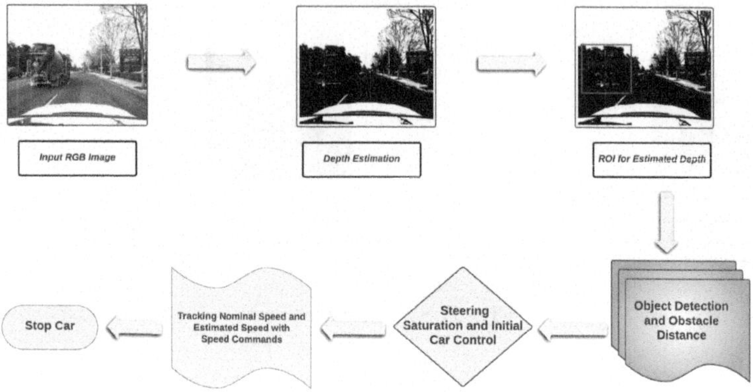

Fig. 2. Block Diagram

2.2 Matlab Simulink Model

A. Lane Detection and Steering Inputs: The first stage in the colour thresholding process is to convert RGB photos to the HSV colour space. A subsystem called HSV Range Selection determines the lowest and highest HSV values in order to isolate a particular colour. Binary picture Creation: The chosen colour regions are highlighted in a binary picture created by the ImageCompare block. Constants are used to apply a rectangular mask on the image, further filtering it. More complex implementations might dynamically modify the mask to enhance performance at speeds more than one metre per second or react to the speed of the vehicle to better estimate lane position[Wang et al., 2023]. Using an Image Find Objects block, the lane locating subsystem looks for blobs that meet a minimum size requirement before classifying them according to size. The steering error is the difference between the centroid of the largest blob and the nominal lane position, which is obtained by the next Matlab function block. The signal outside the subsystem that is utilised to calculate the steering angle is amplified.

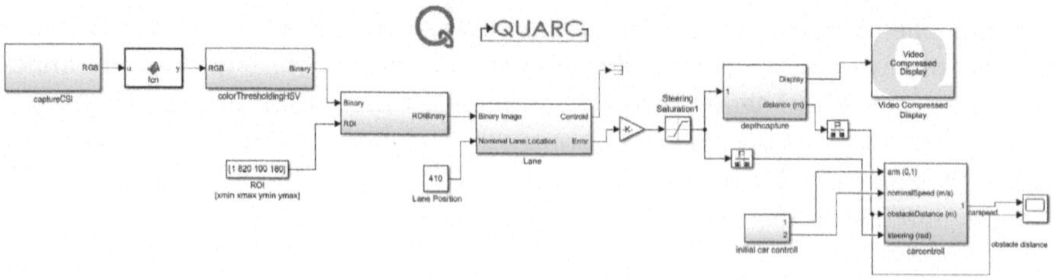

Fig. 3. Simulink Model

B. Obstacle Detection and Distance Estimation: The obstacle detection function extracts a region of interest and a series of points for the border of this region of interest using an input depth image and the desired steering angle. The calculateDistance function receives the depth data for the chosen area. The purpose here is to calculate a distance value based on depth data and specified limits[Sun et al., 2017]. The input taken are depth, minDistance and maxDistance. We find the region of points in the following interval

$$0.05\,m < depth < 2\,m$$

and calculate what the average depth is in the selected region.

$$u_\alpha = depth(depth < maxDistance) \tag{1}$$

$$u = u_\alpha(u_\alpha > minDistance) \tag{2}$$

Equation 1 removes values greater than maxDistance and similarly Eq. 2 removes values less than minDistance. Distance is found by calculating mean of Eq. 2.

$$y = mean(u) \tag{3}$$

C. Speed Control: Based on a commanded nominal distance (m/s) and obstacle distance (m/s), this controller subsystem will modify the system command desired speed. The linear speed command is adjusted so that the QCar slows down until the stop distance is greater than the obstacle distance by using a set stop distance and nominal tracking distance[Zaarane et al., 2020]. Here the input are obstacle distance, stop distance, nominal tracking distance and nominal speed. Output is speed command (*scmd*) in m/s. This speed control takes place in three stages.

- Default speed when no obstacles are present.

$$scmd = nominalspeed \tag{4}$$

- For emergency stop where speed command is set to zero.

$$scmd = 0 \tag{5}$$

- Adaptive Speed Control.

$$scmd = \frac{ns}{(ntd - sd)} * (od - sd) \tag{6}$$

where ns is nominal speed(ns=0.25m/s), ntd is nominal traking distance(ntd=1m), od is obstacle distance and sd is stop distance(sd=0.2m).

D. Speed Control During a Turn: During turning or steering the model reduces the speed so that the car cannot skid. To configure the desiredSpeed (m/s), an enable constant is utilised. Either we can assess the cosine of the steering to the power of eight, or we can pass the linear velocity command directly. Using this backup strategy, the QCar will accelerate in straight stretches of the road and slow down while approaching turns.

E. Speed Estimation: We can obtain counts/s from the motor encoder on the QCar by passing it through four scaling factors. The wheel shaft rotational speed is obtained by passing the motor rotations via a gear ratio in the second scaling term, which also transforms counts/s to rotations/s. The angular speed is multiplied by the wheel radius to obtain an estimate of the logitudinal car speed (m/s) after the third scaling term transforms the shaft speed from rotation/s to rad/s.

$$v = 2 * pi * r * \omega \tag{7}$$

$$v = r * \omega \tag{8}$$

where v is car speed, r ($r = 0.0342$m)is wheel speed and ω is angular speed. Here Eq. 7 in when ω is in rot/s and Eq. 8 is when ω is in rds/s.

F. Throttle Command: The desired throttleCmd(%) signal is produced by a feedforward PI controller and supplied to the QCar's ESC. When comparing the measured and desired speeds of the QCar, the error term is transformed using an integral gain to convert m to % and a proportional gain to convert m/s to %. The arm signal, which is also responsible for activating the motor command, is used to reset the integral in order to prevent integrator windup caused by error accumulation over time. Finally, a feed forward gain is applied to the error term to convert the target speed from m/s to %. When a feedforward gain is used, the controller command is now centred around the feedforward gain's declared target setpoint rather than zero.

3 Results

Figure 4 shows the real time detection of an object. The videoCompressedDisplay Shows the frame of capture depth data with ROI marked in red colour. Similarly Fig. 5 shows that no object is detected. Each pixel in the output of a depth camera has a numerical value assigned to it that indicates its "depth," or distance from the camera. The two extremities of the depth range are usually represented by black and white when these depth values are visualised as different tones of grey.

The spots that are closest to the camera are frequently represented by black as shown in Fig. 4. This is due to the fact that lower numerical values, such as (0,0,0) in an RGB image, are frequently used to represent darkness in images. On the other hand, white frequently indicates the locations that are further away from the camera as shown in Fig. 5. This is due to the fact that higher numerical values (such as 255,255,255 in an RGB image) are frequently used to represent white in images (Table 1).

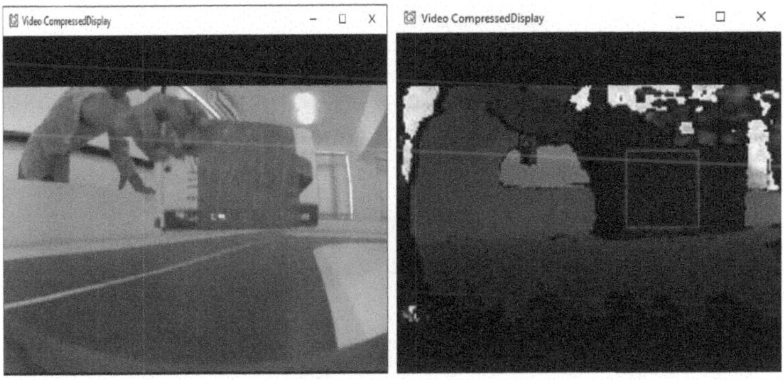

Fig. 4. Obstacle Detection

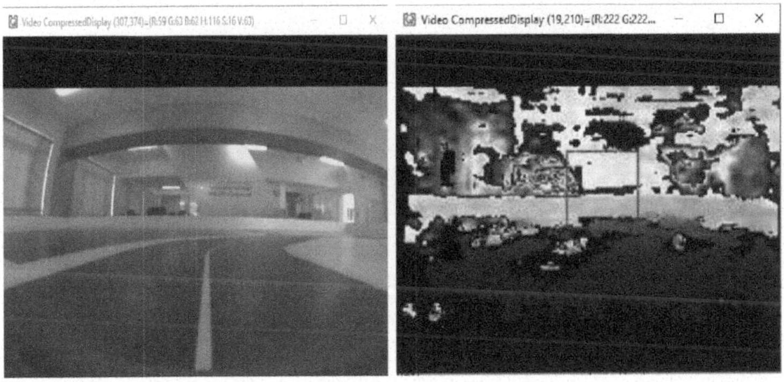

Fig. 5. No Obstacle Detection

The graph depicting the vehicle's speed and object distance as the Q-car gets closer to an item is displayed in Fig. 6. The automobile is initially travelling at a nominal speed of 0.25 m/s. The Q-Car slows down linearly when an object is detected below the nominal tracking distance (2 m) and finally stops when the object is smaller than the stop distance (0.2 m). Figure 6 illustrates the car's behaviour. In Fig. 7, the car's matching throttle response is examined. The throttle reaction or instruction can vary linearly with changes in object distance and is also dependent on that distance. With a throttle instruction of 0%, the Q-Car stops.

Table 1. Comparison Results of Different Methods

Type	mAP_{50-95}	mAP_{50}
yolov5s	37.4	56.8
ODESSA	86.2	87

While evaluating the effectiveness of using RGB images with depth estimation versus implementing yolov5. This comparison aims to demonstrate the advantages of employing depth cameras over relying on yolov5s model.

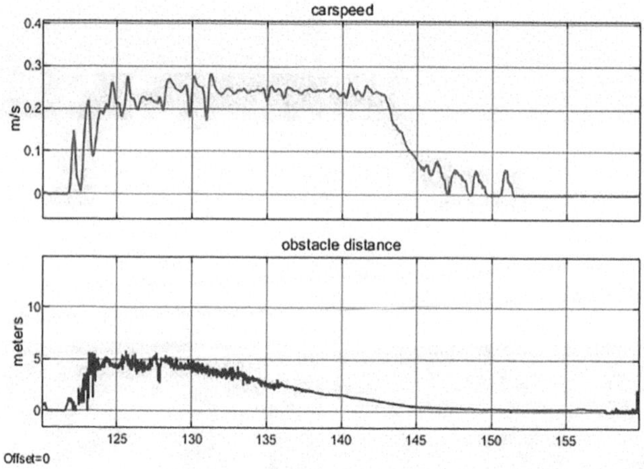

Fig. 6. Comparing Speed and Obstacle distance

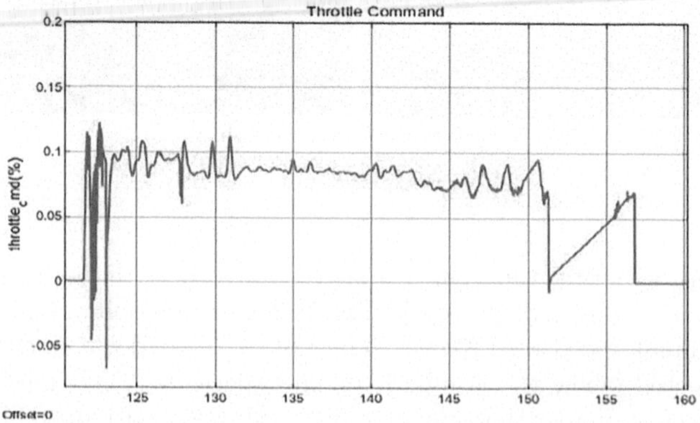

Fig. 7. Throttle response

The Quanser Car(Q-Car) has achieved a accuracy of 87% with a maximum frame rate of 60 fps using the Depth Camera with a Desired Velocity of 0m/s whenever an object is in the track with stop distance.

With respect to the Steering in track with Lane Detection continues to move smooth at 0.25 m/s when an object is not on track within the specified stop distance.

The Quanser Car speed reduces with respect to curvy nature of the track by 0.05m/s depending on the type of the track.

4 Conclusion

With MATLAB-Simulink, the object detection and enhanced safety model is designed and simulated on the Q-Car. The Intel RealSense D400 depth camera is used to detect the object along with measuring the distance. The developed model then gives speed and throttle responses to the Q-car. These responses are plotted. This model generates linearly varying responses and stop the car if distance of the object is less then stop distance. The real time depth capture is also obtained showing the detection model at work. With the use of model-based designing and MATLAB-Simulink software, the entire Object detection and enhanced safety model is simulated and hardware implemented using Quanser car(Q-car).

References

Al-Kaff, A., Garcia, F., Martín Gómez, D., de la Escalera, A., Armingol, J.: Obstacle detection and avoidance system based on monocular camera and size expansion algorithm for uavs. Sensors **17**, 1061 (2017)

Alandkar, L., Gengaje, S.: Study of object detection implementation using matlab (2016)

Arnold, E., Al-Jarrah, O., Dianati, M., Fallah, S., Oxtoby, D., Mouzakitis, A.: A survey on 3d object detection methods for autonomous driving applications. IEEE Trans. Intell. Trans. Syst., 1–14 (2019)

Awano, N.: Approximate depth shape reconstruction for rgb-d images captured from hmds for mixed reality applications. J. Imaging **6**, 11 (2020)

Griffin, B., Corso, J.: Depth from camera motion and object detection (2021)

Lawan, S., Wamdeo, C.: Image recognition using matlab simulink blockset. Inter. J. Comput. Sci. Eng. Appli. **7**, 1–11 (2017)

Sun, C.-C., Wang, Y.-H., Sheu, M.-H.: Fast motion object detection algorithm using complementary depth image on an rgb-d camera. IEEE Sens. J. **17**(17), 5728–5734 (2017)

Vincke, B., Rodriguez Florez, S., Aubert, P.: An open-source scale model platform for teaching autonomous vehicle technologies. Sensors **21**, 3850 (2021)

Wang, Z., Deng, H., Zhang, L.: Obstacle-avoiding path planning and tracking for intelligent vehicles based on kinematic model, pp. 1218–1223 (2023)

Zaarane, A., Slimani, I., Okaishi, W., Issam, A., Hamdoun, A.: Distance measurement system for autonomous vehicles using stereo camera. Array **5**, 100016 (2020)

Lightweight Logarithmic Group Convolution Network with Polarized Attention for Hyperspectral Image Classification

Sobi Jain, Vinod Kumar(✉), Ravi Shankar Singh, Ishika Todwal, and Kenny Patel

Indian institute of Technology (B.H.U.), Varanasi 221005, India
sobi3jain1@gmail.com, {vinodkumar.rs.cse18,ravi.cse}@iitbhu.ac.in, {ishika.todwal.cse19,pkenny.mukeshbhai.cse19}@itbhu.ac.in

Abstract. Hyperspectral image (HSI) classification is a crucial task in various remote sensing applications. Deep learning, particularly Convolutional Neural Networks (CNNs), have emerged as powerful tools for extracting complex features from HSI's high-dimensional data. However, two significant challenges hinder accurate classification: limited labelled training data and reliance solely on spectral information. This paper proposes a novel logarithmic group 3D-CNN architecture specifically designed for HSI classification. Our key contribution is a unique multi-scale spectral-spatial feature extraction approach. Utilizing multi-kernel convolutions arranged in a pyramidal structure, we capture spectral and spatial features at various scales, ensuring comprehensive feature representation. Furthermore, we introduce a novel strategy as a part of spectral-spatial feature extraction by leveraging logarithmic channel division within standard convolutions. This innovative approach significantly reduces the number of model parameters and FLOPs, leading to a lightweight and efficient network. To validate the effectiveness of our proposed architecture, extensive evaluations are conducted on benchmark datasets with varying train-test splits. The results demonstrate that our model performs competitive classification compared to existing state-of-the-art methods. This accomplishment highlights the potential of the logarithmic group 3D-CNN architecture for accurate and efficient HSI classification, particularly in scenarios with limited training data.

Keywords: Logarithmic group convolution neural network · multiscale spectral-spatial feature extraction · polarized attention · hyperspectral image

1 Introduction

Remote sensing technology utilizes specialized sensors to capture hyperspectral images (HSI). These images are distinguished by their high dimensionality, con-

Indian Institute of Technology (BHU) Varanasi.

J. Kakarla et al. (Eds.): CVIP 2024, CCIS 2473, pp. 376–390, 2026.
https://doi.org/10.1007/978-3-031-93688-3_27

taining a multitude of closely spaced, narrow spectral bands that range from the visible spectrum to the short-wave infrared region. The ability of remote sensing sensors to capture data across a wider range of spectral bands (enhanced spectral resolution) has positioned hyperspectral imaging as a powerful technique for generating high-fidelity land-cover data. Moreover, HSI offers a wealth of spectral information compared to their panchromatic and multi-spectral counterparts, enabling finer-grained discrimination of materials and objects within the scene [1]. However, this rich spectral dimensionality presents significant processing challenges due to the need for labeled training data [2]. Feature extraction techniques have emerged as a crucial strategy to address this limitation [3].

In the current scenario, deep learning, especially convolutional neural networks (CNNs), has shown significant potential in extracting features for HSI classification [4,5]. The strategic implementation of spatial weight sharing in CNN's convolutional kernel reduces computational complexity, and integrating activation functions introduces non-linearity to the network. Despite achieving superior results compared to traditional methods, 1-D CNNs are confined to extracting spectral signatures from HSI, with limited utilization of spatial information. In contrast to spectral models, spatial CNNs leverage 2-D maps as input. This approach prioritizes capturing spatial relationships within the hyperspectral image (HSI) data [6]. While 2-D CNNs demonstrably improve classification accuracy by effectively capturing spatial information, this gain comes at the cost of discarding a substantial amount of spectral information. A pixel-wise spectral-spatial CNN was applied to address this challenge, allowing the combined extraction of spectral and spatial features. In contrast to the 2-D CNN model, a 3-D CNN model can capture the combined spatial-spectral features at the same time [7]. Kumar et al. [8] proposed a hybrid 3-D and 2-D CNN model (MDCNN), utilizing 3-D CNN for shallow combined spatial-spectral features and 2-D CNN for abstract spatial texture features.

However, all the above methods tend to overfit under a limited number of labeled training samples. To solve this problem, Liu et al. [9] have proposed the RGCSA module, which involves splitting the input channels into eight groups and passing each group through an RGCA module. Subsequently, the channel groups are further divided into subgroups of eight. Conversely, Wu et al. [10] have introduced the SG-Conv (shuffled group convolution) unit. This model comprises four branches, with half performing conventional convolution and the other half consisting of three convolution layers with different dilation rates. Furthermore, Wang et al. [11] introduce spatial separable convolutional for parameter reduction. It uses different kernel sizes for the vertical and horizontal dimensions, reducing the number of parameters in a CNN and improving generalization performance by avoiding overfitting compared to a standard CNN. Additionally, Gao et al. [12] came up with a unique idea to employ two 2D kernels along X-L and Y-L features together (where (X, Y) denote the spatial dimensions and L is the spectral dimension) instead of a 3D kernel.

This paper explores a novel approach to optimizing network performance while significantly reducing its computational burden. We introduce a pioneering

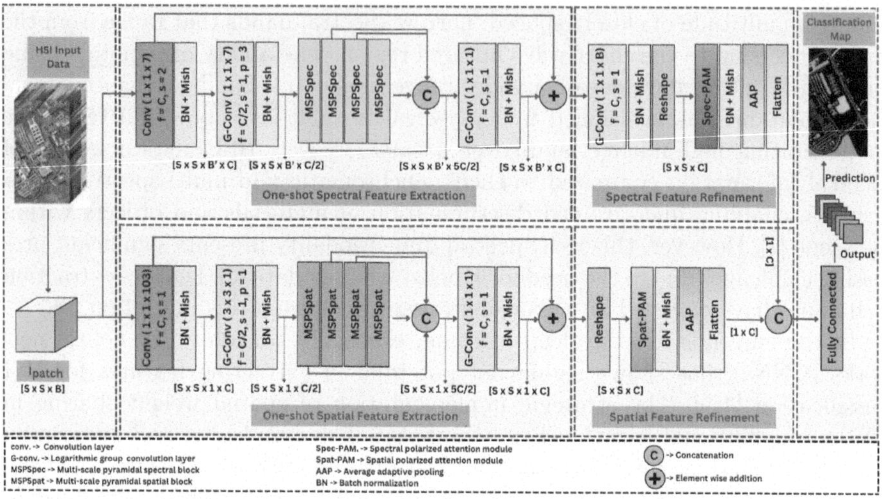

Fig. 1. LLGCN: Illustration of proposed lightweight deep network, which includes: (a) one-shot spectral feature extraction (OSpecFE), (b) one-shot spatial feature extraction (OSpatFE), (c) Spectral polarized attention module (SpecPAM), (d) Spatial polarized attention module (SpatPAM), and (e) a classifier.

pyramidal group 3D-CNN architecture, termed LLGCN (Lightweight Logarithmic Grouped Convolution Network), tailored for HSI classification, focusing on enhancing spectral-spatial feature extraction. In contrast to conventional CNN methodologies, which frequently utilize dimensionality reduction techniques such as PCA [7], our proposed model adopts a multi-scale feature extraction strategy, preserving the intricate spectral details inherent in HSI data. At the core of our architecture are two innovative feature extraction blocks: the multi-scale pyramidal spectral (MSPSpec) and the multi-scale pyramidal spatial (MSPSpat) blocks. These incorporate a custom-designed grouped 3D convolution layer, partitioning input channels using logarithmic distribution $(n/2, n/4, n/8 \ldots)$, reducing model complexity and learnable parameters. Additionally, we introduce two self-attention blocks: the spectral polarized attention module (SpecPAM) and the spatial polarized attention module (SpatPAM), which selectively highlight informative spectral and spatial features. Our contributions to this work are threefold:

1. Building upon the concept of multi-kernel pyramidal convolution, we propose the MSPSpec and MSPSpat blocks for spectral and spatial multi-scale feature extraction. Pyramidal convolution allows feature extraction at multiple scales within the same layer, enabling the network to capture local and global information efficiently. This approach reduces the computational burden of using multiple layers for feature extraction.
2. Our architecture harnesses the power of group convolutions with a logarithmic division of channels, a strategy that revolutionizes spectral and spatial feature

extraction. The logarithmic filter grouping, designed around the filters' non-linear characteristics, reduces parameters in convolution layers and enhances classification performance. This breakthrough approach outperforms uniform filter grouping, inspiring new possibilities for efficient and high-performing network architectures.

3. We have utilized polarized self-attention for spectral and spatial information in parallel. This technique leverages the characteristics of the input feature map to selectively focus on crucial segments, offering a compelling enhancement to standard multi-scale convolutional blocks, especially when operating on high-resolution internal representations.

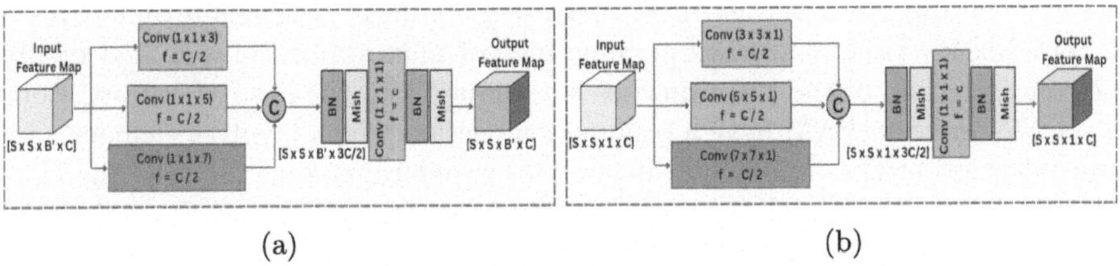

Fig. 2. Illustration of the pyramidal convolution modules(a) MSPSpec module for spectral feature extraction (b)MSPSpat module for spatial feature extraction

The structure of this paper unfolds as follows: Sect. 2 delves into the intricacies of the proposed method. Section 3 showcases the experimental evaluation and analysis that shows the method's efficacy. Finally, Sect. 4 offers concluding remarks that encapsulate the essence of the paper.

2 Proposed Method

This section introduces a novel architecture named LLGCN for HSI classification based on multi-scale features and logarithmic channel group division in 3D convolution. Illustrated in Fig. 1, our architecture comprises five modules: (a) one-shot spectral feature extraction (OSpecFE) module utilizing the spectral pyramidal block and One-shot dense network for spectral feature extraction, (b) one-shot spatial feature extraction (OSpatFE) module utilizing the spatial pyramidal block and One-shot dense network for spatial feature extraction, (c) Spectral polarized attention module (SpecPAM) for refining spectral features, (d) Spatial polarized attention module (SpatPAM) for refining spatial features, and (e) a classifier.

Firstly, we fed HSI data $\mathfrak{S} \in \mathbb{R}^{[H \times W \times B]}$, where H, W, and B are height, width, and the number of bands respectively. The model then extracts input patches, $I_{\text{patch}} \in \mathbb{R}^{[S \times S \times B]}$, where S denotes the spatial size and B denotes the spectral size. These patches are simultaneously fed into the OSpecFE and OSpatFE modules to extract fine-grained multiscale spectral and spatial features using pyramidal convolution. The OSpecFE module comprises a convolution block, a logarithmic grouped convolution block (LGCB), and four MSPSpec blocks. These blocks utilize a one-shot dense network strategy to preserve low-level and hierarchical features, primarily focusing on spectral features. Similarly, the OSpatFE module includes a convolution block, an LGCB, and four MSPSpat blocks, which employ a one-shot dense network strategy to retain low-level and hierarchical features, emphasizing spatial features.

Next, we feed OSpecFE output to the SpecPAM for the feature refinement of the spectral hierarchical and low-level features. SpecPAM contains a dual branch of 2D CNN followed by a series of 2D CNN, normalization and Mish [13] activation layers applied on their concatenation. Parallely, the output obtained fromOSpatFE is fed to the SpatPAM for the feature refinement of the spatial hierarchical and low-level features. SpatPAM similarly contains a dual branch of 2D CNN layers, but average pooling and softmax applied on one and finally the concatenation of the two branches is reshaped into the desired output. Both SpecPAM and SpatPAM have a residual connection which involves element wise multiplication of the input and output tensor before feeding them to the classifier. Finally, the refined feature outputs of the SpecPAM and SpecPAM are concatenated and passed to the classifier.

2.1 Logarithmic Group Convolution Layer

CNNs shine in feature extraction thanks to their multitude of filters, resulting in a vast number of learnable parameters. However, the scarcity of labeled training data for HSI compared to the large number of trainable parameters contributes to overfitting in CNN-based models. To address this, Li et al. [14] propose a convolutional neural network; inspired by his work, we propose a custom 3D CNN layer that uses logarithmic filter grouping that can capture the non-linearity of filter distribution in CNNs. Equation 1 shows the number of parameters used in a 3D CNN layer

$$F_{CNN} = K_v * C_{in} * C_{out} + C_{out} \tag{1}$$

where, K_v, C_{in} and C_{out} are the kernel volume, input channel number and output channel number respectively.

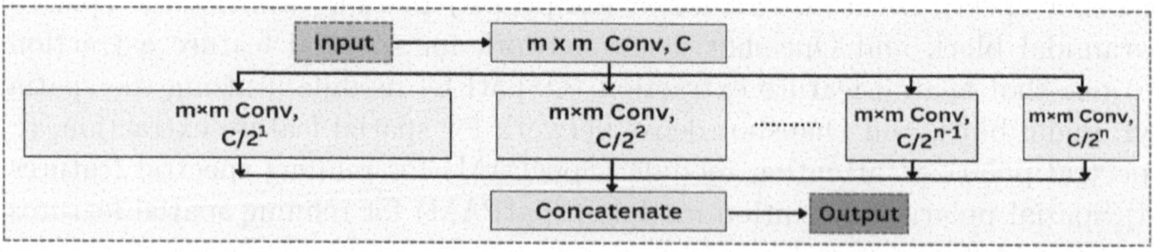

Fig. 3. The logarithmic grouped CNN layer (LG-CNN)

Now considering that the channels are being divided into g groups as a part of the logarithmic grouped convolution, then the size of groups will be $n/2$, $n/4$

... $n/2^{g-1}$ and $n/2^{g-1}$. Equation 2 shows the number of parameters used in the custom logarithmic group CNN (LG_CNN) layer:

$$P_{LG\_CNN} = K_v * (C_{in}/g) * C_{out} + C_{out} \tag{2}$$

The delta between the parameters of the two approaches of performing convolution can be seen in Eq. 3.

$$\Delta_{P_{CNN}-P_{LG\_CNN}} = (g - 1/g)K_v * C_{in} * C_{out} \tag{3}$$

$\Delta_{P_{CNN}-P_{LG\_CNN}} = \frac{2}{3}K_v * C_{in} * C_{out}$ for our model considering we took $g = 3$. Thus, our approach reduces the number of parameters to one-third for each 3D convolution performed in the model. An illustration of the same is depicted in Fig. 3. Similar calculations can prove the reduction in FLOPS too.

2.2 One-Shot Spectral Feature Extraction Module

Our proposed network architecture incorporates a feature extraction approach inspired by the success of ResNet and DenseNet architectures. This approach utilizes one-shot dense blocks for both spectral and spatial feature extraction. In contrast to conventional dense blocks, which concatenate feature maps at every layer, our one-shot blocks streamline this process by performing a single concatenation. This ensures that each block has same amount of input and output feature maps. Moreover, we incorporate skip connections within the one-shot dense blocks, facilitating the extraction of deeper and more holistic features from the hyperspectral image (HSI).

In order to capture both spatial context and spectral information, the network utilizes 3D patch cubes as input. Randomly sampled from the HSI dataset, these cubes are($S \times S \times B$) in dimension, encompassing the central pixel and its surrounding spatial and spectral neighborhood. We start with feeding the data into a 3-D convolution layer with batch normalization (BN) and Mish activation to reduce the dimensionality along the channels. This layer employs a kernel size of $(1 \times 1 \times 7)$, C filters, and a stride of $(1 \times 1 \times 2)$ without padding. Consequently, the resulting feature maps have a size of $(S \times S \times ((B - 7)/2 + 1) \times C)$. Before proceeding to the one-shot segment, another LGCN layer is applied with kernel size $(1 \times 1 \times 7)$ and padding $(0, 0, 3)$ which reduces the number of channels by half and the feature map size becomes $(S \times S \times B', C/2)$.

The spectral extraction block comprises two integral sections: a one-shot connected segment comprising of four MSPSpec blocks and a residual connected segment. In the one-shot connected segment, feature maps are generated and concatenated along the channel dimension. The residual connected section employs a $(1 \times 1 \times 1)$ kernel in the LGCN layer to reduce the channels from $5C/2$ to C. This reduced representation is then element-wise added to the final output of the one-shot connected section resulting in $I_{spec} \in \mathbb{R}^{(S \times S \times B' \times C)}$ as the output.

Multi-scale Pyramidal Spectral Block: The one-shot network designed above is applied to modules called MSPSpec. What sets MSPSpec apart is its unique approach of explicitly separating the kernels into channel-wise components. The multi-scale kernels vary solely along the channel dimension, are a key feature of MSPSpec. This strategy effectively reduces the network's computational complexity. Furthermore, unlike traditional PyConv which segments the input data, MSPSpec leverages the entire input directly, preserving the consistency of the feature maps.

A detailed illustration of the MSPSpec block is provided in Fig. 2 (a). The channel-wise block utilizes three convolutional layers with kernels of size $(1 \times 1 \times 3)$, $(1 \times 1 \times 5)$, and $(1 \times 1 \times 7)$ to harvest multi-scale features from the spectral dimension. These features are then concatenated to achieve feature fusion. Batch Normalization (BN) and Mish activation are subsequently applied to enhance network stability and introduce non-linearity. Finally, an additional LGCN layer with BN and Mish serve to reduce the dimensionality of feature maps, generating the final output.

2.3 One-Shot Spatial Feature Extraction Module

We start with feeding the data into a 3-D convolution layer with batch normalization (BN) and Mish activation to reduce the dimensions of spectral features. This layer employs a kernel of size $(1 \times 1 \times B)$ and C filters. Consequently, the resulting output is of size $(S \times S \times 1 \times C)$. Before proceeding to the one-shot segment, the LGCN layer is applied with kernel size $(3 \times 3 \times 1)$, which reduces the number of channels by half, and the feature map size becomes $(S \times S \times 1 \times C/2)$. The spatial feature extraction block works analogous to the spectral feature extraction block but with MSPSpat block instead of the MSPSpec block and the resulting feature map is $I_{spat} \in \mathbb{R}^{(S \times S \times 1 \times C)}$.

Multi-scale Pyramidal Spatial Block: The one-shot network designed previously has been implemented on modules termed MSPSpat. An in-depth depiction of the MSPSpat block is presented in Fig. 2 (b). The spatial-wise pyramidal convolutional block operates analogously to MSPSpec. The only difference from MSPSpec being the kernel sizes in the pyramid block which are $(7 \times 7 \times 1)$, $(5 \times 5 \times 1)$ and $(3 \times 3 \times 1)$.

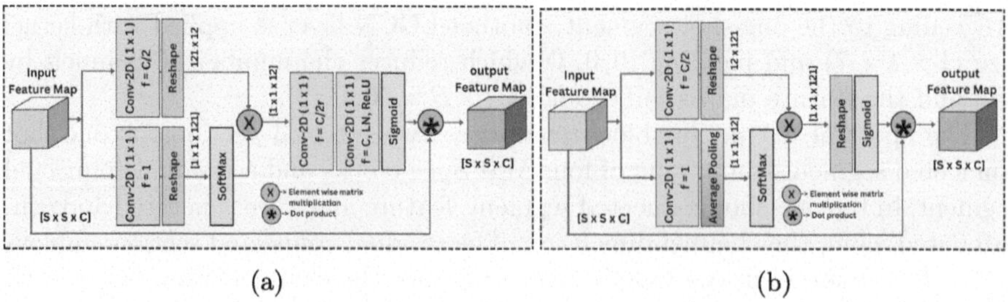

Fig. 4. Illustration of the polarized attention modules(a) Spec-PAM module for spectral features (b)Spat-PAM module for spatial features

2.4 Spectral and Spatial Polarized Attention Module

After the intricate process of spectral and spatial feature extraction, our feature maps have accumulated a rich array of spectral and spatial information. However, it is crucial to recognize that different channels and positions within these feature maps may exert varying influences on classification outcomes. To address this variability, as illustrated in Fig. 4, we have introduced the spectral feature refinement module containing SpecPAM and the spatial feature refinement module containing SpatPAM. These modules serve the dual purpose of amplifying valuable features while dampening non-valuable ones. The input size for both blocks is I_{spec} and I_{spat}. **Spectral feature refinement module** The input I_{spec} undergoes a series of transformations in the spectral feature refinement module given by the Eq. 5

The feature maps, O_{spec_1}, undergo a spectral polarized attention operation using the spec-PAM module as illustrated in Fig. 4 (a)). This module preserves high internal resolution during channel attention calculations by collapsing input tensors along spectral dimensions and introducing non-linearity, aligning the output distribution with characteristics observed in fine-grained regression problems. It consists of a dual-branch architecture, with one branch reducing channels to half and the other to one. Outputs from both branches undergo element-wise matrix multiplication, followed by serial processing through two 2D CNN layers, reducing channels first to $C/2r$ and then to C. The resulting output, O_{spec_2}, is obtained through Sigmoid activation, representing the dot product of the input feature map and the output from the activation layer. Subsequently, the feature maps undergo further operations described in Eq. 4.

$$O_{spec_2} = \mathcal{F}(AvgP(\mathcal{M}h(BN(O_{spec_1})))) \tag{4}$$

where, BN is batch normalisation, $\mathcal{M}h$ is the Mish activation function, $AvgP$ is adaptive average pooling and $\mathcal{F}$ is the flatten layer.

Spatial Feature Refinement Module. The input I_{spat} undergoes a series of transformations in the spectral feature refinement module. Firstly, I_{spat} as input data to a reshape operation is performed to obtain an output O_{spat_1}, of size (S x S x C). The refined feature maps are subjected to a Spat-PAM module, which implements a spatial polarized attention operation, as illustrated in Fig. 4 (b).

$$O_{spec_1}(i,j,k) = \mathcal{R}e(\mathcal{M}h(BN(I_{spec} \circledast K_1(i,j,k)))) \tag{5}$$

where, O_{spec_1} is obtained feature map at i^{th}, j^{th} and k^{th} position. $\circledast$ represents LGCN with kernel K_1, pixel position $(i \times j \times k)$, BN is batch normalisation layer, $\mathcal{R}e$ is reshape and $\mathcal{M}h$ is the Mish activation function.

This module serves the same advantages as SpecPAM but along the spatial dimensions. The module comprises of a dual branch architecture, each branch consisting of a 2D convolution layer. Both the branches reduce the channels to half. One of the branches is subjected to average pooling while the other to reshape. The outputs from both these branches are subjected to element wise matrix multiplication. Sigmoid activation is applied on the resulting output post reshaping. The final output of the module, O_{spat_2} is returned as the dot product of input feature map and output received from the activation layer. Following Spat-PAM, the resulting feature maps undergo a series of operations given in Eq. 6

$$O_{spat_2} = \mathcal{F}(AvgP(\mathcal{M}h(BN(O_{spat_1})))) \tag{6}$$

where, BN is batch normalisation, $\mathcal{M}h$ is the Mish activation function, $AvgP$ is adaptive average pooling and $\mathcal{F}$ is the flatten layer.

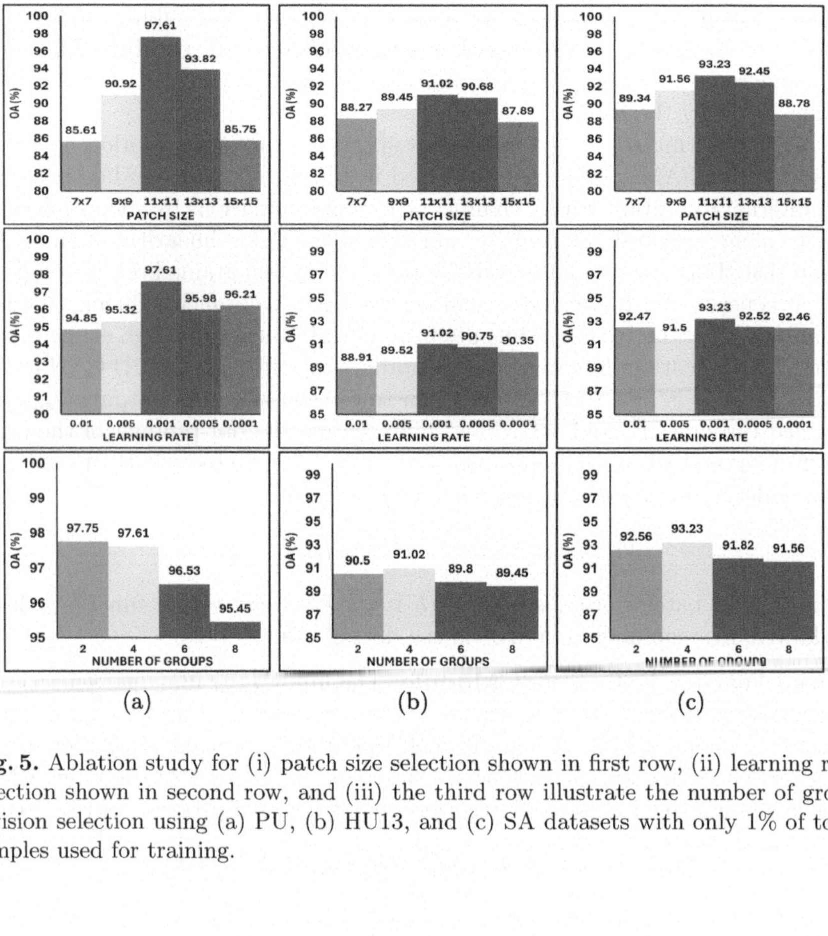

Fig. 5. Ablation study for (i) patch size selection shown in first row, (ii) learning rate selection shown in second row, and (iii) the third row illustrate the number of group division selection using (a) PU, (b) HU13, and (c) SA datasets with only 1% of total samples used for training.

2.5 Feature Fusion and Classification

In order to leverage the complementary information inherent in the enhanced features, we adopt a channel-wise fusion approach, concatenating output feature maps from spectral and spatial modules for a comprehensive representation. These joined maps then enter a linear layer for final classification. Notably, we omit the SoftMax layer due to PyTorch's cross-entropy loss function, simplifying the network architecture and reducing computational overhead.

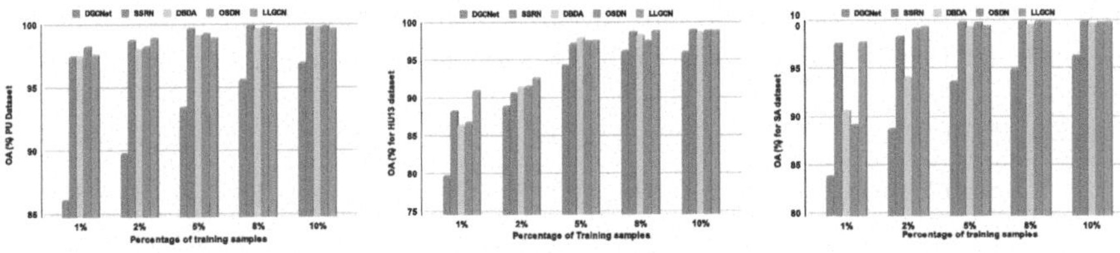

(a) (b) (c)

Fig. 6. Overall accuracy at 1%, 2%, 5%, 8% and 10% train splits.

3 Experimental Results and Analysis

3.1 Datasets

PU (University of Pavia). It is acquired by the ROSIS sensor flown over the University of Pavia campus, with a total of 42,776 samples. It boasts a spatial resolution of 1.3 m per pixel over region of 610×340 pixels. Each pixel comprises of 115 spectral bands spanning the wavelength range of 430 nm to 860 nm. However, to mitigate the impact of noisy spectral information, 12 bands were excluded, resulting in a final set of 103 bands.

HU13 (Houston 2013). It was collected in 2012 over the neighboring area of the University of Houston campus along with the campus. It was released in 2013 as a part of the IEEE GRSS DFC. This dataset consists on 7 classes and has a spatial dimension of 210×954, with 48 spectral bands.

SA (Salinas). It is acquired by the AVIRIS sensor over Salinas Valley region in California and boasts spatial dimensions of 512×217 pixels with a ground resolution of 3.7 m. It comprises 224 spectral bands spanning the wavelength range of 400 to 2500 nm. It provides 16 distinct land-cover types distributed across 54,129 labeled samples.

3.2 Experiments

Parameters. The training process used an initial learning rate of 0.001 and a batch size of 256 samples. Each experiment ran for 200 epochs and iterated ten times. These runs' mean and standard deviation were recorded as the final result. Early stopping was employed to prevent overfitting, halting training if validation accuracy declined for 20 consecutive epochs. This strategy ensures convergence and avoids overfitting.

Performance Comparison. We compare the proposed method with DGC-Net [15], a state-of-the-art model SSRN [16], and two DL models DBDA [17], OSDN [18]. DGCNet dynamically selects the most informative input channels, reducing redundancy and enhancing efficiency for resource-constrained devices. Meanwhile, SSRN addresses declining accuracy in HSI classification with residual blocks and identity connections between convolutional layers. Furthermore,

Table 1. Quantitative performance of various classification methods in terms of OA, AA, and κ, for the PU dataset with Only 1% samples for training.

Classes	DGCNet	SSRN	DBDA	OSDN	LLGCN
1	84.02 ± 0.01	94.94 ± 0.01	97.75 ± 0.01	96.24 ± 0.13	94.14 ± 0.07
2	92.47 ± 0.02	99.29 ± 0.01	99.64 ± 0.01	99.47 ± 0.17	98.88 ± 0.01
3	69.81 ± 0.07	91.44 ± 0.03	98.14 ± 0.01	99.66 ± 0.07	99.82 ± 0.02
4	92.08 ± 0.02	98.99 ± 0.01	98.32 ± 0.01	98.76 ± 0.03	98.20 ± 0.01
5	94.63 ± 0.01	99.47 ± 0.01	98.43 ± 0.01	94.34 ± 2.51	93.94 ± 0.04
6	77.20 ± 0.03	98.49 ± 0.01	99.89 ± 0.01	99.89 ± 0.02	99.24 ± 0.62
7	72.62 ± 0.09	96.87 ± 0.01	100.00 ± 0.00	100 ± 0.00	99.90 ± 0.14
8	71.38 ± 0.02	96.51 ± 0.01	84.85 ± 0.12	93.20 ± 2.21	92.85 ± 0.08
9	98.71 ± 0.01	99.89 ± 0.01	99.61 ± 0.01	99.51 ± 0.02	99.67 ± 0.28
OA(%)	86.13± 0.01	97.49 ± 0.01	97.51 ± 0.01	**98.23 ± 0.23**	97.61 ± 1.56
AA(%)	83.66 ± 0.01	97.32 ± 0.02	97.40 ± 0.01	**97.89 ± 0.01**	97.44 ± 1.83
Kappa	81.44 ± 0.01	97.07 ± 0.01	96.69 ± 0.03	**97.65 ± 0.31**	97.30 ± 2.09
PMs(K)	1046.30	216.54	202.77	49.92	**22.37**
G-FPs	60.19	61.63	51.25	26.28	**11.24**
MMACs	29.67	30.40	25.31	12.88	**5.02**

inspired by DenseNet and 3D-CNN, DBDA uses separate spectral and spatial branches for feature extraction. Finally, OSDN addresses HSI's rich information using separate spectral and spatial features branches. It employs a unique polarized attention mechanism to extract high-quality features efficiently while maintaining model complexity.

3.3 Ablation Studies

Patch Size Selection: To determine the optimal patch size for our model, a series of experiments were conducted utilizing 1% of the SV dataset. Patch sizes in the range [7×7, 9×9, 11×11, 13×13, 15×15] were evaluated. The best results are obtained for the patch size of 11×11 as seen in Fig. 5. Consequently, this patch size was adopted for all subsequent experiments within this study.

Learning Rate Selection: To comprehensively evaluate the model's robustness with different learning rates, we test several values: 0.01, 0.005, 0.001, 0.0005, and 0.0001. The learning rate is crucial for model convergence; a high learning rate can cause the model to overshoot the optimal solution, while a meager rate can result in excessively slow convergence. Therefore, selecting an appropriate learning rate is essential. Our model performs optimally with a learning rate 0.001, as illustrated in Fig. 5.

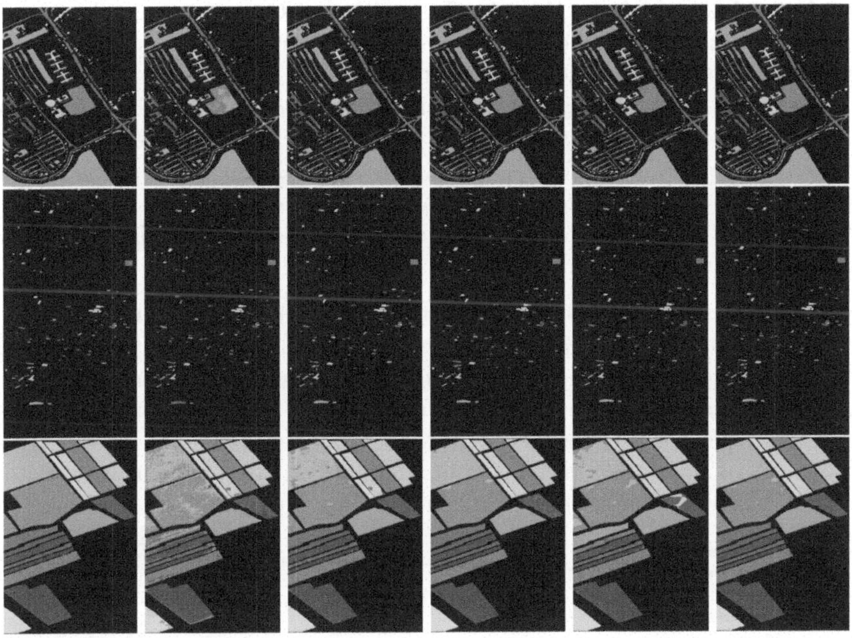
(a) (b) (c) (d) (e) (f)

Fig. 7. Classification results on (i) PU, (ii) HU13 and, (iii) SA, where is (a) Ground truth, and rest are classification maps of (b) DGCNet, (c) SSRN, (d) DBDA, (e) OSDN and (f) LLGCN

Table 2. Quantitative performance of various classification methods in terms of OA, AA, and κ, for the HU13 dataset with Only 1% samples for training.

Classes	DGCNet	SSRN	DBDA	OSDN	LLGCN
1	96.37 ± 1.80	99.21 ± 0.45	95.94 ± 4.06	95.94 ± 4.06	90.88 ± 0.06
2	84.91 ± 10.57	78.59 ± 16.11	91.58 ± 8.42	93.02 ± 5.86	96.72 ± 1.92
3	72.15 ± 18.69	95.56 ± 4.44	77.93 ± 16.56	79.96 ± 20.03	100.00 ± 0.00
4	80.37 ± 7.46	95.88 ± 4.12	90.03 ± 3.48	100.00 ± 0.00	100.00 ± 0.00
5	87.65 ± 1.77	98.85 ± 0.82	88.15 ± 5.04	83.35 ± 2.17	91.79 ± 0.11
6	76.35 ± 0.32	92.85 ± 4.07	98.45 ± 1.55	96.31 ± 0.45	95.88 ± 0.92
7	76.36 ± 8.06	80.44 ± 15.07	81.68 ± 9.11	82.81 ± 15.32	75.74 ± 0.74
OA(%)	79.77 ± 4.89	88.35 ± 1.18	86.51 ± 2.98	86.79 ± 1.05	**91.02 ± 0.56**
AA(%)	82.02 ± 4.13	91.63 ± 2.01	89.11 ± 2.68	90.19 ± 1.17	**93.01 ± 0.35**
Kappa	76.34 ± 5.69	86.35 ± 1.37	84.26 ± 3.47	84.55 ± 1.21	**89.48 ± 0.66**
PMs(K)	1045.10	130.47	104.01	32.38	**20.19**
G-FPs	27.78	27.58	18.06	11.64	**5.21**
MMACs	13.69	13.60	8.89	5.70	**2.47**

Number of Group Selection for Logarithmic Convolution: To comprehensively evaluate the model's robustness with different numbers of groups for logarithmic group convolution, we have tested 2, 3, 4, and 5 values. The number of groups plays a crucial role in balancing the reduction of model parameters with overall accuracy. A higher number of groups reduces parameters more but also lowers accuracy, while fewer groups are less effective in parameter reduction. We found that the three groups offer the best balance, as shown in Fig. 5, significantly decreasing non-trainable parameters while achieving higher accuracy than the two groups.

Sample Selection. The model's robustness was further evaluated using various training split ratios (1%, 2%, 5%, 8%, and 10%) as illustrated in Fig. 6. LLGCN demonstrates competitive performance across these splits, even surpassing alternative methods in specific scenarios. For instance, LLGCN exhibits superior performance on the PU dataset with a 2% training split, and on the HU13 dataset with 1%, 2%, 8% training splits. Similarly, it outperforms competitors on the SA dataset with 2% and 8% training splits. These findings emphasize the generalizability of LLGCN, even under conditions of limited labeled data.

3.4 Results

Running Platform and Evaluation Metrics. The experimental framework leverages Python 3.8.3 and PyTorch (version 2.2.1+cu121). The computations were executed on the Google Colab Pro platform, utilizing a GPU at runtime with a memory limit of 40 GB. To enhance the obtained results, five independent runs were performed for each experiment and report the average of those.

Table 1 and Fig. 7 demonstrates that LLGCN achieves performance on the PU dataset comparable to OSDN, the most accurate method. However, the crucial distinction lies in the substantial reduction of parameters, FLOPs (Floating-Point Operations), and MACs (Multiply-Accumulate Operations) by LLGCN. Specifically, LLGCN achieves reductions of 55.18%, 57.23%, and 58.69%, respectively. This accomplishment underscores the successful development of a lightweight model that maintains competitive performance.

Table 2 and Fig. 7 highlights the dominance of LLGCN on the HU13 dataset. LLGCN not only emerges as the most lightweight model but also surpasses alternative methods in terms of overall accuracy. Compared to DGCNet, SSRN, DBDA, and OSDN, LLGCN exhibits improvements of 11.25%, 2.67%, 4.51%, and 4.23%, respectively, in overall accuracy.

Table 3 and Fig. 7 reveals that LLGCN achieves comparable performance with OSDN in terms of Overall Accuracy (OA), exhibiting a minimal decrease of only 0.39%. However, LLGCN demonstrates superiority in terms of Average Accuracy (AA). Notably, LLGCN achieves significant reductions in computational complexity, diminishing the number of parameters, FLOPs, and MACs by 51.7%, 58%, and 59.5%, respectively.

Table 3. Quantitative performance of various classification methods in terms of OA, AA, and κ, for the SA dataset with Only 1% samples for training.

Classes	DGCNet	SSRN	DBDA	OSDN	LLGCN
1	92.26 ± 2.19	98.14 ± 1.86	100.00 ± 0.00	100.00 ± 0.00	100.00 ± 0.00
2	89.24 ± 8.38	100.00 ± 0.00	97.45 ± 0.43	99.86 ± 0.14	100.00 ± 0.00
3	90.05 ± 6.11	93.60 ± 4.51	98.70 ± 0.14	98.74 ± 0.26	99.84 ± 0.02
4	98.57 ± 0.32	97.80 ± 0.67	93.79 ± 1.79	97.65 ± 1.46	99.03 ± 1.20
5	96.10 ± 3.06	96.76 ± 0.78	91.35 ± 8.03	85.73 ± 6.81	80.86 ± 0.24
6	95.46 ± 0.79	97.91 ± 0.06	100.00 ± 0.00	99.35 ± 0.62	99.97 ± 1.4
7	90.70 ± 0.26	100.00 ± 0.00	97.39 ± 1.00	97.84 ± 0.07	100.00 ± 0.00
8	72.99 ± 4.34	93.88 ± 1.67	72.04 ± 2.42	91.41 ± 6.75	81.98 ± 0.46
9	88.86 ± 1.09	97.36 ± 0.61	96.95 ± 2.56	95.78 ± 3.21	98.14 ± 0.03
10	80.77 ± 0.93	84.76 ± 11.13	84.87 ± 13.29	83.55 ± 16.29	93.56 ± 0.2
11	87.96 ± 0.86	98.69 ± 1.31	49.43 ± 49.43	100.00 ± 0.00	100.00 ± 0.00
12	95.92 ± 2.52	94.59 ± 5.35	98.34 ± 1.66	94.45 ± 0.23	95.68 ± 0.1
13	98.18 ± 1.82	98.91 ± 1.09	100.00 ± 0.00	100.00 ± 0.00	95.07 ± 0.01
14	89.13 ± 2.72	98.85 ± 0.14	91.39 ± 7.65	94.40 ± 1.41	100.00 ± 0.00
15	70.25 ± 2.49	72.39 ± 1.52	85.71 ± 5.92	86.65 ± 3.30	87.82 ± 0.24
16	85.99 ± 0.91	96.54 ± 1.46	100.00 ± 0.00	100.00 ± 0.00	100.00 ± 0.00
OA(%)	83.92 ± 0.20	91.59 ± 4.79	88.50 ± 3.16	**93.62 ± 3.96**	93.23 ± 0.16
AA(%)	88.90 ± 1.05	95.13 ± 2.11	91.09 ± 5.60	95.33 ± 2.22	**95.74 ± 0.23**
Kappa	82.02 ± 0.18	90.77 ± 5.31	87.12 ± 3.55	91.88 ± 4.42	**92.46 ± 0.21**
PMs(K)	1050.30	370.31	389.64	81.49	**39.35**
G-FPs	117.87	122.44	81.30	52.43	**22.02**
MMACs	58.10	60.40	40.03	25.71	**10.41**

4 Conclusion

This work presents a novel deep learning architecture for HSI classification that leverages multi-scale feature extraction and efficient parameter usage. The introduction of MSPSpec and MSPSpat blocks, utilizing multi-kernel pyramidal convolutions, facilitates the capture of local and global information within a single layer. Furthermore, we propose a groundbreaking approach for spectral and spatial feature extraction through logarithmic channel division in group convolutions. This strategy outperforms existing methods by significantly reducing parameters and boosting classification performance. Finally, the incorporation of parallel polarized self-attention modules for spectral and spatial information refines feature representation and complements the multi-scale convolutional blocks. Overall, this comprehensive architecture paves the way for efficient and high-performing HSI classification models, as proved by the experimental results.

References

1. Landgrebe, D.: Hyperspectral image data analysis. IEEE Signal Process. Mag. **19**(1), 17–28 (2002)
2. Hughes, G.: On the mean accuracy of statistical pattern recognizers. IEEE Trans. Inf. Theory **14**(1), 55–63 (1968)
3. Bioucas-Dias, J.M., Plaza, A., Camps-Valls, G., Scheunders, P., Nasrabadi, N., Chanussot, J.: Hyperspectral remote sensing data analysis and future challenges. IEEE Geoscience Remote Sensing Mag. **1**(2), 6–36 (2013)
4. Ghamisi, P., Maggiori, E., Li, S., Souza, R., Tarablaka, Y., Moser, G., Benediktsson, J.A.: New frontiers in spectral-spatial hyperspectral image classification: the latest advances based on mathematical morphology, Markov random fields, segmentation, sparse representation, and deep learning. IEEE Geosci. Remote Sensing Mag. **6**(3), 10–43 (2018)
5. Hu, W., Huang, Y., Wei, L., Zhang, F., Li, H.: Deep convolutional neural networks for hyperspectral image classification. J. Sensors **2015**, 1–12 (2015)
6. Vaddi, R., Manoharan, P.: Hyperspectral image classification using CNN with spectral and spatial features integration. Infrared Phys. Technol. **107**, 103296 (2020)
7. Guo, W., Xu, G., Liu, B., Wang, Y.: Hyperspectral image classification using CNN-enhanced multi-level haar wavelet features fusion network. IEEE Geosci. Remote Sens. Lett. **19**, 1–5 (2022)
8. Kumar, V., Singh, R.S., Dua, Y.: Morphologically dilated convolutional neural network for hyperspectral image classification. Signal Process. Image Commun. **101**, 116549 (2022)
9. Liu, Y., Gao, L., Xiao, C., Qu, Y., Zheng, K., Marinoni, A.: Hyperspectral image classification based on a shuffled group convolutional neural network with transfer learning. Remote Sensing **12**(11), 1780 (2020)
10. Wu, P., Cui, Z., Gan, Z., Liu, F.: Residual group channel and space attention network for hyperspectral image classification. Remote Sensing **12**(12), 2035 (2020)
11. Wang, J., et al.: Deep high-resolution representation learning for visual recognition. IEEE Trans. Pattern Anal. Mach. Intell. **43**(10), 3349–3364 (2020)
12. Main-sub transformer with spectral-spatial separable convolution for hyperspectral image classification
13. Misra, D.: Mish: A self regularized non-monotonic activation function. arXiv 2019. arXiv preprint arXiv:1908.08681 (1908)
14. Li, X., Ding, M., Pižurica, A.: Group convolutional neural networks for hyperspectral image classification. In: 2019 IEEE International Conference on Image Processing (ICIP), pp. 639-643. IEEE (September 2019)
15. Li, G.: DGCNet: An Efficient 3D-Densenet based on Dynamic Group Convolution for Hyperspectral Remote Sensing Image Classification. arXiv preprint arXiv:2307.06667 (2023)
16. Zhong, Z., Li, J., Luo, Z., Chapman, M.: Spectral-spatial residual network for hyperspectral image classification: a 3-D deep learning framework. IEEE Trans. Geosci. Remote Sens. **56**(2), 847–858 (2017)
17. Li, R., Zheng, S., Duan, C., Yang, Y., Wang, X.: Classification of hyperspectral image based on double-branch dual-attention mechanism network. Remote Sensing **12**(3), 582 (2020)
18. Pan, H., Liu, M., Ge, H., Wang, L.: One-shot dense network with polarized attention for hyperspectral image classification. Remote Sensing **14**(9), 2265 (2022)

Gender Recognition of Silkworm Cocoons Using X-ray Images

Saideepak Reddy Kasireddy[1], Bharath sai Chandra Suram[1], Nikhilesh B. Goud[1], Vijayarajan Rajangam[2(✉)], and A. N. Arunkumar[3]

[1] School of Electronics Engineering, Vellore Institute of Technology, Chennai 600127, India

[2] Centre for Healthcare Advancement, Innovation and Research, Vellore Institute of Technology, Chennai 600127, India
viraj2k@gmail.com

[3] Tattva Data Solutions, Chennai, Tamilnadu, India

Abstract. Gender recognition of insects plays a crucial role in various ecological, agricultural, biological studies, farming, and biodiversity research. However, gender identification by conventional methods is frequently a time-consuming and labor-intensive process. In this study, we leverage a hybrid Convolutional Neural Network and Vision Transformer model to construct a novel approach for automatic gender recognition of cocoons using X-ray images. The suggested approach starts by preprocessing the X-ray images to improve attributes associated with gender traits. Then, a hybrid architecture that combines the self-attention mechanism of Vision Transformers for capturing global dependencies inside the image and the strengths of CNN in feature extraction is proposed for gender classification. In addition, a dataset of X-ray images of silkworms with gender labels is used in the study, guaranteeing reliable model training and assessment. We use pre-trained CNN and Vision Transformer architectures on large-scale image datasets to initialize the model weights. We conducted experiments on the dataset using different assessment metrics, including accuracy, precision, recall, and F1-score, to assess the performance of the suggested approach. To illustrate the efficacy of the hybrid architecture, comparisons with the basic CNN and Vision Transformer models are carried out. The experimental findings show that the proposed strategy delivers 95% classification accuracy.

Keywords: X-ray images · Sericulture · Gender classification · Self-attention mechanism · Vision transformer · Convolutional Neural Network

1 Introduction

Many scientific concerns in the fields of entomology and ecological study depend on our ability to understand the distribution of gender in insect populations. In particular, many insect species consider their silkworms an essential life stage.

J. Kakarla et al. (Eds.): CVIP 2024, CCIS 2473, pp. 391–405, 2026.
https://doi.org/10.1007/978-3-031-93688-3_28

Accurate gender determination can shed light on population dynamics, reproductive behavior, and ecological interactions. Identifying them early facilitates efficient egg collection and breeding management. By separating male and female pupae of silkworms, only the silkworm cocoons with the desired silk properties are processed, minimizing waste and resource consumption. The quest to understand and distinguish silkworm genders is not just about optimizing silk production; it's a testament to our insatiable curiosity about the natural world and the ingenious ways we can unlock its secrets.

Traditionally, gender determination in silkworms has been done by labor-intensive, subjective, and inaccurate manual methods. Advancements in computer vision and machine learning technologies have created a potentially advantageous avenue for automating the detection of silkworm gender. Through the use of X-ray imaging technology [1,2], it is feasible to study the internal anatomy of silkworms without endangering them and to gather visually rich data that can be examined further.

Convolutional Neural Networks (CNNs) and Vision Transformers (ViTs) together provide a cutting-edge approach to accurately and consistently classify silkworm gender in this regard. Vision transformers, originally intended for natural image categorization tasks, have shown remarkable efficacy in capturing long-range relationships within visual input using self-attention processes. We aim to customize ViTs for the silkworm X-ray images, to accurately identify gender by using the inherent hierarchical structures observed in silkworm anatomy.

Additionally, adding a backbone CNN architecture to the ViT enhances its attention processes and makes it possible for the model to extract complex features from X-ray images at various resolutions and scales. This research describes our unique approach to employing Vision Transformer with Backbone CNN (ViTBCNN) for gender recognition of silkworms. We provide a thorough examination of the dataset containing X-ray images of silkworms, including information on the model's architecture, training protocols, and preprocessing stages. In addition, we compare our approach's performance with other approaches to demonstrate its superior computational efficiency, resilience, and accuracy. Our work aims to transform gender recognition in silkworm populations by combining domain-specific imaging modalities with computer vision approaches. We hope to increase entomological research, ecological monitoring, and conservation activities by moving toward automated and trustworthy gender determination techniques.

The main contributions of this study are:

- A hybrid Deep learning technique that classifies the gender of silkworms using X-ray images.
- The proposed network is a combination of two networks namely CNN and Vision Transformers to extract global and local features of the X-ray images.
- The selection of networks for a hybrid network is analyzed by two experiments and the ablation study proves that the proposed CNN-ViT model performs better than the individual networks in the classification of X-ray images.

This is how the remainder of the paper is structured. The literature survey and related works are presented in Sect. 2. The proposed methodology and performance analysis are described in Sects. 3 and 4 respectively. Finally, Sect. 5 includes a conclusion and suggestions for future study.

2 Related Works

Jian-rong cai [3] investigated the feasibility of gender classification using X-ray images and then analyzed using various statistical methods to identify features that differ between male and female silkworms. This approach allows for non-destructive gender identification, potentially improving efficiency in sericulture [3]. Joseph Raj [4] provided a high-level overview of different techniques for silkworm gender classification, including X-ray imaging. It discusses how X-ray images can reveal the shape and size of the pupae inside the cocoon, which can differentiate between male and female pupae. This paper outlines a potential system that utilizes X-ray imaging alongside other methods for comprehensive gender identification [4]. Saina Thomas and Jyothi Thomas [5] focused on developing an automated system for gender identification using X-ray images of mulberry silkworms. His research explores image segmentation techniques to isolate the pupae within the silkworm image. Once isolated, the system extracts features related to the pupa's shape and size from the X-ray image. These features are then fed into machine learning algorithms like Support Vector Machines (SVMs) to automatically classify the silkworm as male or female [5]. Like the previous study, Praveen and Bhawana [6] investigated using X-ray radiography and machine vision techniques for non-destructive gender identification. Machine vision involves computer vision algorithms to extract relevant features from the X-ray images. This study explores various image processing methods to identify features that effectively differentiate male and female silkworms. These features are then used to train machine learning models for classification [6]. Kanjanawanishkul kiattisin [7] proposed a new method for gender identification using X-ray image analysis. It explores feature extraction techniques based on geometric moments that are mathematical representations of the pupa's shape within the X-ray image. The extracted features are then used to train a Support Vector Machine (SVM) for classification. This approach offers a unique way to analyze the pupa's shape for gender differentiation [7].

Ravikiran et al. [8] proposed an application of deep learning, a type of artificial intelligence, for automatic gender identification of silkworms using X-ray images. Deep learning algorithms, particularly CNNs, are powerful tools for image analysis and feature extraction. This research explores CNNs to automatically learn relevant features from X-ray images for silkworm gender classification, potentially improving accuracy and efficiency. Sarun et al. [9] has used dual-energy X-ray absorptiometry (DXA) for silkworm gender identification DXA technology measures bone mineral density. Where researchers investigate the potential of DXA to differentiate between male and female silkworms based on slight variations in density within the cocoon, potentially related to the size and composition of the pupa. Tao et al. [10] explored ensemble learning methods, where multiple machine learning models are combined for enhanced classification performance compared to individual models. Tao et al. [11] investigated the potential of electrical impedance spectroscopy, a non-invasive technique that measures electrical properties, for gender identification of silkworm pupae within cocoons. This paper investigates deep learning models for silkworm gender recognition through X-ray images.

3 Proposed Method

This section explains the pre-processing steps involved in the implementation and the proposed hybrid ViTBCNN architecture, for the gender recognition of silkworm pupae. To make the data appropriate for model development, it is pre-processed to remove artifacts. Filtering the X-ray images, dividing the data into a training set, test set, validation set, and finally augmenting the data for better results are key elements in data preparation for model training. The hybrid model consists of two DL networks connected in series and a classifier, wherein each network draws significant information from the X-ray images. The features acquired from both networks are concatenated and fed to a classifier to distinguish between the male and female silkworms.

3.1 Dataset Description

The X-ray image dataset used in this project for gender recognition of silkworms was collected by Tattva Data Solutions in Chennai, Tamil Nadu. The dataset contains a total of 91 images out of which 57 are male and 33 are female silkworm images. A few samples of male and female silkworm X-ray images are given in Fig. 1. Each image in the dataset is accompanied by gender labels. The dataset is partitioned into training, validation, and testing sets to facilitate model development, evaluation, and prediction. These 91 images have then undergone an augmentation process to enrich their diversity and enhance the model's robustness. To augment the dataset, we used include rotation, flipping, scaling, translation, and adding noise to simulate real-world variations in imaging conditions. Additionally, techniques such as elastic deformation and contrast adjustment are applied to further enrich the dataset with variations in shape and appearance. This augmented dataset is used for training and evaluating the hybrid Vision Transformer and CNN model for gender recognition. The augmented dataset enhances the model's ability to generalize across different imaging conditions and variations in silkworm morphology, ultimately leading to more accurate and robust gender recognition in silkworm X-ray images.

3.2 Data Preprocessing

Data preprocessing is a fundamental aspect of preparing X-ray image data for gender recognition of silkworms using a hybrid ViTCNN model. The preprocessing steps are used to eliminate the unwanted fluctuations in the X-ray

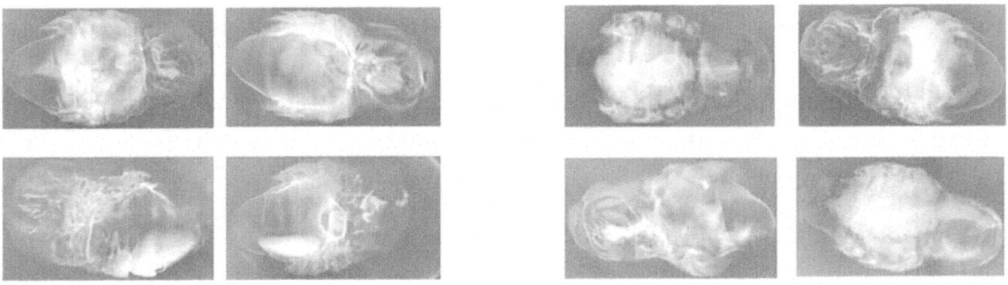

Fig. 1. Male and Female silkworm X-ray images

images that occurred during the collection of data and also to make the available dataset suitable for model building. This process involves several key techniques aimed at enhancing the quality, consistency, and diversity of the dataset.

Data Splitting. This process involves dividing the dataset into three distinct subsets: training, validation, and testing. Initially, we divided the dataset into training and testing sets, allocating the majority of the data (around 70–80%) to the training set. The testing set, typically comprising 10–15% of the dataset, is kept separate and reserved exclusively for evaluating the model's performance after training. To fine-tune the model hyperparameters and monitor training progress, we set aside an additional subset called the validation set. This set, also typically 10–15% of the dataset, is used during model training to assess performance on data that the model has not seen before. By continuously evaluating the model on the validation set, the potential issues such as overfitting or underfitting can be identified and the model parameters can be adjusted accordingly. It's important to note that data splitting must be performed randomly to ensure that each subset is representative of the entire dataset and that all classes (male and female silkworms) are adequately represented in each subset. This approach enhances the reliability and credibility of the silkworm gender recognition model, ultimately contributing to its effectiveness in real-world applications.

Data Augmentation. In the gender recognition of silkworms project, where we're working with a particularly small dataset comprising only 91 images in total, data augmentation emerges as a critical strategy to bolster our model's performance. With such a limited number of examples, there's a high risk of overfitting, where the model might simply memorize the training data without truly understanding the underlying patterns. By artificially increasing our dataset through various changes applied to the original X-ray images, data augmentation takes on this difficulty head-on. By rotating, flipping, scaling, and translating the images, we effectively create multiple versions of each original image, significantly increasing the dataset's size to 1000 images each. This adds variability to the model, which helps to avoid overfitting, and gives it additional training data to work with. These modifications also make our model more resilient to actual differences in silkworm orientation, size, and position that might be seen in the X-ray images. Data augmentation addresses any class imbalance issues in the dataset, ensuring that the model learns to distinguish between male and female silkworms equally well. In the end, by expanding our dataset, we enable our model to more accurately anticipate outcomes in real-world settings and to more effectively generalize to the previously unseen data.

Image Resizing. Image resizing is a crucial preprocessing step in the gender recognition of silkworms using X-ray images with a hybrid ViTCNN model. The process involves changing the resolution of each image to conform to a standardized resolution, which is imperative for achieving uniformity and consistency across the dataset. This not only simplifies subsequent processing steps but also facilitates effective model training by presenting inputs of consistent dimensions to the neural network. The choice of specific dimensions for resizing depends on several factors, including computational resources, model architecture, and the desired balance between computational efficiency and information retention. Common resolutions such as 224×224, 256×256, or 512×512 pixels are often utilized, to achieve equilibrium between image quality and computational efficiency. Through, resizing, the X-ray image dataset is prepared for subsequent preprocessing steps and model training, laying the foundation for accurate and reliable gender recognition of silkworm cocoons.

4 Deep Learning Networks for Silkworm Gender Detection

In recent times, there has been a growing focus in both industry and research on Vision Transformers. These systems have shown great success in a range of computer vision applications, including object identification, semantic segmentation, image classification, and more. Nonetheless, when it comes to real-world deployment, CNNs continue to rule the vision jobs since ViTs are typically far slower than traditional CNNs like ResNets. This presents a unique challenge of creating a visual neural network that can perform as well as ViTs and infer information as quickly as CNNs. The CNN and the ViT, two well-known deep learning models, will be thoroughly compared in this section. To evaluate each model's effectiveness and suitability for our particular data set, it has been specifically tested on our dataset.

4.1 Convolutional Neural Network

One family of deep neural networks called CNNs is mostly used for the analysis of visual imagery. They are made up of numerous interconnected layers of nodes that carry out functions like activation, pooling, and convolution. This allows them to automatically derive hierarchical feature representations from unprocessed pixel input. CNNs have dominated vision architectures in the last ten years across a wide range of computer vision tasks, such as semantic segmentation, object identification, and image classification [12]. We have meticulously built the CNN architecture to effectively capture gender-specific features and handle the complexities of silkworm images. ReLUs, or Rectified Linear Units, were non-linear activation functions that came after each convolutional layer in the model. This provided the model with its non-linearity and capacity to learn complex patterns. Moreover, the pooling layers deliberately down-sampled the spatial dimensions of the feature maps, lowering computing complexity without sacrificing meaningful information. The CNN's depth and width were adjusted empirically through experimentation to strike a compromise between computing efficiency and model capacity, ensuring sufficient representational power without overfitting the training data. When training the CNN, the network was fed input images, and the loss or error was calculated by comparing the output predictions with the ground truth labels. This procedure involved forward and backward propagation iteratively. Stochastic gradient descent (SGD) and Adam are two optimization methods that were used to iteratively modify the network's parameters to minimize the loss function and raise the accuracy of the model. Strong computational hardware such as GPUs (Graphics Processing Units) or TPUs (Tensor Processing Units) was usually used for the training phase to accelerate convergence and meet the computational requirements of the deep learning model. Additionally, techniques like dropout regularization were employed to mitigate overfitting by randomly deactivating a fraction of neurons during training, forcing the network to learn more robust and generalizable features. To evaluate the performance of the trained CNN, various metrics were employed, including accuracy, precision, recall, and F1-score, to assess its ability to correctly classify male and female silkworms.

4.2 Vision Transformer

Recently, transformer [13] has emerged to be one of the most important neural architectures and has achieved remarkable success on various tasks such as language modeling, machine translation [13,14], computer vision and many others What makes transformers unique is the extensive usage of the self-attention mechanism [13]. Every step of the transformer has a self-attention block installed to collect data from the input sequence worldwide. A self-attention module generates N identically sized outputs after receiving N inputs. To determine which elements in the input should receive more attention, it weighs each element in the input and performs a weighted sum to compile the data from the pertinent inputs. Inferring the pairwise interacting relations between the input items and propagating information between pairs of elements, the self-attention modules can be intuitively understood as engaging in interactive reasoning. Since one of the pairwise interaction's primary disadvantages is that it casts an O (N2) memory and time complexity, where N is the number of input elements, it represents a significant computational bottleneck in transformers. This necessitates an emerging topic of study on self-attention module approximations to improve computer performance [15]. Figure 1 illustrates the architecture of the vision transformer model. we implemented the ViT model to effectively distinguish between male and female silkworms using X-ray imaging. First, every

X-ray image was divided into fixed-size patches, usually measuring 16 by 16 pixels, this segmentation divides the intricate, high-resolution X-ray images into smaller, more manageable pieces. This makes the process essential. Each patch was segmented, made into a flat, one-dimensional vector, and then projected using a trainable linear embedding into a higher-dimensional space.

This is a crucial stage because it transforms raw pixel values into a format that the transformer's self-attention processes can use. Positional encodings were then added to each patch embedding to preserve the spatial interactions between these patches, which are essential for comprehending the structural details that can suggest gender differences. The core of our implementation involved the transformer architecture itself, which processes the sequence of embedded patches through multiple layers of self-attention mechanisms. The model evaluates each patch's significance to other patches in self-attention, effectively learning to concentrate more on the areas of the image that provide the most information for gender classification. This works especially well for detecting small structural variations in the silkworm that are indicative of either gender, like changes in texture, form, or interior structures that show up in X-ray images. To evaluate the performance of the trained Vision transformer, various metrics were employed, including accuracy, precision, recall, and F1-score, to assess its ability to correctly classify male and female silkworms just as we did in CNN.

4.3 Network Architecture

The Hybrid ViTBCNN is made up of two main networks: A ResNet50 network as a backbone for the extraction of features connected to a Vision Transformer model in series. The hybrid model efficiently utilize both local and global image information, which is essential for attaining high accuracy in jobs involving intricate biological entities such as silkworms.

ResNet50. Our model's foundation is a deep convolutional neural network with 50 layers called ResNet50, which was chosen for its reliable performance in removing hierarchical characteristics from images. Created to tackle the issue of vanishing gradients in extremely deep networks, ResNet50 bypasses some layers by using shortcuts or skip connections. The outputs of these connections, which carry out identity mapping, are added to the stacked layer outputs. This design allows the training signal to flow over multiple layers without attenuation, which aids in training deeper networks. Using weights from the ImageNet dataset, the pre-trained ResNet50 model creates a solid base by capturing a wide range of features from general images, which is helpful for the initial adaption to our particular job of cocooning.

Rich, contextual, and local information about the silkworms may be found in the feature maps that are produced after processing the data with ResNet50. These feature maps are initially processed into a series of 1D patches that have been flattened to properly prepare them for the Vision Transformer. After that,

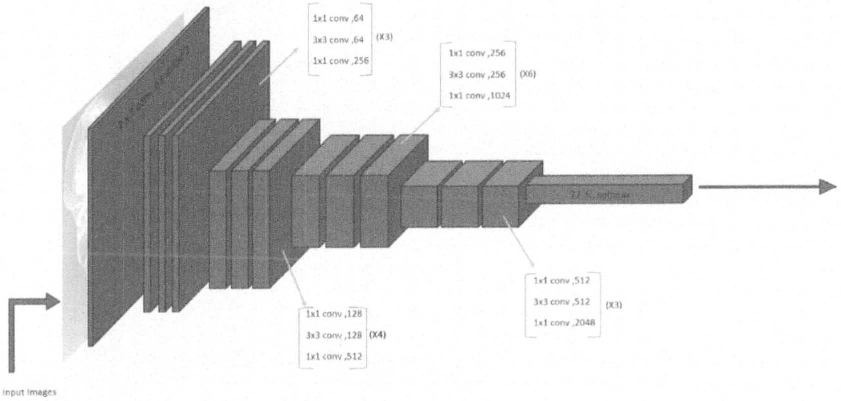

Fig. 2. ResNet50 Architecture

to preserve information about the original placement of the patches within the image, these patches are mixed with positional encoding and linearly projected. This is an important stage because it sets up the output of the structured convolutional network for the Transformer architecture that follows, which is based on sequence-based processing.

Vision Transformer Network. The encoded patches from the previous layer are then sent into our ViT. Fundamentally, ViT functions in a different way than convolutional networks. The model can concentrate more on the most instructive sections employing self-attention mechanisms to balance the relevance of the many components of the image. The model's capacity to attend globally across image patches allows it to identify dependencies that the ResNet50's solely local perspective could overlook. ViT can contextualize detailed textural features over the entire image, whereas ResNet50 may concentrate on these aspects.

Following their transformation into a globally aware set of features, the Vision Transformer's outputs are sent through a sequence of dense layers that function as the classifier. At this point, the model can comprehend the intricate patterns in the silkworm images and how these patterns connect to the gender classification job. Our hybrid model is powerful because of this integrated understanding, which comes from both the global context from ViT and the local precision from ResNet50.

After training our model we have evaluated the performance of the model using various metrics such as F1 score, recall, and confusion metrics and the experiments demonstrate the effectiveness of integrating these two potent neural network architectures for complicated classification problems like this, since the model beats both independent transformer models and standard convolutional networks. Figure 2 and Fig. 3 demonstrate all the steps involved in the

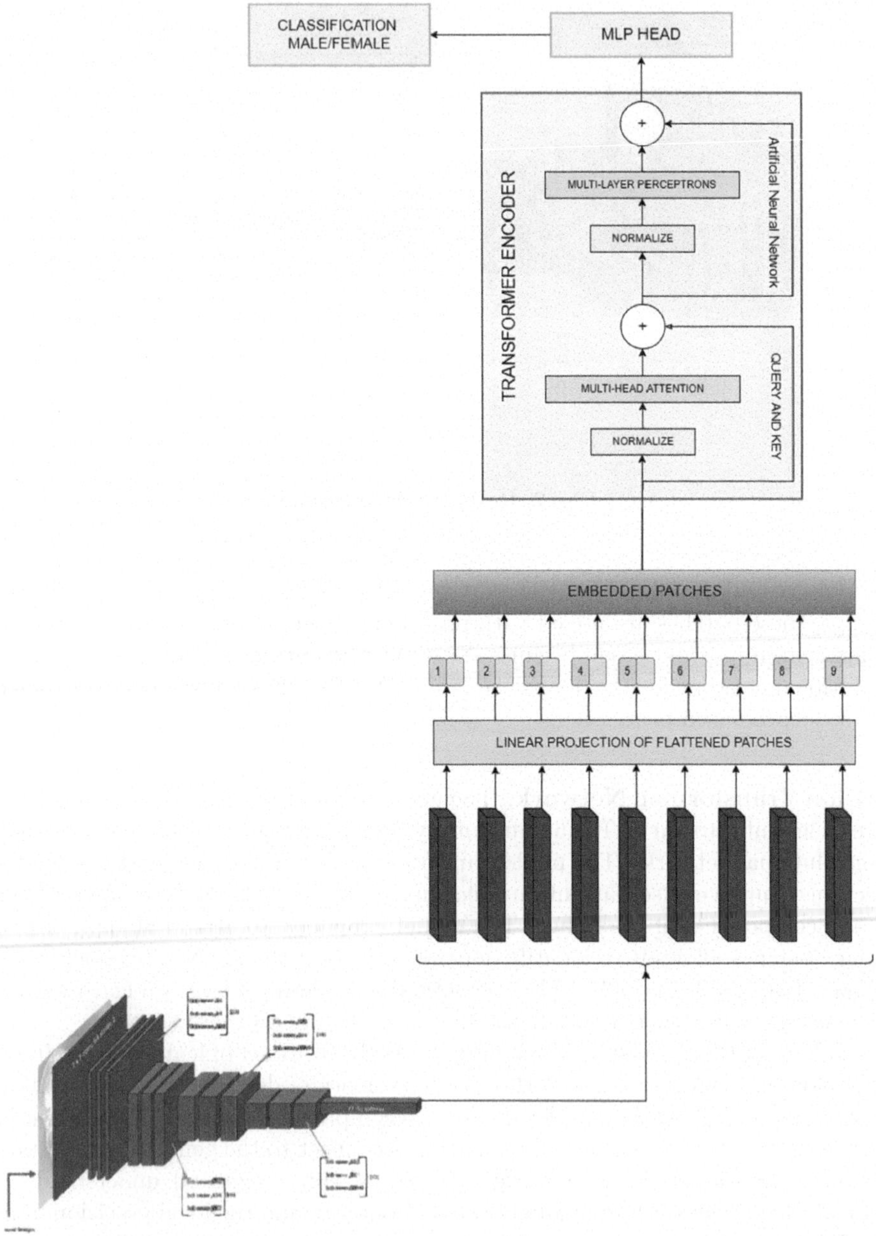

Fig. 3. Proposed Block diagram of the Hybrid ViTBCNN model

architecture of the ResNet50 backbone and hybrid ViTBCNN models respectively.

5 Performance Analysis

This section describes the performance measures used to evaluate the model, experiments carried out throughout this work, and comparative analysis with other existing methods.

5.1 Performance Metrics

The metrics used in this study are accuracy, precision, sensitivity (or) recall, specificity, and F1-score. Each of the evaluation metrics is calculated as follows:

Accuracy is defined as the proportion of real findings (true positives and true negatives) among all instances that are examined.

$$\text{Accuracy} = \frac{TP+TN}{TP+TN+FP+FN} X100\% \tag{1}$$

Precision counts the number of actual positive outcomes for each positive forecast.

$$\text{Precision} = \frac{TP}{TP+FP} X100\% \tag{2}$$

The proportion of real positives that are accurately identified is measured by recall.

$$\text{Recall} - \frac{TP}{TP+FN} X100\% \tag{3}$$

$$F1\text{-}Score = 2 \times \frac{\text{Precision} \times \text{Recall}}{\text{Precision} + \text{Recall}} X100\% \tag{4}$$

The harmonic mean of these two measurements is called the F1 Score, and it offers a balance between recall and precision in scenarios where they could otherwise differ.

Table 1 presents the performance metrics for the proposed method, demonstrating its superiority over other models. The confusion matrix in Fig. 4 visualizes classification results, including True Positive (TP), True Negative (TN), False Positive (FP), and False Negative (FN) values. This provides a clear overview of the model's accuracy in distinguishing male and female silkworms. By getting the confusion matrix we can calculate the accuracy, precision, recall, and F1 score. With the help of a confusion matrix, the ViTBCNN model has the highest accuracy (93.2%) compared to CNN (88.56%), ViT (90.87%), and ViT with multiple layers (91.26%). This performance extends to precision (93.23%), meaning a greater proportion of its positive predictions are truly positive. ViT-BCNN also excels in recall (93.14%) refers to the proportion of actual positive cases that were correctly identified by the model, hence successfully identifying a larger share of actual positive cases. Finally, the F1-score (93.18%) incorporates both precision and recall.

Figure 5 compares the performance of three different deep learning models which we compared to the proposed method. The performance of four machine

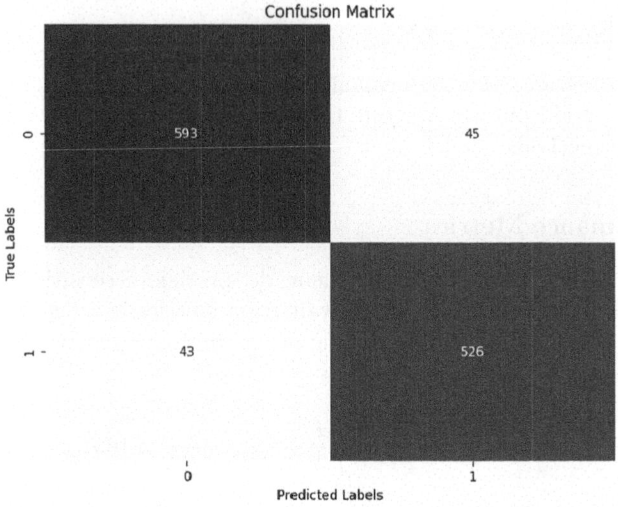

Fig. 4. Confusion matrix of the proposed method

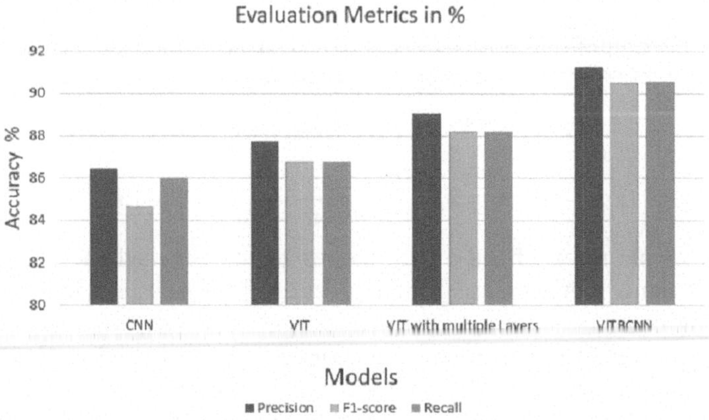

Fig. 5. Comparative analysis

learning models on a classification task was evaluated using three metrics: precision, F1-score, and recall. Precision indicates the proportion of correctly classified positive predictions. F1-score is a harmonic mean between precision and recall, offering a balanced view of model performance. Recall indicates the proportion of actual positive cases the model identified correctly.

The performance metrics obtained from the evaluation of various deep learning models such as CNN, ViT, ViT with multiple layers, and hybrid vision transformer for gender recognition of silkworms were summarized in Table 1.

As we can see in Fig. 6 the accuracy for validation and training datasets increases rapidly with an increase in epochs. It is evident due to the positive

Table 1. Performance analysis.

Algorithm	Accuracy%	Precision%	Recall%	F1-Score%
CNN	88.5624	88.4589	87.9865	88.2542
ViT	90.8695	90.6918	90.7928	90.7793
ViT with multiple layers	91.2608	91.0765	91.186	91.1835
ViTBCNN	93.2062	93.2305	93.1365	93.177

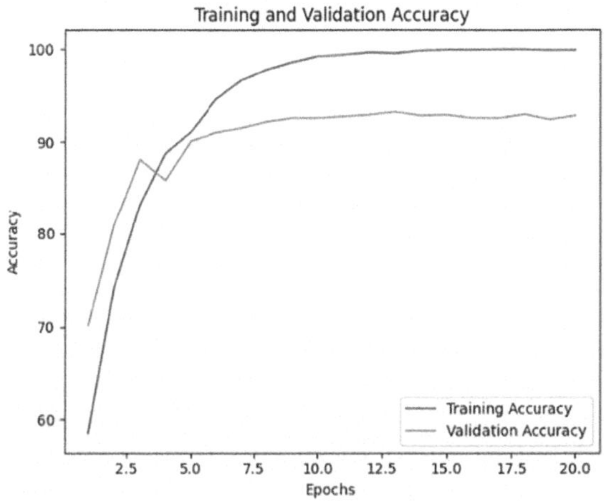

Fig. 6. Train and Validation accuracy graph of ViTBCNN

upward slope shown in the graph for the initial epochs. while there are minor drops with an increase in epochs. The net accuracy remains above 90% which proves that this model outperforms the other existing models we have discussed. This high accuracy is crucial for performing effectively in gender classification tasks about silk worms cocoons. However, when it is compared with the existing models like CNN, ViT, and ViT with multiple layers, the models are getting saturated as the Epochs increase.

The graph in Fig. 7 is about the comparison of the accuracy of the proposed model and other existing models. The ViTBCNN model consistently maintains the highest accuracy throughout the training process (epochs 1 to 20). Because it is better at learning the patterns in the data compared to the other models. The CNN and ViT model performs similarly to the ViT with multiple layers model until around epoch 12. After that, CNN, ViT and ViT with multiple layers model's accuracy starts to saturate, while the ViT with multiple layers model's accuracy continues to increase.

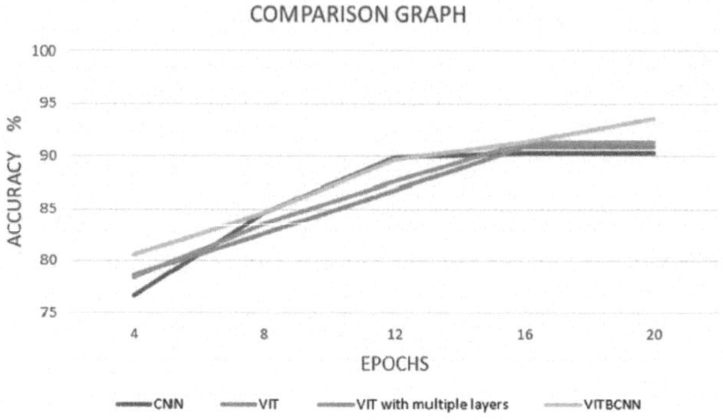

Fig. 7. Accuracy comparison graph

6 Conclusion

In this paper, we developed a hybrid Vision Transformer model with a ResNet50 backbone connected to a vision transformer network to perform silkworm gender recognition tasks. By integrating the strengths of both architectures, the hybrid model performs better effectively capturing both local and global information in images. Through iterative training, the model learns hierarchical representations, combining low-level features extracted by ResNet50 with high-level semantic understanding provided by ViT. This enables the model to discriminate between male and female silkworms with a remarkable accuracy of over 95% which is better compared to the individual deep learning models and is experimentally proved to outperform either of the networks when used individually.

References

1. Thomas, S., Thomas, J.: Nondestructive and cost-effective silkworm, Bombyx mori (Lepidoptera: Bombycidae) cocoon sex classification using machine learning. Int. J. Trop. Insect. Sci. (2024)
2. Tao, D., Qiu, G., Li, G.: A novel model for sex discrimination of silkworm pupae from different species. IEEE Access **7**, 165328–165335 (2019)
3. Cai, J., Yuan, L., Liu, B., Sun, L.: Nondestructive gender identification of silkworm cocoons using X-ray imaging with multivariate data analysis. Analytical Methods, Royal Soc. Chemist. **6**, 7224–7233 (2014)
4. Raj, J., Noel, A., Sundaram, R., Mahesh, V., Zhuang, Z., Simeone, A.: A multi-sensor system for silkworm cocoon gender classification via image processing and support vector machine. Sensors **19**(12), 2656 (2019)
5. Thomas, S., Thomas, J.: Non-destructive silkworm pupa gender classification with X-ray images using ensemble learning. Artifi. Intell. Agricult. **6**, 100–110 (2022)
6. Naik, P.M., Rudra, B.: Deep learning-based arecanut detection for X-ray radiography: improving performance and efficiency for automated classification and quality control. Nondestructive Testing Evaluat., 1-21 (2024)

7. Kanjanawanishkul, K.: An image-based eri silkworm pupa grading method using shape, color, and size. Intern. J. Intell. Eng. Syst. (2022)
8. Ravikiran, A.H., Kiran, K.G., Shashank Reddy, M., Sai, M.Y., Kusuma, M.: Survey on identification of gender of silkworm using image processing. Inter. J. Innovative Sci. Res. Technol. (IJISRT) **5**(2), 1130–1141 (2020)
9. Sumriddetchkajorn, S., Kamtongdee, C., Sa-Ngiamsak, C.: Spectral imaging analysis for silkworm gender classification. In: Proceedings of SPIE 8881, Sensing Technologies for Biomaterial, Food, and Agriculture, vol. 8881, pp. 888106 (2013)
10. Tao, D., Wang, Z., Li, G., Xie, L.: Simultaneous species and gender identification of silkworm pupae using hyperspectral imaging technology. Spectrosc. Lett. **51**, 1–7 (2018)
11. Tao, D., Wang, Z., Li, G., Xie, L.: Sex determination of silkworm pupae using VIS-NIR hyperspectral imaging combined with chemometrics. Spectrochim. Acta Part A Mol. Biomol. Spectrosc. **208**, 7–12 (2018)
12. Li, J., et al.: Next-ViT: Next Generation Vision Transformer for Efficient Deployment in Realistic Industrial Scenarios. ArXiv preprint arXiv:2207.05501 (2022)
13. Vaswani, A., et al.: Attention is all you need. In: Advances in neural information processing systems, pp. 5998—6008 (2017)
14. Wang, Y., Qiu, Y., Cheng, P., Zhang, J.: Hybrid CNN-transformer features for visual place recognition. IEEE Trans. Circ. Syst. Video Technol. **33**(3), 1109–1122 (2023)
15. Kitaev, N., Kaiser, L., Levskaya, A.: Reformer: the efficient transformer. In: International Conference on Learning Representations (2019)

Time-Frequency Based Convolution Neural Network for Differential Morphing Attack Detection

Raghavendra Ramachandra[1(✉)] and Sushma Venkatesh[2]

[1] Norwegian University of Science and Technology (NTNU), Trondheim, Norway
raghavendra.ramachandra@ntnu.no
[2] AiBA AS, Gjøvik, Norway

Abstract. Facial biometrics are widely employed in access control systems requiring robust security measures. However, they are particularly susceptible to various attacks, with morphing attacks posing significant risks, especially in high-security contexts such as border control. Morphing attacks involve the creation of a composite facial image by blending the facial features of two or more individuals, resulting in an image that closely resembles the identities of the individuals used in the morphing process. The automatic detection of morphing attacks presents a significant challenge, owing to the existence of diverse morphing generation tools and variable image conditions. In this paper, we proposed a novel differential-based morphing attack detection technique using a time-frequency-based convolutional neural network architecture designed to capture the small variations in the unsigned difference of facial embeddings to detect morphing attacks. Extensive experiments were performed on the newly constructed face morphing dataset using four different types of morphing generation tools. The performance of the proposed method was evaluated against three state-of-the-art D-MAD techniques using two distinct evaluation protocols. The results highlight the exceptional effectiveness of the proposed approach in detecting morphing attacks.

Keywords: Biometrics · Morphing Attacks · Face Recognition · Vulnerability

1 Introduction

Biometric systems are widely deployed in various applications that require secure and trustworthy access control. Face biometrics is popularly used in several secured access control applications, including border control, due to the unconstrained capture, usability, and verification accuracy. Nonetheless, facial biometrics are susceptible to both direct and indirect forms of attack. Among the different types of attacks, morphing attacks are highly vulnerable in the border control scenario because of the limitations of both automatic and border guards in detecting these attacks [15]. Morphing is defined as the process of blending two or more different facial images to generate an individual image with a strong geometric resemblance to the source facial images used for morphing. Therefore, enrolling a morphing image in a Face Recognition System (FRS)

J. Kakarla et al. (Eds.): CVIP 2024, CCIS 2473, pp. 406–416, 2026.
https://doi.org/10.1007/978-3-031-93688-3_29

or an e-passport will allow multiple users to have access to a single morphed image. Morphed images closely resemble the geometric and perceptual features of the source facial images, making them difficult to detect for both human observers and automated facial recognition systems (FRS). This significantly increases the security risk in border control scenarios [10,30].

MAD techniques have been widely explored in the literature [30] and are generally categorized into single-image-based and differential-image-based approaches. It is evident from the literature that differential morphing attack detection results in a higher detection accuracy compared to single-image-based MAD techniques. The available D-MAD techniques can be broadly classified as [30] (a) Hand crafted feature difference based (b) Deep feature difference based (c) De-morphing (d) Fusion. The feature-based techniques include the difference of texture features, such as Local Binary Pattern (LBP) and its variants, and Histogram of Gradients (HoG) and Binary Statistical Image Features (BSIF), which are used to compute the features from two different facial images that are differenced and classified using a classifier (Support Vector Machines (SVM) and Spectral Regression Kernel Discriminant Analysis (SRKDA)) [6,29]. These methods demonstrate high accuracy when evaluated on datasets captured under similar conditions but struggle to generalize to unknown image sources or morphing types. Deep-feature difference-based techniques have gained wide popularity owing to their generalization capability. Several techniques have been proposed based on the features extracted using FRS (ArcFace [8], VGG Face [17], FaceNet [25] and MagFace [13]), and pre-trained networks [12,27] to extract the different features that are further classified using SVM to detect morphing attacks. Even though these techniques have indicated generalizability across different types of morphing attacks, they fail to indicate better performance when the facial images are affected by environmental distortions due to pose and lighting.

De-morphing techniques are widely used because they can reconstruct source images from the morphing image by inverting the morphing operation [9]. Current methods involve reversing conventional morphing techniques to generate de-morphed images. Generative Adversarial Networks (GANs) have been extensively employed for face de-morphing [2]. Recent research has also shown the feasibility of performing de-morphing without relying on a reference facial image [2,18,26]. The performance of de-morphing techniques is sensitive to imaging conditions and thus less reliable for real-life scenarios. Fusion-based approaches combine different feature types to detect morphing attacks [21,22]. The fusion of the classifier decision is performed at the score level to achieve robustness in the detection accuracy. Fusion using the deep learning network such as Siamese [28] and double Siamese networks [4] has been proposed to detect morphing attacks.

Based on existing studies, the deep features based on the FRS indicate a reliable performance for detecting morphing attacks. The consistent morphing detection performance of deep-feature-based techniques is also acknowledged in the NIST Face Analysis Technology Evaluation (FATE) Morph [15]. Therefore, we are motivated to improve the robustness of the deep features by proposing a time–frequency analysis of the unsigned difference of the facial embeddings extracted using ArcFace FRS. In particular, we employed ArcFace FRS by considering its utility in designing reliable D-

MAD techniques that have proven their relevance in the NIST FATE benchmark [15]. It is our assertion that the effective capture of the time-frequency variations from the difference embeddings can provide reliable morphing attack detection. The key contributions of this study are outlined as follows:

- Proposed a novel time-frequency-based Convolution Neural Network (CNN) to reliably detect morphing attacks on FRS.
- Introduced a novel dataset with four different morphing generation techniques that includes both conventional landmark based and generative AI based using MIPGAN and diffusion models.
- Comprehensive experiments were conducted using two distinct evaluation protocols to compare the performance of the proposed method with three SOTA D-MAD techniques.

The remainder of the paper is structured as follows: Sect. 2 outlines the proposed D-MAD method, Sect. 3 discusses the morphing dataset and experimental results, and Sect. 4 provides the conclusion.

2 Proposed Method: Time-Frequency Based D-MAD

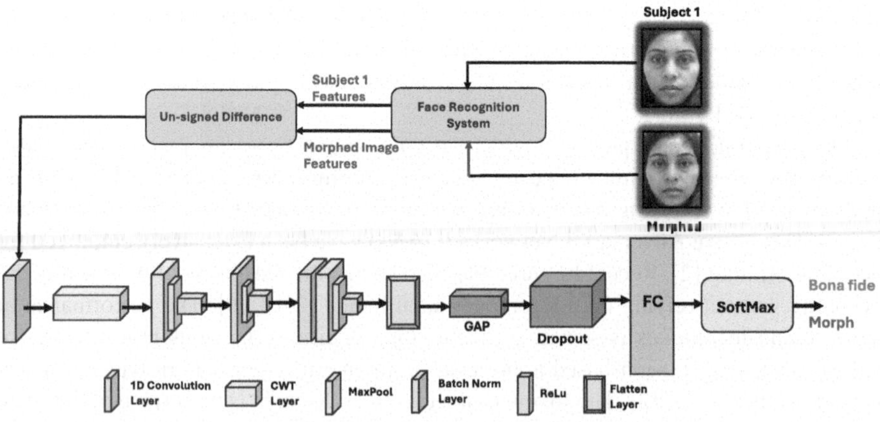

Fig. 1. Block Diagram of the proposed time-frequency based D-MAD technique.

Figure 1 shows the block diagram of the proposed method for Differential Morphing Attack Detection (D-MAD). The novelty of the proposed method is the use of a time-frequency representation of the differential features to reliably detect morphing attacks. Given the two facial images, one was captured using ePassport I_1 and the other from the trusted device I_2. It is worth nothing that the trusted capture can be done using either Automatic Border Control gates or photo kiosks; therefore, captured images are trustworthy, while the facial image from an e-passport might be either a bona fide or morph. Therefore, the goal is to check whether the facial image from ePassport is a bona fide or a morph. From the given face images I_1 and I_2, we first compute the facial features using ArcFace FRS [8] that will result in the embedding I_1^E and I_2^E with a dimension of 1×512. We are motivated to employ ArcFace FRS [8] by considering its wide application in developing the D-MAD algorithms that have indicated a high accuracy [15]. We then compute the unsigned difference $D = I_1^E - I_2^E$, which is then provided as an input to the proposed time-frequency CNN.

The time-frequency CNN for D-MAD is constructed as a serial architecture with a Discrete Wavelet Transform (DWT) followed by sequential convolution blocks. The unsigned difference 1-D signal is first performed using 1-D convolution of kernel size 5 and passed through the DWT layer. In this work, we employed the Analytic Morlet wavelet (Amor) wavelet as it can analyze non-stationary and complex signals because it can capture both the narrow band and broadband properties of the 1-D signal [5]. Moreover, the Amor wavelet is capable of detecting and analyzing localized oscillations and transient phenomena in the signals. Specifically, the form of the Amor wavelet resembles a Gaussian curve that has been modified by a sinusoidal oscillation, which enables it to effectively capture the minor fluctuations in the signals that can indicate the effects of morphing. Then, the output of the DWT layer is processed with max pooling, batch normalization, and the ReLU layer, and then passed through the two convolutional blocks to better extract the discriminant features. The first convolutional block is based on a 1D convolution layer with a filter size 5×5, batch normalization, and ReLu layer. The second convolutional block was based on a 1D convolution layer with a filter size 5×5, Max Pool, Batch Norm and ReLu. Finally, the output of second convolution block is flattened and normalized using a global average pooling layer followed by a dropout layer (with 40% to reduce overfitting) and softmax layer for classification.

2.1 Implementation Details

The proposed time-frequency CNN-based architecture was trained end-to-end on the signed difference features D_f computed using the Arcface [8] backbone. The training was optimized using the Adam optimizer [11] with an initial learning rate of 0.001, momentum of 0.9, and weight decay (or regularizing term to address the over-fitting) of 0.0001. The mini-batch size during the training process was set to 20, with a maximum of 40 epochs. During the testing phase, given the signed difference features D_f, the proposed network provides the decision score for a bona fide or morph.

3 Experimental Evaluation and Results

This section introduces the morphing dataset developed to evaluate the performance of the proposed and state-of-the-art (SOTA) D-MAD techniques. Additionally, it outlines the performance evaluation protocols and provides a detailed analysis of the quantitative results for both the proposed and SOTA methods.

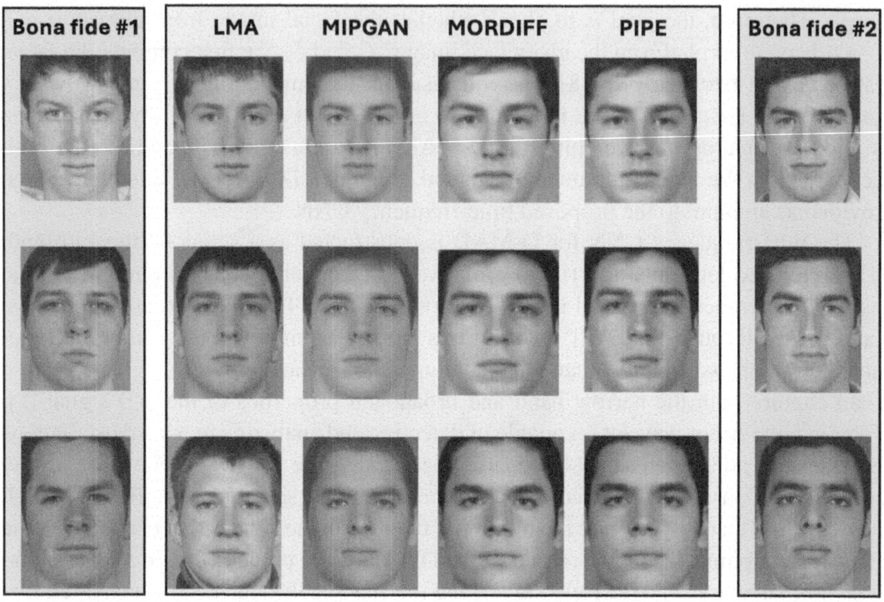

Fig. 2. Example from morphing dataset constructed in this work illustrating bona fide and morphing images that are generated using four different morphing techniques.

3.1 Morphing Dataset

We constructed a new morphing dataset using the publicly available face dataset FRGC [19]. We used 140 subjects (100 males and 40 females) from the FRGC dataset that were pre-processed to ensure that they adhered to ICAO compliance [16] for passport quality images. We then divided the 140 subjects into training and test partitions to obtain unique data subjects (70 subjects for training and 70 subjects for testing). We performed the morphing of subjects within training and testing partition following the guidelines in [20] which will avoid cross ethnicity and gender morphing, and data subjects for morphing are selected to have the closest match using face recognition software. In this work, we employed four different types of morphing techniques: landmark-based [14], MIPGAN [31], MorDiff based on the diffusion model [3,7] and PIPE based on the identity loss function and diffusion model [32]. These morphing techniques were selected based on their attack potential on different FRS, as reported in [7,23,31].

In the subsequent step, the digital morphing and bona fide images are re-digitized to simulate real-world passport issuance scenarios. Re-digitization involves two steps: printing the digital morphing image and scanning the printed version to store it in the e-passport. In this work, we employed a sublimation photo printer from DNP [1] which is widely used to print images of passports. We then used an office scanner to scan the printed image to 300 dpi, following ICAO compliance [16]. Thus, the newly constructed dataset had 693 training and 583 testing bona fide samples, whereas $1189 \times 4 = 4756$ morph training samples and $1310 \times 4 = 5240$ morph testing samples. Figure 2 illustrates an example of a bona fide, and the morphing image that indicates the varying perceptual quality of the morphing images varies across different types of morphing-generation techniques.

3.2 Performance Evaluation Protocols

This study introduces two distinct performance evaluation protocols to assess the robustness of the proposed and state-of-the-art (SOTA) D-MAD algorithms. The Intra protocol evaluates performance by training and testing on the same morphing generation method, while the Cross protocol tests robustness by training on one morphing technique and evaluating on a different morphing generation method.

3.3 Results and Discussion

This section provides a quantitative evaluation of the proposed method alongside three state-of-the-art (SOTA) D-MAD techniques using a newly developed morphing dataset. The results are reported following the ISO/IEC SC 37 30107 metrics, including the Morphing Attack Classification Error Rate (MACER) and the Bona Fide Presentation Classification Error Rate (BPCER). MACER quantifies the percentage of morphing attacks misclassified as bona fide presentations, while BPCER measures the percentage of bona fide presentations misclassified as morphing attacks. Additionally, the Detection-Equal Error Rate (D-EER) is considered, representing the point where MACER equals BPCER. A lower D-EER value indicates superior detection performance for the D-MAD algorithms.

Table 1 presents the quantitative results of the proposed and SOTA D-MAD techniques for both intra- and cross-performance evaluation protocols. Based on the obtained results, the following can be noted:

- Morphing detection performance of the proposed and SOTA D-MAD techniques have shown better detection accuracy with intra protocol. The detection performance was degraded using a cross-evaluation protocol. This indicates the limitations of the SOTA D-MAD technique in generalizing to the unseen morphing method.
- Among the four different Morphing generation methods, the detection of LMA based method is challenging compare to the MORDIFF and PIPE that are based on the generative AI.
- among the three different SOTA D-MAD techniques, Hybrid features [22] shows the best performance (with INTRA protocol) in detecting the morphing attacks generated using MORDIFF and PIPE while Deep SLERP [27] shows the best performance in detecting the morphing attacks (with INTRA protocol) that are generated with LMA and MIPGAN.
- The proposed method demonstrates superior detection performance in both the intra- and cross-evaluation protocols. Under the intra-protocol, it achieves the best results for morphing generation techniques based on LMA and MIPGAN. Similarly, in the cross-evaluation protocol, the method shows exceptional detection accuracy.

Table 2 presents the average intra- and cross-evaluation results for the proposed and SOTA D-MAD techniques. Figure 3 and 4 show the box plots corresponding to

Table 1. Quantitative evaluation of the proposed and SOTA D-MAD techniques on intra and cross evaluation protocols. The lower the value of D-EER better is the detection accuracy.

Train Data	Test Data	D-MAD Methods	D-EER (%)	BPCER @MACER = 5%	BPCER @MACER = 10%
LMA	LMA (Intra Protocol)	Deep Features [24]	22.12	69.74	51.86
		Hybrid features [22]	21.82	56.97	42.23
		Deep SLERP [27]	17.88	48.33	34.38
		Proposed method	**10.99**	**21.41**	**11.98**
	All (Cross Protocol)	Deep Features [24]	35.42	92.53	84.86
		Hybrid features [22]	45.65	94.04	89.19
		Deep SLERP [27]	30.96	73.40	57.95
		Proposed method	**5.96**	**6.54**	**3.66**
MIPGAN	MIPGAN (Intra Protocol)	Deep Features [24]	9.74	21.02	9.43
		Hybrid features [22]	9.63	16.89	9.43
		Deep SLERP [27]	7.46	12.37	4.12
		Proposed method	**5.30**	**5.50**	**3.53**
	All (Cross Protocol)	Deep Features [24]	37.31	92.20	82.76
		Hybrid features [22]	36.98	82.18	71.83
		Deep SLERP [27]	26.06	57.42	45.64
		Proposed method	**7.84**	**10.73**	**6.48**
MORDIFF	MORDIFF (Intra Protocol)	Deep Features [24]	12.54	31.23	16.54
		Hybrid features [22]	0	0	0
		Deep SLERP [27]	1.89	0	0
		Proposed method	**5.53**	**5.89**	**2.94**
	All (Cross Protocol)	Deep Features [24]	31.38	76.48	67.71
		Hybrid features [22]	32.58	89.68	58.61
		Deep SLERP [27]	31.73	55.79	39.94
		Proposed method	**7.01**	**9.62**	**5.30**
PIPE	PIPE (Intra Protocol)	Deep Features [24]	12.97	33.39	16.89
		Hybrid features [22]	0	0	0
		Deep SLERP [27]	3.23	0	0
		Proposed method	**4.92**	**4.91**	**1.76**
	All (Cross Protocol)	Deep Features [24]	30.82	76.35	66.92
		Hybrid features [22]	32.40	62.21	58.54
		Deep SLERP [27]	23.13	55.66	47.67
		Proposed method	**7.77**	**11.39**	**6.59**

Table 2. Quantitative evaluation of the proposed and SOTA D-MAD techniques on intra and cross evaluation protocols.

Evaluation Protocol	D-MAD Algorithms	D-EER (%)	
		Mean	Std. Deviation
Intra	Deep Features [24]	14.34	5.37
	Hybrid features [22]	7.86	10.36
	Deep SLERP [27]	7.61	7.24
	Proposed method	**6.68**	**2.88**
Cross	Deep Features [24]	33.74	3.14
	Hybrid features [22]	36.90	6.26
	Deep SLERP [27]	27.97	4.32
	Proposed method	**7.14**	**0.87**

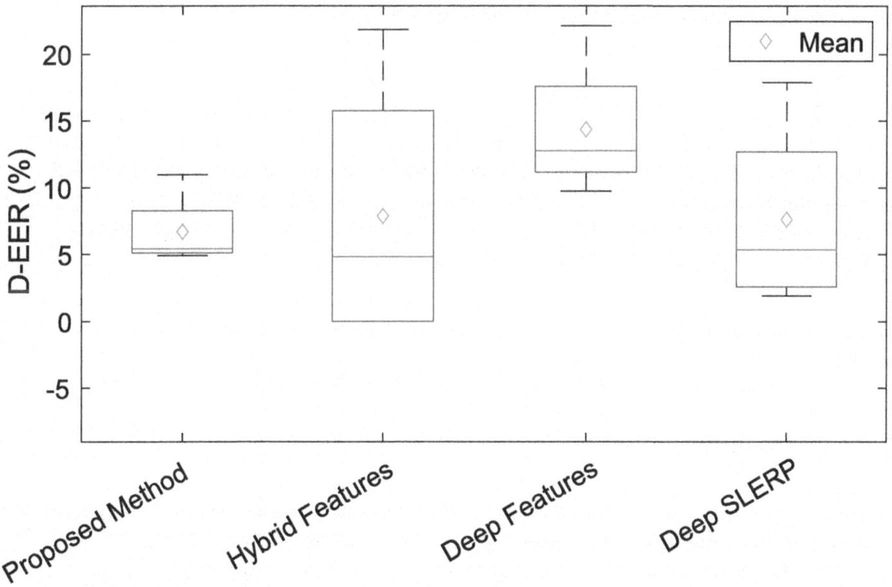

Fig. 3. Box plot showing the mean D-EER of Proposed and SOTA on Intra evaluation protocol. The lower the value of D-EER better is the detection accuracy.

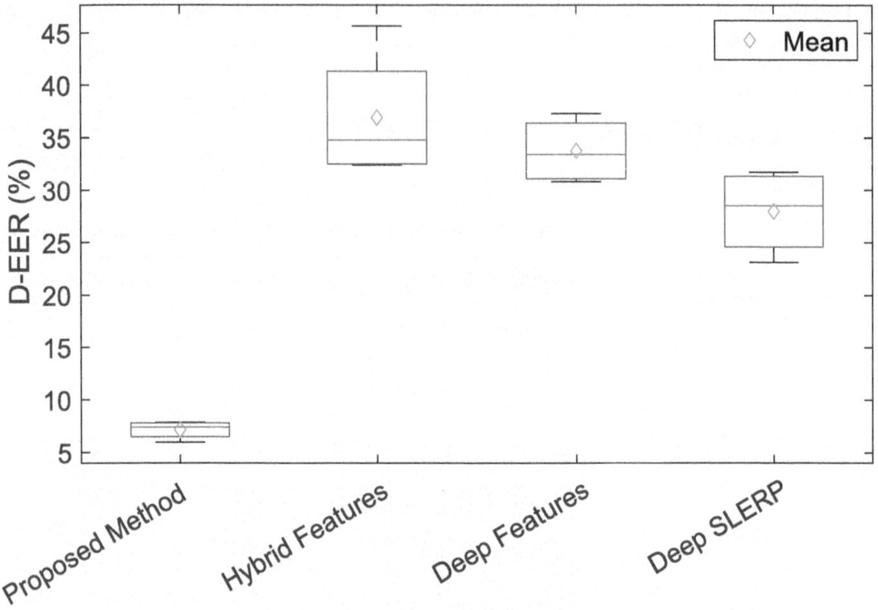

Fig. 4. Box plot showing the mean D-EER of Proposed and SOTA on Cross evaluation protocol. The lower the value of D-EER better is the detection accuracy.

the mean and standard deviation of the D-MAD algorithms with intra- and cross-validations. The results indicate that the proposed method has the best performance for both intra- and cross-protocols. The proposed method indicates a mean D-EER (%) and standard deviation of 6.68 ± 2.88 with intra-and mean D-EER (%) and standard deviation of 7.14 ± 0.87. It is worth noting that the variation in D-EER between intra- and cross-experiments is very small, thus indicating a generalizable variation. Based on the above experimental results, the proposed method emerged as the best performing method for both intra- and cross-evaluation protocols, indicating its efficacy of the proposed method.

4 Conclusion

Accurate detection of morphing attacks in face recognition systems is crucial for enhancing the reliability and security of biometric-based access control systems. Because morphing attacks are targeted to border control applications and passport issuance, the development of automatic morphing detection techniques is essential. In this paper, we present a novel approach for face morphing attack detection using a differential approach that uses two facial images to detect morphing attacks. The proposed time-frequency-based convolution neural networks were trained on the unsigned difference of the facial embedding obtained from the ArcFace backbone. The use of time-frequency information allows the identification of unusually small variations in the unsigned difference embedding features that can identify the morphing images. Extensive experiments were conducted on the newly constructed morphing datasets using four different morphing generation techniques. The quantitative performance computed on two different performance evaluation protocols indicated the best performance of the proposed method compared to three different state-of-the-art D-MAD techniques. Furthermore, the proposed method indicated a consistent performance in both intra- and cross-evaluation protocols, justifying its generalizability to unknown morphing generation types.

References

1. DNP printer (2020). http://dnpphoto.com/en-us/Products/Printers/DS820A. Accessed Oct 2020
2. Banerjee, S., Ross, A.: Conditional identity disentanglement for differential face morph detection. In: 2021 IEEE International Joint Conference on Biometrics (IJCB), pp. 1–8 (2021). https://doi.org/10.1109/IJCB52358.2021.9484355
3. Blasingame, Z., Liu, C.: Leveraging diffusion for strong and high quality face morphing attacks. IEEE Trans. Biom. Behav. Identity Sci. (2024). https://doi.org/10.1109/TBIOM.2024.3349857
4. Borghi, G., Pancisi, E., Ferrara, M., Maltoni, D.: A double siamese framework for differential morphing attack detection. Sensors **21**(10) (2021). https://doi.org/10.3390/s21103466. https://www.mdpi.com/1424-8220/21/10/3466
5. Cohen, M.X.: A better way to define and describe morlet wavelets for time-frequency analysis. Neuroimage **199**, 81–86 (2019)
6. Damer, N., Zienert, S., Wainakh, Y., Saladie, A., Kirchbuchner, F., Kuijper, A.: A multi-detector solution towards an accurate and generalized detection of face morphing attacks. In: 2019 22th International Conference on Information Fusion (FUSION). IEEE (2019)
7. Damer, N., Fang, M., Siebke, P., Kolf, J.N., Huber, M., Boutros, F.: Mordiff: recognition vulnerability and attack detectability of face morphing attacks created by diffusion autoencoders. In: 2023 11th International Workshop on Biometrics and Forensics (IWBF), pp. 1–6 (2023). https://doi.org/10.1109/IWBF57495.2023.10157869
8. Deng, J., Guo, J., Zafeiriou, S.: ArcFace: additive angular margin loss for deep face recognition. In: Conference on Computer Vision and Pattern Recognition (CVPR) (2019)
9. Ferrara, M., Franco, A., Maltoni, D.: Face demorphing. IEEE Trans. Inf. Forensics Secur. **13**(4), 1008–1017 (2018)
10. Godage, S.R., Løvåsdal, F., Venkatesh, S., Raja, K., Ramachandra, R., Busch, C.: Analyzing human observer ability in morphing attack detection–where do we stand? IEEE Trans. Technol. Soc. **4**(2), 125–145 (2023). https://doi.org/10.1109/TTS.2022.3231450
11. Kingma, D.P., Ba, J.: Adam: a method for stochastic optimization. CoRR abs/1412.6980 (2015)
12. Medvedev, I., Shadmand, F., Gonçalves, N.: Mordeephy: face morphing detection via fused classification. arXiv preprint arXiv:2208.03110 (2022)
13. Meng, Q., Zhao, S., Huang, Z., Zhou, F.: MagFace: a universal representation for face recognition and quality assessment (2021)
14. Open CV. https://www.learnopencv.com/face-morph-using-opencv-cpp-python/
15. NIST: FRVT morph web site. https://pages.nist.gov/frvt/html/frvt_morph.html
16. International Civil Aviation Organization: Machine readable passports – part 1 – introduction (2015). http://www.icao.int/publications/Documents/9303_p1_cons_en.pdf

17. Parkhi, O.M., Vedaldi, A., Zisserman, A.: Deep face recognition. British Machine Vision Association, pp. 1–12 (2015)
18. Peng, F., Zhang, L., Long, M.: FD-GAN: face de-morphing generative adversarial network for restoring accomplice's facial image. IEEE Access (2019)
19. Phillips, P.J., et al.: Overview of the face recognition grand challenge. In: 2005 IEEE Computer Society Conference on Computer Vision and Pattern Recognition (CVPR 2005), vol. 1, pp. 947–954 (2005). https://doi.org/10.1109/CVPR.2005.268
20. Raghavendra, R., Raja, K., Venkatesh, S., Busch, C.: Face morphing versus face averaging: vulnerability and detection. In: Proceedings of International Joint Conference on Biometrics (IJCB) (2017)
21. Ramachandra, R., Li, G.: Multimodality for reliable single image based face morphing attack detection. IEEE Access **10**, 82418–82433 (2022)
22. Ramachandra, R., Li, G.: Residual colour scale-space gradients for reference-based face morphing attack detection. In: 2022 25th International Conference on Information Fusion (FUSION), pp. 1–8. IEEE (2022)
23. Reddy, A., Rao, S., Ramachandra, R., Mitra, P.: Extswap: leveraging extended latent mapper for generating high quality face swapping. In: International Conference on Computer Vision and Machine Intelligence (CVMI), pp. 1–8 (2023)
24. Scherhag, U., Rathgeb, C., Merkle, J., Busch, C.: Deep face representations for differential morphing attack detection. IEEE Trans. Inf. Forensics Secur. (2020)
25. Schroff, F., Kalenichenko, D., Philbin, J.: Facenet: a unified embedding for face recognition and clustering. In: Proceedings of the IEEE Conference on Computer Vision and Pattern Recognition, pp. 815–823 (2015)
26. Shukla, N.: Sdemorph: towards better facial de-morphing from single morph. In: 2023 IEEE International Joint Conference on Biometrics (IJCB), pp. 1–9 (2023). https://doi.org/10.1109/IJCB57857.2023.10448779
27. Singh, J.M., Ramachandra, R.: Reliable face morphing attack detection in on-the-fly border control scenario with variation in image resolution and capture distance. In: 2022 IEEE International Joint Conference on Biometrics (IJCB), pp. 1–10. IEEE (2022)
28. Soleymani, S., Chaudhary, B., Dabouei, A., Dawson, J., Nasrabadi, N.: Differential morphed face detection using deep siamese networks. In: International Conference on Pattern Recognition, pp. 560–572. Springer (2021)
29. Venkatesh, S., Raghavendra, R., Raja, K., Busch, C.: Single image face morphing attack detection using ensemble of features. In: 2020 IEEE 23rd International Conference on Information Fusion (FUSION), pp. 1–6. IEEE (2020)
30. Venkatesh, S., Raghavendra, R., Raja, K., Busch, C.: Face morphing attack generation and detection: a comprehensive survey. IEEE Trans. Technol. Soc. **2**(3), 128–145 (2021). https://doi.org/10.1109/TTS.2021.3066254
31. Zhang, H., Venkatesh, S., Raghavendra, R., Raja, K., Damer, N., Busch, C.: MIPGAN–generating strong and high quality morphing attacks using identity prior driven GAN. IEEE Trans. Biom. Behav. Identity Sci. **3**(3), 365–383 (2021). https://doi.org/10.1109/TBIOM.2021.3072349
32. Zhang, H., Ramachandra, R., Raja, K., Busch, C.: Morph-pipe: plugging in identity prior to enhance face morphing attack based on diffusion model. In: Norsk IKT-konferanse for forskning og utdanning (NISK), vol. 3, pp. 1–6 (2023)

RepVGG-GELAN: Enhanced GELAN with VGG-STYLE ConvNets for Brain Tumour Detection

Thennarasi Balakrishnan and Sandeep Singh Sengar(✉)

School of Technologies, Cardiff Metropolitan University, Cardiff, UK
SSSengar@cardiffmet.ac.uk

Abstract. Methods for object detection, especially those utilizing YOLO (You Only Look Once), are known for their impressive ability to balance precision and speed. However, their potential in detecting brain tumours has received limited attention. RepVGG-GELAN, proposed in this study is an advanced YOLO framework enhanced by RepVGG (Reparameterized Convolutional Neural Network), a specialized convolutional method designed for detection particularly emphasizing brain tumours in medical imaging. With RepVGG architecture the model enhances both speed and accuracy of brain tumour detection. The integration of RepVGG within the YOLO framework seeks to optimize both computational efficiency and detection effectiveness. This research incorporates a Generalized Efficient Layer Aggregation Network (GELAN) architecture based on spatial pyramid pooling enhancing the capabilities of RepVGG. Tests on a brain tumour dataset reveal that RepVGG-GELAN exceeds the performance of the RCS-YOLO (Reparameterized Convolution ShuffleNet YOLO) in terms of both precision and processing speed. Notably, RepVGG-GELAN delivers a 4.91% enhancement in precision and a 2.54% improvement in AP50 (Average Precision at IOU=0.5) over the most recent method with a computational efficiency of 240.7 GFLOPs (Giga Floating Point Operations per Second). The proposed RepVGG-GELAN gives positive results demonstrating itself as a state-of-the-art solution for accurate and efficient detection of brain tumour images. The implementation code is publicly available at https://github.com/ThensiB/RepVGG-GELAN.

Keywords: Image detection · Convolution · Generalized Efficient Layer Aggregation Network · Computational efficiency

1 Introduction

With the high rates of sickness and mortality, brain tumors represent a significant global health concern. Brain tumour identification challenges can be effectively resolved with automated detection techniques that make use of state-of-the-art technologies like deep learning algorithms. Incorporating automated detection

J. Kakarla et al. (Eds.): CVIP 2024, CCIS 2473, pp. 417–430, 2026.
https://doi.org/10.1007/978-3-031-93688-3_30

into medical processes has the potential to significantly enhance patient outcomes and medical services by revolutionizing the management of brain tumours, especially as technology develops. The cutting-edge object detection method YOLO divides the input image into a grid while estimating class probabilities and bounding boxes for each grid cell [1]. The application of YOLO in brain tumour detection has significant promise for improving the accuracy, efficiency, and scalability of neuroimaging diagnosis approaches [2,3]. Convolutional Neural Networks (CNN) are widely employed as the primary component of YOLO object identification methods. CNN provides the feature extraction capability needed to recognize objects in an image. Because CNN employs several convolutional and pooling layers to create a hierarchical feature model from raw visual data, they can catch complex patterns and structures that could be indicative of various health problems [4,5]. The VGG deep convolutional neural network architecture was proposed in response to the need for more sophisticated networks with deeper learnable parameters. Further, inside the network max-pooling layers come after several convolutional layers. Their dense hierarchical structure allows for exact detection and diagnosis, consequently, they can recognize complex patterns and features from medical images. VGG architectures are excellent at extracting complicated features and fine-grained information from medical images making them suitable for tasks requiring high-resolution analysis [6]. The objective of ShuffleNet, a more contemporary convolutional neural network architecture is to maximize accuracy while maintaining competitive computational efficiency [7]. This introduces the concept of group convolutions and channel shuffling which drastically reduces processing costs while promoting efficient data flow between channels. ShuffleNet architecture provides a practical combination of precision and performance rendering them ideal for low-power device applications and real-time medical imaging applications [1,8]. The primary concept behind real-time object detection in the YOLO architecture was to use spatially separated bounding boxes with matching class probabilities as a regression task. To boost detection accuracy and speed, YOLOv4 incorporated several enhancements. Using cross-stage partial connections it included the CSPDarknet53 backbone which improved gradient propagation and information flow. With the implementation of AF (Anchor-Free) detection in YOLOv7, anchor boxes were rendered obsolete. This enhanced adaptability and streamlined layout. Additionally, YOLOv7 incorporated Adaptive Convolution which enhanced its ability to capture contextual data by flexible adjustment of the receptive field based on input features. Based on the Reparametrized Convolution and Generalized Efficient Layer Aggregation Network (GELAN), this study suggests a unique YOLO model called RepVGG-GELAN to develop a high-accuracy object detector for medical images. The purpose of RepVGG-GELAN is to combine the advantages of GELAN and RepVGG models for object detection applications. RepVGG offers a simple and efficient architecture with high accuracy, while GELAN provides a lightweight and flexible network design that enhances information flow and reduces information loss. By combining these two architectures, the model achieves high accuracy and efficiency in detecting brain tumors.

The upcoming segments of this paper are structured as, Sect. 2 gives a summary of relevant studies. Section 3 delves into the breif explanation of the proposed RepVGG-GELAN model. Section 4 shows the obtained results with the implementation and analysis of the outcomes. Finally, the Sect. 5 comprises the conclusion part.

2 Literature Review

2.1 RepVGG/RepConv ShuffleNet

Inspired by the RepVGG/RepConv ShuffleNet (RCS) approach utilizes reconfigured convolutional structures to improve feature extraction while minimizing computational expenses [2].

As shown in Fig. 1, a feature division mechanism breaks the incoming array, characterized by the dimensions of $C \times H \times W$ for channels, height, and width, into two arrays of same sizes. During training, each tensor is processed using multiple convolutional blocks. This consists of the 3×3 convolution, 1×1 convolution, and identity branch. Data from both branches is combined upon processing by concatenating the tensors channel-wise. A single tensor is subjected to numerous convolutional steps to collect a huge quantity of feature as training dataset. The model can adapt to various object detection circumstances including those with complicated backgrounds or occlusions because of this diversity in feature learning. A single 3×3 RepConv contains all of the training methods that utilise structural reparameterization during inference. This optimisation allows the model to conclude quicker and with reduced memory use which makes it useful for circumstances requiring immediate actions or low resource availability. By enhancing the interaction of data between the two arrays, the channel rearrangement technique improves the quality of feature mapping. The ability of the channel shuffle operator to properly combine feature information from multiple convolution groups improves the model's performance in feature extraction. The computational cost can be reduced by a factor of $1/g$ with the channel shuffle operator, where "g" represents the overall groups in the aggregated convolutions. Compared to conventional 3×3 convolutions RCS maintains inter-channel data transfer while reducing the computing cost during inference by a factor of two as shown in Fig. 1(b). Consequently, RCS can effectively collect contextual information and spatial connections needed for precise object detection. Using cutting-edge methods including reparameterization, shuffle, and channel splitting, RCS produces outstanding feature representation. RCS provides fast and effective inference which could reduce computational complexity and memory utilization for real-time applications. Because the structure allows for robust representation learning from input data during training it improves the model's capacity to recognize complex patterns [2]. RCS is an excellent option for practical object detection applications since it strikes a compromise between computational efficiency and feature representation through the use of

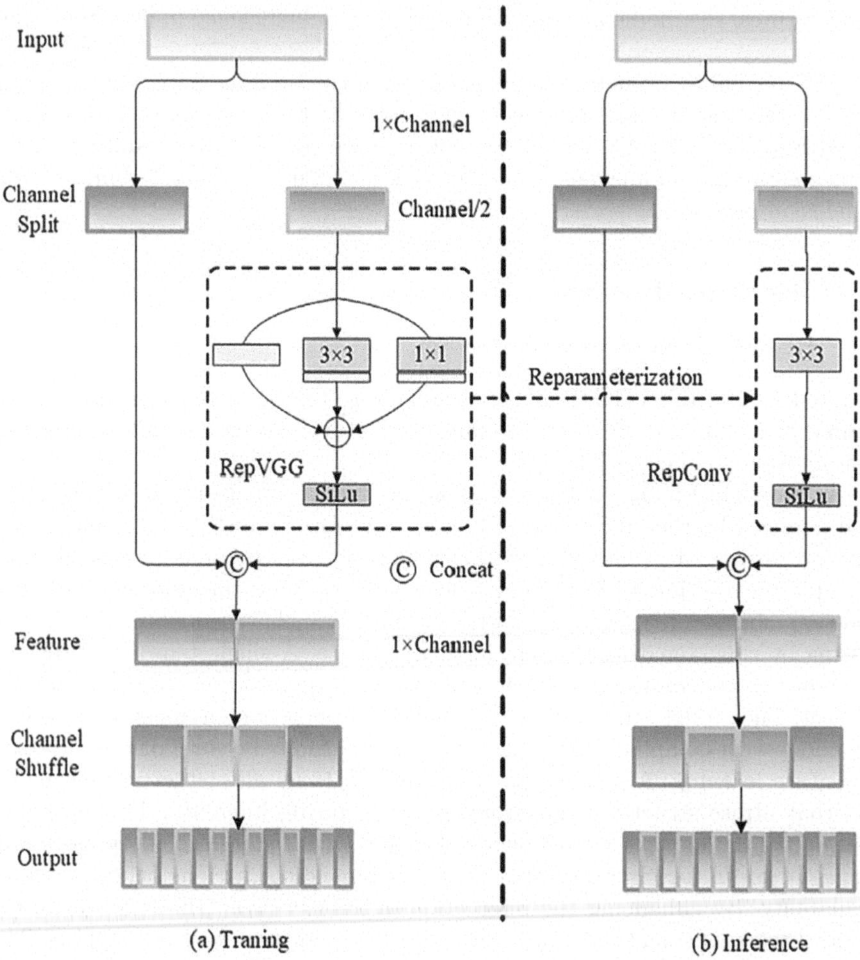

Fig. 1. The RepVGG architecture. (a) during the training phase, (b) during the inference phase (or deployed). Source: (RCS-YOLO: A Fast and High-Accuracy Object Detector for Brain Tumor Detection, 2023)

channel split, shuffle, and reparameterization algorithms. Its versatility in learning different properties, memory optimization, and effective inference makes it an essential tool in computer vision [2,15].

2.2 Generalized Efficient Layer Aggregation Network (GELAN)

GELAN provides a task-dependent advanced method. The input tensor represents an array of images fed into the GELAN object detection model. All images in batches have predetermined channels, heights, and widths [10].

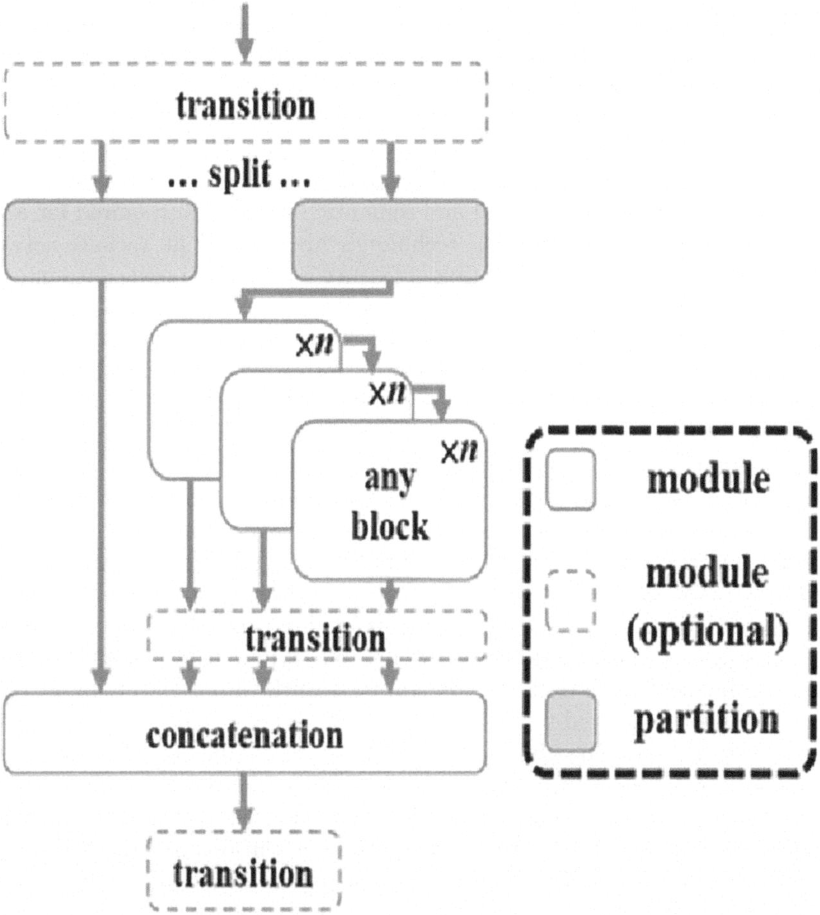

Fig. 2. Generalized Efficient Layer Aggregation Network Architecture Source: (YOLOv9: Learning What You Want to Learn Using Programmable Gradient Information, 2024)

Figure 2 explains the architecture of GELAN, a compact model framework designed around gradient path optimization. The input tensor undergoes many convolutional operations in the backbone layers. In certain circumstances, the number of channels can be increased while the spatial dimensions (height and width) of the feature maps decrease. With the ability of these layers to capture data at varying degrees of complexity, the system can acquire both broad conceptual information and fundamental features needed for detecting objects. As the input tensor passes through the backbone levels hierarchical feature extraction is applied to it. Every layer captures features at various levels of abstraction. After receiving the input tensor SPP (Spatial Pyramid Pooling) blocks process the feature maps to extract multi-scale features. Through adaptive pooling methods, SPP blocks extract features at different spatial resolutions, making them more resilient to object size changes and occlusions. Further, the RepNCSPELAN4 (Rep-Net with Cross-Stage Partial CSP and ELAN) block enhances and refines the feature representations by processing the input tensor. RepNCSPELAN4 blocks integrate convolutional layers to train discriminative features. These architectural components are designed to manage input properties efficiently while preserving the spatial and semantic information required for accurate object detection. Upsampling techniques are applied at various network layers to enhance the spatial resolution of feature maps. Multi-scale data integration is facilitated by combining enlarged feature maps with those from preceding layers. This allows feasibility for the model to preserve fine-grained characteristics and spatial connections which leads to improved object localization and recognition. After the feature maps are evaluated the detection head generates predictions for object detection. The detection head generates bounding boxes, class probabilities, and other relevant information for each object detected in the receiving images. The GELAN's Detect module receives feature maps from different detection layers and uses them to provide class confidence ratings and bounding box predictions. To generate predictions the convolutional layers in the forward pass are applied to the input representation. Class confidence ratings and predictions for bounding box regression are computed using the output from these layers. During inference, the module dynamically computes strides and anchor boxes derived from the configuration of the input feature map. These anchor boxes are employed to decode the bounding box predictions. The anchor boxes and strides are dynamically changed if the input changes. GELAN's modular and flexible architecture allows it to be readily tailored to various datasets and a broad spectrum of object detection applications. The model can detect a large variety of object attributes and spatial correlations due to its reparameterized convolutional blocks, spatial pyramid pooling, and hierarchical structure. Its adaptable structure and inference speed make it ideal for practical implementation across various computer vision tasks from object detection in self-driving vehicles, detecting pedestrians in security monitoring systems and analyzing medical images [10–12].

3 Methodology

The study introduces a new YOLO model, RepVGG-GELAN shown in Fig. 3, built upon the RepVGG/RepConv to develop a precise object detector for medical images. RepVGG-GELAN is crafted to harness the advantages of both RepVGG and GELAN models for identifying objects in various tasks.

RepVGG (Reparametrized VGG) is a simplified convolutional neural network (CNN) framework that unifies depthwise separable convolutions and residual connections. RepVGG blocks provide the starting point of RepVGG-GELAN and are renowned for their ease of use and efficacy in feature extraction. ReLU and identity mappings are combined in these blocks to replace conventional convolutional layers improving training stability and performance [2,7,9,16].

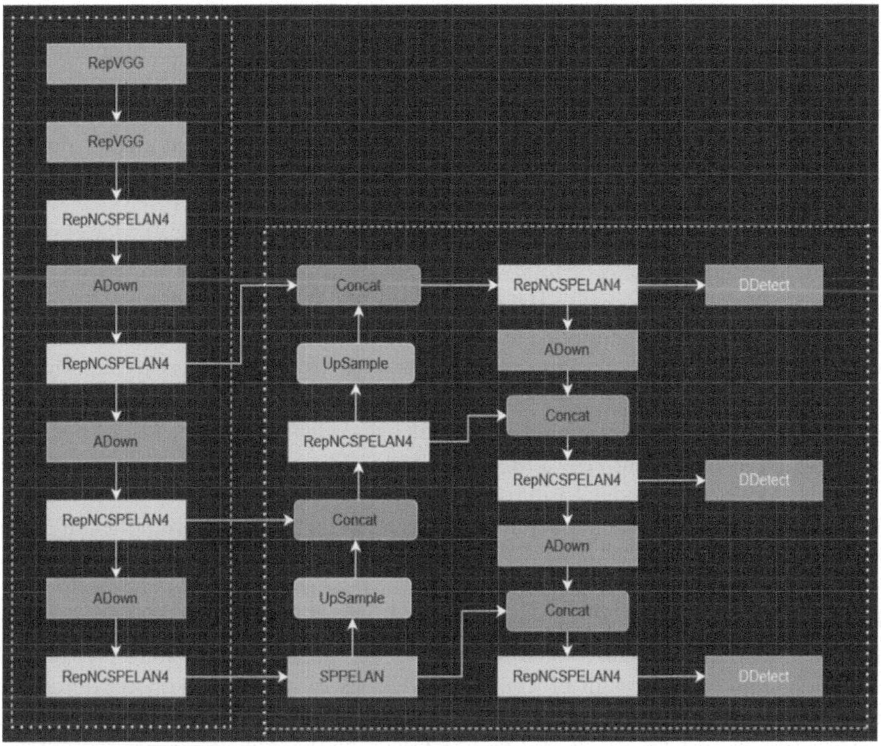

Fig. 3. Proposed RepVGG-GELAN. The architecture of RepVGG-GELAN is mainly comprised of RepVGG and RepNCSPELAN4.

RepNCSPELAN4 (Rep-Net with Cross-Stage Partial CSP and ELAN) is a block architecture that combines Cross-Stage Partial (CSP) connections and ELAN for feature enhancement. It splits the input into two parts processes each part separately with multiple RepNCSP blocks and then concatenates the outputs before passing them through the final convolutional layer. CSP connections facilitate information flow between different stages of the network. ELAN enhances feature representation through attention mechanisms. RepNCSPELAN4 enhances feature representation by combining efficient feature extraction with attention mechanisms. It enables the network to capture and emphasize important features relevant to object detection tasks [10,14,17].

ADown module represents an asymmetric downsampling block. It takes an input tensor x, performs average pooling on one half and max pooling on the other half, applies convolutional operations to each pooled tensor and concatenates the results before returning. This block is useful for downsampling feature maps with different operations on each half [10,17].

Spatial Pyramid Pooling with ELAN consists of a series of convolutions followed by spatial pyramid pooling (SPP) operations where the feature maps are divided into regions of different sizes and the features are pooled from each region separately. The pooled features are merged and fed into another convolutional layer for further processing. This block is useful for capturing multi-scale information from the input feature maps [10,17].

Upsampling and Concatenation operations up-sample feature maps from the backbone and concatenate them with features from previous stages. They enable multi-scale feature fusion and preserve spatial information [10,17].

The DDetect block processes input feature maps through convolutional layers to predict bounding box coordinates and class probabilities. It utilizes predefined anchor boxes and strides for inference. The biases in the detection head are initialized based on the nominal class frequency and image size. Bias initialization helps ensure that the detection head starts with reasonable predictions during training [10,17].

In brain tumor detection capturing multi-scale features is essential as tumors can vary significantly in size and appearance. The spatial pyramid pooling in GELAN allows the model to extract features at different scales improving its robustness to tumor size variations and occlusions. Furthermore, efficient layer aggregation in GELAN enables the model to combine and refine feature representations from different layers leading to more discriminative and comprehensive feature learning. This is particularly beneficial for brain tumor detection where complex patterns and subtle details need to be captured accurately for reliable diagnosis. The overall result of RepVGG-GELAN is an effective object detection architecture that merges the streamlined nature of RepVGG with the advanced feature fusion and handling abilities of GELAN through the combined use of both models' advantages. RepVGG-GELAN seeks to enhance performance, efficiency, and accuracy in difficult detection tasks.

4 Experiments and Results

4.1 Data Collection

To evaluate the proposed RepVGG-GELAN model employed the brain tumour detection 2020 dataset (Br35H) [13], which comprises of 701 images divided into two folders, 'TRAIN' and 'VAL' containing the training and validation images respectively. Each folder has 2 subfolders named labels and images, where the labels of each image are stored in a text file in the labels folder. The .txt format annotations in the folder dataset-Br35H are converted from the original JSON format. Out of these 701 images 500 images were assigned for training, while the other 201 images were set aside for testing. The input image size is set to 640×640. The label boxes of the brain images were normalized and are in the format class, xcenter, ycenter, width, and height.

To further validate the robustness and applicability of the RepVGG-GELAN model across different clinical settings, we conducted additional experiments using a separate brain tumor dataset obtained from Roboflow 't Dataset' [18]. The dataset has 1003 images with auto-orient and resized to 640×640. It has 2 classes: brain tumors and no brain tumour.

4.2 Implementation Details

The RepVGG-GELAN model was developed using the following configurations in Google Colab: Windows 11 as the operating system, Intel Iris Xe as the CPU, PyTorch 1.9.1 as the deep learning framework, NVIDIA GeForce RTX 3090 with 24 GB memory capacity (provided by Google Colab) as the GPU, and the CUDA Toolkit through the Google Colab platform. The model was trained for a maximum of 150 epochs with the number of batches set to 8, the resolution of the image as 640×640 pixels, Stochastic Gradient Descent (SGD) was used with an initial learning Rate of 0.01 as the optimization algorithm and weight decay coefficient 0.0005. Linear warm-up is used in the first three epochs. To prevent overfitting weight decay introduces a penalty term to the loss function by penalizing large weights. Mosaic augmentation is applied to every training sample and is turned off for the last 15 epochs. The Colab environment allows it to be more effective in usage of CUDA for deep learning tasks.

The model loads the configuration from rcs-gelan-c.yaml file with the number of input channels ("ch") 1 and the number of classes ("nc") 1 [0: brain tumour]. Convolutional layers (Conv2d()) and batch normalization layers (BatchNorm2d()) are fused to optimize the inference speed. The input feature maps "x" from each detection layer are concatenated and returned during training. During inference, anchor boxes and strides are computed dynamically if needed. Bounding box predictions and class predictions are extracted from the concatenated output. The IoU (Intersection over Union) is determined by dividing the area of overlap by the area of the combined region. The area is calculated as the product of the widths and heights of the intersecting regions after taking the maximum of zero and the differences between the coordinates. The union area is calculated as the sum of the areas of the individual bounding boxes minus the intersection area. Bounding box coordinates are refined using the Down-sampling Feature Localization (DFL) layer (adjusts the center coordinates and scales the width and height based on learned parameters). The bounding box predictions undergo refinement to improve localization accuracy. Bounding box coordinates are transformed and descaled based on anchor boxes and strides. Class predictions are passed through a sigmoid activation function. The final output consists of the concatenated predictions, which include the transformed bounding box coordinates and the sigmoid-activated class scores.

4.3 Evaluation Metrics

To evaluate the strengths and weaknesses of the model this study uses FLOPs (Floating Point Operations), mAP50 (mean Average Precision at IoU threshold of 0.5), mAP50:95 (mean Average Precision over IoU thresholds from 0.5 to 0.95), precision, and recall as comparative measures of recognition influence in this study. The formulas below are applied to calculate precision and recall at an IoU (Intersection over Union) value 0.5:

$$Precision = TP/(TP + FP) \tag{1}$$

$$Recall = TP/(TP + FN) \quad (2)$$

where FP stands for negative instances mistakenly recognized as positive instances refer to the actual tumors present in the images, FN represents positive instances incorrectly categorized as negative refer to the non-tumor regions in the images and TP signifies positive instances correctly classified as positive. FLOPs, represents number of floating point operations required for inference, help understand the computational cost associated with running the model on different hardware platforms. mAP@0.5 average precision calculated for brain tumour class at a specific IoU (Intersection over Union) threshold of 0.5, considers the precision-recall trade-off for the class and computes the average precision. mAP@0.5:0.95 a more comprehensive metric that evaluates the model's effectiveness over various IoU thresholds offers a broader understanding of the model's ability to localizes objects across different degrees of intersection with actual bounding box regions (Table 1).

Table 1. Quantitative results of RCS-YOLO, YOLOv8 and RepVGG-GELAN on Br35H brain tumor dataset. The best results are shown in bold.

	Precision	Recall	AP50	AP50:95	Parameters (in millions)
RCS-YOLO	0.936	**0.945**	0.946	0.729	45.7
YOLOv8	0.973	0.909	0.957	**0.733**	30.1
RepVGG-GELAN	**0.982**	0.890	**0.970**	0.723	**25.4**

4.4 Results

The RepVGG-GELAN model achieves an outstanding precision score of 0.982 indicating its ability to correctly identify true positive instances while minimizing false positives. Although the recall score of 0.890 is slightly lower compared to other models, it still demonstrates the model's ability in capturing a proportion of true positive cases. RepVGG-GELAN achieves an impressive AP50 score of 0.970 surpassing both RCS-YOLO and YOLOv8, demonstrating its effectiveness in accurately localizing objects with sufficient overlap with ground truth bounding boxes. This metric reflects the model's performance to maintain high precision over various IoU thresholds, particularly at the 50% threshold (commonly used in object detection tasks). With an AP50:95 score of 0.723 RepVGG-GELAN demonstrates consistent performance across various IoU thresholds. While slightly reduced compared to RCS-YOLO and YOLOv8, this metric still reflects the model's robustness in detecting brain tumors across different degrees of intersection between predicted and actual bounding box regions. One of the key strengths of RepVGG-GELAN is its efficiency in model size with only 25.4 million parameters. This streamlined architecture ensures computational efficiency without compromising performance making it well-suited for deployments. The predicted bounding boxes over the input images resulting from the RepVGG-GELAN is shown in Fig. 4.

The second dataset is preprocessed and trained using the same protocols as used with the primary dataset (Br35H). The model was fine-tuned on 80% of the Roboflow dataset and evaluated on the remaining 20%. The results achieved are shown in Table 2 This additional evaluation strengthens the confidence in the RepVGG-GELAN model's robustness and its potential for wide applicability across different clinical settings and data sources.

Table 2. Quantitative results of YOLOv8 and RepVGG-GELAN on Roboflow brain tumor dataset. The best results are shown in bold.

	Precision	Recall	AP50	AP50:95	Parameters (in millions)
YOLOv8	**0.95**	0.877	0.951	0.688	30.1
RepVGG-GELAN	0.898	**0.953**	**0.967**	**0.711**	**25.4**

The reparameterized convolutions from RepVGG enable faster and more stable feature extraction, while GELAN's advanced layer aggregation and multi-scale processing enhance the model's ability to capture intricate details and variations in brain tumor appearances. This synergistic combination of efficiency and representational power makes RepVGG-GELAN a promising solution for accurate and real-time brain tumor detection, potentially improving diagnostic processes and patient outcomes in clinical applications (Table 3).

Table 3. Ablation results on the proposed RepVGG-GELAN module. The best results are shown in bold.

	Precision	Recall	AP50	AP50:95
RepVGG-GELAN (w RepVGG)	**0.982**	0.89	**0.97**	**0.723**
RepVGG-GELAN (w/o RepVGG)	0.964	0.902	0.957	0.722

4.5 Ablation Study

RepVGG-GELAN achieves a higher precision of 0.982 compared to GELAN's precision of 0.964. This indicates that RepVGG-GELAN is more accurate in correctly identifying positive detections leading to a reduction in false positives. Moreover, despite having a slightly lower recall of 0.89 compared to GELAN's recall of 0.902, RepVGG-GELAN achieves a higher mAP50 of 0.97 signifying improved detection accuracy across different thresholds. By leveraging the strengths of both RepVGG and GELAN architectures RepVGG-GELAN achieves higher precision and overall detection performance, making it a more effective and reliable model.

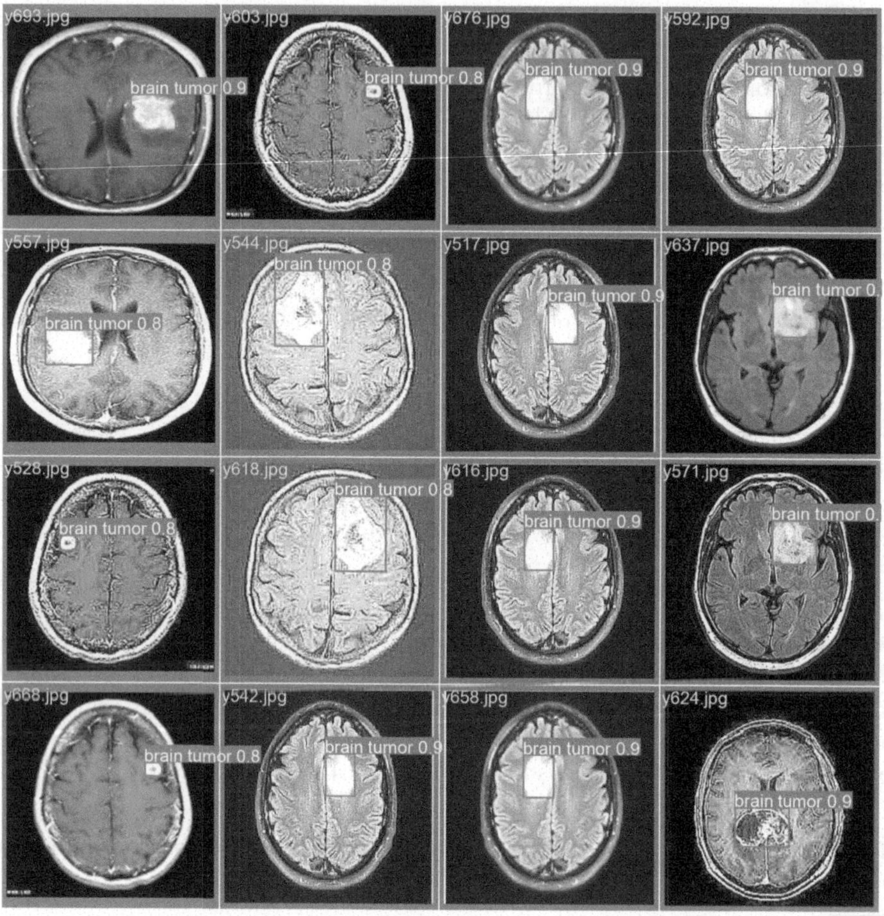

Fig. 4. Sample of the RepVGG-GELAN's prediction on Br35H dataset

5 Conclusion

This study was concentrated on the design and analysis of the RepVGG-YOLO model for the detection of brain tumours in medical imaging data. Incorporating GELAN architecture into RepVGG enhances the performance of the model in capturing relevant attributes from medical imaging data leading to improved tumour detection accuracy. The model was designed to focus on efficiency, leveraging techniques such as structural reparameterization and efficient layer aggregation to optimize resource utilization and inference speed.

6 Future Direction

The practical challenges and the clinical efficacy can be addressed by collaborating with medical professionals and gathering feedback from clinical trials or retrospective studies which can further strengthen the model's credibility and pave the way for its successful adoption in clinical practice.

While the RepVGG-GELAN model aims to improve computational efficiency through techniques like reparameterized convolutions and efficient layer aggregation, the use of sophisticated architectures could still pose challenges in low-resource settings typical of many medical facilities. Exploring model optimization techniques, hardware acceleration, cloud-based solutions, and collaborative efforts can pave the way for making advanced brain tumor detection models more accessible and practical in a wide range of medical facilities, regardless of their resource constraints.

References

1. Terven, J.R., Cordova-Esparaza, D.M.: A comprehensive review of yolo: from YOLOV1 to YOLOV8 and beyond (2023). https://arxiv.org/pdf/2304.00501v1.pdf. Accessed 15 Mar 2024
2. Kang, M., et al.: RCS-YOLO: A Fast and High-Accuracy Object Detector for Brain Tumor Detection. https://arxiv.org/pdf/2307.16412.pdf. Accessed 8 Jan 2024
3. Sengar, S.S., et al.: Multi-planar 3D knee MRI segmentation via UNet inspired architectures. Int. J. Imaging Syst. Technol. **33**(3), 985–998 (2023)
4. Wang, J., et al.: End-to-end object detection with fully convolutional network. In: Proceedings of the IEEE/CVF Conference on Computer Vision and Pat-tern Recognition (CVPR), pp. 15849–15858 (2021). https://arxiv.org/pdf/2012.03544.pdf. Accessed 19 Mar 2024
5. Jain, V., Sengar, S.S., Agastinose Ronickom, J.F.: Age-specific diagnostic classification of ASD using deep learning approaches (2023)
6. Ding, X., et al.: RepVGG: making VGG- style ConvNets great again. In: IEEE/CVF Conference on Computer Vision and Pattern Recognition (CVPR), pp. 13733–13742. IEEE, Piscataway (2021). https://arxiv.org/pdf/2101.03697.pdf. Accessed 8 Mar 2024
7. Liu, Z., et al.: A ConvNet for the 2020s. In: Proceedings of the IEEE/CVF Conference on Computer Vision and Pattern Recognition (CVPR), pp. 11976–11986 (2022). https://arxiv.org/pdf/2201.03545.pdf. Accessed 5 Mar 2024
8. Zhang, X., Zhou, X., Lin, M., Sun, J.: ShuffleNet: an extremely efficient convolutional neural network for mobile devices. In: IEEE/CVF Conference on Computer Vision and Pattern Recognition (CVPR), pp. 6848–6856. IEEE, Piscataway (2018). https://arxiv.org/pdf/1707.01083.pdf. Accessed 12 Mar 2024
9. Wang, C.-Y., et al.: CSPNet: a new backbone that can enhance learning capability of CNN. In: IEEE/CVF Conference on Computer Vision and Pattern Recognition Workshops (CVPRW), pp. 1571–1580. IEEE, Piscataway (2020). https://arxiv.org/pdf/1911.11929.pdf. Accessed 10 Mar 2024
10. Wang, C.-Y., et al.: YOLOv9: A Leap Forward in Object Detection Technology. https://docs.ultralytics.com/models/yolov9/. Accessed 13 Feb 2024
11. Wang, C.-Y., et al.: Designing Network Design Strategies Through Gradient Path Analysis. https://arxiv.org/pdf/2211.04800.pdf. Accessed 17 Mar 2024
12. Wang, C.-Y., et al.: YOLOv7: trainable bag-of-freebies sets new state-of-the-art for real-time object detectors. https://arxiv.org/pdf/2207.02696.pdf. Accessed 17 Mar 2024

13. Hamada, A.: Br35H: brain tumor detection 2020. Kaggle (2020). https://www.kaggle.com/datasets/ahmedhamada0/brain-tumor-detection. Accessed 15 Jan 2024
14. ZainEldin, H., et al.: Brain Tumor Detection and Classification Using Deep Learning and Sine-Cosine Fitness Grey Wolf Optimization. https://www.ncbi.nlm.nih.gov/pmc/articles/PMC9854739/. Accessed 19 Mar 2024
15. Lakshmi, P.B., et al.: Classification of autism spectrum disorder based on brain image data using deep neural networks. In: International Conference on Frontiers of Intelligent Computing: Theory and Applications. Springer, Singapore (2023)
16. Kang, M.: Official implementation of "RCS-YOLO: A Fast and High-Accuracy Object Detector for Brain Tumor Detection". https://github.com/mkang315/RCS-YOLO. Accessed 8 Jan 2024
17. Kin Yiu, W.: Implementation of paper - YOLOv9: Learning What You Want to Learn Using Programmable Gradient Information. https://github.com/WongKinYiu/yolov9. Accessed 28 Feb 2024
18. ronaldo, t Dataset, Roboflow. https://universe.roboflow.com/ronaldo-1dada/t-kabm3. Accessed 17 June 2024

Prompt2LVideos: Exploring Prompts for Understanding Long-Form Multimodal Videos

Soumya Shamarao Jahagirdar, Jayasree Saha(✉), and C. V. Jawahar(✉)

Center for Visual Information Technology, IIIT Hyderabad, Hyderabad, India
{soumya.jahagirdar,jayashree.saha}@research.iiit.ac.in,
jawahar@iiit.ac.in

Abstract. Learning multimodal video understanding typically relies on datasets comprising video clips paired with manually annotated captions. However, this becomes even more challenging when dealing with long-form videos, lasting from minutes to hours, in educational and news domains due to the need for more annotators with subject expertise. Hence, there arises a need for automated solutions. Recent advancements in Large Language Models (LLMs) promise to capture concise and informative content that allows the comprehension of entire videos by leveraging Automatic Speech Recognition (ASR) and Optical Character Recognition (OCR) technologies. ASR provides textual content from audio, while OCR extracts textual content from specific frames. This paper introduces a dataset comprising long-form lectures and news videos. We present baseline approaches to understand their limitations on this dataset and advocate for exploring prompt engineering techniques to comprehend long-form multimodal video datasets comprehensively.

Keywords: Long-form videos · Prompt Engineering · Large Language Models

1 Introduction

Learning representations for video-text fusion poses a significant challenge yet holds paramount importance for comprehensive video comprehension across various real-world applications such as video retrieval, captioning, and video based document retrieval analysis. While multimodal contrastive learning leveraging extensive web-scale datasets has demonstrated efficacy in image-text representation tasks, its application in the video-language domain still needs to be explored, particularly in educational and news contexts. A primary hurdle hindering further exploration in this domain is the need for high-quality video-language datasets suitable for large-scale pretraining. Existing research predominantly relies on datasets such as HowTo100M [24], MSR-VTT [35], YOUCOOK2 [37], etc., utilizing automatically generated transcriptions via automatic speech recognition (ASR) or annotated captions. However, these datasets primarily consist

J. Kakarla et al. (Eds.): CVIP 2024, CCIS 2473, pp. 431–446, 2026.
https://doi.org/10.1007/978-3-031-93688-3_31

of instructional videos focusing on action understanding. The distinct challenges presented by educational and news video content necessitate dedicated attention and dataset curation efforts to facilitate advancements in video-text representation learning within these domains. In education, the focus typically diverges from action understanding, instead emphasizing the transmission of information through mediums like blackboards or PowerPoint presentations. Extracting meaningful insights from these sources poses challenges; solely relying on ASR is insufficient, and acquiring annotations can be complex due to the specialized subject matter knowledge required. Conversely, news videos dynamically convey information through live updates and on-screen graphics.

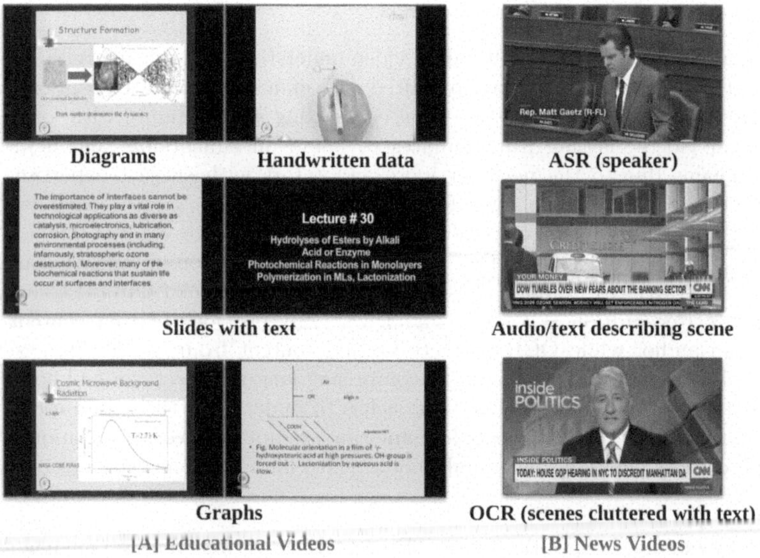

Fig. 1. An illustration showcasing the diverse data found within educational and news videos adds intrigue to these domains. Exploring such data holds promise for advancing long video understanding tasks.

Consequently, comprehending such content practically requires extracting such live updates to be captured in text form related to the frames within the video. Optical Character Recognition (OCR) [2,13,14,23,30], may provide useful information in such cases. Existing video-text repositories typically consist of clips ranging from approximately 2 to 10 s in length, or they are trimmed to fit within this duration in extensive video datasets. However, this duration may prove ineffective for educational and news videos. Processing clips of uniform size across both domains may be challenging, as educational content often requires extended explanations for specific illustrations, spanning several minutes. Conversely, news videos deliver information swiftly, with updates occurring rapidly. Additionally, special news broadcasts may introduce diverse information with each frame, distinguishing them from the content in the analyzed clips. ASR yields extensive textual data, but it may not be optimal for video-text pre-training due to its overwhelming nature. On the other hand, OCR may need more comprehensive information. Merging these sources could result in the loss of valuable data. Therefore, there is a need for processed information that is tailored for optimal video-text comprehension. Recent advancements in natural language processing and computer vision have led to significant progress in developing large language models (LLMs), profoundly impacting tools within the natural language processing domain. Models like ChatGPT [25], LLaVA [20], and others can understand and generate human-like text across diverse contexts. Leveraging LLMs to prompt and extract meaningful insights from raw datasets holds immense potential. This study delves into the extraction of additional information through carefully crafted prompts. The extracted insights offer substantial promise for future tasks, including summarization, keyword extraction, identifying key takeaways, and providing valuable metadata that can be repurposed across a broad spectrum of applications tailored to specific downstream tasks.

This study aims to pinpoint the prevalent challenges associated with comprehending extended video content, particularly within educational and news contexts Fig. 1. Even though captions accompany individual videos, they often need to catch up in capturing every crucial detail within lengthy videos. For instance, videos labeled with "clustering," focusing on partition clustering, may fail to encompass the entire scope or relevance for those seeking information on subspace clustering techniques. Moreover, there are instances where students may seek particular queries, which are eventually discussed within a video rather than as its primary focus. Likewise, news videos encompass a range of topics, often accompanied by captions highlighting key events or breaking news. However, crucial information may only be captured if it coincides with the highlighted segments or breaking news alerts.

In such scenarios, conventional retrieval systems may not yield optimal results. Similarly, videos contain various news, captioned with highlights or breaking news; in such cases, some important information might only be caught if the breaking news or highlights.

Therefore, a way to understand long-form videos is needed. ASR and OCR may provide some helpful information for long-form videos. However, the ASR transcripts are often lengthy and must be more concise to capture meaningful captions for each video clip. Conversely, OCR needs help to extract useful information from complex content, such as equations found in specific educational courses. In summary, our contributions are threefold:

1. We investigate the utility of prompt templates for processing text content derived from both ASR and OCR, enabling the utilization of powerful large language models (LLMs) to generate high-quality video-text data with minimal human intervention.
2. To understand the associated challenges in long-form videos, we have curated the Edu-News dataset to enhance multimodal understanding within the domains of education and news through video-language modeling.

3. The analysis of baseline methods for video-text retrieval aims to comprehend the intricacies of the dataset and actively fosters interest in the research community toward this evolving direction.

The code and dataset are available at https://github.com/soumyasj/Prompt2LVideos

2 Related Works

Video-Language Datasets. Research in the domain of video-language interaction has predominantly concentrated on analyzing movies [26,27,32] and instructional content [1,24,28], notably emphasizing instructional videos related to cooking [7,36]. Despite this emphasis, a limited number of studies [3,4,8,11,22] have explored applications within the educational and news domain, which we outline below. Specifically, certain works [8,22] have delved into methods for localizing and recognizing text within educational settings, particularly on blackboards. Others have examined learner engagement with educational videos [3,4], while another subset of research has focused on segmenting lecture videos [11,29]. News videos [12,15,16] frequently present a complex and multifaceted narrative, often depicting multiple events unfolding simultaneously or in quick succession. While there are some datasets tailored for understanding news content, they typically focus on specific aspects like video timeline modeling or video question answering. Recently, Chou et al. [6] introduced a novel approach with long-form news videos, each encapsulating a single coherent story. These videos comprise action shots capturing real events, interviews with relevant individuals, and footage from related occurrences. However, most of these datasets necessitate manual annotation by annotators to serve specific downstream tasks. We provide a succinct overview of existing datasets in Table 1, offering insights into the scope and characteristics of available resources.

Table 1. A comprehensive description of existing datasets

Dataset	Content	# Videos	Total (hrs)	Annotations & Others
Reuters ViL News	News	1970	50	Subtitle, Caption, Story Keyword
NewsVQA [12]	News	2730	156	QA Pairs
YT-News Timeline	News	300K	-	Timelines
NewsVideo QA [16]	News	3083	-	QA, OCR
LectureVideoDB	Education	-	-	Word bounding boxes and corresponding text ground truths for 5000 frames
AVL Lectures	Education	2350	2200	OCR & Transcripts
Ours	Education+News	5146	1500+	OCR & ASR Transcripts, Caption using Prompts

Prompt Engineering. Prompt engineering [21,34] represents a cutting-edge methodology in natural language processing (NLP), revolutionizing the utilization of large language models (LLMs) by enhancing efficiency and cost-effectiveness. This groundbreaking paradigm stems from the evolution of LLMs, which have revolutionized our natural language comprehension. Their adeptness at discerning linguistic patterns and structures has proved indispensable across language-centric endeavors. Nevertheless, fine-tuning these pre-existing models can be resource-intensive and time-consuming, necessitating substantial annotated data and computational power. In response to this challenge, researchers have embraced prompts to guide model refinement [19,34]. Prompt learning, an innovative framework within NLP, empowers language models to engage in few-shot or even zero-shot learning, seamlessly adapting to novel contexts with minimal labeled data. This methodology, deeply rooted in language modeling, entails directly modeling the probability of text. The meticulous design of prompts tailored to specific downstream tasks is at the core of prompt engineering, effectively steering pre-trained models toward accomplishing desired objectives. Recently, downstream tasks related to images and videos have begun leveraging prompting technology, either through manually crafted prompts or automatically generated prompts, to yield improved results in multimodal learning and enhance zero-shot performance [5,17,33].

3 Edu-News: A Prompt Based Multimodal Dataset

3.1 Data Curation

In the realm of video understanding, predominant research endeavors are concentrated on instructional videos, while educational and news content remains comparatively underexplored despite presenting distinct challenges. Educational videos are characterized by essential elements such as blackboards, PowerPoint presentations, and instructor narration. Conversely, news videos encompass a diverse array of critical information, including breaking news, updates, live coverage, and other significant events (Fig. 2).

Collection Strategies. SWAYAM-NPTEL stands as a flagship initiative by the MHRD, aimed at delivering top-tier education nationwide to all learners. We have meticulously selected a range of diverse courses covering engineering, science, and technology, leveraging the utilization of blackboards and PowerPoint presentations to curate multimodal educational content, enhancing video comprehension for learners. Moreover, we collect news videos mainly categorized into US and World news. They cover various topics, including politics, current affairs, entertainment, and sports. We curate individual YouTube playlists for both news and educational videos.

Statistics. In our analysis of lecture videos, we compile a selection of 35 courses from NPTEL, encompassing a total of 1345 videos, with an average of 38 videos per course. The distribution of courses is illustrated in Fig. 3, which presents a

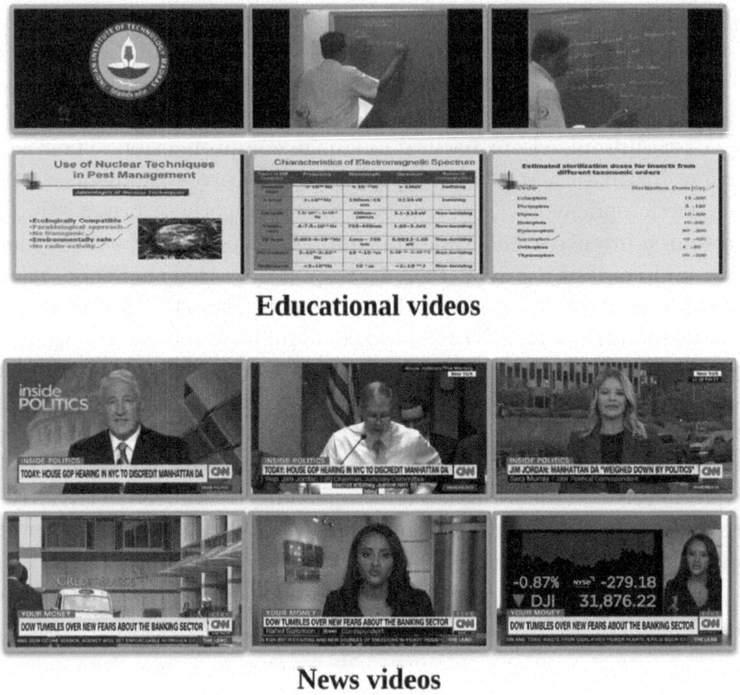

Fig. 2. Edu-News: Dataset for video understanding on educational and news videos.

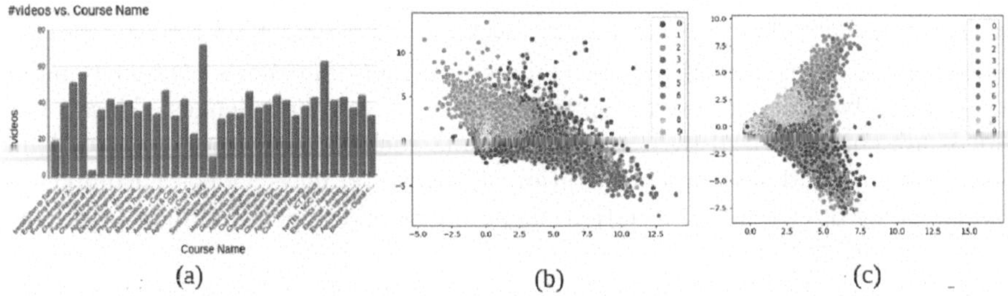

Fig. 3. Insights into the distribution of data investigated in this study are provided. In (a), the distribution of topics in NPTEL videos is illustrated, demonstrating a uniform spread across topics. Notably, the experiments outlined in this work can extend to encompass a broader range of topics and diverse lecture video content. In (b) and (c), we depict the distributions of word embeddings of OCR tokens and transcripts, respectively, in both educational and news videos. We employ clustering techniques with k = 10 clusters to visualize the diverse array of video content types present in the dataset.

bar chart indicating the number of videos across all 35 courses from NPTEL. Similarly, for news videos, we collect approximately 1000 h of content.

Features. Lecture videos undergo content changes less frequently due to the speaker's detailed explanations of concepts or PowerPoint presentations. In contrast, news videos exhibit rapid content turnover, with significant fluctuations in textual content at the frame level. It's essential to pinpoint specific usable and distinct frames to extract OCR-like features. The strategy for selecting frames differs between education and news videos. For long-form education videos averaging around 38 min, we sample one frame per minute, whereas for news videos, we sample one frame per 10 s. We employ the EasyOCR library, an open-source tool [9], to extract OCR content from the chosen frames. Furthermore, we utilize transcripts, subtitles, and closed captions to understand the video content comprehensively. We extract these speech-to-text components by employing the Silero [31] model provided in PyTorch. These transcripts serve a dual purpose: they contribute to the retrieval process and form the foundation for our prompting methodology. In Fig. 4, we show the word cloud of OCR tokens and Transcripts in the dataset.

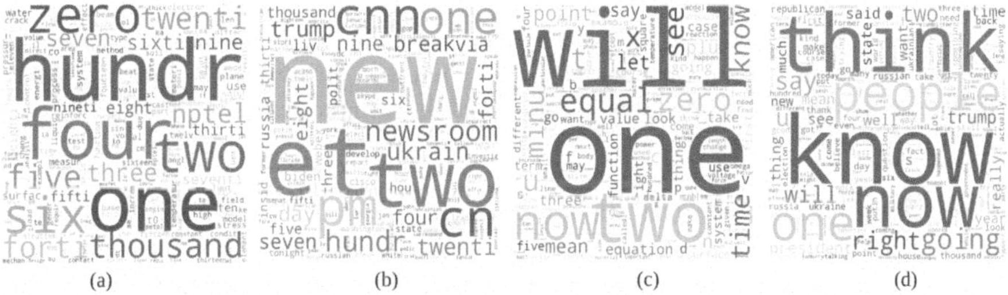

Fig. 4. Word cloud representation of video content in the dataset. (a) Illustrates the word distribution within OCR tokens extracted from (a) NPTEL videos and (b) news videos. Displays the word distribution within transcripts of (c) NPTEL videos and (d) news videos.

3.2 Designing Prompt Templates

As computing capabilities advance, contemporary research increasingly relies on leveraging large language models trained on extensive datasets. One method involves prompting these models with initial text inputs, such as with ChatGPT, Bard, LLaVa, and others, enabling them to produce coherent and contextually relevant content. This approach resembles initiating a creative dialogue with the model, where the input prompt is a guiding seed for generating responses. The resulting data demonstrates the model's proficiency and ability to emulate diverse styles, foster creativity, and offer valuable insights.

In our experiments, we employed large language model: ChatGPT 3.5, developed by OpenAI. This model has been trained on diverse and extensive textual datasets, enabling them to comprehend and generate human-like text across

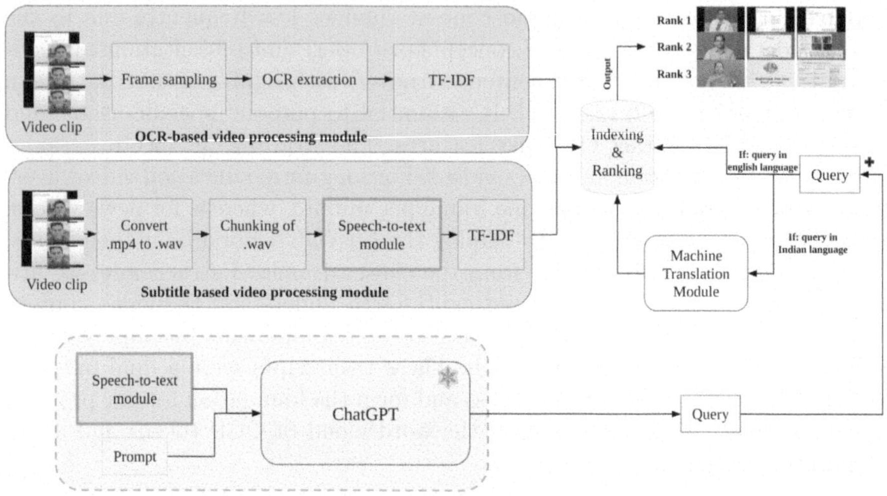

Fig. 5. Pipeline Overview: Initial processing involves leveraging multimodal cues such as OCR tokens and transcripts to analyze long-range videos. Subsequently, retrieval is performed using either captions generated by ChatGPT or alternative queries. Additionally, our system accommodates queries in Indian languages.

various domains and contexts. It can perform multiple tasks, including generating text, translating languages, and providing informative responses to questions. Additionally, It can follow instructions, complete requests thoughtfully, and answer questions comprehensively, even when faced with open-ended and challenging inquiries. Moreover, such models are capable of generating text in different creative formats, such as code, scripts, letters, poems, and more. In this work, we leverage the potential of prompting techniques for generating content in the context of long-range educational and news video understanding. However, these two types of videos vary significantly in content, necessitating the inclusion of tailored prompts to extract the most suitable captions for each video. We establish a distinct set of prompts corresponding to the respective video domains, individualized prompts for educational content, and separate prompts for news content. Depending on the input provided to these models, we further finetune the prompts to capture the necessary essence, ensuring alignment with the unique characteristics of the data at hand. Figures 6 and 7 display the sequential series of prompt templates employed to extract captions from the transcripts generated through ASR for the entire lengthy video.

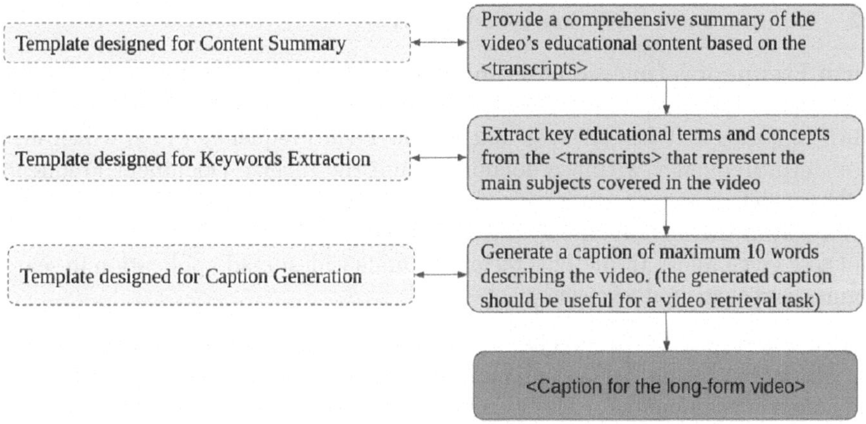

Fig. 6. A collection of prompt templates utilized to generate caption for each video from the transcript generated by ASR outputs extracted from each long-form educational video.

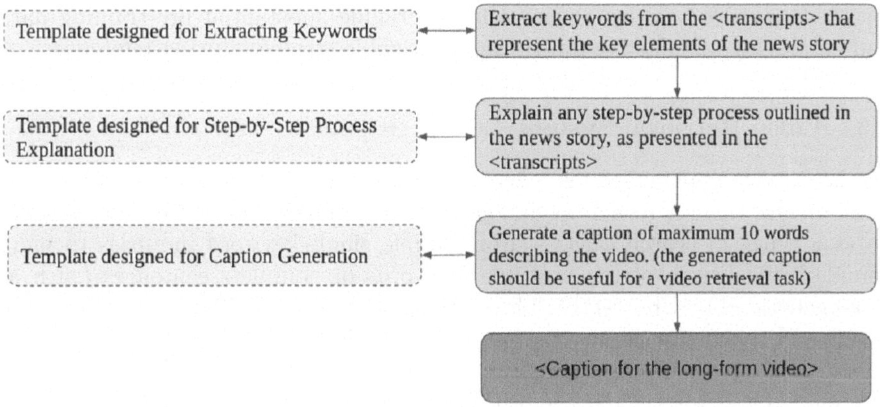

Fig. 7. A collection of prompt templates utilized to generate caption for each video from the transcript generated by ASR outputs extracted from each long-form news videos.

4 Experiments

4.1 Evaluation Setups

We assess our dataset for long-form video retrieval performance with natural language queries. The objective is to identify relevant videos from a vast collection based on textual descriptions. We gauge the effectiveness of our learned embedding using standard recall metrics such as R@1, R@5, and R@10.

4.2 Comparison with State-of-the-Art

Term Frequency-Inverse Document Frequency (TF-IDF). It is a method employed in information retrieval and text mining to assess a document's relevance to a query. It involves calculating the Term Frequency (TF), which measures term frequency within a document, and the Inverse Document Frequency (IDF), which gauges term rarity across the document collection. TF-IDF is derived from these components and is utilized to identify documents most relevant to a given query term. This technique finds widespread application in search engines and text analysis systems.

Dense Passage Retriever (DPR) [10]. The method employs a dense encoder E_p, which transforms any textual passage into $d-$dimensional real-valued vectors and constructs an index for all M passages utilized in retrieval. During inference, DPR utilizes a distinct encoder E_q to map the input question to a d-dimensional vector, retrieving k passages whose vectors closely align with the question vector.

Singularity [18]. The method explores single-frame training methodologies for tasks involving video and language. The study demonstrates state-of-the-art performance in text-to-video retrieval by leveraging substantial pre-training data and employing an effective multi-frame ensemble strategy during inference.

4.3 Video Retrieval System

We present an application for a versatile video retrieval system capable of handling diverse tasks across news and educational domains. Our system accommodates a range of search queries, from simple single-keyword inquiries to more complex searches involving multiple keywords or complete sentences (such as those generated by ChatGPT). The search process is refined by eliminating stopwords and tokenizing sentences, laying the groundwork for our retrieval mechanism. Our approach encompasses two distinct paths, depicted in Fig. 5: one leveraging OCR tokens and the other utilizing transcripts or closed captions. In the OCR path, we preprocess OCR tokens obtained using EasyOCR by removing stopwords, punctuation, and irrelevant details before storing them in a database. These tokens serve as the foundation for our video search engine's functionality. Concurrently, the transcript path involves extracting transcripts or closed captions using a Speech-to-text model, followed by preprocessing to ensure consistency and relevance akin to OCR tokens. For retrieval, OCR tokens and transcripts are separately employed within a TF-IDF-based algorithm. The system provides the flexibility to choose between OCR token-based or speech-to-text-based retrieval. Furthermore, it supports queries in multiple Indian languages, translating them into English before initiating video retrieval operations.

4.4 Quantitative Results

Predominantly existing text-video retrieval systems and datasets work on small-duration videos (approx. 10 sec) and have considered only visual content in the videos to generate captions/queries. Conversely, in the proposed dataset, the news and educational videos span up to approximately 45 min. These videos contain a wide range of content majorly originating from textual (OCR) and audio (transcripts), making it challenging to apply existing SOTA methods. Hence, evaluating such methods could raise concerns about their reliability. It is very important to note that creating precise ground truth data: "video-caption" pairs for lengthy videos is an expensive task. However, we have conducted a comparison of the Dense Passage Retrieval (DPR) text-only model [10] and SINGULARITY [18], a vision-language multimodal method, and its variants against the proposed method TF-IDF-based on this dataset.

We do this by annotating a **test set** of 60 video-caption pairs. We generate captions manually and by ChatGPT. To generate captions using ChatGPT, we prompt it to generate captions using the transcripts of the videos. From Table 2, it can be seen that both DPR and SINGULARITY underperform compared to the proposed method. i) DPR can consider a maximum input size (512) which is insufficient for the context of long-range videos. Hence to evaluate, we randomly sample words from the context and truncate it to the max length. ii) SINGULARITY is a multimodal method. It considers 4 frames at the time of testing to retrieve a video. This results in sparse data usage similar to DPR which is not sufficient to retrieve long-range videos such as educational videos and news videos. On the contrary, a simple non-learning-based TF-IDF-based method can do efficient retrieval by considering information present from multiple frames (both textual and audio in separate and combined forms) throughout the long-range video. It is also important to note that DPR and SINGULARITY are tested for zero-shot performance since, we do not have training data associated for the proposed dataset (Fig. 8).

As seen in Table 2, the utilization of DPR (Dense Passage Retrieval) in this context is multifaceted, as it retrieves outputs based on both Optical Character

Table 2. Quantitative results for a randomly sampled test set of 60 video-caption pairs. Captions are generated by Humans and ChatGPT

Method	Features	Human-caption			ChatGPT-caption		
		R@1	R@5	R@10	R@1	R@5	R@10
Random	-	01.67	11.67	20.00	01.67	11.67	20.00
DPR	OCR	01.67	33.33	20.00	03.33	20.00	30.00
DPR	transcripts	00.00	06.67	18.33	01.67	06.67	13.33
SINGULARITY-5m	visual	16.66	33.33	51.66	16.66	43.33	53.33
SINGULARITY-17m	visual	20.00	40.00	53.33	18.33	43.33	56.66
SINGULARITY-5m-tmp	visual	13.33	43.33	50.00	21.66	40.00	58.33
SINGULARITY-17m-tmp	visual	15.00	33.33	46.66	16.66	38.33	56.66
TF-IDF-based (Ours)	transcripts	38.33	46.67	50.0	**40.00**	48.33	58.33
TF-IDF-based (Ours)	OCR	**40.00**	**51.67**	**60.00**	36.67	**55.00**	**66.67**
TF-IDF-based (Ours)	transcripts+OCR	**40.00**	50.00	56.67	36.67	53.33	61.67

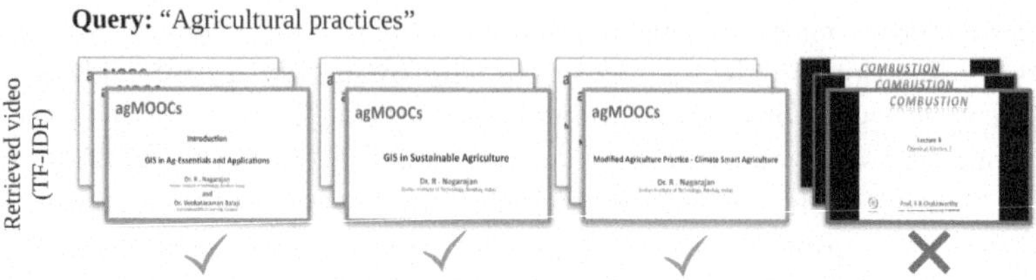

Fig. 8. Results of the proposed method when input is a keyword like "Agricultural practices". It can be seen that the method retrieves relevant videos (shown in green). (Color figure online)

Recognition (OCR) and transcripts, as exemplified in the table. However, a notable challenge lies in the fact that conventional DPR models are typically trained on text corpora with significantly smaller contextual scopes, resulting in cleaner data compared to the complex nature of OCR and transcripts. Singularity, on the other hand, operates as a video retrieval model, primarily trained on 10-second video clips for retrieval purposes, with a focus on the actions depicted within these clips. Yet, when confronted with longer videos, a workaround involves clipping the initial 10 s for retrieval, which poses difficulties due to the disparity between the short clips and the comprehensive captions derived from the entire length of the video. In contrast, TF-IDF (Term Frequency-Inverse Document Frequency) exhibits superior performance, as it encompasses content from the entirety of the video rather than solely focusing on brief segments. Collectively, these challenges underscore the complexity inherent in the proposed dataset, necessitating innovative solutions to address the inherent limitations of existing models and techniques.

4.5 Qualitative Results

In Fig. 9, we illustrate the results obtained from the TF-IDF-based retrieval system. The input query for this retrieval process consists of captions generated

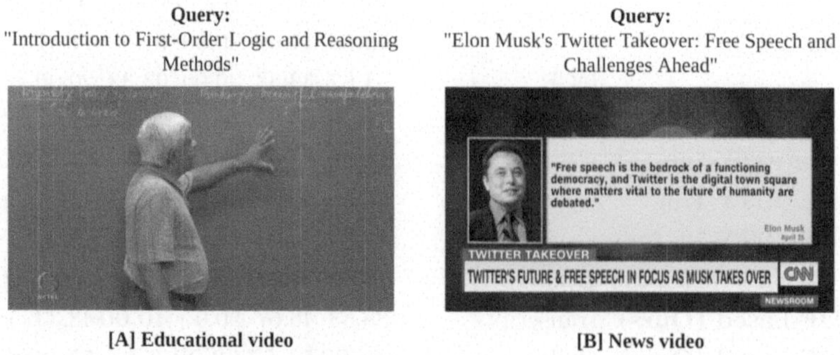

Fig. 9. Results of the proposed method when input is a caption generated by ChatGPT. It can be seen that a simple method can retrieve the desired output.

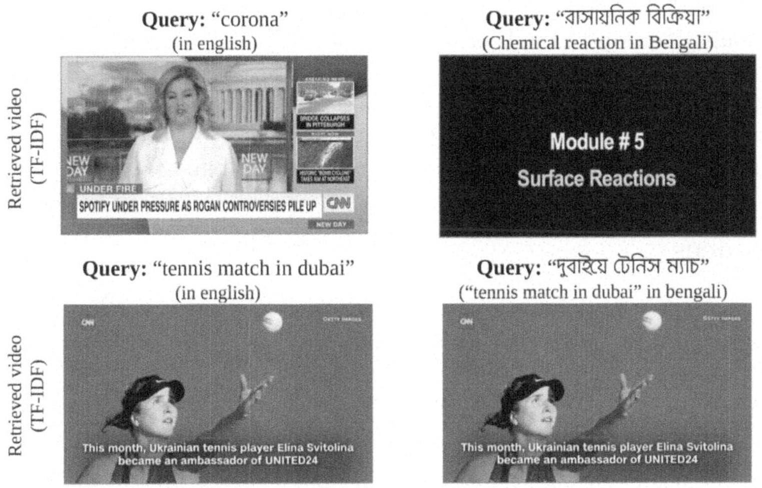

Fig. 10. Qualitative results for queries in Indian languages are showcased. In the first example, the query term "corona" is provided in English. In the second example, we input chemical reactions in Bengali, which the system translates into English for retrieval. In the third and fourth examples, "tennis match in Dubai" is presented in both English and Bengali.

by ChatGPT, derived from the transcripts or closed captions of a diverse range of content, including both news and educational videos. This approach aims to leverage the richness of information embedded within the video content to enhance the accuracy and relevance of the retrieved outputs.

The qualitative results for queries in Indian languages are demonstrated in Fig. 10. In the first instance, the query term "corona" is presented in English, showcasing the system's capability to handle queries in the English language. Moving forward, the second example illustrates the system's proficiency in translating Bengali queries regarding chemical reactions into English for effective retrieval. Expanding further, the third and fourth examples depict queries about "tennis match in Dubai," showcased in both English and Bengali, highlighting the system's versatility in understanding and processing multilingual queries. This diversity underscores the system's adaptability to cater to users across linguistic preferences and aids in fostering inclusive information retrieval experiences.

5 Conclusion

With the rapid advancement of digital media content, there has been a notable surge in the creation of long-form videos online, particularly in education and news. Consequently, comprehending these lengthy videos has garnered increased attention within the research community. We introduce the Edu-news dataset by Utilizing various informational cues, including OCR tokens and transcripts. This dataset is a foundation for exploring potential avenues to augment long-form video comprehension through prompt engineering. Our baseline findings reveal limitations when applied to long-form video datasets. For instance, existing text-based query systems struggle to process large text data efficiently. Additionally, video text retrieval systems exhibit poor quality, as they only consider the initial few seconds of video, resulting in subpar retrieval outputs.

References

1. Alayrac, J.B., Bojanowski, P., Agrawal, N., Sivic, J., Laptev, I., Lacoste-Julien, S.: Unsupervised learning from narrated instruction videos. In: CVPR, pp. 4575–4583. IEEE Computer Society (2016)
2. Biten, A.F., et al.: Scene text visual question answering. In: ICCV, pp. 4290–4300. IEEE (2019)
3. Bulathwela, S., Perez-Ortiz, M., Novak, E., Yilmaz, E., Shawe-Taylor, J.: PEEK: a large dataset of learner engagement with educational videos. CoRR, abs/2109.03154 (2021)
4. Bulathwela, S., Perez-Ortiz, M., Yilmaz, E., Shawe-Taylor, J.: Vlengagement: a dataset of scientific video lectures for evaluating population-based engagement. CoRR, abs/2011.02273 (2020)
5. Chen, H., Wang, X., Chen, H., Song, Z., Jia, J., Zhu, W.: Grounding-prompter: prompting LLM with multimodal information for temporal sentence grounding in long videos. CoRR, abs/2312.17117 (2023)
6. Chou, S.-H., et al.: Multi-modal news understanding with professionally labelled videos (reutersvilnews). CoRR, abs/2401.12419 (2024)
7. Das, P., Xu, C., Doell, R.F., Corso, J.J.: A thousand frames in just a few words: lingual description of videos through latent topics and sparse object stitching. In: CVPR, pp. 2634–2641 (2013)
8. Dutta, K., Mathew, M., Krishnan, P., Jawahar, C.V.: Localizing and recognizing text in lecture videos. In: ICFHR, pp. 235–240. IEEE Computer Society (2018)
9. EasyOCR Developers. EasyOCR: A High Accuracy Real-Time OCR Engine (2024). https://github.com/JaidedAI/EasyOCR
10. Karpukhin, V., et al.: Dense passage retrieval for open-domain question answering. In: EMNLP (1), pp. 6769–6781. Association for Computational Linguistics (2020)
11. Gandhi, A., Biswas, A., Deshmukh, O.: Topic transition in educational videos using visually salient words. In: EDM, pp. 289–296. International Educational Data Mining Society (IEDMS) (2015)
12. Gupta, P., Gupta, M.: Newskvqa: knowledge-aware news video question answering. In: PAKDD (3). Lecture Notes in Computer Science, vol. 13282, pp. 3–15. Springer (2022)
13. Hegde, S., Jahagirdar, S., Gangisetty, S.: Making the V in text-VQA matter. In: CVPR Workshops, pp. 5580–5588. IEEE (2023)
14. Jahagirdar, S., Gangisetty, S., Mishra, A.: Look, read and ask: learning to ask questions by reading text in images. In: Lladós, J., Lopresti, D., Uchida, S. (eds.) ICDAR 2021. LNCS, vol. 12821, pp. 335–349. Springer, Cham (2021). https://doi.org/10.1007/978-3-030-86549-8_22

15. Jahagirdar, S., Mathew, M., Karatzas, D., Jawahar, C.V.: Understanding video scenes through text: insights from text-based video question answering. In: ICCV (Workshops), pp. 4648–4652. IEEE (2023)
16. Jahagirdar, S., Mathew, M., Karatzas, D., Jawahar, C.V.: Watching the news: towards videoqa models that can read. In: WACV, pp. 4430–4439. IEEE (2023)
17. Ju, C., Han, T., Zheng, K., Zhang, Y., Xie, W.: Prompting visual-language models for efficient video understanding. In: ECCV (35). Lecture Notes in Computer Science, vol. 13695, pp. 105–124. Springer (2022)
18. Lei, J., Berg, T.L., Bansal, M.: Revealing single frame bias for video-and-language learning. In: ACL (1), pp. 487–507. Association for Computational Linguistics (2023)
19. Lester, B., Al-Rfou, R., Constant, N.: The power of scale for parameter-efficient prompt tuning. In: EMNLP (1), pp. 3045–3059. Association for Computational Linguistics (2021)
20. Liu, H., Li, C., Wu, Q., Lee, Y.J.: Visual instruction tuning. In: NeurIPS (2023)
21. Liu, P., Yuan, W., Fu, J., Jiang, Z., Hayashi, H., Neubig, G.: Pre-train, prompt, and predict: a systematic survey of prompting methods in natural language processing. ACM Comput. Surv. **55**(9):195:1–195:35 (2023)
22. Mahapatra, D., Mariappan, R., Rajan, V.: Automatic hierarchical table of contents generation for educational videos. In: WWW (Companion Volume), pp. 267–274. ACM (2018)
23. Mathew, M., Karatzas, D., Jawahar, C.V.: Docvqa: a dataset for VQA on document images. In: WACV, pp. 2199–2208. IEEE (2021)
24. Miech, A., Zhukov, D., Alayrac, J. B., Tapaswi, M., Laptev, I., Sivic, J.: Howto100m: learning a text-video embedding by watching hundred million narrated video clips. In: ICCV, pp. 2630–2640. IEEE (2019)
25. OpenAI. Chatgpt: Large-scale language models. https://openai.com/research/chatgpt
26. Papalampidi, P., Keller, F., Lapata, M.: Movie summarization via sparse graph construction. In: AAAI, pp. 13631–13639. AAAI Press (2021)
27. Rohrbach, A., Rohrbach, M., Tandon, N., Schiele, B.: A dataset for movie description. In: CVPR, pp. 3202–3212. IEEE Computer Society (2015)
28. Rouditchenko, A., et al.: Avlnet: learning audio-visual language representations from instructional videos. In: Interspeech, pp. 1584–1588. ISCA (2021)
29. Darshan Singh, S., Gupta, A., Jawahar, C.V., Tapaswi, M.: Unsupervised audio-visual lecture segmentation. In: WACV, pp. 5221–5230. IEEE (2023)
30. Singh, A., et al.: Towards VQA models that can read. In: CVPR, pp. 8317–8326. Computer Vision Foundation/IEEE (2019)
31. Silero Team. Silero models: pre-trained enterprise-grade STT/TTS models and benchmarks (2021). https://github.com/snakers4/silero-models
32. Torabi, A., Tandon, N., Sigal, L.: Learning language-visual embedding for movie understanding with natural-language. CoRR, abs/1609.08124 (2016)
33. Wasim, S.T., Naseer, M., Khan, S., Khan, F.S., Shah, M.: Vita-clip: video and text adaptive CLIP via multimodal prompting. In: CVPR, pp. 23034–23044. IEEE (2023)
34. White, J., et al.: A prompt pattern catalog to enhance prompt engineering with chatgpt. CoRR, abs/2302.11382 (2023)
35. Xu, J., Mei, T., Yao, T., Rui, Y.: MSR-VTT: a large video description dataset for bridging video and language. In: CVPR, pp. 5288–5296. IEEE Computer Society (2016)

36. Zhou, H., Martín-Martín, R., Kapadia, M., Savarese, S., Niebles, J.C.: Procedure-aware pretraining for instructional video understanding. In: CVPR, pp. 10727–10738. IEEE (2023)
37. Zhou, L., Xu, C., Corso, J.J.: Towards automatic learning of procedures from web instructional videos. In: AAAI, pp. 7590–7598. AAAI Press (2018)

First Quantization Matrix Estimation for DJPEG Images: An Adversarial Analysis

Manish Okade(✉)

National Institute of Technology, Rourkela, Rourkela, Odisha, India
okadem@nitrkl.ac.in

Abstract. This paper investigates the role of an intelligent adversary in derailing the advantages offered by machine and deep learning algorithms. The first quantization matrix estimation (FQME) forensic research problem in Double JPEG (DJPEG) compressed images is chosen as an example case study to demonstrate the vulnerabilities of the machine and deep learning algorithms that an intelligent adversary can exploit. DJPEG compression involves two compression cycles: the first compression when the image is initially saved as JPEG and the second compression when a forger manipulates the image and again saves it in the JPEG format. In such cases, the information regarding the first compression is lost in the presence of the second JPEG compression. Specifically, the quantization coefficients are of interest since estimating the quantization coefficients for the first compression, often referred to as the primary quantization estimation, can give information about the history of the image and the possibility of forgery/tampering. Various methods exist for estimating the first quantization coefficients, both statistical and deep learning-based. However, existing works do not evaluate the robustness of these estimation models against adversarial attacks, which is an essential criterion from a security point of view. In this work, a comprehensive adversarial analysis is carried out to show the vulnerabilities of machine and deep learning models for the FQME forensic research problem. Such a detailed security analysis is the need of the hour, and this paper throws light on it from a forensic perspective.

Keywords: Adversarial Attack · DJPEG · Image Forensics · FQME · Adversarial defence

1 Introduction

Multimedia data in today's world are ubiquitous. The internet is full of audio clips, images and videos that are widely shared on many social media platforms. In many instances, there are integrity concerns regarding the multimedia data being circulated. Multimedia forensics focuses on answering integrity concerns by detecting such manipulations. Of particular interest in this paper is image

J. Kakarla et al. (Eds.): CVIP 2024, CCIS 2473, pp. 447–456, 2026.
https://doi.org/10.1007/978-3-031-93688-3_32

forensics, especially JPEG forensics, which focuses on detecting the clues left over by the forger in a JPEG scenario since it is a widely used image compression standard. In JPEG forensics, an interesting case is that of Double JPEG (DJPEG), where a JPEG compressed image is decompressed to replace a certain image region with content from another image, followed by resaving the image as a JPEG image. As a result of two JPEG compressions, there would be a presence of two quantization matrices: the first quantization matrix when the compression took place initially and the second quantization matrix that would be present after the image is possibly forged and resaved. The second compression cycle erases the first quantization matrix. Hence, for evaluating the authenticity, the first quantization matrix needs to be estimated, referred to as the first quantization matrix estimation (FQME) forensic research problem in Double JPEG (DJPEG) compressed images. Figure 1 shows the complete JPEG pipeline. To apply DCT transformation, the image is partitioned into 8×8 blocks. The below equation gives the DCT transform that is applied blockwise.

$$DCT(u,v) = \frac{1}{\sqrt{2N}} C(u)C(v) \sum_{x=0}^{N-1} \sum_{y=0}^{N-1} f(x,y) cos \left[\frac{(2x+1)u\pi}{2N} \right] cos \left[\frac{(2y+1)v\pi}{2N} \right] \tag{1}$$

where $N = 8$ and $C(x) = \frac{1}{\sqrt{2}}$ if $x = 0$ else $1 if x > 0$. In the quantization step, the transformed DCT coefficients are quantized using pre-defined quantization tables specified by the JPEG standard. The 8×8 matrix is denoted by 'Q', which stands for the quantization matrix used in the quantization step of the JPEG standard. When a raw image is subjected to a JPEG compression using quantization matrix Q_1, decompressed with the possible intent of modification, and then compressed back to a JPEG format using quantization matrix Q_2, a double compressed JPEG image is obtained. Q_1 and Q_2 contain 64 coefficients each. The JPEG quality factor is referred to as 'QF'. A 'QF' value specifies a quantization matrix Q according to the JPEG standard. The second compression quality factor is denoted by QF_2, and the first with QF_1.

Researchers have investigated several techniques for the FQME forensic research problem in DJPEG images both conventional and, more recently, deep learning-based. With an increasing focus on deep learning-based methods due to high model accuracy and being end-to-end, they have brought out a lot of advantages that conventional techniques lack, making them the preferred choice of algorithm development. However, a major security threat exists for deep learning models, i.e. the possible presence of an intelligent adversary, which, if it remains unaccounted, could pose severe security threats. Adversaries can easily fool the deep learning models by adding perturbations to the input using various methods. The perturbations, nearly invisible to the human eye, can cause a major performance drop for deep learning models. The paper is a novel attempt to study the adversarial attacks in detail when applied to the FQME forensic research problem in DJPEG images. Alongside adversarial defences are also pro-

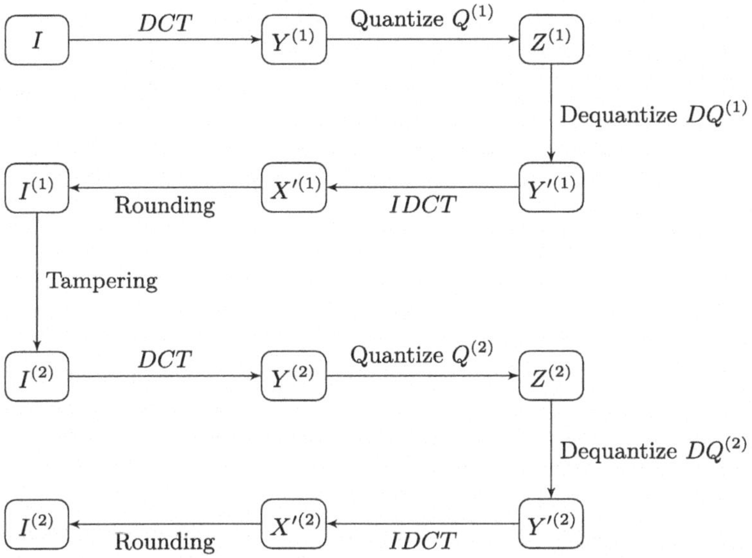

Fig. 1. Block diagram of Double JPEG compression process with tampering operation between the $first^{(1)}$ JPEG and $second^{(2)}$ JPEG compression cycles.

posed to mitigate the ill effects of an adversarial attack launched by an informed adversary.

2 Literature Review

Conventional works on FQME [3,4,6,7] are either DCT domain-based or statistics-based. Farid [6] proposed a forgery detection method by performing a third quantization step and computing the error between DCT coefficients, thereby locating two minima corresponding to the first and second quantization. Galvan et al. [7] improved this method by modelling the split and residual noise and mitigating them via a DCT histogram-based filtering approach, which resulted in accurate first quantization matrix coefficients. However, their DCT histogram filtering approach failed for special cases of split noise. This was improved in [4], where a novel priority assignment and selection strategy was applied to error function values of the second quantisation step's existing and missing multiples, which achieved accurate FQME. Recently, deep learning-based models have gained popularity in image forensics due to the higher accuracy that they offer and their ability to be trained in an end-to-end fashion.

Niu et al. [11] proposed a deep learning model by modifying the dense-net architecture for the FQME forensic research problem. The method achieved good accuracy for all quality factor pairs, and good generalization performance was demonstrated by testing for quality factors different from those in the training stage and on images from different datasets. However, no adversarial analysis

[9,13,14] was carried out, leaving the model vulnerable to attacks by an informed adversary. Along similar lines, Battiato et al. [2] also carried out FQME by utilizing a CNN-based model that employed 1-D histograms of DCT values coupled with a regularization term to improve the estimation accuracy. Still, this model, too, lacked adversarial analysis. A survey of existing problems that have received adversarial attention is available in [12]. It is evident from the survey that although many research problems, like face recognition [1], gait recognition [10], etc., have received attention from an adversarial point of view, the FQME forensic research problem is still left untouched in terms of comprehensive adversarial analysis. Therefore, existing deep learning models for FQME have not been tested under adversarial settings, leaving enough scope for research in the interesting domain of adversarial attacks and defences. Moreover, in image forensics, along with achieving good accuracy, it is also crucial to consider the deep learning model's robustness. While Niu et al. [11] model addressed the model's generalization ability across datasets and quality factors, the model's performance was not studied from the security point of view. Hence, it becomes paramount to understand if the model would continue to show good performance under an adversarial attack. This paper is motivated by the premise of studying the performance of the existing deep learning-based FQME models in an adversarial setting, along with proposing defences to mitigate the possible attacks, thereby achieving secure FQME models.

3 Key Contributions

The key contributions are listed below.

- Detailed performance analysis of existing deep learning-based models for the FQME forensic research problem under an adversarial setting. Two types of adversarial attacks, the Limited-Broyden Fletcher Goldfarb Shanno (L-BFGS) attack and the Fast Gradient Sign Method (FGSM) attacks are launched on existing deep learning-based FQME models to analyze the model's robustness. Inferences are drawn that help in designing good defences.
- Adversarial defences like adversarial retraining are explored to mitigate the drawbacks of the launched adversarial attacks on existing deep learning-based models for the FQME forensic research problem. Overall, such a detailed security analysis of the FQME forensic research problem forms a novel contribution which was lacking in the literature.
- The marriage of forensics with security outlined in the paper, which brings trust in the credibility of image data, is the current need of the hour in the domain of information forensics and security. The paper throws light on these aspects.

4 Adversarial Attacks and Defences: FQME in DJPEG Images

The section is devoted towards a comprehensive security analysis of the FQME forensic research problem in DJPEG images. The first subsection is devoted to understanding the performance of existing deep learning-based methods when adversarially attacked, while the next subsection explores mitigation measures in the form of adversarial defences, also referred to as adversarial countermeasures, that can overcome the attack drawbacks.

4.1 Adversarial Attacks

As an example test case, two existing deep learning-based FQME models are considered, i.e. Niu et al. [11] model, and Battiato et al. [2] model. The two FQME models are adversarially attacked using the Limited-Broyden Fletcher Goldfarb Shanno (L-BFGS) and Fast Gradient Sign Method (FGSM) attacks. The two attacks are chosen to demonstrate the performance drop in the existing deep learning-based FQME models.

L-BFGS Attack: It was the first among the attacks introduced against deep neural networks. L-BFGS attack [9,13,14] is an optimization algorithm belonging to the broad family of quasi-Newton methods. It works by generating adversarial examples using an L-BFGS method to solve the general targeted problem given below, which involves calculating approximate values of adversarial examples by line-searching c > 0.

$$\begin{aligned} \min_{r} \quad & c\|r\|_p + J_\theta(x + r, t) \\ \text{st} \quad & x + r \in [0, 1] \end{aligned} \tag{2}$$

where 'r' represents the perturbation vector, 'x' denotes the original input, and 't' is the target label. J_θ is the loss function, e.g., the cross entropy, 'c' is a suitable constant which finds a compromise between the perturbation magnitude and the attack performance. The L-BFGS attack uses the second-order quasi-Newton method to solve this problem.

FGSM attack: The Fast Gradient Sign Method (FGSM) proposed by Goodfellow et al. [9] is a fast method to generate adversarial examples since the L-BFGS attack was slow due to the utilization of an expensive linear search method to find the optimal value. FGSM performs one step gradient update along the direction of the gradient sign at each pixel, as given below.

$$x' = x + \epsilon * sign[\nabla_x J(\theta, x, y)] \tag{3}$$

where 'x' is the image input, $J(\theta, x, y)$ is the cost function, and $\nabla_x J(\theta, x, y)$ is the gradient of the cost function with respect to the input. The value of ϵ controls the magnitude of perturbation to be added to the image.

4.2 Adversarial Defence

Adversarial defences or countermeasures are basically of two types: reactive and proactive. The former detects adversarial examples after the deep learning model is built, while the latter makes deep neural networks more robust before adversaries generate adversarial examples. Proactive defences have more importance since they account for the presence of an intelligent adversary well in advance. Adversarial retraining is one of the proactive defence strategies explored in this paper for the FQME deep learning models. As outlined earlier, the L-BFGS and FGSM attacks dent the accuracy scores of the existing state-of-the-art FQME deep learning models since they were trained in a non-adversarial setting. In this section, adversarial retraining is adopted in training Niu et al. [11] model and Battiato et al. [2] model. By generating adversarial examples in every step of training and injecting them into the training set of Niu et al. [11] model and Battiato et al. [2] model, it is observed that the adversarial retraining improves the robustness of deep neural networks. The improvement in accuracy achieved for the two state-of-the-art models is shown in the results section. Additionally, by incorporating adversarial retraining, the precision of the two models is improved as it provides some implicit regularization for deep neural networks.

5 Experimental Results

Images for experimentation are taken from two state-of-the-art datasets utilized in image forensics, namely the RAISE dataset [5] and the DRESDEN dataset [8]. In order to have a fair comparison, the experimental methodology followed by the two existing FQME models, i.e. Niu et al. [11] model and Battiato et al. [2] model, are kept unchanged. In other words, the data preparation methodology of both models is followed in letter and spirit. The first 15 quantization matrix coefficients were estimated using both methods in line with prior works. Niu et al. [11] model utilized two cases for training; $QF_1 \in \{60, 65, 70, 75, 80, 85, 90, 95, 98\}$ for $QF_2 = 90$ and $QF_1 \in \{55, 60, 65, 70, 75, 80, 85, 90, 95\}$ for $QF_2 = 80$. 4,00,000 image patches per QF_1 were used for training, and 7440 image patches were taken for testing. Battiato et al. [2] model also utilized $QF_2 = 90$ and $QF_2 = 80$ as Niu et al. [11] and QF_1 as earlier for uniformity. Battiato et al. [2] achieved superiority in their model by including a regularization term that minimized the differences among neighbouring first quantization values. However, neither method accounts for an informed adversary and, as a result, lacks security aspects, which is of paramount importance and the focus of the work reported in this paper.

5.1 Adversarial Attack Analysis

Two types of adversarial attacks, i.e. L-BFGS and FGSM, are launched on Niu et al. [11] method and Battiato et al. [2] method to test the robustness of the FQME models. A set of 1000 images is chosen randomly from the RAISE and DRESDEN datasets. Adversarial examples are generated using the L-BFGS attack method by line-searching c > 0, which generates the perturbed test images. While generating the perturbed samples in an L-BFGS attack, it is observed that the method is slow because it is designed to find the smallest possible attack perturbation. On similar lines, for the FGSM attack, ϵ is chosen as '0.005' to be in the range $\epsilon \in [0, 0.01]$. For each of these images, the perturbation value is calculated by utilizing the sign of the gradient of the cost function with respect to the input, multiplied by the ϵ value to control the magnitude, i.e. given in Eq. (3). This perturbation is then added to the original image to generate adversarial images.

Niu et al. [11] and Battiato et al. [2] models are tested on the generated adversarial images to obtain the accuracy scores. Table 1 and Table 2 show the accuracy scores obtained for the two adversarial attack types when applied to the existing state-of-the-art FQME models for $QF_2 = 90$ and $QF_2 = 80$, respectively. As observed, there is a drop in accuracy for both methods in general when adversarial images are utilized to test the built models, signifying vulnerability to attacks from an informed adversary. In particular, it is observed from the two tables that the FGSM attack is stronger than the L-BFGS attack for $QF_2 = 90$ and $QF_2 = 80$. This is due to parameter ϵ, which controls the magnitude of the perturbation in the FGSM attack. Another important observation from the two tables is that $QF_2 = 90$ performs better than $QF_2 = 80$ in no attack and the two attack types. This is because lower QF_2 values are detrimental to the FQME process due to heavier post-compression, as observed from the mean accuracy scores.

Table 1. Accuracy scores for 'No Attack', L-BFGS and FGSM attack with $QF_2 = 90$.

QF_1	No Attack		L-BFGS attack		FGSM attack	
	Niu's model [11]	Battiato's model [2]	Niu's model [11]	Battiato's model [2]	Niu's model [11]	Battiato's model [2]
55	0.00	0.80	0.00	0.55	0.00	0.42
60	0.64	0.86	0.45	0.52	0.36	0.41
65	0.54	0.84	0.37	0.50	0.28	0.40
70	0.66	0.88	0.44	0.53	0.37	0.42
75	0.77	0.89	0.49	0.55	0.38	0.43
80	0.81	0.87	0.52	0.51	0.41	0.42
85	0.81	0.90	0.53	0.57	0.42	0.45
90	0.02	0.12	0.00	0.00	0.00	0.00
95	0.78	0.62	0.48	0.45	0.36	0.34
98	0.76	0.76	0.47	0.48	0.35	0.37
Mean	0.58	0.75	0.38	0.46	0.29	0.36

5.2 Adversarial Defence: Retraining

As observed in the earlier subsection, the performance of existing FQME models deteriorates in the presence of an informed adversary, i.e. L-BFGS and FGSM attacks. The role of adversarial defence or countermeasures is to counter and mitigate the effects of such an informed attack. In this paper, adversarial retraining

Table 2. Accuracy scores for 'No Attack', L-BFGS and FGSM attack with $QF_2 = 80$

QF_1	No Attack		L-BFGS attack		FGSM attack	
	Niu's model [11]	Battiato's model [2]	Niu's model [11]	Battiato's model [2]	Niu's model [11]	Battiato's model [2]
55	0.24	0.61	0.11	0.55	0.07	0.42
60	0.50	0.65	0.39	0.57	0.28	0.44
65	0.31	0.71	0.22	0.60	0.13	0.49
70	0.50	0.82	0.39	0.71	0.28	0.59
75	0.15	0.65	0.06	0.54	0.00	0.43
80	0.00	0.05	0.00	0.00	0.00	0.00
85	0.04	0.53	0.00	0.41	0.00	0.30
90	0.48	0.40	0.36	0.29	0.24	0.18
95	0.95	0.35	0.77	0.22	0.61	0.14
98	0.21	0.43	0.09	0.31	0.00	0.19
Mean	0.33	0.52	0.23	0.42	0.16	0.31

is the defence that is chosen among the various defences to mitigate adversarial attacks. The motivation for choosing adversarial retraining stems from the fact that it is intuitive and also has good attack mitigation capabilities, especially for the L-BFGS and FGSM attacks. Adversarial retraining works on the concept of including adversarial samples in the training dataset during model training. This helps the model learn in the presence of adversarial samples. More details of adversarial retraining can be referred to in [13].

Adversarial samples are included in the training set, and both the models Niu et al. [11] and Battiato et al. [2] are retrained. The retraining is carried out by exactly following the training steps outlined earlier, with the only difference being that the training set is no longer pristine but contains the perturbed adversarial images. Table 3 shows the performance analysis after incorporating the adversarial retraining defence strategy. As observed, the accuracy drop is mitigated for L-BFGS and FGSM attacks when adversarial retraining is adopted as a countermeasure, i.e. there is an improvement in the accuracy score values for the two models in both the attack cases. However, it is to be noted that the adversarial retrained models are sub-optimal when compared with the no-attack scenario, signifying that accounting for the presence of an informed adversary does have an overhead. In other words, it is to be noted that the no-attack scenario achieves the best accuracy in comparison to the adversarial defence scenario, which is the price attributed to incorporating adversarial analysis. However, the price paid for incorporating adversarial analysis is still acceptable since the deep learning models are more resilient to attacks, which is the need of the hour.

Table 3. Accuracy scores for adversarial retaining defence strategy

QF_1	$QF_2 = 90$ (Adversarial retraining)				$QF_2 = 80$ (Adversarial retraining)			
	L-BFGS		FGSM		L-BFGS		FGSM	
	Niu's model [11]	Battiato's model [2]	Niu's model [11]	Battiato's model [2]	Niu's model [11]	Battiato's model [2]	Niu's model [11]	Battiato's model [2]
55	0.00	0.61	0.00	0.66	0.18	0.58	0.22	0.55
60	0.55	0.65	0.53	0.71	0.44	0.61	0.46	0.57
65	0.47	0.71	0.42	0.70	0.27	0.66	0.27	0.66
70	0.55	0.82	0.51	0.74	0.44	0.75	0.45	0.75
75	0.65	0.65	0.62	0.76	0.11	0.61	0.11	0.56
80	0.72	0.05	0.70	0.74	0.00	0.00	0.00	0.00
85	0.77	0.53	0.70	0.79	0.02	0.47	0.02	0.42
90	0.01	0.40	0.01	0.00	0.45	0.37	0.45	0.35
95	0.66	0.35	0.67	0.51	0.86	0.30	0.84	0.29
98	0.65	0.43	0.66	0.65	0.17	0.38	0.17	0.36
Mean	0.50	0.52	0.48	0.65	0.24	0.61	0.29	0.45

6 Conclusions

This paper provides a detailed adversarial analysis of existing deep learning-based FQME models. Two types of adversarial attacks, namely L-BFGS and FGSM, were studied along with adversarial retraining countermeasures to mitigate the two attack types. It was shown that existing FQME models were vulnerable to attacks from an intelligent adversary, thereby calling researchers in the domain of forensics and security to propose models accounting for the presence of adversaries. Among the two attacks, FGSM was found to be more effective as it was fast along with being deceptive in comparison to L-BFGS. The tunable ϵ parameter in the FGSM attack rendered it more effective than the L-BFGS. Adversarial retraining was explored as a defence strategy to mitigate the two attack types, which provided good resilience. However, as expected, the FQME models could not achieve no-attack accuracy when the retraining defence was applied, signifying the price paid for achieving resilience. Although there was a drop in accuracy for adversary-aware models, as seen in the countermeasure subsection, researchers can trade off the drop in accuracy to achieve more secure models. The paper highlighted the importance of achieving security coupled with good accuracy for deep learning-based FQME models, which had not received enough attention in the literature.

Acknowledgments. This work is supported by ANRF (formerly SERB), Government of India, under grant number MTR/2023/000106.

References

1. Alparslan, Y., Keim-Shenk, J., Khade, S., Greenstadt, R.: Adversarial attacks on convolutional neural networks in facial recognition domain. CoRR abs/2001.11137 (2020). https://arxiv.org/abs/2001.11137
2. Battiato, S., Giudice, O., Guarnera, F., Puglisi, G.: CNN-based first quantization estimation of double compressed JPEG images. J. Vis. Commun. Image Represent. **89**, 103635 (2022). https://doi.org/10.1016/j.jvcir.2022.103635. https://www.sciencedirect.com/science/article/pii/S1047320322001559

3. Bianchi, T., Piva, A.: Image forgery localization via block-grained analysis of JPEG artifacts. IEEE Trans. Inf. Forensics Secur. **7**, 1003–1017 (2012). https://doi.org/10.1109/TIFS.2012.2187516
4. Dalmia, N., Okade, M.: Robust first quantization matrix estimation based on filtering of recompression artifacts for non-aligned double compressed JPEG images. Signal Process. Image Commun. **61** (2017). https://doi.org/10.1016/j.image.2017.10.011
5. Dang-Nguyen, D.T., Pasquini, C., Conotter, V., Boato, G.: RAISE: a raw images dataset for digital image forensics. In: Proceedings of the 6th ACM Multimedia Systems Conference, MMSys 2015, pp. 219–224. Association for Computing Machinery, New York (2015). https://doi.org/10.1145/2713168.2713194
6. Farid, H.: Exposing digital forgeries from JPEG ghosts. IEEE Trans. Inf. Forensics Secur. **4**(1), 154–160 (2009). https://doi.org/10.1109/TIFS.2008.2012215
7. Galvan, F., Puglisi, G., Bruna, A.R., Battiato, S.: First quantization matrix estimation from double compressed JPEG images. IEEE Trans. Inf. Forensics Secur. **9**(8), 1299–1310 (2014). https://doi.org/10.1109/TIFS.2014.2330312
8. Gloe, T., Böhme, R.: The dresden image database for benchmarking digital image forensics. J. Digit. Forensic Pract. **3**(2-4), 150–159 (2010). https://doi.org/10.1080/15567281.2010.531500
9. Goodfellow, I., Shlens, J., Szegedy, C.: Explaining and harnessing adversarial examples. arXiv:1412.6572 (2014)
10. Jia, M., Yang, H., Huang, D., Wang, Y.: Attacking gait recognition systems via silhouette guided GANs (2019). https://api.semanticscholar.org/CorpusID:204837725
11. Niu, Y., Tondi, B., Zhao, Y., Barni, M.: Primary quantization matrix estimation of double compressed JPEG images via CNN. IEEE Signal Process. Lett. **27**, 191–195 (2020). https://doi.org/10.1109/LSP.2019.2962997
12. Ozdag, M.: Adversarial attacks and defenses against deep neural networks: a survey. Procedia Comput. Sci. **140**, 152–161 (2018)
13. Szegedy, C., et al.: Intriguing properties of neural networks. In: International Conference on Learning Representations (2014). http://arxiv.org/abs/1312.6100
14. Yuan, X., He, P., Zhu, Q., Li, X.: Adversarial examples: attacks and defenses for deep learning (2018)

3D Feature Pooling Module and Attention Mechanism for Liver and Tumor Segmentation

Rinku Rabidas[1(✉)], Tanish[1], Shubham Kumar[1], Sandeep Mandia[2], and Amarjit Roy[3]

[1] Department of ECE, Assam University Silchar, Silchar, Assam, India
rabidas.rinku@gmail.com

[2] Department of ECE, Thapar Institute of Engineering and Technology, Patiala, Punjab, India

[3] Department of EE, Ghani Khan Choudhury Institute of Engineering and Technology, Malda, West Bengal, India

Abstract. Accurate segmentation of liver and tumors from medical imaging is critical for effective diagnosis and treatment planning in hepatic diseases. This paper introduces robust 3D deep learning architectures tailored for precise delineation of liver and tumor regions from Computed Tomography (CT) scans. Our approach is based on the encoder-decoder framework integrating specialized attention mechanisms and a Modified 3D Feature Pooling Module (MFPM) in U-Net architecture to handle the intrinsic challenges posed by the variable size & shape of tumors and the heterogeneous texture of liver tissues. Our methodology begins with a meticulous preprocessing stage that enhances image contrast and normalizes intensity distributions, followed by data augmentation to ensure robust model training. Leveraging the 3D spatial context, the proposed architecture employs attention-enhanced U-Net variants and a MFPM module, allowing for high-resolution feature extraction and multi-scale analysis essential for distinguishing complex anatomical structures. Experimental results obtained by investigation on Liver Tumor Segmentation Challenge (LiTS) dataset demonstrate that our models achieve the superior performance in terms of Dice Score Coefficient (DSC), Precision, Recall, and F2 with values 0.92, 0.91, 0.91, and 0.91, respectively for liver segmentation while the same for tumor lesions are 0.70, 0.68, 0.73, and 0.72, respectively.

The proposed architectures exhibit exceptional capability in the segmentation of liver and tumors when compared with other contemporary models in terms of accuracy and efficiency. This work not only advances the state-of-the-art in medical image segmentation, but also suggests a scalable approach for other complex segmentation tasks in medical imaging.

Keywords: Segmentation · Liver · Tumor lesion · MFPM · Attention module · 3D Deep learning Networks

J. Kakarla et al. (Eds.): CVIP 2024, CCIS 2473, pp. 457–468, 2026.
https://doi.org/10.1007/978-3-031-93688-3_33

1 Introduction

Liver is a vital organ in a human body and is under threat due to lifestyle, fooding habits etc. Liver cancer is frequent now a days and has taken a large number of lives every year. Globally, it is the sixth common cancer; 5th among men and 9th among women. Around 900,000 new cases detected in 2020 only and has high mortality rate also [3]. Detection an diagnosis, at the early stage, can reduce the mortality significantly, but in early stages, it has no visible symptoms which causes a challenge in detection. Computed tomography (CT) scans are preferred for liver and tumor localization. Precise outlining of liver and its tumors can be of great help in preparing the diagnosis plans. Manual segmentation is time taking and is dependent on the expertise of the radiologists. It emphasizes the need of an automatic systems where less intensity variation in liver and its surrounding regions and variable size make it a difficult task. Tumor is considered more challenging than liver due to its varying shape, size, and number in a patient or different patients. The intensity distribution in and around the tumor is low due to which the boundary is difficult to be drawn, consequently limits the outcome of several methods. To mitigate these issues, various methods are proposed which may categorized as either traditional machine learning or deep learning techniques. Traditional machine learning approaches have shown limited performance as it mainly relies on hand crafted features in contrast to the deep learning methodologies which has achieved remarkable outcome especially in medical imaging.

In this regard, fully convolutional neural networks (FCNs) are proposed for liver and tumor segmentation [16]. Ronneberger introduced U-Net architecture which is quite popular in segmentation mainly due to encoder-decoder arrangement in symmetrical structure [15]. U-Net model is adopted in liver and lesion outlining using 2D and 3D images. Although the computational complexity involved to handle 2D data is lower as compared to 3D, the context in z axis is missed out which impacts the performance of the system adversely. Several modifications of U-Net are also presented by changing the skip connection path. Li et al. [9] introduced the fusion approach by combining the 2D DenseUnet features with the 3D for liver and tumor segmentation. Jiang et al. [7] uses short and long skip connections with attention mechanism in cascade form for the outlining. Based on the U-Net architecture, U^n-Net presented in [17] where convolutional features are taken as skip connections due to which information transfer to the decoder node is more. V-Net introduced by Milletari et al. [11] incorporates the same encoder-decoder in 3D images. Also, a comparison of U-Net, V-Net, and FPN (Feature Pyramid Network) for segmentation is presented by Reza et al. [14] where FPN network performs better. Multi-scale Attention-Net, MA-Net, is proposed by Fan et al. [5] where dual attention mechanism increases feature representation capability for liver and tumors segmentation.

Considering the significance of 3D architecture in analyzing the anomalies especially in 3D structures, this paper introduces 3D deep learning architectures to segment the liver and tumor as well. The encoder-decoder framework, U-Net, integrated with specialized attention mechanisms and a Modified 3D Feature

Pooling Module (MFPM) handles the intrinsic challenges posed by the variable size and shape of tumors and the heterogeneous texture of liver tissues. The attention mechanisms specifically improve segmentation precision for smaller and irregularly shaped tumors by focusing computational efforts on salient features while MFPM effectively captures spatial hierarchies crucial for comprehensive liver segmentation due to which the proposed architectures provide satisfactory proficiency in outlining the liver and tumors.

The rest of the paper is organized as follows. Section 2 elaborates the Dataset, Methodology has been described in Sect. 3 followed by Experimental Set up, Result, and discussions in Sect. 4. Finally the work is concluded in Sect. 5.

2 Dataset

The experiments are conducted using the LiTS dataset from the MICCAI 2017 for liver tumor segmentation challenge. This dataset contains 131 CT scans which are labeled while 70 scans does not have the ground truth [2]. Hence, 131 volumes are leveraged for both training and testing purposes. The number of slices in each volumes varies. Since the collection of scans is done at different places with distinct scanners, the in-plane resolution is varying between 0.55 mm and 1.0 mm having spacing between the slices in the range of 0.45 mm to 6.0 mm.

3 Methodology

The proposed approach for the segmentation of liver and lesions is two step process where initially the liver is outlined upon which the lesions are marked. The methodology initiates with preprocessing the images with contrast enhancement followed by data augmentation. These enhanced images are utilized as an input to the introduced deep learning architectures to segment the liver region. The liver regions are cropped out as volume of Interest (VOI) which further acts as an input to the model for the segmentation of tumors. The overall procedure of the introduced approach is demonstrated in Fig. 1.

3.1 Preprocessing

In order to remove the irrelevant information, the intensity distribution in all the scans are limited in the range of [−100 400] HU for liver segmentation while the same for the tumors are [−200 250] HU. The intensity values for both segmentation are normalized in the range of [0 1]. To ease burden of computational complexity, the scans are resized to 128×128 and patches of 64 images are formed with the scans along the z-axis. To ensure optimal learning and generalization of the model, data augmentation is performed by rotating the images by 90°, 180°, and 270°, as well as horizontal and vertical flipping them. Since the proposed approach leverages the 3D images for tumor segmentation, the precise delineation of the Volume of Interest (VOI) within the liver is crucial step that significantly influences the accuracy and efficiency of tumor segmentation. Hence, the largest bounding box that encapsulates the liver segmentation mask across all slices is considered as VOI.

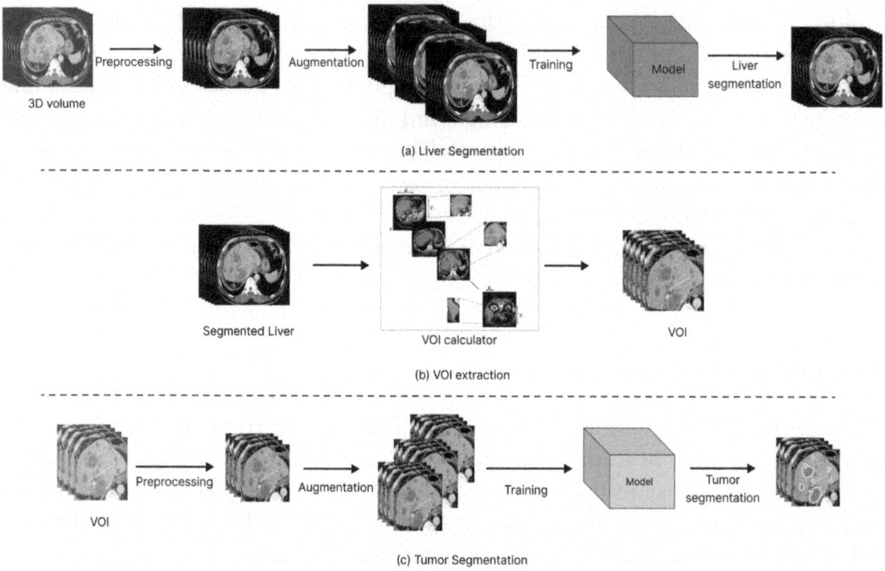

Fig. 1. Proposed flow diagram for the segmentation of liver and tumor lesions.

3.2 Proposed Architectures for Segmentation

Central to our methodology is the development of different architectures, each designed to address the challenges of accurately segmenting liver and tumor regions. Considering the success of encoder-decoder type of arrangement in segmentation, the introduced architectures exploits the U-Net architecture [15] as its base model and various modifications are proposed as below.

Attention Enhanced U-Net (AE UNET). At the core of U-Net architecture lies the integration of attention mechanisms, which are pivotal in refining the model's focus on pertinent features within the imaging data. The attention modules, positioned in the decoder side, taking skip connections as key and output of upsampling layers as its query, employ a gating mechanism to weigh the relevance of features at different levels of abstraction as shown in Fig. 2 while the stage wise details of the proposed framework is summarized in Table 1. This selective focus is instrumental in suppressing irrelevant information, thereby improving the clarity and precision of the segmentation boundaries.

Table 1. Stage-wise Architecture Summary of Attention-Enhanced U-Net Architecture (AE-UNET).

Stage	Encoder	Skip Connection	Decoder	Fully Connected
1	3D Conv + ReLU + Pooling	-	Up-sampling + 3D Conv + ReLU	3D Conv
2	3D Conv + ReLU + Pooling	Attention + Copy	Up-sampling + 3D Conv + ReLU	-
3	3D Conv + ReLU + Pooling	Attention + Copy	Up-sampling + 3D Conv + ReLU	-
4	3D Conv + ReLU + Pooling	Attention + Copy	Up-sampling + 3D Conv + ReLU	-
5	3D Conv + ReLU	-	-	-

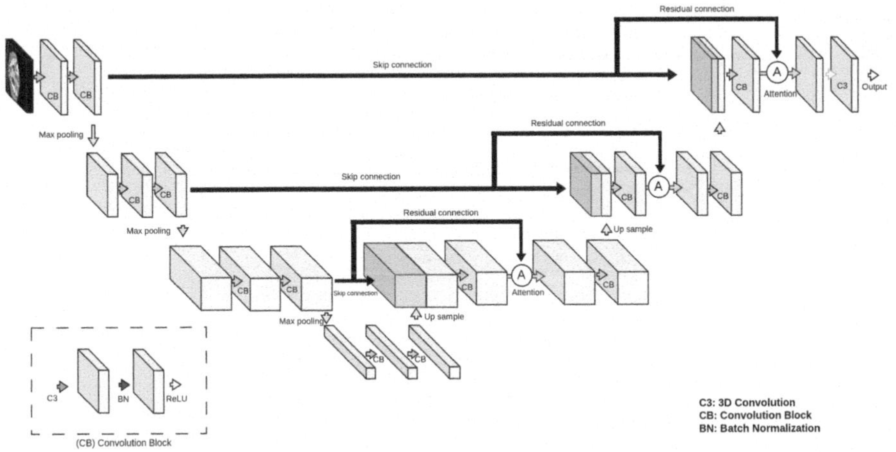

Fig. 2. Schematic of the Attention-Enhanced U-Net (AE-UNET), highlighting the placement of attention blocks within the encoder-decoder structure.

Modified Attention-Enhanced U-Net (MAE-UNET): This architecture is modified version of AE-UNET where convolutional blocks are placed before and after the traditional attention mechanism which are connected together with skip connections as illustrated in Fig. 3. The stage wise details of the proposed framework is also summarized in Table 2. This modification ensures that original features are not lost during processing and addresses a common issue in standard U-Net models where important features might be diluted through successive layers of pooling and convolution. This architecture utilizes blocks of convolution both prior to and following the attention mechanism to prepare the features for attention processing and refine them post-attention. The details abot the architecture is mentioned in Table 2. This approach ensures a comprehensive

Table 2. Stage-wise Architecture Summary of Modified Attention U-Net Architecture (MAE-UNET)

Stage	Encoder	Skip Connection	Decoder	Fully Connected
1	Conv3D + ReLU + Pooling	-	UpSampling3D + Concatenate + Conv3D + BatchNorm + ReLU	Conv3D
2	Conv3D + ReLU + Pooling	Attention + upSampled	UpSampling3D + Concatenate + Conv3D + BatchNorm + ReLU	-
3	Conv3D + ReLU + Pooling	Attention + upSampled	UpSampling3D + Concatenate + Conv3D + BatchNorm + ReLU	-
4	Conv3D + ReLU + Pooling	Attention + upSampled	UpSampling3D + Concatenate + Conv3D + BatchNorm + ReLU	-
5	Conv3D + ReLU	-	-	-

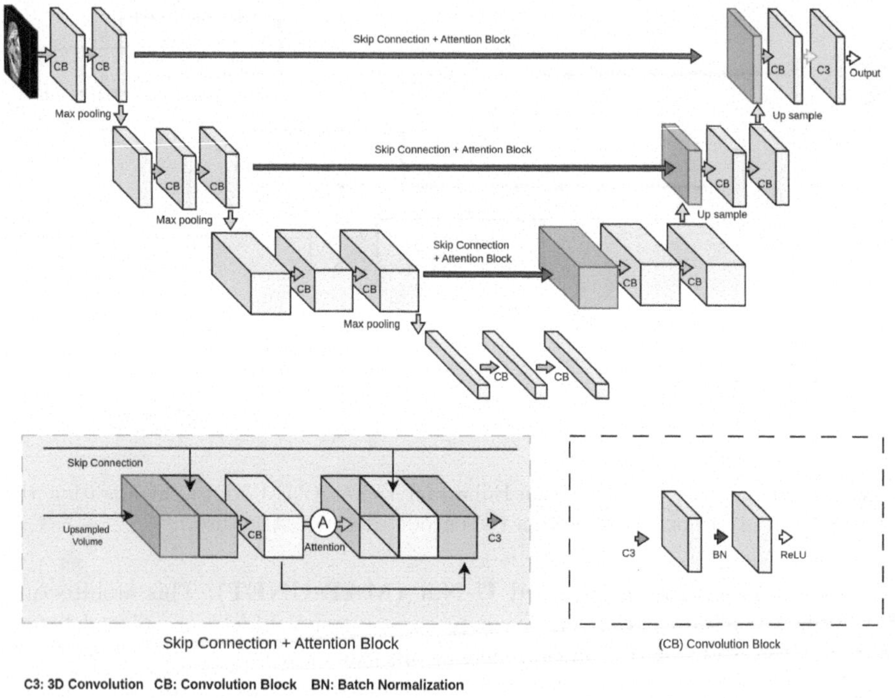

Fig. 3. Diagram of the Modified Attention-Enhanced U-Net (MAE-UNET), displaying the sequence of convolutional and attention layers.

feature enhancement that supports better segmentation outcomes, especially in complex scenarios like variable object sizes or high noise levels in the images.

Modified 3D Feature Pooling Module with U-Net (MFPM-UNET): The introduction of a 3D Feature Pyramid Module into the U-Net architecture represents a significant advancement in processing volumetric medical data. 2D MFPM has been widely exploited in computer vision applications [13], but 3D MFPM is introduced and integrated with U-Net architecture in this work to handles the intrinsic challenges of 3D imaging, such as the analysis of spatial hierarchies and the integration of features across varying scales. Figure 4 presents the proposed framework whose details are provided in Table 3. Since, 3D MFPM facilitates a more comprehensive understanding of the spatial relationships within the data, MFPM component enhances the network's ability to discern and segment anatomical structures with high precision, catering to the diverse sizes and shapes encountered.

4 Experimental Set Up, Result, and Discussions

To evaluate the efficiency of the proposed approach, LiTS 2017 dataset is employed and divided in the ratio of 80:10:10 for training, validation, and test, respectively. During training, the model parameters are adam optimizer with a learning rate of $1e^{-4}$; Dice loss and cross-entropy loss are chosen for their effectiveness in handling the imbalance between the liver and tumor regions versus the background; Batch size of 8 with number of epochs set to 100. The training was conducted using Kaggle's Tesla P100 GPUs.

Table 3. Stage-wise Architecture Summary of Modified 3D Feature Pooling Module (MFPM) with U-Net Architecture (MFPM-UNET).

Stage	Encoder	Skip Connection	Decoder	Additional Layers	Fully Connected
1	Conv3D + BatchNorm + ReLU	-	UpSampling3D + Concatenate + Conv3D + ReLU	MFPM with Decoder (stage 1)	Concatenate (Additional Layers) + Conv3D (to num classes)
2	Conv3D (non-dilated) + Conv3D (dilated)	Concatenate + BatchNorm + ReLU (with dil)	UpSampling3D + Conv3D + ReLU	MFPM with Decoder (stage 2)	-
3	Conv3D + BatchNorm + ReLU + MaxPooling	-	-	MFPM with Decoder (stage 3)	-
4	Conv3D (non-dilated) + Conv3D (dilated)	Concatenate + BatchNorm + ReLU (with dil)	UpSampling3D + Concatenate + Conv3D + ReLU	MFPM with Decoder (stage 4)	-
5	Conv3D + BatchNorm + ReLU + MaxPooling	Conv3D + MFPM	-	-	-

To establish the effectiveness of the proposed architectures, the models are trained rigorously and testing performance is evaluated in terms of Dice Score C oefficient (DSC), Precision, Recall, F2, Dice Loss (DL), Jaccard Score, Hausdorff Distance (HD), Mean Absolute Error (MAE), and Mean Square error (MSE) as mentioned in the Tables 4 and 5, respectively for liver and tumor segmentation. Given the importance of Dice coefficient (DSC), Precision, Recall, F2, Dice Loss (DL) in evaluating the effectiveness of a CAD model, the performance of the U-Net with MFPM architecture renders the best outcome in case of outlining the livers while the same for liver tumors is Attention with U-Net as observed from the Tables 4 and 5. F2, Recall, Precision, and DSC values obtained for liver segmentation via U-Net with MFPM is 0.9136, 0.9138, 0.9131, and 0.1581, respectively while the same for tumor are 0.7221, 0.7313,0.6879, and 0.3349, respectively obtained via Attention enhanced U-Net. The sample output of the introduced models are also demonstrated in Figs. 5 and 6 for liver and tumor segmentation, respectively where Contour in red color indicates the predicted outcome of the models while the same in blue represents the ground truth. The outcomes listed in Tables 4 and 5 are promising and competitive in nature. In case of attention with U-Net, some features are assigned higher weights while

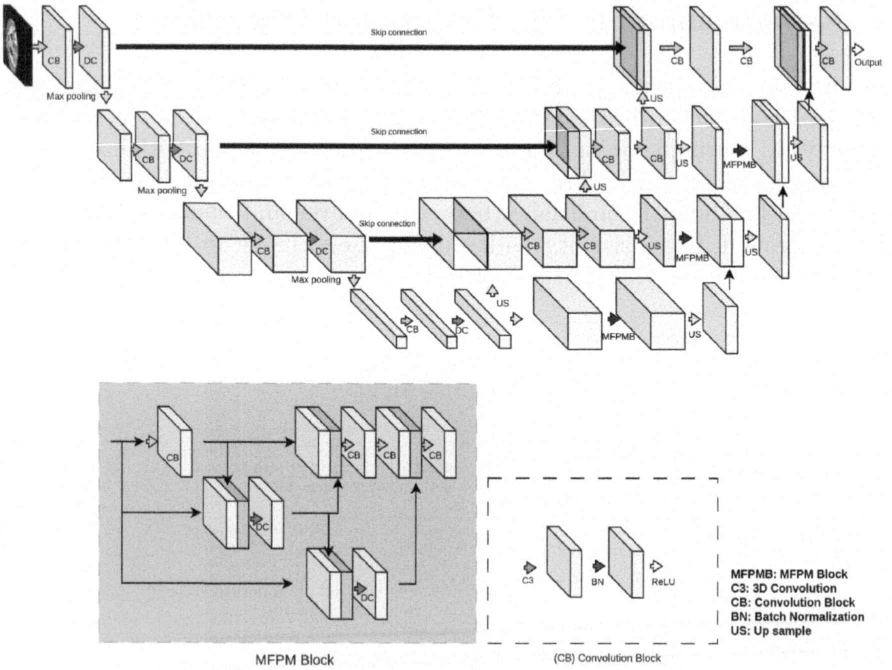

Fig. 4. Detailed architectural diagram of U-Net with Modified 3D Feature Pooling Module (MFPM), highlighting the integration and workflow of the feature processing module within the traditional U-Net structure.

the others are discarded due to which it is more effective in case of small tumor lesions while the U-net with MFPM shows better results in case of liver due to larger spatial region and multi-resolution analysis is more effective. The best results measured are also compared with the some of the relevant schemes in the state-of-the-art as listed in Table 6 and it can be summarized that the outcomes are satisfactory and competitive in nature.

Table 4. The performance of the proposed architectures in Liver segmentation

Model	Dice Loss	Jaccard Score	Hausdorff Distance	Dice Score	F2	Recall	Precision	MAE	MSE
AE-UNET	**0.1362**	0.9167	**8.8671**	0.9162	0.9019	0.9034	0.8962	0.0068	**0.0016**
MAE-UNET	0.1635	**0.9347**	8.3461	**0.9279**	0.9054	0.9061	0.9029	**0.0012**	0.0028
MFPM-UNET	0.1581	0.8861	8.5976	0.9231	**0.9136**	**0.9138**	**0.9131**	0.0035	0.0024

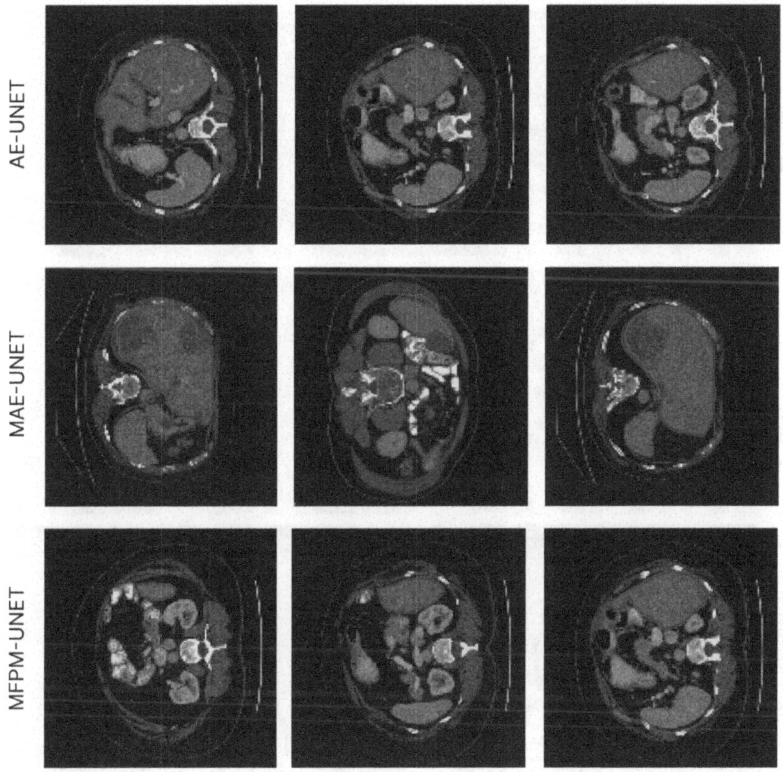

Fig. 5. Illustration of segmented contours of the liver using the introduced models. The contour in blue color represents the ground truth, while the contour in red color indicates the predicted segmented liver part. (Color figure online)

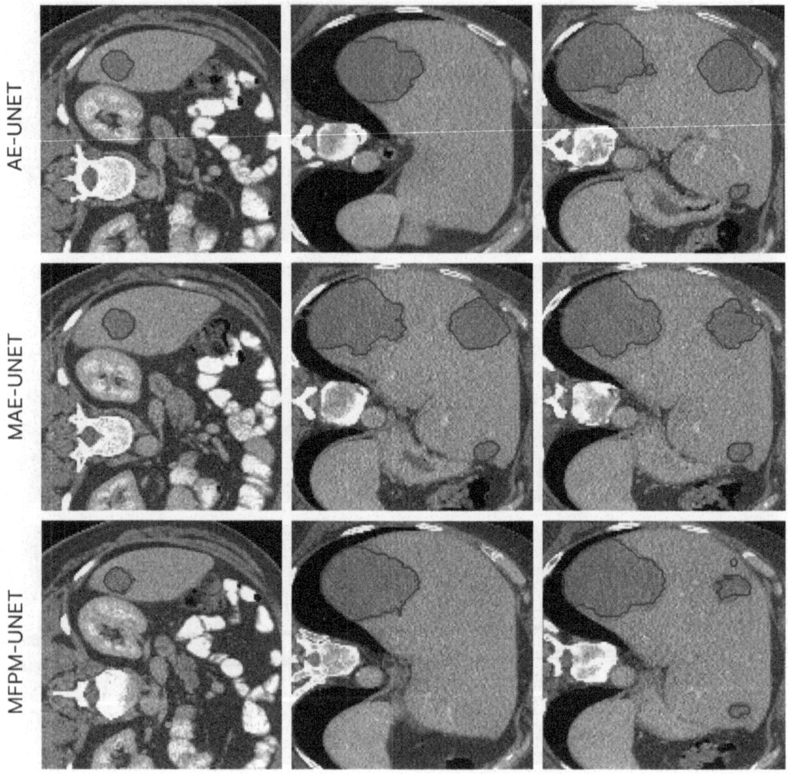

Fig. 6. Illustration of segmented contours of liver tumors using the introduced models. The contour in blue color represents the ground truth, while the contour in red color indicates the predicted segmented tumor part. (Color figure online)

Table 5. The performance of the proposed architectures in Liver Tumor segmentation

Model	Dice Loss	Jaccard Score	Hausdorff Distance	Dice Score	F2	Recall	Precision	MAE	MSE
AE-UNET	**0.3349**	**0.7167**	**7.9783**	**0.7053**	**0.7221**	0.7313	**0.6879**	**0.0154**	0.0325
MAE-UNET	0.3621	0.7092	7.2694	0.6921	0.7198	**0.7394**	0.6512	0.0197	**0.0315**
MFPM-UNET	0.3786	0.6827	6.9891	0.6554	0.6897	0.6612	0.6332	0.0215	0.0394

Table 6. The comparison of proposed model with other relevant state-of-the-art methods

Model	DSC_{Liver}	DSC_{Tumor}	HD_{Liver}	HD_{Tumor}
Unet (Ronneberger et al., 2015) [15]	0.93	0.36	6.52	5.49
AHC-Net (jiang et al., 2019) [8]	0.94	0.62	-	-
Unet + level set (Omar et al., 2020) [1]	0.95	0.70	-	-
3D-UNet + Model ensemble (Fernandez et al., 2021) [6]	-	0.611	-	16.86
S-Net (luan et al., 2021) [10]	-	0.647	-	-
Vision-transformer (R. Mojtahedi et al., 2022) [12]	0.88	0.53	-	-
mt-b (Tschuchnig et al., 2023) [18]	0.84	-	-	-
TD-NET (Shuanhu et al., 2023) [4]	-	0.709	-	7.563
AE-UNET	**0.92**	**0.71**	**8.86**	**7.97**
MAE-UNET	**0.93**	**0.69**	**8.34**	**7.26**
MFPM-UNET	**0.92**	**0.65**	**8.59**	**6.98**

5 Conclusion

This research highlights the differential impacts of employing U-Net with the Modified 3D Feature Pooling Module (MFPM) and attention mechanisms in the segmentation of liver and liver tumors. The observations clearly demonstrate that for liver segmentation, the integration of MFPM with U-Net architecture outperforms other methods. This effectiveness is attributed to MFPM's capability to conduct multiresolution analysis, crucial for comprehending and segmenting the liver with its large and well-defined structure. By effectively integrating features at various scales, MFPM enhances the model's ability to capture the spatial and structural complexities inherent in liver imaging. In contrast, for tumor segmentation, usually smaller in size, U-Net architectures augmented with attention mechanisms have shown superior performance. These attention mechanisms improve the precision of segmentation by focusing the model's computational resources on the most relevant features within the image. This focus is particularly vital for small-sized tumors, where precise delineation is necessary to accurately capture and diagnose pathological changes. The attention-based models provide a refined sensitivity to subtle discrepancies within the imaging data, a critical factor in the effective identification and segmentation of tumors. The introduced frameworks shows competitiveness in performance evaluation when compared with other methodologies. Assessment of the proposed networks can be extended to larger datasets and other medical imaging problems.

References

1. Alirr, O.I.: Deep learning and level set approach for liver and tumor segmentation from CT scans. J. Appl. Clin. Med. Phys. **21**(10), 200–209 (2020)
2. Bilic, P., et al.: The liver tumor segmentation benchmark (LITS). Med. Image Anal. **84**, 102680 (2023)

3. Cancer, Trends: Liver cancer statistics (2020). https://www.wcrf.org/cancer-trends/liver-cancer-statistics/. Accessed 10 Jan 2024
4. Di, S., Zhao, Y.Q., Liao, M., Zhang, F., Li, X.: TD-net: a hybrid end-to-end network for automatic liver tumor segmentation from CT images. IEEE J. Biomed. Health Inform. **27**(3), 1163–1172 (2023). https://doi.org/10.1109/JBHI.2022.3181974
5. Fan, T., Wang, G., Li, Y., Wang, H.: MA-net: a multi-scale attention network for liver and tumor segmentation. IEEE Access **8**, 179656–179665 (2020)
6. Fernández, J.G., Fortunati, V., Mehrkanoon, S.: Exploring automatic liver tumor segmentation using deep learning. In: 2021 International Joint Conference on Neural Networks (IJCNN), pp. 1–8 (2021). https://doi.org/10.1109/IJCNN52387.2021.9533649
7. Jiang, H., Shi, T., Bai, Z., Huang, L.: Ahcnet: an application of attention mechanism and hybrid connection for liver tumor segmentation in CT volumes. IEEE Access **7**, 24898–24909 (2019)
8. Jiang, H., Shi, T., Bai, Z., Huang, L.: Ahcnet: an application of attention mechanism and hybrid connection for liver tumor segmentation in CT volumes. IEEE Access (2019)
9. Li, X., Chen, H., Qi, X., Dou, Q., Fu, C.W., Heng, P.A.: H-DenseUNet: hybrid densely connected UNet for liver and tumor segmentation from CT volumes. IEEE Trans. Med. Imaging **37**(12), 2663–2674 (2018)
10. Luan, S., Xue, X., Ding, Y., Wei, W., Zhu, B.: Adaptive attention convolutional neural network for liver tumor segmentation. Front. Oncol. **11**, 680807 (2021)
11. Milletari, F., Navab, N., Ahmadi, S.: V-net: fully convolutional neural networks for volumetric medical image segmentation. CoRR abs/1606.04797 (2016). http://arxiv.org/abs/1606.04797
12. Mojtahedi, R., Hamghalam, M., Do, R.K.G., Simpson, A.L.: Towards Optimal Patch Size in Vision Transformers for Tumor Segmentation, pp. 110–120. Springer (2022)
13. Rabidas, R., Ravi, D.K., Pradhan, S., Moudgollya, R., Ganguly, A.: Investigation and improvement of VGG based encoder-decoder architecture for background subtraction. In: 2020 Advanced Communication Technologies and Signal Processing (ACTS), pp. 1–6 (2020)
14. Reza, S.M., et al.: Deep learning for automated liver segmentation to aid in the study of infectious diseases in nonhuman primates. Acad. Radiol. **28**, S37–S44 (2021)
15. Ronneberger, O., Fischer, P., Brox, T.: U-net: convolutional networks for biomedical image segmentation. In: Navab, N., Hornegger, J., Wells, W.M., Frangi, A.F. (eds.) Medical Image Computing and Computer-Assisted Intervention – MICCAI 2015, pp. 234–241. Springer, Cham (2015)
16. Sun, C., et al.: Automatic segmentation of liver tumors from multiphase contrast-enhanced CT images based on FCNs. Artif. Intell. Med. **83**, 58–66 (2017)
17. Tran, S.T., Cheng, C.H., Liu, D.G.: A multiple layer U-Net, Un-Net, for liver and liver tumor segmentation in CT. IEEE Access **9**, 3752–3764 (2021)
18. Tschuchnig, M.E., Coste-Marin, J., Steininger, P., Gadermayr, M.: Multi-task learning to improve semantic segmentation of CBCT scans using image reconstruction (2023)

Author Index

J. Kakarla et al. (Eds.): CVIP 2024, CCIS 2473, pp. 469–470, 2026.
https://doi.org/10.1007/978-3-031-93688-3

The manufacturer's authorised representative in the EU is Springer Nature Customer Service Centre GmbH, Europaplatz 3, 69115 Heidelberg, Germany. If you have any concerns regarding our products, please contact ProductSafety@springernature.com

Printed and bound by CPI Group (UK) Ltd, Croydon, CR0 4YY
30/09/2026
02225585-0015